Cooking with Class

Published by
The Parents' Council
Charlotte Latin Schools, Inc.
Charlotte, North Carolina

The Parents' Council of Charlotte Latin Schools grate-
fully dedicates this book to the people who made it
possible -- Virginia Golding, Ellen Knott, and Georgia
Miller. Its conception was a result of their enthusiasm, its
production of their perserverence, and its completion of
their commitment. Their ability to keep things in
perspective and the wonderful sense of humor that each
displayed made an ambitious project a pleasurable
endeavor.

First Printing   10,000 books   November 1982
Second Printing   10,000 books   October 1985
Third Printing   10,000 books   April 1990
Fourth Printing   10,000 books   October 1994
(new cover design)

©1982 Charlotte Latin Schools Parents Council

To order additional copies, see order blank in back of book

ISBN: 0-9615616-0-2

Printed in the USA by
WIMMER
The Wimmer Companies, Inc.
Memphis • Dallas

FOREWORD

The Cookbook Committee wishes to express most sincerely our gratitude for the overwhelming response to "Cooking with Class" and for the enthusiastic support of the Parents' Council members, board and president.

We extend grateful appreciation to all who contributed their favorite recipes and gave unselfishly of their time to help make this book an exciting reality.

We wish to thank our families for their patience, who after a full cookbook workday were served less than gourmet meals far past the usual dinner hour.

This is a wonderful collection of over 1200 recipes from the kitchens of parents, teachers, friends and relatives. That every recipe contributed could not be used is our only regret. Lack of space, the large number received, and the similarity of many prevented us from printing many more recipes. The multiple listing of contributors after a recipe indicates that recipes submitted were similar, but not necessarily identical. Not all recipes included are original, but many are.

The word "class" has several meanings and connotations: "a group whose members have at least one attribute in common"; "a division by quality"; "high style in manner." "Cooking with Class" represents all these things. It is our aim that this book will become your favorite collection of recipes to be used over and over again by the novice as well as the most accomplished cook. May it bring you cooking at its very best. Perhaps it will become your constant kitchen companion— the cookbook you will turn to before any other on your shelf. And when you serve these special favorites to your friends you will hear, "May I have your recipe?" Happy cooking— with class!

A special "thank you" to our dedicated friends whose enthusiasm was endless and help invaluable— Betty Holland, Sophie Godwin, Edith Wellborn, Dot Nicholls, Margaret Van Sciver, Kathy Jackson, G. B. Adams, Carol Ledford, Carolina Compositors, Inc. and Printcrafters of the Carolinas, Inc.

> Virginia Golding
> Ellen Knott
> Georgia Miller

 The napkin and flower symbol refers to recipes also included in the first Charlotte Latin Cookbook.

EDITORIAL STAFF

EDITOR

Mrs. John G. Golding

CO-EDITORS

Mrs. Benjamin F. Knott and Mrs. George Miller

PARENTS' COUNCIL PRESIDENTS

Mrs. Calvin Holland, 1982

Mrs. B. D. Farmer, III 1985

ART DESIGN

Mrs. Daniel J. Wellborn

DESIGN CONSULTANT

Donald McDonald

SECTION CO-ORDINATORS: Mrs. Robert L. Alphin, Mrs. D. T. Bridges, Jr., Mrs. William B. Brown, Mrs. Burt S. Davis, III, Mrs. Sophie Godwin, Mrs. Calvin Holland, Mrs. Richard A. Jones, Mrs. Richard L. Kennedy, Mrs. Mandy Martin, Mrs. Donald G. Murfee, Mrs. Thomas H. Nicholls, Mrs. G. Don Roberson, Mrs. Verner Stanley, Jr., Mrs. William C. Sugg, Mrs. Robert Vinroot, Mrs. F. Arthur Webb, III.

ADDITIONAL TESTERS: Mrs. Martin L. Brackett, Jr., Mrs. Patrick N. Calhoun, Mrs. James H. Carson, Jr., Mrs. Carol Coleman, Mrs. E. H. Copeland, Jr., Mrs. Sharon Culp, Miss Susan Cunningham, Mrs. John G. Golding, Mrs. Isaac Grainger, III, Mrs. Erskine Harkey, Mrs. Calvin Holland, Mrs. Mahmood Hosseinian, Mrs. Benjamin F. Knott, Mrs. Scott Lea, Mrs. Malcolm McLean, Mrs. John A. McLeod, Jr., Mrs. Sally McMillen, Mrs. John C. Mahoney, III, Mrs. J. P. Merrill, Mrs. George Miller, Mrs. James D. Monteith, Mrs. Thomas F. Moore, Jr., Mrs. Gayanne Mraz, Mrs. Neal A. Rutherford, Jr., Mrs. Barbara Schischa, Mrs. Les Schwelling, Mrs. William D. Simerville, Mrs. Edward F. Shaver, Jr., Mrs. William H. Skidmore, Mrs. Pat Viser, Mrs. Hamlin L. Wade, Mrs. Charles E. Warner, Mrs. Bart Willis, Mrs. John A. Young, Mrs. John P. Zeola.

PROOFREADING AND TYPING: Mrs. Elizabeth H. Capitano, Mrs. James G. Culp, Jr., Mrs. W. S. Edge, Mrs. Sophie Godwin, Mrs. Ben T. Johnson, Mrs. James W. Kiser, Mrs. Thomas F. Moore, Jr., Mrs. Thomas H. Nicholls, Mrs. G. D. Privette, Mrs. Peter G. Rielly, Mrs. Neal A. Rutherford, Jr., Mrs. Les Schwelling, Mrs. Pat Viser.

INDEX

Mrs. Thomas H. Nicholls, Mrs. William F. Medearis, Mrs. E. H. Copeland, Jr.

MARKETING

Mrs. Claude Hamilton, Mrs. James H. Barnhardt, Jr., Mrs. Jerry A. Thompson

DISTRIBUTION

Mrs. Mark B. Edwards, Mrs. Robert G. Williams, Mr. Thomas H. Nicholls

TITLE CREDIT

Mrs. Ronald A. Marcus

INTRODUCTION

Some nearly-remembered quotations emerge from the recesses of the dim past:

"A school marches on its stomach."

"Students are what they eat."

"Give a student a fish, and he'll eat for a day; teach him how to use a cookbook, and he'll eat for a lifetime."

Finally, *"The way to a student's heart is through his stomach."*

In a world that seems to have a plethora of fine cookbooks, another emerges to take its rightful place among them. *Cooking with Class* is Charlotte Latin's contribution to the world.

Like everything else at Charlotte Latin, this volume is the result of thousands of hours of volunteers who care about the School and who care enough to bring you the finest in culinary delights to be.

Unlike most cookbooks, however, all entree recipes and most of the other entries in this book have been both tested and tasted. Only those products that passed the "taste of thyme" were included.

It was only fitting that an introduction to a cookbook be written with tongue in cheek.

Enjoy!

Ned Fox

Edward J. Fox, Jr.
Headmaster

Charlotte Latin is an independent coeducational day school that is the product of her parents for their children, her students.

TABLE OF CONTENTS

Beverages & hors d'oeuvres

M.E. Welborn

ICED TEA
Marvelous picnic drink and will keep 2 or 3 days

8 cups water
12 small tea bags
10 whole cloves
1-1/2 cups sugar
1 large can lemonade concentrate

Bring first three ingredients to a boil and set aside to steep for 5 minutes. Then add sugar and lemonade concentrate. Put in gallon container and add enough water to make 1 gallon of tea. Serve with a sprig of mint.

Sue Ellen Biswell (Mrs. C.D.)

EASY ICED TEA

1 large carton (2 lb.) Lipton
   Instant Tea with lemon and
   sugar
2 cups unsweetened pineapple
   juice
water

Into one gallon container measure 6 or 7 scoops of tea mix (scoop comes with mix). Add pineapple juice. Mix well. Add water to complete gallon. Mix again thoroughly.

Shirley Benfield (Mrs. R.H.)

"SMOOTHY"
Let your children try this frozen as a popsicle.

1 carton Mandarin Orange Yogurt
1 banana
1/4 cup orange juice
1/2 cup cracked ice (3-4 ice cubes)

Combine all ingredients in bowl of food processor or blender; process until smooth. Can pour in small containers and freeze like popsicles. Makes 1 large glass.

Ellen Knott (Mrs. B.F.)

ROSEMARY'S ORANGE CAESAR
Could be addictive!

1 (6 oz.) can frozen orange juice
1 cup milk
1 cup water
10-12 ice cubes
1/2 cup sugar
1 tsp. vanilla

Combine all ingredients in blender. Blend until smooth, about 30 seconds. Serve immediately. Serves 4-6.

Peggy Buchanan (Mrs. D. Douglas)
Mary Frances Gray (Mrs. Gene)

SLUSH

Great for a summer party

2 packages cherry Kool Aid
1/2 gallon water
2 cups sugar
2 large cans pineapple juice
1 small can frozen orange juice
1 large bottle ginger ale

Mix first 5 ingredients together and freeze. Thaw to slush. Pour ginger ale over slush. Serves 20.

Linda Miller (Mrs. W.R.)

SUMMER FRUIT PUNCH

Refreshing!

1 quart can pineapple juice
1 quart can orange juice
1 quart apple juice
2 quarts ginger ale
large lump of ice or ice ring
slices of orange (optional)
fresh mint (optional)

Mix the juices and let stand for an hour or two to blend the flavors. Pour in ginger ale just before serving. Serve over ice. Garnish with fresh mint and slices of orange. Fifty to 60 servings.

Kay Roberson (Mrs. G.D.)

PERKED CRANBERRY PUNCH

Try this for a meeting instead of coffee

2 quarts cranberry juice
*2 quarts unsweetened pineapple
    juice
1 quart water
2/3 cups light brown sugar
1 Tbsp. whole cloves
1 Tbsp. whole allspice
4 cinnamon sticks
2 lemons quartered
*For a sweeter punch, use
    sweetened pineapple juice

Place juices in bottom of 30 cup electric percolator. Place remaining ingredients in basket. Perk 30 minutes or until light signals. Makes 5 quarts. Serves 25.

Myrtle Ussery (Mrs. Albert M.)
Submitted by Carol Barreau

HOT FRUIT PUNCH
Good at a buffet table to offer variety

3 cups orange juice
1 quart cranberry juice (not
    cocktail)
1 12-oz. can light beer (optional)
2 apples cored, peeled and sliced
    thin, or your favorite (within
    limits!) fruit
1/4 cup (or less, depending on
    your preference) brown sugar
    (liquid is easier to pour)
1 stick cinnamon
1/2 tsp. ginger (optional)
1/2 tsp. nutmeg
4 orange slices, or more, as garnish

Combine all ingredients but oranges. Heat on very low in crock pot, or on very low on stove for 1 hour. After it is well heated, it may be served or kept warm. Garnish with orange slice. Can be made ahead and refrigerated. Do not freeze. Makes 2 quarts.

Anne Szymanski (Mrs. Louis)

FRUIT PUNCH

5 cups sugar
3 cups water
1 6-oz. can frozen lemon juice
1 6-oz. can frozen orange juice,
    diluted
1 46-oz. can unsweetened
    pineapple juice
7 bananas, mashed
food coloring (optional)
5 quarts ginger ale

Boil sugar and water together; cool. Add all juices; mix well. Add bananas and food coloring. Freeze in 1-quart containers. Add 1 quart ginger ale to 1 quart frozen mixture. Let fruit mixture thaw slightly before mixing. Yield: 35 to 48 cups.

Ann Copeland (Mrs. E.H., Jr.)

PARTY PUNCH

1 quart orange juice, chilled
1 quart cranberry juice, chilled
2 (33.8 oz.) bottles ginger ale,
    chilled
1 32-oz. bottle champagne, chilled
fresh strawberries (optional)

Combine orange juice and cranberry juice in punch bowl. Gently stir in ginger ale and champagne. Garnish punch with fresh strawberries, if desired. Yield: about 20 cups.

Betty Holland (Mrs. Calvin)

HOT CRANBERRY PUNCH
This is great for Christmas parties—buffets—everyone likes it!

3 qts. cranberry juice cocktail
2 (6 oz.) cans frozen orange juice
   concentrate
1 can pineapple juice
2 cups water
1-1/2 cup cinnamon red hot
   candies
1 cup brown sugar

Combine juices and water in an automatic percolator. Place sugar and cinnamon candies in basket. Allow to go through perk cycle. Makes 42 4-oz. cups.

Carol Barreau (Mrs. E.H.)

WASSAIL PUNCH
This tangy, warm punch substitutes vitamin C for alcohol to everyone's delight on a wintry evening.

2 gallons apple cider
2 quarts (64 oz.) orange juice
2 quarts pineapple juice
   (unsweetened)
2 cups lemon juice, freshly
   squeezed
30 whole cloves
8 cinnnamon sticks
2 cups sugar
5 small oranges (for decoration)

Cook 5 small oranges in water for 10 minutes. Meanwhile, pour remaining ingredients into large 3-gallon cooking pot. Bring to slow boil, stirring to dissolve sugar. Reduce heat and simmer for 10 minutes. Remove cooked oranges from heat. Put small knife point at bottom of each orange and insert a cinnamon stick from large pot into each. Add several cloves to each orange. Skim remaining cloves from punch. Pour a portion of punch into punch bowl, allowing remainder to keep warm on low heat for future additions. Float oranges in punch bowl. Yield: 75 servings.

Carole Woodring (Mrs. E.M. Berg)

HOME-MADE SANGRIA
Impresses even the non punch-lovers.

1 pint orange juice
1 cup water
1 cup red wine (more to taste)
1 cup sugar
2 Tbsp. lemon juice
1/4 cup club soda
1/2 cup grenadine syrup
2 or 3 sliced oranges

Dissolve sugar in water. Combine with other liquids. Add the grenadine syrup. Add ice cubes and orange slices. Stir well. Looks nice in punch bowl or clear glass pitcher. Add a little red food coloring if desired, for more color. Yield: 10 4-oz. cups.

Lin Tillman (Mrs. L.W.)

MICROWAVE HOT BUTTERED RUM

If you don't have a microwave, heat apple cider and combine with other ingredients

2 oz. (1/4 cup) dark rum
1 tsp. unpacked light brown sugar
2/3 cup apple cider, room
   temperature
slice of sweet butter
mace to taste

Combine rum and sugar in a hot toddy glass or mug; blend well. Pour in cider until glass is 2/3 full, blend well. Cook on high, uncovered, 2 minutes. Top with butter and sprinkle lightly with mace. Give each guest a spoon for stirring the butter and mace into the drink. Makes 1 drink.

Virginia Golding (Mrs. John G.)

ORANGE FROST

Has quite a distinctive taste and guests will always inquire as to the make-up.

package Libby's Orange Frost
   (when lucky, Harris Teeter
   has this in their produce
   department)
6 ice cubes or 1 cup cracked ice
2 oz. vodka (optional)
16 oz. orange juice

Pour 2 cups orange juice into blender. Add package mix and 6 good-sized ice cubes or 1 cup cracked ice. A little vodka goes nicely here also if it's not for a "P.G." group. Blend on high for 30 seconds.

Lin Tillman (Mrs. L.W.)

ORANGE CHABLIS MORNING DRINK

Perfect for brunch

1 large can frozen orange juice
3 cans of Chablis wine
   or
1 large can frozen orange juice
1 can water
2 cans of Chablis wine

Mix either of the above together and serve over cracked ice. Recipe chosen depends on how "strong" you like your drink. Serves 8.

Ellen Knott (Mrs. B.F.)

FROZEN MARGARITAS

Margarita salt
1 (6-oz.) can frozen limeade (still
    frozen and undiluted)
6 oz. tequila
1/4 cup Triple Sec
ice

Rub rim of glass with lime and dip in Margarita salt. Put frozen limeade, tequila and Triple Sec in blender and add ice until about 3/4 full. Blend. Yield: 14 ozs.

Pat Vinroot (Mrs. Robert)

HUMMERS
One sip and you'll hum!

MOCHA:
1 ounce Kahlua
1 ounce creme de cacao
2 scoops vanilla ice cream

GOLDEN CADILLAC:
1 ounce Galliano
1 ounce white creme de cacao
2 scoops vanilla ice cream

PINK SQUIRREL:
1 ounce white creme de cacao
1 ounce creme de almond
2 scoops vanilla ice cream

BROWN VELVET:
1 ounce Triple Sec
1 ounce brown creme de cacao
2 scoops vanilla ice cream

MINT PATTY:
1 ounce green creme de menthe
1 ounce white creme de cacao
2 scoops vanilla ice cream

SPANISH:
1 ounce Kahlua
1 ounce white rum
2 scoops vanilla ice cream

BRANDY PILLOW:
2 ounces brandy
1 scoop lemon ice cream
1 scoop orange sherbet

ANGEL WINGS
1 ounce creme de menthe
1 ounce brandy
2 scoops vanilla ice cream

ROCKY MOUNTAIN:
1 ounce brandy
1/2 ounce white creme de cacao
1/2 ounce creme de menthe
2 scoops chocolate chip ice cream

BRANDY ALEXANDER:
1 ounce brown creme de cacao
1 ounce brandy
2 scoops vanilla ice cream
dash nutmeg

Let ice cream soften a little. Put all ingredients in blender and blend. One sip and you'll hum! Makes 2 servings.

The Committee

SHERRY SOURS

1 bottle Taylor's pale dry sherry
1 6-oz. can lemonade
4 Tbsp. fresh lemon juice
  or lime juice

Combine and blend well. Pour over crushed ice in wine glasses. Serves 8.

The Committee

BLOODY MARY

*3/4 cup (1 large can)
  tomato juice
1 tsp. (8) Worcestershire sauce
1 Tbsp. (8) lemon or lime juice
1 jigger (12 to 16 oz.) vodka
dash (8) of Tobasco (optional)
stalks of celery
* First amount equals one portion.
  Amount in parenthesis equals
  eight portions.

Mix together first three ingredients. Add vodka and Tobasco last. Stir well. Serve over ice cubes in tall glasses. Garnish with celery stalks if desired. Serves 1 or 8.

Virginia Golding (Mrs. John G.)

JANE'S EGG NOG
"Can do one day ahead"

1 dozen eggs, large
2 cups bourbon
10 Tbsp. 4X sugar
1 pint whipping cream
1 pint milk
nutmeg

Separate eggs; whip egg whites. Beat egg yolks and very slowly dribble bourbon in, add sugar and beat. Whip the cream. Fold all ingredients together. If it is too thick, add a little more milk. Chill several hours and stir before serving. Sprinkle a ittle nutmeg on top of each cup. Serves about 24.

Jane C. Jones

MOCK BOURSIN
"Must do ahead"

8 oz. whipped butter, softened
16 oz. cream cheese, softened
2 cloves garlic, pressed
1/2 tsp. oregano
1/4 tsp. basil
1/4 tsp. dill weed
1/4 tsp. marjoram
1/4 tsp. black pepper
1/4 tsp. thyme

Mix all ingredients thoroughly in food processor, but be careful not to overmix. Refrigerate overnight. Serve with assorted crackers.

Virginia Golding (Mrs. John G.)

BRIE EN CROUTE
A super "make-ahead" appetizer!

3 small rounds Brie Cheese
1 package frozen patty shells
1 egg yolk, beaten

Roll out 2 patty shells for each Brie. Place Brie on top of one round of pastry and roll up sides. Cut circle in second round with empty Brie container. Place this round on top of Brie. Use remaining pastry for strips to wrap around the top edge and crimp to join top edges and folded up sides. Brush with egg yolk. This can be frozen at this point. Bake at 450 degrees for 10 minutes, then reduce heat to 350 degrees and bake for 20 minutes more or until crust is lightly browned. Cut into wedges and serve with crackers or fruit. Sliced unpeeled apples or pears are particularly good.

Wilhelmina Cunningham (Mrs. John A.)

CAMEMBERT AUX NOIX
Easy to prepare, this is my favorite touch of sophistication for a cheese board,

1/4 cup butter
1/4 cup ground pecans
Few drops of tabasco sauce
2 Tbsp. lemon juice (fresh)
1 8-oz. wheel French Camembert
  or Brie (chilled)

Cream softened butter until light and fluffy. Blend in nuts, tabasco and lemon. Cut Camembert in half, horizontally, while still firm. Spread with butter mixture. Chill in refrigerator one hour until filling is firm. Slice in thin wedges and serve on toast points. Approximately 16 wedges.

Carole Woodring (Mrs. E. M. Berg)

HOT BACON AND CHEESE HORS D'OEUVRES

Men, in particular, love these. Processor makes it easy.

1/2 lb. raw bacon, cut in small
    pieces
1 medium onion, cut in small
    pieces
1/2 lb. sharp cheese, cut in small
    pieces
Worcestershire sauce
Party rye bread (1-1/2 packages,
    approx.)

Preheat oven to 400 degrees. Put first three ingredients in food processor or through meat grinder. Add a few drops of Worcestershire sauce. Mix and spread on party rye bread. Put in shallow baking pan and bake about 10 minutes until brown and bubbly. Can store in freezer in small batches and take out as needed. Serves 8 to 10.

Ellen Knott (Mrs. B. F.)

MUSHROOM CANAPES

"So easy and delicious. These go in a hurry."

1 can French fried onion rings
1 cup mayonnaise
1/2 cup grated Parmesan cheese
1 4-oz. can mushrooms, pieces
    and stems

Drain mushrooms and mix all ingredients. Spread on bread slices and broil until bubbly. Party rye is great, or pumpernickel.

Janie Mayhew (Mrs. J. M.)

CHEESE AND MUSHROOM TOAST

Super as an hors d'oeuvre or a hot open-faced sandwich

2 Tbsp. butter
1/4 pound mushrooms, sliced
1 small onion, chopped
1/4 cup parsley, minced
1 cup Swiss cheese, shredded
1/3 cup Parmesan cheese, grated
2 tsp. Dijon mustard
1/2 tsp. salt
1/8 tsp. thyme
1/2 cup mayonnaise
6 slices bread, buttered
    and toasted
6 Tbsp. Parmesan cheese,
    grated

Saute mushrooms and onions in butter. If too much liquid, pour off. Mix other ingredients except bread and 6 Tbsp. Parmesan cheese. Stir that mixture into mushroom mixture. Spread equal portions on bread that has been lightly toasted and buttered on both sides. Sprinkle each slice with 1 Tbsp. Parmesan cheese and quarter. Broil 5 inches from heat until cheese bubbles and browns. Makes 24 squares. Also delicious on halved slices of toast and served as a hot open-faced sandwich. Makes 12 halves.

Ellen Knott (Mrs. B. F.)

TOASTED CHEESE ROUNDS

1/2 cup Parmesan cheese, grated
1 cup mayonnaise
1/2 cup onion, chopped
Dash Worcestershire sauce
salt
pepper
1 loaf Pepperidge Farm
    Party Rye bread

Mix ingredients well. Spread over entire slice of bread. Broil on cookie sheet until bubbly. Serve warm. Makes 40 rounds.

Janet Rubin (Mrs. Stephen)

CURRIED CHEESE APPETIZERS

1-1/2 cups shredded sharp cheese
1/2 cup mayonnaise
1/2 cup green onion, finely
    chopped
1/2 cup ripe olives, finely chopped
1/2 teaspoon curry powder
Triscuits

Blend first five ingredients. Spread by teaspoons onto Triscuits. Broil until cheese melts. Makes 5 dozen.

Grace Sanders (Mrs. E. G.)

CHEESE CASHEW WAFERS

1 lb. extra sharp cheddar
    cheese
1/2 lb. butter, softened
1/4 to 1/2 Tbsp. cayenne
2 Tbsp. salt
1 cup flour
2 cups dry roasted cashews,
    or if desired, substitute
    dry roasted mixed nuts
paprika

Grate or shred cheese. In electric mixer, beat until creamy. Add butter. Continue beating. Add pepper and salt. Add 2 to 3 tablespoons flour. Blend well. Add flour until mixture becomes soft dough and can be rolled into balls without sticking to fingers. The less flour used, the better the pastry. Add finely chopped but not ground nuts. Form into small balls. Flatten with fork on greased cookie sheet. (Dust hands and fork with flour.) Bake at 325 degrees for 20 to 30 minutes until slightly tan. Sprinkle with paprika while hot, after removal from oven. Better after first day. Makes about 8 dozen. Garlic or onion powder may be added for variation.

Ellen Knott (Mrs. B.F.)

FRIED CHEESE

One-inch cubes of Mozzarella,
  Swiss, Monterey Jack, or
  Camembert cheese
1 egg
2 Tbsp. water
Italian seasoned bread crumbs
hot oil (in mini-fryer)

Dip cheese cubes in beaten egg mixed with water. Coat with bread crumbs and let dry. Preheat oil to 375 degrees. With slotted spoon or fry basket, lower cheese into oil and fry until coating is crisp. Do not prick cheese with fork. Serve immediately with apple or pear slices or with grapes.

Pam Allen (Mrs. John R.)

CHEESE DATE GOODIES
Takes some time, but really good! Keeps great in a tin !

Pastry:
1 stick butter
2 cups sharp cheese
1-1/2 cups flour
1 tsp. salt
dash of red pepper

Filling:
1 8-oz. package chopped
  and pitted dates
1/2 cup brown sugar, packed
1/4 cup water
1/2 cup chopped pecans
  (added after filling is cooked)

Grate cheese and mix with other pastry ingredients until dough can be rolled. Mix filling in saucepan and cook until thick and fairly dry. Add nuts. Roll out dough and cut with small biscuit cutter. Put small amount of filling on 1/2 the cheese biscuit. Fold over other side and mash edges together. Bake on a cookie sheet at 325 degrees for 15-20 minutes. Makes 2-3 dozen.
Helpful hint: I use a baby's cereal spoon (heaping) to measure filling onto biscuit and use a baby's fork to mash the edges together.

Kay Roberson (Mrs. G. Don)

"ART'S" CHEESE BALL

1 8-oz. package Philadelphia
  cream cheese (softened)
1 to 1-1/2 wedges real "Danish
  Blue" cheese (softened)
1/2 tsp. Worcestershire sauce
2 tsp. grated onion
chopped pecans.
chopped parsley

Let cheeses soften and blend them together with Worchestershire sauce and onion. Form into a ball or a roll and wrap in waxed paper. Let harden in refrigerator several hours or over night. Then roll in nuts and parsley which have been mixed together. (If you form into a roll, you need to double the recipe.)

Barby Goode (Mrs. David J.)

CHEESE FILLED DIAMOND PASTRIES
(Bourekakia)
Lots of fun to make!

1 8-ounce package cream cheese
1/2 pound feta cheese
2 cups large-curd cottage cheese
3 egg yolks
2 Tbsp. minced parsley
1 cup (1/2 lb.) butter
About 24 sheets filo dough
    (about 2/3 of a 1 lb. box)

Beat together cream cheese, feta cheese, cottage cheese, egg yolks and parsley until well blended and creamy. Melt butter in small pan; set aside. Lay out 3 sheets of filo (keep remaining sheets covered with plastic). Lightly brush 1 sheet with butter, using a wide pastry brush or something similar. Lay on second sheet and brush with butter; repeat for third sheet. Spoon a 1/2 inch wide ribbon of cheese mixture along one side of dough. Starting with that same side, roll up in a jelly-roll fashion, tucking in ends as you go, to encase filling. Place seam side down on an ungreased baking sheet. Repeat, making 7 more rolls and placing them about 1 inch apart (you'll need two baking sheets). Bake, uncovered, in a 375 degree oven for 15 minutes or until puffed and lightly browned. If you are planning to serve them that day, let cool 15 minutes; then slice on the diagonal about 2 inches apart, making diamond-shaped pieces. If you want to serve the following day, cover and chill (or for longer storage, wrap airtight and freeze). To reheat (thaw if frozen), bake at 350 degrees until thoroughly heated. Makes 4 dozen appetizers.

Betsy Knott

CHEESE BALL

1 lb. Velveeta Cheese
    (small box)
1/2 lb. soft Cheddar
    (grated) sharp
1 small package Roquefort or
    bleu cheese
4 small packages cream cheese
    (3 oz. size)
1 small onion, grated
1 tsp. horseradish (or less)
1 tsp. Worcestershire sauce
chopped nuts

Let cheese soften, add onion, horseradish, and sauce. Mix with mixer. Chill. Roll in chopped nuts. Serve with crackers. This freezes nicely. Yield: 2 medium balls.

Joyce Summerville (Mrs. W. Kelly)
Similar recipe submitted by Carole Goodwin

JULIA'S CHEESE BALL

1 8-oz. cream cheese
1 4-oz. bleu cheese
1 8-oz. jar Cheese Whiz
1 3-oz. cream cheese with chives
1/2 tsp. garlic powder
dash paprika
drop or two Tabasco
1/4 tsp. Worcestershire sauce
1 cup chopped pecans

Have cheese at room temperature. Mix well all ingredients except nuts. Chill for several hours or overnight. Form into a ball and roll in chopped pecans. Can be frozen.

Julia Warner (Mrs. C. E.)
Similar recipe submitted by B. J. Miller
(Mrs. Henry F., III)

CHEESE CHUT-NUT MOLD

"This combination sounds strange, but this is my most-requested recipe."

11 oz. cream cheese
1-1/2 oz. box of raisins
(lunch box size)
3 Tbsp. sour cream
1 Tbsp. curry powder
1 scant cup salted
cocktail peanuts
1/2 lb. (9 or so slices) crisp-
fried bacon, crumbled
1/2 cup chopped green onion
1 10-oz. jar of Raffetto's
Chut-Nut
Angel Flake coconut (may use
fresh grated)
artichoke petals (optional)

Mix together all of the ingredients (do not use a mixer), reserving one-half jar of chutney. Form into a ball. Refrigerate. Frost with strained chutney and sprinkle with coconut. Serve with rye crackers. For flair . . . garnish with freshly-cooked artichoke petals to surround the mold. Can be prepared ahead. Freezes only moderately well. Serves 15.

Virginia Golding (Mrs. John G.)

PINEAPPLE CHEESE BALL

2 8-oz. cream cheese, softened
1 small can crushed drained
pineapple (8-1/4 oz.)
1 green pepper, minced
1 onion, minced
1 Tbsp. seasoned salt
1 cup chopped pecans

Combine all ingredients until well blended. Add nuts and mix well. To serve — cut pineapple in half lengthwise and hollow out. Mound cheese mixture in each half and sprinkle a few more chopped nuts on top. Serve with assorted crackers. Make 24 hours ahead.

La McLeod (Mrs. J. A.)

CHEESE SHRIMP BALL

1 8-oz. softened cream cheese
1/2 tsp. minced onion
1 Tbsp. catsup
1/2 Tbsp. Worcestershire sauce
1/2 tsp. cayenne pepper
1/4 tsp. salt
1/8 tsp. black pepper
1/8 tsp. Tabasco sauce
1 5-0z. can deveined shrimp
    or a little more

Mix all ingredients except shrimp. Fold in about 1/2 of shrimp—saving some for decoration. Form into ball. Decorate ball with remaining shrimp and sprinkle lightly with parsley. Refrigerate for 24 hours before serving. Serve with Triscuits.

Sue Ellen Biswell (Mrs. C. D.)

CHEESE PIE
Deliciously spicy!

1 4-oz. can hot chilies (Old
    El Paso green chilies)
10 oz. grated Kraft sharp cheese
4 whole eggs, beaten

Put chopped chilies in bottom of greased pie pan or greased 9 x 9 inch square pan. Fill with grated cheese and pour egg on top. Let stand 3 hours. Baked at 325 degrees for 1 hour. Let set a few minutes and cut into small squares or wedges. Yield: 25 appetizers.

Nancy Langston (Mrs. J.T.)

"BEST EVER" CHEESE RING
Good combination of flavors. Men love it!

1 pound sharp cheddar cheese,
    grated
1 cup pecans, chopped
3/4 cup mayonnaise
1 medium onion, grated
1 clove garlic, pressed
    (or dash of garlic salt)
1/2 tsp. Tabasco
1 cup strawberry preserves

Combine all ingredients except preserves and mix well. Chill. Put into ring mold. At serving time unmold and fill center with strawberry preserves. Serve with crackers. Can prepare a day before serving.

Jocelyn Rose (Mrs. L.L., Jr.)

HOT ARTICHOKE DIP

1 14-oz. can artichokes,
    drained and chopped
1 clove garlic, mashed, or
    4 drops of garlic juice
    (optional)
1 cup Hellman's mayonnaise
1/2 tsp. Worcestershire sauce
    (optional)
1 cup grated Parmesan cheese
    (freshly grated is best)
Freshly ground pepper to taste
Paprika or minced parsley to taste

Combine all ingredients in small greased baking dish. Bake 20 to 25 minutes. Serve hot with Triscuits, taco-flavored chips, or onion crackers. Serves 8-10.
Variation: Can add 1 4-oz. can chopped green chilies (seeded if you do not want it too hot).

Jean Bridges (Mrs. D.T.B., Jr.)
Cherrill Ferguson (Mrs. Paul A.)
Peggy Hormberg (Mrs. R.H.)
Ann Jones (Mrs. R.A.)
Laura Roddey (Mrs. John H., Jr.)

SPINACH DIP
Versatile—use for dip or salad

1 10-oz. package frozen
    chopped spinach
1 cup mayonnaise
1 cup sour cream
1 medium onion, chopped
1 5 oz. can water chestnuts,
    chopped
1 (1-5/8) oz. package vegetable
    soup mix (Knorr)
Parmesan cheese

Thaw spinach; place on paper towels and press until barely moist. Combine spinach, mayonnaise, sour cream, onion, water chestnuts and vegetable soup mix. Stir well. Cover and chill mixture several hours. Serve with crackers or raw vegetables. Try stuffing a tomato, or topping a thick slice of tomato, with mixture and place on lettuce leaf for a nice luncheon salad feature. Sprinkle with Parmesan cheese if desired. Yield: 3 cups.

Hilda Hemby (Mrs. T.E., Jr.)
Paula Klein (Mrs. R.A.)

HOT BROCCOLI DIP

3 stalks celery, chopped
    medium fine
1/2 large chopped onion
1 pkg. frozen chopped broccoli
1 4-oz. can mushrooms, drained
    (pieces or button)
1 can cream of mushroom soup
1 roll Kraft garlic cheese
toasted almonds (optional)

Saute celery, onion and mushroom pieces in butter. Cook broccoli as directed on package (don't overcook) and drain well. Add mushroom soup to above ingredients. Melt cheese in double boiler. Combine all in chafing dish and serve. Serves 12. This may also be served as a vegetable. Freezes beautifully. Dip with Fritos, Doritos or put in miniature patty shells or toast cups.

Beverly Keller (Mrs. Guy)

CUCUMBER DIP

1 pint sour cream
1 pkg. dry onion salad dressing
    mix (buy at Reid's)
2 Tbsp. lemon juice
1/2 tsp. Worcestershire sauce
4 slices bacon, crisply
    cooked and crumbled
1/2 cup very finely chopped
    cucumber
2 Tbsp. finely chopped pimiento

Combine all ingredients. Refrigerate 30 minutes or longer before serving with potato or corn chips. Yield: 2-1/2 cups.

Sharon Edge (Mrs. W.S.)

CHIFFONADE DIP

1/4 cup minced pimiento
1/4 cup minced parsley
3 Tbsp. minced onion
1/8 tsp. Tabasco
2 chopped hard-boiled eggs
1/4 cup mayonnaise
1/4 cup minced green pepper
1/4 tsp. salt
1/2 tsp. garlic salt

Combine and chill until blended. Serve with raw vegetables or chips for dipping.

Margaret Pitts

SOUR CREAM DIP
"Best with home-made curry powder"

1/2 cup sour cream
1/2 cup ripe olives, chopped
1/2 cup mayonnaise
2 Tbsp. snipped chives
1 tsp. Worcestershire sauce
1/2 tsp. prepared mustard
*1/2 tsp. curry powder (home-
    made is best)
*(See index for recipe)

Mix. Refrigerate. Serve with raw vegetables.

Margaret Pitts

CURRIED EGG DIP FOR VEGETABLES

"Use leftover dip for cooked vegetables."

1/4 tsp. Tabasco
1/2 tsp. curry powder
1/4 tsp. dry mustard
1/2 tsp. salt
1/2 cup mayonnaise
1-1/2 Tbsp. finely chopped onion
1/2 cup finely chopped celery
1 tsp. minced parsley
1/4 cup sour cream
4 hard-boiled eggs, finely chopped

Combine Tabasco, curry powder, dry mustard, and salt. Stir into mayonnaise and sour cream. Combine onion, celery, and parsley; stir into first mixture. Fold in eggs. Chill until ready to serve. Makes about 2 cups of dip. Good with carrots, cucumbers, cauliflower, etc.

Ellen Knott (Mrs. B. F.)

SAYRE MEYER'S CHUTNEY CASHEW DIP

A hit at every cocktail party!

8 oz. cream cheese, softened
2/3 cup sour cream
1 cup chutney, chopped
    and drained
1 cup cashews, cut in half
3 tsp. curry powder
Ritz crackers

Mix cream cheese, sour cream, chutney, cashews and curry powder. Serve with Ritz crackers. Serves 8.

Lynn Wheeler (Mrs. Joseph G.)

RESI'S PROCRASTINATION DIP

"Can be made at the last minute!"

1 8-oz. cream cheese, softened
1 8-oz. sharp cheddar cheese
    grated
1 10-oz. can Old El Paso
    tomatoes and green chilies,
    drained (save liquid)
garlic salt to taste

Blend cheeses, drained tomatoes, green chilies and garlic salt. Beat with mixer or wire whisk, adding liquid as needed to get desired consistency. Serve with corn chips, potato chips, or crackers.

Resi Golding

17

SPICY SOUTH-OF-THE-BORDER DIP

This is easy, delicious and serves a large crowd.
Rotel can be found at Reid's.

1 can ROTEL Tomatoes and
   Green Chilies (no substitute)
2 pound package Velveeta
1 can chili with or without beans

Melt Velveeta in top of double boiler. Drain Rotel, reserving liquid. Add drained Rotel and heated chili to Velveeta. Stir Rotel liquid to get desired consistency for dip. Serve with Triscuits, wide Fritos, Tostados, etc.

Charlotte Arrendel (Mrs. C.W.)

CLAM DIP

1 can (10 oz.) cream of celery
   soup
8 oz. cream cheese, softened
1 6-1/2 oz. can minced clams,
   drained
1/2 cup finely chopped cucumber
1/2 cup finely chopped
   mushrooms
1/4 cup minced green onion
1 Tbsp. Worcestershire sauce
1/4 tsp. dried dill, crushed

Using electric mixer, blend soup into cheese *just until smooth.* Overbeating makes it too runny. Add clams, cucumber, mushrooms, onion juice, Worcestershire sauce and dill. Blend well. Chill before serving. Serve with crackers, raw vegetables or chips. Yield: 3 cups.

Judy Ranson (Mrs. R.C.)

HOT CRAB MEAT DIP

Delicious! People think you have prepared an elegant crab dish!

1 8-oz. package Philadelphia
   cream cheese, softened
1 can crab meat (back fin)
salt and pepper to taste
1 Tbsp. milk
1 Tbsp. mayonnaise
1 tsp. Worcestershire sauce
2 Tbsp. grated onion
2 Tbsp. horseradish (optional)

Mix all together and bake in 375 degree oven for 15 minutes. Nice to use an attractive small ovenproof dish in which the dip can be baked and served. Serves 8-10

Cherril Ferguson (Mrs. Paul A.)
Barby Goode (Mrs. David J.)

HOT CHEESE DIP

"Positively one of my most sought-after recipes. Surely wish I'd thought it up."

1 10-1/2 oz. can Frito bean dip
1 8-oz. package cream cheese
1/2 cup grated jack cheese
1/2 cup grated cheddar cheese
1 cup sour cream
1/2 cup chopped onion
1-1/4 oz. packet taco season-
    ing mix
15-20 dashes Tabasco

Let cream cheese soften at room temperature. Combine all ingredients and bake at 350 degrees for 20 minutes in 1-1/2 quart round casserole. Serve with Fritos. Yield: about 5 cups.

Gensie

PEGGY'S HOT CHILI DIP

1/2 pound ground beef
1/4 cup chopped onions
1/4 cup catsup
1/2 tsp. salt
8 oz. can red kidney beans
    and liquid, mashed
1 tsp. chili powder
1/2 cup shredded sharp cheese
1/4 cup black olives, chopped
    (optional)

Brown beef and onions together; then drain. Add other ingredients except cheese and olives, and bring to a boil. Transfer to chafing dish; top with cheese and olives. Serve with large-size Fritos. Flavor improves if prepared a day ahead. Serves six.

Georgia Miller (Mrs. George)

LAYERED NACHO DIP

This hor d'oeuvre is absolutely great!

1 16-oz. can refried beans
1/2 (1.25) package Taco
    Seasoning Mix
1 6-oz. carton avocado dip
1 8-oz. carton commercial
    sour cream
1 4-1/2 oz. can chopped ripe
    olives
2 large tomatoes, chopped
1 small onion, diced
1 4-oz. can chopped
    green chilies
1-1/2 cup or 6 oz. shredded
    Monterey Jack cheese

Combine beans with seasoning. Spread bean mix evenly in 12x8x2 dish. Layer remaining ingredients in order listed. Serve with large Mexican chip (Doritos). Makes 6 cups and goes quickly. Serves 12.

Judy Pence

*   *   *

Variation: Use 1 ripe avocado mashed, in place of 6 oz. carton avocado dip. Heat for 15 minutes at 325 degrees.

Dale E. Yaged

*   *   *

Variation: Use 1 package Taco seasoning mix.

Joan Kar (Mrs. A.K.)

SHRIMP MOUSSE

1 can tomato soup
1 8-oz. cream cheese
1 cup mayonnaise
2 pkgs. Knox gelatin (slight)
1/2 cup cold water
3/4 cup grated onion
3/4 cup chopped celery
salt to taste
1-1/4 lb. cooked shrimp

Boil soup, add cream cheese and beat until cream cheese melts. Dissolve gelatin in cold water. Add to soup. Add remaining ingredients and pour into mold. (I use a fish mold.) Unmold on a bed of lettuce. Use an olive for the eye. Serves 50 with 2 boxes of crackers.

Anne Thrift (Mrs. Charles B., III)

DIP FOR FRUIT

1 cup sour cream
1 Tbsp. gelatin
1/4 cup sugar
1/2 tsp. vanilla
1 cup heavy cream, whipped
bite-size pieces of fruit

In top of double boiler over hot water, mix sour cream, gelatin and sugar until gelatin dissolves and sugar melts. Stir in vanilla. Cool mixture. Fold in whipped cream. Refrigerate until ready to use. Yield: 3 cups dip.

Libby Morrison (Mrs. Jack)

EGG MOLD WITH CAVIAR
ELEGANT!

1 Tbsp. plain gelatin
2 tsp. lemon juice
2 Tbsp. cold water
8 hard-boiled eggs, chopped
1 cup Hellman's mayonnaise
1 tsp. Worcestershire sauce
1/4 tsp. Dijon mustard
salt and pepper to taste
1/2 cup chopped green onions
    (or to taste)
3-1/2 or 4 oz. jar red or black
    caviar

Cook first three ingredients in Pyrex cup set in pan of water over low heat until gelatin is dissolved. Combine with remaining ingredients, excluding green onions and caviar. Turn into round, oiled mold and chill until set. Unmold on serving platter. Put chopped green onions on top and caviar around base. Serve with onion-flavored melba toast rounds. Serves 15.

Catherine Collins (Mrs. Quincy)

SONOMA CRAB DIP
"Men seem to love this dish."

1 cup mayonnaise
1 tsp. minced onion
1/4 tsp. Worcestershire sauce
2 Tbsp. finely chopped
    green pepper
1/4 cup sherry
1 lb. crabmeat (I use backfin, but
    canned may be used)

Combine all ingredients, stirring lightly. Serve chilled with crisp crackers. Yield: 2-1/2 cups.

Nancy Langston (Mrs. J.T.)

SHRIMP DIP
"Good for a large group"

16 oz. cream cheese
1/2 pint Miracle Whip
2 lbs. chopped shrimp
1 clove minced garlic
small chopped onion
1/2 bottle French dressing
6 drops horseradish
juice of 1 lemon
1-1/4 tsp. sugar
1 tsp. Worcestershire sauce
1 tsp. Accent
salt and pepper to taste

Let cream cheese come to room temperature. Add remaining ingredients. Chill and serve with crackers. Best when made in advance. Yield: approximately 7 cups.

Barbara Stutts (Mrs. Clyde)

SHRIMP WRECK
"Tastes best when made earlier in the day."

1 can shrimp, 6-7 oz. size
1 cup sharp grated cheese
1/3 cup finely chopped onion
1 cup mayonnaise
1 tsp. Worcestershire sauce

Put shrimp, cheese and onion on board and chop. Add remaining ingredients and mix well (do not put in blender). Chill. Serve with crackers or chips. Yield: 2-3/4 cups.

Ellen Knott (Mrs. B.F.)

IMPERIAL CRAB DIP

"One day I was out of crabmeat when guests dropped in so I tried a can of shrimp. It was delicious; everyone loved it."

1 8-oz. package cream cheese,
    room temperature
1/4 cup onion, chopped fine
1/3 tsp. horseradish
1 tsp. milk or dry vermouth,
    or 1 Tbsp. lemon juice
1 6-1/2 oz. can crabmeat, drained
1 package slivered almonds

Mix all ingredients except almonds and pour into a greased baking dish (one you can serve it in). Top with almonds. Bake at 275 degrees for 25-30 minutes. Serve at once with Wheat Thins or any other crackers you like. Keep warm on an electric warming tray or candle warmer. To prepare as a spread, use only 4 oz. cream cheese. You can vary this recipe by adding green pepper, green onion, or a pinch of herbs. Yield: 2-1/2 cups.

Microwave: Soften cream cheese in microwave for 15 seconds, then add other ingredients. Heat on high until bubbly, stirring each minute for about 3 minutes.
Gensie

Variation: Substitute 2 tsp. Worcestershire sauce for horseradish and carefully brown almonds first.
Anne Zeola (Mrs. J.P.)

OVEN-BAKED CRAB DIP

This is great!

2 (8 oz.) packages cream cheese,
    softened
1/3 cup mayonnaise
1 Tbsp. powdered sugar
1 Tbsp. chablis
1/2 tsp. onion juice
1/2 tsp. prepared mustard
1/4 tsp. garlic salt
1/4 tsp. salt
1 8-oz. crabmeat, or more to taste
chopped fresh parsley

Combine first 8 ingredients; mix well. Stir in crabmeat. Spoon crabmeat mixture into a lightly greased 9 inch pie dish. Bake for 15 minutes at 375 degrees. Sprinkle on parsley. Serve warm with your favorite crackers. Yield: 2-3/4 cups.

Hilda Hemby (Mrs. T.E. Jr.)

SALMON MOUSSE
"Food processor makes it easy."

3/4 Tbsp. gelatin
1 Tbsp. lemon juice
1 small onion
1/2 cup boiling water
1/3 cup mayonnaise
1/8 tsp. paprika
1/2 tsp. dill
8 oz. can pink salmon
1/2 cup heavy cream.

Open salmon can and take out large bones and dark skin. Empty gelatin into water and lemon juice. Pour into food processor fitted with metal blade. Put in onion and blend. Put in all other ingredients except cream; blend. Add cream, blend. Pour into greased fish mold. Chill. After unmolding, decorate fish. Use cut olives for eyes, almonds or cucumbers can be used for scales.

Jean Davis (Mrs. Burton)

SHRIMP REMOULADE IN ASPIC RING
This sounds long-winded, but it is easy to make, delicious, low in calories, and is pretty, too! Can also be used as a salad for a buffet supper supreme.

Aspic:
4 cups tomato juice
1/2 cup onion, chopped
1/4 cup celery leaves, chopped
2 Tbsp. brown sugar
1 tsp. salt
4 whole cloves
2 Tbsp. unflavored gelatin,
   mixed with 1/4 cup cold water
3 Tbsp. lemon juice
1 cup celery stalks, chopped fine

Simmer tomato juice, onion, celery leaves, brown sugar, salt and cloves for 5 minutes. Strain. Mix gelatin with water and dissolve in the hot tomato mixture, then add lemon juice. Chill until partially set. Add chopped celery, pour into a greased ring mold, and chill until set.

Shrimp Remoulade:
1/2 cup white or wine vinegar
1 cup olive oil
6 Tbsp. prepared mustard
1 tsp. paprika
1 cup green onion, chopped
3 Tbsp. parsley, chopped
4 Tbsp. anchovy paste
1 Tbsp. horseradish
4-5 drops Tabasco sauce
3 lbs. shrimp, cooked
   shelled and chilled

Mix vinegar and oil in blender. Add all other ingredients except shrimp, and blend. Refrigerate this sauce in a glass jar or bowl overnight. When ready to serve, place the shrimp in the center of the aspic ring which has been unmolded on lettuce leaves. Pour the remoulade sauce over the shrimp. Garnish with fresh dills or parsley. Serve with crackers, a spreader, and picks, so guests can spread some aspic on a cracker, and place a shrimp on top.

Gensie

ARTICHOKE SQUARES
Always a hit! Serve hot or cold

1 can (10-oz.) artichoke hearts,
  drained and chopped
1 small onion, chopped
1 clove garlic, minced
butter
4 eggs, beaten
1/4 cup fine dry bread crumbs
1/8 tsp. each pepper, oregano,
  Tabasco
1/4 tsp. salt
2 cups cheddar cheese, shredded
2 Tbsp. parsley, minced

Saute onions and garlic in a little butter until limp. Add eggs, crumbs and seasonings. Add other ingredients. Pour into 8 x 8 greased pan and bake at 350 degrees until set, or about 30 minutes. Cut in small squares. Can be refrigerated and heated before serving. Yield: 25 squares.

Linda Miller (Mrs. W.R.)

SHRIMP-STUFFED ARTICHOKES
"Lots of trouble—but everyone loves them.
Can be prepared early and heated."

4 large artichokes
lemon
salt
1 lb. raw shrimp
1/2 lb. butter
6 cups fresh bread crumbs
1 cup chopped onions
4 tsp. chopped garlic
2 cups freshly-grated Parmesan
1/2 cup chopped parsley
2 tsp. grated lemon peel
1/2 cup Creole (or other)
  sauce
4 Tbsp. butter

Trim artichokes. Rub cuts with lemon. Cook with 1/2 lemon in boiling salted water. Boil 15 minutes until bases are done. Drain. Clean and dry cooked shrimp. Chop all but 4 shrimp finely. Melt butter. Add crumbs and stir over heat until golden. Scrape into bowl. Melt the 4 Tbsp. butter and add onions and garlic. Stir until clear, add to other ingredients. Toss gently. Stuff artichokes. Start at base. Fold foil up and around chokes. Twist together at top and stand up in pot with water. Boil. Cover and steam 20 minutes. Put 1 shrimp on top. Pass sauce for dip.

CREOLE SAUCE FOR SHRIMP-STUFFED ARTICHOKES

2 Tbsp. tarragon vinegar
1 tsp. paprika
1/2 tsp. brown mustard
1/2 tsp. salt
1/4 tsp. Cayenne pepper
6 Tbsp. olive oil.

Combine all ingredients. Serves four.

Dot Nicholls (Mrs. T.H.)

STUFFED CUCUMBERS
Unusual—Good

1 2-oz. can anchovy fillet or 2 ozs.
    anchovy paste
2 3-oz. pkg. cream cheese
1 tsp. dill weed
1 tsp. grated green onion
1 Tbsp. mayonnaise
1/16 tsp. cayenne pepper
sour cream
chervil
6 cucumbers (small)

Peel and cut small cucumbers into halves. Scoop out center and drain well on paper towels. Blend above ingredients and fill cucumbers. Cut each half in two. Spread sour cream on top and sprinkle with chervil. Makes 2 dozen hors d'oeuvres.

Teny Sugg (Mrs. William)

POTATO SKINS

large Idaho baking potatoes
melted butter
salt
coarsely ground pepper
onion or garlic salt (optional)
grated Cheddar cheese
sour cream with chives

Prick potatoes with fork before baking. Bake the potatoes until soft (do not wrap in foil or grease them for baking). Scoop out almost all of the potato but leave a little on the peel. (If you leave too much potato they will not be crisp.) Cut the skins into strips about 3 inches long and 1 inch wide. Coat each piece completely with the melted butter and sprinkle with the seasoning of your choice and Cheddar cheese. Place on an ungreased jelly-roll pan and bake at 400 degrees for 10 minutes or until crisp. May dip skins in sour cream with chives.

The Committee

SPINACH BALLS

2 10-oz. boxes chopped spinach
2 cups Pepperidge Farm herb
    stuffing mix
2 onions, finely chopped
6 eggs, beaten
3/4 cup melted butter
1/2 cup grated Parmesan cheese
1 Tbsp. garlic salt
1/2 tsp. thyme
pepper to taste

Cook spinach; drain and squeeze. Mix all ingredients together. Form into balls, using 1 teaspoon of mixture. Bake at 350 degrees on lightly greased cookie sheet 20 minutes. May be frozen up to two months. Makes 4 to 5 dozen.

Janet Rubin (Mrs. Stephen)

EGGPLANT ROLLS
"Good appetizer for a dinner party"

1/2 cup grated Parmesan cheese
1 cup grated Mozzarella cheese
1/3 cup ricotta cheese
1 egg
1 Tbsp. chopped parsley
1 egg white, stiffly beaten
2 Tbsp. flour
1/2 tsp. baking powder
1/4 tsp. salt
2 eggs
1 cup milk
1 Tbsp. oil
1 eggplant
1/4 cup oil
Flour for dredging

Preheat oven to 375 degrees. Mix cheeses, 1 egg, and parsley. Fold in stiffly beaten egg white and chill for 2 hours. Sift 2 Tbsp. flour, baking powder and salt; add eggs, milk and 1 Tbsp. oil, and beat until the batter is smooth. Peel eggplant and cut into half-inch slices. Dredge each slice in flour and dip in batter. Fry in oil until lightly browned, and drain on paper towels. Place a spoonful of cheese mixture in center of each slice. Roll up and arrange folded side down in a shallow, buttered baking dish. Bake about 15 minutes in 375 degree oven. When cold, cut into bite-size pieces and serve as appetizers. Can also serve whole and warm as a vegetable.

Barbara Schischa

SPINACH BROWNIES
Can be made ahead and frozen. Simply reheat.

1 cup flour
1 tsp. salt
1 tsp. soda
2 beaten eggs
1 cup milk
1/4 cup melted margarine
1/2 cup chopped onion
1 lb. cheddar cheese, grated
1 pkg. frozen spinach, thawed and
   drained

Mix together flour, salt and soda. Mix eggs, milk and margarine together and add to flour mixture. Then add onion, cheese and spinach. Mix well and place in a greased 8 x 11 pan. Bake at 350 degrees for 30-35 minutes. Cut in squares and serve warm. Yield: 60 brownies by making 6 slices one way and 10 the other. Can be frozen after cooking. If frozen, reheat at 350 for 10 minutes.

Rickey Springs (Mrs. Eli B., Jr.)

SOMERSET SPREAD

1 lb. sharp cheddar cheese, grated
1/2 lb. cream cheese, room
   temperature
1/2 cup full-bodied dry red wine
   (Zinfandel or Petite Sirah)
1/4 cup chopped chives
2 Tbsp. cognac or brandy

Combine all ingredients in large bowl or food processor, until smooth and spreadable. Spoon into crock, cover tightly and chill several hours or overnight. Will last 2 to 3 weeks. Do not freeze. Serve with cocktail rye, crackers or breadsticks.

Frances Breckett (Mrs. Martin L., Jr.)

COCKTAIL MUSHROOMS
A real favorite!

2 lbs. large fresh mushrooms
1 cup butter, melted
3 Tbsp. marjoram
3 tsp. chopped fresh chives
1 to 1-1/2 tsp. salt
sprinkling of fresh ground pepper
1 cup chicken bouillon
1/2 cup dry white wine

Put mushrooms in a casserole. Combine butter with marjoram, chives, salt and pepper. Add bouillon and wine. Stir well and pour over mushrooms. Cover and bake at 350 degrees for 20 minutes. Serves 8 to 10.

Nancy Little (Mrs. T.M.)

MARINATED MUSHROOMS
If possible, use fresh mushrooms.

2/3 cup tarragon vinegar
1/2 cup salad oil
1 medium clove garlic, minced
1 Tbsp. sugar
1-1/2 tsp. salt
dash freshly-ground pepper
2 Tbsp. water
dash bottled hot pepper sauce
1 medium onion, sliced and separated into rings
2 (6 oz.) cans broiled mushroom crowns, drained, or 2 pints fresh mushrooms washed and trimmed

Combine all ingredients except onions and mushrooms. Pour over the onions and mushrooms. Cover and refrigerate for at least 8 hours. Stir several times. Drain and serve as a relish or appetizer.

Virginia Golding (Mrs. John G.)

MUSHROOM CAVIAR

1/2 cup green onions with a bit of the tops, chopped
2 Tbsp. butter
1 cup mushrooms, chopped
1 Tbsp. lemon juice
salt, pepper, dash of Tabasco
dill weed, chopped
1/3 cup sour cream

Saute onions in butter for one minute; add mushrooms, lemon juice, salt, pepper and Tabasco. Saute 4 minutes, stirring occasionally. Remove from heat. Stir in dill and sour cream. Serve with Triscuits or wheat crackers.

Margaret L. Pitts

STUFFED MUSHROOMS
"Low calorie—good with cocktails"

1/2 to 1 lb. fresh mushrooms
1/2 cup diced green pepper
1/2 cup diced onion
3 Tbsp. butter
2 slices white bread
1/2 tsp. salt
1/2 tsp. pepper
1/2 tsp. thyme
1/2 tsp. sage
Parmesan cheese

Wash mushrooms, remove stems and dice, Saute stems, green pepper and onion in butter. Trim crusts from 2 slices of bread and pull into small pieces. Stir into saute mixture. Remove from heat. Add salt, pepper, thyme and sage. Moisten with water if dry. Pack into mushroom caps. Sprinkle with Parmesan cheese and place in buttered pan. Bake for 15 minutes at 350 degrees.

Rickey Springs (Mrs. Eli B., Jr.)

STUFFED MUSHROOMS FROM TULSA
Excellent cocktail fare

Fresh mushrooms
hot sausage, uncooked
Tabasco sauce
Worcestershire sauce
grated Parmesan cheese

Wash and remove stems from mushrooms. Fill each mushroom cap with hot sausage. Place on cookie sheet with sides. Put a dash of Tabasco sauce on each. Put several dashes of Worcestershire sauce on each. Sprinkle generously with Parmesan cheese. Bake each cookie sheet 30 minutes at 325 degrees. Cool and drain. Serve immediately or freeze until needed. Place on cookie sheets and heat in 350 degree oven 8-10 minutes. Serve immediately.

B.J. Miller (Mrs. H.F.,III)

CURRIED CHUTNEY SPREAD
Neat for several Christmas gifts or hostess gifts, prepared in small crystal bowls covered with saran and topped with a bow.

2 8-oz. packages of cream cheese
1/2 cup Major Grey's chutney
1/2 cup chopped almonds, toasted
1 tsp. curry powder
1/2 tsp. dry mustard

Bring cream cheese to room temperature. Mix all ingredients together well. Pack in a crock or Tupperware-covered bowl. Chill. Serve with crackers or use mixture to stuff dates or cut celery. Can be prepared a week ahead. Do not freeze. Yield: 3 cups.

Beverly Michaux (Mrs. Roy)

SPINACH PIE
(Spanakopita)
"Spinach and cheeses at their best"

4 10-oz. pkg. frozen spinach
(chopped)
1 lb. feta cheese
1 lb. cottage cheese
1/2 cup grated Romano cheese
10 eggs
5 Tbsp. fresh parsley (chopped)
7 scallions (chopped)
3 Tbsp. vegetable oil
1-1/2 tsp. dill, chopped
1 tsp. salt (omit if feta is salty)
1/2 tsp. pepper
1 to 1/2 Tbsp. butter, melted and
clarified
16 sheets filo pastry

Thaw spinach—press with paper towels until dry. Place filo in refrigerator to thaw. (Refer to directions on box in using filo.) Mix all remaining ingredients (except butter and filo) with drained spinach until well blended. In buttered 11 x 14 inch baking dish, arrange 9 sheets of filo—each individually buttered with a pastry brush—spread spinach-cheese mixture evenly over filo. Top with 7 more sheets of filo—each individually buttered. Preheat oven to 350 degrees. Cut through top layer of filo into desired serving pieces. Bake for 45 to 60 minutes until lightly brown. Cool and cut through entire mixture before serving. Serves 32.

Aphroula Anderson (Mrs. Jimmie)

ZUCCHINI APPETIZERS

3 cups grated zucchini, unpared,
or 3 cups unpared thinly
sliced zucchini
1 cup Bisquick
1/2 cup finely chopped onion
1/2 cup grated Parmesan cheese
2 Tbsp. snipped parsley
1/2 tsp. salt
1/2 tsp marjoram or oregano
dash black pepper
1 clove garlic, finely chopped
1/2 cup vegetable oil
4 eggs, slightly beaten

Grease a 9 x 13 pan. Mix all ingredients together. Spread in pan. Bake 25 to 30 minutes. Let "set" for 2 or 3 minutes. Cut through with sharp knife into 2 x 1-inch rectangles. Serve warm. May be made ahead and frozen for parties: bake, cut and cool, then spread, not touching, on a flat surface to freeze individually. Pack carefully into freezer container placing a sheet of waxed or foil paper between each layer. Yield: 4 dozen.

Kathleen Boyce (Mrs. Richard N.)
Frances Brackett (Mrs. Martin L., Jr.)

MARINATED SHRIMP

May use a 4 to 5 pound bag of frozen, cooked shrimp from Butler's Seafood Market

4 to 5 lbs. cooked, cleaned shrimp
3 or 4 medium onions, sliced
1 cup tarragon vinegar
2 cups salad oil
1 10-oz. bottle Durkee's Sauce
1 Tbsp. sugar
1 tsp. salt
bay leaves

Layer shrimp, onions, and bay leaves in large glass or ceramic jar or bowl. Mix tarragon vinegar, oil, Durkee's Sauce, sugar and salt. Pour over shrimp, gently stirring and turning jar to coat shrimp. Chill for 24 hours. Drain off some of the marinade to serve. Hors d'oeuvres for up to 30 persons.

Julia Lackey (Mrs. R.S.)

MARINATED SHRIMP

2 lbs. cooked shrimp
1 cup tomato soup
1 cup Wesson oil
3/4 cup vinegar
1 tsp. garlic powder or garlic salt
1/2 tsp. dry mustard
1/2 tsp. Worcestershire sauce
red pepper or paprika to taste
1 onion, sliced
1 lemon, thinly sliced
1 large bay leaf

In a bowl place one layer of shrimp and thinly sliced onions and lemon. Mix remaining ingredients. Pour half of the marinade. Then repeat. Refrigerate until ready to use. Best made at least one day in advance of using. Serves 8 to 10.

Georgia Miller (Mrs. George)

SESAME CHICKEN BITS

These are great to bake ahead and freeze.

1/3 cup sesame seeds
2 cups bread crumbs
4 chicken breast halves, boned and
 skinned
flour
1 to 2 eggs, beaten
1/2 cup melted butter

Mix sesame seeds and bread crumbs together. Cut each chicken breast in about 5 to 7 pieces, depending on size of breasts. Dust chicken pieces with flour, then dip into egg, then sesame and bread crumb mixture. Arrange in single layer on greased baking sheet (or aluminum foil). Pour melted butter over top. Bake at 350 degrees for 15-20 minutes. I always put a sweet and sour sauce in a little dish and pass it with the chicken stacked around it. (I like the yellow sauce better than the red.) Can be frozen. Simply thaw and reheat for 5 minutes. Serves 12.

Rickey Springs (Mrs. Eli B., Jr.)

ORIENTAL CHICKEN WINGS
These freeze well in marinade after they are cooked.

1/2 tsp. salt
1/4 cup soy sauce
1/4 cup apricot nectar
2 Tbsp. sugar
1/4 tsp. Accent
1/2 tsp. ginger
1 clove garlic, minced
5 drops Tabasco
1 tsp. lemon juice
8-12 chicken wings

Cut wing tips off and discard. Cut wings in half, like small drumsticks. Mix remaining ingredients and marinate chicken overnight in refrigerator. Bake 1 hour at 350 degrees in marinade. Serves 6-8.

Linda McAlexander (Mrs. Sam. L.)
Similar recipe submitted by Karen Schwelling (Mrs. L.J.)

BACON-WRAPPED WATER CHESTNUTS

1 8-oz. can water chestnuts
1/4 cup dark rum
2 Tbsp. soy sauce
16 strips bacon

Marinate chestnuts in rum-soy sauce mixture for at least 2 hours. Cut bacon in half and wrap half piece of bacon around a chestnut. Secure with toothpick. Bake at 400 degrees for 20 minutes or until bacon is cooked. Yield: 32 appetizers. Note: May cut large chestnuts in half.

Jean Davis (Mrs. Burton S.,III)

RUMAKI
"This recipe came from Peg Smiler when I took a cooking class from her."

18 water chestnuts, halved
18 chicken livers, halved
18 slices bacon, halved
1 Tbsp. dried onion chips
1 cup soy sauce
1/2 tsp. ginger
1/2 tsp. curry powder

Wrap a piece of water chestnut and half chicken liver together in a strip of bacon. Fasten with a tooth pick. Marinate 6 to 8 hours. Drain, broil until bacon is crisp, about 3 to 4 minutes on each side. Yield: 3 dozen appetizers.

Gensie

GINNY'S HOT CLAM SPREAD

"This tastes too good to be so easy to make."

1 or 2 cans minced clams (6-1/2 oz.), drained
8 oz. cream cheese
1 tsp. Worcestershire sauce
1/2 cup sour cream
2 Tbsp. mayonnaise
1/2 medium onion, chopped
1/2 lb. MILD cheddar cheese, grated

Reserve 1/2 the cheese. Mix all the ingredients except reserved cheese. Place mixture in a pie plate, evenly and top with reserved cheese. Bake at 350 degrees for 20 minutes and serve immediately with Pepperidge Farm Butter Thins (crackers). Makes 4 or 5 cups dip depending on 1 or 2 cans minced clams.

Karen Schwelling (Mrs. L.J.)

PENNY'S CRAB HORS D'OEUVRE

"Looks messy—tastes terrific"

1 8-oz. block cream cheese
1 can white crab meat (6-1/2 oz.) or fresh

Cocktail sauce:
1 cup chili sauce (bottled)
1 Tbsp. lemon juice
2 Tbsp. horseradish, or to taste
1 tsp. Worcestershire sauce
1 dash of Tabasco, or to taste

Slice cream cheese lengthwise. Place 2 halves side by side. Spread crab on top of cream cheese. Pour sauce over all. Serve with crackers on plate with spreaders. The sauce can be prepared ahead. Good with cocktails. Yield: 15 to 20 servings.

Penny Gregory (Mrs. Thomas R.)

CRAB SPREAD

Guests always enjoy this hors d'oeuvre—looks like you worked so hard!

8 oz. cream cheese
2 Tbsp. Worcestershire sauce
1 Tbsp. lemon juice
2 Tbsp. mayonnaise
1/2 onion, chopped
1/4 tsp. garlic salt
1/2 10-oz. bottle chili sauce
1 6-oz. pkg. frozen crabmeat, thawed and drained
parsley for garnish

Mix first 6 ingredients; put in dish and allow to set up in refrigerator. Pour chili sauce over cream cheese mixture. Sprinkle crabmeat on top just before serving. Garnish with parsley. Serve with crackers. Serves 8.

Peggy Hormberg (Mrs. R.H.)

Similar recipe submitted by B.J. Miller (Mrs. H.F.,III)

CRAB PATE
This is always a hit!

1 can cream of mushroom soup
1 envelope unflavored gelatin
3 Tbsp. cold water
3/4 cup mayonnaise
1 8-oz. pkg. cream cheese,
    softened
1 6-1/2 oz. can crabmeat, drained
    and flaked
1 small onion, grated
1 cup finely chopped celery

Heat soup in medium saucepan over low heat; remove from heat. Dissolve gelatin in cold water; add to soup, stirring well. Add next 5 ingredients and mix well. Spoon into oiled 4-cup mold. Chill until firm. Unmold and garnish with parsley sprigs. Serve with assorted crackers. Yield: 4 cups.

Nancy Wohlbruck (Mrs. Everett L.)

SNOW-CAPPED PATE
For that special occasion

1/2 cup chopped onion
1 small clove garlic, crushed
1/4 cup butter
1 lb. chicken livers
2 tsp. all-purpose flour
1/4 tsp. dried crushed thyme
2 dashes pepper
2 Tbsp. dry sherry
2 3-oz. cream cheese, cubed and
    softened
3 Tbsp. milk
1/2 cup (packed) stemmed parsley
    sprigs
1/2 cup pecans

Cook onion and garlic in butter until tender. Add livers; cook, covered, over low heat until no longer pink, about 7-8 minutes. Stir in flour, salt, thyme, and pepper. Add sherry; cook and stir 1 minute. Transfer to blender container; blend until smooth. Mold in small greased bowl. Chill overnight. Unmold. Blend cream cheese and milk until smooth. Spread over mold. Chill until serving time. Chop and mix parsley and nuts. Sprinkle atop pate. Serve with assorted crackers. Prepare 2 days in advance to blend flavors. Do not freeze. Serves 12.

Jean Webb (Mrs. F.A.,III)

HOT CHIPPED BEEF SPREAD

1 8-oz. package cream cheese
2 Tbsp. milk
1 2-1/2 oz. jar chipped beef
dash salt
1/4 cup chopped green pepper
1/2 tsp. garlic powder
2 Tbsp. dry onion flakes
1/4 tsp. pepper
1/2 cup sour cream
1/2 cup chopped pecans

Cream the cream cheese and 2 Tbsp. milk. Stir in small jar of chipped beef. Add a dash of salt. Add green pepper (bell pepper), garlic powder, dry onion flakes, and fold in 1/2 cup sour cream. Pour into small baking dish. Sprinkle with 1/2 cup chopped pecans. Bake in preheated 350 degree oven for 10 minutes. Serve warm with party rye and and crackers.

Libby Morrison (Mrs. Jack)
Janis Rikard (Mrs. William)

DEVILED EGGS WITH CRABMEAT

4 eggs, hard-cooked
1/4 cup crabmeat
3/4 cup Parmesan cheese
1 Tbsp. butter
1-1/2 Tbsp. mayonnaise
1 Tbsp. each: chives and parsley
1/2 tsp. Worcestershire sauce

Split hard-cooked eggs in half, remove yolk. Mash yolk and mix with all ingredients. Stuff eggs with filling. Put small piece of parsley on top. Yield: 8 appetizers.

Jean Davis (Mrs. Burton S.,III)

CRABMEAT/CHEESE MUFFINS
Good to keep bags of these in the freezer ready to pull out for those unexpected times.

6 to 10 muffins, halved, with each half cut into quarters (48-80 pieces)—will depend on how thick mixture is spread on bread pieces:
1 stick butter, softened
1 jar Old English sharp cheddar cheese
1-1/2 tsp. mayonnaise
1 tsp. garlic salt
1 7-oz. can crabmeat

Rinse, drain and pick out shells in crabmeat. Mix crabmeat with other ingredients. Blend well. Spread on muffin quarters. Put quarters on cookie sheet. Freeze quarters on cookie sheets. Remove frozen quarters to plastic bag, seal and store in freezer. When ready to serve, place quarters on cookie sheet and broil until puffed, bubbly, and slightly golden brown. Crabmeat/Cheese muffins MUST be frozen at least 30 minutes before broiling.

B. J. Miller (Mrs. U.F.,III)

Variation: Add a dash of tabasco sauce, shake of parsley.
Suggest leaving muffin halves uncut and serving as sandwiches.

Anne Thrift (Mrs. Charles B.,III)

CRABMEAT IN CHAFING DISH
Nice hot hors d'oeuvre

2 6-1/2 oz. cans of crab meat, drained, rinsed and picked
1 can mushroom soup
1 (4-1/2 oz.) can sliced mushrooms, drained (reserve some liquid)
1 can artichoke hearts
1 cup grated cheddar cheese
1/4 cup sherry
dash of Tabasco

Slice artichoke hearts. Combine all ingredients and heat. Serve hot from chafing dish with melba toast points or patty shells. If mixture seems too thick, add more soup or mushroom liquid. Serves 12.

Ellen Knott (Mrs. B.F.)

CRABMEAT RAMEKINS
A festive way to begin any meal and is absolutely delicious!

1 lb. lump crabmeat
6 pieces bacon
1 tsp. dry mustard
1/2 tsp. paprika
1/2 tsp. celery salt
1/2 tsp. Tabasco
1/2 cup chili sauce
1 tsp. tarragon vinegar
1-1/2 cups mayonnaise

Preheat oven to 400 degrees. Divide crabmeat into seafood shells; top with fried bacon. Blend together all other ingredients. Spoon on top of crabmeat and bacon. Bake until sauce bubbles— about 10 minutes. Serves 6.

Sandy Hamilton (Mrs. C.E.)

OYSTER LOAF
Elegant hors d'oeuvre

2 8-oz. pkg. cream cheese,
  softened
2 3-3/4 oz. cans smoked oysters
1/4 cup milk or cream
2-3 Tbsp. mayonnaise
1 Tbsp. lemon juice
1 Tbsp. Worcestershire sauce
dash Tabasco
salt to taste
garlic powder to taste
chopped parsley
paprika
chopped pecans

Cream the cheese and chop the oysters. Mix all above ingredients except parsley and paprika. Cover and refrigerate for several hours. Form 1 loaf or 2 small ones. Cover with parsley and paprika. Serve with buttery sesame seed crackers. Serves 12-15.

Nancy Crutchfield (Mrs. E.E., Jr.)
Genevieve Cummings (Mrs. T.E.)

STUFFED CLAM SHELLS
Really delicious—get clam shells from seafood market

1 cup crushed Ritz crackers
1-1/2 cups minced clams,
  including liquid
2 tsp. grated Parmesan cheese
1/4 stick melted butter or
  margarine
1 small grated onion
lots of garlic powder

Mix by hand and stuff into clam shells. Cook in preheated 350 degree oven 20 to 25 minutes. Can freeze before or after cooking.

Pat Nesbit (Mrs. W.M.)

HOT DOGS A LA BOURBON
"So easy to prepare"

3/4 cup bourbon
1-1/2 cups brown sugar
1-1/2 cups catsup
1 Tbsp. chopped onion
4 or 5 hot dogs cut in 1-inch pieces

Mix all the ingredients together and cook on medium low heat until the hot dog pieces are coated with the sauce that has cooked down (about an hour). Serve in a chafing dish with toothpicks. Yield: 16 to 20 appetizers.

Arnita Kee

HOT DOGS COOKED IN BEER
"Crock pot is handy when making these"

1 lb. Oscar Meyer all-beef wieners
1 can beer
1/2 cup chili sauce
1/2 cup brown sugar

Cut up wieners into bite-sized pieces. Simmer in beer until beer is gone—1 to 3 hours. Add chili sauce and brown sugar and simmer 30 minutes. Keep warm in fondue pot or crock pot. Use toothpicks for serving. Yield: 32 appetizers.

Joan Kar (Mrs. A.K.)

MINI PIZZA HORS D'OEUVRES
This is an easy "do ahead" recipe—one of those things to keep on hand in your freezer.

1 lb. sausage
1 lb. ground beef
1 lb. Velveeta cheese
1 tsp. basil
1 tsp. oregano
1/4 tsp. garlic powder
1-2 Tbsp. parsley flakes
2 loaves (small round slices) party
  rye bread

Brown meats and drain. Stir in Velveeta until it melts. Add remaining ingredients except bread. Spread on small party rye slices. To freeze: At this point freeze the bread on cookie sheets. When frozen solid, store in bags or container in freezer. Bake at 350 degrees for 15-20 minutes. Yield: approximately 6 dozen.

Yvonne Rayburn (Mrs. C. Richard, Jr.)

PIZZA SMACKS
This recipe is easily cut in half.

1 lb. mild cheddar cheese (diced fine)
2 4-oz. cans chopped mushrooms
1/2 cup Wesson oil
2 medium onions (chopped fine)
2 tsp. oregano
2 tsp. garlic salt
2 4-oz. cans tomato sauce
party rye bread

Mix together all of the above, except rye rounds. Toast rye rounds for 10 minutes at 350 degrees. Spoon mixture on rye rounds and put in oven until cheese melts. Serves many.

Sue Anderson (Mrs. R.D.)

TWO-BITE PIZZA
Great fun for children to make for lunch—or grand as an appetizer!

1 lb. sausage
1 cup onions, chopped
1-1/2 shredded sharp cheese
1/2 cup Parmesan cheese
1-1/2 tsp. oregano
1 tsp. garlic salt
1 can tomato paste (6 oz.)
1 can tomato sauce (8 oz.)
2 cans Pillsbury's flaky biscuits
sliced mozzarella cheese

Simmer sausage until half done. Add onions and cook until both are done. Drain well. Add sharp and Parmesan cheeses, oregano, garlic salt, tomato paste, and sauce. Simmer 20 minutes. Take 12 biscuits from 1 can and separate each biscuit into 4 layers. Place 1 tsp. pizza mixture on top of each. Freeze if desired. When ready to serve put mozzarella cheese on top. Bake on cookie sheet for 10 minutes at 400 degrees.

Anne Thrift (Mrs. Charles B., III)

PARTY SALAMI
A fun thing to make. Most unusual!

4 lbs. of ground beef (maximum fat content 25%)
1/4 cup curing salt (hard to find in Charlotte except in summer—my mother sends it to me from Illinois)
2 Tbsp. liquid smoke
1-1/2 tsp. garlic powder
1-1/2 tsp. ground pepper, or
2 tsp. whole black pepper

Mix above ingredients in large container. Cover and chill for 24 hours (can be left longer). Take used soup can, cut off both ends, put salami mixture into mold and push out. Place logs on broiler pan with a rack and bake in a 225 degree oven for 4 hours. Remove from oven. Pat rolls well with paper towel. Cool slightly. Wrap in foil and refrigerate or freeze. Makes about 3 pounds. Slice thin and serve with cheese and crackers. Makes 5 rolls. Excellent to make and freeze for later.

Donna Rasmussen (Mrs. D.W.)

CONNIE'S WAIKIKI MEATBALLS
Deliciously different meatball recipe

1-1/2 lbs. ground beef, lean
2/3 cup cracker crumbs
1/3 cup minced onions
1 egg
1-1/2 tsp. salt
1/4 tsp. ginger
1/4 cup milk
1 Tbsp. shortening
2 Tbsp. cornstarch
1 can (13-1/2 oz) crushed
    pineapple, drained, reserving
    the juice
1/2 cup brown sugar
1/3 cup vinegar
1 Tbsp. soy sauce
1/3 cup finely chopped green
    pepper

Mix thoroughly beef, crumbs, onions, egg, salt, ginger and milk. Shape into balls. Heat shortening in large skillet; brown and cook. Drain meatballs and wipe skillet. Mix cornstarch and sugar. Stir in pineapple juice, vinegar and soy sauce. Stir until mixture is smooth. Pour into skillet and cook over medium heat, stirring constantly until it thickens and boils. Add pineapple, green pepper, and meatballs. Heat through. If using as a main dish, double sauce recipe and serve over rice. Meatballs may be made ahead and frozen and sauce made the day you wish to serve.

B.J. Miller (Mrs. H.F.,III)

CHEVDA
This is a wonderful "munch" or cocktail nibble, especially for the holidays.

oil for frying
1 Tbsp. sesame seeds
4 Tbsp. coconut
3 oz. raisins
3 oz. peanuts
2 oz. cashew nuts
2 cups rice krispies
1/2 cup corn flakes
1/2 cup shoestring potatoes
1/2 cup Chinese fried noodles
1/2 tsp. turmeric powder
1 tsp. red pepper (or less)
1-1/2 tsp. coriander powder
1-1/2 tsp. cumin powder

Heat oil. Over low heat, carefully brown sesame seeds, coconut and raisins. Add other ingredients and cook briefly, but mix thoroughly. Cool. Store in jars. Makes 4-1/2 cups.

Gensie

HEALTH SNACKS
So good—and an added bonus—good for you

1-1/2 cups peanut butter
1/4 cup carob powder
1/2 lb. chopped almonds (toasted)
1 cup dates or raisins
3 tsp. vanilla
1/2 cup honey

Mix well. Form into balls. Roll each ball in toasted sesame seeds. If dates are used they should be cut in pieces. These may be refrigerated to last longer. Also, they may be frozen.

Margaret L. Pitts

COCKTAIL PECANS
If any are left, store in air-tight container!

4 cups shelled pecan halves
1 - 1-3/8 oz. envelope dried onion
    soup mix
1/4 cup buttery-flavored oil
2 tsp. salt

Toast pecans in shallow roasting pan at 300 degrees in oven 30 minutes. Empty soup mix into plastic bag and crush with a rolling pin. Combine soup mix with oil. Stir in nuts. Return to oven and roast mixture for 15 minutes, stirring often. Remove from oven and spread on paper towel. Sprinkle with salt. Store in air-tight container.

Betty Holland (Mrs. Calvin)

OLD-FASHIONED CARAMEL CORN
Great for parties!

2 cups light brown sugar, firmly
    packed
1/2 cup light corn syrup
1/2 lb. margarine or butter
1/4 tsp. cream of tartar
1 tsp. salt
1 tsp. baking soda
6 quarts popped popcorn

In large saucepan, combine sugar, corn syrup, margarine, cream of tartar and salt. Bring to boil, stirring over medium high heat. Stirring constantly, boil rapidly to hard-ball stage, 260 degrees on candy thermometer (about 5 minutes). Remove from heat. Stir in baking soda quickly but thoroughly; pour immediately over popcorn in large turkey roaster. Stir gently until well coated. Bake at 200 degrees for 1 hour, stirring every 15 minutes. Turn out at once on waxed paper and spread to cool. Break apart and store in airtight container.

Cheryl L. Hosse

*   *   *

Variation: Omit cream of tartar; use 7 to 8 quarts popcorn.

Missy Bridges

SESAME-CHEESE POPCORN

Perfect for the crowd watching football games on TV

1/2 cup melted butter
2 Tbsp. sesame seeds
1 1-1/4 oz.) envelope cheese sauce
  mix
1/2 tsp. salt
4 quarts popped popcorn

Combine butter and sesame seeds in a small saucepan. Heat slowly until butter has melted; set mixture aside. Sprinkle cheese sauce mix and salt over popcorn. Drizzle butter mixture over popcorn, tossing well to coat popcorn evenly.

Del Fox (Mrs. Jerry)

GREATEST GRANOLA

2-1/2 cups uncooked rolled oats
1/2 cup sliced almonds
1/2 cup shredded coconut
1/2 cup sesame seeds
1/2 cup shelled sunflower seeds
1/4 cup flour
1/4 cup instant nonfat dry milk
  solids
1/4 cup wheat germ
2 Tbsp. packed brown sugar
1/2 tsp. ground cinnamon
1/2 cup safflower oil
1/2 cup honey
1/2 tsp. salt
1/2 cup dark raisins

Heat oven to 350 degrees. Combine first ten ingredients in a large bowl. Mix oil, honey and salt in small bowl. Pour honey mixture over oat mixture and combine thoroughly. Spread in 13 x 9 x 2 inch pan. Bake until toasted, 30 to 35 minutes, stirring every 10 minutes. Stir in raisins; bake 10 minutes. Cool in pan on wire rack. Store in airtight container. Makes 6 cups.

Resi Golding

Soups

& sandwiches

Wellborn

ARTICHOKE AND OYSTER SOUP

24 oysters
6 shallots or 1 large onion
4 cloves garlic, minced
1/2 stick butter
2 Tbsp. flour
3 cups scalded milk
2 cups chicken stock
1 15-oz. can artichoke hearts with
    liquid, chopped fine or put in
    food processor
2 Tbsp. parsley
1/2 tsp. thyme
salt and pepper to taste

Brown shallots and garlic lightly in butter. Add flour and cook 3 minutes. Add milk and chicken stock; mix well. Stir in artichoke hearts, parsley, thyme and salt and pepper to taste. Simmer 30 minutes. Add oysters with liquid and cook until oysters curl. Serves 4.

Hilda Hemby (Mrs. T.E., Jr.)

BLACK BEAN SOUP
Boys love this.

1 lb. dried black beans
1 large green pepper, chopped
1 large onion, chopped
5 cloves garlic, minced
1/3 cup olive oil
1/2 cup pimiento-stuffed olives,
    sliced
1/4 cup dry white wine
3 Tbsp. vinegar
1 bay leaf
1 tsp. ground oregano
1/2 tsp. salt
1/2 tsp. pepper
1 tsp. ground cumin

Sort and wash beans. Cover with 2 inches water above beans and soak overnight. Saute green pepper, onion and garlic in olive oil until tender and stir into beans. Add next 8 ingredients, stirring into mixture well. Cover and bring to a boil; reduce heat. Simmer 2-3 hours or until done — add water if needed. Remove and discard bay leaf. Serve over hot cooked rice. Top with cheese, chopped onion, etc. Serves 10. Freezes well.

Betty Holland (Mrs. Calvin)

BROCCOLI BISQUE

Delicious and easy to make a day or two ahead for a dinner party

2 10-oz. pkg. frozen chopped
  broccoli
1 medium onion, quartered
2 13-oz. cans chicken broth
2 Tbsp. margarine
1 to 2 tsp. curry powder
2 Tbsp. lime juice
8 lemon slices
1 Tbsp. chopped chives
1 tsp. salt
dash pepper
1/2 cup sour cream

Place broccoli, broth, onion, margarine, salt, curry powder and pepper into large saucepan. Cook until tender, 8-12 minutes. Place mixture in blender, blend until smooth. Stir in lime juice. Cover and refrigerate for at least 4 hours. Top with a lemon slice, then a spoonful of sour cream and a sprinkling of chives. Serves 8.

Susan Murfee (Mrs. D.G.)

CREAM OF BROCCOLI SOUP

This is my own combination of several recipes and I really recommend it!

2 cups chicken stock
1/3 bunch or 1 cup fresh broccoli,
  chopped and steamed "al
  dente"
1/2 onion, chopped
1/4 cup chopped parsley
salt and freshly-ground pepper to
  taste
1 cup cream (I use half and half)
1 Tbsp. arrowroot

In a large saucepan or Dutch oven with a vegetable steamer rack, steam the broccoli and onion over the broth so that all vegetable juices will be conserved. Save broth in pan and transfer vegetables to food processor bowl or blender; add a little broth and blend. Return to saucepan with other broth and all other ingredients. Heat, stirring. Add arrowroot (or instant mashed potatoes) to thicken to desired consistency. Serve hot. Serves 4.

Nancy Little (Mrs. T.M.)

BEST BROCCOLI SOUP

Everyone who tastes this always wants the recipe.

1-1/2 lbs. broccoli (approx-
    imately), cut up
2 cups water
3/4 cups thinly-sliced celery
1/2 cup chopped onion
2 Tbsp. butter
2 Tbsp. flour
2-1/2 cups water
1 Tbsp. MBT instant chicken
    bouillon
3/4 tsp. salt
1/8 tsp. pepper
dash of ground nutmeg
1/2 cup whipping cream
grated cheese (optional)

Heat 2 cups water to boiling in 3-quart saucepan or Dutch oven. Add broccoli, celery and onion. Cover and cook until tender, about 10 minutes; do not drain. Place broccoli mixture in blender container or food processor; cover and blend until of uniform consistency. Heat butter in 3-quart saucepan over low heat until melted. Stir in flour. Cook, stirring constantly until mixture is smooth and bubbly. Remove from heat; stir in 2-1/2 cups water. Heat to boiling, stirring constantly. Boil and stir 1 minute. Stir in broccoli mixture, bouillon, salt, pepper and nutmeg. Heat just to boiling. Stir in cream; heat but do not boil. Serve with grated cheese. Serves 8. May be frozen.

Virginia Golding (Mrs. John G.)
Linda Miller (Mrs. W.R.)

CARROT SOUP

This is easy with a blender or food processor. Gets raves!

4 medium onions, chopped
    coarsely
4 cups carrots, chopped coarsely
5 Tbsp. butter
4 Tbsp. flour
5 cups beef broth (I use Herb-Ox)
4 whole cloves
3 cups milk
salt, and pepper to taste
nutmeg

Melt butter in 4-quart pot. Saute vegetables until onion is transparent (about 5-10 minutes). Blend in flour and 2 cups beef broth. Mix until smooth. Add rest of broth and cloves. Simmer 30 minutes. Discard the cloves and whirl in blender until pureed, 3/4 cup at a time. Stir in the milk. Heat until hot. Do not boil. Sprinkle with nutmeg. Serves 6.

Dale E. Yaged (Mrs. D.)

QUICK CLAM CHOWDER

1 can minced clams (6-1/2
or 10-1/2 oz.)
1 can condensed clam chowder
(15 oz.)
1 can evaporated milk (13 oz.)
1 can cream of potato soup
(10-3/4 oz.)
1/2 soup can of milk
2 Tbsp. butter
dash in parsley flakes, nutmeg,
salt, and pepper

Mix all together and heat. May sprinkle crumbled bacon on top. Makes five 8-oz. servings. May be frozen.

Wynne McLean (Mrs. Malcolm)

COPYCAT CLAM CHOWDER

One of our ALL-TIME favorite recipes—from a native New Englander

6 slices of bacon
1 cup diced sweet onion
8 oz. bottle of clam juice
3 cups pared and diced potatoes
4 Tbsp. flour
3 cups light cream
1 tsp. salt
pepper to taste
1 cup milk
2 8-oz. cans minced clams

In a large, wide saucepan or Dutch oven, gently fry the bacon until crisp; remove bacon, drain on paper towel and crumble. To the bacon drippings add the onion; fry gently, stirring often, until a rich, dark golden brown. With a slotted spoon remove the onion. Drain the liquid from the clams (reserve the clams) and add to the drippings in the saucepan along with bottled clam juice and the potato. Boil gently, covered, until potato is tender. Gradually stir about a cup of the cream into the flour, keeping smooth; add to the potato mixture with the remaining cream, the drained clams and salt and pepper. Cook over moderately low heat, stirring constantly (try not to let it boil) until thickened. Stir in milk, bacon and onion; heat through. Serves 8 to 10.

Donna Rasmussen (Mrs. D.W.)

Linda Rodman (Mrs. M.L.)

Variation: Pinch of thyme, curry to taste, chives and parsley may be added.

NEW ENGLAND FISH CHOWDER

2 lbs. haddock (or red snapper or
   trout)
2 cups water
2 oz. salt pork, diced
2 onions, sliced
4 large potatoes, peeled and diced
   (the red variety is best)
1 cup celery, chopped
1 bay leaf, crumbled
salt and freshly-ground black
   pepper
1 qt. milk
2 Tbsp. butter

Simmer haddock in water for 15 minutes. (Cooking time should be reduced when using substitute fish because haddock has firmer texture and takes longer to cook.) Drain fish, reserving broth. Remove bones from fish and cut into bite-size pieces. Saute diced salt pork until crisp. Remove from pan and set aside. Saute onions in pork fat until golden brown. Add fish, potatoes, celery, bay leaf, salt and freshly-ground black pepper. Pour in reserved fish broth plus enough boiling water to make 3 cups of liquid. Simmer for 30 minutes. Stir in milk and butter, and simmer for 5 more minutes. Adjust seasonings. Add diced salt pork. Serves 6.

Gensie

SHE-CRAB SOUP

This goes well with a spinach salad and hard rolls.

1 stick butter (do not substitute
   margarine)
1 lb. king crab meat
3 or 4 onions, finely chopped
8 drops Tabasco
1/2 tsp. MSG
1 tsp. salt, pepper to taste
1 tsp. nutmeg
5 tsp. paprika
1/4 cup flour
2 quarts half and half

Melt butter over low heat. Saute onions until tender but not brown. Add crab meat and saute with onions for a few minutes. Add Tabasco, MSG, salt and pepper, nutmeg and paprika and mix well. Mix flour and half and half, then add to crab meat mixture, stirring constantly. Bring to a boil and serve at once. Serves 8.

Sue Ellen Biswell (Mrs. C.D.)

ERMA'S CREOLE GUMBO
From a New Orleans Creole cook

1/2 cup butter
4 small onions
1/4 cup flour
1/2 lb. okra, sliced
2-1/2 cups tomatoes
2 lbs. shrimp, or 1 lb. shrimp and
 1 lb. crab meat
2 qts. chicken broth (can be made
 with bouillon cubes)
salt, pepper, cayenne pepper to
 taste
bay leaf
parsley, hot sauce such as Tabasco

Brown chopped onions in melted butter. Stir in flour until smooth and lightly browned (this is the roux). Add okra, tomatoes, bay leaf, broth, salt and peppers. Bring mixture to a boil, stiring constantly. Simmer for 1 hour. Add shrimp and cook for 15 to 20 minutes. Serve in soup bowls over cooked rice. Garnish with parsley. Pass hot sauce. Serves 6.

Shirley Snead (Mrs. Henry T.)

SEAFOOD GUMBO

1/2 cup chopped onions
1 cup chopped celery
1/2 stick butter
6 cups chicken broth
1 pkg. frozen chopped okra
1 pound shelled, deveined shrimp
 (fresh or frozen, raw or
 cooked)
1 pound crab meat (fresh or
 frozen
1 pint oysters
salt and pepper
2 Tbsp. chopped parlsey
cooked rice

Saute 1/2 cup chopped onions and 1 cup chopped celery in 1/2 stick butter until clear. Add six cups chicken broth and one pkg. frozen chopped okra. Bring to a boil and simmer 10 minutes. Add the shrimp, crab meat and oysters (drained). Bring to a boil and simmer 10 minutes. Taste and adjust seasonings. Add salt and pepper to taste and 2 Tbsp. parsley. (Don't let seafood cook a long time—this toughens it.) If you are making this ahead of time, cook as directed, remove from heat and reheat at serving time.) Ladle gumbo into large flat soup bowls and put 1/2 cup cooked rice in middle of bowl. It's great with crusty French bread and butter or corn muffins. A glass of cold beer or a chilled glass of a dry white wine goes nicely with this gumbo. Serves 6.

Gayanne Mraz

CORN SOUP
Good soup! So easy!

2 (17 oz.) cans cream-style corn
1/2-1 cup half-and-half (depending on thickness desired)
1 small onion, chopped
salt and pepper
1 Tbsp. butter

Blend ingredients in blender. Place mixture in double boiler. Add 1 Tbsp. butter and heat thoroughly. Serves 3.

Peggy Buchanan (Mrs. D. Douglas)

CUCUMBER SOUP

3 cucumbers, peeled, seeded and coarsely chopped
1/2 cup chopped onions
1 clove garlic, minced
2 cups chicken broth
2 cups sour cream
3 Tbs. white wine vinegar
salt and white pepper to taste
garnishes

Place cucumbers, onions, garlic and chicken broth in blender or food processor. Process until well blended. Place cucumber mixture in large container and stir in sour cream, vinegar, salt and white pepper. Chill. Serve with following garnishes of your choice: 1 hard-cooked egg, chopped; 1 tomato, diced; 1 avocado, diced; green onions, chopped; one cup croutons.

Virginia Golding (Mrs. John G.)

EASY, MAKE-AHEAD GAZPACHO
(Spanish Cold Soup) Make in blender

1 clove garlic
1/2 small onion, sliced
1/2 green pepper, seeded and sliced
3 ripe tomatoes, quartered, or 1 16-oz. can of tomatoes
1 small cucumber, peeled, sliced and seeded
1 tsp. salt
1/4 tsp. pepper
2 Tbsp. olive oil
3 Tbsp. wine vinegar
1/2 cup ice water or a few ice cubes
croutons
sour cream

Put all ingredients into blender container, except croutons and sour cream. Cover and blend for 3 seconds, or until the last slice of cucumber is pulled down into cutting blades. Chill in refrigerator, or pour into soup bowls and serve with an ice cube in center of each serving. Serve with toasted croutons. A spoon of sour cream adds an extra pleasure for variety. Serves 6.

Penelope (Penny) Gregory (Mrs. Thomas R.)

GAZPACHO

1 cup chopped, peeled tomato
1 cup finely chopped green pepper
1 cup diced celery
1 cup diced cucumber
1/4 cup minced green onion
2 Tbsp. parsley flakes
1 tsp. chives
1 tsp. fresh chopped basil
1 small clove garlic, minced
1/4 cup red wine vinegar

1/4 cup Bertolli olive oil
1 tsp. salt
1 tsp. pepper
1 tsp. Worcestershire sauce
2 cups tomato juice
1 tsp. sugar
1/8 tsp. Tabasco sauce
1 tsp. lemon juice (optional)
sour cream (optional

Mix all ingredients together and chill. Top with sour cream. Yield: 6 servings.

The Committee

LENTIL SOUP

1 lb. dried lentils
1/4 lb. bacon, diced
2 medium onions, thinly sliced
2 carrots, scraped and thinly sliced
1 cup celery, thinly sliced
2 bay leaves
1/4 tsp. dried thyme
salt and pepper to taste
2 qts. water
1 large potato, peeled and grated
1 meaty ham bone

Soak lentils overnight in plenty of water to cover. Drain. In a large kettle saute bacon, onions and carrots until onions are golden. Add the drained lentils, celery, bay leaves, thyme, salt, pepper and the 2 quarts of water. Add the grated potato and the ham bone. Cover and simmer for 3 or 4 hours. Discard bay leaves. Cut meat from ham bone and return to kettle. Adjust seasonings, Reheat, if necessary. Serves 6 to 8.

Gensie

DIET MUSHROOM SOUP

Make this when you are in a hurry, and on a diet! About 20 calories per serving

1 can Campbell's beef bouillon
    soup
1/4 cup spring onions, or 1 small
    onion
4 or 6 fresh mushrooms or 4 oz.
    can chopped or sliced
season: pepper to taste (careful!)
3/4 cup water

Chop onions and slice mushrooms and boil in 1/4 cup bouillon soup in a 1-1/2 quart saucepan for 2 or 3 minutes. Add rest of soup and water and seasoning pepper. Serves 4.

Peggy Young (Mrs. John A.)

FRENCH ONION SOUP

This soup is good for an evening meal.

1/2 cup butter
7 cups thinly sliced onions
3 Tbsp. plain flour
salt to taste if needed
1/2 tsp. black pepper
grated Parmesan cheese
2 cans of consomme
1 can beef broth
2 cans of water
6 thick slices of French bread,
   toasted and very dry
6 thin slices of Swiss cheese or
   Gruyere cheese

Melt butter, add the onions and saute over very low heat, stirring occasionally for 20 minutes. Add the flour and mix until smooth. Add the stock, stirring constantly. Add the pepper, cover and cook over low heat for 30 minutes. Add salt now, if needed. Grate or break pieces of cheese to cover bottom of each oven-proof soup bowl, pour soup over it, place the toasted bread on top and cover with Parmesan cheese. Place in a 375 degree oven for 5 minutes, then under the broiler for a minute to brown cheese. Soup can be made a day or two before serving. Serves 6.

Carolyn Bailey (Mrs. J.M.)

ONION SOUP

This is so easy, but tastes like you have been cooking all day.

1 box (2 packages) Lipton Onion
   Soup
1 package brown gravy mix
2 quarts plus 2 cups boiling water
3 or 4 red onions, thinly sliced
5 Tbsp. butter
1 loaf French bread, cubed
6 oz. Monterey Jack cheese,
   shredded
6 oz. Mozzarella cheese,
   shredded

Mix water with onion soup and gravy mix. Saute onions in 3 Tbsp. butter. Add onions to soup, saving butter, and add 2 Tbsp. butter. Slice and cube French bread, adding this to melted butter. Brown bread in hot oven until crisp. To serve, put a little of both cheeses and some bread cubes in soup bowl, pour hot soup over this. Stir to melt cheese. This serves 8.

Linda Miller (Mrs. W.R.)

POTAGE ESAU

This recipe for a hearty soup was inspired by the story of Esau in the Bible "Then Jacob gave Esau bread and pottage of lentils"

—Genesis 25:34

4 Tbsp. chopped salt pork
1 cup finely chopped onion
1 tsp. chopped garlic
1 lb. dried lentils
1/2 cup raw rice
11 cups beef broth, fresh or canned
salt, if desired
freshly ground pepper
1 bay leaf
1 cup heavy cream
2 Tbsp. butter

Place pork fat in pot and cook briefly to render but not brown the fat. Add onion and cook slowly, stirring frequently, about 5 minutes. Add garlic and lentils and stir. Add the rice and broth. Add salt and pepper to taste, and bay leaf. Bring to a boil and simmer uncovered about 45 minutes or until lentils are tender. Scoop out one cup of lentils and set aside. Put the soup through a food mill or sieve to remove the outer skin of the lentils. Then blend the puree of lentils in an electric blender until smooth. (Do this in small batches.) As the soup is blended, return to the pot and add the reserved cup of lentils. Bring to a boil. Add the cream and return to a simmer. Swirl in butter. Serve piping hot. 8-10 servings.

Gensie

HIGH-PROTEIN SOUP

This is almost a meal in itself and is nice to have following a game at school—when everything needs to be done ahead!

8 cups chicken or turkey broth
    (preferably home made)
3/4 cup dried lentils
3/4 cup dried garbanzo beans
    (soaked overnight)
1/2 cup brown rice
3/4 cup chopped celery, carrots,
    and green onions (tops, too)
2 cups canned tomatoes or equi-
    valent fresh
2 Tbsp. lemon juice
1 Tbsp. vinegar
2 bay leaves
1 tsp. basil
1 garlic clove, minced
salt and pepper to taste

Cook garbanzo beans in broth (with bay leaves) for about 45 minutes. Add other vegetables, lentils, rice and seasonings. Bring to a slow boil and cook until rice is done—about 45 minutes to 1 hour more. If it becomes too thick, add a little water. Freezes well. 5-6 servings.

Anna Stanley (Mrs. V.E., Jr.)

PUMPKIN SOUP

2 Tbsp. butter
2 Tbsp. minced onion
2 Tbsp. flour
1/2 tsp. paprika
1/4 tsp. nutmeg
1 can (13-3/4 oz.) chicken broth
(1-3/4 cups)
2 cups milk
1 cup cooked pumpkin
1 egg yolk
1 cup heavy cream
2 to 3 Tbsp. dry sherry
garnish: toasted pumpkin seeds

Melt butter and saute onion until transparent. Blend in flour, paprika and nutmeg. Gradually add chicken broth and milk. Cook, stirring, until soup thickens and comes to a boil. Stir in the pumpkin and transfer the soup to the top of a double boiler. Cook over water for about 25 minutes. Beat egg yolk with heavy cream in a bowl. Gradually beat a small amount of the hot soup into the egg mixture, and pour back into the remaining soup. Stir in sherry. Serve either hot or thoroughly chilled, garnished with toasted pumpkin seeds. Serves 6.

Virginia Golding (Mrs. John G.)

SAUSAGE-BEAN CHOWDER

Great for a winter supper

1lb. bulk hot pork sausage
2 (16 oz.) cans kidney beans,
undrained
2 (14-1/2 oz.) cans stewed
tomatoes, undrained
2 cups tomato juice
1 large onion, chopped
1 bay leaf
1 tsp. salt
1/2 tsp. garlic salt
1/2 tsp. chili powder
1/2 tsp. thyme
1/4 tsp. pepper
1 cup whole kernel corn
1 stalk celery, chopped
1 green pepper, chopped

Brown sausage, drain. Combine all ingredients in large kettle. Simmer covered for 1 to 2 hours. Remove bay leaf. Serves 10 to 12.
Variation: Can substitute 1 to 2 cups diced potatoes for 1 cup whole kernel corn and omit chili powder.

Betty Holland (Mrs. Calvin)

Ellen Knott (Mrs. B.F.)

SPINACH SOUP

Very quick and easy, and a favorite of my children. Also good for bridge luncheon.

1 10-oz. pkg. frozen chopped
   spinach, or fresh spinach
1/4 cup onions, chopped
5 fresh mushrooms, sliced or
   chopped (optional)
1 Tbsp. butter
1 10-3/4 oz. can Campbell's
   chicken broth with 1/2 can
   water
1/2 to 3/4 cup milk
1/8 tsp seasoning salt
1/2 tsp. dried chopped parsley
salt to taste

Saute onions in butter. Cook spinach according to directions, or cook fresh spinach just until limp. (Can saute mushrooms with onions, just until tender.) To the onions add cooked spinach and can of broth with water. Add milk, including spinach broth. Add seasonings and heat to boiling point. Do not boil. 4 servings.

Peggy Young (Mrs. John A.)

TOMATO-CUCUMBER-AVOCADO BISQUE

This is SO Good—do not omit avocado

4 Tbsp. butter
4 Tbsp. flour
1 large onion, chopped
4 cups tomatoes, peeled and
   chopped
4 cups cucumber, peeled and
   chopped
4 cups chicken broth
1 ripe avocado, peeled and diced
salt and freshly-ground pepper
1 cup heavy cream (optional)

Melt butter in saucepan. Add onion and stir until transparent. Blend in the flour until smooth. Add tomatoes and cucumbers, whisking rapidly. When well blended, add chicken broth and seasoning. Simmer 30 minutes. Pour into blender container and blend until smooth. If it is to be served cold, strain the soup. If served hot, return to stove and heat. Add diced avocado. Also add the cream if you desire. 8 servings.

Virginia Golding (Mrs. John G.)

VEGETABLE SOUP

Just vegetables, and what makes this a little different is the yellow turnip or rutabaga.

2 large onions, chopped, and
    sauteed
1/4 lb. butter
4 large carrots, sliced
1 small, yellow turnip, cubed
6 large stalks celery, thinly sliced
4 large red potatoes, cubed
6 sprigs parsley, finely chopped
1 small bay leaf
1/4 tsp. thyme
1 Tbsp. salt
1/4 tsp. freshly ground pepper
3 quarts water

Saute onions in butter. Add to all the other ingredients in a soup kettle and simmer 1-1/2 hours. Serves many!

Gensie

MY VEGETABLE SOUP

2 pounds lean ground round
2 29-oz. cans tomatoes (not whole)
3 to 4 tomato cans of water
1 package frozen or fresh baby
    lima beans
1 package frozen or fresh corn
6 to 8 carrots, scraped and sliced
2 or 3 Idaho potatoes, peeled and
    diced
1 large onion, chopped
1 Tbsp. salt (or more to taste)
1 to 2 tsp. black pepper
1 tsp. sugar
1/2 cup milk (or more)
1 cup coarsely shredded cabbage
    (optional)

Bring tomatoes and water to a boil in a Dutch oven or very large, heavy container. (May divide base and make it in two containers.) Keep heat on medium-high and add ground round, dropping it in a little at a time at different places over rolling surface of tomato mixture. Simmer for 5 minutes after adding salt, pepper, and sugar. Add lima beans, corn, carrots, potatoes and onions. Simmer on medium-low until carrots are tender. At end of cooking time add cabbage and cook until cabbage is clear and tender. Turn off heat and when soup mixture has stopped simmering, add milk, stirring well to blend. Serves many. Can freeze for future use. Best the second day after flavors have blender together.
Note: Sugar and milk add flavor and cut the sharp, acid taste. May omit cabbage according to personal preference.

Ellen Knott (Mrs. B. F.)

COLD OR FROZEN ZUCCHINI SOUP

2 Tbsp. olive oil
2 Tbsp. butter
2 onions, thinly sliced
1 clove garlic, minced
6 small or 3 medium zucchini,
    sliced
5 cups chicken broth
2 Tbsp. mixed fresh herbs, finely
    chopped (parsley, chives,
    oregano, basil, dill) or
2 or 3 Tsp. lemon juice
salt and pepper to taste.

Heat oil and butter in a large pot. Add onion and garlic and cook over low heat about 10 minutes. Do not allow to turn brown. Add zucchini and continue cooking five minutes longer, stirring occasionally. Add chicken broth and simmer, covered, for 15 minutes or until squash is just tender. Puree in blender or food processor. Add herbs, lemon juice, salt and pepper. Chill or freeze as desired. Serve cold. 6-8 servings.

Beverly Nance (Mrs. James)

ETTA'S TOMATO SOUP

1/2 stick butter, no substitute
1/4 cup fresh olive oil (Bertolli)
2 garlic cloves put through press
    (use only part that goes
    through press)
1 cup chopped onion
1/2 tsp. dried basil
2-1/2 lbs. (minimum) fresh
    tomatoes, cored and pureed in
    food processor, or 1 lb. 12 oz.
    can plus 16 oz. can
    Contadino's tomatoes
3 cups College Inn chicken broth
1/4 cup freshly grated real Italian
    Parmesan cheese
salt and pepper to taste
1/2 cup sour cream (optional)
1/2 cup whipping cream (optional)
sliced French bread (optional)
Gruyere cheese, grated (optional)

In heavy skillet, saute garlic and onions in melted butter plus oil until soft. Add tomatoes, basil and chicken stock. Simmer 25 to 30 minutes. Add Parmesan cheese and let melt. Stir and cool for a few minutes, then pour by small batches into food processor and puree. This soup is great at this point, but in the French manner, it is garnished with Creme Fraiche: Mix 1/2 cup sour cream and 1/2 cup whipping cream, unwhipped, into a small bowl; let this ferment outside refrigerator 3 to 4 hours. Refrigerate. Add a dollop to each bowl when serving. I have also served this soup garnished with a slice of French bread (dried in oven) plus grated Gruyere cheese on top— like onion soup. Serves 3 to 4.

Julia Wade (Mrs. Hamlin)

RAISIN SANDWICH SPREAD
Try this spread with peanut butter instead of jelly—you'll like it!

1 cup chopped raisins
1 cup sugar
1 cup mayonnaise
1 egg
1 cup chopped nuts (optional)
juice of 1 lemon

Place all ingredients in top of double boiler. Cook until thick and smooth. Keep refrigerated. Makes about 1 quart.

Edna E. Sewell (Mrs. R.P.)

SWEET SANDWICH SPREAD
Delicious for a garden party or tea menu

2 cups chopped dates (or 1 cup
    dates and 1 cup chopped
    raisins)
1 small can crushed pineapple
24 large marshmallows
juice of 1 lemon
1/2 cup mayonnaise
1 cup finely chopped nuts

Put chopped dates, pineapple, marshmallows and lemon juice in double boiler. Heat, stirring constantly until marshmallows are melted. Cool. Stir in mayonnaise and chopped nuts. Mix 2 or 3 days ahead and keep refrigerated. Spread sandwiches the night before and keep covered in refrigerator. Makes about 1 quart.

Edna E. Sewell (Mrs. R.P.)

TEA PARTY SANDWICHES
"These are always served at the Meredith alumni tea."

1 8-oz. cream cheese, softened
1 3-oz. cream cheese, softened
4 Tbsp. milk
1 Tbsp. Worcestershire sauce
12 oz. crumbled cooked bacon
1 loaf white sandwich bread
1 loaf "autumn grain" type
    sandwich bread
pimiento-stuffed olives for garnish

Combine first five ingredients. Spread mixture on white bread slice. Top with a slice of brown bread. Cut off crusts. Cut into thirds. Top each sandwich with a slice of olive. These can be made a day ahead and refrigerated. Be sure to cover with a damp paper towel. I have frozen these but they are not quite as good as when freshly made. Makes 100 finger sandwiches.

Jean Webb (Mrs. F.A., III)

HAM AND POPPY SEED DELIGHTS
Jeannie's friends requested this recipe.

1/2 lb. butter, softened
3 Tbsp. prepared mustard
3 Tbsp. poppy seeds
1 tsp. Worcestershire sauce
1 medium onion, finely diced
sliced boiled ham
processed Swiss cheese or
natural Swiss cheese
3 pkg. Pepperidge Farm Party
    Rolls

Combine first 5 ingredients. Horizontally slice all 20 rolls at a time, leaving them attached. Spread both sliced sides of rolls with the butter-poppy-seed mixture. Put 1 layer of ham and 1 layer of cheese between rolls, cutting ham and cheese to fit as necessary. Another layer of ham may be added as desired if ham is sliced very thinly. Separate rolls by slicing with a bread knife or other sharp knife. Place on a cookie sheet and bake 10 to 12 minutes at 400 degrees. Makes 60 small sandwiches or appetizers. May be prepared ahead and refrigerated, or frozen, for a short period of time before baking.

Virginia Golding (Mrs. John G.)

HEARTHSIDE SANDWICH LOAF

1 - 1-lb. 2 oz.loaf French bread
1/2 cup butter, softened
1/3 cup minced onion
3 Tbsp. mustard
1 Tbsp. poppy seeds
2 tsp. lemon juice
few drops Tabasco
12 slices Swiss cheese
6 slices bacon

Make diagonal cuts in bread almost to bottom. Place on greased cookie sheet. Combine butter, onion, mustard, poppy seeds, lemon juice, Tabasco, and blend. Reserve about 3 Tbsp. for later use. Spread remaining mixture on cut surfaces of bread. Place cheese slices in bread cuts so they "poke out" at top. Spread reserved mixture on top and sides of loaf. Bake 30 minutes at 350 degrees F. Cook bacon and lay slices on top of loaf when done. Remove loaf and cut through to serve. 4 to 6 servings.

Joyce W. Summerville

JUMBO BURGERS

2 lbs. ground beef (1 lb. is four
    patties)
1 cup grated Cheddar cheese
3/4 cup chopped onion

Mix all ingredients in large mixing bowl. Roll into large patties. Place patties on broiler pan and broil 5 minutes on one side. Turn and broil another 5 minutes or until done. Serve on buttered hamburger rolls.

Meredith McLeod

HAMBURGER BENEDICT

All you need is a salad for a super supper.

1 lb. ground round steak (a must)
4 slices bread, crusts removed, or
4 English muffin halves
butter
1 tomato (firm), peeled and diced
2 cups Bearnaise sauce

Saute bread in butter until each side is just browned. Place in warming oven with the diced tomato. Grill or broil round steak, which has been shaped into 4 patties, to desired doneness. Keep warm while preparing Bearnaise sauce. Quickly place bread on a heated platter; top with diced tomato and meat patties and pour sauce over all. Serves 4.

BEARNAISE SAUCE FOR HAMBURGER BENEDICT

6 egg yolks
4 Tbsp. lemon juice
1 cup melted butter
4 Tbsp. hot water
1/2 tsp. salt
1/8 tsp. cayenne pepper
3 tsp. finely chopped parsley
2 tsp. finely chopped tarragon

In top of double boiler over hot water, beat egg yolks with a wooden spoon until smooth. Add remaining ingredients and beat until sauce thickens. Spoon over patties.

Ellen Knott (Mrs. B.F.)

GLORIFIED HAMBURGERS

"Good with or without a bun"

1-1/2 lbs. lean ground beef
1 cup sour cream
1 Tbsp. instant onion
1-1/2 tsp. salt
1-1/4 cups corn flake crumbs

Mix. May be grilled over charcoal or any other way you cook hamburgers.

Margaret Pitts

BURGUNDY BURGERS

1 cup soft bread crumbs
3/4 cup burgundy wine
2 lbs. lean ground beef
1 4-oz. can mushrooms (stems and
   pieces)
2 tsp. onion salt
1 tsp. dry mustard
1 tsp. Worcestershire sauce
1/4 tsp. garlic powder
1/4 tsp. pepper

Grill and serve on buns. Makes 8 burgers.

Pat Vinroot (Mrs. Robert)

SPOONBURGERS

"Your family will never know about the okra. Good for 'crowds' and teenagers."

2 lbs. ground beef
2 Tbsp. fat
2/3 cup chopped onion
2 Tbsp. catsup
1 Tbsp. prepared mustard
1 tsp. salt
1/8 tsp. pepper
2 cans condensed chicken gumbo
    soup, undiluted
8 hamburger buns

Brown meat in hot fat in skillet over low direct heat. Add onion and continue cooking until onion is nicely browned. Stir in remaining ingredients, except buns. Place cover on skillet and simmer over direct heat for 30 minutes. Spoon over buns. Serves 8.

Ellen Knott (Mrs. B.F.)

SLOPPY JOES

"Good with baked potato and salad for a simple summer entree."

1 lb. ground beef
1 cup Kraft Barbeque Sauce
1/4 cup chopped onion
1/4 cup chopped green pepper
hamburger buns
Velveeta cheese

Brown ground beef. Stir in barbeque sauce, onion, and green pepper and cook, covered, for 15 minutes. Spoon on bottom half of buns. Top with a slice of Velveeta and broil until cheese is melted. Serves 4.

Max Ussery

BARBECUED BEEF SANDWICHES

Good Saturday lunch—can be prepared ahead and reheated.

1-1/2 lbs. stewing beef
1 cup ketchup
3 tsp. mustard
3 Tbsp. vinegar
5 tsp. Worcestershire sauce
1 diced onion
1/8 cup sugar
hamburger buns

Cook beef 2-1/2 hours in 325-350 degree oven, adding water as needed. When tender, shred and add remaining ingredients. Serve on hamburger rolls. Serves 4.

Liz Lowry (Mrs. W.F.)

ROSEMARY'S OPEN-FACE STEAK SANDWICHES
"This recipe comes from the best cook I know."

flank steak
1/3 cup oil
2/3 cup beer
1/2 tsp. garlic powder
salt and pepper
French bread, sliced and toasted
onion slices
butter
paprika
1 cup sour cream
horseradish, to taste

Pierce steak with fork. Marinate for several hours in oil, beer, garlic powder, salt and pepper. Half way through marinating time, turn steak and pierce again. Broil steak and slice thin. Place on French bread slices. Top with onion slices which have been sauteed in butter and a good amount of paprika. Combine sour cream and horseradish. Top onions and meat with sauce.

Peggy Buchanan (Mrs. D. Douglas)

TURKEY DEVONSHIRE
Similar to the "Hot Dorsey"—doubles or triples nicely

4 slices buttered toast
sliced turkey
3 Tbsp. butter
2 Tbsp. flour
1/4 tsp. salt
1/4 tsp. dry mustard
dash cayenne
1 cup milk
1-1/2 cups grated Cheddar cheese
1/4 lb. bacon, cooked
paprika

Butter individual shallow baking dishes or oven-proof plates. In each, put buttered toast cut to fit. Arrange turkey on toast. In saucepan, make cheese sauce by melting butter, adding flour and cooking until bubbly. Add salt, mustard and cayenne. Remove from heat and blend in milk. Stir in 1 cup of grated cheese and return to low heat, stirring until cheese melts. Pour sauce over turkey. Sprinkle with remaining cheese and paprika. Dot with butter and bake 15 minutes. Garnish with strips of bacon; put under broiler just long enough to brown lightly. Serves 2.

Ellen Knott (Mrs. B.F.)

HAM FINGERS
A sandwich that men like. Good for lunch boxes and picnics as well as for party menus.

1 cup ground cooked ham
1/2 cup shredded natural Swiss
    cheese
3 Tbsp. mayonnaise
1/2 tsp. prepared mustard
20 slices (1 loaf) raisin bread
soft butter or margarine

Mix ham, cheese, mayonnaise and mustard together. Spread slices of raisin bread with soft butter or margarine. Spread half the slices with ham mixture; top with remaining bread. Trim crusts. Cut each into 3 "fingers." Cover with plastic wrap or aluminum foil. Chill. Yield 30 finger sandwiches.

Edna E. Sewell (Mrs. R.P.)

CRAB ON RUSK

1/2 stick butter
1 large package Philly cream cheese
1 Tbsp. minced onion
1 Tbsp. lemon juice
1 Tbsp. Worcestershire sauce
1 can crab meat
6 cheese slices
6 tomato slices
6 bacon slices, cooked slightly
6 Holland rusks

Mix together first five ingredients. Blend in can of crab meat. Place on Holland rusks in this order: crab mixture, a slice of sharp cheese, a slice of tomato, and a piece of slightly cooked bacon. Put in 325 degree oven for 20 minutes. Serves 6.

Susan Trotter (Mrs. George)

Betty Dale Archer (Mrs. John M., III)

OYSTER SANDWICH
Fast and easy

1 loaf French bread, or
4-5 French rolls
1 pt. or more oysters, floured
2 firm tomatoes, sliced
6-8 bacon slices
1/3 cup mayonnasie
2 Tbsp. horseradish
salt and pepper to taste

Slice French bread lengthwise and remove some of the center of the bread. In a frying pan cook bacon until crisp. Remove bacon; do not wash pan. Then cook floured oysters. Remove these and fry tomatoes. Layer French bread in above order and top with mayonnaise/horseradish mixture. Add salt and pepper. Cover with other half of French bread. Cut into slices. Serves 4-5. Can be made ahead and reheated.

Georgia Miller (Mrs. George J.)

FRENCH-TOASTED SALMON SANDWICH
"With a slice of tomato and a few potato chips, it's a festive lunch!"

6 slices white bread
1 7-oz. can pink salmon
2 to 3 Tbsp. mayonnaise
1/2 tsp. onion juice, or dash of onion salt
1 egg
1/2 cup milk
Crisco for frying

In a pie plate mix egg and milk and juice from salmon, and set aside. Crumble salmon, removing small bones and black skin. Combine mayonnaise, onion and fish and spread on 3 slices of bread. Cover with 3 remaining slices. Dip each sandwich quickly into egg/milk mixture and fry on each side until lightly brown. Serves 3.

Margaret Van Sciver (Mrs. Richard)

VEGETABLE SANDWICHES

"Good for any party occasion"

2 large carrots
2 stalks celery
2 cucumbers
1 small onion
1 pint Kraft mayonnaise
1 Tbsp. lemon juice
1 envelope unflavored gelatin
1/4 cup water
bread

Finely chop carrots, celery, cucumbers and onion. Mix vegetables in large bowl. Dissolve gelatin in water in top of double boiler over cold water. Turn on heat and let water in lower pan boil for about 2 minutes, stirring constantly. (Mixture will become thick, then thin again.) Combine mayonnaise, lemon juice, and gelatin mixture with vegetables and mix well. Refrigerate at least 24 hours. Cut each bread slice into 3 long pieces. Spread filling on and top with another bread slice. Yield: about 80 finger sandwiches. Can be made ahead of time and stored, well wrapped, in refrigerator until serving time.

Carolyn Tomlin (Mrs. M.G.)

VEGETABLE SANDWICH MIX

"Can serve on crackers, too"

2 small onions, quartered
1 green pepper, quartered
2 medium cucumbers, peeled and
    quartered
2 carrots, scraped and coarsely
    chopped
1 cup mayonnaise (Duke's)
2 pkg. Knox unflavored gelatin
salt and pepper to taste

Put onions, green pepper and cucumbers into blender. Cover with water. Turn on, then off quickly several times. Add chopped carrots. Blend by turning blender on and off quickly several times. Drain water off vegetables, being certain to reserve 3-4 Tbsp. of the liquid. Put the reserved liquid in a saucepan and heat well but do not boil. Put the gelatin in a cup and spoon in just enough of the heated liquid to dissolve, then pour into rest of hot liquid in saucepan. Stir for 2 minutes until completely dissolved. Add to vegetable mixture along with 1 cup of Duke's mayonnaise and salt and pepper to taste. Mix well. Refrigerate for 3 hours before serving as sandwich spread or on crackers. Yield: 2 pints.

Sara Lowe (Mrs. F. Robbins)

PITA SANDWICHES

1 lb. lean ground beef
1 large onion, chopped
2 cloves garlic, minced
1 Tbsp. vegetable oil
1 16-oz. can tomatoes
1/2 cup stuffed sliced olives
2 Tbsp. chopped almonds
1 tsp. capers
1 tsp. chili powder
1/4 tsp. salt
1/8 tsp. pepper
4 pita or pocket bread

In large skillet cook and stir beef, onion and garlic in oil until meat loses its color. Add remaining ingredients except pita bread. Reduce heat and simmer 30 minutes, stirring occasionally. Cut a large slit in side of pita breads; fill with meat mixture. Serves 4.

Sophie Godwin

HOT DOGS CREOLE

2 Tbsp. margarine
1/4 cup chopped onion
1/4 cup chopped celery
1/3 cup Madeira wine
2 tsp. Dijon mustard
1 Tbsp. Worcestershire sauce
1/2 cup chili sauce
1 tsp. brown sugar
1/8 tsp. cayenne pepper
dash Tabasco sauce
8 frankfurters
8 buns

In a skillet, saute onion and celery in margarine until lightly brown. Add remaining sauce ingredients and simmer 5 minutes. Prick the skins of frankfurters, place them in the sauce, cover and simmer slowly about 15 minutes until thoroughly heated. Lightly butter buns and warm in moderate oven. Place frankfurters in buns and spoon on sauce. Serves 8.

Betty Holland (Mrs. Calvin)

Salads

M.E.Wellborn

CRANBERRY WALDORF SALAD

So good, especially on holidays!

2 cups raw cranberries
3 cups miniature marshmallows
3/4 cup sugar
2 cups diced, unpared tart apples
3/4 cup broken walnuts
1/4 tsp. salt
1 cup seedless green grapes
1 cup whipping cream, whipped

Grind cranberries and combine with marshmallows and sugar. Cover and chill overnight. Add apples, grapes, walnuts and salt. Fold in whipped cream. Chill. Serve in large bowl or individual lettuce cups. Garnish with clusters of grapes if desired. Serves 8-10.

Ellen Knott (Mrs. B.F.)

Variation: Omit green grapes and use 1 medium container Cool Whip in place of whipped cream.

Judy Bryson (Mrs. R.C.)

EASY YEAR-ROUND FRUIT SALAD

1 12-oz. carton small-curd cottage
    cheese
1 cup small marshmallows
1 12-oz. can pineapple chunks
    with juice
1 3-oz. package peach gelatin
    (or other desired flavor)
1 8-oz. carton Cool Whip

Mix all ingredients. Refrigerate 1 to 2 hours or overnight before serving. Serves 6.

Virginia Golding (Mrs. John G.)

OVERNIGHT FRUIT SALAD

1 lemon
1 cup Royal Anne cherries
1 cup pineapple chunks
30 marshmallows
1/2 pint whipping cream
yolks of 4 eggs
1/4 tsp. prepared mustard
1/4 tsp. salt

Beat egg yolks, add juice of 1 lemon, 1/4 tsp. prepared mustard, 1/4 tsp. salt. Heat mixture on *very low* burner until thickened — cool. Mix with cream that has been whipped. Combine in a bowl the Royal Anne cherries (pitted), pineapple chunks and marshmallows (cut into bite size). Pour dressing over fruit and refrigerate overnight. Serves 10-12.

Judy Beise (Mrs. D.W.)

24-HOUR FRUIT SALAD

2 cups dark fresh sweet cherries, or
    seedless grapes
2 cups miniature marshmallows
2 cups pineapple chunks, drained
    (reserve liquid for sauce)
2 cans (11 oz.) mandarin oranges,
    drained
1 package slivered almonds,
    toasted
SAUCE:
3 egg yolks, beaten slightly
dash salt
1/4 lb. butter
2 Tbsp. sugar
2 Tbsp. pineapple syrup
1 cup heavy cream, whipped

Combine fruit and marshmallows. Combine ingredients for sauce, and heat until thick. Cool and fold in whipped cream. Mix with fruit and add nuts. Make 24 hours ahead. Chill. Stir again before serving. Serves 8.

Myrtle B. Ussery (Mrs. Albert M.)

QUEEN CHARLOTTE FLUFF
EASY!

1 3-oz. package dry orange gelatin
1 8-oz. can undrained crushed
    pineapple
8 oz. carton sour cream
8 oz. carton Cool Whip
canned Mandarin oranges, peaches
    or fruit cocktail, drained

Mix first 4 ingredients. Stir in drained fruit. Refrigerate. Serves 6.
Note: Can also be used as a dessert. Various other flavors of gelatin can be substituted for orange, as desired.

Virginia Golding (Mrs. John G.)

MRS. LITTLE'S APRICOT NECTAR SALAD
Very tasty in a new and different way!

1 #2 can crushed pineapple, drain
    juice and reserve
1 orange, 1 lemon—grate rind,
    reserve; squeeze and strain
    juice, reserve
1 large can apricot nectar
1 3-oz. pkg. Jello, apricot flavor
1 3-oz. pkg. Jello, lemon flavor
1/2 cup blanched, slivered
    almonds

Follow above directions for pineapple, orange, lemon juice, and add apricot nectar to make 3-3/4 cups. Heat 2 cups (of the 3-3/4 cup total) and dissolve the 2 pkg. of Jello in this. Add remaining 1-3/4 cups cold juice and refrigerate until partially jelled. Add crushed pineapple, orange and lemon rind and the almonds. Put in large mold or 12 individual molds to set in refrigerator.

Nancy Little (Mrs. T.M.)

APRICOT-CHEESE SALAD

1 can (20 oz.) apricots, drained
    and chopped
1 can (29 oz.) crushed pineapple,
    drained
2 pkg. (3 oz.) orange Jello
juice from apricots and pineapple
3/4 to 1 cup mini marshmallows
1/2 cup sugar
3 Tbsp. flour
1 beaten egg
2 Tbsp. butter
1 cup whipping cream, whipped
3/4 cup grated cheddar cheese

Combine juices from apricots and pineapple with enough water to make 3 cups of liquid, and heat to boiling. Dissolve Jello in liquid and cool. Fold in fruit and marshmallows. Pour into a 9x13 pyrex dish. When firm, spread with a cooked topping made as follows: Combine sugar, flour and egg. Cook in double boiler until thick. Add butter and cool. Fold in whipped cream. Spread on salad. Top with cheese.

Betty Bradley
Mary Sue Patten (Mrs. Robert)
Barbara Stutts (Mrs. Clyde)

CORAL SALAD

Crisp apples make a nice texture.

1 3-oz. package strawberry Jello
1 3-oz. pkg. lemon Jello
1 medium can crushed pineapple,
    drained; reserve juice
water
3 tart eating apples (Winesap),
    cored and grated
1/2 cup chopped pecans
1/2 pint sour cream
1 8-oz. carton Cool Whip
pinch of salt

Dissolve Jello in 2 cups boiling liquid (use pineapple juice and enough water to equal 2 cups). Grate apples on coarse grater (you want long slivers). Add apples, pineapple and nuts to partially-set Jello. Add Cool Whip and salt to sour cream and fold all into Jello. Pour into molds and refrigerate. Serves 12.

Barby Ross Goode (Mrs. David)

APPLE CRUNCH SALAD

This could also be used as a dessert.

1 6-oz. package strawberry Jello
1 20-oz. can crushed pineapple
2 large apples, peeled, cored
    and chopped
1 pint whipping cream, whipped
1 cup pecans, chopped

Drain crushed pineapple and reserve juice. To juice add enough water to make 4 cups. Heat 2 of the cups of liquid to boiling. Add Jello and stir until dissolved. Add remaining 2 cups of liquid. Place in refrigerator and leave until slightly set. Whip cream and fold into gelatin along with other ingredients. Stir until well combined.
Note: It is important that gelatin be partially set up before stirring in other ingredients or the mixture will separate with the whipped cream on top.

Nita Street (Mrs. Frank)

TART CHERRY SALAD

1 small package cherry Jello
1 cup sugar
1 # 2 can (or approximate equi-
    valent) sour cherries
1 #2 can (or approximate equi-
    valent) crushed pineapple
juice of 2 oranges and 1 lemon
1 cup chopped pecans

Drain well the cherries and pineapple; reserve juices. Combine 4 different fruit juices with 1 cup sugar in saucepan; bring to a boil; boil 5 minutes. Pour over cherry Jello, stir until dissolved. When Jello is partially chilled, add fruit and nuts. Chill thoroughly. Serves 6-8

Shelly Brown (Mrs. C.E.)

CHERRY PIE SALAD

1 6-oz. pkg. cherry Jello
2 cups boiling water
1 can cherry pie filling
1 20-oz. can crushed pineapple,
    undrained
TOPPING:
8 oz. cream cheese
1 tsp. vanilla extract
1 cup sour cream
1/4 cup sugar

Dissolve Jello in boiling water. Add cherry pie filling and crushed pineapple. Put in 8-cup pyrex casserole and refrigerate. Beat in mixer the softened cream cheese, vanilla, sour cream and sugar. Spread over congealed mixture and chill. Serves 8.

Variation: Grape Jello and blueberry pie filling may be substituted for cherry.

Beverly Hance (Mrs. James)

LEMON CREAM MOLD
A colorful, refreshing salad

1 pkg. (3 oz.) lemon-flavored
　　gelatin
1/2 cup sugar
1/8 tsp. salt
1 cup boiling water
1 can (6 oz.) frozen lemonade con-
　　centrate
1 cup whipping cream, whipped
cantaloupe balls, watermelon
　　balls, honeydew melon balls,
　　strawberries, blueberries and
　　raspberries

Blend gelatin, sugar and salt in a bowl. Add boiling water and stir until dissolved. Stir in lemonade concentrate. Chill until mixture has a jelly-like consistency. Fold whipped cream into lemon mixture; pour into a 4-cup ring mold or 6 to 8 individual molds. Unmold and fill center with fresh fruit of your choice. Can garnish with mint leaves. Serves 6-8.

Ellen Knott (Mrs. B.F.)

LEMONADE SALAD
Nice dressing accompaniment

1 large can fruit cocktail
1 3-oz. package lemon gelatin
1 3-oz. can thawed lemonade.
1/2 cup chopped pecans
1/2 cup sugar

Drain juice from fruit cocktail into a saucepan. Add enough water to make 1-1/2 cups liquid; add sugar. Heat until very hot but not boiling. Add gelatin and stir until well dissolved. Remove from heat and let cool 5 minutes. Stir in thawed lemonade—reserving 1 Tbsp. for dressing. Add fruit cocktail and pecans. Cool until slightly thickened and pour into a slightly oiled mold or dish. Chill until firm. Serve with Lemonade Dressing. Serves 6.

LEMONADE DRESSING

2 Tbsp. sugar
1/2 cup sour cream
1 Tbsp. lemonade (reserved from
　　above)
1/2 cup Hellman's mayonnaise

Blend all ingredients. May pass during serving or spread over salad.

Ellen Knott (Mrs. B. F.)

GEORGIA PEACH ASPIC

1 envelope unflavored gelatin
1/4 cup cold water
2 3-oz. pkgs. peach-flavored
    gelatin
1-1/4 cups boiling water
1 cup orange juice
grated rind of 1 lemon
3 Tbsp. lemon juice
1-1/2 cup pureed fresh Georgia
    peaches
1/4 cup sugar, if necessary
CREAM CHEESE DRESSING:
1 3-oz. pkg. cream cheese
1 Tbsp. mayonnaise
1 peach, pureed

Soften plain gelatin in 1/4 cup cold water. Dissolve both unflavored and peach gelatine in 1-1/4 cups boiling water. Add orange juice, rind of lemon and lemon juice. Add pureed peaches; sweeten, if necessary. Pour into 1-1/2 quart mold and chill until set. Serve with Cream Cheese Dressing.
DRESSING:
Beat the cream cheese until smooth. Add mayonnaise, blending well. Add pureed peach; mix well. Serve over salad. Serves 8.

Libby Morrison (Mrs. Jack)

SPICY PEACH JELLO SALAD

2 (16-oz.) cans sliced peaches
    (juice pack, drained; save
    juice)
1 6-oz. pkg. peach Jello
1-2 tsp. each cinnamon, ground
    cloves, nutmeg and ginger
2 cups boiling water
2 cups peach juice (add enough
    water to make 2 cups)
2 Tbsp. cider vinegar
mayonnaise

In saucepan, dissolve gelatin and spices in boiling water. Pour into flat 2 quart pyrex dish. Add peach juice and vinegar. Mix. Add peaches, chill until set. To serve, cut into squares, place on lettuce and top with mayonnaise. Serves 8-10.

Peggy Buchanan (Mrs. D. Douglas)

SPICED PEACH SALAD

2 pkgs. lemon Jello
1/2 cup nuts
4 oranges, juice and chopped pulp
1 large jar spiced peaches
1 small jar maraschino cherries
1/2 cup water

Cut up peaches and save all juice. Add 1/2 cup water to peach and orange juices, heat and add to Jello. Quarter the cherries. Combine all ingredients and pour into ring mold. Chill until set. Serves 8.

Gayanne Mraz

PINEAPPLE CREAM CHEESE SALAD
Good with baked ham

4 3-oz. pkgs. cream cheese,
   softened
1 29-1/2 oz. can sliced pineapple,
   drained and juice reserved
2 Tbsp. cold water
1 envelope (1 Tbsp.) unflavored
   gelatin
1 cup mayonnaise
1 cup chopped blanched almonds
1/4 tsp. dried green onion
1/2 tsp. Worcestershire sauce
1/2 tsp. salt
3/4 tsp. Beau Monde seasoning
3 dashes cayenne pepper
1 cup whipping cream, whipped

In a large mixing bowl beat cream cheese until light and fluffy. Cut pineapple into bite-sized pieces. Dissolve gelatin in cold water. Heat pineapple juice in saucepan and add dissolved gelatin to it; cool. Add mayonnaise to cream cheese along with pineapple juice and gelatin mixture. Add almonds and seasonings. Fold in whipped cream. Lightly grease 2 large oblong casseroles with mayonnaise and spoon mixture into them. Chill until set, cut into slices and serve. Yield: 20 to 22 servings.

Ellen Knott (Mrs. B.F.)

SALAD DELIGHT
Adds color to any meal and is delicious!

2 pkgs. raspberry Jello
2 cups hot water
2 cups cold water
2 small cans pineapple chunks or
   one large can, drained (save
   liquid)
4 bananas, sliced
2 cups small marshmallows
TOPPING:
pineapple juice plus water to make
   2 cups
4 rounded Tbsp. flour
1 cup sugar
2 eggs, beaten
dash salt
1 cup whipped cream.

Combine Jello with hot water. When dissolved, add 2 cups cold water. Let partially set and add fruits and marshmallows. Put in large flat 9x12 baking dish and congeal. Add flour mixed with sugar, beaten eggs and salt to juice and water. Cook and stir until thickened. Chill. Fold in whipped cream. Put topping on congealed Jello. Serves 10-12. All can be prepared ahead of serving and stores well.

Betty Holland (Mrs. Calvin)

MRS. CLELAND'S RASPBERRY-CRANBERRY SALAD

1 small pkg. raspberry Jello
1-1/2 cups water
1 can mandarin orange sections, drained
1 small can crushed pineapple, undrained
1 small can jellied cranberry sauce (cut into small bits)
1/3 cup chopped English walnuts or pecans

Dissolve Jello in 1 cup boiling water. Add 1/2 cup cold water. Add drained orange sections, undrained pineapple, cranberry sauce and nuts. Put into 6 individual molds or 1 larger mold and congeal. Serve with mayonnaise. Serves 6.

Julia Warner (Mrs. C.E.)

Variation: Omit Mandarin orange sections.

Anita Shapiro (Mrs. Marvin)

CRANBERRY-CREAM SALAD
Side dish or accompaniment to picnic-type lunch

3 oz. cherry gelatin
1 cup hot water
1 lb. can whole cranberry sauce
1/2 cup celery, minced
1/4 cup chopped walnuts
1 cup sour cream
greens for salad in individual dishes if you are not serving from a large bowl

Dissolve gelatin in water. Chill until thick but not firm. Break up cranberry sauce. Stir sauce, celery and nuts into gelatin mix. Fold in the sour cream. Chill until ready to use. Unmold onto greens to serve. Serves 4-6.

Anne Szymanski (Mrs. Louis)

ELEGANT MOLDED FRUIT

1 l-lb. can pineapple chunks
1 1-lb. can pitted Bing cherries
2 6-oz. pkgs. strawberry Jello
2 1-lb. cans whole cranberry sauce
1 large pkg (plastic bag) whole strawberries, partially defrosted

Drain the pineapple chunks and pitted cherries. Measure the juice and add water to make two cups. Bring to boil, remove from heat, add Jello and stir. Add the pineapple, cherries and cranberry sauce. When it begins to thicken, add the strawberries. Put into 11-cup mold and refrigerate until congealed. Serves 15 or more.

Virginia Golding (Mrs. John G.)

RIBBON MOLD

It is eye-catching and tastes good, too.

3 3-oz. pkgs. raspberry Jello
2 3-oz. pkgs. lime Jello
2 3-oz. pkgs. lemon Jello
1 can evaporated milk

Dissolve 1 pkg. raspberry Jello in 1 cup boiling water and put in pan (9x13) in refrigerator to set. Dissolve 1 pkg. raspberry Jello in 1 cup boiling water and put aside to cool, but not set. Then, add 1/2 cup evaporated milk and pour over plain raspberry Jello that is set. Follow same with other flavors, ending with plain raspberry Jello on top. (Can use other flavors.) Makes 28 half-cup servings.

Karen Schwelling (Mrs. L.J.)

FROZEN BANANA SALAD

2 large bananas, mashed
2 Tbsp. lemon juice
3/4 cup sugar
2 cups sour cream
2 Tbsp. chopped cherries
    (maraschino)
1 #2 can pineapple, undrained
1/2 cup chopped pecans or
    walnuts

Mix and let freeze. Cut into squares to serve.

Mytle B. Ussery (Mrs. Albert M.)

FROZEN CHERRY SALAD

1 large can crushed pineapple,
    drained
1 can cherry pie filling (Thank You
    brand)
1 can Eagle Brand milk
1 large container Cool Whip

Mix well and put into large container. Freeze 24 hours before serving. Serves 8.

Stephany Alphin (Mrs. R.L.)

FROZEN FRUIT SALAD

16 large marshmallows
1 #2 can crushed pineapple (drain
   and reserve juice)
1/2 cup sliced almonds
2 pkgs. Dream Whip
1 large jar maraschino cherries,
   sliced
2 eggs
2 level Tbsp. flour
3 Tbsp. vinegar

Combine juice from drained pineapple, eggs, flour and vinegar in saucepan. Stir over heat until thick and smooth. Add marshmallows and let melt. Add pineapple and almonds. Refrigerate for a few hours. Beat both packages of Dream Whip according to package directions and fold into pineapple mixture. Add sliced cherries. Freeze overnight. Cut into squares to serve on lettuce leaf. Garnish with banana slices if desired. Serves 12 to 18.

Nancy Sibley (Mrs. W.A.L., Jr.)

FROZEN FRUIT SALAD

2 ripe bananas
1 can whole cranberry sauce
1 13-1/2 oz. can crushed pineapple
1 package Dream Whip
1 can Eagle Brand milk

Make Dream Whip according to package directions. Mash bananas and combine all ingredients including the juice of canned pineapple. Freeze in muffin tins lined with cupcake liners. Remove papers and serve on lettuce. 24 servings.

Darlene Thomas Beard (Mrs. John N.)

FROZEN YOGURT FRUIT SALAD

1 8-oz. carton peach yogurt
1 8-oz. carton sour cream
3/4 cup sugar
juice of large lemon
2 bananas, sliced
1 8-1/4 oz. can crushed pineapple,
   drained
1/4 cup maraschino cherries,
   sliced
dash salt
1/4 cup chopped nuts (optional)
mayonnaise

Mix yogurt, sour cream and sugar together. Add other ingredients and stir well. Pour into oiled mold (individual or other) and freeze. Take out of freezer and let stand at room temperature 30-45 minutes. Slice and serve on lettuce leaf with mayonnaise as a topping.

Libby Morrison (Mrs. Jack)

FROZEN ORANGE PECAN MOLD

1 8-oz. pkg. cream cheese, softened
1 tsp. grated orange peel
1 8-1/4 oz. can crushed pineapple,
*   drained*
1/2 cup pecans
1/2 cup (4 oz.) chopped dates
1/2 cup (4 oz.) maraschino cherries
1 cup heavy cream, whipped
1 Tbsp. sugar
1/4 cup orange juice

Dissolve the sugar in the orange juice; add cream cheese. Beat until fluffy (no lumps). Stir in nuts and fruits; fold in whipped cream. Pack into individual molds and freeze. Serve on orange slice with half cherry on top. Serves 14.
Note: For large groups, freeze in orange juice cans. One recipe makes 2 16-oz. cans. Allow to sit out 15 to 20 minutes. Rip can off. Slice in 7 servings per 16 oz. can, or 5 servings per 12 oz. can. Place in freezer to reharden until serving time.

Georgia Miller (Mrs. George)

PAPER CUP FROZEN FRUIT SALAD

"I have put these in a zip-lock bag in the freezer for up to one month."

2 cups dairy sour cream
2 Tbs. lemon juice
1/2 cup sugar
1/8 tsp. salt
1 can crushed pineapple, drained
1 or 2 bananas, diced
4 drops red food color
1/2 cup chopped pecans
1 1-lb. can pitted Bing cherries,
*   drained, or*
3 Tbsp. maraschino cherries,
*   drained and chopped*

Combine sour cream, lemon juice, sugar, salt, crushed pineapple, banana pieces, and enough red food color to give a pretty pink tint. Lightly fold in nuts and cherries. Spoon into fluted paper muffin cups (large size) which have been placed in 3-inch muffin pans. Freeze. Cover with plastic wrap or put in a plastic bag and store in the freezer. Remove from freezer about 15 minutes before serving to allow paper cups to loosen from salad. Peel off paper cups and place salad on greens. Fills 12 large paper muffin cups.

Ellen Knott (Mrs. B.F.)
Linda Miller (Mrs. W.R.)

BEET SALAD

This is different, and good

1 pkg. lemon Jello
1 envelope gelatin
3/4 cup beet juice
3 Tbsp. vinegar
1/2 tsp. salt
2 tsp. grated onion
1 Tbsp. prepared horseradish
3/4 cup diced celery
1 cup cooked, diced beets (reserve
    juice)

Dissolve gelatin in 1 Tbsp. cold water. Then dissolve both gelatin and Jello in 1 cup hot water. Add beet juice, vinegar, salt, onion, and horseradish. Chill. When slightly thickened, fold in celery and beets. Pour into mold or molds to congeal. Serves 6-8.

Myrtle B. Ussery (Mrs. Albert M.)

CHARLOTTE'S DINNER SALAD MOLD

1 can tomato soup
1 envelope gelatin
1 pint cottage cottage
1/2 to 2/3 cup mayonnaise
1/4 tsp. onion salt
1 avocado, sliced
1 can artichoke hearts, drained
    and quartered
1 10-oz. can asparagus, drained

Soften gelatin in 1/4 cup water and let stand a few minutes. Heat soup and dissolve the gelatin mixture in the hot soup. Cool slightly. Add cottage cheese, mayonnaise and salt. Pour into ring mold. Add vegatables evenly to mold and press in to submerge. Chill until congealed. Serves 8.

Virginia Golding (Mrs. John G.)

CUCUMBER-LIME ASPIC

1 3-oz. pkg. lime Jello
2/3 cup boiling water
2 Tbsp. white vinegar or lemon
    juice
1 small white onion, grated
1/4 tsp. salt
dash of pepper
1/2 cup sour cream
1/2 cup mayonnaise
1 cup unpeeled, shredded
    cucumber

Dissolve gelatin in water; add vinegar. Cool slightly. Add seasonings, onion, mayonnaise and sour cream. Blend well. Stir in cucumber. Turn into fancy 1-quart mold. Refrigerate. Serves 6.

Myrtle B. Ussery (Mrs. Albert M.)

CUCUMBER RING SALAD
This is so refreshing on a hot summer day.

1 3-oz. pkg. lime Jello
1 cup boiling water
3/4 cup water
3 Tbsp. lemon juice
1 cucumber, thinly sliced
1 envelope unflavored gelatin
2 Tbsp. sugar
3/4 tsp. salt
3/4 cup water
2 Tbsp. lemon juice
1 8-oz. pkg. cream cheese,
    softened and cubed
4 cucumbers (small)
1 cup mayonnaise
3 Tbsp. finely-chopped onions
1/4 cup snipped parsley

Dissolve lime Jello in boiling water; add the first 3/4 cup water and 3 Tbsp. lemon juice. Pour into a deep 6-1/2 cup ring mold. Chill until partially set. Arrange overlapping slices of cucumber in bottom. Press into gelatin. Chill until almost firm. Meanwhile mix the envelope of unflavored gelatin, sugar and salt in saucepan. Add the second 3/4 cup water; stir over low heat until dissolved. Stir in 2 Tbsp. lemon juice. Gradually beat hot gelatin mixture into cream cheese until smooth. Pare and halve cucumbers, remove seeds. Grind or shred cucumbers and drain (1-1/2 cups). Add cucumbers, mayonnaise, onion, and parsley to cheese mixture. Pour over almost-firm gelatin in mold. Chill until firm. Unmold and decorate with cherry tomatoes and fresh parsley. Makes 8-10 servings.

Linda H. McAlexander (Mrs. Sam L.)

HEALTH SALAD

1 small bunch carrots, grated
2 cups chopped cabbage (or
    grated)
2 cups chopped celery
1 large green pepper, chopped
1 medium onion, grated
1-1/2 cups mayonnaise
4 Tbsp. sugar
3 Tbsp. vinegar
salt to taste (I add red pepper)
1/2 cup chopped pecans can be
    added
2 envelopes plain gelatin
1/2 cup cold water

Soften gelatin in 1/2 cup cold water in teacup. Then heat in top of double boiler until gelatin is dissolved. Mix remaining ingredients into gelatin. Put in large mold or 12 individual molds. Refrigerate until firm.

Betty Hight (Mrs. M.L.)

MOLDED SPINACH-CHEESE SALAD

1 pkg. lemon Jello
1-1/2 Tbsp. vinegar
1/2 cup mayonnaise
1/4 tsp. salt
1 Tbsp. minced onion
1 pkg. frozen, chopped spinach,
    thawed and drained well
3/4 cup cottage cheese

Dissolve Jello in 3/4 cup hot water. Add 1 cup cold water. Add vinegar, mayonnaise and salt. Chill in freezer. When slightly set, beat with electric beater until fluffy. Add onion, spinach and cottage cheese. Pour into mold and refrigerate until firm. Unmold. Serve with lettuce greens. Serves 6.

Sally McMillan

SPRING SALAD MOLD

If you have a Cuisinart Food Processor, use the French-fry attachment to chop the vegetables, except onions.

2 Tbsp. unflavored gelatin
1/2 cup cold water
1/2 green pepper
5 stalks celery
3 carrots
4 green onions
1/2 cup vinegar
1 28-oz. can whole, peeled
    tomatoes (or 2 cans Del
    Monte wedges or
    Contandino slices)
1/4 cup sugar
1/2 tsp. salt
cucumbers, tomatoes, avocado

Soak gelatin in cold water. Chop pepper, celery, and carrots very fine, and slice green onions very, very thin. Quarter tomatoes and place in saucepan and bring to a boil. Add gelatin and dissolve. Let cool and add remaining ingredients. Mix well and pour into a greased 6-cup ring mold (or make individual molds). Place your favorite dressing in the center of the large mold and garnish with sliced cucumbers, tomatoes and avocado. Serves 8.

Virginia Golding (Mrs. John G.)

SWEET AND SOUR ASPIC

1/3 cup sugar
1/2 cup water
1/4 tsp. vinegar (wine or tarragon)
1/8 tsp. salt
1 envelope plain gelatin
1/4 cup cold water
1/2 cup celery, chopped
1/2 cup pecans
1 small jar pimientos, diced
1/2 cup asparagus, cut in 1"
　　lengths
1/4 cup lemon juice
1 tsp. onion, grated
water chestnuts, sliced (optional)

In a saucepan blend together sugar, water, vinegar and salt. Bring to a boil. Soften gelatin in cold water and add to sugar-vinegar mixture. Place celery, pecans, pimientos, asparagus, lemon juice, water chestnuts and onion in shallow greased pan. Add heated mixture and chill in refrigerator until set. Serve on lettuce and garnish with mayonnaise and paprika. Serves 4-6. Can be doubled.

Ellen Knott (Mrs. B.F.)

TOMATO ASPIC

2 envelopes unflavored gelatin
2-1/4 cups tomato juice (#2 can)
1/2 tsp. onion salt
1 tsp. sugar
1 tsp. Worcestershire sauce
1/4 cup lemon juice
dash of Tabasco
1 small pkg. cream cheese
1/4 cup pecans, chopped
1/4 cup green pepper, chopped

Sprinkle gelatin on 1/2 of the tomato juice in a small saucepan over low heat. Have remaining tomato juice chilled. Stir until gelatin is *completely* dissolved. Remove saucepan from heat and add salt, sugar, Worcestershire, lemon juice and Tabasco. Add chilled tomato juice at the last. Stir. Pour into individual molds. Chill until slightly jelled. Mix cream cheese, pecans and green pepper and add to the center of the aspic when slightly thickened. When completely jelled, unmold on crisp greens. Serves 6. This is an easy recipe — is delicious with fried chicken. Can be done two or three days before needed.

Fefe Booth (Mrs. Richard B.)

TOMATO ASPIC

4 cups V-8 juice
1 small onion, thinly sliced
3 celery stalks with leaves, coarsely cut
1 bay leaf
6 peppercorns
1 tsp. salt
2 Tbsp. vinegar
1 Tbsp. sugar
dash allspice
1 tsp. Worcestershire sauce
2 envelopes Knox gelatin
1/2 cup sliced olives and/or small shrimp

Soften gelatin in 1/2 cup V-8 juice. Combine remaining V-8 and ingredients except olives/shrimp. Heat to boiling—simmer 10 minutes. Strain. Add softened gelatin and stir until dissolved. Pour into mold. When partially set, stir in olives/shrimp. Chill until set. Serves 8-10.

Peggy Buchanan (Mrs. D. Douglas)
Guerry B. Russell (Mrs. Don J.)

COLD ASPARAGUS WITH MUSTARD SAUCE

Beautiful at Easter time—as a salad or vegetable

2 lbs. asparagus (fresh), stems trimmed
1 hard-cooked egg yolk
1 raw egg yolk
1-1/2 tsp. Dijon mustard
1/2 cup olive oil
1/2 tsp salt
1/4 tsp. white pepper
1-1/2 Tbsp. white wine vinegar
1 Tbsp. minced hard-cooked egg white

Cook asparagus in boiling salted water to cover, until crisp-tender (5-7 minutes). Drain and place in a large bowl of ice water. Drain on paper towels. Place on serving platter and refrigerate, covered, several hours. Mash cooked egg yolk in small bowl with raw yolk and mustard until smooth. Gradually whisk in oil until smooth. Combine vinegar, salt and pepper, add to oil mixture. Whisk until smooth. Spoon over asparagus and garnish with chopped egg whites. 4-6 servings.

Susan Rielly (Mrs. P.C.)

AVOCADO SALAD

1/2 cup olive or vegetable oil
1/4 cup red wine vinegar
1 clove garlic, crushed
1 tsp. salt
1/4 tsp. pepper
1/4 tsp. dry mustard
3 avocados, sliced
1 onion, thinly sliced
pimientos, cut in strips
lettuce

Combine first 6 ingredients in a jar and shake well. Place lettuce leaves on a pretty plate. Arrange avocados, onion and pimientos on lettuce and pour dressing over. Can use individual plates as well. Serves 4-6.

Liz Medearis (Mrs. Wm. F., Jr.)

BROCCOLI SALAD

1 bunch broccoli, chopped
1 medium onion, chopped
1/2 to 3/4 cup olives, chopped
4 hard-cooked eggs, chopped
1/2 to 2/3 cup mayonnaise,
    depending on taste
1 Tbsp. vinegar

Combine broccoli, onion, olives and eggs. Mix vinegar and mayonnaise and stir into broccoli mixture. Refrigerate several hours for flavors to blend. Serves 6-8.

Sally Gaddy (Mrs. C.E.)
Linda Hawfield (Mrs. Ben)

EASY BROCCOLI SALAD
An easy, do-ahead recipe; gets rave reviews!

2 bunches broccoli, fresh
6 egg
1 envelope Ranch dressing

Prepare Ranch dressing as directed on envelope and refrigerate. Hard-cook 6 eggs and refrigerate. Steam broccoli pieces (3" florets) and refrigerate. Crumble eggs and arrange over broccoli in casserole. Pour Ranch dressing over broccoli and eggs when ready to serve.

Linda Rowe (Mrs. Wm.)

CAULIFLOWER SALAD

1 large head cauliflower
1/2 lb. bacon, cooked and
    crumbled
3 medium tomatoes, diced
1 small bunch green onions
    chopped (3 with some tops)
1 cup diced Cheddar cheese
1/2 cup pimiento stuffed olives,
    sliced
1/2 cup mayonnaise

Remove outer green leaves and break cauliflower into florets; wash them thoroughly. Toss cauliflower with the remaining ingredients. Can chill or serve at room temperature. Yield: 10 servings.

Ellen Knott (Mrs. B.F.)

CAROL SLUDER'S CAULIFLOWER AND BROCCOLI TOSS
A favorite with ham or beef at a buffet

1 head cauliflower
1 bunch broccoli
1 medium onion, chopped or
    sliced
DRESSING:
1/2 cup salad oil
1/2 cup mayonnaise
1/3 cup white wine vinegar
1/3 cup sugar
1/2 tsp. salt
dash pepper
paprika

Cut the very tips of broccoli and cauliflower to size of the end of your finger and add sliced onion (or use green onions sliced). Marinate in dressing overnight or at least 8 hours. Serve in crystal bowl garnished with lettuce. Serves 12.

Gensie

Variation: Add 3 carrots, thinly sliced.

Eloise Dellinger (Mrs. H. Stephen)

MARINATED CUCUMBER SALAD

7 cups sliced cucumbers
1 cup chopped onions
1 medium green pepper, chopped
1 Tbsp. salt
1 Tbsp. celery seed
2 cups sugar
1 cup vinegar

Combine cucumbers, onions and pepper in a large bowl. Heat vinegar and sugar until sugar dissolves. Cool. Pour mixture over vegetables. Cover and refrigerate overnight. Stir several times. Serves 8.

Judy Bryson (Mrs. R.C., Jr.)

MARINATED VEGETABLE SALAD

Tastes better each day!

1 head cauliflower cut into florets
1 large bell pepper cut into rings
1 bottle green olives with pimientos, drained
1 can black olives, pitted
4 carrots, cut into half-dollars
1 container cherry tomatoes
1 can whole mushrooms, drained
1 pkg. Good Seasons Italian dressing

Place all vegetables except tomatoes into a plastic bag. Mix Good Seasons Italian dressing. Pour entire bottle over vegetables. Seal bag and refrigerate at least one day. Empty bag into large bowl, mix in tomatoes. Sprinkle with Parmesan cheese just before serving. Serves 10-12.

Linda Miller (Mrs. W.R.)

GREEK TOMATO SALAD

3 large ripe tomatoes
12 ripe olives, pitted
3/4 cup feta cheese
3 Tbsp. wine vinegar
1/2 cup olive oil
1/2 tsp. oregano
1/2 tsp. thyme
salt and pepper to taste
1 garlic clove

Cut tomatoes to bite size. Slice olives in halves. Crumble cheese coarsely. Rub bowl with garlic. Add tomatoes, olives and cheese. Make marinade from remaining ingredients. Toss all together. Marinate at least 4 hours or overnight. Serve at room temperature. Serves 3 to 4.

Beverly Hance (Mrs. James)

SHOE PEG CORN SALAD

2 16 oz. cans shoe peg corn, drained
1 2 oz. jar chopped pimiento, drained
1/2 cup chopped green pepper
1/2 cup chopped onion
2 stalks chopped celery
1/2 cup sugar
1/2 cup vegetable oil
1/2 cup vinegar
1 tsp. salt
1/2 tsp. pepper

Mix together corn, pimiento, green pepper, onions and celery. Combine sugar, oil, vinegar, salt and pepper. Pour over vegetables; cover and chill overnight. Drain vegetables well before serving. Makes 6-8 servings.

Lillie Huss

GRANDMOTHER'S REFRIGERATOR SLAW

1 large head cabbage
4 medium onions
1 green bell pepper
1 red bell pepper or can of
    pimientos
1 pt. vinegar
2-1/2 cups sugar
1 tsp. mustard seed
1-1/2 tsp. celery seed
1/2 tsp. turmeric
1/2 tsp. salt

Bring to boil vinegar, sugar, mustard seed, celery seed, turmeric and salt. Set aside to cool. Chop cabbage, onions and peppers. Pour cooled mixture over vegetables in glass dish or crock. Cover and let stand in refrigerator 24 hours before serving. Keeps indefinitely in refrigerator. Serves 12.

Linda Dowd (Mrs. J. Kenneth)

MARINATED SLAW
SO good, and keeps well for days

Thinly slice the following:
1 large cabbage
1 large onion (optional)
1 large green pepper
carrots, enough for color
1 cup sugar—mix with above and
    set aside
Mix and bring to a boil:
1 Tbsp. salt
1 tsp. dry mustard
1 tsp. celery seed
pepper
3/4 cup salad oil
1 cup vinegar

Pour cooked mixture over vegetables. Put in airtight container (glass is best) and do not stir or uncover for at least four hours (preferably overnight). Keep refrigerated until ready to serve. Serves 12.

Peggy Buchanan (Mrs. D. Douglas)
Shila Elden (Mrs. D. J.)
Donna Hanna (Mrs. R.T.)
Linda Hawfield (Mrs. Ben)

POPPY SEED COLE SLAW

This is absolutely delicious and real zippy!

1 medium head shredded cabbage
2 to 3 stalks chopped celery
1 small minced onion
DRESSING:
2 Tbsp. salad dressing (heaping)
2 Tbsp. white wine vinegar
1/3 cup sugar
1 Tbsp. poppy seeds
4 oz. commercial sour cream
salt and pepper

Mix dressing ingredients together and pour over cabbage, celery and onion. Mix well. Add more sour cream if needed. Serves 8.

Marsha Cagle (Mrs. P.C.)

ARTICHOKE SALAD

1 9-oz. pkg. frozen artichoke
  hearts
6 cups salad greens: lettuce, romaine, spinach, etc.
DRESSING:
1/2 cup olive or salad oil
1/3 cup vinegar
2 Tbsp. water
4 thin slices onion
1 Tbsp. sugar
1 clove garlic, crushed
1/4 tsp. celery seed
1/2 tsp. salt
dash pepper

Mix dressing in saucepan. Bring to a boil. Add artichoke hearts. Cook until tender according to time on package. Cool and chill until serving time. Drain artichokes, reserving dressing. Add artichokes to salad greens and toss with enough reserved dressing to coat greens. Serves 6.

Julia Lackey (Mrs. R.S.)

ETTA'S WANDA SALAD

1 head lettuce
1 can mandarin oranges, drained
1 cup coconut, toasted in butter
1/2 cup croutons
15-20 cherry tomatoes, halved
1 can baby shrimp, drained
Vietoff's Peppercream

Break lettuce into bite-size pieces and place in large bowl. Arrange other ingredients on top in pie-wedge fashion. Add Vietoff's Peppercream (see index) and serve immediately.
NOTE: Salad can be arranged ahead of time but add croutons just before dressing or they will become soggy.)

Julia Wade (Mrs. Hamlin)

BEET, ONION SALAD TOSS

6 cups assorted greens (iceberg or
    Boston lettuce, romaine,
    spinach, endive, etc.)
1 16 oz., can sliced beets,
    well drained
1 small Bermuda onion,
    thinly sliced
1/2 cup salad oil
2 Tbsp. lemon juice
1 Tbsp. white vinegar
1/4 tsp. garlic powder
1 tsp. caraway seeds
1/4 tsp. salt
dash pepper

Place green salad in large bowl, arranging beets and onions (separated into rings) over greens. In jar, combine salad oil, lemon juice, vinegar, garlic powder, caraway seeds, salt and pepper. Just before serving, drizzle over salad, toss and serve. Serves 6.

Stella Thurston (Mrs. Doc J.)

CAESAR SALAD

This recipe came from a famous restaurant in San Francisco. The elegance of a fine cuisine can be captured by preparing this delicious salad at the table.

2 large heads romaine lettuce
5 slices bread
7 garlic cloves
1 stick butter
1/4 tsp. dry mustard
1/2 tsp. salt
1/4 tsp. black pepper
4 oz. Roquefort cheese
2 oz. anchovies, cut (optional)
6 Tbsp. olive oil
juice of two lemons
2 raw eggs
croutons

Preparation ahead:
Wash two large heads of romaine and pat each leaf dry. Break the leaves into pieces and chill for at least two hours. Rub a large wooden salad bowl with two cloves of garlic and place in refrigerator several hours ahead. Make croutons by toasting 5 pieces of bread; then cut the toast into 1/2" squares. Simmer 5 peeled cloves of garlic until tender; mash the cloves; then add one stick of butter until melted. Pour garlic butter over croutons; tossing well. Bake in a 350 degree oven 5-10 minutes or until crisp. Croutons may be made several days ahead and kept chilled in the refrigerator.
Place the romaine in the chilled salad bowl and add the remaining ingredients. Toss the salad well and serve immediately. Serves 8.

Anne Zeola (Mrs. John P.)

LIZ'S CAESAR SALAD

"This is our 'house' salad. It is different and our guests have always loved it!"

2 Tbsp. lemon juice
2 cloves garlic
3 slices white bread, toasted
1/4 cup crumbled bleu cheese
salt and ground pepper
2 Tbsp. wine vinegar
2 small heads romaine lettuce, or
     1 large
1/3 cup olive oil
3 Tbsp. Parmesan cheese

Combine vinegar and lemon juice in cup. Mash and chop garlic and add to cup. Let this set out for at least 2 hours. Wash and tear lettuce into 2" pieces. Cube toast. Put all ingredients together in bowl and toss. Add salt and pepper. Serve on chilled salad plates. Serves 6-8.

Maryann R. Berry (Mrs. W.P.)

EASY SPINACH-LETTUCE SALAD

1 lb. fresh spinach, torn
1/2 head iceberg lettuce, torn
4 slices bacon, cooked and
     crumbled, or 4 Tbsp. Oscar
     Meyer's canned "Bacon Bits"
1/2 cup vegetable oil
1/4 cup cider vinegar
2 Tbsp. sugar
1 Tbsp. poppy seeds
1 Tbsp. onion juice (bottled—
     found in the spice section of
     store)
1 tsp. salt
3/4 cup large-curd cottage cheese

Wash spinach and tear into pieces (remove tough stalks). Combine with lettuce and bacon in a large bowl; toss lightly. Combine next 7 ingredients in a jar. Cover and shake vigorously. Pour over salad and toss. Serves 8.

Kay Roberson (Mrs. G. Don)

KATHERINE'S SALAD

combination of fresh spinach and
     fresh, crisp lettuce
canned mandarin orange slices,
     well drained
thinly sliced red onions
toasted almonds, slivered or sliced
*Berry's Salad Dressing
see index

Combine in desired proportions and serve with Berry's salad dressing.

Katherine Moore (Mrs. Peter)

ORIENTAL SPINACH SALAD

2 pkg. fresh spinach (wash,
  remove coarse stems, crisp
  overnight)
4 hard-boiled eggs, sliced
8 strips bacon, cooked and
  crumbled
1 can water chestnuts, drained and
  sliced
1 can bean sprouts, drained
1 cup sliced fresh mushrooms
  (optional)
DRESSING:
1 medium red onion
1/3 cup catsup
1 cup salad oil
1 Tbsp. Worcestershire sauce
1 tsp. salt
3/4 cup (or less) sugar
1/4 cup vinegar

Tear the spinach into bite-sized pieces before tossing salad. Add hard-boiled eggs, bacon, water chestnuts and bean sprouts. Toss gently, then toss again in the dressing which has been liquified in the blender or food processor. Serves 8-10.

Carol S. Barreau (Mrs. E.H.)
Gensie
Nancy Little (Mrs. T.M.)
Mary Lou Scholl (Mrs. Ken)

SPINACH AND CABBAGE SALAD
Pleasing to the eye

1 large package fresh spinach
1 small head red cabbage
6-8 slices bacon, cooked and
  broken
5-6 hard-boiled eggs, chopped
DRESSING:
1 clove garlic, crushed
1 Tbsp. Parmesan cheese
1 tsp. mustard
salt and pepper
1 cup oil
1/2 cup wine vinegar.

Combine first four ingredients and serve with dressing of ingredients listed. Serves 10-12

Beverly Hance (Mrs. James)

SPINACH SALAD

1 pkg. spinach, torn
3/4 cup sliced almonds, toasted
5 slices bacon (reserve drippings)
2 Tbsp. orange juice
2 Tbsp. vinegar
2 Tbsp. red currant jelly

Rinse, trim and dry spinach. Toast almonds and set aside. Fry bacon until crisp, drain and crumble. FOR DRESSING, add 3 Tbsp. bacon drippings, orange juice, vinegar and jelly. Bring to boil. Sprinkle bacon and almonds over beds of spinach and drizzle with dressing. Makes 4 servings (1/2 cup dressing).

Georgia Miller (Mrs. George)

TOSSED GREEN SALAD

As you well know, the secret to a great salad is crisp, cold greens.
This method insures it.

6 Tbsp. olive oil
2 Tbsp. white wine vinegar with tarragon
1/2 tsp. salt
1 small clove garlic, minced
1 small head Boston lettuce
2 heads Bibb lettuce
3 stalks Belgian endive
1/2 bunch watercress
2 Tbsp. chopped parsley
2 Tbsp. chopped chives
2 Tbsp. chopped fresh dill, or 1 tsp. dried dill
2 tsp. chopped fresh thyme leaves or 1/2 tsp. dried thyme
1 medium avocado

Combine the olive oil, vinegar, salt and garlic in bottom of your salad bowl. Wash lettuce leaves and dry very well. Tear into bite-sized pieces over dressing. Do not toss. Wash endive, dry and slice over lettuce. Wash watercress and discard stems. Add to lettuce. Sprinkle parsley, chives, dill and thyme over top of leaves. Cover bowl tightly with plastic wrap and chill in refrigerator several hours. Just before serving, peel and slice avocado and add to greens. Toss all gently but well. Serves 8.

Gensie

MACARONI SALAD

4 cups cooked macaroni
   (1/2 lb. raw)
2 cups diced tomatoes
1 cup grated cheese
1 scant cup mayonnaise
1/4 cup sliced stuffed olives
2 Tbsp. grated onion
garlic salt if desired
1/8 tsp. red pepper

Cook macaroni until done. Mix all ingredients together, folding in tomatoes last. Better made ahead of time — seasonings meld. Serves 4-6.

Betty Hight (Mrs. M.L.)

RICE SALAD

Lovely for a summer supper buffet

2 cups cooked rice
1/2 cup Italian salad dressing
1/2 cup mayonnaise or Miracle
   Whip
In a blender or food processor,
   shred the following:
1 medium cucumber
1 stalk celery (large)
1 medium tomato or two small
   ones
1 medium green pepper
1/4 cup green onion
1 large carrot
several large radishes
1/4 head cabbage

Cook rice a day ahead and marinate overnight in Italian dressing (I use Good Seasons). Next day, add mayonnaise to undrained rice mixture, stirring until combined. Add vegetables and put mixture into ring mold. Cover and place in refrigerator for at least 4 hours. When ready to serve, unmold onto fresh lettuce leaves and fill center with cherry tomatoes. Serves 8-10.

Syble Carson (Mrs. James H., Jr.)

RICE AND ARTICHOKE SALAD
This tastes even better the second day.

1 cup regular rice
2 cups chicken bouillon or broth
1/3 cup chopped green pepper
1/3 cup chopped green onions
1 small jar marinated artichoke
    hearts
1 tsp. capers
1 tsp. curry powder (or less,
    to taste)
2/3 cup mayonnaise or salad
    dressing

Cook rice in chicken broth; cool. Meanwhile, drain artichokes (reserving liquid) and cut into small pieces. Chop pepper and green onions. Add artichokes, pepper and onion to cooled rice. Mix together the mayonnaise, reserved marinade, curry powder and capers. Add rice to mixture. Mix and chill thoroughly. Serves 6.

Patsy Farmer (Mrs. B.D.,III)

CRAB AND RICE SALAD
A really good make-ahead seafood dish for entree or salad

1 7-1/2 oz. can crab meat (or 1
    6-oz. package frozen crab, or
    1/2 lb. fresh crab meat,
    backfin or regular)
4 cups cooked Uncle Ben's rice
1 10-oz. pkg. frozen small green
    peas, barely cooked
5 stalks celery, chopped or thinly
    sliced
1/2 cup sliced green onions
1/2 cup sour cream
1 1/4 cups mayonnaise
1 Tbsp. Spice Island salad
    seasoning
curry powder for garnish
1 Tbsp. fresh lemon juice
salt and pepper to taste
lettuce leaves

Combine crab, rice, peas, celery, green onions, sour cream, mayonnaise, salad seasoning, lemon juice, salt and pepper to taste. Chill 24 hours. Serve on lettuce leaves and sprinkle lightly with curry powder. Serves 6-8.

Ellen Knott (Mrs. B.F.)

SALAD NICOISE

2 cups fresh green beans, cooked
    only until crisp-tender (or use
    frozen)
1/2 lb. fresh mushrooms
salt and fresh-ground pepper
1 large or 2 small avocados
2 cans (7 oz.) best quality tuna
    packed in oil
1 2-oz. can flat anchovy filets
1 ripe tomato (1/2 lb.)
Rind of 1 lemon, cut in very fine
    strips
1 peeled, thinly sliced cucumber
1 small red onion, peeled
8 black olives
8 stuffed green olives
6 Tbsp. olive oil
2 Tbsp. red wine vinegar
1 tsp. finely-chopped garlic
2 Tbsp. finely-chopped parsley
2 hard-cooked eggs, peeled and
    quartered
lettuce

Thinly slice mushrooms (3 cups). Put in large bowl; add lemon juice, salt and pepper. Toss. Add avocados. Drain tuna and add. Drain anchovies and add. Dice tomato and add. Slice onion and add with lemon rind and olives. Blend dressing ingredients and pour over. Toss well, being careful tt leave vegetables intact. Garnish with hard-cooked egg quarters and parsley. Serves 6.

Ada Offerdahl (Mrs. John)

TUNA MOUSSE

Great for a cool luncheon!

2 envelopes unflavored gelatin
1/2 cup cold water
1 cup mayonnaise
2 7-oz. cans tuna, drained
1/2 cup celery, finely diced
1/4 cup stuffed olives, chopped
1 Tbsp. chives, finely chopped
2 Tbsp. lemon juice
1-1/2 tsp. horseradish
1/4 tsp salt.
1/4 tsp. paprika
1 cup heavy cream, whipped
dash Tabasco

Soften gelatin in cold water; dissolve over boiling water. Stir in mayonnaise. Add remaining ingredients except cream. Mix well. Chill slightly. Fold in whipped cream. Pour into 10x6x1" pan and chill until firm. Cut into squares and serve on greens. Serves 8. Good served with Cold Spiced Fruit (see index).

Jane W. Lucas (Mrs. R.T.)

CHICKEN SALAD

This chicken salad is moist and flavorful.

2-1/2 lb. chicken breasts
1 pkg. Good Seasons Old Fash-
    ioned French Dressing Mix
*1/4 cup rice vinegar (not rice wine
    vinegar)
celery, sliced
almonds, sliced and toasted
mayonnaise
fresh-ground pepper
(halved green grapes may be
    substituted for celery)
*rice vinegar can be found in
    Japanese food stores

The day before: prepare French dressing according to package directions, substituting rice vinegar for regular vinegar. Cook chicken. Remove
meat from bones and cut into bite-sized pieces.
Pour dressing over chicken. Toss. Cover and
refrigerate overnight. Next morning, add remaining ingredients according to your individual
taste. Chill until serving time. Serve on leaf
lettuce. Sprinkle with paprika for color. Serves 6.

Peggy Buchanan (Mrs. D.Douglas)

CHICKEN SALAD

2-1/2 cups chicken, cut up
1 cup chopped celery
1 cup pineapple chunks
1 cup seedless grapes
1/2 cup toasted nuts
1 tsp. salt
1 tsp. sugar
3/4 tsp. curry powder
1 cup mayonnaise
1 cup whipping cream, whipped

Mix together in order listed, carefully folding in
the whipped cream last. Serves 6-8

Shirley Benfield (Mrs. Robert)
Jane Ives (Mrs. Buddy)

Variation: Omit curry powder and add 1 tsp.
minced onions.

Linda Miller (Mrs. W.R.)

CHICKEN SALAD

Serve on a salad plate with tomatoes, hard-cooked egg slices and avocados.

2-1/2 cups diced cooked chicken
1 cup small seedless green grapes
1 tsp. minced onions
1 cup finely-cut celery
1 cup chopped nuts
1 tsp. salt
1 cup Kraft mayonnaise
1/2 cup heavy cream whipped

Combine ingredients; chill. Serve on greens
garnished with thin slices of pickles. Serves 8.
Note: Tester suggests this chicken salad complements Spiced Peach Mold; see index.

Linda Miller (Mrs. W.R.)

CHUTNEY CHICKEN SALAD

1 cup mayonnaise
1/2 cup chutney, chopped
1 tsp. curry powder
2 tsp. grated lime peel
1/4 cup fresh lime juice
1/2 tsp. salt
4 cups diced white meat of chicken
    or turkey
1/2 fresh pineapple, cut in bite-
    sized pieces
1/2 cup thinly-sliced green onions
3/4 cup slivered almonds, toasted

Combine mayonnaise, chutney, curry powder, lime peel, lime juice and salt. Toss with other ingredients except almonds. Refrigerate until serving, then sprinkle with almonds. Should not be mixed any longer than 2 to 3 hours before serving.

The Committee

CURRY CHICKEN SALAD
"Make a day ahead"

2 cups mayonnaise
2 Tbsp. lemon juice
2-1/2 Tbsp. Kikkoman soy sauce
1 rounded Tbsp. curry powder (or
    less to taste)
1 Tbsp. onion juice
1 Tbsp. chutney, chopped
3 cups diced white meat of chicken
    or turkey
1-1/2 cups chopped celery
1 6-oz. can water chestnuts,
    drained and sliced
2 cups seedless white grapes
1 1-lb. can pineapple chunks, **well**-
    drained
3/4 cup slivered almonds, toasted

Combine mayonnaise, lemon juice, soy sauce, curry powder, onion juice and chutney. Toss with remaining ingredients except almonds. Refrigerate overnight. Sprinkle with almonds. Nice served in pineapple halves. Serves 8.

The Committee

MANDARIN CHICKEN SALAD

2 or 3 cups cooked chicken, diced
1 Tbsp. minced onion
1 tsp. salt
2 Tbsp. lemon juice
1 cup thinly-sliced celery
1 cup seedless grapes
1/3 cup mayonnaise
1 11-oz. can mandarin oranges
1/2 cup toasted slivered almonds

Combine first 7 ingredients. Chill. Just before serving, gently toss in mandarin oranges. Garnish with toasted almonds. Serves 8.

Nancy Wohlbruck (Mrs. Everett L.)

WONTON CHICKEN SALAD

5 half chicken breasts, boiled
2 dozen wonton skins cut into
    strips 1/2 wide and deep fried
    until golden
3 or 4 large stalks celery, chopped
5 or 6 green onions, chopped
SALAD DRESSING:
8 Tbsp. vinegar
6 Tbsp. sugar
2 Tbsp. vegetable oil
1 T. sesame oil
1 tsp. salt

Cut boiled chicken breasts into bite-sized pieces. Mix salad dressing ingredients together and put chicken breasts into it. The chicken should soak in the sauce 2 to 4 hours. Add celery and green onions to chicken in sauce. Just before serving, add wonton skins (deep fried) and toss. Salad may be made in advance. Serves 8 to 10.

Georgia Miller (Mrs. George)

CHICKEN AND LOBSTER LA BELLE DAME

3 whole chicken breasts
salt, celery salt, onion salt
1/2 tsp. fresh black pepper,
    divided
1 clove garlic
1 8-oz. pkg. frozen lobster tails
1 cup Hellman's mayonnaise
4 Tbsp. chopped chives
2 Tbsp. tomato sauce
2 tsp. prepared mustard
1/2 cup heavy cream
1 can black olives, pitted (divided)
1 stalk celery, finely diced
4 Tbsp. chopped parsley
1 cucumber

Cook chicken breasts in water to which celery salt, onion salt, the minced garlic clove and 1/4 tsp. pepper have been added. Pull from bones and cut into medium-sized pieces. Cook lobster tails according to package directions and dice. Mix mayonnaise, chives and tomato sauce and add to chicken and lobster. Add mustard, remaining pepper, salt to taste, cream and half of the black olives (sliced) to the mayonnaise mixture. Place chicken and lobster in a shallow salad bowl. Sprinkle with parsley and celery. Slice cucumbers thinly and arrange in overlapping circles on outer edge of bowl. Place remaining olives in a mound in the center. Serve slightly chilled.

Lynn Lewis

93

SUPER SALAD

Exactly what the name implies—a super salad.

1 large head lettuce, washed, broken in pieces
1 bunch watercress, if available If not, use butter lettuce
3 hard-boiled eggs, sliced
12-14 slices crisp-fried, crumbled bacon
1/3 cup crumbled Roquefort or bleu cheese

4 medium tomatoes, peeled and diced
2 medium avocados, peeled and diced
4 boned chicken breasts, cooked and cut in chunks
1 Tbsp. chopped chives
1 cup slivered, toasted almonds

Mix above ingredients. Use the following French dressing.

FRENCH DRESSING

1 tsp. salt
dash cayenne
1/4 tsp. Worcestershire
1 Tbsp. finely-minced onion
2 Tbsp. vinegar
6 Tbsp. salad oil.

Combine in bowl. Beat with rotary beater. Shake before serving. Makes 1/2 cup.

Ellen Knott (Mrs. B.F.)

MUSHROOM, HAM AND ARTICHOKE SALAD

2 Tbsp. lemon juice
1/2 lb. fresh mushrooms, thinly sliced
2 slices boiled ham, cut into thin strips
1 14-oz. can artichoke hearts, drained and coarsely chopped
2 Tbsp. minced onions
1/2 cup olive oil
1/4 cup wine vinegar
1 tsp. salt
pepper to taste

Sprinkle lemon juice over mushrooms. Arrange mushrooms, ham and artichokes on a serving platter. Mix onion, olive oil, vinegar, salt and pepper. Pour over salad and chill. Serves 4 to 6.

Linda Miller (Mrs. W.R.)

TACO SALAD

A complete dinner! Fun and good!

1 lb. ground beef
1 pkg. taco seasoning
water
1 can kidney beans, drained and
    rinsed
1 head lettuce
2 medium tomatoes, chopped
1/2 lb. grated Cheddar cheese
4 oz. Thousand Island dressing
1/2 large bag of Doritos

Brown beef and prepare taco sauce as directed. Break lettuce into bowl. Add warm beef, beans, tomatoes and cheese. Toss with salad dressing. Add Doritos and toss lightly. Makes 3 to 4 servings.

Linde Mullis (Mrs. W.F.)

CELERY SEED DRESSING FOR FRESH FRUITS

1/2 cup sugar
1 tsp. dry mustard
1 tsp. paprika
1/4 tsp. salt
1 tsp. celery seeds
1/3 cup honey
5 Tbsp. vinegar
1 Tbsp. lemon juice
1 cup salad oil.

Mix the dry ingredients. Add the remaining ingredients, oil last. Keep in a jar in the refrigerator. Let come to room temperature and shake well before using. Yield: 1-3/4 cups.

Barbara Stutts (Mrs. Clyde)

NEIMAN MARCUS POPPY SEED DRESSING

1-1/4 cups sugar
2 tsp. dry mustard
2 tsp. salt
2/3 cup vinegar
1 Tbsp. onion juice
2 cups salad oil (Wesson Oil)
2 Tbsp. poppy seeds

Mix sugar, mustard, salt and vinegar. Add onion juice and mix well (use hand mixer). Slowly add oil, beating constantly until thick. Add poppy seeds and mix again. Keeps indefinitely in the refrigerator. Stir well if it separates. Yield: 3-1/2 cups.

Sallie Wooten (Mrs. F.M.)

POPPY SEED DRESSING WITH HONEY

For fruit salad

1/2 cup sugar
1 tsp. dry mustard
1 tsp. paprika
1 tsp. poppy seeds
1/4 tsp. salt
1/3 cup honey
1/4 cup white vinegar
2 tsp. lemon juice
3/4 cup Wesson oil

Mix first five ingredients well. Add combined honey, vinegar and lemon juice. Beat well, with mixer, then add oil very slowly. Store in refrigerator. Makes 1 pint. Note: Can add 1 tsp. grated onion or 1 tsp. onion juice.

Stephany Alphin (Mrs. R.L.)
Barby Ross Goode (Mrs. D.J.)
Arnita Kee

YOGURT DRESSING FOR FRUIT SALAD

Delicious over fresh fruit salad

8 Tbsp. vanilla yogurt
4 Tbsp. unsweetened pineapple
    juice
2 tsp. cherry juice
1 Tbsp. mayonnaise (Hellman's)
2 packets Sweet 'n Low
sprinkle of pecans

Put yogurt in mixing bowl and add pineapple juice. Blend well with a whisk. Add other ingredients and blend until smooth. Serves 4.

Barby Ross Goode (Mrs. David J.)

BERRY'S SALAD DRESSING

Featured in "Bon Appetit." From Berry's Restaurant in Winston Salem, N.C.

1/2 cup sugar
2 Tbsp. sesame seeds
2 Tbsp. poppy seeds
1-1/2 tsp. minced onion
1/4 tsp. Worcestershire sauce
1/4 tsp. paprika
1/2 cup vegetable oil
1/4 cup cider vinegar

Mix well and store until ready to use. Yield: about 1 cup. Note: I would suggest using 2 bags of fresh spinach and 1 pint of halved fresh strawberries for this dressing recipe. Good on Katherine's Salad (see index) or any fruit salad.

Virginia Golding (Mrs. John G.)

BEV'S SALAD DRESSING

2 cloves garlic
1/4 cup sugar
1/4 cup salad oil
1/4 cup vinegar
2 tsp. salt
bleu cheese, crumbled

Mince garlic and add sugar, salad oil, vinegar and salt. Whisk together and pour over Boston lettuce. Sprinkle bleu cheese on top, to taste. Yield: 1/2 cup.

Beverly Hance (Mrs. James)

BIG MARGARET'S SPINACH SALAD DRESSING

This dressing is so easy, and gets nothing but raves.
It keeps for weeks in the refrigerator.

2 large onions, chopped
1 Tbsp. sugar
2 tsp. salt
1 tsp. pepper
2 tsp. celery seeds
6 tsp. prepared mustard
2/3 cup vinegar
2 cups salad oil.

Combine all ingredients in a jar and shake well until thoroughly blended. Yield: about 4 cups.

Deede Grainger (Mrs. Isaac B.)

BRASS DOOR DRESSING

Delicious, especially on spinach salads

1-1/4 cup mayonnaise
1/2 cup vegetable oil
1/4 cup honey
1/4 cup prepared mustard
3 Tbsp. fresh lemon juice
2 spring onions, finely chopped
1 Tbsp. chopped fresh parsley
1 tsp. celery seeds
1/4 tsp. dry mustard
1/4 tsp. curry powder

Thoroughly combine all ingredients in air-tight container. Shake well. Chill. Yield: 2-3/4 cups.

Carole Moore (Mrs. Thos. F., Jr.)

SUZANNE ROYSTER'S SPINACH SALAD DRESSING
"Low-calorie"

1/4 cup sugar (or less)
1 tsp. salt
1 tsp. dry mustard
1 tsp. poppy seeds
1 Tbsp. onion juice
3/4 cup cottage cheese
1/4 cup vinegar (apple cider)
1 cup salad oil

Place in blender and slowly add 1 cup salad oil, blending on slow speed while adding oil. Makes about 2 cups.

Georgia Miller (Mrs. George)

CAESAR SALAD DRESSING
Excellent!

4 Tbsp. lemon juice
1/4 cup olive oil
1/2 tsp. ground pepper
1 tsp. Worcestershire sauce
1/2 tsp. garlic powder
1/2 tsp. salt
1 egg, beaten
1/2 cup grated Parmesan cheese

Put all ingredients in a glass pint jar. Shake thoroughly and refrigerate several hours. Before using, shake well again. Serve over Romaine lettuce and toss with croutons. Yield: enough for one large salad.

B. J. Miller (Mrs. H.F., III)

COLESLAW DRESSING

1-1/2 cup mayonnaise
1/2 cup half and half
1/2 cup buttermilk
1/2 cup sugar
1/3 cup white vinegar
dash pepper
celery seed

Blend with hand mixer and mix with finely chopped cabbage. Can store in refrigerator and use as needed.

Georgia Miller (Mrs. George)

SALAD DRESSING
Nice to have in refrigerator at all times

1 can tomato soup (Campbell's)
1/2 cup Wesson oil
2/3 cup vinegar
3/4 cup sugar
1 tsp. salt
1 tsp. dry mustard
1/4 tsp. red pepper

Mix all ingredients in blender. When well mixed, put in quart jar and store in refrigerator. Yield: almost a quart.

Ann Copeland (Mrs. E.H., Jr.)

HONEY-LEMON FRENCH DRESSING
This is great on spinach and also excellent marinade for vegetables, meat and fish.

1/3 cup lemon juice (fresh)
1/2 cup salad oil
1 tsp. salt
1 tsp. paprika
2 Tbsp. honey
1/2 tsp. celery seed
1 clove garlic (optional)

Combine all ingredients and shake well before serving. Yield: 1 cup.

Variation: To make sweet French dressing, add additional 1/2 cup honey.

Carolyn Adams (Mrs. G.B., Jr.)

NONA JANE'S FRENCH DRESSING: PHILADELPHIA
"Very Special"

1 tsp. salt
1/4 tsp. paprika
1/2 tsp. dry mustard (I use
　　Coleman's)
3 or 4 Tbsp. sugar
dash pepper
1/3 cup olive oil
1/4 cup tarragon vinegar
1/4 cup white vinegar
4 Tbsp. ketchup
juice of 1/2 lemon
dash of Worcestershire sauce

Blend thoroughly in blender and store in covered jar in refrigerator. Yield: 1 cup.

Nancy Little (Mrs. T.M.)

SEA CAPTAIN'S RESTAURANT
BLEU CHEESE DRESSING

A specialty from Sea Captain's Restaurant in Murrell's Inlet, S.C.
Great to make in this quantity for Christmas presents.

1-1/2 lbs. bleu cheese
1 Tbsp. garlic powder
1/2 cup chopped onion
1 quart mayonnaise
3-1/2 quarts sour cream (Sealtest)
1/2 cup lemon juice
1/2 tsp. white pepper
1 cup cider vinegar
1/4 cup salt (about, or less to taste)

Grind cheese, garlic and onion and add to mayonnaise. In mixer, beat on low speed for two minutes. Add remaining ingredients and mix two more minutes. Yield: 1-1/2 gallons.

Anne Thrift (Mrs. Charles B., III)

SEAFOOD SALAD DRESSING

2 cups Hellman's mayonnaise
1/4 cup fresh parsley
1/4 cup onion
1/4 cup green pepper
1/4 cup chili sauce
1/4 cup Heinz catsup
1/4 cup sweet pickle
1/4 cup sour pickle
2 hard-boiled eggs
Tabasco and Worcestershire to
  taste

Finely chop vegetables, pickles and eggs. Mix all ingredients well and chill. Great with seafood, especially shrimp. Yield: 4 cups.

Betty Hight (Mrs. M.S.)

ROQUEFORT DRESSING

1/2 lb. Roquefort cheese,
  crumbled
1-3/4 cups half-and-half cream
2 cups mayonnaise (1 pt.),
  homemade or bought
1/4 tsp. salt
1/4 cup lemon juice
1 tsp. Worcestershire sauce
3 dashes Tabasco sauce
1/2 tsp. garlic powder

Place all ingredients in deep bowl of electric mixer. Mix at low speed until smooth and well blended. Pour into a jar and keep refrigerated. If a thicker dressing is desired, cut down on cream and mayonnaise. Yield: 5 cups.

Ellen Knott (Mrs. B.F.)

THOUSAND ISLAND DRESSING

1 cup mayonnaise
1/4 cup chili sauce
2 hard-boiled eggs, quartered
1/4 medium green pepper
1/2 medium stalk celery, sliced
1 tsp. paprika
1/2 tsp salt

Put ingredients in blender container. Blend until combined and green pepper, celery and onion are finely chopped. Makes two cups.

Jean Bridges (Mrs. D.T., Jr.)

THOUSAND ISLAND DRESSING
"Also good with seafood"

1 cup Hellman's mayonnaise
1/2 cup Heinz tomato catsup
1/2 cup chopped pickles
1 Tbsp. minced onion
1 tsp. chili powder
1/4 tsp. garlic salt
1/4 tsp. Tabasco sauce
1/8 tsp. pepper

Mix all ingredients and refrigerate. Yield: 1 pint. (Good with salad greens and seafood, particularly crabmeat.)

The Committee

VIETOFF'S PEPPERCREAM

2 cups mayonnaise
1/4 to 1/2 cup vinegar
1/2 cup Parmesan cheese
dash Tabasco
2 Tbsp. lemon juice
1 Tbsp. onion juice
1/2 tsp. garlic powder
lots of black pepper, freshly
*   ground if possible*

Mix in blender.

Julia Wade (Mrs. Hamlin)

FRENCH SALAD DRESSING FOR TOSSED GREEN SALAD

2 tsp. Kosher salt
1 tsp. freshly-cracked white pepper
1/2 tsp. freshly-cracked black pepper
1/4 tsp. granulated sugar
1/2 tsp. dry mustard
1 Tbsp. Dijon mustard
1 tsp. lemon juice
2 tsp. finely-chopped garlic (or put through press)
5 Tbsp. tarragon wine vinegar
2 Tbsp. olive oil
10 Tbsp. vegetable oil
1 raw egg
1/2 cup light cream (half-and-half)

To change the dressing to make a "Sauce Vinaigrette" add the following:
1 finely chopped hard-boiled egg
1 Tbsp. finely-chopped chives
1 Tbsp. finely-chopped parsley
2 tsp. finely-chopped green olives
1 Tbsp. small, well-drained capers

Put into blender jar in order given. Blend; then chill before using.

Serve over cooked asparagus or other cooked vegetables.

Gensie

CREAMY ITALIAN DRESSING FOR TOSSED GREEN SALAD

1/3 cup tarragon wine vinegar
1 tsp. salt
1/2 tsp. sugar
1 tsp. dry mustard
1 tsp. paprika
1/4 tsp. freshly-ground pepper
2/3 cup salad oil
1 clove garlic, minced (or put through press)
2 tsp. drained capers
1/2 tsp. dried oregano
1/2 tsp. minced parsley
2/3 cup mayonnaise
2/3 cup sour cream

Combine all ingredients in blender. Blend. Yield 2/3 cup.

Gensie

Vegetables

M.E. Wellborn

ARTICHOKES WITH SPICY VINAIGRETTE SAUCE

1. Wash 6 artichokes in cold water. Drain. Cut stems flush with base. Remove any small discolored outer leaves. Rub cut surface with lemon. Cut 1 inch off top of each, cutting straight across. Snip 1/4 inch off tip of each leaf with kitchen shears.
2. Tie with clean, white string to keep shape during cooking. In stainless steel or enamel kettle, bring large amount of water to boil. Add 2 tsp. salt and 2 Tbsp. lemon juice or vinegar to each quart of water. Add artichokes, stem side down. Set plate on top to keep submerged. Bring back to boil then simmer 25-30 minutes or until stem end pierces easily with knife.
3. Remove from water. Turn upside down to drain if served hot. Cool in cold water if served cold. Remove string; spread leaves apart. Pull out small prickly purple leaves in center.
4. Remove fuzzy choke from the inside; discard. If desired, put purple leaves on top of the artichoke. To eat, pull off leaves one by one and dip fleshy part in sauce. Pull between teeth to scrape off pulp. When all leaves are eaten, cut the heart and dip in sauce.

SPICY VINAIGRETTE SAUCE

1/4 cup wine or tarragon vinegar
1/2 tsp. garlic salt
1/4 tsp. black pepper
1 tsp. dry mustard
1 tsp. instant minced onion
3/4 cup oil

Mix first 6 ingredients. Gradually beat in oil. Let stand 1 hour before serving. Makes 1 cup.

The Committee

ASPARAGUS AU MAISON

2 lbs. fresh asparagus
SAUCE
1 tsp. lemon juice
1/2 cup dry white wine
3 egg yolks
salt and pepper to taste
sugar to taste
1/2 cup grated sharp Cheddar
    cheese

Clean and trim the asparagus and simmer until tender (about 8 to 10 minutes). Mix remaining ingredients together in top of a double boiler over low heat; beat with wire whisk until sauce doubles in volume. Spread drained asparagus in a 1-1/2 quart baking dish and pour sauce over; sprinkle with 1/2 cup sharp grated cheddar cheese and broil until bubbly. Serves 6.

Pam Allen (Mrs. John R.)

ASPARAGUS CASSEROLE

2-1/2 cups cracker crumbs
1 No. 2 can asparagus (reserve liquid)
1/2 lb. grated cheese
1 can mushroom soup
2 hard-boiled eggs
1/2 stick margarine

Drain asparagus and mix liquid with soup. Mix cracker crumbs and cheese. In a 2 qt. casserole dish start with a layer of crumbs and then layer with 1/2 the asparagus, then 1 egg sliced and 1/2 soup mixture. Repeat, ending with cracker-cheese mixture. Dot top with 1/2 stick margarine. Bake 20 minutes at 350 degrees. Serve 4 to 6.

Grace McBride (Mrs. J.W.)

ASPARAGUS IN CHEESE SAUCE

1-1/3 cup (1/2 lb.) diced cheddar cheese
2/3 cup milk
1 tsp. Worcestershire sauce
1/8 tsp. salt
dash cayenne pepper
3 slices cooked bacon, crumbled
3/4 cup buttered crumbs
*2-1/4 cups asparagus, canned or fresh-cooked
*Note: Can sustitute green beans for asparagus

Combine cheese, milk, Worcestershire sauce, salt and cayenne pepper. Cook over simmering water until smooth and well blended. Put asparagus into a 1 qt. casserole. Pour sauce over. Top with combined bacon and crumbs. Bake 20 to 30 minutes at 350 degrees. Serves 4 to 6.

Jean Bridges (Mrs. D.T., Jr.)

ARLIE'S BEANS

2 large (30 oz.) cans kidney beans, drained
8 strips bacon
2 cups chopped onions
2 green peppers, chopped
1 20-oz. bottle catsup
1 cup brown sugar
2 fresh, chopped tomatoes
salt to taste

Put 4 strips of bacon on the bottom of the casserole. Add half the beans and cover with the chopped foods. Add other half of drained beans, then brown sugar, catsup and salt, and top with 4 strips of bacon. Bake at least 3 hours at 300 degrees. Serves 12.

Caren Hollenbeck (Mrs. J.I.)

BAKED BEANS FOR A CROWD

3 large (28 oz.) cans pork 'n beans
1 large (21 oz.) can kidney beans
1 large (21 oz.) can northern beans
1 lb. bacon, fried and crumbled
2 medium onions, chopped
2 cups catsup
1 lb. brown sugar
1 Tbsp. dry mustard
1/2 green pepper, chopped
3 pickles, chopped, or
1/3 cup pickle relish

Combine all ingredients and bake at 350 degrees for 1 hour. Serves 30.

Sharon Edge (Mrs. W.S.)

BARBECUE BEANS

2 slices bacon, chopped
1/2 lb. ground chuck
1 small onion, chopped
1 2-lb. can pork and beans
1 1-lb. can kidney beans, drained
    and rinsed
1/4 cup brown sugar
1/2 cup catsup
2 Tbsp. Worcestershire sauce

Fry bacon and drain. Saute ground chuck and onions; drain. Add remaining ingredients. Place in 3 qt. casserole and bake at 375 degrees for 45 minutes. Serves 6-8.

Sandy Chase (Mrs. E.R.)

BOSTON BAKED BEANS

1 qt. navy or pea beans
3/4 lb. fat bacon or salt pork
1/3 cup molasses
1 Tbsp. salt
3 Tbsp. sugar
1/2 tsp. mustard
boiling water
1/2 tsp. baking soda

Pick over beans and soak overnight in cold water. In the morning drain and cover with fresh water containing baking soda. Cook slowly, simmering beans 10-15 minutes. Drain beans and rinse in cold water. Scald and scrape the pork and cut in thin slices. Pour beans into pot and place layer of pork every 1/2 inch, using beans to bury pork. Mix salt, sugar, mustard, molasses and cup of boiling water and pour over beans, adding enough boiling water to cover beans. Cover pot and bake 6 hours in 250 degree oven. Uncover during last 1/2 hour of cooking. Add water as needed.

Mary Jane Gilmore (Mrs. S.T.)

CASSEROLE OF BLACK BEANS
A good meatless meal.

1 lb. dried black beans
1/2 tsp. soda
1-1/2 cups coarsely-chopped
onions
2 large cloves garlic, minced
3 stalks celery, coarsely chopped
1 medium carrot, scraped and
chopped
1-1/2 Tbsp. salt
1/2 tsp. black pepper, freshly
ground
2 bay leaves
1/4 tsp. oregano
1 Tbsp. parsley, chopped
dash cayenne
4 Tbsp. butter
2 oz. dark rum
sour cream

Rinse beans and pick over. Cover with water and 1/2 tsp. soda. Let stand overnight, drain and rinse. Add next nine ingredients and just enough water to cover. Simmer, covered, over heat for 2 hours, stirring occasionally. Correct seasoning, adding a bit of cayenne. Remove bay leaves and turn bean mixture into casserole. Stir in butter and dark rum. Cover, bake at 350 degrees for 1 hour or more — until tender. Serve with side dish of sour cream. Serves 4-6.

Gensie

GREAT GREEN BEANS
Particularly handy with leftover green beans.

3 stalks celery, cut diagonally into
1/2 inch pieces
2 Tbsp. margarine or butter
1 Tbsp. cornstarch
3/4 cup chicken bouillon
2 Tbsp. soy sauce
2 tsp. sesame seeds, toasted
dash garlic salt
1 lb. fresh green beans, cooked and
drained
chopped parsley

Saute celery in margarine until tender. Combine cornstarch, bouillon, soy sauce, sesame seeds and garlic salt; add to celery and stir constantly over medium heat until thickened. Add green beans, stir and heat thoroughly. Garnish with parsley. Serves 4 to 6.

Carole Moore (Mrs. Thomas F., Jr.)

GREEN BEAN CASSEROLE

1 cup cracker crumbs
1 can (1 lb.) tomatoes
3 Tbsp. flour
1 can mushroom soup
1 cup sour cream
1 can l-lb. drained green beans
1 small onion, chopped
1 tsp. salt
2 tsp. butter
1/8 tsp. pepper
4 slices bacon, fried crisp

Sprinkle half the cracker crumbs on bottom of buttered 1-1/2 qt. casserole. Drain juice from tomatoes, reserve. Blend flour and tomato juice. Stir in soup, sour cream, onion, salt, pepper and crumbled bacon. Mix with beans and tomatoes. Sprinkle remaining crumbs on top and dot with butter. Bake at 350 degrees for 30 minutes. Serves 6.

Mary Lou Scholl (Mrs. Ken)

GREEN BEANS SUPREME

"Goes well with beef or poultry; also pork.
It is one of my family's favorites."

2 cans (1-lb. each) French-style
green beans
1-1/2 cups sour cream (large size)
3/4 cups grated Colby cheese
2 Tbsp. brown sugar
2 Tbsp. flour
1 Tbsp. grated onion
1 tsp. salt
1/4 tsp. pepper
1/2 tsp. Cavender's seasoning
(Greek seasoning)
1 can water chestnuts, drained and
sliced
1 4-oz. can sliced mushrooms,
drained
3/4 cup cornflake crumbs
4 Tbsp. melted butter

Saute cornflake crumbs in melted butter and set aside. Drain beans well. In large bowl combine sour cream, cheese, brown sugar, flour, onion and seasonings. Next, carefully fold in drained beans, water chestnuts and mushrooms. Spoon mixture into buttered 2-1/2 qt. casserole dish. Sprinkle sauteed cornflake crumbs over top of mixture. Bake at 350 degrees for 30 minutes. Serves 8. Can be made a day before serving.

Mandy Martin

Fresh tomatoes keep longer when placed with their stem ends down.

BROCCOLI CASSEROLE I

Very good!

2 pkgs. (10 oz.) frozen chopped
　broccoli
1 can cream of mushroom soup
1/2 cup mayonnaise
1/2 cup minced fresh onion
1 cup grated sharp Cheddar cheese
2 beaten eggs
　cheese cracker crumbs

Cook broccoli 5 minutes in boiling water, drain and put in colander and steam over boiling water 10 minutes. Mix mushroom soup, mayonnaise, onion, cheese, eggs and broccoli. Put into a 1-1/2 qt. casserole dish and sprinkle with cheese cracker crumbs. Bake 20 minutes at 400 degrees. This is better if made up and refrigerated a day before it is baked. Serves 8.

Hazel Harris
B.J. Miller (Mrs. H.F., III)
Variation: Substitute 2 boxes chopped spinach for broccoli.
Georgia Miller (Mrs. George)

BROCCOLI CASSEROLE II

Contains both vegetable and starch.

1 Tbsp. butter
1/2 cup onion, chopped
2 10-oz. boxes frozen chopped
　broccoli
3 oz. Velveeta cheese, diced
1 can cream of celery soup
1 cup prepared Minute Rice

Saute onion in butter. Prepare rice according to box directions for 1 cup of rice. Cook broccoli according to package directions; drain. Add onion, rice, cheese and soup to broccoli and mix well. Bake in greased 1 qt. casserole at 350 degrees for 45 minutes. Serves 6.

Deidre Witt (Mrs. L.P.)

BROCCOLI DELIGHT

1-1/2 lbs. fresh broccoli
1/3 cup fresh bread crumbs
1/2 cup minced onion
3 Tbsp. olive oil
1 garlic clove, mashed
salt and pepper
6-8 pieces bacon

Blanch broccoli. Cook bacon, drain and crumble. Saute bread crumbs in same pan. Put aside. Cook onions in oil in same pan until tender. Stir in garlic, chopped broccoli, salt and pepper. Toss until warmed. Add bacon and crumbs. Toss gently and serve. Can be cooked ahead, then tossed and reheated. Serves 6.

Dot Nicholls (Mrs. T.H.)

NAN'S BROCCOLI PUFF

6 unbeaten eggs
2 lbs. cottage cheese
6 Tbsp. flour
1/2 lb. cheddar cheese, diced
1 pkg. frozen chopped broccoli,
    uncooked
1/4 lb. butter
2 green onions and tops, chopped

Thaw the frozen broccoli quickly by placing in a colander and running hot water over it. Separate pieces with a fork and drain well. Have all ingredients at room temperature. In order listed, layer ingredients in the large bowl of the mixer and beat until well blended. Pour into a greased 9x12 inch baking dish and bake for 1 hour at 350 degrees or until a knife comes out clean. It should be golden brown and bubbly on top. Let set at room temperature for 10 minutes before serving.

Gayanne Mraz

SCALLOPED BROCCOLI CASSEROLE

1 10-oz. pkg. frozen chopped
    broccoli
3 Tbsp. melted butter or
    margarine
1/4 cup finely-chopped onion
1 16-oz. can cream-style corn
1 beaten egg
1/2 cup coarse saltine cracker
    crumbs (12 crackers)
1/2 tsp. salt
dash black pepper

Cook broccoli for 6 minutes. Drain well. Add onion, melted butter, corn, salt and pepper. Beat in egg. Fold in crumbs and place in 1 qt. casserole. Cook in 350 degree oven until set, about 50 minutes to an hour. Serves 4-6.

VARIATION
    Use as topping:
4 Tbsp. melted butter
2 slices chopped, cooked bacon
1 cup Pepperidge Farm herb
    stuffing

Mix butter, bacon and stuffing. Spread over vegetable mixture. Cook at 350 degrees 50-60 min. or until set.

Ellen Knott (Mrs. B.F.)

STIR-FRY BROCCOLI

1/4 cup boiling water
2 Tbsp. soy sauce
1 Tbsp. dry sherry
1 tsp. sugar
1/4 tsp. salt
1 bunch fresh broccoli
small onion, chopped

Combine first 5 ingredients, stir well. Set aside. Coat wok or skillet with oil. Heat at medium high temperature for 2 minutes, add broccoli and stir-fry for 2 minutes. (Note: If vegetable such as carrots is substituted, cooking time may be increased, but vegetables should be crisp.) Add onion and stir-fry for 3 minutes. Add soy sauce mixture, reduce heat to low and cook for 5 minutes. Serves 4.

Note: This recipe can be altered by substituting other vegetables, such as cauliflower, sliced carrots, mushrooms and others, or by combining any of the above.

Libby Preston

APPLE AND KRAUT BAKE

This blends a more favorable ingredient (apple) with a less favorable ingredient (kraut) for those who may not usually like kraut.

1 can (1 lb. 11 oz.) sauerkraut,
    drained and rinsed
1 cup applesauce (unspiced)
1/2 cup chopped onion (optional)
1 tsp. instant beef broth granules
    or from envelope)
2 tsp. caraway seeds

Combine all ingredients and place in a baking dish. Cover. Bake 35 minutes at 350 degrees. Uncover; bake 5 minutes more at 350 degrees. Serves 6-8.

Anne Szymanski (Mrs. Louis)

CABBAGE CASSEROLE

3 tsp. butter
1/2 cup onions, chopped
3 Tbsp. flour
1 can (1 lb.) tomatoes, broken up
2 tsp. Worcestershire sauce
1-1/2 tsp. salt
1 Tbsp. sugar
1/2 tsp. thyme
1/2 tsp. pepper
6 cups cabbage, chopped or cut up
3 slices buttered bread made into
    crumbs
1/4 lb. sharp cheese, cubed

Make a sauce of butter, onions and flour. Stir in tomatoes, Worcestershire sauce, salt, sugar, thyme and pepper. Cook slowly, mixing well. Boil cabbage for 5 minutes in water, drain and mix together with sauce. Place in a large casserole. Mix half of cheese with cabbage mixture and mix or toss other half of cheese with breadcrumbs and sprinkle over cabbage mixture. Bake at 350 degrees for 20 to 30 minutes. Serves 8-10.

Grace McBride (Mrs. J.W.)

SAUTEED CABBAGE

1/2 small head cabbage, about 1 lb.
4 Tbsp. butter
2 whole cloves
salt and freshly-ground pepper to taste

Quarter cabbage and cut away core. Cut each quarter crosswise into very thin slices. There should be about six cups. Heat butter in a skillet and add remaining ingredients. Cook, stirring often, without browning—about 15 minutes. Serves 4.

Ada Offerdahl (Mrs. John)

SWEET-SOUR CABBAGE
"Goes well with roast pork"

1 large onion
4 cloves
5 Tbsp. butter or margarine
1 small head cabbage (about 1-1/2 lbs.) sliced thin
1 small bay leaf
1 Tbsp. red wine vinegar
2 tsp. sugar
2 cups broth from boiled beef, OR
2 cups canned beef broth
salt and freshly-ground pepper to taste
1/4 cup currant jelly
2 cooking apples, peeled and chopped

Cut onion in half; stud one half with cloves and mince other half. Melt butter in large skillet, add cabbage, onion, apples, bay leaf, vinegar and sugar. Cover and cook until moisture is absorbed, about 15 minutes. Add 1 cup broth, cover and cook until cabbage is crisp-tender, about 20 minutes. Add more broth if mixture becomes too dry. Discard onion with cloves and bay leaf. Stir in 1/2 cup more broth or enough to moisten, plus jelly. Adjust seasoning and sprinkle with salt and pepper. Serves 6.

Ada Offerdahl (Mrs. John)

CARROTS WITH GREEN GRAPES
This is a delicious vegetable to serve with highly-seasoned food such as a curry or Mexican dish.

8 medium carrots
2 Tbsp. butter
1 Tbsp. sugar
1 tsp. salt
2 cups seedless green grapes
1/4 tsp. dried tarragon leaves
1/2 cup sour cream
2 Tbsp. water

Cut carrots crosswise into halves. Cut each half lengthwise into 1/2 inch strips. Heat 1 inch salted water (1/2 tsp. salt to 1 cup water) to boiling. Add carrots. Cover and cook until crisp-tender, about 5 minutes; drain. Melt butter in 10-inch skillet over medium-high heat. Add carrots, sugar and salt; cook and stir 5 minutes. Stir in grapes and tarragon; heat until hot. Remove from heat; stir in sour cream and water. Serves 6.

Gensie

CARROT SOUFFLE

". . . for one who says 'I do not eat carrots'!"

1 lb. carrots, peeled and sliced
1/2 cup melted butter
3 eggs
1/2 cup sugar
3 Tbsp. flour
1 tsp. baking powder
1/2 tsp. vanilla

Cook carrots in boiling, salted water until tender; drain. Combine carrots and butter in blender; blend until smooth. Add remaining ingredients and blend well. Spoon into lightly-greased 1-qt. shallow dish. (May separate eggs and add beaten egg whites for fluffiness.) Bake at 350 degrees for 45 minutes. Serves 6-8.

Janice Mayhew (Mrs. J.M.)

CRANBERRIED CARROTS

Goes well with poultry

1 can whole jellied cranberry sauce
4 Tbsp. brown sugar
1/4 cup margarine
20 oz. pkg. frozen crinkle-cut
    carrots

Preheat oven to 350 degrees. Combine all ingredients in a buttered baking dish. Bake at 350 degrees for 20 to 30 minutes, until carrots are tender. Serves 4 to 6.

Barbara Schischa

FESTIVE CARROT RING

Superb! A favorite with men.

2 cups mashed cooked carrots*
1 cup cracker crumbs
1 cup milk
3/4 cup grated sharp Cheddar
    cheese
3 eggs
1 cup soft butter
1/4 cup grated onion
1 tsp. salt
1/4 tsp. pepper
1/8 tsp. cayenne
Garnish: two 10-oz. pkgs. frozen
    peas, cooked as pkg. directs

*About 1 lb. fresh carrots, cut up,
    and cooked until tender.
    Mash thoroughly.

Combine carrots, crumbs, milk, cheese, butter, onion and seasonings. Beat eggs until puffy. Fold into carrot mixture. Pour into well-greased 1-1/2 qt. ring mold. Bake at 350 degrees for 40 to 45 minutes. Turn out onto warm platter. Fill center with cooked peas. Garnish outside of ring with parsley. Serves 8-12.

Ellen Knott (Mrs. B.F.)

HAWAIIAN CARROTS
Colorful and delicious

1 pound carrots, peeled and
    diagonally sliced
1 medium-sized green pepper,
    chopped coarsely
1/3 cup sugar
1 tsp. cornstarch
1/2 tsp. salt
1 (8-oz.) can pineapple chunks
2 tsp. vinegar
2 tsp. soy sauce

Cook carrots, covered, in a small amount of boiling water until tender. Add green pepper; cook 3 minutes. Drain. Combine sugar, cornstarch and salt in a medium saucepan. Drain pineapple and reserve juice. Add water to reserved pineapple juice to make 1/3 cup liquid; stir into sugar mixture. Stir in vinegar and soy sauce; cook over low heat until bubbly, stirring constantly. Stir in vegetables and pineapple; cook until heated throughout. Serves 6 to 8.

Virginia Golding (Mrs. John G.)

SWEET HERBED CARROTS
For microwave oven

4 cups (about 1 lb.) sliced carrots
1 large stalk celery, chopped
1 small onion, sliced
1/4 tsp. dill weed
2 Tbsp. sugar
1/3 cup white wine

Place all ingredients in a bowl, cover tightly with plastic wrap. Cook in microwave on high for 5 minutes, stirring once. Lower power to 70 percent (med. high) and cook 10 more minutes, stirring once half way through the time, or until carrots are tender-crisp. Serves 4-6.

Carolyn Adams (Mrs. G.B., Jr.)

ZESTY CARROTS

8 medium carrots, sliced
1/4 cup water
2 Tbsp. grated onion
2 Tbsp. horseradish
1/2 cup mayonnaise
1/2 tsp. salt
1/4 tsp. pepper
1/4 cup cracker crumbs
1 Tbsp. butter
dash of paprika

Cook carrots until tender; drain and place in shallow baking dish. Mix water, onion, horseradish, mayonnaise, salt and pepper; pour over carrots. Mix crumbs, butter and paprika; sprinkle over top. Bake at 325 degrees for 15 minutes. Serves 4-6.

Bonnie Phillips (Mrs. H.M.)

CAULIFLOWER WITH DILLY SHRIMP SAUCE

Serve with an entree other than sea food.

2 Tbsp. melted butter
2 Tbsp. all-purpose flour
1-1/2 cups milk
1/4 tsp. salt
dash of pepper
1/2 tsp. dried dill weed
1 medium head of cauliflower
1 cup small cooked shrimp

Combine butter and flour in saucepan. Add milk to make white sauce. Add salt, pepper, dill weed and shrimp. Stir well. Meanwhile cook cauliflower whole. Drain. Pour sauce over and garnish with additional shrimp. Serves 4-6.

Virginia Golding (Mrs. John G.)

CHEESE-FROSTED CAULIFLOWER

Even kids like this.

1 large cauliflower
1 can cream of celery soup
sharp cheese
paprika

Wash cauliflower and trim base. Precook whole in boiling salted water for 15 min. Drain. Place in greased baking dish. Empty can of soup on cauliflower. Grate enough cheese to cover cauliflower. Sprinkle with paprika. Bake at 375 degrees for 10-15 minutes. Serves 4-5.

Judy Ranson (Mrs. R.C.)

HUNGARIAN CAULIFLOWER

4 Tbsp. butter
4 Tbsp. flour
1/2 tsp. salt
1/4 tsp. pepper
1 cup sour cream
1 cup water
1 tsp. dill seed
1 head cauliflower
dry bread crumbs

Preheat oven to 400 degrees. Heat butter, stir in flour, salt and pepper. Remove from heat; add sour cream, water and dill seeds. Return to heat and boil for one minute. Separate the cauliflower into florets. Arrange in square baking dish. Cover with sauce, sprinkle with bread crumbs and bake 40-45 minutes. Serves 4-6.

Barbara Schischa

CREOLE CORN

3 slices bacon, finely chopped
3/4 cup chopped onions
10 ears fresh corn, cut from cob
4 ripe tomatoes, peeled and
    chopped
1/3 cup chopped green pepper
1 tsp. salt
1 tsp. freshly-ground black pepper

Saute bacon until about half done, then add onions and cook, stirring until transparent. Add corn and cook about 10 minutes, stirring constantly. Add tomatoes and green pepper and cook 10 minutes more, until very soft. Add salt and pepper. May be served as is or stuffed into tomatoes or green peppers. Serves 6-8.

Anna Stanley (Mrs. Verner)

CORN FRITTERS

salad oil
2 eggs
1 can (16 oz.) whole corn, drained
1 cup flour
3/4 tsp. salt
1 tsp. baking powder
1/4 cup milk
syrup or confectioner's sugar

Heat one-half inch of oil in a skillet. In a bowl, with a fork, stir one tablespoon of salad oil and next six ingredients. Drop by tablespoonful into hot oil. Fry 3-5 minutes. Serve with hot syrup or dusted with confectioner's sugar. Serves 6.

Gail Golding (Mrs. James N.)

GREAT-GRANDMOTHER BOW'S CORN PUDDING
Old-fashioned goodness!

1/2 cup sugar
1 tsp. salt, scant
3 Tbsp. flour
2 cups milk
3 eggs
1 can (No. 303) white shoe-peg
    sweet corn, drained

In mixing bowl, mix well the sugar, salt, flour and 1 cup milk. In separate bowl, beat eggs. Add beaten eggs and one more cup milk to other ingredients. Add drained corn and mix well. Pour into a buttered 1-3/4 quart dish. Dot top with butter, using approximately 2 Tbsp. Bake 1 hour in a 350 degree preheated oven. Serves 6-8.

B. J. Miller (Mrs. H.F., III)

CORN PUDDING

3 eggs
2 cups milk
1/2 cup light cream
1 Tbsp. sugar
1 tsp. salt
3 cups drained whole kernel corn
  (canned or cooked frozen or
  fresh)
1/4 cup bread crumbs
2 Tbsp. butter, melted

Preheat oven to 350 degrees. Grease 1-1/2 qt. casserole. Beat eggs until light and fluffy. Add milk, cream, sugar and salt. Stir in corn, bread crumbs and butter. Pour into prepared casserole. Bake at 350 degrees for 50 to 60 minutes. Serves 6.

Mayree Kay Miller (Mrs. J.J.)

CUCUMBERS WITH SOUR CREAM DRESSING
"A good accompaniment."

4 medium cucumbers
1-1/4 tsp. salt
1 cup thick sour cream
2 Tbsp. white vinegar
2 tsp. minced onion
1/4 tsp. sugar
dash freshly-ground black pepper

Peel and slice cucumbers and sprinkle with 1 tsp. salt. Let stand for 30 minutes; then press out excess water between pieces of cheesecloth. Combine remaining ingredients and mix with cucumbers. Serves 6-8. This is a good way to use excess summer garden cucumbers.

Ellen Knott (Mrs. B.F.)

CRISPY EGGPLANT
This goes well with anything—a good meat substitute if you have an occasional 'veggie' meal, as we do!"

1/2 cup Hellman's mayonnaise
1 Tbsp. finely-minced onion
1/4 tsp. salt
1/3 cup Pepperidge Farm Seasoned
  Dressing crumbs
1/3 cup Parmesan cheese
2 tsp. dried Italian seasoning
1 1-lb. eggplant, unpeeled

Mix first 3 ingredients. Mix next 3 together. Wash and dry eggplant and slice into 1/2 inch slices (not necessary to peel). Spread each slice with mayonnaise on both sides and roll in crumb mixture. Place in a shallow roasting pan and bake at 425 degrees for 15 minutes—until lightly browned. Serves 4 to 6.

Anna Stanley (Mrs. Verner E.)

EGGPLANT CASSEROLE

1/2 medium onion, chopped
1/2 green pepper, chopped
3 stalks celery, chopped
2 Tbsp. oil
1 16-oz. can tomatoes, sieved
1/2 tsp. Worcestershire sauce
1/2 tsp. salt (or to taste)
1/8 tsp. pepper
1 large eggplant
1/4 pound grated Cheddar cheese

Saute first 3 ingredients in cooking oil until onion is golden. Add tomatoes, Worcestershire, salt and pepper. Simmer. Peel and cube eggplant and cook in salted water until almost done but still firm. Drain and add to tomato mixture. Simmer about 5 more minutes. Put in a buttered casserole, mix in 3/4 of the cheese and sprinkle remaining cheese over the top. Dot with butter and bake about 15 minutes in a 350 degree oven, or until cheese is melted and bubbly. This may be prepared ahead and refrigerated until time to pop into oven. Serves 6-8.

Cathy Bradford (Mrs. W.Z., Jr.)

MUSHROOM CASSEROLE
Different!

1 lb. sliced fresh mushrooms
2 tsp. beef bouillon granules
2 Tbsp. flour
1/2 cup water
1/2 cup milk
TOPPING:
1/2 cup bread crumbs
3/4 cup Parmesan cheese

Slice mushrooms, place in buttered 1-1/2 qt. casserole dish. Put bouillon, flour and water into pan—make a paste. Stirring, add milk and bring to a slow boil. Pour sauce over mushrooms. Top with topping—dot with butter. Bake at 350 degrees for 40 minutes. Serves 4-6.

Dale E. Yaged

MUSHROOMS POLONAISE

1-1/2 lbs fresh mushrooms, sliced
1/2 cup butter
1 onion, minced
2 Tbsp. flour
1 cup sour cream
1/4 cup whipping cream
salt and pepper to taste
1/4 tsp. nutmeg
2 Tbsp. minced parsley
1/4 cup bread crumbs tossed in
    1/4 cup butter

Saute mushrooms in butter until lightly browned. Add onion; cook until soft. Stir in flour. Cook until thick, stirring constantly. Stir in other ingredients except crumbs. Pour into buttered casserole. Top with bread crumbs. Bake at 325 degrees for 35 minutes or until brown. Serves 6.

Ellen Knott (Mrs. B.F.)
Virginia Golding (Mrs. John G.)

GRANDMOTHER BARNES' STUFFED MUSHROOMS

If you like garlic, these are the best stuffed mushrooms ever!

1 lb. large, fresh mushrooms
1 cup finely-chopped pecans
1/4 cup melted BUTTER
4 Tbsp. chopped parsley (fresh or
    dried)
1 large clove garlic, mashed
1/4 tsp. thyme
1/2 tsp. salt
dash pepper
1/2 cups whipping cream*

Rinse mushrooms and remove stems. Arrange hollow side up in 9x13 pan. Chop the stems and mix with all the rest of the ingredients except the cream. Heap this mixture into the mushroom caps. (I use a baby feeding spoon.) Pour unwhipped whipping cream over all. Bake at 350 degrees for 20 minutes. Baste with cream once or twice during baking. Serves 6-8.
*If freezing, do so without the cream. Remove from freezer, add cream. Bake about 10 minutes longer.

Marg Barnes (Mrs. R.W.)

STUFFED MUSHROOMS

Great to serve with game dinners.

2 lbs. large white mushrooms,
    rinsed and stems removed
1 lb. bulk sausage
1 can cheddar cheese soup
Italian bread crumbs

Cook sausage in frying pan and break into small pieces. Drain fat. Add about half a can of cheddar cheese soup, undiluted, and sprinkle bread crumbs to desired consistency to handle easily (the cheese will bind ingredients). Stuff the mushroom buttons. Bake at 425 degrees for about 5 to 7 minutes.

Libby Morrison (Mrs. Jack)

CHOW YUK

Orientals appreciate vegetables for their own sakes. This combination is pleasing in taste, shape, texture and color.

1 7-oz. pkg. frozen (or fresh)
    Chinese pea pods
1 qt. thinly sliced broccoli, stems
    and tops
1/2 cup sliced water chestnuts
1/2 cup sliced green onions
1 Tbsp. slivered fresh ginger, or
1 tsp. ground ginger
2 Tbsp. peanut oil
2 Tbsp. soy sauce
3 Tbsp. pale dry Sherry

Thaw pea pods. Prepare next 4 ingredients and refrigerate all until ready to cook. Heat peanut oil in wok or electric frying pan set at 425 degrees. Saute ginger 1 to 2 minutes, stirring frequently. Add broccoli and water chestnuts. Stir in soy sauce and Sherry. Cover and cook 2 to 3 minutes, stirring occasionally. Remove cover; add pea pods and green onions; stirring until heated through. Turn into heated serving dish. Serves 6.

Gensie

LEEKS WITH SWISS CHEESE

8 large leeks
8 slices bacon, cut into 2-inch
    pieces
1 cup water
1/8 tsp. ground thyme
3 Tbsp. butter
2 Tbsp. flour
1 cup milk
1 egg yolk
1/2 cup heavy cream
2 Tbsp. grated Swiss cheese
salt and pepper to taste

Preheat oven to 375 degrees. Trim off root ends of leeks. Cut off tops, leaving 1 to 2 inches of light green. Cut the stalks in half lengthwise and wash thoroughly under running water, holding the leaves apart. Again, cut in half lengthwise, then into 2-inch pieces. Brown bacon in a skillet. Drain fat. Add leeks, water, salt, pepper and thyme. Cover tightly and cook until leeks are tender and water has evaporated, about 20-25 minutes. Melt the butter in a saucepan and stir in flour with a whisk until smooth. Add milk, stirring and cooking until it comes to a boil. Cook 5 minutes. Stir egg yolk and cream together and mix into the white sauce. Combine the sauce and leeks. Pour all into a lightly buttered, 9 to 10 inch pie plate or shallow casserole. Sprinkle with the cheese and bake 20 minutes or until golden. Serves 6.

Virginia Golding (Mrs. John G.)

HEAVENLY ONIONS

2 large Bermuda onions
2 Tbsp. butter
1/2 lb. Muenster or Swiss cheese
10-3/4 oz. can cream of mush-
    room soup
1/2 cup milk
1 Tbsp. soy sauce
1 cup buttered crumbs
1/4 tsp. freshly-ground pepper

Peel and slice onions. Separate into rings and saute in butter with pepper until transparent. Place onions in a shallow baking pan or casserole. Cover with cheese. In a separate bowl, combine soup with the milk and soy. Pour over cheese and onions. Top with crumbs. Bake for 40 minutes at 350 degrees. Serves 4 to 6.

Gensie

To keep sweet white onions such as Vidalias fresh longer, tie them in a stocking with a knot between each onion so they do not touch, and hang from a hook.

SPINACH-STUFFED ONIONS

2 pkgs. frozen, chopped spinach
2 3-oz. pkgs. cream cheese,
    softened
2 eggs
2 slices bread with crusts removed,
    crumbled
1/2 cup grated Parmesan cheese
1/4 cup liquid from cooking
    spinach
2 large flat white onions
1/2 tsp. nutmeg

Cook spinach. Drain and save 1/4 cup liquid. Beat together the cream cheese and eggs until light. Add remaining ingredients except spinach. Mix well. Add spinach and stir. Peel onions and cut in half crosswise. Separate to form shells. Cutting the "core" out with a paring knife helps in separating them. One can get about 6 shells per onion. Place in a greased baking dish. Fill in base of shells with smaller onion pieces. Put a larger piece over the hole left in separating process. Spoon in the mixture. Bake at 350 degrees for 35-40 minutes, or until shells are soft and filling is set. Makes 12 shells.

Jean Rowe (Mrs. William)

STIR-FRIED SNOW PEAS AND WATER CHESTNUTS
"Cannot be prepared ahead."

2 lbs. fresh snow peas
3 bunches young green onions,
    sliced diagonally
6 Tbsp. butter
2 cans water chestnuts, sliced
salt, freshly-ground pepper and
    Accent, to taste
1 Tbsp. soy sauce (Kikkoman)

Pull off strings and break off ends of snow peas. Heat butter in large skillet or wok. Add onions and saute over medium heat 2 or 3 minutes. Add snow peas, water chestnuts and seasonings. Continue sauteing 2 to 3 minutes more until peas are hot but crisp. Stir in soy sauce and serve immediately. Serves 8.
Note: If fresh snow peas are unavailable, use frozen peas. Thaw, dry them, and follow same procedure.

Virginia Golding (Mrs. John G.)

SPINACH AND ARTICHOKE CASSEROLE
Rich, but excellent side dish with steak or roast

2 10-oz. pkgs. frozen chopped
    spinach
1 can artichokes
1/2 cup melted butter
1 8-oz. pkg. cream cheese,
    softened
1 tsp. lemon juice
saltine cracker crumbs

Heat oven to 350 degrees. Cook spinach and drain well. Add butter, cream cheese and lemon juice to spinach. Chop artichokes and place in bottom of casserole dish. Cover with spinach mixture and top with crumbs (toss crumbs with extra melted butter). Bake for 25 minutes uncovered, until bubbly. Serves 6.

Carole Moore (Mrs. Thomas F. Jr.)

SPINACH CASSEROLE I

2 pkgs. frozen chopped spinach
1 pkg. Lipton onion soup
1 8-oz. carton sour cream
grated cheddar cheese

Cook spinach according to package directions and drain. Mix with onion soup and sour cream. Pour into greased 1-1/2 casserole. Cover with grated cheese. Bake at 375 degrees until cheese is lightly brown and casserole is bubbly. Serves 4 to 6.

Pat Gatlin (Mrs. Leon)

SPINACH CASSEROLE II

1 pkg. frozen chopped spinach
1/2 cup water
1 tsp. sugar
1 egg
1 cup grated sharp cheese
1 can cream of chicken soup
3 Tbsp. melted butter
dash of garlic salt
dash of red pepper
2 slices of bread, cubed

Cook spinach until thawed, using 1/2 cup water and 1 tsp. sugar. Drain thoroughly, mashing out all liquid. Combine soup, egg, cheese and spinach in greased 1-1/2 qt. casserole. Toss bread cubes in butter to which garlic and red pepper have been added. Place on top of spinach and bake in a 350 degree oven for 1 hour. Serves 6.

Mary Ann Thomas (Mrs. John G.)

DELUXE BAKED SPINACH
Even reluctant spinach eaters will like this tasty dish.

2 10-oz. pkgs. frozen chopped
   spinach
3 Tbsp. butter or margarine
2 Tbsp. minced onion
3 Tbsp. flour
1 cup milk
3 hard-boiled eggs, finely chopped
1/4 tsp. nutmeg
1/2 tsp. salt
1/4 tsp. pepper
1/2 cup shredded sharp Cheddar
   cheese
1/2 cup fine soft bread crumbs
2 to 3 Tbsp. melted butter or
   margarine
paprika

Cook spinach according to package directions and drain well—press out as much liquid as possible. Cook onion in melted butter until transparent. Make a white sauce by blending flour well with butter and stirring in milk. Season with nutmeg, salt and pepper. Mix spinach and eggs well with white sauce and place in buttered baking dish. Top with mixture of cheese and crumbs. Drizzle butter over top and sprinkle with paprika. Bake at 375 degrees for 15-20 minutes. Serves 6-8.

Hilda Rutherford (Mrs. N.A.)

MARY FEE'S SPINACH CASSEROLE
Great side dish from Evanston, Illinois

2 pkg. frozen chopped spinach
  (partially thawed and
  cooked)
1 can water chestnuts, drained and
  sliced
1 pkg. frozen Welsh rarebit,
  thawed
8 slices cooked chopped bacon
1/2 can onion rings

Combine well-drained spinach, chestnuts and 1/3 of the rarebit in medium-sized casserole. Top with bacon. Spread remaining rarebit on top, then onion rings. Bake at 350 degrees for about 20 minutes. Serves 6 to 8.

Nancy Little (Mrs. T.M.)

SPINACH MADELEINE
This is spicy!

2 pkgs. chopped spinach
4 Tbsp. butter
2 Tbsp. flour
2 Tbsp. chopped onion
1/2 cup evaporated milk
1/2 cup vegetable liquid
1/2 tsp. pepper
3/4 tsp. celery salt
3/4 tsp. garlic salt
salt to taste
6 oz. Jalepenos cheese
1 tsp. Worcestershire sauce
red pepper to taste
bread crumbs (optional)

Cook spinach according to directions. Reserve liquid. Melt butter in saucepan over low heat. Add flour, stirring until blended and smooth, but not brown. Add onion and cook until soft. Add liquid slowly. Cook until smooth and thick. Add seasonings and cheese which has been cut up into small pieces. Stir until melted. Combine with cooked spinach. Put into casserole, cover with bread crumbs and bake at 350 degrees for 30 minutes or until bubbly. Serves 6.

Mary Lou Bethune (Mrs. W.H.)

SPINACH PIE
Great for lunch or brunch—a quiche without a crust

10 oz. sharp Cheddar cheese,
  grated
10 oz. pkg. chopped frozen
  spinach
2 Tbsp. flour
4 eggs, beaten
1 cup milk
salt and pepper

Cook spinach and drain well. Toss cheese with flour. Add eggs, milk, salt, pepper and spinach. Pour into greased 9 inch pie pan. Bake 40 minutes at 350 degrees until set. Serves 6.

Linda Miller (Mrs. W.R.)

EASY SPINACH SOUFFLE
Quick, easy, few calories; but good

2 pkgs. frozen chopped spinach
2 eggs, beaten
2 cups cottage cheese, small curd
   (A & P's is best)
1/3 cup Parmesan cheese, grated

Cook spinach as directed on package. Drain well; squeeze out excess water. Add remaining ingredients. Put in greased 2-qt. pyrex dish. Cook at 350 degrees for 30-40 minutes. Sprinkle extra Parmesan cheese on top. Serves 8-10.

Mary Maletis

MEME'S SQUASH SOUFFLE
Special touch is "homemade" white sauce

2 lbs. yellow squash
2 eggs
1 onion, grated
1/2 lb. New York State cheese,
   grated
2 cups white sauce (recipe follows)
bread crumbs

Cook squash; drain and mash. Add beaten eggs, grated cheese and white sauce. Cook in top of double boiler for 1 hour with the lid on, stirring occasionally. Put in greased 2-qt. casserole. Top with bread crumbs. Bake at 375 degrees abour 25-30 minutes until crumbs are brown.

THICK WHITE SAUCE

6 Tbsp. butter
8 Tbsp. flour
2 cups milk
1/2 tsp. salt

Melt butter; blend in flour. Add slowly the 2 cups milk and salt. Stir constantly. When thickened, stir into squash.

Betty Dale Archer (Mrs. J.M., III)
Georgia Miller (Mrs. George)

Variation: Use 1 can mushroom soup and 1 cup fresh breadcrumbs in squash mixture for white sauce and place 4 bacon strips on the top of casserole.

SQUASH CASSEROLE

2 lbs. yellow squash
1 medium onion, chopped, or to
   taste
2 eggs
1 stick butter or margarine
1 cup bread crumbs, divided
1 Tbsp. sugar (or to taste)
1 tsp. salt (or to taste)
grated cheese or crumbled bacon
   (optional)

Cook squash and onion until tender. Drain partially. mash squash and add 1/2 cup bread crumbs, sugar, salt, eggs and butter. Pour into a 1-1/2 qt. casserole. Add remaining crumbs, dot with butter. If you wish, add grated cheese or crumbled bacon to topping. Bake at 325 degrees for 30 minutes. Serves 6.

Linda Hawfield (Mrs. Ben)

SOUFFLED SQUASH

2 lbs. small tender yellow squash
6 Tbsp. butter, divided
1/2 tsp. salt
1 green onion chopped, with some
    of the tops, OR
1 tsp. dried green onion
1/2 tsp. black pepper
1/3 cup celery, finely chopped
1/4 cup onion, finely chopped
1/4 cup green pepper, finely
    chopped
2 large eggs
1 Tbsp. milk
1 Tbsp. honey
salt to taste
1 tsp. baking powder
1/8 tsp. Tabasco
1 tsp. Worcestershire sauce
1 tsp. all-purpose flour
3 Tbsp. fine cracker crumbs OR
3 Tbsp. finely grated Cheddar
    cheese

Wash unpeeled squash and slice as thinly as possible and place in saucepan with 3 Tbsp. butter, salt, green onion and pepper. Cover and simmer over low heat for 25 minutes or until squash is tender. Mash squash in large bowl and add celery, onion and green pepper. Combine lightly beaten eggs with milk, honey, salt, baking powder, Tabasco, Worcestershire sauce and flour; fold into squash mixture. Add more salt if needed. Grease souffle dish or cups with butter and fill with mixture. Top with cracker crumbs and dot with remaining butter. Place in a pan of hot water which is at least 1 inch deep. Bake in a preheated 350 degree oven for 30 minutes for cups and about 45 minutes for souffle dish, or until light brown and bubbling. Serves 6.

Ellen Knott (Mrs. B.F.)

SAVORY STUFFED ZUCCHINI

Serve with steak from the grill.
The cayenne pepper gives this dish a unique taste.

6 small and thin zucchini
salt
1/4 cup butter or margarine
1 clove garlic, split
1 medium onion, chopped
1 cup chopped fresh tomato, skin
    removed
1 cup cooked white rice
1/2 tsp. dried oregano leaves
1/8 tsp. cayenne pepper
1/2 cup grated Parmesan cheese

Wash zucchini, cut off stems, cut in half lengthwise. In small amount of water with 1/2 tsp. salt cook zucchini 5 minutes or until tender. Drain. Scoop out seeds and discard. In hot butter saute garlic until golden—discard. Add onion, brown until golden, add tomato, rice, oregano, 1 tsp. salt and cayenne pepper. Mix well. Preheat oven to 350 degrees; sprinkle inside of zucchini with salt. Fill with rice mixture. Sprinkle with Parmesan cheese, arrange in single layer in buttered baking dish and bake uncovered 15 minutes. Put under broiler for 1 or 2 minutes to brown top. Serves 8-10.

Mary Ann Falciani (Mrs. R.B.)

ZUCCHINI CASSEROLE

1 cup red Italian onion rings
1 cup green pepper strips
1/4 cup butter
2 cups zucchini, cut in 1 inch slices
4 tomatoes, peeled and cut in wedges
salt and pepper
Parmesan cheese

Saute onion rings and pepper strips in butter. When vegetables begin to take color add zucchini and saute about 5 minutes longer. Add tomatoes and cook until tomatoes are soft (about 5 minutes). Season with freshly-ground black pepper and salt. Turn the vegetables into a casserole and sprinkle with Parmesan cheese. Just before serving time, bake in a 375 degree oven until topping browns and vegetables are hot. Serves 6.

Cathy Bradford (Mrs. W.Z., Jr.)

ZUCCHINI AND CHEESE CASSEROLE

3 cups finely **grated** zucchini
1 cup cracker crumbs
1 cup grated cheese
2 beaten eggs
2 Tbsp. chopped onion
2 Tbsp. chopped chives
3 Tbsp. melted butter or margarine
1/2 cup sour cream

Combine all the ingredients and put into a well-buttered 3 qt. casserole. Bake for one hour at 350 degrees. Serves 6.

Ellen Knott (Mrs. B.F.)

ZUCCHINI SQUASH CASSEROLE

10 zucchini squash
1/2 cup butter, softened or melted
3/4 cup Cheddar cheese, grated
1/4 cup Gruyere cheese, grated
1 cup sour cream
1/2 tsp. salt
1/4 cup chives
1/2 tsp. paprika
1 cup crumbs
Parmesan cheese

Preheat oven to 350 degrees. Slice zucchini in hunks. Cook for a few minutes in boiling salted water. Drain thoroughly. Make a sauce from the butter, Cheddar cheese, Gruyere, sour cream, salt, chives and paprika. Put squash in a 3-qt. casserole dish. Pour sauce over the top. Sprinkle crumbs on this. Dot with butter. Grate Parmesan cheese on top. Bake until heated through. Serves 8.

Libby Morrison (Mrs. Jack)

ZUCCHINI FRITTERS

Great as a different use for zucchini

2 cups flour
1 tsp. baking powder
1 egg
2 Tbsp. olive oil
1-1/4 cup milk (divided)
1/2 tsp. salt
1/4 tsp. pepper
1 cup grated Cheddar cheese
3 medium zucchini, grated and
　　drained
2 crushed cloves garlic
2 Tbsp. finely-chopped onion
1 Tbsp. minced parsley
oil for frying
salt
Parmesan cheese (optional)

Sift flour and baking powder. Mix egg, olive oil, 1/2 cup milk, salt and pepper. Beat and add flour mixture. Add Cheddar and rest of milk to make smooth batter. Blend in zucchini, garlic, onion and parsley. Heat oil in deep fryer and drop in batter. Fry until golden (4 or 5 minutes per fritter) and keep warm in oven. Also good sprinkled with Parmesan cheese. Salt and serve at once. Makes 1 doz. fritters or 3 doz. appetizers.

Dot Nicholls (Mrs. T.H.)

ZUCCHINI ROUNDS

Like a cheesy pancake

1/3 cup biscuit mix
1/3 cup grated Parmesan cheese
1/8 tsp. pepper
2 eggs, slightly beated
2 cups shredded, unpared zucchini
1/4 cup minced onion
butter

In mixing bowl, stir together biscuit mix, cheese and pepper. Stir in beaten eggs, just until mixture is moistened. Fold in zucchini and onion. In 10-inch skillet melt butter over medium heat. Using 2 Tbsp. of mixture for each round, cook four rounds at a time until brown. Keep warm in ovenproof container while cooking remaining rounds. Serves 6.

Ellen Knott (Mrs. B.F.)

Use a pinch of sugar when cooking all vegetables. A pinch of baking soda in green vegetables is always nice to bring out the flavor.

ZUCCHINI SOUFFLE

3 lbs. grated zucchini (5 to 6
    zucchini)
1 med onion, grated
1/4 cup fresh parsley
1 clove garlic, mashed (optional)
1 cup Bisquick
1/2 cup Wesson oil
1/2 tsp. seasoned salt
1/2 cup Parmesan cheese
5 eggs, beaten
1 Tbsp. butter or margarine
mint (optional). If fresh, use up to
    1/2 cup; if dried, use 1 tsp.

Mix grated zucchini, onion, parsley, mint, garlic, Bisquick, oil, salt and cheese. Beat lightly. Add beaten eggs. Pour into greased 9x13 inch or 8x11 pan. Drizzle top with butter or margarine. Bake approx. 35 minutes at 350 degrees. Cut in 3 inch squares.

Note: Yellow squash may be substituted for zucchini.

Betty Forlidas (Mrs. Philip)

TOMATOES STUFFED WITH ARTICHOKE HEARTS

When you need a splash of color, or the perfect accompaniment on a party plate, try this!

2 16-oz. cans whole peeled
    tomatoes, drained
1 tsp. salt
1/4 tsp. freshly-ground black
    pepper
1/2 tsp. sugar
1 tsp. sweet basil
1 can (14 oz.) can artichoke hearts,
    drained and rinsed
butter or margarine
1 cup seasoned Italian bread
    crumbs
3/4 cup grated Parmesan cheese

Butter a 10x6-1/2x2 inch casserole. Cross-cut tomatoes so they can hold an artichoke heart. Place tomatoes, properly spaced in the casserole. Blend salt, pepper, sugar and basil; sprinkle over tops and sides of tomatoes. Allow tomatoes to stand 15 minutes. Place one artichoke heart in the center of each tomato and top with a generous pat of butter. Combine bread crumbs and Parmesan cheese. Sprinkle half of the crumb/cheese mixture over tops and sides of tomatoes; bake in a pre-heated 400 degree oven for 10 minutes; then sprinkle remaining crumb mixture over tomato tops and turn dial to broil. Cook 2 or 3 minutes or until golden brown. Serve HOT. Serves 6 to 8.

Ellen Knott (Mrs. B.F.)

TOMATOES STUFFED WITH MUSHROOMS
Great for buffets!

8 firm, ripe tomatoes
1-1/2 lbs. mushrooms, sliced
1/2 cup melted butter or
    margarine
4 tsp. all-purpose flour
1 (8 oz.) carton sour cream
1 (3 oz.) pkg. Roquefort cheese
1/4 tsp. ground oregano
1 tsp. chopped parsley
2 Tbsp. dry sherry (or white wine)
salt and pepper to taste
paprika (optional)

Cut a slice from top of each tomato; scoop out pulp, leaving shell intact. Invert tomatoes and drain. Saute mushrooms in butter until tender; drain. Combine sour cream, flour, cheese, oregano, parsley and sherry over low heat until smooth and thickened, stirring constantly. Add mushrooms, salt and pepper; stir well. Spoon mixture into tomato shells, and place in shallow baking pan. Sprinkle with paprika. Bake at 375 degrees for 15 to 20 minutes. Serves 8.

Georgia Miller (Mrs. George)

SPINACH-STUFFED TOMATOES
Good and easy

6 small, firm tomatoes
1 container frozen Stouffer's
    spinach souffle, thawed
lemon pepper
oregano
6 fresh mushroom caps

Cut tops off tomatoes. Spoon out pulp. (Save to put in soup, meat loaf or spaghetti sauce.) Turn upside down on paper towel to drain. Sprinkle inside of tomato with pepper and oregano. Fill with thawed spinach. Bake at 350 degrees for 15 to 20 minutes. Place buttered mushroom cap on top for last 8 minutes. Serves 6.

Teny Sugg (Mrs. Wm. C.)

STEWED TOMATO CASSEROLE
"My very favorite vegetable!"

1 16-oz. can stewed tomatoes
1 can tomato soup
1/2 cup warm water
3/4 cup light brown sugar
    (packed)
1/4 tsp. salt
1 stick butter (not margarine),
    melted
5 slices bread, cut in cubes

Melt butter in skillet over medium heat. Stir the cubed bread into the butter. Stir until bread cubes become slightly brown and toasted. Set aside. Mix soup, water, tomatoes, brown sugar and salt in bowl. Add toasted bread cubes and mix well. Put into a 2 qt. buttered casserole dish and bake at 350 degrees for 30 minutes. Serves 6.

Mandy Martin

TOMATO BAKE

1 28-oz. can whole tomatoes
1 small grated onion
1 10-oz. pkg. Mozzarella cheese, grated
1 10-oz. pkg. Swiss cheese, grated
1 cup seasoned croutons
butter

Drain tomatoes and place into casserole dish. Add grated onion. Place grated cheeses on top. Cover with croutons and dot with butter. Bake at 350 degrees for 1 hour. Serves 4 to 6.

Jean Skidmore (Mrs. W.H.)

TOMATO-CHEESE CASSEROLE

Simple, but sparks up a ho-hum meal—good with leftovers

1 can Durkee's French-fried onion rings
1 16-0z. can stewed tomatoes
1-1/2 cups grated Cheddar cheese
Parmesan cheese

Layer in casserole. Sprinkle Parmesan cheese on top. May want to put onion rings on top with cheeses. Bake at 350 degrees until bubbly, 20 to 30 minutes. Serves 6.

Tonia Fuller (Mrs. Edwin W.)

TOMATO PUDDING

1 cup celery, chopped
1 medium onion, chopped
3 Tbsp. butter
1 heaping Tbsp. flour
2 1-lb. cans stewed tomatoes (with green pepper)
2-1/2 cups bread cubes, toasted, or 2-1/2 cups Brownberry croutons
1 tsp. salt
1/2 tsp. pepper
1 Tbsp. sugar
1 tsp. prepared mustard
3/4 cup grated Cheddar cheese

Saute celery and onion in butter just until tender. In same pan blend in the flour, mixing well. Add the tomatoes, salt, pepper, sugar and mustard. Stir in 1-1/2 cups of the bread cubes last. Turn into well-greased 1-1/2 quart casserole and bake at 350 degrees for 30 minutes. Remove from oven and put remaining 1 cup of croutons on top of casserole. Sprinkle with cheese and bake 10 minutes longer. Serves 6.

The Committee

CHARLOTTE'S VEGETABLE CASSEROLE

There are no specific measurements in this recipe, but it's delicious and you can hardly miss!

zucchini, washed, unpeeled and sliced
tomatoes, peeled and sliced
onions, peeled and thinly sliced
salt and pepper to taste
butter
Parmesan cheese (freshly grated, if possible)

In a large deep casserole layer the zucchini, tomatoes and onions. Sprinkle each layer with salt and pepper to taste and dot with butter; then top liberally with Parmesan cheese. Cover and bake in preheated 350 degree oven for 30 to 60 minutes, depending on amount of vegetables used. Remove cover during last few minutes of baking.

VARIATION:

1 yellow squash, washed, unpeeled and sliced
1 zucchini, washed, unpeeled and sliced
1 onion, peeled and thinly sliced
2 tomatoes, peeled, sliced and added separately
dill weed
butter and oil
salt and pepper
Parmesan cheese

Layer all vegetables except one of the tomatoes in a deep casserole, adding a little oil (about 2 Tbsp.), dill weed, salt and pepper between layers. Halfway through cooking stir and add the other tomato, dot with butter and add more cheese. Cook at 350 degrees for 40 minutes. Sprinkle with Parmesan cheese during last 5 minutes.

The Committee

RATATOUILLE

This is a good change from green beans and broccoli.

2 medium onions, sliced
2 cloves garlic, chopped
1/4 cup cooking oil
2 small zucchini, cut in 1/2 inch slices
3 medium tomatoes, diced
1 small eggplant, peeled and cubed (1 inch cubes)
1 large green pepper, cut in strips
2 Tbsp. chopped parsley
2 tsp. salt
1/2 tsp. basil leaves
1/8 tsp. pepper

Saute onions and garlic in hot oil until tender (do not brown). Add remaining ingredients. Cover and cook 15 minutes. Uncover and continue cooking 40 minutes or until vegetables are tender and juice is thickened. Stir occasionally. Serves 8.

Helen S. Burns

VEGETABLE HODGEPODGE CASSEROLE

1 box each (9 or 10 oz. each) frozen
    lima beans, cauliflower,
    green peas and cut green
    beans
salt
1 4-oz. can sliced mushrooms,
    drained
3/4 cup butter
1/2 cup flour
1 tsp. dry mustard
1 cup light cream
1 cup chicken stock
2 Tbsp. prepared horseradish
1/2 cup slivered almonds
2 cups soft stale-bread crumbs

Cook each vegetable separately in boiling, salted water as directed on the label. Drain and add mushrooms. Melt 1/2 cup butter and blend in flour and dry mustard. Gradually add liquids. Cook and stir until thickened. Add the horseradish and salt to taste. Brown the almonds in the remaining butter; add crumbs and toss. Sprinkle over vegetable mixture in 9x13 casserole dish. Bake in 400 degree oven until hot and bubbly. Serves 10-12.

Judith F. Kennedy (Mrs. Richard L.)

MIXED VEGETABLES

Serve at Thanksgiving or Christmas because it serves several!

1 10-oz. pkg. frozen butter beans
1 10-oz. pkg. frozen green beans
1-10 oz. pkg. frozen green peas

Prepare vegetables according to directions on packages. Drain well. Add salt, pepper and butter to taste. Serve with following sauce:

SAUCE:
1/2 cup mayonnaise
1/2 cup sour cream
1 tsp. chives (fresh or freeze-dried)
2 hard-boiled, grated eggs
1/2 tsp. Worcestershire sauce

Combine and mix with cooked vegetables in a large saucepan. Heat for a short time over moderate temperature. Sauce may be mixed the day before serving. Serves 10 to 12.

Mary Lou Scholl (Mrs. Ken)

MIXED VEGETABLE MEDLEY WITH SAUCE

A special-occasion vegetable casserole for holidays or company. Given to me long ago by a special friend.

1 10 oz. pkg. frozen English peas
1 10-oz. pkg. frozen baby lima beans
1 10-oz. pkg. French-cut green beans
1 cup mayonnaise
3 hard-boiled eggs
3 Tbsp. lemon juice
2 Tbsp. minced onion
1 tsp. Worcestershire sauce
1 tsp. prepared mustard
1/4 tsp. garlic salt
3 or 4 dashes Tabasco

Cook vegetables in boiling salted water according to package directions. Drain. Combine remaining ingredients in a saucepan over low heat and cook until warm, not *too hot* because mayonnaise will separate. Pour over well-drained vegetables; mix well. Yield: 8 to 10 servings. Nice touch to put in pre-warmed serving dish or platter. Serves 8-10.

Ellen Knott (Mrs. B.F.)

NOEL'S VEGETABLE CASSEROLE

Good with any meat. Doubles or triples nicely for a crowd

1 can (1 lb.) French green beans
1 can (1 lb.) shoe-peg corn
1/2 cup chopped celery
1/2 cup chopped onion
1 small container pimientos
1 can celery soup
1/2 cup sour cream

TOPPING:
1 cup grated Cheddar cheese
1 cup nip-cheese crackers, crushed
1/2 cup butter, melted
1/2 cup toasted almonds

Mix vegetables, soup and sour cream together. Pour into well-greased 2-qt. casserole. Melt butter and combine with cheese, cracker crumbs and almonds. Sprinkle on top of casserole and bake at 350 degrees for 45 minutes or until bubbly. Serves 4-6.

Ellen Knott (Mrs. B.F.)

BAKED OATMEAL

A good, nourishing winter breakfast!

1 cup oatmeal
2 cups milk
1/4 tsp. salt
1/2 cup chopped apples (or dates
   or raisins)
3 Tbsp. brown sugar, honey
   or maple syrup
1 Tbsp. butter
1/4 tsp. cinnamon (optional)

Scald milk, add butter and stir to melt. Add the other ingredients and mix well. Pour into a greased 1-1/2 qt. casserole and bake at 350 degrees for 20 minutes.

Anna Stanley (Mrs. Verner E.)

BARLEY AND PINE NUT CASSEROLE

Different! Goes well with poultry and lamb.

1 cup pearl barley
6 Tbsp. butter
2 oz. (1/3 cup) pine nuts
1 cup chopped green onions
1/2 cup chopped fresh parsley (or
   2-1/2 Tbsp. dried)
1/4 tsp. salt
1/4 tsp. pepper
3-1/3 cups chicken broth

Rinse barley in cold water and drain. In a 10-inch skillet, heat butter and brown pine nuts. Remove and reserve. Next, saute green onions and barley until lightly toasted. Remove from heat. Stir in nuts, parsley, salt and pepper. Spoon into ungreased 2 qt. casserole. Heat broth to boiling and pour over barley mixture. Stir to blend well. Bake uncovered for 1 hour and 10 minutes at 350 degrees. Serves 6.

Georgia Miller (Mrs. George)

LENTIL-WHEAT CASSEROLE

Let's get out of the habit of cooking the same old recipes. Your family will love this.

1/2 cup lentils, rinsed
2 cups water
1 tsp. salt
3 Tbsp. olive oil
1 small onion, chopped
1/4 lb. mushrooms, sliced
1/2 cup bulgar cracked wheat
unflavored yogurt
sliced green onions, including part
   of the tops

Combine the lentils, water, and salt in a saucepan. Bring to a boil, cover and simmer for 20 minutes; set aside. Heat the oil in a 10-inch frying pan over medium heat; saute onion, mushrooms and wheat until onion is soft (about 5 minutes). Pour lentils and water over wheat, bring to a boil, cover and simmer for 15 minutes or until wheat is just tender. Serve with yogurt and green onions to spoon on top. Serves 4.

Gensie

CHEESE GRITS I

1 cup regular grits
1 cup milk
1 stick butter
1 cup chopped Gruyere cheese
    (Swiss, garlic or other cheeses
    can be used)
2 eggs
1/2 cup grated Parmesan cheese

After cooking grits in salted water as per package directions, add butter and cheese. Mix well. Beat eggs and milk together and combine with grits mixture. (More milk may be added if mixture is too thick.) Pour into well-greased 2-qt. casserole and top with the Parmesan cheese. Bake until bubbly at 350 degrees for 50 to 60 minutes. Serves 6-8.

Betty Dale Archer (Mrs. J.M., III)

CHEESE GRITS II

1-1/2 cups quick-cooking grits
6 cups water
1 tsp. salt
1 tsp. seasoning salt
1 stick butter
1 lb. Velveeta cheese
2 or 3 drops Tabasco
3 beaten eggs

Cook grits according to directions on box. Remove from heat and add butter, cheese, seasoning salt and Tabasco. Cool. Add beaten eggs. Pour into 3-qt. casserole and bake uncovered at 375 degrees for 1 hour. Serves 6-8.

Mary Kay Grieg (Mrs. John H.)

GOURMET POTATO CASSEROLE
Easy and good!

4 or 5 large baking potatoes
salt, pepper, paprika
butter
1 small carton Velveeta cheese
1 small carton sour cream
1 Tbsp. chopped chives or onion

In top of double boiler melt cheese. Add sour cream and chives (or onion); set aside. Peel, slice and cook potatoes in slightly salted water until tender. *Drain well.* Place potatoes in 1-1/2 qt. buttered casserole. Add salt and pepper to taste. Dot with butter. Pour cheese sauce over potatoes, sprinkle with paprika and bake in 350 degree oven 15 to 20 minutes, until bubbly. Serves 6.

Teny Sugg (Mrs. Wm. C.)

HASH-BROWN POTATO CASSEROLE

Easy and delicious. Use two pyrex dishes—bake one and freeze one.

1 large bag (2 lbs.) Ore-Ida frozen
    hash-brown potatoes
2 cans cream of potato soup
8 oz. grated Cheddar cheese
1 8-oz. carton sour cream
1/2 tsp. garlic salt
1/2 cup Parmesan cheese

Mix potatoes, soup, sour cream, Cheddar cheese and garlic salt together in a large mixing bowl. Pour into a buttered 2-1/2 qt. casserole, 8-3/4 x 13-1/2 x 1-1/2 inch dish, or 2 - 8 x 8 inch square pyrex dishes. Dot with butter. Sprinkle top with Parmesan cheese. Bake uncovered 1 hour at 350 degrees. This casserole can be frozen before baking. To serve, place frozen casserole in cold oven, set temperature to 350 degrees and cook covered 1 hour and uncovered an additional 30 minutes. Serves 8.

B.J. Miller (Mrs. H.F. III)

HERBED POTATOES

8 cups diced potatoes
1/2 cup margarine
1 onion, minced
1 cup chopped celery and leaves
1/4 cup parsley
2 tsp. salt
2 tsp. poultry seasoning
1/4 tsp. pepper

Cook potatoes in small amount of boiling water for 5 minutes. Drain. Place in shallow baking dish. Melt margarine. Saute onions, celery and parsley a few minutes. Stir in seasonings. Pour mixture over potatoes. This dish may be refrigerated at this point for baking at a later hour. Bake 30 minutes at 375 degrees. Serves 8.

Betty O. Harkey (Mrs. E.L.)

POTATO CASSEROLE

"From an old cookbook"

6 medium potatoes
3 strips bacon
1 medium onion, chopped
1 can cream of mushroom soup
2 cups grated Cheddar cheese
salt and pepper

Cook potatoes in water until tender. Cool, peel and dice. Fry bacon in skillet and drain on paper towel. Saute onion in bacon drippings until golden. Add onions and any bacon drippings to potatoes. Sprinkle with salt and pepper. Add mushroom soup, cheese and crumbled bacon. Place in buttered 2 qt. casserole. Bake at 350 degrees for at least 20 minutes or until hot through. Serves 8.

Nancy Diffee (Mrs. Jim)

POTATO CASSEROLE SUPREME

One of the very best potato casseroles!

8 medium baking potatoes
1/2 cup butter or margarine
2-1/2 tsp. salt
1/4 tsp. pepper
2/3 cup warm milk
1-1/2 cups shredded Cheddar
  cheese
1 cup (1/2 pint) heavy cream,
  whipped

Peel and boil potatoes until tender. Drain and beat in a large bowl with electric mixer until fluffy, adding butter, seasonings and milk. Check seasonings and add more salt if necessary. Turn into a 9x13 casserole. Fold cheese into whipped cream and spread over potatoes for topping. Bake at 350 degrees for about 25 minutes—only until golden brown. Can be made ahead and topping added just before baking. Serves 8-10.

Nancy Wohlbruck (Mrs. Everett)

SAUTEED POTATO CUBES

So good!

1-1/2 pounds potatoes, peeled
Salt and freshly-ground pepper to
  taste
1/3 cup peanut, vegetable or corn
  oil
2 Tbsp. butter

Cut the potatoes into half-inch slices. Cut the slices into half-inch strips. Cut the strips into half-inch cubes. As the cubes are formed, drop them into cold water to prevent discoloration. Drain potatoes and add them to a saucepan. Add water to cover, and salt to taste. Bring to the boil and let simmer about 2 minutes. Drain. Heat the oil in a skillet, preferably one with rounded sides. Add the potatoes. Add salt and pepper to taste. Cook, shaking the skillet and stirring occasionally, so that the potatoes cook evenly. When stirring, stir gently so that pieces do not break. Cook about 10 minutes or until the potato cubes are nicely browned. Drain the potatoes into a colander. Return them to the skillet and add the butter. Toss the potatoes in the butter, cooking over high heat about 5 minutes. Serves four.

Virginia Golding (Mrs. John G.)

SCALLOPED POTATOES
Great with ham!

1/3 cup butter or margarine
1/2 cup minced onion
1/3 cup flour
3 cups milk
2-1/2 cups (10 oz.) grated Cheddar
  cheese
1 Tbsp. salt
1/4 tsp. dry mustard
10 cups thinly-sliced Irish potatoes
1/4 tsp. paprika

Melt butter or margarine in medium saucepan. Add onion; saute until soft, 2 to 3 minutes. Stir in flour, cook over low heat one minute. Gradually add milk, stirring constantly. Cook over medium heat until slightly thickened and beginning to boil. Add 1 cup cheese, the salt and mustard. Remove from heat; stir until cheese is melted. Arrange half the potato slices in 13x9 inch greased baking dish. Pour half the sauce over potatoes in dish. Arrange remaining potato slices in dish and pour on remaining sauce. Cover with foil and bake at 350 degrees for 1 hour or until potatoes are fork-tender. Uncover, sprinkle with remaining 1-1/2 cups cheese and paprika. Continue baking until cheese is melted. Makes 10-12 servings.

Carole Goodwin

SWISS POTATOES
Children love these for a change.

4 potatoes
1 stick butter
salt and pepper

Put 2 to 3 Tbsp. butter in heavy frying pan. Slice peeled potatoes in thin rounds (as for Potatoes Anna). Layer in pan with butter on top and salt and pepper. Turn when bottom starts to brown. They'll separate enough to brown both sides. Serves 4-6.

Dot Nicholls (Mrs. T.H.)

"LIKKER" PUDDING
Delicious with turkey

2-1/2 cups milk
3 medium sweet potatoes
2 cups sugar
2 tsp. cinnamon
3 eggs
1/4 stick butter
1/2 cup blanched, slivered
  almonds
1/2 cup whiskey or rum (rum is
  better)

Put milk into 2 qt. casserole. Grate potatoes, adding to milk as you grate to prevent potatoes from turning dark. Beat eggs well and add sugar gradually. Add cinnamon and almonds and mix well with potatoes. Dot generously with butter and bake in a 300 degree oven for 2 hours. Just before serving pour whiskey or rum over pudding. Serves 6.

Stella Thurston (Mrs. Doc. J.)

SWEET POTATO CASSEROLE

3 to 4 cups mashed sweet potatoes
1 cup sugar
pinch of salt
2 tsps. vanilla
3 eggs
1/2 cup milk
1/2 stick butter, melted
TOPPING:
1/3 cup flour
1/3 stick butter
1 cup brown sugar
1 cup nuts
1/2 cup coconut (optional)

Cook sweet potatoes and mash. Mix all the above ingredients (except topping) with mixer until smooth. Pour into greased 2-qt. casserole. Mix topping ingredients; pour topping over this and bake 35 minutes at 350 degrees. Serves 8.

Jane Craven (Mrs. Jesse)
Nancy Langston (Mrs. J.T.)

Variation: Kathy Demas (Mrs. Ronald G.) omits topping.

SWEET POTATO AND ORANGE CASSEROLE
Good at Christmas or Thanksgiving—great with turkey!

2 (1 lb. cans) sweet potatoes,
  drained
1/3 cup firmly-packed brown
  sugar
1/4 cup melted butter
1/4 cup pecans, finely chopped
1/2 tsp. salt
2 Tbsp. rum (or sherry)
1 (11 oz.) can mandarin oranges,
  drained

Mash sweet potatoes and beat in 1/4 cup brown sugar, half the butter, the salt and rum. Fold in oranges and turn into buttered 2-qt. casserole. Mix together pecans and remaining brown sugar and butter; sprinkle over top. Bake at 375 degrees for 30 minutes. Serves 6-8.

Sonja Edwards (Mrs. W.D., Jr.)

BAKED RICE

A most colorful rice dish—superb with barbecue meals.

1 cup Uncle Ben's Converted Rice
2-1/4 cup chicken stock
1/2 tsp. marjoram
1/3 cup butter or margarine,
    chopped up
2 Tbsp. butter or oil
1 onion, diced
5 mushrooms, sliced thick
1 garlic clove, mashed
1/4 cup pine nuts
2 peeled tomatoes, chopped
1/2 green pepper, chopped
1/2 cup cooked green peas
4 Tbsp. raisins

Butter a casserole dish. Mix in rice, stock, marjoram and butter. Bake uncovered 45 minutes in a 350 degree oven. Stir and bake for 30 minutes more, still uncovered, and it will be moist and fluffy when done. Now prepare and toss remaining ingredients in the following way: Heat butter or oil in frying pan and saute nuts until tan; remove to a dish. Add onions and garlic to pan and saute until tender; add mushrooms and cook 2 minutes. Toss in green peppers, tomatoes, peas and raisins. Cook very quickly and toss all this into the rice with a long cooking fork. Place rice on a large platter and serve. Serves 6-8.

Georgia Miller (Mrs. George)

BONNIE'S ARROZ CON JOCOQUI

"This recipe comes from northern Mexico."

4 cups cooked rice
4 cups sour cream
1 lb. Monterey Jack cheese,
    shredded
3 small cans chopped green chilies
    (only 2 cans if you buy the
    already chopped)
1/2 lb. Cheddar cheese, shredded
salt and pepper to taste

Mix sour cream, rice, chilies, salt and pepper. Layer this mixture and Jack cheese, beginning and ending with rice mixture, in a 3-qt. casserole. Top with shredded Cheddar cheese. Bake at 350 degrees for 30 minutes. Serves 12.

Brenda Monteith (Mrs. James D.)

BROWN RICE

1 cup rice
4 Tbsp. butter or margarine
1 can mushrooms, drained and
    chopped
1 can onion soup
1 soup can water
4 Tbsp. soy sauce

Brown the rice in butter until golden. Add remaining ingredients, cover and simmer until fluffy, approximately 45 minutes. Serves 4-6.

Eleanor Minor (Mrs. Wm. N.)

BROWN RICE STRATA
A great company dish

2-2/3 cups water
1 cup brown rice
2 tsp. salt
1 Tbsp. butter or margarine
1 (10 oz.) pkg. frozen broccoli, thawed
1/2 cup slivered almonds
2 Tbsp. chopped pimiento
8 oz. shredded sharp cheese (or more if you wish)
3 eggs
1-1/2 cups milk
1 Tbsp. minced onion
1 tsp. Dijon mustard

Bring water to boil in medium saucepan. Add rice, 1 tsp. salt and the butter. Cover tightly and cook over low heat until all water is absorbed, approximately 50 minutes. Spoon 2 cups rice into greased pan. Press excess moisture from broccoli; arrange evenly over rice. Sprinle almonds over broccoli; dot with pimiento. Sprinkle with about 3/4 cup cheese. Spoon on remaining rice in even layer. Combine eggs, milk, onion, mustard and remaining 1 tsp. salt. Pour over rice mixture. Sprinkle remaining cheese on top; cover and refrigerate at least 2 hours. Uncover and bake at 300 degrees until top is brown—about 1-1/4 hours. Let stand 5 minutes before cutting into squares to serve. Serves 6.

Carolyn Adams (Mrs. G.B., Jr.)

GREEN RICE

1 10-oz. pkg. chopped broccoli
1/2 cup chopped celery
1/2 cup chopped onion
1/4 lb. margarine
1 10-1/2 oz. can mushroom soup
1 8-oz. jar Cheese Whiz
1-1/2 cup cooked rice

Cooked chopped broccoli about 5 minutes; drain. Saute celery and onion in margarine. When tender, add to broccoli. Add mushroom soup, cheese and rice. Mix well. Pour into a flat casserole (7-1/2x11-1/2), cover and bake 45 minutes at 375 degrees. Serves 6-8.

Julia Warner (Mrs. C.E.)

NATURAL VEGETABLE CASSEROLE
Good for a meatless meal

1 cup brown rice
3 medium zucchini, thinly sliced
12 oz. Monterey Jack cheese, shredded
2 cups sour cream
1 tsp. oregano
1/2 small onion, finely chopped
1 tsp. garlic salt
3 tomatoes, sliced

Cook rice according to package directions for making 2 cups of rice. Lightly grease pan; spread cooked rice across bottom of pan. Place a layer of thinly-sliced zucchini, then sliced tomatoes over rice. Mix sour cream, onions and garlic salt together. Spread on top of tomatoes. Sprinkle top with the cheese and oregano. Bake at 350 degrees until brown on top. Cut into squares and serve. Serves 6.

Dale E. Yaged

ORANGE CASHEW RICE

3 Tbsp. butter
2/3 cup diced celery
2 Tbsp. finely-chopped onions
1-1/2 cups water
juice from drained mandarin
    oranges plus orange juice to
    make 1 cup
2 Tbsp. orange rind
1-1/4 tsp salt
1 cup uncooked rice
1 11-oz. can mandarin oranges,
    drained, juice reserved
1 cup cashew nuts
parsley

Melt butter; add celery, onions, water, orange juice, orange rind and salt. Bring to boil; add rice slowly and cover. Reduce heat; cook 25-30 minutes. Gently stir in orange sections and cashew nuts. Garnish with parsley. Serves 6.

Linda Miller (Mrs. W.R.)

RISOTTO PRIMAVERA

This has to be a spring dish because it needs fresh vegetables to be special!

1/4 lb. asparagus
1 small zucchini
1/4 cup tender fresh green peas
1/2 cup butter
1 small onion, chopped
2 cups rice
5 cups beef broth
1/2 lb. mushrooms, sauteed
1 green pepper, roasted and
    chopped
1-1/2 cups fresh tomatoes,
    chopped
freshly-grated Parmesan cheese

Trim asparagus, scrub zucchini and cut each into small pieces about 1 inch long. Shell peas. Cook each vegetable separately until barely tender (about 3 minutes for asparagus, 2 for zucchini and 1 minute for peas); drain. Saute onion in butter and add rice, lightly browning. Add broth and bring to simmer. Stir frequently. When half done (about 8 minutes) stir in vegetables and continue cooking until rice is tender (15 minutes total). Spoon into serving dish and top with Parmesan cheese. Serves 6-8.

Anna Stanley (Mrs. V.E., Jr.)

VEGETABLE PILAU

An authentic, easy, not spicy-hot, Indian dish

1 cup long-grain rice
1 stick margarine or butter
2 cardamon pods (whole)
2 whole cloves
1 to 2 inch cinnamon stick
2 whole bay leaves
1/2 pkg. frozen peas and carrots,
   thawed
1 tsp. salt
1/4 cup raw cashews
2 cups water

Melt margarine in 2 qt. saucepan. After foam subsides, add cardamon, cloves, cinnamon, bay leaves and cashews; saute over moderate heat for 3 minutes. Add rice and saute until grains turn white. Watch carefully and stir to prevent scorching. Add vegetables to rice and stir. Add 2 cups water and salt. Bring to full boil. *Do not stir again.* Cover and cook on simmer for 20 minutes. Delicious! Serves 4.

Beverly Patnaik (Mrs. P.K.)

WILD RICE IN A CASSEROLE

There are so many menus that wild rice complements!

1 cup wild rice, soaked overnight
1 10-1/2 oz. can consomme,
   undiluted
4 Tbsp. butter
1/2 lb. mushrooms, sliced
1-1/2 cups finely-chopped celery
1 bunch green onions, sliced
1 6-oz. can water chestnuts,
   drained and sliced (optional)
1/2 cup vermouth
butter

Rinse wild rice well and drain. Combine with consomme in a large saucepan and simmer, uncovered, until liquid is absorbed, about 30 minutes. In a skillet, melt butter and saute vegetables until limp. Combine with cooked rice and place in a buttered, 2-qt. casserole. Refrigerate until ready to use. When ready to heat, add vermouth and dot with butter. Bake, covered, in 350 degree oven for 30-40 minutes. Serves 6.

The Committee

MUSHROOM-RICE RING

1 cup chopped mushrooms
3 Tbsp. butter
1/4 tsp. nutmeg
5 to 6 cups cooked long-grain
   white rice

In a medium skillet, saute the chopped mushrooms in the butter until tender but not brown. Season with nutmeg. Combine mushrooms and rice and turn into a well-buttered 5 to 6 cup ring mold, pressing mixture down gently. Turn out at once on a warm serving plate or keep the mold warm in a pan of hot water until ready to serve. Fill center with, and place around the ring, green vegetables such as green peas, Chinese pea pods or broccoli. Serves 6-8.

The Committee

Eggs
Cheese
& Pasta

EASY CHEESE SOUFFLE

This is easy and light. It makes a great Sunday night supper.

12 slices day-old bread
1/2 lb. Cheddar cheese, thinly sliced
4 eggs
2-1/2 cups milk
1 tsp. Dijon-style mustard
1 tsp. salt

Cut crusts from bread. Put 6 slices in bottom of greased 9 x 13 baking dish. Cover with cheese slices, then remaining bread slices. Beat together eggs, milk, mustard and salt. Pour over casserole. Let stand one hour at room temperature (or cover and refrigerate over night to use for breakfast). Bake at 325 degrees for 50-60 minutes. Serve immediately. Serves 6.

Peggy Buchanan (Mrs. D. Douglas)

QUICK SWISS SOUFFLE

Fantastic for a brunch!

2-1/2 cups cubed white bread (no crusts)
2-1/2 cups Swiss cheese, shredded
8 strips of bacon slightly precooked and cut in quarters
4 eggs
3/4 tsp. dry mustard
2-1/4 cups milk
1/2 cup milk
1 can cream of mushroom soup

Grease a 9 x 13 pan. Mix the bread cubes with the Swiss cheese and place in pan. Lay bacon strips on top of bread and cheese. Slightly beat the eggs. Mix eggs with dry mustard and 2-1/4 cup milk. Pour over all and refrigerate overnight. Next day, mix 1/2 cup milk with 1 can cream of mushroom soup. Pour over other ingredients. Bake 1-1/2 hours at 300 degrees. Serves 8.

Marg Barnes (Mrs. R.W.)

FAST CHEESE RABBIT

Last minute supper before a game!

1/2 lb. grated sharp cheese
1 can condensed cream of mushroom soup
1/3 cup ripe, pitted olives, sliced
a touch of chopped green pepper
English muffins or toast cut in triangles

Melt cheese with undiluted soup in top of a double boiler; after heating thoroughly add olives and pepper. Heat another few minutes and serve on toast or split English muffins.
Can add to this if desired: tuna, cooked shrimp, cooked ham; or cooked slices of bacon can top this dish.

Beverly Michaux (Mrs. Roy)

CHEESE FONDUE
Fun for Mt. house and cold weather

1 clove garlic
1-1/2 cups dry white wine
1 Tbsp. lemon juice
1/2 lb. Swiss cheese
1/2 lb. Gruyere cheese
flour
nutmeg and pepper
2 loaves good, crusty, French
    bread

Grate and mix cheeses. Dredge in flour. Rub pot with cut garlic. Add wine and heat until wine is hot but not boiling. Add lemon juice. Stir cheese in slowly until creamy. Add nutmeg and pepper to taste. Bring to a boil — place on lighted burner. Cube French bread in 1-inch cubes. Dip in fondue.

Ann Snider

TAHOE BRUNCH
Perfect for brunch

12 slices white bread, crusts
    removed
2 to 3 Tbsp. soft butter
1/2 cup butter
1/2 lb. fresh mushrooms, trimmed
    and sliced
2 cups thinly sliced yellow onions
salt and pepper
1-1/2 lbs. mild Italian sausage
1 lb. cheddar cheese, grated
5 eggs
2-1/2 cups milk
1 Tbsp. Dijon mustard
1 tsp. dry mustard
1 tsp. nutmeg
2 Tbsp. chopped fresh parsley

Butter bread with softened butter — set aside. In large skillet, melt 1/2 cup butter and brown mushrooms and onions over medium heat 5-8 minutes. Add salt and pepper to taste. In another pan, cook sausage and cut into bite-sized pieces. In an 11 x13 casserole, layer half the bread, then mushroom mixture, sausage and cheese. Repeat layers. In bowl mix eggs, milk, mustards, nutmeg, 1 tsp salt and 1/8 tsp. pepper. Pour over sausage-cheese layers. Refrigerate overnight. When ready to bake, sprinkle with parsley. Bake at 350 degrees for 1 hour. Serves 8-10.

Sally McMillen (Mrs. Bruce)

When combining beaten egg whites with heavier mixtures, it is best to pour the heavier mixture onto the beaten egg whites. Fold just until there are no streaks remaining in the mixture. Do not stir — this forces the air out of the whites.

SAUSAGE-EGG-CHEESE CASSEROLE
An easy breakfast, brunch or late-night casserole

1 lb. hot sausage or bacon
6-8 eggs
2 cups milk
1 tsp. dry mustard
1 tsp salt
1 cup sharp cheese, grated
2-4 slices of bread, cubed, or 1 cup
   fresh bread crumbs, not
   toasted

Saute sausage or bacon and drain. Grease 9 x 13 casserole and put bread cubes in bottom of casserole. Crumble sausage or bacon over bread. Beat eggs, milk, mustard and salt together and pour over meat. Sprinkle with cheese. Cover and refrigerate overnight, or freeze. Bake for 1 hour at 350 degrees. (Takes about 1 hour cooking time whether frozen or not.) Serves 8.

Virginia Golding (Mrs. John G.)
Peggy Hormberg (Mrs. R.H.)
Susan Justice (Mrs. M.E.)
Judy Ranson (Mrs. Richard C.)
Laura Roddey (Mrs. John H.)
Mary Anne Thomas (Mrs. John G.)

CHRISTMAS BREAKFAST
This makes such a nice big meal with such little effort!

7 slices white bread (regular, not
   thin)
2 pkg. (4 oz. each) shredded
   cheddar cheese
6 eggs
3 cups milk
1/2 tsp salt
1/4 tsp. pepper
1 tsp. mustard
3 strips bacon, or more as desired,
   cut in half

Trim crust from bread and crumble the bread. Mix bread and cheese and spread in bottom of 11 x 13 dish. Beat eggs and milk together and stir in salt, pepper and mustard. Put this over bread and cheese. Lay bacon on top. Refrigerate overnight. Bake uncovered at 350 degrees for 50-55 minutes. Remove from oven just after everyone sits down at the table. Serves 6.

Hazel Harris (Mrs. T.C.)

Eggs separate better when cold, but beat better at room temperature.

SAUSAGE BREAKFAST CASSEROLE
Great for large family breakfast or party brunch

2 lbs. bulk sausage—1 mild, 1 hot
6-7 slices white bread, crusts removed; spread with oleo and cubed
2 or more cups shredded sharp cheese
7-8 eggs
2-1/2 cups milk
1 tsp. salt
1 tsp. dry mustard

Cook sausage until done, stirring to crumble well. Remove grease while cooking, then drain well on paper towels. Place buttered bread into 3 qt. casserole baking dish. Sprinkle with sausage and top with cheese. Combine remaining ingredients and beat well. Pour over mixture in baking dish and chill *at least* 8-12 hours. Bake at 350 degrees for 40-45 minutes. Serves 12.
Variations: Can use 1-1/2 lb. ham, bacon or Canadian bacon.
Can use 1 cup grated cheddar cheese and 1 cup cubed Swiss cheese.

Georgia Miller (Mrs. George)
Rickey Springs (Mrs. Eli B., Jr.)

COUNTRY EGGS AND SAUSAGE
Sour cream makes the difference

1/2 lb. (2 cups) grated sharp cheddar cheese
1/2 tsp. dry mustard
1/2 tsp. paprika
1 tsp. salt
1 cup sour cream
1 lb. sausage, cooked, drained, and crumbled
12 eggs

Grease an 8 x 11 casserole. Put cooked sausage in bottom of casserole. Cover with half the cheese and half the sour cream mixed with seasonings. Beat eggs. Pour over casserole. Top with drops of the rest of the sour cream and seasonings mixture and the rest of the sharp cheese. Bake uncovered for 35 minutes in a 350 degree oven. Serves 6-8.

Linde Mullis (Mrs. W.F.)

BAKED EGGS GRUYERE
A company dish, easy enough for any day

12 oz. Gruyere cheese, shredded
10 crisp-cooked bacon slices, crumbled
6 eggs
1/2 cup half and half
1/2 tsp. salt
1/8 tsp. pepper

Preheat oven to 350 degrees. Generously butter 10 x 6 x 2 baking dish. Cover bottom of dish with shredded cheese. Crumble bacon over cheese. Make "nests" for eggs with back of a large spoon. Break eggs, one at a time, into small bowl. Carefully transfer each egg into its "nest," taking care not to break the yolk. Pour half and half over the eggs. Sprinkle with salt and pepper. Bake about 20 minutes until eggs are set. Cut in squares and serve. If prepared the night before, cover tightly so that eggs will not dry out. Serves 6.

Eloise Dellinger

CHILI RELLENO PUFF
Simple, quick and delicious

1 7-oz. can whole green chiles
2 cups shredded Monterey Jack
    cheese
6 eggs, slightly beaten
3/4 cup milk
1 Tbsp. flour
1 tsp. baking powder
1-1/2 tsp. parsley
1/2 tsp. seasoned salt
1/2 tsp. garlic powder
1 cup shredded Cheddar cheese

CHILI SAUCE
1 8-oz. can tomato sauce
1/4 cup hot picante sauce
1 tsp. oregano

Grease 9 x 9 baking dish. Layer split chiles and Jack cheese in dish. Combine eggs, milk, flour, baking powder, garlic powder, salt and parsley; mix well. Pour over chiles and Jack cheese. Top with Cheddar cheese. Bake at 350 degrees for 40-45 minutes until puffed and brown. Serve with chile sauce; heat combined tomato sauce, picante sauce and oregano for 5 minutes. 4-6 servings.

Margie Tice (Mrs. John R.)

CORINNA'S BAKED CURRIED EGGS
Can be made hours before serving

6 Tbsp. butter or margarine
16 eggs
2 cups prepared white sauce (your
    favorite recipe)
1 Tbsp. curry powder (or less as
    desired)
1 Tbsp. salt
1/2 tsp. pepper
1/4 cup toasted sliced almonds
1 8-0z. pkg. cream cheese

Melt butter or margarine and cream cheese in a 12 inch skillet. Beat together eggs, white sauce, curry powder, salt and pepper. Pour egg mixture into skillet, stirring constantly, with a fork or rubber spatula. Continue to stir until eggs are just setting but still soft and not dry. Pour eggs into a buttered two-quart baking dish and sprinkle with almonds.

About 15 minutes before you're ready to serve, place scrambled eggs in a preheated oven at 400 degrees. Bake about 10 minutes or until heated through. Top can be lightly browned. Serves 8-10.

Note: Curry can be eliminated.

Variations: Omit curry and substitute thinly-sliced Montery Jack or Swiss cheese, and buttered bread crumbs for the almonds.

Deede Grainger (Mrs. Isaac B., III)

EGG DISH DELICIOUS
Unusual and delicious

6 eggs, hard boiled
1 lb. onions, sliced
4 Tbsp. butter
white sauce (recipe follows)
1/2 cup sharp cheese, grated for sauce
3/4 cup sharp cheese, grated for topping
bread crumbs (optional)
paprika

Slice eggs in four slices each. Place in a greased shallow dish. Slice onions very thin and saute ever so gently in butter. They must cook but not brown. Make white sauce and season well. Add grated cheese. Put onions on top of eggs and pour white sauce over all. Cover with sprinkling of bread crumbs, if desired, and grated cheese. Place in 350 degree oven for 15-20 minutes. Sprinkle with paprika. Serves 6-8.

Ellen Knott (Mrs. B.F.)

CREAM OR WHITE SAUCE FOR EGG DISH DELICIOUS

4 Tbsp. butter
3 Tbsp. flour
2 cups milk
salt
pepper

Melt butter in saucepan over medium heat or in double boiler. Blend in flour, using wire whisk or slotted spoon. Continue stirring while slowly adding milk, salt and pepper. Cook until right consistency. Pour over onions and eggs.

Ellen Knott (Mrs. B.F.)

QUICHE UNIQUE
Easy and truly unique

3/4 cup shredded Swiss cheese
3/4 cup shredded Mozzarella cheese
1/2 cup Monterey Jack cheese
1 Tbsp. green onion, chopped
1 9-inch unbaked pie shell
3 eggs, beaten
1 cup half and half
1/2 tsp. salt
1/4 tsp. oregano
parsley

Combine cheeses and onion; sprinkle in pie crust. Combine eggs, half and half, salt, oregano and a touch of parsley. Mix well and pour into pie shell. Bake at 350 degrees for 45 minutes. Allow to stand 10 minutes before cutting.

Kathleen Golding Boyce (Mrs. R.N.)

QUICHE
Good use for leftovers

2 or 3 eggs, slightly beaten
1 cup grated Swiss cheese
1 cup milk
1 cup sliced mushrooms
2 tsp. parsley flakes
1/8 tsp. red pepper
pinch of nutmeg
pinch of oregano
1 to 1-1/2 cups meat or vegetable filling (cooked and drained sausage, ham bits, crumbled bacon, shrimp, crabmeat, broccoli, spinach, zucchini, etc.)
1 unbaked deep dish pie shell or 2 regular pie shells.

Cook pie shell about 6 minutes at 350 degrees. Combine eggs, cheese, milk, mushrooms, parsley flakes, red pepper, nutmeg and oregano. Put filling on bottom of crust. Pour liquid mixture over filling. Bake at 350 degrees for 45 minutes. Serves 6-8.

Bonnie Phillips (Mrs. H.M.)

SWISS QUICHE WITH CRAB MEAT SAUCE

unbaked 9-inch pastry shell
4 eggs, separated
1-1/2 cups light cream
1/2 tsp. salt
1/8 tsp. ground nutmeg
6 oz. natural Swiss cheese, shredded (1-1/2 cups)

Bake pricked pastry shell at 450 degrees for 7 minutes. Remove and reduce heat to 350 degrees. Slightly beat the egg yolks and add the cream, salt and nutmeg. Beat the egg whites until stiff peaks form. Fold into the egg yolk mixture, then fold in the cheese. Pour into the pastry shell. Bake at 350 degrees for 45-50 minutes, or until a knife inserted comes out clean. Let stand 5 minutes. Serve with Ham or Crab Meat Sauce.

CRAB MEAT SAUCE

1 cup crab meat, or 7-oz. can, drained and flaked
2 Tbsp. butter
1 Tbsp. flour
1/8 tsp. salt
1 cup light cream

Heat the crab in the butter, blend in the flour and salt, then add the cream. Cook and stir until thickened.

Beverly Hance (Mrs. James)

QUICHE AUX CHAMPIGNONS
An excellent mushroom quiche

4 Tbsp. butter
2 Tbsp. shallots, minced
1 cup sliced mushrooms
lemon juice
salt and pepper
2 cups heavy cream
3 eggs
dash nutmeg
Pastry shell, partially cooked
    (8-10 minutes)
1/4 cup grated Gruyere cheese

Preheat oven to 375 degrees. Cook shallots gently in butter about 2 minutes. Sprinkle mushrooms with lemon juice and add to shallots. Stir about 3 minutes. Add salt, pepper and one cup of cream. Simmer slowly 15-20 minutes, until liquid has almost evaporated and mushrooms are lightly colored. Meanwhile, lightly beat eggs with remaining cup of cream, nutmeg, salt and pepper. Add mushroom mixture and correct seasonings. Pour mixture into partially cooked pastry shell. Sprinkle top with cheese. Bake 25 to 30 minutes until quiche is puffed and brown. Serves 4-6.

Jane Craven (Mrs. J.C.)

BROCCOLI QUICHE

1 pkg. frozen chopped broccoli
1 or 2 onions, chopped
2 Tbsp. butter
1/2 cup butter
1/4 cup flour
1 cup milk
1/2 tsp. salt
1/8 tsp. pepper
1/2 tsp. dill
4 eggs, beaten
1-1/2 cup Cheddar or Swiss cheese
    (I like a combination best)
1/2 cup Parmesan cheese
1 deep-dish pie shell or 2 regular
    pie shells

Cook broccoli according to package directions. Meanwhile saute onion in 2 Tbsp. butter. In medium saucepan, melt 1/2 cup butter. Stir in flour; then add milk slowly; cook slowly until mixture has thickened into a white sauce. Add salt, pepper, dill. Remove from heat. Add eggs, Cheddar and/or Swiss cheese, and drained broccoli. Stir until cheese is melted. Pour into unbaked pie shell and cook at 350 degrees for 30 minutes. Sprinkle with Parmesan cheese and cook 10 minutes more. Serves 4-6.

Kathleen Boyce (Mrs. R.N.)

Use a moderate to low temperature with exact timing when cooking eggs. High temperature and long cooking time will cause egg whites to become tough or rubbery. Yolks will become tough and their surface will turn greyish green.

SPINACH SOUFFLE QUICHE
"Short-cut quiche"

1 deep-dish 9-inch frozen pie shell, thawed
1 pkg. Stouffers frozen spinach souffle, thawed
2 eggs, lightly beaten
3 Tbsp. milk
2 tsp. chopped onion
1/2 cup sliced canned mushrooms
3/4 cup cooked and crumbled Italian sausage, or plain sausage
3/4 cup grated Swiss cheese

Bake pie shell for 10 minutes at 400 degrees. Reduce heat to 375. Mix remaining ingredients together and bake at 375 degrees for 35-40 minutes.

Betty Cobb (Mrs. J.O.)

MARGARET'S FAVORITE SPINACH QUICHE

1 pkg. spinach, frozen
1-1/2 cups plain yogurt
3 eggs
a little nutmeg
Grated Swiss cheese, a cup or more
1 pie crust in 10 inch pan

Partially bake pie crust in 400 degree oven, about 8-10 minutes on lower rack. It should look a little brown. Steam and drain spinach. Don't cook it too long. Beat eggs, add yogurt and nutmeg and mix well. While piecrust is still warm, put in well-drained spinach, then egg and yogurt mixture. Sprinkle grated cheese on top. Cut strips of aluminum foil and fold over edge of crust to keep it from burning. Cook in lower part of oven for 25 to 40 minutes at 350 to 425 degrees, depending on how quickly you need it. It's done when it looks firm and brownish in the middle. (This would probably fit into 2 purchased pie crusts.)

Sally Hughes (Mrs. Benjamin)

SALLY'S PIE CRUST

2 cups unbleached flour
3/4 to 1 cup Crisco
1 tsp salt
3 to 6 Tbsp. very cold water

In a mixing bowl put flour, salt and half the Crisco and beat with a mixer on low speed. Add rest of Crisco and beat again. Start with 3 Tbsp. water. Add to dough mixture and knead with hands, adding enough water so dough sticks together. Refrigerate until cool. Roll dough out between 2 sheets of waxed paper. Put in 10 inch pie pan, fluting edges.

Sally Hughes (Mrs. Benjamin)

ZUCCHINI CRESCENT PIE
$100,000 winner!

4 cups thinly sliced zucchini
1 cup chopped onion
1/2 cup butter or margarine
1/2 chopped parsley or 2 Tbsp.
    flakes
1/2 tsp. salt
1/2 tsp. pepper
1/4 tsp. garlic powder
1/4 tsp. basil
1/4 tsp. oregano leaves
2 beaten eggs
8 oz. (2 cups) grated Mozzarella
    cheese
8 oz. can Pillsbury Crescent Din-
    ner Rolls
2 tsp. mustard

Cook and stir the zucchini and onion in the half-cup butter for 10 minutes. Stir in parsley, salt, pepper, garlic powder, basil and oregano. Combine 2 beaten eggs and Mozzarella cheese; stir into zucchini mixture and set aside. Separate rolls into 8 triangles. Place in ungreased 10 inch pie pan. Press over bottom and up sides to form crust. Spread crust with prepared mustard. Pour vegetable mixture into crust. Bake in preheated 375 degree oven for 18-20 minutes or until set. Cover crust with foil during the last 10 minutes. Let stand 10 minutes before serving.

Judy Ranson (Mrs. R. C.)

SAVANNAH QUICHE
Given me by a friend from Savannah—good for lunch or brunch

1 9-inch pie shell, deep dish
2 fresh tomatoes
salt and pepper
flour
2 Tbsp. oil
1 cup onions, chopped
3 slices provolone cheese, broken
    into bite-size pieces
2 eggs, beaten
3/4 cup heavy cream
1 cup Swiss cheese, grated

Brown pie shell in 350 degree oven for 5 minutes. Remove pie shell and turn oven to 375 degrees. Peel and slice tomatoes, about 4 slices each tomato. Salt and pepper and dip in flour. Saute in oil. Remove and drain. Place tomatoes and onions in bottom of pie shell. Cover with provolone cheese. Mix cream and eggs together, pour into pie shell. Sprinkle Swiss cheese on top. Cook at 375 degrees for 35 to 40 minutes.

Ellen Knott (Mrs. B.F.)

Cook cheese at a low temperature as it becomes stringy when subjected to high heat.

CHEESE TORTE

1-1/2 cups bread crumbs
1 stick butter plus 6 Tbsp.
10 oz. Edam or Gouda cheese
3 tomatoes, sliced horizontally
mushrooms (if desired)

Butter quiche dish or pie pan. Grate 4 oz. Edam or Gouda cheese. Mix with 1 stick melted butter and 1-1/2 cups soft bread crumbs. Press into pie pan to form crust. Grate remaining 6 oz. of cheese on top of crust. Slice tomatoes horizontally into pie crust until filled. Add sauteed mushrooms on top of tomatoes if desired, using 2 Tbsp. of butter, and pour over all. Bake at 325 degrees for about 25 minutes. Serves 6.

Tonia Fuller (Mrs. E. W.)
Laura Roddey (Mrs. John H.)

HAM AND CHEESE PIE (QUICHE)

The mayonnaise in this recipe makes it especially good.
This can be cut in small pieces for lots of hors d'oeuvres.

3/4 cup Hellman's mayonnaise
3/4 cup milk
2 eggs, beaten
1 Tbsp. cornstarch
1-1/2 cups cooked ham (use good quality ham) cubed or shredded
1-1/2 cups Kraft's bulk Swiss cheese, grated
chopped onion to taste
pepper
1 unbaked deep-dish pie shell (Pet Ritz) or make your own

Mix together mayonnaise, milk, beaten eggs and corn starch until smooth. Stir in ham, cheese, onions and pepper. Place in pie shell. Bake at 350 degrees for 35 to 40 minutes until golden brown and puffy. May be cooked and reheated. Quiche can be mixed and frozen before cooking.

Beverly Hance (Mrs. James)

HAMBURGER QUICHE

1 unbaked 9 inch pie shell
1/2 lb. ground beef
1/2 cup mayonnaise
1/2 cup milk
2 eggs
1 Tbsp. cornstarch
1-1/2 cup cubed Cheddar or Swiss cheese
1/3 cup sliced green onions
dash pepper

Brown meat, drain off fat. Blend next 4 ingredients until smooth. Stir in remaining ingredients. Turn into shell. Bake in preheated 350 degree oven for 40 minutes. Serves 6.

Caroline Carriker (Mrs. John H.)

CURRIED DEVILED EGGS

"Deviled eggs with a difference"

9 hard-boiled eggs
3 Tbsp. mayonnaise
2 Tbsp. melted butter
few drops Worcestershire sauce
1 tsp. curry powder (or less according to taste)
1-1/2 tsp. white vinegar
1/3 tsp. dry mustard (Coleman's is best)
parsley for garnish

Halve hard-boiled eggs and scoop yolks into a bowl. Sieve or mash yolks and mix in all the remaining ingredients except parsley. Place some of the mixture in each egg half. Garnish with a snip of fresh parsley. Makes 18 halves.

Nancy Little (Mrs. T.H.)

HOT DEVILED EGGS

Prepare as many eggs as needed and make sauce accordingly.

10-12 hard-boiled eggs
horseradish mustard or horseradish and mustard
Worcestershire sauce
mayonnaise
red pepper
garlic salt
white sauce (recipe follows)

Devil 10-12 hard-boiled eggs with any amount of the above ingredients (except white sauce), to taste. Place in container large enough to hold egg halves. Make white sauce and pour over eggs. Heat in 350 degree oven until hot and bubbly.

WHITE SAUCE FOR HOT DEVILED EGGS

2 Tbsp. margarine
2 Tbsp. flour
red pepper
1 cup cold milk
1 tsp. Worcestershire sauce
1 cup grated sharp cheese

Melt margarine, add flour and seasonings. Then add milk, stirring constantly over medium heat. Add cheese and stir until melted. Pour over eggs and heat in 350 degree oven until hot and bubbly.

Ann Copeland (Mrs. E.H., Jr.)

For perfect hard-boiled eggs every time: Place eggs in large saucepan with enough tap water to cover by 1 inch; bring to boil, uncovered; remove from heat, put lid on and let rest for 17 minutes. Drain eggs promptly and rinse thoroughly in cold water. To remove shell: crack all over by tapping gently: roll egg between hands to loosen shell; then peel, starting at the large end. Hold egg under cold running water to help ease off shell.

TEASED EGGS WITH SHRIMP

6 extra large hard-boiled eggs or
   8 large
2 Tbsp. butter
2 Tbsp. flour
1 cup milk
3/4 tsp. salt
2 tsp. horseradish
2 cups sour cream
1 lb. cut up cooked shrimp
2 Tbsp. grated onion
salt and pepper to taste

Cut hard-boiled eggs lengthwise and put in shallow baking dish after removing yolks. Set yolks aside. Make white sauce by melting 2 Tbsp. butter, adding flour and mixing well. Add milk and salt, stirring constantly. When thick, stir in 2 tsp. horseradish. Take off heat and add 2 cups sour cream. Set aside and mash egg yolks. To yolks add cut up, cooked shrimp, grated onion and salt and pepper to taste. Mix 1/4 cup white sauce with egg mixture. Stuff egg whites and cover with remaining white sauce. Makes 12 or 16 halves.

Georgia Miller (Mrs. George)

CHEESE BAKED GRITS (GNOCCHI)
Twice cooked makes them even better

1 qt. milk
1-1/3 sticks butter
1 tsp. salt
1/8 tsp. pepper
1/2 tsp. red pepper (optional)
1 cup grits (quick cooking)
1 cup grated Swiss cheese
1/3 cup grated Parmesan cheese

Bring milk and 1 stick of butter to a slow boil. Stir in grits, cover, reduce heat and cook 3 to 5 minutes, stirring occasionally. Remove from heat; add 1 tsp. salt, 1/8 tsp. pepper, and 1/2 tsp. red pepper if desired. Beat hard with electric beater for 5 minutes, no less, until creamy. Pour in oiled 9 x 13 pan. Refrigerate until firm. Cut in rectangular pieces; arrange like fallen dominos. Pour remaining 1/3 cup melted butter over grits. Sprinkle with 1 cup grated Swiss cheese and 1/3 cup Parmesan cheese. At this point, can be refrigerated for a day. Bake at 400 degrees for 25 to 30 minutes until browned. Serves 6 to 8.

Tonia Fuller (Mrs. E. W.)
Sally McMillan (Mrs. Bruce)

BLINTZ CASSEROLE

Be sure to include this for your next brunch.

FILLING:
2 lbs. ricotta cheese
2 eggs
1/4 cup sugar
1/8 tsp. salt
1/4 cup lemon juice
8 oz. cream cheese, softened

BATTER:
1/2 lb. margarine, melted
1/2 cup sugar
2 eggs
1 cup sifted flour
3 tsp. baking powder
1/8 tsp salt
1/4 cup milk
1 tsp. vanilla

Put all ingredients for filling in mixer and blend well. Set aside. Mix batter ingredients by hand and spoon half of batter into a well-greased 9 x 13 x 2 inch pan. Top this with the filling—spreading, not mixing. Spread remaining batter over the filling. Bake at 300 degrees for 1-1/2 hours. Serves 12.

Libby Morrison (Mrs. Jack)

CRUSTY NOODLE RING

"We love pasta—this is a favorite side dish for a dinner party."

1/4 cup butter
1/2 cup dark brown sugar
1 cup pecan halves
1/2 lb. broad noodles
2 eggs, slightly beaten
1/2 cup butter, melted
1/2 tsp. cinnamon
1/3 cup sugar
1/2 tsp salt

Spray a 6-cup ring mold with Pam. Melt butter in bottom of mold. Add brown sugar, pressing into bottom of the mold. Place pecan halves firmly into brown sugar to form a pattern. Boil noodles until barely tender. Drain well and combine with other ingredients. Spread into prepared mold over the pecan mixture. Bake for 1 hour at 350 degrees. Unmold and garnish. Serves 6.

Ellen Knott (Mrs. B.F.)

GOURMET NOODLES

1 stick margarine or butter
1 small can mushrooms, drained
1/4 cup chopped onion
1/4 cup chopped almonds
1 clove garlic
1 Tbsp. lemon juice
1 can beef consomme
1 4-oz. pkg. thin noodles

Saute first six ingredients for 7 minutes. Add beef consomme. Bring to a boil. Add noodles. Cook on medium heat for 5 minutes, covered. Pour into dish and serve immediately. Serves 6.

Arnita Kee

BAKED HUNGARIAN NOODLES

1 lb. fine noodles
4 cups cream-style cottage cheese
4 cups sour cream
1 cup minced onion
3 or 4 cloves garlic, minced
4 Tbsp. Worcestershire sauce
4 dashes Tabasco sauce
4 Tbsp. poppy seeds
2 tsp. salt
freshly-ground pepper to taste
paprika
freshly-grated Parmesan cheese

Cook noodles in boiling, salted water until tender. Drain. Combine the noodles with th remaining ingredients except the paprika and Parmesan cheese. Approximately 30 minutes before serving, bake in buttered casseroles at 350 degrees until hot. Sprinkle with paprika and serve with Parmesan cheese. Serves 24. May be prepared ahead.

The Committee

NOODLE KUGEL (Pudding)
May be served along with meat as a side dish, or used as a dessert.

2 eggs, beaten
3 Tbsp. sugar
1/4 tsp. cinnamon
pinch of salt
1/2 lb. noodles (broad), cooked
    and drained
1 cup shredded tart apples
1/4 cup raisins
1/4 cup chopped nuts
4 Tbsp. melted butter

Combine eggs, sugar, cinnamon and salt. Add to noodles. Add apples, raisins, nuts and melted butter. Mix thoroughly. Place in a well-greased 1-1/2 qt. casserole. Bake at 400 degrees until brown on top (about 1 hour). Serves 6.
Note: Other fruits such as crushed pineapple, apricots, peaches, etc., may be substituted for the apples.

Ruth Solomon (Mrs. A.M.)

NOODLE PUDDING — KUGEL (Sweet)
"Always a hit! Everyone asks for the recipe."

8 oz. pkg. old fashioned noodles
8 oz. container of sour cream
16 oz. container of cottage cheese
3 eggs
1 cup sugar
1 tsp. vanilla
cinnamon
butter or margarine

Cook noodles according to package directions. Drain and rinse. Using mixer at medium speed, mix together all ingredients, except noodles, until fluffy. Add cooked noodles. Mix and pour into greased 9x9 square pan. Top with pats of butter or margarine. Sprinkle with cinnamon. Bake at 350 degrees for one hour. Serves 8-10.

Susan O. Kaye (Mrs. B.J.)

FETTUCCINI ALFREDO
Good with beef as a side dish

2 8-oz. pkg. thin egg noodles
   (fettuccini)
1 stick butter
1 cup heavy cream
1 cup Parmesan cheese
freshly-ground pepper

Cook noodles according to directions, being sure not to overcook. Drain and return to pot. Add butter and cream and mix well. Add cheese and toss lightly. Spoon into chafing dish or casserole which can be warmed. Serve with freshly-ground pepper. Serves 8. Good with green salad and white wine alone or salad, red wine and a good steak.

Ellen Knott (Mrs. B.F.)

FETTUCINE FERRARI

1 lb. fettuccine
1/2 cup butter
1 bunch green onions, chopped
1 or 2 cloves garlic, minced
1 cup cherry tomatoes, quartered
5 oz. ham, cut in 1/4 inch cubes
1 egg yolk
1/4 cup heavy cream
1/2 cup freshly-grated Parmesan
   cheese
salt to taste
freshly-ground pepper to taste

In a large kettle, cook the fettuccine in boiling, salted water until it has reached the "al dente" stage, still firm to the bite. Drain thoroughly. Melt the butter in a medium skillet. Add the scallions and garlic, cooking gently until onions are tender. Add the tomatoes and saute for 1 to 2 minutes. Add ham to heat through. Beat the egg yolk and then beat the cream into the egg only until well mixed. Slowly stir into the tomato and ham mixture with a flat whisk and cook just until thickened and well blended. Add remaining ingredients and remove from heat. Add the sauce to the hot fettuccine, toss, and serve immediately on warm plates. Serves 4 to 6.

The Committee

GOURMET MACARONI AND CHEESE

8 oz. pkg. macaroni, cooked
3 eggs, slightly beaten
1 can (13 oz.) evaporated milk
3 drops Tabasco sauce
2 tsp. salt
2 heaping tsp. dry mustard
1 stick (1/2 cup) butter
1 lb. N.Y. State sharp Cheddar
    cheese, grated
Pepperidge Farm stuffing
    (optional)

Combine eggs, evaporated milk, 3/4 cup water, and seasonings. Add cooked and drained macaroni. Stir in butter until it melts; stir in cheese. Pour into large 2-1/2 qt. casserole and sprinkle Parmesan cheese on top. (Can also put some Pepperidge Farm stuffing mix on top.) Sprinkle with paprika. Bake at 350 degrees for 45 minutes or until lightly browned and bubbly. Serves 8. May be made ahead and refrigerated.

Susan Rielly (Mrs. P.C.)

FLORENTINE MANICOTTI
A good and easy Sunday night supper

1/2 cup chopped onion
1 clove garlic, minced
1 Tbsp. butter
2 10-oz. pkgs. frozen chopped
    spinach, cooked and drained
1 lb. cottage cheese
1 4-oz. pkg. shredded Mozzarella
    cheese
1/2 cup Parmesan cheese, grated
3 beaten eggs
1/2 Tbsp. lemon juice (fresh)
3/4 tsp. salt
dash pepper
12 large manicotti noodles,
    cooked and drained
1 16-oz. jar spaghetti sauce

Saute garlic and onion in butter. Combine this with spinach, cheeses, eggs, lemon juice, salt and pepper; mix well. Fill cooked noodles with spinach mixture. Place in a 13x9 inch baking dish. Cover and bake at 350 degrees for 40 minutes. Heat spaghetti sauce; pour over noodles. Sprinkle with additional Parmesan cheese. Freezes beautifully. Serves 6.

Peggy D. Young (Mrs. John A.)

SPAGHETTINI ESTIVI (Summer Spaghetti)

A delicious, inexpensive, meatless meal. The sauce may be made ahead of time.

*1 large (28 oz.) can whole
tomatoes, drained
2 Tbsp. fresh chopped parsley
1 tsp. basil
scant 1/4 cup fresh lemon juice
4 Tbsp. olive oil
3 cloves garlic, minced
1 tsp. salt
1/2 tsp. pepper
1 lb. spaghettini, cooked
2 Tbsp. butter*

Coarsely chop drained tomatoes. Add next 7 ingredients (can use Cuisinart) to bowl and mix well. Cook spaghetti, drain and quickly toss with butter so that spaghetti stays hot. Add 1/2 sauce and toss again. Serve remaining sauce over individual servings. Serves 4.

Donna K. Alpert (Mrs. Eric D.)

TAGLIARINI WITH EGGPLANT SAUCE

*6 large tomatoes—peeled, seeded
and coarsely chopped
1 large eggplant (about 1-1/4 lbs.)
cut into 1/2 inch cubes
1/4 cup olive oil
2 cloves garlic, pressed or minced
2 small green peppers, diced
1/4 cup water
2 Tbsp. capers
1 cup chopped fresh basil (or
1/4 cup dry)
6 to 8 anchovy fillets, chopped
1 can pitted ripe olives, drained
salt
1/4 tsp. crushed red pepper
1 to 1-1/4 lbs. dry tagliarina (very
thin noodles)*

In large 5-qt. kettle, heat oil; add garlic and eggplant, stirring constantly for 1 minute. Stir in peppers. Reduce heat and add water. Cover and cook until tender (6 to 8 minutes). Add capers, basil, anchovies, crushed red pepper, olives and tomatoes. Boil uncovered until sauce thickens— 15 to 20 minutes. Salt to taste. Meanwhile, cook tagliarini in boiling salted water according to package directions. Drain; serve with eggplant sauce.

Gensie

LAZY LASAGNA
"I usually double this recipe and freeze half in a 2-qt. casserole."

8 oz. package egg noodles
1 cup (8 oz.) ricotta or creamed cottage cheese
2/3 cup shredded mozzarella cheese
1/3 cup grated Parmesan cheese
2-1/2 cups prepared spaghetti sauce

Cook noodles, drain and rinse. Mix noodles, ricotta, mozzarella and Parmesan cheeses together in large bowl. In 2-qt. oblong baking dish, spoon enough sauce to cover bottom. Layer noodle mixture and sauce—repeat, ending with sauce. Bake 25-30 minutes at 375 degrees. Serves 4.

Vivian Stanley (Mrs. J.S.)

SPINACH LASAGNA
This recipe will make Popeye converts of spinach haters.

1 16-oz. carton ricotta or small-curd cottage cheese
1-1/2 cups shredded mozzarella cheese
1 egg, lightly beaten
1 10-oz. pkg. frozen chopped spinach, thawed and drained
1 tsp. salt
1/8 tsp. pepper
3/4 tsp. oregano
2 15-1/2 oz. jars spaghetti sauce
1 8-oz. pkg. lasagna noodles, uncooked
1 cup water

Thaw spinach and drain. Combine ricotta cheese, 1 cup mozzarella cheese, egg, spinach, salt, pepper and oregano. Mix well. Grease baking dish. Spread 1/2 cup spaghetti sauce in bottom. Place 1/3 of the lasagna noodles over sauce. Spread with half the cheese mixture. Repeat layers. Top with remaining noodles, spaghetti sauce, and 1/2 cup mozzarella cheese. Pour 1 cup water into sauce jars, shake, and pour around edges of dish. Cover tightly with aluminum foil. Bake at 350 degrees for 1 hour and 15 minutes. Let stand 15 minutes before serving. Serves 6-8.

Laura McMaster (Mrs. J.C.)

GOURMET MUSHROOMS AND NOODLES
Good accompaniment to beef

1/2 cup butter
1/2 lb. fresh mushrooms, sliced
1/3 cup onion, chopped
1/2 cup sliced almonds
1 clove garlic, minced
1 can beef consomme
1 Tbsp. lemon juice
4 oz. medium noodles

Melt butter. Cook mushrooms, onion, almonds and garlic in butter over *low* heat for 10 minutes. Add remaining ingredients and cook until noodles are tender—about 10 minutes. Serves 4. Doubles nicely.

Dot Nicholls (Mrs. T.H.)

CHEESY NOODLES

1 8-oz. pkg. cream cheese,
   softened
1 cup sour cream
1 cup cottage cheese
1 8-oz. pkg. small noodles
1/3 cup diced green onions, with
   tops
1 tsp. salt
1/4 tsp. pepper
dash cayenne
1/4 tsp. garlic salt
2 tsp. Worcestershire sauce
1 cup bread crumbs
1/4 cup melted butter

Cook noodles according to package directions. Mix cream cheese, sour cream and cottage cheese. Add remaining ingredients, except bread crumbs and butter, and blend with noodles. Place in buttered 2-qt. covered casserole and top with bread crumbs and butter. Bake at 350 degrees for 10 minutes. Remove cover and bake 10 minutes longer. Serves 4.

Betty Holland (Mrs. Calvin)

MACARONI AND CHEESE

1/2 lb. pkg. macaroni (elbow,
   short lengths, or wide
   macaroni, as preferred)
2 Tbsp. butter or margarine
2 Tbsp. flour
3/4 tsp. salt
1/8 tsp. freshly-ground black
   pepper
2 cups milk
1 to 2 cups (1/4 to 1/2 lb.) cheese,
   cubed, shredded or crumbled
buttered bread crumbs (optional)

Cook macaroni in rapidly boiling salted water, using at least 4 quarts water. When tender, drain well. Melt butter, stir in flour and cook until it bubbles. Add salt and pepper; then slowly stir in milk and cook until smooth. Add 1 cup cheese; stir until partially melted. Place macaroni in layers with the cheese sauce; over the top place remaining cheese or bread crumbs tossed with melted butter (using 2 Tbsp. butter to 1/2 cup bread crumbs). Bake uncovered at 400 degrees for 20 to 25 minutes. Serves 4.

The Committee

Meats

GOURMET HAMBURGER CASSEROLE

1 lb. lean ground chuck
1 cup chopped onion
1 clove garlic, crushed
1 tsp. salt
3 cups (4 oz.) medium noodles
1 can (2-1/2 cups) tomato juice
1-1/2 tsp. Worcestershire sauce
1-1/2 tsp. celery salt
dash pepper
1 can condensed beef broth
1/2 cup water
1/3 cup chopped green pepper
1 cup sour cream
1 4-oz. can sliced mushrooms

Place beef, onion, garlic and salt in electric skillet. Heat to 350 degrees. Cook and stir until beef is browned. Add noodles. Combine tomato juice, Worcestershire sauce, celery salt, salt, pepper, beef broth and water. Pour over noodles. Cover. Simmer at 220 degrees for 20 minutes, stirring occasionally. Add green pepper. Cover, cook 10 minutes or until noodles are tender. Stir in mushrooms and sour cream, heat. Can be prepared ahead and reheated. Serves 6.

Virginia Golding (Mrs. John G.)

HAMBURGER CASSEROLE

1 lb. hamburger
2 carrots
2 onions
2 stalks celery
2 potatoes
1 can tomato soup
1/2 can water
salt and pepper to taste
Worcestershire sauce (optional)

Dice vegetables and mix with hamburger. Add tomato soup and water. Salt and pepper to taste. Add Worcestershire sauce if desired. Bake 2 hours at 325 degrees. Serves 4.

Joyce W. Summerville (Mrs. W. Kelly)

JOE'S SPECIAL

1 lb. ground beef
1/2 cup chopped onions
1 can (4 oz.) sliced mushrooms, drained
1 pkg. (10 oz.) frozen chopped spinach, thawed
1 tsp. garlic salt
1 tsp. salt
1/4 to 1/2 tsp. oregano, basil or marjoram
4 eggs, beaten

Brown the ground beef until crumbly. Drain off the fat. Add onions, mushrooms, spinach, garlic salt, salt and oregano or basil or marjoram. Cook and stir for about 4 minutes or until the onions are tender and the spinach is cooked. Add eggs and cook until the eggs are set. Serves 4-5.

Georgia Miller (Mrs. George)

AWARDS NIGHT CASSEROLE

1-1/2 lbs. ground beef
1/2 lb. ground lean pork
1/2 cup chopped onion, or more
1/2 cup chopped green pepper, or
  more
2 cans tomato soup
1 can mushroom soup
1 can cream of celery soup
1 tsp. salt
1/2 tsp. pepper
1 16-oz. pkg. medium noodles
1 cup grated sharp cheese

Put ground beef, pork, onions and green pepper into skillet and cook until meat is brown. Put in colander and drain off fat. Return to skillet and add soups and spices. Cook noodles. Alternate noodles and meat in large casserole (at least 3 qt.), sprinkle with grated cheese and cook for 45 minutes at 350 degrees. Serve with green salad and light dessert. Serves 12.

Jayne Withers (Mrs. Philip)

BEEF AND CABBAGE

1/2 head cabbage, sliced or
  shredded
1/2 cup raw rice
1 can beef consomme
1 medium onion, chopped
1 lb. ground beef or sausage
seasoned salt
pepper

Spread shredded cabbage evenly in a 2-qt. greased casserole. Sprinkle rice over cabbage. Brown meat and onion. Drain if necessary and pour over cabbage and rice. Add consomme and sprinkle with seasoned salt and pepper. Cook covered at 350 degrees for 45 minutes. Serves 4-6.

Hilda Hemby (Mrs. T.E., Jr.)

CHINESE CASSEROLE

1 lb. hamburger (or half
  hamburger and half sausage)
1 large onion, sliced
1 can Chinese vegetables, drained
1 green pepper, sliced
1 can Chinese noodles
1 can mushroom soup
1 can chicken and rice soup
1/3 can water for each can of soup
1 Tbsp. soy sauce
1 can water chestnuts, cut in little
  pieces
grated Cheddar cheese

Brown hamburger with onions. Add remainder of ingredients. Place in lightly buttered casserole dish and sprinkle with Cheddar cheese. Bake at 350 degrees for 1 hour. May be frozen. Serves 6.

Hilda Hemby (Mrs. T.E., Jr.)

MOUSSAKA
This is a great main dish.

3 medium eggplants
1 cup butter
3 large onions, finely chopped
2 lbs. ground beef or lamb
3 Tbsp. tomato paste
1/2 cup red wine
1/2 cup chopped parsley
1/4 tsp. cinnamon
salt and freshly-ground pepper

CREAM SAUCE
6 Tbsp. flour
1 quart milk
4 eggs, beaten
dash nutmeg
2 cups ricotta cheese
1 cup fine bread crumbs
1 cup grated Parmesan cheese

Peel eggplants and cut into slices 1/2 inch thick. Brown slices quickly in 4 Tbsp. butter and set aside. Heat 4 Tbsp. butter in same skillet and cook onions until brown. Add ground meat and cook 10 minutes. Combine tomato paste with wine, parsley, cinnamon, salt and pepper. Stir this mixture into meat and simmer over low heat until all liquid is absorbed, stirring often.
Preheat oven to 375 degrees.
Make a white sauce by melting 8 Tbsp. butter and blending in the flour, stirring with a wire whisk. Meanwhile, bring milk to a boil and add it gradually to butter/flour mixture, stirring constantly. When mixture is thickened and smooth, remove from heat. Cool slightly and stir in beaten eggs, nutmeg and ricotta cheese.
Grease 11 x 16 pan and sprinkle bottom lightly with bread crumbs. Arrange alternate layers of eggplant and meat sauce in pan, sprinkling each layer with Parmesan cheese and bread crumbs. Pour ricotta cheese sauce over top and bake 1 hour or until top is golden. Remove from oven and cool 20 minutes before serving. Cut into squares and serve. Freezes well.
The flavor of this dish improves if made a day ahead.

Carolyn Adams (Mrs. Geroge B., Jr.)

Similar recipe submitted by:
Peggy Hormberg (Mrs. R.H.)

Peggy Hormberg suggests a combination of eggplant and potatoes, or all potatoes if your family doesn't like eggplant.

Salt is neither an herb nor a spice; it is a mineral which is essential to life. Its role is not to give a special taste of its own to food, but to intensify natural flavors.

STUFFED GREEN PEPPERS

4 or 5 large green peppers
3 Tbsp. butter or margarine
1 small onion, finely chopped
1/2 cup raw rice
1 lb. ground beef chuck
1-1/2 tsp. salt
1/4 tsp. pepper
1 egg
2 Tbsp. butter or margarine
2 Tbsp. flour
1 18 oz. can tomato juice

Cut each pepper in half. Cut membranes and seed from inside. Place peppers in a bowl and add boiling water to cover. Drain, set aside. Melt 3 Tbsp. butter in a skillet and add the onions and rice. Cook about 5 minutes. Place meat in a bowl. Blend rice, onion, salt, pepper, and egg into the meat. Fill the green peppers with the meat mixture. Melt the 2 Tbsp. butter in a saucepan over moderately low heat. Add flour and blend. Slowly add tomato juice. Cook, stirring constantly, until mixture thickens — about 5 minutes. Remove from heat. Place peppers in a casserole dish. Pour sauce over all. Bake 1-1/4 hours at 350 degrees. Freezes well. Serves 4-5.

Mary Robinson (Mrs. R.F.)

GATEAU DE CREPES

2 eggs, beaten
2 tsp. sugar
1 cup flour
1-1/4 cup milk
1/8 tsp. salt
4 tsp. melted butter

FILLING:
3 Tbsp. olive oil
1/2 cup onion, chopped
1 lb. ground beef
1 tsp. salt
1 clove garlic, crushed
1 Tbsp. dry oregano
1 Tbsp. dry basil
2 8-oz. cans tomato sauce
1 lb. ricotta cheese
1 egg, well beaten

Mix dry ingredients, add milk and beat until smooth. Add beaten eggs and butter. Let stand 3 hours or over night in refrigerator. Heat and grease small frying pan. Pour in enough butter to cover bottom, cook until brown, turn and cook other side. Makes at least 12 crepes.

Heat oil. Add onions and cook until soft. Add meat, salt, garlic, basil and oregano. Cook until brown. Add tomato sauce, and boil. Add a few teaspoons water if necessary. Cover, reduce heat, and simmer for 45 minutes.

Blend cheese and egg with fork. Center a crepe in 8-inch round ovenproof baking dish. Spread with meat sauce. Cover with a crepe. Spread with cheese mixture. Alternate layers until crepes are used. Bake at 350 degrees for 20-30 minutes. Cut into wedges. Serves 10 to 12.

Mary Liz Maletis (Mrs. James)

STUFFED PEPPERS

The general rule of wine cooking is to use the wine which is normally served with the dish—red with meat, whites with fish and fowl, and sweet with fruit. This recipe successfully violates the rule.

2 lbs. ground chuck
2 Tbsp. olive oil
2 tsp. salt
1-1/2 cups chopped onions
1 pkg. Italian salad dressing mix
1 cup raw rice
2 8-oz. cans tomato sauce
1 cup dry white dinner wine
6 large green peppers
1/4 cup water
2 cups grated sharp Cheddar cheese

Preheat oven to 350 degrees. Saute ground chuck in olive oil until well browned but not dry. Sprinkle with salt during browning. Stir in onions and rice. Cook until onions are just limp. Blend in dry salad dressing mix. Add tomato sauce and wine. Cook on low heat for 10 minutes. Remove from heat. Cut peppers into halves; scoop out seeds and large membranes. Place peppers cut side up in a large baking dish. Spoon meat filling into peppers, heaping up well. Pour water into bottom of pan. Cover and bake 55 to 60 minutes. Remove cover; sprinkle with grated cheese and return to oven 5 to 10 minutes longer until cheese is melted. Can be prepared the night before and refrigerated until ready to bake. Serves 6.

Gensie

BEEF-IN-A-BLANKET

These reheat nicely in the microwave.

1 lb. ground chuck
1 small onion, chopped
1/2 medium green pepper, chopped
1/2 tsp. salt
1/4 tsp. hickory smoked salt
1/4 tsp. basil
2 pkg. (8 count each) crescent rolls

SAUCE
1 can cream of mushroom soup
6 oz. sharp Cheddar cheese, grated
1/2 cup cottage cheese, sieved or blended
1 tsp. hickory smoked Worcestershire sauce
1 can (3 or 4 oz.) sliced mushrooms

Brown meat in skillet. When some grease forms (or add some if necessary), turn down heat and add the onions, pepper, salt and basil. After the meat is brown and onion and green pepper soft, pour off any excess grease.

Separate the rolls into 16 triangles. Place approximately 1-1/2 Tbsp. filling in center of each triangle. Fold up points and press side edges together to seal. Bake on lightly greased cookie sheet 11-13 minutes at 375 degrees. Remove to serving platter and spoon on sauce. (If you have a large baking/serving dish, bake in it.)

SAUCE:
Put all ingredients into saucepan over low heat. Stir occasionally until cheese is melted. Pour over "rolls" and top each with a parsley sprig, chopped chives or pimiento strips. Serves 5 to 8.

Guerry Barnett Russell (Mrs. Don J.)

BEEF AND BEAN BAR-B-QUE

1 lb. hamburger
1/4 cup diced green pepper
1/4 cup diced onion
1/2 cup diced celery
1 8-oz. can tomato sauce
1/2 cup water
1 No. 2-1/2 can Campbell's
    Pork and Beans
2 Tbsp. brown sugar
2 Tbsp. vinegar
salt and pepper to taste

Brown meat with vegetables. Add remaining ingredients except beans. Simmer 5 to 10 minutes. Add beans. Put in 13 x 9 casserole and bake at 375 degrees for 45 minutes. Can prepare the day before. Serves 8.

Mary Lou Scholl (Mrs. Ken)

CROCK POT BEAN DINNER

1/2 to 1 lb. ground beef
3/4 lb. bacon
1 cup chopped onion
1 cup catsup
1/4 cup brown sugar
1 Tbsp. liquid smoke
3 Tbsp. white vinegar
1 tsp. salt
dash of pepper
2 cans (1 lb. 15-oz. size) pork and
    beans
1 can (1 lb.) kidney beans, drained
1 can (1 lb.) lima beans, drained

Brown ground beef, then drain. Brown bacon, drain and crumble or cut into small pieces. Cook onions in remaining fat. Drain all well. Combine the first 9 ingredients. All this may be prepared well ahead, or even frozen for later use.
When ready to prepare the meal, combine all 12 ingredients. Place in crock pot, and stir together. Cover and cook on low heat 4 to 9 hours. Leftovers may be frozen. Serves 12.

Charlotte Arrendell (Mrs. C.W.)

SNOOPY BURGERS
Kids love these!

5 lbs. ground chuck
1 cup applesauce
1 cup Ritz cracker crumbs (use
    food processor)
3 Tbsp. Worcestershire sauce
1 envelope onion soup mix
3 tsp. Tabasco sauce
1 tsp. garlic salt.

Mix in large bowl with hands and pat out in *5 oz. burgers. Oven broil or charcoal grill. Can be frozen cooked or uncooked. Yield: about 18 five-ounce burgers.
*I use a postage scale for uniformity. Sometimes I cook all of them on the grill and then put them in the freezer. They reheat beautifully in the microwave oven.

Kay Roberson (Mrs. G. Don)

CHEESEBURGER PIE

1 lb. ground beef
1/2 tsp. oregano
1 tsp. salt
1/4 tsp. pepper
1/4 cup chopped onion
1/4 cup chopped green pepper
   (optional)
1/2 cup dry bread crumbs
1 8-oz. can tomato sauce

CHEESE TOPPING:
8 oz. mellow Cheddar cheese,
   grated
1 egg, beaten
1/4 cup milk
1/2 tsp each: salt, dry mustard,
   Worcestershire sauce

SAUCE:
1/2 8-oz. can tomato sauce and
   equal amount of chili sauce

Heat oven to 425 degrees. Brown beef in small amount of fat. Mix in all other ingredients except cheese topping and sauce. Spread into 9-inch pie shell. Mix together ingredients in cheese topping and spread over filling. Bake about 30 minutes. Serve in wedges with the sauce. Serves 4-6.

Doris Edwards (Mrs. Mark B.)

IMPOSSIBLE LASAGNE PIE

1/2 cup creamed cottage cheese
1/4 cup Parmesan cheese
1 lb. ground beef
1 tsp. oregano leaves
1/2 tsp basil leaves
1 (5 oz.) can tomato paste
1 cup shredded mozzarella cheese,
   divided
1 cup milk
2/3 cup Bisquick baking mix
2 eggs
1 tsp. salt
1/4 tsp. pepper

Preheat oven to 400 degrees. Grease 10 x 1-1/2 pie plate. Cook ground beef and drain. Layer cottage and Parmesan cheeses in plate. Mix beef, herbs, paste and 1/2 cup mozzarella; spoon on top. Beat milk, baking mix, eggs, salt and pepper for 15 seconds in blender on high or 1 minute with hand beater. Pour into plate. Bake until knife inserted between center and edge comes out clean — 30 to 35 minutes. Sprinkle with remaining mozzarella. Serves 6.

Pat Gatlin (Mrs. Leon)

BURRITOS

1 lb. ground beef
12 oz. Colby, Longhorn or Monterey Jack cheese, grated and divided
1 head lettuce, cut up
1 small onion, or 5 spring onions, cut up
2 tomatoes, diced
1 can Old El Paso tomatoes and chilies
1 can Old El Paso refried beans
1 jar Old El Paso hot or mild taco sauce
flour tortillas

Brown ground beef and drain. Mix refried beans and tomatoes and chilies in pan over low heat; add ground beef. Keep warm over low heat. Mix lettuce, tomatoes, onion and 8 oz. cheese (setting aside 4 oz. of cheese) in large bowl. Take the salad mixture and roll up about 1/2 cup in each flour tortilla; then place in pyrex dish. Spread the ground beef mixture over the tortillas; sprinkle with remaining cheese. Heat until the cheese melts. Serves 6-8.

Jean Skidmore (Mrs. W.H.)

QUICK AND EASY CHILI CON CARNE

1-1/2 lb. ground beef
1 medium onion, chopped
1 pkg. French's Chili-O seasoning
15 oz. can Hormel Chili with no beans
15 oz. can Luck's pinto beans
16 oz. can stewed tomatoes
1/2 cup water (optional)

Brown ground beef and onion. Drain off fat. Add tomatoes, then seasoning. Mix together. Add beans and stir in canned chili. Add water if desired. Simmer 10 minutes (I usually let it sit in the refrigerator overnight, or freeze in serving sizes for later use.) Serves 6-8.

Elizabeth Fox (Mrs. E.J.)

CHILI PILE-UPS
Teenagers love it!

1 large bag regular Fritos
1 recipe favorite chili
2 cups shredded cheese
2 heads shredded lettuce
3 chopped tomatoes
1 chopped onion
1 16-oz. container sour cream
guacamole (optional)

Put each of the above ingredients in bowls so that each person can stack their own "chili pile-up" according to taste. Begin with Fritos on the bottom and stack according to ingredients listed above, in that order. Nice to serve as a buffet meal. Serves 6.

Beverly Michaux (Mrs. Roy H.)

CHILI CON CARNE

2 Tbsp. shortening
2 cloves garlic
2 or 3 large onions, sliced
1/2 green pepper, seeded and
    chopped
1 Tbsp. chili powder
1/2 tsp. cumin
1/2 tsp. oregano
1 lb. ground meat
1 1-lb. can peeled tomatoes, or
    1 8-oz. can tomato sauce
1 1-lb. can red kidney beans, with
    liquid
1 cup water or broth
salt

Heat shortening to sizzling, add split garlic cloves and onions; cook until soft. Mash garlic into fat with tines of fork. Add green pepper, chili powder, cumin and oregano; cook 2 minutes. Add ground meat. Cook, stirring, until it loses its pink color. Add tomatoes (or sauce) and kidney beans with liquid. Add water or beef broth made with stock concentrate, and salt to taste. (If broth is used, salt may not be necessary.) Simmer, covered, about 40 minutes. Serve with rice and a green salad. Makes 6 servings.

For 2 or 3 servings, prepare full recipe, freeze the rest for another time — it will taste still better when reheated.

Georgia Miller (Mrs. George)

MUSTA CIOLI

This combines the best features of chili and spaghetti.

2 Tbsp. bacon drippings
2 large onions, chopped
2 lbs. ground beef
1 stalk chopped celery
1 bell pepper, chopped
1 (3-1/2 oz.) can mushrooms and
    liquid
2 (6 oz.) cans tomato paste
2 buds garlic
2 bay leaves
1 tsp. pepper
dash red pepper
3/4 oz. chili powder
18 oz. water
3/4 lbs. cooked noodles
cheese

Put celery and bell pepper in a little water and simmer until tender. Brown onion in bacon drippings and add meat to brown lightly. Add to this all other ingredients (except the noodles and cheese). Cook 45 minutes; then add noodles. Cheese can be put on top. Serves 8.

Noble Dillard

MEAT BALLS

1 lb. ground meat
1 medium onion, finely grated
1 egg, slightly beaten
1 tsp. oregano
1 tsp. salt
1/2 tsp. pepper
1 tsp. tomato paste
1/2 cup bread crumbs
3 Tbsp. oil

SAUCE:
2 Tbsp. tomato paste
2 Tbsp. vinegar
1/2 tsp. allspice
dash salt and pepper

In a bowl combine onion, oregano, ground meat, bread crumbs, egg, tomato paste, salt and pepper. Knead lightly. Form into small balls, approximately 30. Fry in oil in a shallow pan for 10-15 minutes, turning until brown; remove from pan and place in a serving dish.

In the same pan add ingredients for the sauce: tomato paste, vinegar, allspice, salt and pepper. Bring to a quick boil and pour over meat balls. Serve hot.

Mrs. John Miller

PIA LINDSTROM'S SWEDISH MEATBALLS

1/2 cup fresh white bread crumbs
1/2 cup milk
1/2 lb. ground beef
1/4 lb. ground veal
1/4 lb. ground pork
1 egg, slightly beaten
3 Tbsp. chopped onion
1-1/2 tsp. salt
1/4 tsp. white pepper
1/4 tsp. allspice
2 Tbsp. butter or margarine
2 Tbsp. flour
1 beef bouillon cube
boiling water
1/2 cup light cream
1/2 cup milk
1 Tbsp. snipped fresh dill, OR 2
    tsp. dried dill weed

In a small bowl, soak bread crumbs in milk about 5 minutes.

In a large bowl combine meats, egg, onion, salt, pepper, allspice and bread mixture. Toss gently with fork just to combine. Using hands, gently shape mixture into 30 meatballs.

In large skillet, in hot butter, saute meatballs, half at a time, until they are all browned and cooked all the way through—about 10 minutes. Remove meatballs as they are cooked, and place in a large bowl. Remove the skillet from heat.

Add flour into bacon grease, stirring until smooth. Add bouillon cube, stir in 3/4 cup boiling water. Bring to boiling over medium heat, stirring until bouillon is dissolved and mixture is smooth. Add cream and milk. Simmer gently, stirring, for 3 minutes. Add meatballs to sauce; toss gently to coat well. Simmer, covered, 5 minutes, or until heated through. To serve, sprinkle with dill. Makes 4 to 6 servings. The flavor improves if made the night before and reheated. Freezes well.

Jean Rowe (Mrs. William)

SWEET-SOUR MEAT BALLS

1/2 cup bread crumbs
1/4 cup milk
1/2 tsp. salt
1 lb. ground beef
butter
2 tsp. sugar
1 cup catsup
2 Tbsp. Worcestershire sauce
2 Tbsp. cider vinegar

Mix together bread crumbs, milk, salt and ground beef. Shape into balls about 1/2 oz. each and brown in butter. Arrange in baking pan. Combine sugar with catsup, Worcestershire sauce and vinegar. Pour sauce over meat balls; cover, bake at 375 degrees for 45 minutes. Rice or noodles make a nice accompaniment. Yield: 36 miniature meat balls.

Pat Gatlin (Mrs. Leon)

CURRIED BEEF AND MACARONI

1-1/2 lbs. lean ground beef
1 cup uncooked elbow macaroni
2 strips bacon
1/2 cup chopped onions
1/2 cup chopped green pepper
1 1-lb. can tomato wedges, drained
   (reserve juice)
1/4 cup red wine
1 clove garlic, minced
dash Worcestershire sauce
1 tsp. curry powder
1/2 tsp. sugar
1/2 bay leaf
salt to taste

Cook macaroni and drain. In skillet cook bacon and remove. Saute onions and peppers in bacon grease. Add beef and cook until brown. Chop drained tomato wedges and add along with other ingredients, except tomato juice. Simmer for 20 minutes. Add macaroni, toss and put into casserole dish. Sprinkle bacon on top. Add 1/4 cup tomato juice just before cooking at 375 degrees for 30 minutes. Serves 6.

Etta Nelson (Mrs. James)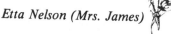

MEAT LOAF WITH CHUTNEY

3 lbs. ground beef
salt and pepper
2 cups diced green onion
   (some tops)
1-1/2 cups diced green pepper
1 cup vinegar
1 cup brown sugar
1 cup Major Gray's chutney
2 eggs, beaten slightly
1 large onion, sliced in rings
1 can beef broth

Season the ground beef with salt and pepper. Mix with the green onion and green pepper. Simmer the vinegar, brown sugar and chutney for 20 minutes on low heat. Cool. Blend in with the meat; add eggs. Form into a loaf and place in a roasting pan which has been greased. Pour the broth over the loaf and bake at 325 degrees for 1 hour and 15 minutes. Place the onion rings on top and baste with the broth. Cook for 30 minutes longer. Serves 8.

The Committee

MOZARELLA MEAT LOAF

1 to 1-1/2 lbs. ground beef
2 Tbsp. onion, chopped
2 Tbsp. bell pepper, chopped
1 egg
1/2 cup milk
2 slices bread, in crumbs, OR
1-1/2 cups croutons, in crumbs
salt and pepper to taste
1/2 tsp. Worcestershire sauce
10-12 oz. shredded mozzarella cheese
1 12-oz. can tomato sauce (Heinz Spicy Herb Sauce is best)

Mix together all ingredients except cheese and sauce. On a long piece of double-fold wax paper, press the meat mixture into a rectangle twice as wide as your rectangular dish. Spread cheese on one half of meat loaf. Lift wax paper's edge and fold other side of meat loaf over cheese side and seal edges and cracks. Place in greased dish. Bake 35 to 45 minutes in a 375 degree oven until it begins to brown. Drain grease, pour tomato sauce over, and return to oven to bake another 10 minutes. Serves 6.

Lin Tillman (Mrs. L.W.)

MEAT LOAF

1-1/2 to 2 lbs. ground beef chuck
2 eggs
2 Tbsp. dehydrated onion flakes
1 can Van Camp's Spanish rice
salt and pepper to taste
3/4 cup catsup, divided
6 strips bacon

Grease 9 x 9 casserole dish. Combine all ingredients except bacon and only 1/4 cup of the catsup. Turn into casserole dish, put remaining catsup over top and add bacon strips. Cook, uncovered, at 375 degrees for 1 hour. Serves 6-8.

Helen Seymour (Mrs. J. Gordon)

BEARD'S CASSEROLE

1 8-oz. box Kraft macaroni and cheese
1/4 cup butter
1/2 cup milk
1 can mushroom soup
1 to 1-1/2 lb. ground chuck
salt, pepper, garlic powder, onion powder
Optional: 1/4 onion chopped, 1/4 green pepper, chopped, few olives, sliced, grated cheese

Cook macaroni 10 minutes in boiling salted water, rinse and drain. Brown ground meat, adding salt, pepper, garlic powder, onion powder plus onion and green pepper if used. Melt butter in sauce pan. Remove from heat to blend in packaged cheese mixture in Kraft box. Add milk; cook over medium heat a few minutes until thicker. Add soup and macaroni, mixing well. Pour into buttered casserole. Put meat on top and heat until bubbly. Grated cheese should be added on top before heating. May be prepared ahead and heated later. Freezes well. Serves 6.

Darlene Beard (Mrs. John N.)

LASAGNA

1 lb. lean ground beef
1/4 cup chopped onions
2 minced garlic cloves
1 No. 2-1/2 can tomatoes
2 '6-oz.' cans tomato paste
2 tsp. salt
1 tsp. dried basil
1/2 tsp. dried oregano
1/4 tsp. pepper
1/2 bay leaf
1 '8-oz. pkg. lasagna noodles
1 lb. ricotta cheese
1 lb. mozzarella cheese, sliced
1/2 cup Parmesan cheese
2 Tbsp. olive oil.

Brown beef in hot olive oil. Add onion and garlic and cook until transparent. Add next 7 ingredients. Cover and simmer for 1 hour or until sauce thickens. Meanwhile, cook lasagna according to directions; drain. Slice mozzarella. In shallow rectangular dish 7 x 12 x 2 spread 1/4 of sauce, cover with lasagna noodles, layer of ricotta, 1/3 of the mozzarella and 1/3 of the Parmesan. Repeat layers, ending with sauce and Parmesan. Bake at 350 degrees for 30-40 minutes. Serves 6.

Beverly Shaver (Mrs. E.F.)

CRESCENT LASAGNE

2 lbs. ground beef
1 medium onion, chopped
1/2 clove garlic (I use dried garlic)
salt and pepper to taste
1 Tbsp. dried parsley flakes
1/2 tsp. basil leaves
1/2 tsp. oregano leaves
1 6-oz. can tomato paste
1 12-oz. carton small-curd cottage
    cheese
1 egg, beaten
1/4 cup grated Parmesan cheese
    (or more if desired)
3 cans Pillsbury Crescent Rolls
1 6-oz. pkg. mozzarella cheese
sesame seeds

Brown together the beef, onion, garlic, salt and pepper. Drain fat and add parsley flakes, basil, oregano and tomato paste. Stir together and simmer for 5 minutes. Set aside.

Use 1-1/2 cans Crescent Rolls to form the bottom crust. Place 3 rectangles (1-1/2 cans) on ungreased cookie sheet. Press perforations together. Place 1/2 of meat mixture down the center of the bottom crust to about 1 inch from sides and ends. Spread the cheese mixture on top of this. Put remainder of meat mixture on this. Top with sliced mozzarella cheese. (I use a 6-oz. package of Kraft sliced mozzarella cheese).

Fold the sides of the bottom crust up. Make the top crust from the remaining 3 rectangles of crescent rolls (1-1/2 cans). Press perforations together, press edges together to seal.

Brush top and sides with milk and sprinkle with sesame seeds. Bake at 375 degrees for 20-25 minutes or until golden brown. Serves 6-8.

Gloria Anderson (Mrs. Vernon)

LASAGNA CASSEROLE

2 tsp. Lawry's seasoned salt
1-1/4 lb. ground chuck
2 cloves garlic, crushed
1/2 tsp. pepper
1 No. 2-1/2 can tomatoes (3-1/2 cups)
1 8 oz. can tomato sauce
1/2 lb. lasagna noodles
1 pkg. Lawry's spaghetti sauce mix (yellow package)
1/2 lb. mozzarella cheese, sliced
1/2 lb. ricotta cheese, OR creamed cottage cheese
1/2 cup grated Parmesan cheese

In seasoned salt, in hot dutch oven or deep kettle, brown ground chuck. Add crushed garlic and pepper; simmer slowly for about 10 minutes, uncovered. Stir in tomatoes, tomato sauce and spaghetti sauce mix; cover and simmer 30 minutes. Meanwhile, cook noodles in boiling, salted water until tender; drain, rinse. Preheat oven to 350 degrees. In 12 x 8 x 2 inch baking dish, pour 1/3 of the sauce. Cover with noodles, then slices of mozarella and spoonfuls of ricotta. Repeat layers, ending with sauce and Parmesan cheese. Bake about 20 minutes. Can prepare ahead. Freezes beautifully. Serves 6-8.

Virginia Golding (Mrs. John H.)

EASY LASAGNA

1 to 1-1/2 lbs. ground beef
1 envelope onion soup mix
3 small cans tomato sauce
dash of Texas Pete hot sauce and Worcestershire sauce
8 oz. egg noodles
mozzarella cheese (and other kinds you might have)

Saute meat, add soup mixture, tomato sauce and seasoning. Cook noodles and put half in a 13 x 9 pyrex dish; add half of meat mixture, and cheeses. Repeat layer and add lots of cheese on top. Bake at 350 degrees for 30 minutes. Freezes well. Serves 10.

Ann Copeland (Mrs. E.H., Jr.)

MOZETTI

1 lb. ground veal or beef
1 lb. ground pork
2 large green peppers, chopped
3 10-3/4 oz. cans tomato soup
1 8-oz. can mushrooms, drained
1 bunch celery, chopped
1 large can Parmesan cheese
1 lb. chopped onions
12 oz. pkg. egg noodles, cooked as directed
salt and pepper to taste

Saute meat in a little margarine until brown; add celery, pepper, salt, mushrooms and onions. Put drained ingredients in a large pan (I use a roasting pan with lid) and add all other ingredients except cheese. Mix well. Add cooked noodles. Add half of the can of cheese in mixture and the other half on top. Cook at 350 degrees for 30 to 45 minutes, until heated through and bubbly. Freezes well. Serves 12 to 15.

Ann Copeland (Mrs. E.H., Jr.)

JUAN MARZETTI

1 4-oz. pkg. wide noodles
2 Tbsp. butter
1-1/2 lbs. ground beef
1 large onion, diced
1/2 green pepper, diced
1 4-oz. can mushrooms and juice
1 tsp. salt
1/4 tsp. pepper
1/4 tsp. oregano
1 10-3/4 oz. can tomato soup
1/3 can water
1 8-oz. can tomato sauce
1 Tbsp. Worcestershire sauce
1/2 lb. sharp cheese, grated
1/2 cup sliced ripe olives
1/2 cup sliced pecans or water
chestnuts.

Cook noodles and drain. Brown meat in butter; add onion and green pepper and cook until soft. Drain. Add other ingredients. Layer with noodles in casserole. Bake at 375 degrees for 45 minutes.

Note: Tester used a combination of other cheeses such as mozzarella, Parmesan and Cheese Whiz instead of sharp cheddar and recommended it for a change.

Mary Lou Lindsey

MANICOTTI

1 box manicotti shells
1 container ricotta cheese
1 egg
1/4 cup chopped parsley

SAUCE I
1/4 cup butter, melted
1/4 cup flour
2 cubes bouillon (beef)
1-1/2 cups milk

SAUCE II
1 15-1/2 oz. jar Ragu spaghetti
sauce with mushrooms
1 lb. ground beef
1/4 cup onion, chopped
1 clove garlic, mashed
1/4 cup butter
2 tsp. basil
1 large pkg. shredded mozzarella
cheese

Cook manicotti shells. Mix ricotta, egg, and parsley. Fill shells and arrange in baking dish.

SAUCE I: Blend flour and bouillon with melted butter. Stir in milk. Heat to boiling and cook 1 minute. Pour over manicotti shells.

SAUCE II: Saute onion and garlic in butter. Add ground beef and cook until browned. Drain. Add spaghetti sauce and basil. Pour over Sauce I. Top with mozzarella. Bake at 350 degrees for 30 minutes. Serves 6-8.

Anne Jones (Mrs. Richard)

MEAT PIE

1 lb. ground beef
1 envelope spaghetti sauce
1 6 oz. can tomato paste
3/4 cup water
1 (9-inch) deep-dish crust
Parmesan cheese to taste
2 cups mozzarella cheese

Brown beef and drain. Add sauce mix, tomato paste and water. Simmer 5 minutes. Put half of meat mixture into pie crust. Sprinkle with Parmesan cheese and 1 cup of mozzarella. Add remaining meat and sprinkle with more Parmesan and remaining 1 cup of mozzarella. Bake until cheese melts (15 to 20 minutes) at 400 degrees. Serves 6.

Myrtle Ussery (Mrs. Albert)

NATCHIDOCHES MEAT PIES

Great to pull out of the freezer

1 lb. hot sausage
3 lbs. ground beef
1 onion, chopped
3 scallions, chopped
1/2 cup parsley, chopped
2 stalks celery, chopped
salt and pepper to taste
Worcestershire, Tabasco to taste
pie crust (3 covered pies) OR crescent rolls

Brown meat. Add vegetables and seasonings and cook until done. Make (or buy) pie crust — enough for 3 covered pies. May also use crescent rolls; approximately 6 cans. Roll out for small pies. Fill with meat mixture. Fold over and press edges together with tines of fork. At this point, you may wrap separately and freeze. Fry in deep fat or bake at 350 degrees for 15 to 20 minutes or until done. We prefer them baked. If baking after freezing, take out of freezer early to thaw. Serves 20 to 27.

Dot Nicholls (Mrs. T.H.)

PIZZA BY THE YARD

Wonderful for a crowd of hungry teenagers

1 (18-inch loaf) French bread
1 lb. lean ground beef
1/3 cup grated Parmesan cheese
1/2 cup finely chopped onion
1/4 cup finely chopped olives
    (optional)
1 tsp. oregano
salt and pepper to taste
1 6 oz. can tomato paste
3 tomatoes, sliced
sliced mozzarella cheese

Split French bread in half lengthwise. Mix next 7 ingredients and spread on both halves of bread, covering edges well (so they will not burn). Broil 12 minutes. Arrange alternate and overlapping slices of cheese and tomato on top of meat, and broil 2 minutes more. Slice in serving size portions and feed to a hungry crowd. The entire loaf may be frozen without the cheese and tomato. Thaw completely before broiling. Serves 8.

The Committee

DEEP CRUST PIZZA A LA PILLSBURY

This is guaranteed to be popular with all true pizza lovers.

SAUCE:
8 oz. can (1 cup) tomato sauce OR
11 oz. can pizza sauce

MEAT:
1 lb. ground beef or sausage, cooked and drained; OR
1/2 lb. sliced pepperoni

SEASONINGS:
1 Tbsp. chopped parsley or chives,
1 to 2 tsp. oregano or Italian seasoning
1 tsp. salt
1/4 to 1/2 tsp. fennel seed or sweet basil
1/4 tsp. pepper

TOPPINGS:
(Use up to 1 cup total): sliced, chopped or whole mushrooms, onions, green pepper, olives, green chilies, bacon

CHEESES
1-1/2 cup (6 oz.) shredded mozzarella, Cheddar, Monterey Jack, Swiss or American cheese
Pillsbury Hot Roll Mix

Preheat oven to 425 degrees, move oven rack to lowest position. Grease bottom and sides of 13 x 9-inch pan or 12-inch pizza pan.* In large bowl dissolve yeast in 1 cup warm water, add flour mixture; blend well. With greased fingers, press dough into greased pan forming a high rim around edge. Use sauce, meat, seasonings, toppings and cheese from suggested ingredients. Bake at 425 degrees for 25-35 minutes until crust is golden brown. Let stand 5 minutes before cutting.

*Tip: For thin crust pizza, use 15 x 10-inch pan. Bake 20-30 minutes. Serves 6.

Kathleen Boyce (Mrs. R.N.)

NOODLE PLEASER
Also pleasing to the palate!

6 oz. cream cheese, softened
8 oz. sour cream
1-1/2 to 2 lbs. ground chuck
2 medium onions, chopped
1/2 tsp. granulated garlic
1-1/2 tsp. salt
1-1/2 tsp. sugar
dash of pepper
2 15-oz. cans tomato sauce
1 12-oz. package wide noodles
1 cup shredded Cheddar cheese

Combine cream cheese and sour cream. Mix well and set aside. Brown ground chuck. Add onion, garlic, salt, sugar, pepper and tomato sauce. Cover and simmer on low heat for 20 minutes. Cook noodles, rinse and drain. Layer half the noodles in a greased 2-1/2 or 3 qt. casserole. Spread with half the cream cheese mixture. Top with half the meat sauce. Repeat layers. Top with cheese. Bake at 350 degrees for 20-30 minutes or until bubbly. Better when prepared ahead and refrigerated. Freezes well. Serves 8-10.

Linda Brown (Mrs. William B.)

STUFFED GIANT SHELLS

1 lb. ground beef
1 large onion, chopped
1 clove garlic, chopped
8 oz. mozzarella cheese, shredded
1/2 cup Italian-style bread crumbs
1/4 cup chopped parsley
1 beaten egg
18 giant shells (macaroni)
3 15-1/2 oz. jars spaghetti sauce
   (reserve 1/2 jar to use when
   reheating leftovers)
1/3 cup dry red wine
1/2 cup grated Parmesan cheese

Brown meat, onion and garlic. Drain. Cool. Stir in mozzarella cheese, bread crumbs, parsley and egg. Season with salt and pepper. Cook shells in boiling salted water until almost tender, about 15 minutes. Drain. Use meat mixture to stuff shells. Spoon a quarter of sauce over bottom of 13 x 9 pyrex dish. Place shells on top of sauce side by side in a single layer. Mix wine with remaining sauce and pour over shells. Sprinkle with Parmesan cheese. Bake at 400 degrees for 20-25 minutes. Freezes well. Serves 6.

Kathleen Boyce (Mrs. R.N.)

GREEK MACARONI AND MEAT CASSEROLE (PASTITSIO)

Make this casserole ahead of time and reheat it for the best flavor.

MEAT FILLING
2 large onions, finely chopped
1 clove garlic, finely chopped
2 to 3 Tbsp. butter or olive oil
2 lbs. lean ground beef or lamb, or
    a combination of the two
3 oz. canned tomato paste
1 cup dry red wine
1/4 tsp. grated orange zest
    (no white)
1 tsp. ground nutmeg
1 tsp. ground cinnamon
1 tsp. ground allspice
salt and pepper to taste
2 eggs, well beaten
1-1/2 cups grated Kefalotyri
    cheese, or substitute
    Parmesan or Kasseri
1/4 cup fine bread crumbs

MACARONI
1 lb. elbow macaroni or ziti
2 to 3 Tbsp. butter

CREAM SAUCE
8 Tbsp. butter
7 Tbsp. flour
1 qt. warm milk
salt and white pepper to taste
4 egg yolks
1-1/2 cups grated Kefalotyri
    cheese, or substitute
    Parmesan or Kasseri

TOPPING
1/2 cup fine bread crumbs
grated nutmeg
additional butter

In a large skillet, saute onions and garlic in butter until they are barely soft. Crumble meat into the pan and stir-fry until it has lost all its pinkness. Tilt the skillet and spoon off all the fat. Stir in the tomato paste, wine, and spices. Bring to a simmer and cook, covered, until all the juices have been absorbed, about 45 minutes. Stir occasionally to prevent sticking. Remove the mixture from heat and when it is thoroughly cool, stir in the eggs, grated cheese and bread crumbs.

Cook the macaroni according to package directions until tender, al dente. Drain it thoroughly and toss with butter. Cover and set aside while you prepare the cream sauce.

In a large, heavy saucepan, melt 8 Tbsp. of butter. Gradually stir in the flour and cook, stirring, over medium heat until the roux has lost its floury taste. Do not let it brown. Gradually pour in the warm milk, stirring continually. Bring the sauce to a bubble and simmer until it becomes as thick as heavy cream. Stir often to prevent sticking or scorching. Remove from the heat. Add salt and pepper. Stir some of the hot sauce into the beaten yolks to warm them. Whisk the yolks into the sauce. When the sauce has cooled, blend in the grated cheese.

Generously butter a baking dish about 15 x 10 x 3 inches, and sprinkle a few bread crumbs on the bottom. Spread half of the macaroni on the bottom. Cover with the meat filling. Pour about half of the cream sauce over the meat, then add the remaining macaroni in an even layer. Pour the last of the sauce over all and sprinkle the top of the casserole with about 1/2 cup fine bread crumbs, some nutmeg and dots of butter. Bake in a 350 degree oven for about 1 hour, until the casserole is set and the top is golden brown. Let stand for 15 minutes. Cut into square serving pieces. To freeze, cool, cover with aluminum foil and freeze. Reheat the dish, covered, in a 350 degree oven for about 1-3/4 hours or until the middle is piping hot. Freezes well. Serves 6 to 8.

Gensie

BAKED SPAGHETTI

1 8-oz. pkg. thin spaghetti
1 12-oz. pkg. link sausage
1 medium onion, chopped
1 bell pepper, chopped
1 lb. ground beef
1 16-oz. can tomatoes
1 can water
1 6-oz. can tomato paste
1 tsp. salt
1 tsp. garlic salt
1 4-oz. can mushrooms
pepper, Tabasco, Worcestershire
    sauce to taste
Parmesan cheese

Fry sausage, remove from pan, leaving about 2 tsp. drippings for browning onions and pepper. Add meat, continue cooking until it loses its red color. Add remaining ingredients, cutting link sausage into small pieces. Grease casserole; put in a layer of meat sauce and a layer of broken uncooked spaghetti, until casserole is filled. Store in refrigerator until ready to cook, or bake in 350 degree oven for 1 hour. Serve with Parmesan cheese topping. Serves 8.

Grace McBride (Mrs. J.W.)

SPAGHETTI CASSEROLE

Flavors blend better when prepared ahead. Nice for a crowd

12 oz. cottage cheese
8 oz. sour cream
8 oz. cream cheese
1/3 cup minced spring onion
12 oz. cooked spaghetti
10 oz. frozen spinach, thawed
    (optional)
1 lb. ground beef, cooked and
    drained
1/2 bell pepper, chopped
16 oz. can tomatoes
6 oz. tomato paste
8 oz. tomato sauce
1 tsp. garlic salt
1 tsp. oregano
salt and pepper as desired
Parmesan cheese

When cheeses are at room temperature, blend well with onion. While spaghetti is cooking, prepare sauce with remaining ingredients, except spinach. Layer 1/2 spaghetti, 1/2 sauce, all the cheese mixture, then remaining 1/2 spaghetti and 1/2 sauce. Top generously with Parmesan cheese. If spinach is used, it is spread on first layer of sauce. Bake in 350 degree oven for 30 minutes. Cooking time will be a little longer if casserole is cold. May be prepared one day ahead. Freezes well. Serves 8-10.

Jackie Plott (Mrs. C.W.)

SPAGHETTI WITH MEAT SAUCE

If you have a Cuisinart Food Processor, use the French-fry attachment to chop the vegetables.

2 Tbsp. salad oil
1-1/4 to 1-1/2 lbs. lean ground
    beef
1 large onion, chopped
1 clove garlic, minced
1/2 cup celery, chopped
1 green pepper, diced
2 tsp. salt—or to taste
1 6 oz. can tomato paste
2 cups tomato juice (use more or
    less to get desired con-
    sistency)
1 tsp. chili powder
1/8 tsp. cayenne pepper
1/8 tsp. curry powder
cooked spaghetti noodles
Parmesan cheese

Heat heavy Dutch oven and add salad oil. Brown beef. Add onion, garlic, celery, pepper and salt. Add combined tomato paste, tomato juice and seasonings. Cover and simmer until thick and done—one to two hours. Serve over cooked spaghetti noodles. Sprinkle with Parmesan cheese. Sauce may be frozen. I always triple the recipe and freeze the remaining sauce. Makes four servings.

Virginia Golding (Mrs. John G.)

SPICY MEAT LOAF

1 lb. Neeses' hot or mild bulk
    sausage (I use hot)
2 lbs. very best quality ground
    chuck
1 pkg. Good Seasons Onion Salad
    Dressing Mix (Reid's)
1 cup coarsely crumbled soda
    crackers
1/2 cup dry white dinner wine

Preheat oven to 375 degrees. Combine all ingredients in a large mixing bowl, mixing well. To shape, pack down into a small bowl; bake in an 8 x 8 inch cake pan. Bake 1 hour until browned. Serves 6. Serve with horseradish sauce (optional).

HORSERADISH SAUCE:
1/2 cup sour cream
3 Tbsp. vinegar
1/4 tsp. salt
2 Tbsp. prepared horseradish
few grains pepper

Blend all ingredients.

Virginia Golding (Mrs. John G.)

BEEF STEW
Perfect for a cold day

2 lbs. stew beef
1/4 cup cooking oil
1-1/2 cups chopped onions
1 1 lb. can tomatoes, cut up
1 Tbsp. quick-cooking tapioca
1 10-1/2 oz. can beef broth
1 clove garlic, minced
1 Tbsp. parsley flakes
2-1/2 tsp. salt
1/4 tsp. pepper
1 bay leaf
6 medium carrots, peeled, cut in
    pieces
3 medium potatoes, peeled, cut in
    pieces
1/2 cup chopped celery

Brown beef in oil. Add all ingredients except vegetables. Bring mixture to a boil. Put in a 3-quart casserole with tight-fitting lid and cook at 350 degrees for 1-1/2 hours. Add vegetables and cook 1 hour longer or until vegetables are tender. Can cook in crockpot on low for 8-12 hours or on high for 5-6 hours. Add vegetables at the beginning. Serves 6-8.

Helen Burns (Mrs. J. Gordon)

BEEF/VEAL SAUTE

2 lbs. stew beef
1 lb. boneless veal for stew
butter
olive oil
dill weed
1/2 cup canned bouillon
1/2 cup consomme
garlic salt
Beau Monde salt
salt, pepper and flour
1 pkg. frozen artichoke hearts
1/2 lb. fresh mushrooms
1/2 cup red wine

Lightly flour and brown meat cubes in small amount of butter and olive oil. Add small amounts of dill, garlic salt, beau monde and salt and pepper. After meat is brown, add 1/2 cup wine, 2 Tbsp. dill weed, 1/2 cup undiluted bouillon and 1/2 cup consomme. Cook at low heat and allow to simmer for 2 hours. Add artichoke hearts and mushrooms (sliced and sauteed in butter). Cook 45 minutes longer. Serves 4-6.

Georgia Miller (Mrs. George)

BURGUNDY STUPENDOUS "NO PEEK" STEW

2 lbs. beef stew meat
1 can cream of mushroom soup
2 4-oz. cans mushrooms,
*   undrained*
1 pkg. dry onion soup mix
1/2 cup Burgundy wine

Mix soups, Burgundy wine and mushrooms. Add beef stew meat. Place in a 2-quart container with a tight-fitting lid. Bake at 350 degrees for 2-1/2 to 3 hours. Do not peek! Can also prepare in a crock-pot. Cook on low for 8-12 hours or on high for 5-6 hours. May be doubled for large model crock-pots. Serves 6-8.

Linda Miller (Mrs. W.R.)

VARIATION: Substitute 1 cup ginger ale for Burgundy wine. Cook as above.

Jane McColl (Mrs. H.L.)

CHRISTMAS SHOPPING STEW

2 lbs. lean chuck, cut into cubes
1 cup chopped celery
2 cups canned tomatoes
2 onions, thinly sliced
4 carrots, peeled and thinly sliced
1 4-oz. can water chestnuts, sliced
*   and drained*
1-1/2 tsp. sugar
2 Tbsp. minute tapioca
1/4 cup dry red or white wine
*   (optional)*
salt and pepper to taste

Place all ingredients in Dutch oven or other large container. Cover. Bake at 225 degrees for 5 hours. Serve with rice or noodles. Serves 6-8.

Barbara Stutts (Mrs. Clyde)

MAKE-AHEAD SOPHISTICATED STEW

3 lbs. lean round steak, cut into
    bite-size pieces
flour, salt and pepper
6 strips of bacon
2 cloves garlic, finely minced
1 oz. brandy, warm
12 small whole mushrooms
1 cup condensed beef bouillon
1-1/2 cups dry red wine
12 small peeled white onions
12 small carrots, peeled and sliced
6 slightly bruised peppercorns
4 whole cloves
1 bay leaf, crumbled
2 Tbsp. chopped, fresh parsley
1/4 tsp. dried marjoram
1/4 tsp. thyme

Shake beef cubes in seasoned flour in plastic bag until coated. Fry bacon in large skillet until brown but not crisp. Cut bacon into 1-inch pieces and place in heavy baking dish. Cook garlic in bacon fat for 1 minute. Add cubed beef and brown quickly on all sides. Pour brandy in skillet, ignite, and when flame dies remove meat and put in casserole. Brown mushrooms and add to casserole. Put bouillon and *one* cup of red wine into skillet and bring to boil; loosen particles on bottom and add liquid to casserole. Add to casserole the onions, carrots, peppercorns, cloves, bay leaf, parsley, marjoram and thyme. Pour remaining 1/2 cup red wine over casserole ingredients. Cover and bake at 300 degrees for 2 hours. Refrigerate. Next day spoon some liquid from bottom of casserole over meat and heat in 300 degree oven, covered, for 1 hour. Serve with rice or noodles. Serves 8 to 10.

Virginia Golding (Mrs. John G.)

BASIC BEEF

2 lbs. stew beef
1 can onion soup
1/2 can water

Combine ingredients in a 2-quart container with a tight-fitting lid. Cover and cook at 350 degrees for 3-4 hours. Serve over rice or noodles if desired. Serves 6-8.

VARIATIONS:
1. Add 1 small can tomato sauce after draining some of the beef liquid, if desired.

2. Add 1 8-oz. carton sour cream and sherry or wine to taste.

Lucy Anderson (Mrs. D.L.)

EASY BEEF POT PIE

2 lbs. stew beef
2 Tbsp. flour
1 pkg. brown gravy mix
2 medium onions, sliced
2 cups sliced raw potatoes
1 cup sliced raw carrots
1-1/2 cups water
1-1/2 tsp. salt
1/4 tsp. pepper
1 9-inch frozen pie crust

Place meat on bottom of round 3-quart baking dish. Sprinkle with flour and gravy mix and stir to coat. Add carrots, potatoes and onions (in that order). Combine water, salt, pepper and Worcestershire sauce. Pour over meat and vegetables. Place pie crust on top. Cut slits to let steam escape. Bake at 400 degrees for 20 minutes. Lower heat to 350 degrees and bake for 2 hours. Serves 4.

Linda Brown (Mrs. Wm. B.)

BEEF BURGUNDY

1-1/2 lbs. round steak, cubed
3 Tbsp. oil
4 Tbsp. flour
3 cups water
3 beef bouillon cubes
1 cup red wine
1 bay leaf
2 tsp. salt
1/2 tsp. fresh ground black pepper
1 tsp. thyme
1/2 tsp. marjoram
2 large onions, cut up
1 cup sliced fresh mushrooms
cooked white rice (Uncle Ben's is
    best)

Brown meat in oil. Add flour all at once. Add all other ingredients except mushrooms. Simmer on low heat for about 3 hours. During last 30 minutes, add mushrooms. Serve over cooked rice. Serves 6.

Ellen Knott (Mrs. B.F.)

BEEF STROGANOFF

2 lbs. beef filet or top sirloin,
    cut into thin strips
1 onion, grated
butter to saute
1/2 lb. fresh mushrooms, sliced
    (may be canned)
1/4 cup white wine
2 pinches basil
1 to 2 cups sour cream
salt and pepper to taste

Saute grated onion in butter until transparent. Add salt, pepper and meat; brown for several minutes. Place onion and meat on platter and keep warm. Add more butter to frying pan; stir in mushrooms and saute, adding 1/4 cup wine and basil. Return meat and onions to mushroom mixture; then add sour cream, additional salt and pepper if needed. Serve with rice or buttered flat noodles. Serves 6.

Sophie Sly (Mrs. Richard)

BEEF STROGANOFF

1-1/2 lbs. round steak
1/4 cup oil
1/4 to 1/2 lb. sliced mushrooms,
    or 1 4-oz. can
3/4 cup chopped onions
1 tsp. salt
3 Tbsp. flour
1 10-1/2 oz. can beef broth or
    2 bouillon cubes dissolved in
    1-1/2 cups hot water
8 oz. carton sour cream
1/2 cup Sherry

Cut steak into 1/4 inch strips. Brown in large skillet in hot oil. Push meat to side of skillet and add mushrooms and onions. Cook until tender but not brown. Stir in beef broth; cover and simmer for 1 hour or until meat is tender (do not overcook meat). Add Sherry. Combine flour with sour cream. Stir into mixture. Simmer uncovered for 15 minutes. May freeze before adding sour cream. Serve over rice or noodles. Serves 5 to 6.

Betty Cobb (Mrs. J.O.)

BARBECUED BEEF

Good Saturday lunch or Sunday supper

1-1/2 lbs. stew beef
1 cup catsup
3 tsp. mustard
3 Tbsp. vinegar
5 tsp. Worcestershire sauce
1 diced onion
1/8 cup sugar

Cook beef 2-1/2 hours in 350 degree oven, adding water as needed. When tender, shred and add remaining ingredients. Serve on hamburger rolls. Can be prepared ahead and reheated. Freezes well. Serves 4.

Liz Lowry (Mrs. W.F.)

BARBECUED LONDON BROIL ON BUNS

1 cup catsup
1-1/2 cups water
1 clove garlic, minced
2 Tbsp. prepared mustard
2 Tbsp. Worcestershire sauce
3 Tbsp. cooking oil
1 tsp. seasoned salt
1/4 tsp. seasoned pepper
1 tsp. onion powder (or salt)
2 flank steaks
meat tenderizer

BUTTER SPREAD:
1/4 lb. bleu cheese
1/2 cup butter
1/2 clove garlic, crushed
2 Tbsp. prepared mustard
1/2 tsp. salt
dash pepper
10 onion buns

ONION GARNISH
3 red onions, sliced thinly
boiling water
1 cup vinegar
1 cup water
1/2 cup sugar
1/2 tsp. salt
1/8 tsp. pepper

Combine first 9 ingredients. Pour over meat and marinate several hours or overnight. Charcoal broil medium rare and slice thinly. Then cream bleu cheese and butter. Season with garlic clove, mustard, salt and pepper. Spread on both sides of *warm* buns. Separate onion rings and cover with boiling water. Combine vinegar, water, sugar and salt. Drain hot water off onions and add above mixture. Marinate and chill 1 hour or more. When ready to serve, put slices of steak on warm buns which have been spread with bleu cheese butter. Add crisp onion rings. Makes 10 sandwiches.

Teny Sugg (Mrs. W.C.)

RIC'S ORIGINAL MARINATED BARBECUED STEAK

4 10-to-12 oz. well-trimmed
  rib-eye steaks
1 Tbsp. Worcestershire sauce
1 Tbsp. Teriyaki sauce
1 2-oz. bottle Kitchen Bouquet
1 Tbsp. Lea and Perrins steak
  sauce
3 to 4 Tbsp. flour to thicken
  mixture

Mix all ingredients except steaks together in measuring cup. Pour marinade into shallow pan large enough to hold steaks. Dry each steak with paper towel. Place in marinade and turn to coat completely. May grill immediately but better if marinated 1 to 2 hours at room temperature. Cook on charcoal grill or gas grill, turned to high, 4 to 6 minutes per inch per side for medium rare, spooning marinade over top before turning. Finished steaks should have a somewhat black, crusty exterior. Delicious! Serves 4.

Ric Alpert

LOUISE'S ORIENTAL BEEF

3 lbs. lean round steak, cut
    1/2 inch thick
2 Tbsp. cooking oil
water
1/3 cup soy sauce
2 tsp. sugar
1/2 tsp. pepper
1 green pepper, cut in strips, then
    in 1/2 inch lengths
8 green onions, cut in 1/2 inch
    pieces
1 clove garlic, minced
3 carrots, cut in strips and then in
    1/2 inch lengths
1/2 lb. fresh mushrooms
1 8-oz. can water chestnuts, sliced
2 Tbsp. cornstarch
1/2 cup bouillon

Partially freeze meat; then cut into 3 to 4 inch strips and brown in cooking oil in large Dutch oven. Pour drippings into a cup and add enough water to equal 1 cup. Combine with soy sauce, sugar, pepper and garlic. Add to meat, cover and cook 45 minutes. Add peppers, onions, carrots, mushrooms and water chestnuts to mixture. Cover and continue cooking 15 minutes. Combine cornstarch and bouillon and thicken mixture. Serve over rice. Serves 8.

Barby Goode (Mrs. David J.)

ONE LONG HOP

1 lb. round steak, half frozen
1/4 cup soy sauce
1 tsp. sugar
2 tomatoes, cut into 1-inch cubes
2 green peppers, cut into 1-inch
    cubes
1/4 cup oil
1/2 tsp. ginger
1 clove garlic, finely chopped
1 Tbsp. cornstarch
2 tsp. soy sauce

Cut round steak into thin strips and marinate for 48 hours in 1/4 cup soy sauce and 1 tsp. sugar. In 2 Tbsp. oil saute meat for 3-5 minutes. Remove meat from pan. Add more oil and saute ginger, garlic and green peppers for 3 minutes. Remove garlic. Add tomatoes and saute another minute. Thicken immediately with cornstarch mixed with 2 tsp. soy sauce. Return meat to pan, and cook one more minute. Serve over rice. Serves 3 to 4.

Georgia Miller (Mrs. George)

STIR-FRIED PEPPER STEAK

1 tsp. Accent
1 Tbsp. soy sauce
1 tsp. sugar
1/2 tsp. salt
dash pepper
1 Tbsp. cornstarch
2 Tbsp. Sherry wine
few drops sesame oil
few gratings fresh ginger
1 clove garlic, minced
1 Tbsp. oil to coat meat
1 lb. flank, rump or sirloin steak,
  cut against grain of meat in
  slices 1 x 2 x 1/8 inch thick
1 tsp. salt
3/4 cup broth or water (I use
  broth)
1 Tbsp. cornstarch
1 Tbsp. soy sauce
2 Tbsp. oil for frying, divided
2 cups green peppers, sliced
  in strips 1/2 inch wide
1/2 cup water chestnuts, thinly
  sliced
1 small onion, halved and cut in
  strips 1/2 inch wide

1. Soak beef in first eleven ingredients. Let stand 15 minutes.
2. Heat wok on high heat. Add 1 Tbsp. oil; slosh around. Add peppers, water chestnuts and onions. Toss-fry for 2 minutes. Remove to platter.
3. Clean wok. Heat on high heat. Add remaining 1 Tbsp. oil; slosh around. Add marinated beef; keep tossing for about 3 minutes. Keep beef pinkish.
4. Add salt, broth, cornstarch and soy sauce. Toss-fry for about 1 minute. Add precooked vegetables. Stir and toss-fry until heated through—about 1 more minute. Serves 4.

Virginia Golding (Mrs. John G.)

STRIP STEAK

4 Tbsp. butter
1 medium onion
1 4-oz. can mushrooms (or use
  fresh), reserve juice
1-1/2 lbs. top sirloin steak
2 Tbsp. flour
1 can beef consomme
1 consomme can water
3 Tbsp. prepared mustard
4 Tbsp. brown sugar
1 to 2 Tbsp. Worcestershire sauce
1 beef bouillon cube
salt and pepper

Trim fat from steak and slice thinly. Saute onions and mushrooms in butter for 5 minutes. Add steak strips and brown them. Blend in flour and remove from heat. Add consomme, water, mustard, brown sugar, Worcestershire sauce, salt and pepper. Return to medium heat, cover and simmer until tender — 45 minutes to 1 hour. Serve over prepared egg noodles. Serves 4-6.

Mary Liz Maletis (Mrs. James)

SHISH KABOB ISTANBUL

1 sirloin steak (5 lbs., or 2 smaller
    ones)

MARINADE:
2 bay leaves
1/2 tsp. pepper
1 Tbsp. Worcestershire sauce
1 garlic clove, crushed
2 cups Burgundy wine
1 small onion, chopped

SAUCE:
1 cup chili sauce
1/2 cup catsup
2 tsp. pickle relish
2 tsp. honey
2 tsp. vinegar

COATING:
1 cup Italian seasoned bread
    crumbs
1 tsp. salt
2 Tbsp. oil

Trim fat from steak and cut into 1-1/2 inch cubes. Marinate 3 hours, turning occasionally. Combine bread crumbs and salt; shake meat cubes in mixture. Thread on skewers and sprinkle with oil. Broil 2 to 3 inches from heat, turning once, about 20 minutes or until done. Serve with hot sauce. Serves 8.

NOTE: Tester recommends cooking on grill, also.

Linda Rowe (Mrs. William)

MARINATED STEAK KABOBS
A good summertime entree

1 cup chopped onion
1/2 cup vegetable oil
1/4 cup lemon juice
1/4 cup soy sauce
1 Tbsp. Worcestershire sauce
1 tsp. prepared mustard
1-1/2 lbs. sirloin steak, cut into
    2-inch cubes
1 large green pepper, cut into
    1-inch pieces
2 medium onions, quartered
2 medium tomatoes, quartered, or
    18 cocktail tomatoes.

Saute onion in oil; remove from heat. Stir in lemon juice, soy sauce, Worcestershire sauce and mustard; pour over meat and vegetables. Cover and marinate overnight in refrigerator, or at least five hours. Remove from marinade and alternate meat and vegetables on skewers. Grill 5 minutes on each side over medium coals or until desired degree of doneness, brushing frequently with marinade. Yield: 4 large skewers or 6 smaller ones.

Ellen Knott (Mrs. B.F.)

FLANK STEAK TERIYAKI BARBECUE

2 lbs. flank steak
3/4 cup Wesson Oil
1/2 cup soy sauce
2 Tbsp. honey
2 Tbsp. vinegar
1 tsp. ginger
1 tsp. garlic powder
1 scallion, top included, finely chopped

Cut steak into 1/2 inch strips. Roll and secure each with a toothpick. Rolls are approximately 3 inches in diameter. Combine all other ingredients in a blender. Pour over steak rolls and marinate for 8 hours. Barbecue over medium fire for 10 minutes on each side.

Georgia Miller (Mrs. George)

MARINATED FLANK STEAK

1/2 cup soy sauce
6 Tbsp. honey
1/4 cup white vinegar
2 tsp. garlic powder
2 tsp. ground ginger
1 cup Crisco or Wesson oil
2 onions, chopped
1 flank steak

Mix all ingredients together, except for flank steak. Pour marinade over steak and cover. Leave overnight. Cook over grill, basting with the marinade. Cook for 5 minutes per side. *Do not overcook!* Cut diagonally to serve. Serves 4.

Barby Goode (Mrs. David J.)

BEEF ROLLS

2 round steaks, cut 1/4 inch thick
prepared mustard
salt and pepper
2 medium onions, chopped
4 strips bacon, cut into small pieces
1 dill pickle, finely chopped
3 Tbsp. oil
red wine
1/2 cup sour cream
2 Tbsp. flour

Cut each steak in half; pound to tenderize. Spread each piece with mustard and sprinkle with salt and pepper. Place bacon, onion and dill pickle on top. Roll each piece and secure with toothpicks. Heat oil in a Dutch oven and brown meat on all sides. Cover rolls with wine, cover pot and simmer about 1-1/2 hours, until rolls are tender. Combine 2 Tbsp. flour with 1/4 cup water; add to stock and simmer until thickened. Add sour cream, and heat through. Serves 4.

Virginia Golding (Mrs. John G.)

LONDON BROIL
Superb flavor!

1 London Broil or flank steak (2
  lbs.)
2 Tbsp. salad oil
2 tsp. chopped parsley
2 Tbsp. Worcestershire sauce
1 clove garlic crushed, or
5-6 drops garlic juice
1 tsp. salt
1 tsp. lemon juice
1/2 tsp. pepper
sauteed mushrooms

Mix marinade ingredients together and pour over steak. Cover and marinate at least 2 hours — overnight is better. Turn occasionally. Drain and reserve marinade. Broil steak for 5 minutes. Turn and brush with marinade. Broil 5 minutes longer, or to desired degree of doneness. Remove steak to carving board and slice thinly on the diagonal and across the grain. Can serve on heated platter. Sauteed mushrooms are a nice accompaniment. Serves 4 to 6.

Ellen Knott (Mrs. B.F.)

SWISS STEAK SUPREME

1/2 Tbsp. butter
2 lbs. round steak, sliced thin
1 pkg. onion soup mix
1/2 lb. fresh mushrooms, sliced
1 green pepper, sliced
fresh ground black pepper
1 16 oz. can tomatoes, drained
  and chopped, reserve juice
1/4 tsp. salt
1 Tbsp. A-1 sauce
1 Tbsp. cornstarch
1 Tbsp. chopped parsley

Butter large 10-inch casserole. Arrange strips of meat in casserole, overlapping each piece. Sprinkle with soup mix, mushrooms, green pepper, black pepper, tomatoes and salt. Mix A-1 sauce and cornstarch in 1/2 cup tomato juice. Pour over meat. Cover casserole with foil and seal tightly. Bake at 375 degrees for 2 hours. Sprinkle with parsley and serve with buttered noodles. Serves 4.

Ellen Knott (Mrs. B.F.)

To reheat rare meat, line a baking pan with greens (lettuce, etc.). Layer leftover meat slices on top, then blanket with additional leaves. Warm about 10 minutes in slow oven.

GOURMET BEEF ELEGANTE

This recipe takes very little work, and yet it is a gourmet's delight!
Serve with Caesar Salad and mashed potatoes.

1 3-lb. beef rump roast
1 6-oz. can tomato paste
2 cups cold chicken stock
1/4 cup dry sherry
1 cup dry white wine
1 stalk celery, chopped
1 bay leaf
1/2 tsp. oregano
1 large onion, sliced
2 Tbsp. finely chopped caraway
* seed*
3 Tbsp. flour
1 cup cold water
salt and pepper to taste
1/2 cup sour cream

Cover beef rump with tomato paste. Place beef in bowl with chicken stock, wines, onion, celery, bay leaf and oregano. Marinate overnight, turning once. Remove beef from liquid; reserve marinade. Place beef in roasting pan. Bake at 450 degrees for 30-40 minutes or until beef is brown. Remove from oven; add marinade. Simmer beef over low heat; add caraway seeds. Blend flour and cold water. Add slowly to simmering liquid; add seasonings. Cook for 2 hours and 30 minutes or until tender. Remove onion, celery and bay leaf. Stir in sour cream slowly. Serve sauce over mashed potatoes. Serves 4 to 6.

Anne Zeola (Mrs. John P.)

SAUERBRATEN

1 boneless rump roast, about 4 lbs.
4 cups water
2 cups red wine vinegar
2 Tbsp. sugar
1 medium-size onion,
* finely chopped*
3/4 cup finely-chopped celery
1/4 tsp. salt
pinch of pepper
1 tsp. mixed pickling spices
2 Tbsp. vegetable shortening
24 crushed ginger snaps
* (1-1/2 cups crumbs)*

Trim meat of all but a thin layer of fat. Place in large glass bowl. Add water, vinegar, sugar, onion, celery, salt, pepper and pickling spices, stirring to mix. Cover with plastic wrap; refrigerate 4 or 5 days, turning meat each day.

Remove meat from marinade; reserve marinade. Pat meat dry with paper toweling. Heat shortening in Dutch oven. Brown meat on all sides (about 15 minutes). Remove fat from pan.

Pour marinade over meat. Roast uncovered in 350 degree oven for 30 minutes. Cover; continue roasting 2-1/2 to 3 hours longer, until meat is tender. Remove meat to platter. Strain marinade; remove fat. Return marinade to pan. Stir in ginger snap crumbs. Heat until thickened; strain again. Slice meat and serve with gravy. Nice with potato pancakes and red cabbage. Serves 6 to 8.

Ada Offerdahl (Mrs. John)

BEEF POT ROAST WITH BEER

3-1/2 lb. rump roast
2 Tbsp. dried onion flakes
1 12-oz. can beer
garlic salt to taste, sprinkled
    over roast
2 onions, sliced
1 bay leaf
1/2 tsp. thyme
2 Tbsp. brown sugar
4 bouillon cubes
1 tsp. parsley flakes
4 garlic cloves, minced
1/4 cup flour
1 cup water

Marinate roast in next three ingredients for 8 hours or overnight. Then brown roast in 1/4 cup oil. Add onions and garlic and saute until clear. Add bay leaf, beef marinade, thyme, bouillon and parsley. Cover and simmer in 350 degree oven for 2-1/2 to 3 hours. Make paste of 1/4 cup flour and 1 cup water and add to sauce. Remove bay leaf. Add salt and pepper to taste.

The Committee

POT ROAST PERFECT

1 3-lb. beef chuck roast, brisket
    rump or round roast
1 can cream of mushroom soup
1 envelope onion soup mix
1/4 tsp. pepper
1/2 tsp. thyme
1 Tbsp. parsley flakes
1 Tbsp. Worcestershire sauce
1 Tbsp. steak sauce

Place sheet of aluminum foil, long enough to fold over roast and seal edges, into a 13 x 9 casserole dish. Place beef on foil. Combine all ingredients, stir and pour over meat, spreading to cover. Fold foil over and crimp edges to seal securely. Bake at 350 degrees for 3 to 3-1/2 hours or until tender. Spoon juices over roast. Slice and serve with juices over rice or poppy seed noodles. Serve 6.

Ellen Knott (Mrs. B.F.)

To degrease accumulated fat from surface of hot liquids such as stocks, sauces or soups, put in refrigerator to cool until the fat on the surface has solidified and can easily be removed.

FILET OF BEEF IN PHYLLO WITH MADEIRA

3 lbs. filet, trimmed
salt
2 Tbsp. butter
1/2 lb. mushrooms, minced
2 shallots, minced
1 pkg. phyllo (filo)
1/2 cup melted butter

MADEIRA SAUCE
3 Tbsp. butter
1-1/2 Tbsp. flour
3/4 cup beef stock
1 tsp. Kitchen Bouquet
1/4 cup Madeira wine

Preheat oven to 400 degrees. Rub filet with salt. Sear in butter until brown on all sides. Set aside. Saute mushrooms and shallots until soft. Layer 12 pieces phyllo, brushing each with butter. Spread 1/2 mushroom mixture on pastry and put filet on top. Spread other 1/2 of mushroom mixture on top of filet. Spread 6 more sheets of phyllo with butter, layer them and place on top of filet. Fold phyllo around filet. Put in buttered baking pan and bake 40 to 45 minutes until brown and flaky. Serve with Madeira Sauce. May be frozen. Serves 4.

MADEIRA SAUCE: Melt butter, stir in flour and cook for 5 minutes. Add other ingredients. Cook until thickened and serve. Makes 1-1/2 cups.

NOTE: This sauce is also good with sauteed mushrooms added and spread on Filet Mignon or other kinds of steaks.

Dot Nichols (Mrs. T.H.)

FILET OF BEEF WITH GREEN PEPPERCORN SAUCE
For your very special guests! Serve on heated plates.

4 lb. filet, trimmed and tied
2 Tbsp. oil
salt and pepper to taste
3 Tbsp. Cognac
1-1/2 cups brown stock
    or bouillon
1 cup heavy cream
3 Tbsp. green peppercorns,
    packed in brine, well-drained
lemon juice
3 Tbsp. butter

In a large, heavy skillet, brown the filet well on all sides in the oil over moderately high heat. Transfer the meat to an oval gratin dish and roast uncovered 20-25 minutes in a 450 degree oven for rare (140 degrees on meat thermometer). Transfer the meat to a serving platter and let it rest for 10 minutes. Meanwhile make the sauce. Pour off fat from the skillet, add Cognac and flame, shaking the pan until the flames go out, and stirring in the brown bits. Add the stock and cream. Reduce over moderately high heat to 2 cups. Add the peppercorns, lemon juice, salt and pepper to taste. Remove pan from heat and swirl in butter, softened and cut into bits. Slice meat and re-form into filet. Pour some of the sauce over, then serve remaining in a sauce boat. Serves 6.

Virginia Golding (Mrs. John G.)

VERY SPECIAL FILET MIGNON

This is an elegant, easy recipe that is not hard to do at the last minute if the rest of the dinner is prepared in advance.

8 filets mignon
2 Tbsp. butter
2 Tbsp. oil
salt, fresh-ground pepper and
    Accent to taste
1/2 cup brandy
1 cup heavy cream
1-1/2 Tbsp. Worcestershire sauce
1-1/2 Tbsp. Dijon-style mustard
2 cloves garlic, crushed
1 tsp. parsley, chopped

Heat butter and oil in large skillet. Saute steaks about 5 or 6 minutes per side for rare. Transfer to a heated platter and season to taste. Pour off fat in pan and add brandy, warmed. Ignite and shake until flames go out.

Combine cream, Worcestershire sauce, mustard, garlic and parsley and add to pan. Cook until hot but do not boil. Spoon over steaks and serve. Serves 8.

Virginia Golding (Mrs. John G.)

BEEF TENDERLOIN

1/2 cup butter
1 Tbsp. vermouth
1 medium onion, chopped
3/4 cup celery chopped (some
    leaves)
1 4 oz. can B & B mushrooms,
    drained, or 6 oz. fresh mush-
    room pieces
1 can water chestnuts, sliced
1 medium green pepper, diced
2 cups soft bread crumbs
1 tsp. salt
1/2 tsp. pepper
1/2 tsp. basil
1/2 tsp. parsley flakes
3 lbs. beef tenderloin, well
    trimmed
5 strips lean bacon, cut in halves

Melt butter in skillet over low heat; add vermouth. Saute onion, celery, mushrooms, water chestnuts and green peppers in butter mixture for about 5 minutes. Put bread crumbs in a bowl and add the salt, pepper, basil, parsley and sauteed vegetable mixture. Mix until well blended, stirring lightly.

Make a lengthwise cut 3/4 of the way through the tenderloin. Put stuffing in pocket. Fasten pocket together with wooden toothpicks. Place bacon strips diagonally across the top, covering the picks and the pocket. Place in an oblong 13 x 9 inch casserole dish and bake uncovered at 325 degrees for 1 hour or until desired doneness. Serves 6-8.

The Committee

BARBECUED BRISKET OF BEEF

5 to 6 lb. fresh beef brisket
1 tsp. celery salt
1 tsp. onion salt
1 tsp. garlic salt
pepper
2 tsp. Worcestershire sauce
2 or 3 Tbsp. liquid smoke
1 bottle prepared barbecued sauce

Thoroughly pierce meat with a fork. Sprinkle with pepper, celery, onion and garlic salts and liquid smoke. Let soak overnight in marinade, turning once or twice. Wrap meat in heavy-duty foil and bake 5 hours at 275 degrees. Let cool and slice thinly. Pour Worcestershire sauce and barbecue sauce over meat, return to oven and heat slowly for 1 hour at 275 degrees. Serve when meat has been reheated. Leftovers make delicious barbecue sandwiches.

Judy Beise (Mrs. D.W.)
Nancy Harper (Mrs. R.N.)

VARIATION: Use 1 whole bottle liquid smoke and 1 small bottle of *smoked* barbecue sauce instead of amounts listed.

SPICY CORNED BEEF—PEPPERY PASTRAMI

The first night I serve as corned beef with cabbage, carrots, boiled potatoes and corn bread. The next night I serve as pastrami sandwiches.

4 to 5 lbs. **corned** beef brisket
instant **seasoned** meat tenderizer
1/3 cup red wine vinegar
2 cloves garlic, cut in halves
4 whole cloves
6 dry red chili peppers
1 Tbsp. sugar
1 Tbsp. whole pickling spice
1/2 tsp. liquid smoke
2 Tbsp. cracked black pepper

Moisten meat and sprinkle with tenderizer. Pierce meat deeply with a sharp fork. Into a large bowl or pot add remaining ingredients, except black pepper. Pour in 3 quarts warm water. Add meat, cover and refrigerate overnight. Simmer in large pot until tender—2-1/2 to 3 hours. Remove meat and cut in half. Save liquid. Slice half of the meat paper thin and serve as corned beef.

To serve as peppery pastrami sandwiches: Place remaining half of meat in glass baking dish. Press black pepper into top and sices of meat. Add enough of the reserved liquid to cover bottom of baking dish. Bake uncovered about 30 minutes at 350 degrees. Slice thinly. Place on rye bread which has been spread with sauce made of equal parts of prepared mustard, mayonnaise and horseradish sauce. Serve with cole slaw and French fries.

Teny Sugg (Mrs. W.C.)

REUBEN CASSEROLE

1-3/4 cups sauerkraut (drained)
1-1/2 lbs. corned beef, sliced
    paper-thin
1/2 lb. Swiss cheese, grated
3 to 4 Tbsp. Thousand Island
    dressing
2 medium-size tomatoes, thinly
    sliced

TOPPING:
1 stick butter
1/2 Tbsp. caraway seeds
1-1/2 cups crumbled Keebler
    rye crackers

In a 9 x 13 inch or a 2-quart pan layer the sauerkraut, corned beef, Swiss cheese, Thousand Island dressing and tomatoes. Sprinkle crumbled topping on top. Bake at 350 degrees for 35 to 45 minutes. Cover with aluminum foil for more than half of the cooking time. Serves 6 to 8.

NOTE: In a pinch I have gotten corned beef at Big Star delicatessen instead of cooking my own.

Georgia Miller (Mrs. George)

REUBEN PIE

This is an easy luncheon or Sunday supper

1 egg, beaten
1/3 cup evaporated milk
3/4 cup rye bread crumbs
1/4 cup chopped onion
1/4 tsp. salt
dash pepper
1/2 tsp. prepared mustard
1 8-oz. can sauerkraut, drained
    and snipped
12 oz. corned beef, chopped
6 oz. Swiss cheese, grated
pastry for 1 10-inch pie crust

In mixing bowl combine first 7 ingredients. Then add sauerkraut and corned beef. Mix well. Place 1/2 of meat mixture in pie shell and sprinkle with 1/2 the cheese. Cover with remaining meat mixture; top with remaining cheese. Bake at 400 degrees for 25 to 30 minutes. Serves 6 to 8.

Shirley Benfield (Mrs. R.H.)

Shape hamburgers lightly, with little pressure. They will be jucier.

BUTTERFLIED LEG OF LAMB

1 6-7 lb. leg of lamb, butterflied
1 cup dry red wine
1 cup beef broth
3 Tbsp. orange marmalade
2 Tbsp. red wine vinegar
1 Tbsp. minced dried onion
1 Tbsp. dried marjoram
1 Tbsp. dried rosemary
1 large bay lead, crumbled
1 tsp. seasoned salt
1/4 tsp. ginger
1 clove garlic, crushed

Place lamb in a shallow roasting pan, fat side down. Combine remaining ingredients in a 2-quart saucepan and simmer, uncovered, for 20 minutes. Pour the hot mixture over the lamb and marinate at room temperature for 6-8 hours. Turn often.

BARBECUE METHOD: Place meat over medium-hot coals, fat side up, for 30-45 minutes. Turn several times, being careful not to pierce meat. Brush frequently with marinade.

OVEN METHOD: Preheat oven to 425 degrees. Place meat, fat side up, under broiler, about 4 inches from heat. Broil 10 minutes per side. Transfer meat to preheated oven for 15 minutes. On a slight diagonal, carve meat in fairly thin slices. Serves 6-8.

Georgia Miller (Mrs. George)

BURGUNDY-STYLE LAMB AND BEAN STEW
One of our favorite winter meals. Serve with a tossed salad.

1/2 lb. dried beans such as baby lima, pea or navy beans
2 lamb shanks, about 1 lb. each, split in half
2 lbs. breast of lamb with bones in
1/4 lb. salt pork
salt and freshly-ground pepper to taste
1 cup coarsely chopped leeks or green onions
1 cup coarsely chopped onions
1 cup coarsely chopped carrots
2 cups canned tomatoes, preferably Italian plum variety
4 cups water
3 sprigs fresh thyme or 1/2 tsp. dried
1 bay leaf

Soak the beans overnight in cold water to cover. Have butcher split the lamb shanks in half. Cut the breast of lamb with bones into 2 or 3 inch squares. Cut the salt pork into small cubes and place in a heavy metal Dutch oven. Cook, stirring until pork is rendered of its fat. Add the lamb shanks and breast of lamb, salt and pepper to taste. Cook, stirring frequently, until browned all over, about 10 minutes. Add the leeks, onions and carrots and stir. Cook, stirring occasionally, about 5 minutes. Drain the beans and add to the casserole. Add the tomatoes, water, thyme, bay leaf, salt and pepper to taste. Cover and cook about 1 hour and 45 minutes until the meat and beans are tender. Uncover and cook 15 minutes longer. Serve piping hot in casserole. Serves 6-8.

Gensie

VINEYARD LAMB

5-6 lb. leg of lamb
2 slivered garlic cloves
1 cup brandy
1 tsp. ground cumin
1-1/2 Tbsp. salt
2 tsp. pepper
1/4 cup sherry
1/4 cup dry red wine

Remove fell; trim excess fat. Cut slits on surface and insert garlic. Drench cloth with 1/2 cup brandy. Wrap around lamb and cover with foil. Marinate at room temperature for 2 hours. Mix spices and press into lamb. Place fat side up in a shallow pan. Cook at 450 degrees for 20 minutes. Lower to 350 degrees. Baste with wine mixture. Roast 40-60 minutes, basting 2 or 3 times. Warm 1/2 cup brandy. Ignite and pour flaming over lamb. Serve at once. Serves 6-8.

Dot Nicholls (Mrs. T.H.)

LAMB SHANK AND PILAF CASSEROLE
Serve with a crisp tossed salad

2 lamb shanks
2 Tbsp. butter
1 garlic clove, finely minced
1 medium onion, chopped
2 tsp. salt
1/4 tsp. freshly-ground pepper
2 Tbsp. butter
1 cup raw, long-grain rice
4-6 Tbsp. pine nuts
juice of 1/2 fresh lemon
1 Tbsp. parsley

Trim fat from lamb shanks. In heavy pot, brown in butter on all sides, add garlic and onions. Saute until soft. Add 2-1/2 cups water, 1 tsp. salt and 1/4 tsp. pepper. Bring to boiling. Cover. Simmer 1-1/2 hours. Melt butter to bubbling in a skillet. Saute pine nuts and rice in 2 Tbsp. butter. Stir constantly until butter is light amber in color and begins to foam between the kernels. Add remaining salt. Set aside. Remove shanks from pan. Measure broth. Add enough water, if necessary, to make 2-1/2 cups. Return shanks to broth. Add lemon and parsley. Bring to a boil. Stir in sauteed rice and nuts. Simmer covered, 20 minutes. Allow to stand, covered, 10 minutes. Serves 2 to 4.

Gensie

Instant mashed potatoes make a great thickening agent for gravies and stews and will not lump.

LAMB LOUISE

Must be prepared the night before you serve it.

1 boned leg of lamb (about 6 lbs.),
   reserve bones
1/4 lb. butter (room temperature)
1 tsp. garlic powder
1 tsp. monosodium glutamate
   (Accent)
1 tsp. salt
1 tsp. cayenne pepper
fresh, chopped parsley

GRAVY
1/2 pint sour cream
3/4 tsp. saffron
1 tsp. cornstarch
1 bottle capers (drained)
paprika

Ask your butcher to bone the lamb and include the bones in the package. The night before, cut off most of the fat from the lamb. Cream together butter, garlic powder, monosodium glutamate, salt and cayenne pepper, and spread over the roast, inside and out. On a double thickness of aluminum foil, place the bones with the roast around them. Wrap tightly and refrigerate overnight. On the following day, remove from refrigerator 2 hours before time to roast. Do not unwrap. Bake, *wrapped*, in a shallow roasting pan in a 375 degree oven, allowing 35 minutes per pound for medium or 45 minutes for well-done meat. Thirty minutes before the roast is done, remove from oven. Unwrap carefully and strain juices into a saucepan. Turn the oven up to 400 degrees, discard the bones, place the roast in the open foil in the pan and return to oven to brown for 30 minutes.

To the strained lamb juice in the pan, add the sour cream and saffron. Bring to a boil, stirring constantly. Mix the cornstarch with 3 Tbsp. cold water, add to mixture and boil gently for 4 minutes. Add the drained capers and cook for a minute more. Pour gravy in warmed gravy boat and sprinkle with paprika.

Serve with poppy seed noodles or with rice. As an accompaniment I serve peach halves filled with chutney, baked in a 300 degree oven for 30 minutes.

Gensie

BAKED COUNTRY HAM

1 12 to 20 lb. country ham
1 cup brown sugar
1/2 cup honey
2 Tbsp. dry mustard
whole cloves

Soak ham in water for 1-1/2 days. Remove from water, scrub well with stiff brush and place in a tightly-covered roaster, skin side down. Add one quart of water. Bake at 325 degrees for 15 minutes per pound. Start counting time when placed in oven. *Or* can put in roaster, cover with water and simmer 30 minutes per pound on top of stove. If oven baking, turn ham skin side up for the last hour. When cooking time is up, add enough water (hot) to come well up on the ham. Put back in oven overnight with oven turned off. In the morning, take ham out of water, pat dry with paper towels and remove the skin. Cut off most of the fat, leaving 1/4 inch of the fat to score. Mix the sugar, honey and mustard and spread over the fat. Stick a whole clove in each scored section. Bake at 350 degrees until lightly browned.

If cooking on top of the stove, cool ham in the water you cooked it in. Remove from water, skin, score fat, spread with basting mixture. Add cloves, and bake at 350 degrees until lightly browned.

Betty Hight (Mrs. M.L.)

HAM AND CHEESE SANDWICH SOUFFLE
So good—a nice change from the usual cheese strata
Must do ahead.

16 slices white Pepperidge Farm
    regular-sliced bread, crusts
    removed
8 thin slices ham
8 slices cheese
6 eggs
3 cups milk
1 tsp. dry mustard
1 stick butter
2-1/2 cups crushed corn flakes

Place 8 slices of bread, side by side, in a buttered 9-x-10 inch baking dish. Lay a slice of ham, then a slice of cheese, then the other 8 slices of bread to make a sandwich.
Mix the beaten eggs, milk and mustard. Pour over all. Let stand overnight in the refrigerator. Next day, melt the butter and add cornflakes. Sprinkle over the top of casserole. Bake at 350 degrees for 35-45 minutes or until bubbly and a knife inserted in center comes out clean. Cut in squares, sandwich size, and serve hot. Serves 8.

Ellen Knott (Mrs. B.F.)

HOT HAM AND ASPARAGUS SANDWICH

2 slices bread—white or rye,
  homemade is best
2 slices Swiss cheese
2 slices baked ham
8 asparagus spears
1 cup mayonnaise
1 Tbsp. horseradish

Preheat oven to 400 degrees. Layer all except mayonnaise and horseradish. Bake 10 to 15 minutes. Mix mayonnaise and horseradish; heat until warm. Pour over sandwiches. May increase as often as desired. Serves 2.

Betty Holland (Mrs. Calvin)

MAIN DISH CAULIFLOWER AND HAM
A nice use for left-over ham

1 large head cauliflower
1-1/2 to 2 cups chopped cooked
  ham
1/2 cup butter or margarine
1/4 cup all-purpose flour
1-1/2 cups milk
1/2 lb. medium Cheddar
  cheese, diced
1 cup bread crumbs
2 Tbsp. melted butter or
  margarine
paprika

Remove large outer leaves and break cauliflower into florets; wash thoroughly. Place in small amount of boiling, salted water; cover and cook 20 minutes or just until tender. Drain well. Place in lightly greased 2-quart casserole and sprinkle with chopped ham. Melt 1/2 cup butter in heavy saucepan; blend in flour and cook until bubbly. Gradually add milk; cook over medium heat, stirring constantly, until thickened and bubbly. Add cheese, stirring until melted. Spoon sauce over cauliflower and ham. Combine bread crumbs and remaining butter; spoon over sauce. Bake at 350 degrees for 30 minutes. Yield: 6 servings.

Ellen Knott (Mrs. B.F.)

HAM DIVAN SANDWICH

4 thick slices French bread
butter
1 cup mayonnaise
1 cup Parmesan cheese
1 Tbsp. lemon juice
1/4 cup red onion, chopped
1 lb. broccoli or 1 pkg. frozen
  broccoli spears
4 slices baked ham.

Butter bread; toast. Mix mayonnaise, cheese, lemon juice and onion. Cook broccoli until almost tender. Drain well. Place ham on toast. Put broccoli over ham and cover with sauce. Bake at 400 degrees for about 15 minutes. Serves 4.

Dot Nicholls (Mrs. T.H.)

GRUYERE-GLAZED PORK CHOPS

4 loin pork chops, cut 1 inch thick
    and trimmed of excess fat
1 Tbsp. olive oil
1 Tbsp. butter
1/2 tsp. salt
1/8 tsp. pepper
1/2 cup dry white wine (or apple
    cider or apple juice)
1-1/2 cups finely-grated Gruyere
    cheese
1 Tbsp. prepared Dijon mustard
1/4 cup heavy cream
    or evaporated milk

Preheat oven to 350 degrees. Brown chops 4 to 5 minutes on a side in oil and butter in a large flameproof casserole over moderately high heat; drain. Sprinkle with salt and pepper, add wine and bake uncovered 50-60 minutes until chops are tender. Meanwhile, blend together cheese, mustard, and cream (mixture will not be smooth). When chops are tender, spread top of each with cheese mixture and broil 3 inches from heat 2-3 minutes until lightly speckled with brown. (Casserole liquid can be served in a gravy boat or saved for stock.) Serves 4.

Noble Dillard

CHINESE PORK CHOPS

This is the dinner answer on a busy day.

1 small box Uncle Ben's Wild Rice
    with Herb Seasonings (or
    Comet Brown & Wild Rice
    with Seasonings)
1 can mushroom soup
1 can Chinese vegetables, drained
1-1/3 soup cans of water
6 pork chops

Combine all ingredients and pour into large casserole dish. Put 6 raw pork chops (or chicken breasts) on top. Bake at 350 degrees for 1 hour. That's it! Serves 4-6.

Mary Sue Patten (Mrs. Robert)

BAKED PORK CHOPS

8 pork chops (not thin)
8 tomato slices
8 onion slices
8 green pepper rings (inside
    scooped out)
1-1/2 cups cooked rice
salt, pepper to taste

Flour and brown chops. Place in rectangular pyrex baking dish. Salt and pepper to taste. On each chop place 1 slice onion. Add enough (about 1/2 cup) warm water to keep from sticking. Cover tightly with foil. Bake at 325 degrees for 2-1/2 hours or longer. For the last hour of cooking, cover onion slices with tomato and green pepper slices. Place small mound of rice on top. Re-cover and continue last hour of cooking. May need a little more water to keep pork chops tender. Serves 6-8.

Betty Archer (Mrs. John M., III)

PORK CHOP CASSEROLE
This also works well with chicken.

6 pork chops
1 cup uncooked rice (not instant)
1 beef bouillon cube
1 can cream of mushroom soup
1/2 pkg. Lipton Onion Soup mix
1-1/2 cups water

Brown pork chops. Place uncooked rice in casserole dish. Dissolve bouillon cube in 1-1/2 cups water. Pour over rice. Place browned pork chops on top. Sprinkle 1/2 pkg. onion soup mix over rice and pork chops. Pour cream of mushroom soup, diluted with 1/2 can water, over pork chops. Cover; bake at 325 degrees for 1 hour and 15 minutes. Serves 6.

Jan Smith (Mrs. M.H.)

NORWEGIAN PORK CHOPS WITH CARAWAY APPLES
Sweet apples and pungent caraway seeds give a surprising lilt to this sage-scented pork chop casserole.

8 pork chops, 1/2 to 3/4 inch thick
flour
sage to taste
salt and pepper to taste
3 Tbsp. vegetable oil for frying
8 medium-sized apples, peeled, cored and sliced in 1/4 inch rings
2 tsp. caraway seeds
1/4 cup apple juice

Dust the pork chops lightly with the flour and shake off any excess. Sprinkle each chop with ground sage, salt and pepper on both sides. Heat about 3 Tbsp. oil in a large skillet. Brown the chops lightly on both sides and set aside. Butter a large, shallow baking dish and spread half the apples over the bottom. Sprinkle with salt and pepper if you like, and then add about half the caraway seeds, crushed slightly with the back of a spoon. Lay the pork chops over the apples and top with the remaining apples and caraway seeds. Deglaze the skillet with the apple juice and pour over all. Cover and bake at 350 degrees for about one hour. Baste occasionally with the pan juices. Serves 6-8.

Gensie

ORIENTAL HASH

2 Tbsp. oil
dash garlic powder
1-1/2 cups cubed pork
2 cups cooked rice
3 Tbsp. soy sauce
2 well-beaten eggs
2 cups shredded lettuce

Heat oil in skillet. Add garlic powder and pork. Cook until meat is brown. Add cooked rice and soy sauce. Cook ten minutes, stirring occasionally. Mix in beaten eggs and cook 1 minute longer, stirring frequently. Remove from heat. Add shredded lettuce; toss together. Serve immediately. Serves 3-4.

Georgia Miller (Mrs. George)

SOKEEN LOKE'S MALAYAN PORK CHOPS

4 fairly thick lean pork chops
2 medium onions, sliced
salt and pepper to taste
2 Tbsp. cornstarch
2 cups water
4 Tbsp. soy sauce
2-3 Tbsp. shortening

Melt shortening in skillet and fry onions until lightly browned. Remove onions and brown chops. Remove chops and pour off fat. Combine remaining ingredients and pour into skillet. Stir vigorously and cook until thickened. Return chops to gravy. Cover and simmer slowly until chops are tender, about 30 minutes. Add onions and heat thoroughly. Serve over rice. Especially good with fresh pineapple. Serves 4.

Gayanne Mraz

STUFFED BLACK WALNUT PORK CHOPS

4 1-inch-thick pork chops, slit to
  bone for stuffing
1 small pkg. herbed stuffing mix
1/2 cup black walnuts, chopped
1/2 cup chopped celery
1/2 cup chopped onion
1 stick margarine
1 cup water
salt and pepper to taste
4 Tbsp. cooking oil
1/4 cup flour

MARINADE:
4 Tbsp. soy sauce
1/2 tsp. garlic salt
1/2 tsp. sugar
1/4 tsp. MSG

Prepare dressing by melting margarine in boiling water. Add onions, celery and packaged mix. Toss walnuts lightly into mixture.

Marinate chops 10 minutes in marinade ingredients. Add as much of the walnut dressing to each chop as possible, stuffing carefully. Skewer or close chops with toothpicks. Coat each chop with salt, pepper and flour. Brown just lightly in hot oil. In casserole dish put remaining dressing mix on bottom. Layer stuffed, browned chops on top and bake 30-40 minutes at 350 degrees. Serves 4.

Bobbye Howell (Mrs. Billy Shaw, Jr.)

When opening a package of bacon, roll it into a long tube. This loosens the slices and keeps them from sticking.

COUNTRY SAUSAGE AU GRATIN

1 lb. Polish sausage, smoked
  (cut into 1/2 inch slices)
1 large onion, chopped
1 Tbsp. oil
1 pkg. au gratin potatoes
2-1/2 cups water
1/4 tsp. pepper
4 carrots cut into 2 inch strips
1 pkg. frozen chopped broccoli
  (thawed and drained)
1 cup shredded Cheddar cheese
  (4 oz.)

Cook sausage, oil and onions in skillet for 5 minutes. Stir in potatoes and sauce mix (packet), with water and pepper. Bring to a boil and reduce heat. Simmer covered 10 minutes. Stir in broccoli and cheese. Cover and cook 10 minutes more. Serves 4-5.

Carol S. Barreau (Mrs. E.H.)

NEW ENGLAND SAUSAGE DINNER

1-1/2 lbs. kulbassa, Polish or
  smoked sausage
4 large potatoes, peeled and cut
  in halves
1 lb. carrots, cut in 2 inch pieces
1 medium head cabbage,
  quartered
6 small onions, peeled and left
  whole
water to cover (approx. 4 cups)
1/4 cup flour
1/4 cup brown sugar
1/4 cup apple cider vinegar
2 tsp. dry mustard
1 tsp. salt
1/2 to 1 tsp. pepper
dash of garlic salt

Cut sausage in 2-inch pieces. Put in pan with carrots, potatoes and water. Cook approximately 10 minutes. Add cabbage and onion. Cook until tender — about 20 minutes. Combine flour, brown sugar, vinegar, mustard, salt, pepper and garlic. Remove sausage and vegetables; keep warm. Add flour mixture to broth. Cook until thickened. Return sausage and vegetables to broth. Heat through. Serves 6.

Nita Street (Mrs. Frank)

DEEP DISH PIZZA

1 pie crust (deep dish)
1 lb. sausage
3/4 cup chopped onions
4 eggs
1/2 cup milk
1/2 tsp. oregano
1/8 tsp. pepper
1 cup shredded Cheddar cheese
   (4 oz.)
1 cup shredded mozzarella cheese
1/2 cup pizza sauce

Brown pie crust slightly. Brown sausage and onion (cook completely). Drain in colander. Combine eggs, milk and seasonings. Beat well. Add to sausage and onion mixture. Add shredded Cheddar cheese and pour into pie shell. Bake at 375 degrees for 25 to 30 minutes or until filling is set. Take out of oven, spread pizza sauce on top, sprinkle with mozzarella cheese and return to oven until cheese melts. Serves 4-6.

Linda Hagemeyer (Mrs. R.H., Jr.)

SAUSAGE/SUMMER SQUASH SPECIAL

1 lb. pork sausage
1 clove garlic
4 cups sliced yellow squash
1/2 cup dry bread crumbs
1/2 cup grated Parmesan cheese
1/2 cup milk
1 Tbsp. chopped parsley
1/2 tsp. whole oregano
1/2 tsp. salt
2 eggs, beaten

Saute sausage and garlic until sausage is browned. Drain. Cook squash in small amount of boiling water until tender; drain. Combine sausage, squash and remaining ingredients; blend well. Spoon mixture into a lightly-greased 10 x 6 baking dish. Bake at 325 degrees for 20 minutes. Serves 6.

Susan Murfee (Mrs. Donald G.)

SWEET AND SOUR PORK

3 cups cooked pork, cubed or cut
   in strips
2 Tbsp. butter
1/4 cup brown sugar
2 Tbsp. cornstarch
1/2 tsp. salt
1/4 to 1/3 cup vinegar
1 cup pineapple juice
1 Tbsp. soy sauce
1/2 cup green pepper, cut in strips
1/2 cup or more pineapple chunks
1/2 medium onion, sliced

Mix brown sugar, cornstarch and salt in saucepan. Blend in vinegar, pineapple juice, soy sauce and melted butter.
Cook over low heat; stir until smooth and sauce thickens. Pour over pork and let stand 10 minutes. Add pepper, onions and pineapple that have been sauteed in butter. Serve over rice. Serves 4-6.

Liz Medearis (Mrs. W.D., Jr.)

SWEET AND SOUR PORK

2 lbs. lean pork cut into 1/2 inch
   cubes
1/4 cup vegetable oil
1 cup chicken bouillon
2 green peppers, cut into eighths
1 cup pineapple chunks
3 Tbsp. cornstarch
2 to 3 Tbsp. soy sauce
1/2 cup vinegar
1/2 cup sugar
1/2 tsp. salt
1/4 tsp. pepper
small portion crystallized
   ginger, cut fine

Roll pork in flour, brown on all sides in hot oil. Add 1/2 cup chicken bouillon; cover and simmer 15 minutes. Add green pepper and pineapple and simmer 10 minutes longer. Combine remaining 1/2 cup chicken bouillon, cornstarch, soy sauce, vinegar, sugar, salt and pepper, and ginger. Add slowly to pork mixture. Cook until sauce thickens, stirring. Serve over hot rice. Makes 6 servings.

Joyce W. Summerville (W. Kelly)

BARBECUED SPARERIBS

3 lbs. meaty country spareribs
   (pork)
1 onion, sliced
2 stalks celery with tops
1 Tbsp. salt
1 tsp. pepper

BARBECUE SAUCE
1 cup catsup
3/4 cup soy sauce
4 Tbsp. Worcestershire sauce
1 Tbsp. horseradish
1/2 tsp. garlic juice
2 Tbsp. brown sugar
2 Tbsp. oil (olive is best)
1/4 tsp. salt
1/4 tsp. pepper
dash Tabasco sauce
1-1/2 cups apple juice

Mix all sauce ingredients together and set aside. In a large pot, cover the ribs with water and add the onion, celery, salt and pepper. Boil until the ribs are tender when pierced with a fork, but not coming off the bones. Remove from water, drain well and put into a pan large enough to be able to pour sauce over all ribs. Bake at 350 degrees for 15 to 20 minutes, basting often. Serves 6.

Ellen Knott (Mrs. B.F.)

STIR-FRIED PORK

1 clove garlic, minced
1 tsp. Sherry wine
few grains fresh ginger
1-1/2 Tbsp. soy sauce
1 tsp. corn starch
3/4 tsp. sugar
1/4 tsp. sesame oil
1/2 tsp. salt
dash Accent (optional)
2 tsp. oil to coat meat
1/2 lb. (or more) pork tenderloin,
*   sliced like matchsticks*
1/2 large onion
1 large green pepper
1 cup fresh oriental pea pods, or
*   substitute fresh green beans*
1/2 cup celery
2 Tbsp. oil for frying, divided
salt to taste

1. Marinate pork in first eleven ingredients for 15 minutes. Stir to mix flavors.
2. Heat wok on high. Add 1 Tbsp. oil; slosh around. Add all vegetables, sliced like matchsticks. Toss-fry for 1 minute; salt slightly.
3. Remove from wok to platter. Clean wok. Reheat on high and add additional 1 Tbsp. oil and slosh around. Add marinated meat. Toss-fry meat until cooked, about 3 to 4 minutes.
4. Add about 2 Tbsp. water. Continue to toss-fry 1 more minute. Add precooked vegetables. Keep toss-frying until heated through, about 1 minute. Serve with soy sauce. May be poured over pan-fried noodles for a change. Serves 4.

Virginia Golding (Mrs. John G.)

PORK BRAISE AU WHISKEY

3 lb. pork loin, boned and tied
18 prunes
1-1/2 to 2 cups beef bouillon
1/2 lb. smoked ham in thin slices
1/2 cup Dijon mustard
2/3 cup dark brown sugar
2 Tbsp. peanut oil
2/3 cup Bourbon whiskey
salt and pepper to taste
bouquet garni of thyme, sage,
*   and parsley*
watercress
cornstarch

Preheat oven to 375 degrees. Steep prunes in 1 cup warm bouillon. Cut ham into strips and insert into pork loin with sharp knife. Paint meat with mustard and roll it in brown sugar. Brown meat in heavy casserole in peanut oil for 10 to 15 minutes. Sugar will carmelize (do not burn). Pour half of whiskey over meat and flame. Add 1/2 cup of remaining bouillon. Cook covered in oven for 1-3/4 hours. Turn meat halfway through cooking time. Season with salt and pepper, add bouquet garni and lower oven to 350 degrees. Add prunes 10 minutes before cooking is complete. Skim off and discard fat.

Bring pan juices to boil, add remaining whiskey and stir. To thicken, boil and add cornstarch mixed with cold stock. Season to taste. Decorate with prunes and watercress. Serves 8.

Georgia Miller (Mrs. George)

PORK TENDERLOIN L'ORANGE
A dressed-up dish for a hurry-up gourmet

1-1/2 to 2 lbs. pork tenderloin,
    sliced 3/4 inch thick
2 Tbsp. butter
1/2 cup chopped onion
1 tsp. salt
1/4 tsp. pepper
1/2 cup white wine (Chablis)
1 can (10-12 oz.) mandarin orange
    slices
1 cup orange juice
2 Tbsp. sugar
1 Tbsp. parsley
2 tsp. cornstarch
1 Tbsp. water
4 cups cooked rice

Saute tenderloin slices in butter until golden. Remove from pan. Add onion to pan and cook with salt and pepper until tender. Return meat to pan.

Mix wine, orange juice, sugar, and parsley. Pour over meat. Cover and simmer 45 minutes. Remove meat. Mix cornstarch and water. Add to sauce. Cook until thick. Add drained orange slices; cook 1 minute. Arrange pork on rice. Pour sauce over all. Serves 6. Electric frying pan is perfect to use.

Eloise Dellinger (Mrs. H.S.)

KALUA OVEN PORK
A native of Honolulu gave me this recipe. It is wonderful for barbeque.

1 pork roast (I like the large end
    of the loin)
2 tsp. liquid smoke
sea salt
pepper

Rub roast vigorously with sea salt. Place on double thickness of heavy foil. Top with 2 tsp. liquid smoke. Close foil carefully, leaving a little room for the liquid which forms. Bake 5 hours at 275 degrees. Remove meat from the bones. Pour the broth over it. This makes wonderful sandwiches with or without barbeque sauce.

NOTE: To remove grease from broth, place in refrigerator until fat can easily be removed.

Gensie

ITALIAN VEAL AND PEPPERS
Can be prepared early in the day

1-1/2 lbs. veal for stewing
2/3 cup white wine
5 Tbsp. oil
6 Tbsp. butter
1 large onion, sliced
4 large green peppers, cut into
   1 inch strips
1 can (1 lb. 4 oz.) whole tomatoes,
   chopped
salt and pepper to taste
1 medium can sliced mushrooms,
   or use fresh

Cut veal into 1-1/2 inch cubes. Melt butter in skillet (not teflon). Brown veal for 10 minutes. Add tomatoes, salt and pepper. Cover and simmer for 30 minutes. In another pan saute onions and peppers in oil until tender. Stir to prevent burning. Mix with veal. Add wine and mushrooms, cover and simmer for 15 more minutes on low heat. Serve over rice. Serves 4-6.

Mary Ann Felciani

VEAL FRANCAISE
For an economical treat, substitute chicken breasts for veal.

1 lb. veal scaloppine
1 stick butter
1 lb. mushrooms
1/2 cup Gallo sherry
1/2 cup Swanson chicken broth
1 egg
flour
1 lemon
2 rounded tsp. parsley

Dredge veal in slightly beaten egg, then flour. Saute in butter, over medium heat, until golden. Reserve cooked veal, leaving drippings in pan. Add sherry, chicken broth, parsley and 3/4 of mushrooms, cut bite size. (Use the rest of the mushrooms to garnish salad). Cook over high heat, covered at first to cook the mushrooms. After a few minutes, remove cover and continue to cook over high heat, until fairly thickened.

Pour mushrooms and sauce over meat on platter. Garnish with 6 lemon wedges. It is essential for each person to apply lemon juice instead of salt and pepper.

Serve with saffron or herb rice, a salad of leaf lettuce, and your favorite white wine.

Richard Malnati

VEAL PARMIGIANO I

4 veal cutlets or 1 lb. veal
3 Tbsp. butter or margarine
1/2 cup grated Parmesan cheese
4 slices mozzarella cheese
1 or 2 eggs, lightly beaten
1/2 tsp. salt
dash pepper
1 8-oz. can tomato sauce
1/2 tsp. crushed oregano
dash onion salt

Melt butter in a 6 x 10 baking dish. Combine Parmesan cheese, salt and pepper. Cut veal into 4 serving pieces. Dip in egg, then Parmesan cheese mixed with salt and pepper. Place in baking dish. Bake at 400 degrees for 20 mintues. Turn meat; continue baking 15 to 20 minutes or until tender. In a saucepan combine tomato sauce, oregano and onion salt. Heat just to boiling, stirring frequently. Pour sauce over meat. Top each piece of veal with mozzarella cheese. Return to oven 3 to 5 minutes to melt cheese. Serve over buttered noodles. Serves 4.

Stevie Keown (Mrs. M.G.)

VEAL PARMESAN II

SAUCE:
2 onions
2 cloves garlic
1 pkg. garlic cheese dressing
(Good Seasons)
dash red pepper
sprinkle Italian dressing
basil leaves
Parmesan cheese
2 8-oz. cans tomato sauce
1 4-oz. can tomato paste
1/2 cup water

FOR MEAT PREPARATION:
3 Tbsp. oil
6 veal cutlets
1 egg, beaten
1 cup bread crumbs
1/2 cup Parmesan cheese
6 slices mozzarella cheese

Saute onions and garlic cloves in 2 Tbsp. oil until onions are tender. Remove garlic cloves, add the rest of sauce ingredients. Simmer for 1/2 hour.

Bread veal cutlets by dipping in egg first then in bread crumbs and Parmesan mixture. Brown cutlets in oil. Cover with mozzarella cheese and sauce. Cover; simmer for 1-1/2 hours. Serves 6.

Libby Preston (Mrs. James)

VEAL SCALOPPINE I

This recipe is from the St. George's Hotel, Rome.

1-1/2 lbs. veal cutlet, sliced 1/4
   inch thick and cut into 8
   pieces
1/4 cup flour
1/2 tsp. salt and black pepper
4 Tbsp. butter
1/2 lb. fresh mushrooms or
   1 6-oz. can
1/2 cup beef bouillon
1/4 cup Madeira wine
1 Tbsp. parsley, chopped
1 Tbsp. tarragon vinegar

Dip veal cutlets in flour, salt and pepper. Brown in butter and add mushrooms. Saute mushrooms with veal until a little brown. Simmer 40-50 minutes. Remove veal and mushrooms to a hot platter. Add the bouillon and wine to the drippings and pour sauce over veal and mushrooms. Sprinkle with parsley and vinegar. Serves 6-8.

Noble Dillard

VEAL SCALOPPINE II

1 to 1-1/2 lbs. veal cutlets which
   have been put through
   tenderizing machine
2 to 4 Tbsp. oil
1 to 2 Tbsp. butter
1/2 cup flour
salt and pepper to taste
1 cup beef bouillon
1/4 tsp. rosemary
1/2 tsp. Kitchen Bouquet
1-1/2 Tbsp. lemon juice
parsley
1 cup white wine or dry vermouth
   (I use vermouth)

Dredge veal in mixture of flour, salt and pepper. Saute in 2 Tbsp. oil and 1 Tbsp. butter. Mix bouillon with rosemary and Kitchen Bouquet. When meat is brown, add bouillon mixture. Add lemon to taste, fresh parsley and wine. Simmer 40-50 minutes, covered. Remove veal and add more wine for sauce if needed. Strain and pour over meat. Garnish with fresh parsley. Serves 6-8.

Virginia Golding (Mrs. John G.)

VEAL SCALOPPINE WITH CHEESE

2 lbs. veal scaloppine
1/2 cup butter
3 Tbsp. sherry or marsala
1 Tbsp. flour
1/2 cup milk
1/2 cup water
1 beef bouillon cube
dash nutmeg, pepper
1/2 lb. Swiss or Gruyere cheese,
  sliced

Heat 6 Tbsp. butter, add veal and brown. Add wine and cook a few seconds. Remove from heat. SAUCE: Melt remaining butter in a saucepan, add flour and whisk. Bring water and milk to boil in another saucepan and dissolve bouillon cube. Add all at once to butter/flour mixture stirring until smooth and thick. Add pepper and nutmeg. Place veal in shallow, ovenproof dish. Add drippings. Top with sauce and cheese on top. Before serving, cook at 425 degrees for 20 minutes. Serves 6-8.

Frances Brackett (Mrs. Martin L., Jr.)

VEAL PAPRIKA

3-1/2 lbs. boneless veal cut into 1/2
  inch cubes
6 slices bacon, cut in small pieces
1 medium onion, chopped
5 cups chicken broth (or 3 cans of
  broth)
3 Tbsp. paprika
salt to taste
3 Tbsp. flour
1/2 cup water
1 cup sour cream
toasted almonds for garnish

Cook bacon with veal and onions until golden brown. Add chicken broth, paprika and salt. Cover and simmer until veal is tender, about 1-1/2 hours. Mix flour with water and stir into veal until thickened, stirring constantly. Add sour cream, stirring until well blended. Garnish with almonds. Serve with rice or noodles. Serves 8.

Helen Lampus (Mrs. A.G.)

SAUSAGE PASTA SUPPER

3 Tbsp. butter
1 medium onion, chopped
1 medium green pepper, chopped
1/2 lb. fresh mushrooms, sliced
2 cups fresh vegetable (sliced zucchini is great)
1/2 tsp. garlic salt
1/2 tsp. oregano
1 lb. Kielbasa sausage (Hillshire Farms)
1/2 cup Parmesan cheese
8 oz. thin spaghetti, cooked

Stir-fry in skillet first 7 ingredients until barely tender. Add sausage which has been cut in bite-size pieces; heat through but not long enough to overcook vegetables. Stir in cheese. Serve over buttered pasta with additional cheese. Yields 4 to 6 servings.

Betty Holland (Mrs. Calvin)

RED BEANS AND RICE

1/2 stick butter
1/2 to 1 lb. Italian sausage, cut in 1-inch slices
2 15-oz. cans Van Camp's New Orleans kidney beans
1 large onion, chopped
1/2 cup celery, chopped
1 small green pepper, chopped
2 Tbsp. parsley
1/3 cup green onion tops, chopped
2 Tbsp. catsup
1-1/2 tsp. Worcestershire sauce
1 8-oz. can tomato sauce
1 to 2 tsp. chili powder
1/8 tsp. red pepper
salt to taste
cooked rice

Saute sausage in butter for 5 minutes. Remove sausage and saute all vegetables until wilted. Add beans, sausage and remaining ingredients. Cover and simmer about 20-30 minutes. Serve over rice. Serves 6.

NOTE: Can substitute bacon, 8 strips, for sausage. Use bacon drippings for sauteing vegetables.

Jane C. Jones

Poultry

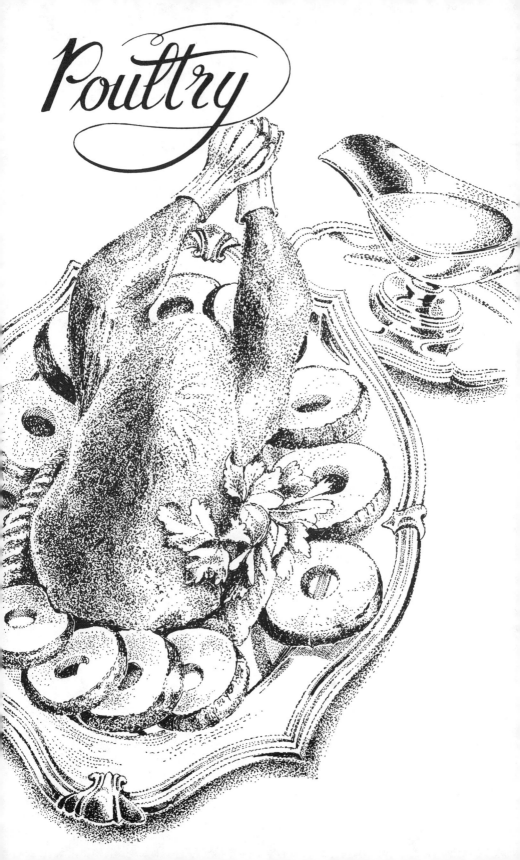

CHICKEN AMBASSADOR

This is easy. For a family meal you may omit the artichokes.

6-8 large chicken breasts
1 tsp. salt
1 tsp. poultry seasoning (more
    if desired)
paprika
1/2 cup melted butter
1 can beef consomme
1/2 cup sherry
1/2 lb. mushrooms, sliced
2 Tbsp. butter
2 10-oz. cans artichoke hearts,
    halved

Season chicken with salt, poultry seasoning and paprika. Spread in dish, skin side up. Baste with combined butter and consomme. Bake at 325 degrees for 1 hour, basting every 20 minutes. Add sherry to pan drippings. Bake and baste for 1/2 hour. Saute sliced mushrooms in 2 Tbsp. butter. Remove chicken to a warm platter. Combine drippings, mushrooms and artichoke hearts. Heat and pour over chicken. Serves 6-8.

Genevieve Cummings (Mrs. T.E.)

CHICKEN-ARTICHOKE CASSEROLE

1 broiler-fryer chicken, cut
    in parts
4 Tbsp. butter
1 Tbsp. cooking oil
1 pkg. (8 oz.) fresh mushrooms,
    sliced
1 Tbsp. flour
1 can cream of chicken soup
1 cup dry white wine
1 cup water
1/2 cup cream
1 tsp. salt
1/4 tsp. tarragon leaves
1/4 tsp. pepper
1 can (15 oz.) artichoke hearts,
    drained
6 green onions, green and white
    parts included, chopped
2 Tbsp. chopped parsley.

In large frypan place butter and oil and heat to medium temperature, until butter melts. Add chicken and cook, turning, about 10 minutes or until brown on all sides. Remove chicken and place in baking pan or casserole. In same frypan saute mushrooms about 5 minutes or until tender. Stir in flour. Add soup, wine, and water; simmer, stirring, about 10 minutes or until sauce thickens. Stir in cream, salt, tarragon and pepper; pour over chicken. Bake, uncovered, in 350 degree oven for 60 minutes. Mix in artichoke hearts, green onions and parsley. Bake about 5 more minutes or until chicken is tender. Serves 4. Three pounds of chicken breasts may be substituted for whole chicken.

Virginia Golding (Mrs. John G.)

A 3-1/2 lb. chicken will yield about 3 cups cooked cubed chicken.

CHICKEN-ASPARAGUS CASSEROLE
Easy and good!

12 slices of cooked chicken
2 15-oz. cans of asparagus
    (drained)
2 cans Campbell's cream of
    mushroom soup, undiluted
1 cup heavy cream
1 tsp. curry powder
4 drops Tabasco sauce (Texas
    Pete)
4 Tbsp. chopped pimiento
Parmesan cheese
paprika

Place asparagus in greased 2-quart baking dish. Arrange cooked chicken slices over. Combine soup, cream, curry and Tabasco in saucepan and heat — stirring until smooth. Add pimiento. Pour over chicken. Sprinkle with lots of Parmesan cheese. Top with paprika. Bake in 350 degree oven for 20 minutes. May be prepared ahead. Serves 4.

NOTE: Tester suggests using large bite-size pieces of chicken and asparagus pieces. Worked well for a buffet casserole for it eliminated the use of a knife.

Sophie Godwin

CHICKEN BROCCOLI CASSEROLE

3/4 cup mayonnaise
1/3 cup flour
1/2 cup onion, chopped
1 clove garlic, chopped
2-1/4 cups milk
1 cup shredded Swiss cheese
7 oz. spaghetti, cooked and
    drained
1/3 cup white wine or sherry
    (optional)
2 cups cooked chicken
1 10-oz. package chopped broc-
    coli, thawed and drained
1 cup sliced almonds,
    lightly toasted
1 cup sliced mushrooms
chopped pimiento
salt and pepper to taste

In medium saucepan, combine mayonnaise, flour and seasonings. Gradually add milk. Cook over low heat until thickened. Stir constantly. Add cheese and wine. Stir until cheese melts. In a large bowl combine remainder of ingredients with mayonnaise/cheese mixture. Toss lightly. Pour into buttered 8 x 10 inch baking dish. Top with additional almonds, if desired. Bake at 350 degrees until hot and bubbly.

NOTE: Tester suggests varying by substituting sharp Cheddar cheese for Swiss and using more onion and garlic. She thought chopped celery and green pepper would add taste, texture and color.

Eileen Antonelli (Mrs. G.A.)

CHICKEN WITH ARTICHOKES

1 chicken, cut up (or 6 or 8 of
    your favorite pieces)
oil
seasoned flour
1/2 lb. fresh mushrooms
    (cut in half if large)
1 can artichoke hearts, drained
2 cloves garlic, minced
1-1/4 tsp. salt
1/2 tsp. oregano
1/2 tsp. pepper
2 cups canned or fresh tomatoes
1/2 cup sherry

Preheat oven to 350 degrees. Flour chicken and brown slightly in oil. Place in large casserole dish or Dutch oven adding mushrooms and artichokes. Combine tomatoes with garlic and spices, pour over chicken. Cover casserole and bake 1-1/2 hours, basting often. Add sherry during last few minutes of cooking. Serve on rice. Serves 6.

Liz Medearis (Mrs. W.F., Jr.)

ELEGANT CHICKEN

8 chicken breasts, skinned and
    boned
salt
1/4 cup melted butter or
    margarine
2 (9 oz.) pkgs. frozen artichoke
    hearts, thawed and halved
1/2 lb. fresh mushrooms, sliced
1/4 cup melted butter or
    margarine
3 Tbsp. all-purpose flour
1-1/2 cups chicken broth
1/3 cup sherry

Sprinkle chicken with salt and brown in 1/4 cup butter. Arrange chicken in shallow baking dish. Add artichokes and set aside. Saute mushrooms in 1/4 cup butter. Sprinkle flour over mushrooms, stirring until blended. Gradually add broth and sherry, stirring constantly. Simmer 5 minutes and pour over chicken. Bake *covered* at 375 degrees for 45 minutes.

Nancy Wohlbruck (Mrs. Everett L.)

Two whole chicken breasts (10 oz. each) will yield about 2 cups cooked chicken.

CHICKEN-BROCCOLI CASSEROLE

6 chicken breasts, cooked
3 pkgs. frozen broccoli spears, or
   asparagus (or use fresh)
3 cans Campbell's creamy
   chicken-mushroom soup
1 1/2 cups Hellman's mayonnaise
2 tsp. lemon juice
6 Tbsp. sherry
3/4 cup shredded sharp Cheddar
   cheese
3/4 cup soft bread crumbs
2 Tbsp. melted butter

Arrange cooked vegetable in 13 x 9 inch casserole. Cut chicken into large bite-size pieces and place over vegetable. Mix together soup, mayonnaise, lemon juice and sherry and pour over all. Sprinkle with cheese, then crumbs and drizzle melted butter over the top. Bake at 350 degrees, covered, about 1 hour, until bubbly. If prepared ahead and refrigerated for a time, allow to come to room temperature before baking, or add 15 minutes to baking time. Serves 8.

Nancy Little (Mrs. T.M.)

CHICKEN DIVAN

3 whole chicken breasts (6 halves)
celery, carrots, peppercorns for
   boiling chicken
2 10-oz. pkgs. frozen broccoli
   spears
2 cans cream of chicken soup
1 cup mayonnaise
1 8-oz. carton sour cream
1 cup sharp Cheddar cheese,
   grated
1 Tbsp. lemon juice
1 tsp. curry powder
salt and pepper to taste
1/2 cup Parmesan cheese, grated
paprika
butter

Cooked chicken breasts in water for 30 minutes with some celery, carrots and peppercorns. Cut into bite-size pieces. Cook broccoli according to package directions. Mix the rest of the ingredients except for Parmesan cheese and paprika. Grease a 3-quart casserole and arrange broccoli on bottom. Sprinkle with Parmesan cheese. Layer the chicken next and sprinkle with more Parmesan cheese. Top with sauce, sprinkle with more Parmesan cheese and then paprika. Dot with butter. Bake at 350 degrees for 30 to 40 minutes. Serves 8.

Georgia Miller (Mrs. George)

CHICKEN-GREEN BEAN CASSEROLE

2-1/2 cups Pepperidge Farm
    Stuffing Mix
1/4 cup melted butter
1/2 cup chicken broth
1 1-lb. can French-style green
    beans, drained
1/3 to 1/2 cup slivered almonds,
    toasted
1 can cream of chicken soup
1 can chicken broth
2 cups cooked chicken pieces (or
    2 whole chicken breasts,
    cooked and cut up)
pepper to taste

Mix stuffing, melted butter and the 1/2 cup chicken broth. Line a 2-quart pyrex casserole with 1/2 of the mixture. Cover with beans, pepper and almonds. Place pieces of chicken on top. Pour over this the soup and broth, mixed together. Cover with remaining dressing mixture. Bake, covered, at 350 degrees for 45 minutes. Uncover last 5 minutes to brown. Serves 8.

Carolyn Tomlin (Mrs. M.G.)

EASY CHICKEN WITH ONIONS

1 large fryer, cut up
1/2 tsp. salt
1/2 tsp. pepper
12 to 16 tiny onions, peeled, or
    1 8-oz. can onions
1 can mushroom soup
2 Tbsp. cooking sherry
1/2 cup sharp cheese, grated

Place chicken in shallow baking dish. Sprinkle with salt and pepper; add onions. Mix soup and sherry; pour over chicken. Sprinkle with cheese. Bake uncovered for 45 minutes at 350 degree. Uncover and bake 30 to 45 minutes or until done. Serves 4 to 6.

Mickie Turner (Mrs. Cliff)

BOOZED-UP CHICKEN
Very good "2-day make ahead" chicken dish

1/4 cup dry vermouth
1/4 cup sweet vermouth
1 pkg. onion soup mix
1 small bottle Italian salad
    dressing
8-10 deboned, skinned chicken
    breasts (may use fewer
    chicken pieces)
1 bay leaf
2 jars mushrooms

In a blender, mix 1/4 cup dry vermouth, 1/4 cup sweet vermouth, onion soup mix, and bottle of Italian salad dressing. Put the above mixture in a large cooking bag along with chicken, bay leaf, and mushrooms. Refrigerate in bag for 2 days before cooking. Cook 1 hour and 25 minutes at 325 degrees. Serve over rice. Serves 8-10.

B.J. Miller (Mrs. H.F., III)

CASSOULET

4 slices bacon
8 chicken breast halves
1 onion, chopped
1/2 lb. fresh mushrooms, sliced
1 cup vermouth
1/4 cup parsley
1 bay leaf
salt and pepper to taste
2 15-oz. cans navy beans, drained
8 chicken thighs
2 lbs. smoked sausage
1 green pepper, chopped
8 oz. can tomato puree
1/8 tsp. ground cloves
1/4 tsp. thyme
1 tsp. dried garlic flakes
1 tsp. basil

Fry the bacon. Drain and set aside. Brown chicken in bacon fat and set aside. Cut sausage in chunks and brown with onion, green pepper and mushrooms. Combine all ingredients except beans in skillet. Simmer slowly for 40 minutes, uncovered. Add beans and mix. Transfer to serving casserole. (May be prepared ahead to this point.) Bake, covered, for one hour at 325 degrees. Serves 8.

Georgia Miller (Mrs. George)

CHICKEN A LA BASQUE
A simple, flavorful recipe

4 large double chicken breasts or
    1 frying chicken, disjointed
2 Tbsp. butter
2 Tbsp. olive oil
2 cups sliced fresh mushrooms
4 tsp. garlic salt
2 tsp. oregano
1 tsp. paprika
1/2 cup sliced green onions
1 cup white dinner wine

Wipe chicken well. Melt butter in a large skillet; add olive oil. Saute mushrooms until golden; remove and reserve. Brown chicken well on both sides. Sprinkle with garlic salt, oregano, paprika and onions. Top with reserved mushrooms and add wine. Cover and simmer 45 minutes until chicken is tender and flavors blended. Makes 4 generous servings.

Virginia Golding (Mrs. John G.)

CHICKEN IN WINE SAUCE

*chicken breasts—whole, split or boned, according to preference
Lawry's seasoned salt
1 can cream of mushroom soup
Holland House White Cooking Wine

*1 can of soup covers about 6 breasts

Wash breasts, pat dry with paper towels and place in baking dish. Sprinkle with seasoned salt. Slather with mushroom soup. Pour cooking wine about half way up the dish. Bake uncovered at 350 degrees for about an hour or until chicken is tender and sauce is bubbly.

Beverly Hance (Mrs. James)

VARIATION: Use 6 to 8 chicken breasts, boned and skinned. Use 4 oz. can sliced mushrooms instead of 1 can mushroom soup; 6 to 8 slices Muenster cheese.

Sprinkle chicken with seasoned salt; brown in butter and add mushrooms. Cover with white wine and steam slowly in covered pan for 45 minutes. Just before serving place a slice of cheese on each chicken breast. Sauce may be served over rice.

Janice Mayhew (Mrs. J.M.)

CAROLYN'S CHICKEN AND VEGETABLES IN WINE
You can visit with your guests while your dinner cooks.

4-6 boned chicken breasts
1 stick butter (not margarine)
4 Tbsp. white wine
4 Tbsp. lemon juice
3 large carrots, cut in finger-size pieces
1 large onion, sliced and ringed
1 lb. green beans
1 cup sliced, raw mushrooms
1 clove garlic
fresh parsley

Melt butter in heavy fry pan with cover. Add wine and lemon juice and chicken. Brown chicken, then turn down heat to simmer 1/2 hour. Add vegetables in order given. Crush garlic over vegetables and sprinkle with fresh chopped parsley. Cover and continue cooking for 45 minutes or longer. Serves 4 to 6.

Mary O. McElveen (Mrs. G.A., III)

CHICKEN WITH FRESH VEGETABLES

4 broiler-fryer chicken breast
    quarters
3 Tbsp. butter
3 large zucchini
3 large tomatoes
1 cup chopped green onions
1 tsp. lemon juice
1 tsp. salt
1/2 tsp. pepper

In large frypan place butter and melt over medium-high heat. Add chicken and brown on all sides for about 30 minutes. Slice zucchini lengthwise and cut in 1-inch pieces; cut tomatoes into 1-inch chunks. Stir in green onions, zucchini, and tomatoes. Reduce heat to low; add lemon juice, salt and pepper. Cook, uncovered, about 20 minutes or until fork can be inserted in chicken with ease. Makes 4 servings.

Betty Holland (Mrs. Calvin)

COQ AU VIN

2 chickens, cut up
3 Tbsp. butter
1-1/2 cups pearl onions
6 shallots, minced
4 Tbsp. flour
2 Tbsp. fresh chervil (optional)
1 sprig thyme
pepper, freshly ground
3 cups dry red wine
3 Tbsp. olive oil
1/4 lb. bacon, minced
2 carrots, chopped
2 garlic cloves, minced
4 tsp. parsley, minced
1 bay leaf
2 Tbsp. salt
2 Tbsp. brandy
1 lb. sliced mushrooms

In a heavy casserole, heat butter and oil. Add bacon, onions, carrots, shallots and garlic and brown lightly. Push vegetables aside and brown the chicken. Add the flour, parsley, chervil, bay leaf, thyme, salt and pepper and stir. Add brandy and stir. Add wine and simmer for 5 minutes. Place covered casserole in moderate oven (325 degrees) for 50 minutes. Add the sliced mushrooms to the casserole. Cover and bake another 5 to 10 minutes. Serve with buttered noodles and salad. Serves 8.

Georgia Miller (Mrs. George)

SPIRITED CHICKEN

Brandy combined with white wine makes this an elegant company dish.

1/2 lb. sliced fresh mushrooms
1/4 cup butter
6 large chicken breasts
1 tsp. salt
1/2 tsp. thyme
1/4 cup brandy
1 cup dry white dinner wine
2 Tbsp. cornstarch
1/3 cup water
1/2 cup chopped green onions,
    stems and tops

Saute mushrooms in butter in a large skillet. Remove mushrooms and reserve. Brown chicken well. Sprinkle with salt during browning. Crush thyme between fingers and sprinkle over chicken. Remove from heat; pour brandy over all and light. Spoon liquid over chicken until flame dies. Add wine, cover and simmer 35 minutes until chicken is tender. Remove chicken to a heated serving platter. Skim excess fat from juices. Stir cornstarch into water; add pan juices and heat, stirring constantly, until mixture thickens and boils. Stir in reserved mushrooms and green onions. Cook 1 minute. Spoon over chicken and serve at once. Serves 6.

Virginia Golding (Mrs. John G.)

CHICKEN MAUI

8 whole chicken breasts, boned
8 pineapple slices
honey
sesame seeds
oil
salt

STUFFING:
1/2 lb. lean beef
1/2 lb. sausage
1/2 onion, chopped
2 eggs, beaten
2 oz. soy sauce
4 slices white bread,
    soaked in milk
1 small can water chestnuts, sliced
1/2 tsp. ginger

Combine all the ingredients for stuffing, blending them well. Place stuffing in each breast, secure with toothpicks if necessary. Brush each breast lightly with oil and salt to taste. In a large baking pan place chicken breasts on pineapple slices. Bake for 35 minutes at 350 degrees. Glaze with honey and sesame seeds. Continue baking for another 40 minutes. Serves 4 or 8.

Helen Lampus (Mrs. A.G.)

CHICKEN-PEACH AMANDINE

1/4 cup butter or margarine
4 chicken breasts
1/2 tsp. salt
3 green onions, sliced
1/2 cup slivered almonds
1/2 tsp. tarragon
1/2 cup chopped parsley
1 1-lb. can peach halves
1/2 cup grated Parmesan cheese
paprika

Melt butter or margarine in skillet. Add chicken and brown slightly. Then place chicken in baking dish. To drippings add salt, onions, almonds, tarragon and parsley. Stir mixture and pour over chicken. Cover and bake in 350 degree oven for 45 minutes. Uncover, add peach halves around chicken. Sprinkle Parmesan cheese over all and bake 15 minutes more. Sprinkle with paprika. Serves 4.

NOTE: Can substitute apricot halves.

Muriel Sandbo (Mrs. Robert O.)

FRUITED CHICKEN BREASTS
One of the best "easy" chicken recipes

8 chicken breast halves, cleaned
    and skinned
2 cans Mandarin oranges, drained
1 large can whole berry cranberry
    sauce
1/2 bottle Kraft Miracle French
    Dressing or Russian Dressing
1 envelope Lipton onion soup mix

Place chicken breast halves in large baking container. Mix remaining ingredients together and pour evenly over breasts. Can be prepared ahead to this point and refrigerated. When ready to cook, place oranges around breasts. Cover with foil and bake at 325 degrees for 1 hour. Makes 8 servings.
NOTE: Some recipes call for 1 bottle salad dressing. I find the thicker consistency of the sauce makes a nicer coating on the chicken pieces and the sauce doesn't all run off into the pan.

Ellen Knott (Mrs. B.F.)

HAWAIIAN CHICKEN

6-8 chicken breasts
1/2 tsp. salt
1/2 cup flour
3 Tbsp. cooking oil
1 onion, sliced
1 can (1 lb. 4 oz.) pineapple tidbits,
  drained (reserve juice)
1/3 cup soy sauce
1/3 cup water
1/4 cup honey
1/3 cup vinegar
1 can mushrooms (4 oz.)
1 green pepper, cut in strips
1/2 cup toasted slivered almonds

Salt and flour chicken and brown in oil. Add onion and pineapple juice. Simmer 15 minutes. Add soy sauce, water, honey and vinegar. Simmer 30 minutes. Add pineapple, mushrooms and pepper strips. Simmer 5 minutes. Garnish with toasted almonds. Serve over or with hot cooked rice. Serves 6-8.

Georgia Miller (Mrs. George)

HONOLULU KABOBS

6 chicken breast halves, boned and
  cut into 1 inch cubes
1 1-lb. can pineapple chunks,
  drained (reserve juice)
green peppers, sliced
cherry tomatoes
fresh mushrooms
water chestnuts

MARINADE:
1/2 cup pineapple juice
1/2 cup soy sauce
1/4 cup cooking oil
1 tsp. dry mustard
1 Tbsp. brown sugar
2 tsp. ground ginger
1 tsp. garlic salt
1/4 tsp. pepper

Simmer marinade ingredients in saucepan for 5 minutes. Cool. Combine with cubes of chicken and marinate for 1 hour.

Thread chicken, pineapple chunks, green pepper slices, water chestnuts, cherry tomatoes and mushrooms on skewers. Grill for 20 minutes on low gas setting or low charcoal heat, basting with remaining sauce. Serves 4 to 6.

NOTE: For best results, use *wooden* skewers.

Libby Morrison (Mrs. Jack)

ANNA-MARIE'S LEMON CHICKEN

3 whole chicken breasts, skinned,
    boned, and cut in half
juice of 1 lemon
1 tsp. grated fresh ginger, or
    1/4 tsp. ground ginger
1 clove garlic, put through the
    garlic press, or 1/4 tsp. garlic
    powder
2 Tbsp. cornstarch
2 Tbsp. vegetable oil
1 Tbsp. water
1 lb. snow peas, cleaned and left in
    ice water for 5 minutes, or
1 head broccoli, peeled and cut up,
    or
2 pkgs. frozen broccoli spears
salt and pepper to taste
1 cup chicken broth

Cut the chicken breasts into thin strips, put them into a bowl and add the lemon juice, garlic, ginger, 1 Tbsp. oil, cornstarch and water. Combine all these ingredients and let them marinate for about 10 minutes.

Heat the 1 Tbsp. vegetable oil in a heavy saute pan. When the oil is very hot add the drained snow peas or broccoli, season with salt and pepper, and stir them constantly for 2 minutes, then remove and put them aside. Then add the marinated chicken breasts into the hot pan; season them with salt and pepper; stir them constantly for about 3 minutes. Then add the chicken broth, bring it to a boil, add the snow peas or broccoli, combine and serve. Serves 4 to 6.

NOTE: Water chestnuts may be added for a nice touch.

The Committee

SPICED CHICKEN

1/4 cup flour
1 tsp. salt
1/8 tsp. pepper
1/4 cup oil
1 frying chicken, cut up
1-1/2 cups orange sections
orange juice
2 Tbsp. brown sugar
2 Tbsp vinegar
1/2 tsp. nutmeg
1 clove garlic
1/2 tsp. crushed basil leaves

Coat chicken parts with flour, salt and pepper. Brown in 1/4 cup oil. Drain orange sections, reserving juice. Add enough juice to make 1 cup. Mix juice, sugar, vinegar, nutmeg, garlic and basil in saucepan. Bring to boil and simmer 10 minutes. Remove clove of garlic.

Put browned chicken parts in oven pan or skillet and pour sauce over. Cook 1 hour or until chicken is tender. Put orange sections on top of chicken for last 15 minutes of cooking. Serves 4 or 5.

Peggy Young (Mrs. John)

SUNSHINE CHICKEN WITH POACHED ORANGES

A national prize-winning recipe

8 chicken thighs
8 chicken drumsticks
1 tsp. salt
1 tsp. basil
1 tsp. monosodium glutamate
1/2 tsp. freshly-ground pepper
1/2 cup soy sauce
1/2 cup catsup
1/4 cup honey
1/4 cup corn oil
2 cloves garlic, crushed

Sprinkle chicken with salt, basil, MSG and pepper. In a bowl mix together the soy sauce, catsup, honey, corn oil and garlic. Place chicken in a single layer (I skin my chicken first) in a shallow baking dish. Baste with sauce. Bake uncovered, basting frequently until a fork can be inserted with ease. Serve with poached oranges as directed below. Remaining basting sauce should be mixed with sauce from poached oranges and served in a separate bowl. Garnish with parsley or watercress.

POACHED ORANGES

3/4 cup water
1-1/2 cup sugar
3 Tbsp. orange rind, slivered
6 navel oranges, peeled remove membrane, cut in wedges
2 Tbsp. orange liqueur (Grand Marnier)

In saucepan mix water, sugar and orange rind over medium heat. Cook until slightly thickened (about 8 minutes). Place orange wedges in syrup. Reduce heat and cook on low heat about 3 minutes until they are warm. Remove from heat; add liqueur. Can refrigerate, but best served warm. Serves 8.

Ellen Knott (Mrs. B.F.)

SUSAN'S FAVORITE "ORANGE" CHICKEN

So convenient because it makes its own rice and sauce!

1 cup Uncle Ben's long grain rice (not quick-cook kind)
4 large chicken breasts

SAUCE:
1 can Campbell's Golden Mushroom soup
1/4 soup can sherry
3/4 soup can orange juice

Butter the baking dish. Evenly sprinkle the rice on the bottom. Place the chicken breasts on top of rice. Mix sauce and pour over all. Cover with foil and bake at 350 degrees for 1 hour or until rice absorbs liquid and chicken is done. Can prepare early in the day and refrigerate until baking time. Serves 4.

Nancy Little (Mrs. T.M.)

SWEET AND SAUCY CHICKEN
Another "good and easy"

8 chicken breasts
1 bottle Russian salad dressing
1 envelope Lipton's onion soup
    mix
1 jar (10 oz.) apricot preserves

Mix salad dressing, soup mix and preserves. Arrange chicken, which has been skinned and patted dry, in a large pyrex dish or baking pan. Spoon sauce over chicken and bake uncovered at 350 degrees for 1 hour.

Georgia Miller (Mrs. George)

SWEET AND SOUR CHICKEN

1 lb. boneless chicken breasts, cut
    in cubes
3 Tbsp. soy sauce (Kikkoman)
1 Tbsp. sherry
1/4 tsp. pepper
1/4 tsp. garlic powder
1 small egg
4 to 6 Tbsp. cornstarch
2 cups vegetable oil for deep frying

In medium bowl mix chicken with soy sauce, sherry, pepper, garlic and egg. Add cornstarch and mix well. If coating is not thick enough, add more cornstarch. Heat oil to 375 degrees in an electric fry pan. Carefully drop chicken in, one piece at a time. Fry until golden brown.

SAUCE:
1 cup pineapple chunks
1 cup pineapple syrup
1/2 cup sugar
1/4 cup catsup
1/4 cup vinegar
2 Tbsp. cornstarch
1 Tbsp. soy sauce (Kikkoman)
1/2 green bell pepper, cut in bite
    size pieces

SAUCE: In a saucepan add all ingredients except green bell pepper. Bring mixture to a boil while stirring. Add green pepper and mix in cooked chicken.

Pat Vinroot (Mrs. Robert)

EASY CHICKEN A LA KING

There are no specific measurements for this recipe, but it's easy and tasty
Use chicken or turkey.

1 can cream of mushroom or
    cream of chicken soup
milk to thin soup (perhaps 1/4 to
    1/2 cup)
sherry (about 2 Tbsp.)
chopped pimientos (small jar)
4 oz. can mushrooms, drained, or
    sauteed fresh mushrooms
garlic salt to taste
pinch of nutmeg
toasted almonds (about 1/4 cup)
leftover chicken or turkey

Pour soup into heavy saucepan; add milk and sherry to get desired consistency. Whisk until smooth. Add remaining ingredients except poultry; heat. Just before serving, add poultry and heat but do not boil. Serve over rice, Chinese noodles, toasted English muffins or Holland rusk.

Virginia Golding (Mrs. John G.)

ROAST ALMOND CHICKEN

You'll get compliments for very little work.

10-12 chicken breast halves
salt and pepper
1 5-oz. pkg. slivered or sliced
    almonds
1 can cream of mushroom soup
1 can cream of chicken soup
1 can cream of celery soup
1/4 cup dry white wine
Parmesan cheese

Wash chicken breasts, skin and pat dry with paper towels. Lightly salt and pepper pieces and put into a buttered 13 x 9 inch baking dish. Cover with 2/3 of the almonds. Combine the 3 soups, mix with wine and pour over chicken. Sprinkle generously with Parmesan cheese and remainder of almonds and bake, covered with foil, at 350 degrees for 2 hours. May be prepared ahead and heated at the last minute. Serves 6-8.

Fefe Booth (Mrs. R.B.)

When a recipe calls for boiled or cooked chicken, this is the easiest, most flavorful way: Place 2 chickens or equivalent pieces in a large container with 6 cups hot water, 1 Tbsp. salt, 2 tsp. onion salt, 1 tsp. celery salt, and peppercorns, if desired. Simmer for 1 to 1-1/2 hours. Remove from bones and use with your favorite recipe specifying cooked chicken.

CHICKEN AMANDINE

8 whole chicken breasts (8 lbs.)
   halved, skinned and boned
3 eggs
1 cup unsifted, all-purpose flour
1 cup milk
1 tsp. grated lemon peel
2 tsp. salt
1/4 tsp. pepper
3 cups dried bread crumbs
2 cups sliced almonds
1/2 tsp. tarragon, crushed
12 Tbsp. (3/4 cup) butter or
   margarine
4 Tbsp. salad oil
2 cups chicken broth
1/4 cup lemon juice
3 Tbsp. minced parsley
lemon wedges for garnish
parsley for garnish.

Using the bottom of a small saucepan, slightly flatten chicken breast halves between 2 sheets of waxed paper. Set aside.

BATTER:

In a blender container combine eggs, flour, milk, lemon peel, 1 tsp. salt and pepper. Cover and blend until smooth. Place chicken in a large, shallow dish. Pour batter over chicken and stir until chicken is well coated. Cover and refrigerate at least 30 minutes or overnight.

PREPARATION:

Combine bread crumbs, almonds, remaining 1 tsp. salt and tarragon on a large tray or pan. Remove chicken from batter, draining well. Coat chicken evenly in bread mixture. Set aside on waxed paper in a single layer. In a large skillet, heat 2 Tbsp. butter or margarine and 1 Tbsp. oil until foamy. Add 4 chicken breasts and saute 5 minutes on each side, turning once. Place chicken on paper towels in large baking pan; keep warm. Wipe out skillet with paper towels. Repeat sauteing 3 more times with remaining chicken. To skillet, add chicken broth and lemon juice; heat to simmer. Stir in remaining 4 Tbsp. butter or margarine. (May be prepared in advance to this point. Place chicken as it is cooked into 200 degree oven. Keeps up to 3 hours.) Leave sauce in skillet and cover; remove from heat. Set aside. At serving time, heat sauce to boiling. Season to taste; stir in parsley.

To serve, arrange chicken on serving platter. Spoon sauce over chicken. Garnish with lemon wedges and parsley. Serve 16.

Noble Dillard

CHICKEN BALLS
Ideal for serving dinner guests

1/2 cup chopped celery
1/4 cup chopped onion
2 Tbsp. butter
2 Tbsp. flour
1/4 cup chicken broth
2 cups cooked rice
2 cups chopped cooked chicken
1/2 cup shredded Cheddar cheese
1 beaten egg
1/2 tsp. salt
1/2 tsp. chili powder, or less
1/4 tsp. poultry seasoning, or less
1-1/2 cup cornflake crumbs
1 can condensed cream of
    mushroom soup
1/4 cup milk

Cook celery and onion in butter until tender. Blend in flour; add broth. Cook and stir until thick. Stir in rice, chicken, cheese, egg and seasonings. Form into balls approximately 1-1/4 inches in diameter. Roll in cornflake crumbs. Bake in 350 degree oven 25 to 30 minutes. Heat remaining ingredients. Serve over balls. Six servings.

NOTE: Tester suggests adding can of mushroom soup and milk to chicken mixture. Put into a 2 quart greased casserole, top with cornflake crumbs and bake at 350 degrees for 25 minutes.

Martha M. Goodwin (Mrs. W.B.)

BAKED CHICKEN ROLLS
Uses 3 meats—chicken, ham and bacon

8-10 chicken breasts, boned
salt and pepper to taste
garlic powder
oregano
8-10 slices **baked** ham
16-20 slices lean bacon
2 cups sour cream
2 cans cream of mushroom soup
juice of 2 lemons or 5 Tbsp. lemon
    juice
1/2 lb. fresh mushrooms, sliced
2 Tbsp. butter
paprika

Season chicken breasts on both sides with salt, pepper, garlic powder and oregano. Set aside. Partially fry bacon. Place a slice of ham over each breast and roll up. Wrap 2 pieces of bacon around each breast and secure with toothpicks. Place in a greased 3 quart casserole.
Mix mushroom soup with sour cream and lemon juice. Pour over chicken rolls and bake at 300 to 325 degrees for 2 hours. Broil briefly, watching carefully to crisp bacon. Saute mushrooms in butter and spoon over chicken. Sprinkle with paprika. Serves 8 to 10.

Ellen Knott (Mrs. B.F.)

BAKED CHICKEN BREASTS WITH CASHEWS

8 chicken breast halves, skinned
garlic salt to taste
1 stick butter, divided
    (not margarine)
1 Tbsp. paprika
1 Tbsp. lemon juice
1/2 lb. (or more) fresh
    mushrooms, sliced
1/2 tsp. Worcestershire sauce
1/4 cup sherry
1 cup cashew halves (6-1/4 oz. can
    Planter's will do)
2 Tbsp. flour
1/2 cup sour cream

Wash chicken breasts, skin and pat dry with paper towels. Season by sprinkling with garlic salt. Melt 1/2 stick butter in shallow dish. Stir in paprika and lemon juice. Dip chicken in mixture. Place in large baking dish and bake at 350 degrees for 30 minutes. While chicken is baking, saute mushrooms in remaining 1/2 stick butter. Add Worcestershire sauce and wine. When 30 minutes are up, spoon mushroom mixture over chicken. Sprinkle with cashews. Bake 30 minutes longer. For extra tender chicken, cover with foil and bake for 20 to 30 minutes longer. Remove chicken from casserole, thicken sauce with flour and stir in sour cream. Serve sauce over chicken breasts. Serves 6 to 8.

Ellen Knott (Mrs. B.F.)

BLUSHING CHICKEN

4 chicken breasts, split in halves
1 tsp. Accent
1/2 cup butter or margarine
1/2 cup dry white wine
1-1/2 cups red currant jelly
1 cup dairy sour cream

Wash chicken, drain and pat dry. Sprinkle with Accent. Melt butter or margarine in electric skillet. Cook chicken slowly at 360 degrees to a golden brown, turning to brown evenly. Add wine to chicken. Cover and cook slowly for 15 minutes at 300 degrees. Melt currant jelly in pan juices, basting chicken thoroughly. Cook 15 minutes longer, uncovered, at 300 degrees. Turn frequently and baste until chicken is fork-tender. Add sour cream to saucepan and blend well until thoroughly heated. Serve, spooning sauce generously over chicken. Serves 4 to 6.

Virginia Golding (Mrs. John G.)

CHEESY CHICKEN CASSEROLE

6 chicken breasts or one 4-lb.
   chicken
2 10-oz. pkgs. frozen broccoli
1-3/4 cup milk
2 8-oz. pkg. cream cheese
1 tsp. salt
1 tsp. garlic salt
1-1/2 cups Parmesan cheese
1 can French fried onion rings

Cook or bake chicken. Cut into bite size pieces. Cook broccoli about 4 minutes. Place broccoli in greased 2-quart casserole. In blender, mix milk, cream cheese, 3/4 cup Parmesan cheese, salt and garlic salt. Pour 1/2 of this sauce over broccoli. Add chicken and pour remainder of sauce over. Sprinkle with remaining Parmesan cheese. Bake at 350 degrees for 30 minutes. Garnish with onion rings and return to oven for 5 minutes. Can be frozen before or after baking. Serves 6-8.

Faye Thurston (Mrs. W.H.)

CHEESE GLAZED CHICKEN

6 large chicken breasts
2 Tbsp. flour
1 tsp. paprika
1-1/2 tsp. salt
2 Tbsp. butter
1/4 cup dry sherry
1 tsp. cornstarch
3/4 cup light cream
1/3 cup sauterne
1 Tbsp. lemon juice
1/2 cup grated Swiss cheese

Skin chicken. Put in bag and shake with flour, paprika and 1 tsp. salt. Brown in butter and oil over moderate heat. Add sherry. Cover and simmer until tender — 25 minutes. Blend cornstarch with cream and remaining 1/2 tsp. salt. Stir into pan drippings and continue cooking until thickened slightly. Add wine and lemon juice. Heat a few minutes longer. Sprinkle on cheese. Cover and let stand 5 minutes or run under broiler to brown.

Jean Rowe (Mrs. William)

CHICKEN CHIP AND BAKE

Good and easy recipe to make for those covered dish dinners or luncheons

2 cups cooked and cubed chicken
2 cups celery, sliced thin
2 Tbsp. diced onion
salt to taste
1 Tbsp. lemon juice
1/2 cup toasted sliced almonds
1 cup mayonnaise
1 cup shredded Cheddar cheese
1 cup crushed potato chips

In a large mixing bowl stir well the chicken, celery, onion, salt, lemon juice and almonds. Mix in mayonnaise. Put in 13 x 9 inch pyrex dish. Sprinkle cheese on top. Bake in preheated oven at 350 degrees until heated through, approximately 20-30 minutes. Sprinkle crushed potato chips on top. Put casserole back in oven and let chips brown. Serves 6-8.

B.J. Miller (Mrs. H.F., III)

DIJON CHICKEN

6 whole chicken breasts, halved
    (12 pieces)
salt and pepper to taste
garlic powder to taste
1-1/2 cups commercial sour cream
1-1/2 cups Dijon mustard
1 8-oz. pkg. Italian style bread
    crumbs
parsley

Lightly sprinkle chicken with salt, pepper and garlic powder.
Combine sour cream and mustard in a shallow dish, mixing well. Dip each chicken breast into mustard mixture and dredge in bread crumbs. Arrange chicken in a single layer in a large baking pan. Bake at 375 degrees for about 50 minutes or until tender. Garnish with parsley. Serves 6 or 12.

Ellen Knott (Mrs. B.F)

IMPERIAL HERBED CHICKEN
Variations of a favorite way to prepare chicken

I
1 cut-up 2-1/2 to 3 lb. fryer,
    skinned
*1-1/2 cups stale bread crumbs, or
1-1/2 cups seasoned Italian bread
    crumbs
1/2 cup Parmesan cheese
2 Tbsp. parsley
1 tsp. salt
dash pepper
several dashes garlic salt
1 stick butter, melted
*Crumb mixture also good as
    coating for pork chops.
II
7 or 8 boned chicken breasts
2/3 (8 oz.) bag Pepperidge Farm
    herb seasoned bread crumbs
several dashes garlic powder
2/3 cup Parmesan cheese
1 stick margarine, melted
III
8 chicken breasts, skinned
2 cups crushed corn flakes
1/2 cup Parmesan cheese
1 tsp. **each** thyme, oregano, chop-
    ped parsley and rosemary
1 tsp. **each** garlic powder, salt
    and pepper
1 stick margarine

Combine all ingredients in any of the above variations, except chicken and butter or margarine. Melt butter or margarine. Dip chicken pieces in melted butter or margarine to coat and then in combined crumb mixture. Place in greased 13 x 9 baking dish. Bake covered at 350 degrees for 1 hour.

I Dixie Denny (Mrs. T.E.)
II Sue Ellen Biswell (Mrs. C.D.)
III Maria Blount (Mrs. J.A.)

KENTUCKY FRIED CHICKEN

3 lbs. chicken parts
2 pkgs. Italian salad dressing mix
4 Tbsp. flour
1/2 cup lemon juice
2 tsp. seasoned salt
2 Tbsp. butter, softened
1-1/2 cups pancake mix
1-1/2 tsp. paprika
1/2 tsp. sage
1/2 tsp. pepper
1 cup milk
24 oz. Mazola oil

Wipe chicken dry after washing. Combine salad dressing mix, flour, lemon juice, seasoned salt and butter into a paste and coat the chicken evenly. Stack pieces in a bowl. Cover and refrigerate for several hours. Combine pancake mix with spices. Dip chicken in milk and then into pancake mixture. Dust off excess. Heat oil in large skillet and fry pieces until golden brown, about 4 to 5 minutes on each side. Place chicken in shallow pan and spooon any remaining milk over pieces. Seal with foil. Bake in preheated oven at 350 degrees for one hour. Uncover and bake 10 to 15 minutes at 400 degrees to crisp chicken. Serves 6.

The Committee

BECKY'S MICROWAVE CHICKEN
Quick and easy

1 2-1/2 to 3 lb. chicken, cut up
1 onion, sliced
1/2 lemon, sliced
1/4 tsp. cayenne pepper

SAUCE:
1/4 cup Worcestershire sauce
1/2 cup catsup
1/2 cup water
1/2 tsp. Tabasco
1 tsp. salt
1 tsp. chili powder
1/2 tsp. garlic powder

Make the sauce first by combining all the sauce ingredients in a 4-cup measure and cook on high for 4 minutes. Season the chicken pieces with 1/4 tsp. cayenne pepper. Cook on high 8 minutes with sliced lemon and onion on top of the pieces. Pour sauce over chicken. Cook 30 minutes. Serves 4 to 5.

NOTE: May be covered with Saran wrap during the last 10-15 minutes of cooking time if chicken seems dry.

Gensie

CHICKEN ORIENTAL

Cooking in a double boiler allows you to "hold" this until serving time.

CREAM SAUCE
1/2 cup butter
1/2 cup flour
2-1/2 tsp. salt
1/2 tsp. pepper
1 cup half and half, or
evaporated milk
3 cups milk
2 cups chicken broth (or stock)

2 cups cooked chicken, coarsely
  chopped
1/4 cup green pepper, finely
  chopped, sauteed in butter
  (optional)
1 cup fresh mushrooms, sliced,
  sauteed in butter
1/2 cup blanched almonds
1 can water chestnuts, sliced
1 small jar pimiento, chopped
1/4 cup sherry

Melt butter in top of double boiler, add flour, salt and pepper and blend well. Add remaining sauce ingredients. Stir until smooth and cook over hot water for 30 minutes. Just before serving, add remiaining ingredients and heat well. This is good served over Chinese noodles, egg noodles, rice or in a pastry shell. Very good served over a cheese souffle. Freezes well. Serves 8 to 10.

Ellen Knott (Mrs. B.F.)

OVEN-FRIED CHICKEN

The easiest way to fry chicken, plus no mess!

1/2 cup flour
1 tsp. salt
1/4 tsp. pepper
2 tsp. paprika
1/2 cup shortening (half butter)
2 to 3 lb. frying chicken, cut into
  pieces or 2 to 3 lbs. breasts,
  thighs, etc.

Heat oven to 425 degrees (hot). Mix flour, salt, pepper and paprika in paper bag. Place shortening in pan and set in oven to melt. Shake 2 pieces of chicken at a time in bag to coat thoroughly. Place chicken, skin side down, in single layer in hot shortening. Bake 30 minutes. Turn skin side up and bake another 30 minutes. Serves 4-6.

Linda Miller (Mrs. W.R.)

SESAME CHICKEN

2 tsp. margarine or butter
2 tsp. olive oil
8 chicken breasts, boned (skin on)
seasoned flour (in plastic bag add
    garlic powder, salt and
    pepper)
sesame seeds
3 tsp. minced green onions
1/2 cup dry white wine

Preheat oven to 375 degrees. Put butter and olive oil in baking pan (pyrex preferable) and melt in warm oven. When melted, remove and cool, but do not allow to harden. Shake chicken in seasoned flour. Coat floured pieces with cooled oil and arrange skin side down without touching. Sprinkle generously with sesame seeds and bake for 30 minutes. When brown, turn and sprinkle with seeds and minced onions. Add wine and cook for 45 minutes, basting occasionally. Serves 8.

Georgia Miller (Mrs. George)

STUFFED BANTAMS

It's actually preferable to assemble at least a day ahead. Flavors are enhanced.

8 chicken breasts, boned,
    in one piece
salt
monosodium glutamate
1 beaten egg
1 cup herb stuffing mix
1 can cream of mushroom soup,
    divided
1 6-1/2 oz. can drained, flaked
    crab meat
1 Tbsp. lemon juice
1/4 cup chopped green pepper
2 tsp. Worcestershire sauce
1 tsp. prepared mustard
1/4 tsp. salt
1/4 cup salad oil
1 tsp. Kitchen Bouquet
1/4 tsp. onion juice
dash pepper

Sprinkle inside of chicken breasts with salt and monosodium glutamate. Top with a filling made of mixture of the egg, stuffing, *one-half cup* of the soup, the crab, and next 5 ingredients. Skewer each bantam closed. Broil over hot coals (or bake in a 350 degree oven) for 30 minutes or until tender (45 minutes maximum), turning frequently. During the last 15 minutes, brush with a basting sauce made of the remaining soup with the salad oil, Kitchen Bouquet, onion juice and pepper. Bantams may be completely assembled a day ahead and refrigerated. Assembled bantams also freeze well. Serves 8.

NOTE: A metal basket for the grill works well for this recipe.

Jean Webb (Mrs. F.A.)

BAKED CHICKEN BREASTS SUPREME
A super "make-ahead" chicken dish

12 chicken breast pieces
2 cups dairy sour cream
1/4 cup lemon juice
4 tsp. Worcestershire sauce
4 tsp. celery salt
2 tsp. paprika
4 cloves garlic, minced
4 tsp. salt
1/2 tsp. pepper
1-3/4 to 2 cups unseasoned bread
   crumbs
3/4 cup butter
1 pkg. frozen green peas, rinsed
   and drained

Cut breasts in half and wipe with a damp towel. In a large bowl combine sour cream with lemon juice, Worcestershire sauce, celery salt, paprika, garlic, salt and pepper. Mix well. Add chicken, coating each piece well. Let stand covered in refrigerator at least 24 hours.

Next day, preheat oven to 350 degrees. Remove chicken from sour cream mixture. Roll in crumbs, coating evenly. Arrange in a single layer in large shallow baking dish. Bake chicken uncovered for 45 minutes. Spoon rest of butter over chicken and add green peas. Bake 15 minutes longer or until chicken is tender and nicely browned. Serves 6 or 12.

Ellen Knott (Mrs. B.F.)

TEXAS CHICKEN

2 chickens, cut in pieces
2 cloves garlic, chopped
salt, pepper, cayenne to taste
1 cup buttermilk
1 egg
1/2 cup unbleached flour
nutmeg, cayenne, cinnamon,
   cumin
1 cup vegetable oil
1/2 cup corn oil
1/2 cup peanut oil

Cut up chicken and have at room temperature. Mix together garlic, salt, pepper, cayenne, buttermilk and egg; marinate chicken pieces in mixture for 2 hours. Season flour with nutmeg, cayenne, cinnamon and cumin to taste. Drain chicken pieces and roll in seasoned flour. Mix oils in deep fryer and heat to 340 degrees. Fry pieces until done. Serves 4 to 6.

Mary Liz Maletis (Mrs. James)

The slower you defrost frozen chicken the less moisture loss you will have.

ROLLED CHICKEN WASHINGTON

Great to prepare ahead for a large dinner party

1 3-oz. can chopped mushrooms,
    drained
2 Tbsp. butter or margarine
2 Tbsp. all-purpose flour
1/2 cup half-and-half
1/4 tsp. salt
dash cayenne pepper
1-1/4 cup shredded sharp
    Cheddar cheese
6 or 7 boned whole chicken breasts
all-purpose flour
2 slightly beaten eggs
3/4 cup fine dry bread crumbs

CHEESE FILLING: Cook mushrooms in butter about 5 minutes. Blend in flour; stir in cream. Add salt and cayenne; cook and stir until mixture becomes very thick. Stir in cheese, cook over very low heat, stirring constantly, until cheese is melted. Turn mixture into pie plate. Cover, chill thoroughly about 1 hour.

ASSEMBLY: Cut the firm cheese mixture into 6 or 7 equal portions; shape it into short sticks. Place a stick on each boned chicken breast. Tucking the sides, roll chicken as for jelly roll. Press to seal well. Dust the chicken rolls with flour; dip in slightly beaten eggs then roll in bread crumbs. Cover and chill chicken roll at least one hour or overnight. Bake 45 minutes at 375 degrees.

Libby Morrison (Mrs. Jack)

CHICKEN WELLINGTON

Good to have on hand in freezer

12 chicken breast halves, boned
salt and pepper
6 oz. long grain and wild rice mix
    (Uncle Ben's)
1/4 cup grated orange peel
2 eggs, separated
3 8-oz. cans crescent rolls
1 Tbsp. water
20 oz. red currant jelly
1 Tbsp. mustard
3 Tbsp. port wine
1/4 cup lemon juice

Preheat oven to 375 degrees. Pound breasts until thin. Sprinkle with salt and pepper. Cook rice by directions for dry rice. Add peel; cool. Beat egg whites to soft peaks. Fold into rice. Roll 2 triangles of dough into a circle. Repeat for 12 circles. Put breast in center. Top with 1/4 cup rice. Roll chicken as jelly roll. Bring dough over chicken. Moisten edge with a little water, crimp and seal. Put seam down on baking sheet. Beat yolk and 1 Tbsp. water. Brush each roll. Bake uncovered 50 minutes or until tender. Cover with foil if they brown too quickly. Heat jelly; stir in mustard, wine and juice. Serve warm over chicken. Serves 12. May be prepared early and refrigerated or frozen.

Dot Nicholls (Mrs. T.H.)

WEIGHT WATCHERS CHICKEN BAKE
You think it has been fried!

6 to 8 chicken pieces, skin removed
1/3 cup non-fat dry milk
2 tsp. chicken or beef bouillon
2 tsp. paprika
1 tsp. salt
1/2 tsp. pepper
1/2 tsp dry mustard

Combine all ingredients except chicken. Coat chicken in mixture. Place in greased 13 x 9 inch baking pan and bake at 325 degrees for 45 to 55 minutes or until forked done. Can also use coating mixture on fish fillets. Bake at 400 degrees for 20 minutes. Serves 6 to 8.

NOTE: Nice to mix ahead and keep on hand for busy days.

Anne Thrift (Mrs. Charles B. III)

CHICKEN AMANDINE

1 8-oz. pkg. Uncle Ben's long grain
   and wild rice
10 Tbsp. butter or margarine,
   divided
1/2 lb. fresh mushrooms, sliced
3 to 4 cups cooked chicken
   or turkey
1/2 cup chopped onion
1/4 cup flour
1/2 cup chicken broth
1 cup half-and-half
2 Tbsp. minced parsley
1 tsp. salt, 1/4 tsp. pepper
1/4 cup sherry
1/2 cup ripe olives, sliced
1/2 cup slivered almonds

Prepare rice by directions on box, using only 1/2 pkg. of seasonings. Spread rice on bottom of 2-quart baking dish. Brown mushrooms in 2 Tbsp. butter and spread on rice. Melt remaining butter and cook onions. Add flour and stir until bubbling. Stir in chicken broth and half-and-half. Stir constantly until thickened. Add parsley, salt and pepper. Distribute chicken over mushrooms. Sprinkle sherry and ripe olives over this. Pour sauce over top. Sprinkle almonds and paprika. Bake at 350 degrees for 30 to 40 minutes. Serves 6. Can be prepared early in day, refrigerated and baked at serving time.

Tester suggested using entire package of wild rice seasoning.

Linda Hawfield (Mrs. Ben)

COMPANY CHICKEN CASSEROLE

3 cups cooked rice
2 whole fryers without giblets
1 Tbsp. salt
1/2 lb. sliced fresh mushrooms
1/2 stick butter, divided
1/2 cup slivered almonds

SAUCE:
1/2 stick butter
1/4 cup flour
1 cup cream (or milk)
8 oz. carton sour cream
juice of 1 lemon
2 egg yolks
1/2 cup cooled chicken stock
1/2 tsp. grated nutmeg
1 Tbsp. sherry
dash of red pepper
salt to taste
pinch of thyme and/or sage

Cook fryers in salted water until done (about 40 minutes). Reserve stock. Remove meat from bones in bite-size pieces. Saute fresh mushrooms in 1/4 stick butter over medium heat for 1 minute. Set aside. Saute almonds in 1/4 stick butter. Set aside.

Make sauce by melting 1/2 stick butter in large pan; blend in 1/4 cup flour; smooth in cream; stir in sour cream. Then slowly stir in, to maintain creamy consistency, the juice of 1 lemon, 2 beaten egg yolks which have been whisked with 1/2 cup cooled chicken stock. Then season with nutmeg, sherry, red pepper, salt, thyme and/or sage.

To assemble, layer the following in a 2-quart casserole: rice, chicken, mushrooms, sauce and drained almonds. Sprinkle lightly with salt, if desired. Bake at 350 degrees for 30 minutes or until bubbling.

Connie Connelly (Mrs. Charles W., Jr.)

CHICKEN AND DRESSING CASSEROLE

1-1/2 pkgs. (8 oz.) Pepperidge
    Farm cornbread dressing mix
1-1/2 sticks margarine
1 chicken—cooked, boned
    and cut up
1 can cream of mushroom soup
1 can cream of chicken soup
2 cans chicken broth

Melt margarine. Mix crumbs and margarine together. Pour 1/2 of crumbs in a 9 x 13 inch baking dish. Put cut-up chicken over crumbs. Mix both soups with 2 cans chicken broth. Pour over chicken and top with remaining crumbs. Dot with butter and bake at 350 degrees for 30 minutes. May prepare ahead. Serves 10 to 12.

La McLeod (Mrs. J.A.)

DRESSED-UP CHICKEN CASSEROLE
Might become a standby

*1 pkg. Pepperidge Farm
  stuffing mix
1 stick margarine, melted
2 to 3 cups cooked chicken, diced
  (3-4 chicken breasts)
1 can cream of chicken soup
1 8-oz. carton sour cream
1/2 pkg. slivered almonds or
  1/2 can water chestnuts,
  sliced (or more if desired)
1-3/4 cup chicken broth (reserved
  from cooking chicken)*

Cook chicken in water until done, using celery tops and onions for flavor. Remove chicken from the bone and dice, making sure to reserve broth. Mix melted margarine with stuffing mix. Use half of this mixture to cover bottom of 7-1/2 x 12 inch baking dish. Put over this the cut-up chicken. Combine thoroughly the chicken soup and sour cream and spread evenly over the chicken. Cover with the remainder of the stuffing mix. Dot with almonds or water chestnuts. Pour chicken broth over all, distributing evenly. Bake at 350 degrees for 30 minutes. May prepare ahead except for adding chicken broth just before baking. Serves 6 to 8.

Ellen Knott (Mrs. B.F.)

CHICKEN-WILD RICE CASSEROLE
Prize-winning recipe from the Miami Herald

*2 chickens (3 lbs. each)
1 cup water
1 cup dry sherry
1-1/2 tsp. salt
1 tsp. curry powder
1/2 cup sliced celery
1 lb. fresh mushrooms
1/4 cup butter or margarine
2 pkgs. (6 oz. each) Uncle Ben's
  wild rice mix
2 cups sour cream
2 cans cream of mushroom soup*

Place chicken in a deep kettle. Add water, sherry, salt, curry powder, onion and celery. Bring to boil; cover tightly. Reduce heat; simmer one hour. Remove from heat, strain broth. Refrigerate broth and chicken at once. When chicken is cool, remove meat from bones; discard skin. Cut into bite size pieces. Wash mushrooms, pat dry. Saute in butter until brown. (Reserve enough to circle top of casserole.) Measure chicken broth; use as part of liquid for cooking rice, following directions for firm rice. Combine chicken, rice and mushrooms (except those reserved for top) in a 3-1/2 or 4 qt. casserole. Blend sour cream and undiluted mushroom soup. Toss together with chicken mixture. Arrange reserved mushrooms in a circle on top of casserole. Cover; refrigerate (overnight if need be). Heat at 350 degrees for one hour. May be frozen.

Great for company because it can be done the day before. Makes 8 to 10 servings.

Sallie Wooten (Mrs. F.M.)

CHICKEN-RICE CASSEROLE
Another easy and quick one

1 cup rice (uncooked)
1 envelope dry onion soup
1 can cream of mushroom
    (or chicken) soup
1 soup can water
1 cut-up chicken

Mix first **4** ingredients; place chicken parts on top. Dot with butter and sprinkle generously with Parmesan cheese. Bake covered at 325 degrees for 45 minutes. Uncover and cook 45 more minutes. Makes 4 to 6 servings.

Pat Gatlin (Mrs. Leon)

CHICKEN AND RICE CASSEROLE

3 cups diced, cooked chicken
1 can cream of mushroom soup
3/4 cup mayonnaise
1-1/4 cups diced celery
1 pkg. R.M. Quigg's brand yellow
    rice
1 Tbsp. grated onion
2 Tbsp. lemon juice
3/4 tsp. salt
1/3 cup slivered almonds
buttered bread crumbs or
    stuffing mix

Cook rice according to package directions. Mix all of the ingredients together and put in greased casserole. Sprinkle bread crumbs or stuffing mix on top. Bake at 325 degrees for 30 minutes. Serves 8. Can be prepared ahead and heated when ready to serve. Do not freeze.

Doris Walker (Mrs. James E.)

CHICKEN-RICE CASSEROLE
This is my husband's very favorite chicken dish.

2 cups diced cooked chicken
1/2 cup cooked rice
2 to 3 Tbsp. chopped onion
1/2 cup toasted almonds
1 10-oz. can cream of chicken soup
sherry, to taste
1 cup water chestnuts, chopped
3/4 cup mayonnaise (or less)
2 Tbsp. butter
1 cup herbed stuffing mix

Combine rice, almonds, onions, chicken and water chestnuts; toss lightly. Mix soup and mayonnaise; add to chicken mixture and stir. Place in 1-1/2 qt. casserole. Cover with stuffing mix and melted butter. Bake 30 minutes at 325 degrees. This can be made in advance and frozen without topping. Makes 6 to 8 servings.

Kathleen Boyce (Mrs. R.N.)

CHICKEN SPECTACULAR

4 or more cups cooked chicken breasts, cut into bite-size pieces
1 box (6-3/4 oz.) Uncle Ben's long grain and wild rice mix (regular, not instant)
1 can cream of celery soup
1 large jar sliced pimientos
1 large onion, chopped
2 10-oz. pkgs. frozen French-style green beans
1 cup Hellman's mayonnaise
1 can water chestnuts, drained and sliced
salt and pepper to taste
Parmesan cheese
paprika

Cook rice according to package directions. Cook green beans slightly and drain. In a 3-quart casserole place one layer of chicken. Mix all other ingredients except remaining chicken; spread over chicken layer in casserole. Place and slightly press down the remaining chicken over this mixture. Sprinkle Parmesan cheese and paprika on top. Bake in preheated 350 degree oven for 30 to 40 minutes. May prepare ahead. Serves 8 to 10. The secret of this casserole is to be generous with the chicken.

Jane Lucas (Mrs. R.T.)

VARIATION: Use 2 boxes long grain and wild rice mix instead of 1 box. Use 2 cans cream of mushroom soup instead of 1 can cream of celery soup. Use 2 cups Hellman's mayonnaise instead of 1 cup. Other ingredients remain the same. Prepare by combining all ingredients except Parmesan cheese and paprika. Sprinkle these over top and bake for 30 to 40 minutes at 350 degrees. Serves 8 to 10.

Peggy Buchanan (Mrs. D. Douglas)

CHICKEN CASSEROLE SHERRILL
Most unusual but good—can be doubled easily.

6 chicken breasts, boiled, boned, diced
4 or 5 drops garlic juice
1/2 stick butter
1/2 pound mushrooms, sliced
1/2 cup chopped onion
3 Tbsp. chopped green pepper
1 cup chopped pecans
3 cups chicken broth
1 cup uncooked rice (wild or Uncle Ben's herbed or mixed)
1 cup salami, chopped
salt and pepper

Cook chicken breasts with onion pieces and celery. Remove from the bones and chop in small pieces. Saute mushrooms and onions in butter and garlic. Put all ingredients in a 3-quart casserole. Cook covered for 1 hour at 325 degrees. Serves 6.

Ellen Knott (Mrs. B.F.)

CHICKEN SALAD CASSEROLE

4 cups cubed chicken
1 can cream of chicken soup
1/4 cup diced sweet pickle
3/4 cup mayonnaise
1/2 cup sour cream
2 Tbsp. minced onion
1 tsp. salt
1/2 tsp. pepper
1 Tbsp. lemon juice
1 cup grated sharp cheese
1 cup crushed potato chips

Combine all ingredients except cheese and potato chips. Put into greased 2-quart casserole. Top with cheese and chips. Bake at 350 degrees for 25 to 30 minutes.

Betty Holland (Mrs. Calvin)

CHICKEN-SAUSAGE-WILD RICE CASSEROLE
Wonderful party dish—makes 2 casseroles.

1 (5-lb.) chicken or 2 (2-1/2 lb.)
   fryers
2 (6-3/4 oz.) pkgs. quick-cooking
   long grain and wild rice with
   seasoning packet
1 lb. hot sausage
4 large onions, chopped
*2 green peppers, chopped
4 stalks celery, chopped
1 can mushrooms
3 or 4 cans cream of mushroom
   soup
bread crumbs
butter
*May use just green pepper and
   celery, or just mushrooms, or
   a combination of both,

Cook rice in chicken stock after chicken has been cooked and removed from bones. Cut in bite-size pieces. Cook rice according to package directions, substituting chicken stock for water. Fry sausage, drain. Saute vegetables and/or mushrooms in butter. Add soup to sauteed mixture and sausage. Divide soup mixture between 2 greased 13 x 9 inch baking dishes or pans. Top with chicken. Put rice on top of chicken. Put dabs of butter and bread crumbs on top of rice. Cover with foil and bake at 350 degrees for 30 minutes or until bubbly. Freezes beautifully. Serves 14 to 16.

Carol Barreau (Mrs. E.H.)
Judy Ranson (Mrs. R.C.)

TURKEY CASSEROLE

4 cups cooked turkey breast, cut
    into large cubes
1 cup Hellman's mayonnaise
1 cup sour cream
1/3 jar hamburger or piccalilli
    relish, drained
2 Tbsp. finely-chopped onion
1/2 tsp. salt
1-1/4 cup milk
4 oz. whole pimientos, drained
    and chopped
8 oz. pkg. "Cheese-Its"
2 Tbsp. melted mutter
buttered bread crumbs

Mix mayonnaise, sour cream, relish, onions, salt, milk and pimineto with turkey pieces. Crumble cheese crackers. In greased 8 x 8 inch pan, layer: 1/3 of cracker crumbs, 1/2 of turkey mixture; then another 1/3 of cracker crumbs, remainder of turkey mixture, and lastly the remaining cracker crumbs. Sprinkle bread crumbs, mixed with butter, on top. Refrigerate overnight. Bake at 350 degrees for 30 to 35 minutes. Freezes extremely well.

Sophie Sly (Mrs. Richard)

CHICKEN CURRY

Nice for entertaining since it can be made ahead

1/3 cup butter
3 Tbsp. chopped onion
3 Tbsp. chopped celery
3 Tbsp. chopped green apple
12 peppercorns
1 bay leaf
1/3 cup sifted flour
2-1/2 tsp. curry powder
1 tsp. MSG
1/4 tsp. sugar
1/8 tsp. nutmeg
2-1/2 cups milk
2 tsp. lemon juice
1/2 tsp. Worcestershire sauce,
    divided
1/4 cup cream
2 Tbsp. sherry
3 cups chicken, cut in pieces
Condiments:
hard-boiled eggs (chopped),
    shredded coconut, finely-
    chopped peanuts, chopped
    cooked bacon bits, crushed
    pineapple, India relish,
    chopped green onions,
    chutney

Heat 1/3 cup butter in heavy 2 qt. saucepan. Add onion, celery, apple, peppercorns and bay leaf — cook over medium heat until lightly browned, stirring occasionally. Blend in mixture of flour, curry powder, MSG, sugar, nutmeg. Heat until mixture bubbles. Remove from heat, add milk gradually, stirring constantly. Return to heat, bring rapidly to boiling. Stirring constantly, cook until mixture thickens. Cook 1 to 2 minutes longer. Remove from heat and stir in lemon juice and Worcestershire sauce. Strain mixture through a fine sieve, pressing vegetables against sieve to extract all sauce. Blend in cream, sherry and 1/4 tsp. Worcestershire sauce. Add chicken and cook over medium heat until thoroughly heated; or refrigerate and reheat when ready to serve. Serve with condiments and rice.

Cathy Bradford (Mrs. W.Z., Jr.)

SOPHIE'S CHICKEN CURRY

1 large chicken, boiled, deboned and cubed (reserve broth)
1 bouillon cube
5 Tbsp. butter
1/2 cup minced onion
6 Tbsp. flour
2 tsp. curry powder, or less
1 tsp. salt
1 tsp. sugar
1/4 tsp. ginger
2 cups milk

Melt butter and add onions; simmer until tender. Stir in flour, curry powder, salt, sugar and ginger. Dissolve bouillon cube in chicken stock and slowly add, alternately with milk, to first mixture. Cook until thickened. Add chicken. Sauce should cling to chicken. Serve with rice and add choice of condiments in separate dishes. Serves 4.

TOPPINGS:
fruit chutney, chopped olives, shredded coconut, dark raisins, salted peanuts or cashews, chopped onions

Georgia Miller (Mrs. George)

CHICKEN DIABLO

1 3-lb. chicken, cut up
4 Tbsp. butter
1/2 cup honey
1/4 cup prepared mustard
1 tsp. salt
1 tsp. curry powder

Wash chicken and remove skin. Melt butter in pan; stir in remaining ingredients. Roll chicken in butter mixture. Arrange chicken in 13 x 9 inch casserole, meaty side up. Pour remaining liquid over chicken. Bake 1 hour in 375 degree oven or until richly glazed. Serves 4 to 6.

Mary Lou Bethune (Mrs. W.H.)

BAKED CHICKEN MUSHROOM SANDWICH

8 slices sandwich bread
4 Tbsp. butter, softened
4 cups chopped chicken
1 10- oz. can cream of mushroom soup
3/4 cup milk
1/2 cup Parmesan cheese
8 slices crisp bacon
12 mushroom caps or 1 (4 oz. or 8 oz.) can mushrooms

Trim bread; spread with butter. Make 4 sandwiches, using chicken as filling. Place in 8 x 9 inch baking dish. Combine soup and milk; blend well. Pour over sandwiches, sprinkle with cheese. Bake 15 to 20 minutes. Top with bacon and mushrooms. Makes 4 sandwiches.

Virginia Golding (Mrs. John G.)

CREPES DE POLLO

*3 fryers equalling 10 lbs. or
    equivalent chicken breasts*
6 cups water
1 Tbsp. salt
2 tsp. onion salt
1 tsp. celery salt
*4 cups Swiss or sharp Cheddar
    cheese, grated*
2 Tbsp. onion, grated
2 Jalapeno peppers, chopped
3 pimientos, chopped
*16 oz. whipping cream, combined
    with*
16 oz. light (coffee) cream
*24 crepes, prepared ahead (see
    recipe below)*

Cook chickens until done in the water to which salt, onion salt and celery salt have been added. Cool, bone and chop. Add cheese, chopped Jalapenos, grated onion, pimiento. To this, add 2 cups of the combined creams. Put filling in the center of each crepe and roll. Lay in buttered shallow baking dish and pour the rest of the cream over them. Sprinkle with grated cheese. Bake at 350 degrees for 20 minutes. Makes 24 crepes.

BATTER FOR ENTREE CREPES

1 cup cold water
1 cup cold milk
4 eggs
1/2 tsp. salt
2 cups sifted all-purpose flour
4 Tbsp. melted butter

Put the liquids, eggs and salt into a blender jar. Add the flour and then the butter. Cover and blend at top speed for 1 minute. If bits of flour adhere to sides of jar, dislodge with a rubber scraper and blend for 2 or 3 seconds more. Cover and refrigerate for at least 2 hours.

The batter should be a very light cream, just thick enough to coat a wooden spoon. If, after making your first crepe, it seems too heavy, beat in a bit of water, a spoonful at a time. Your cooked crepe should be about 1/16 inch thick.

From Mastering the Art of French Cooking by Child, Bertholle and Beck.

Gensie

ENCHILADAS DIEGO

Pumpkin seeds add a crunchy garnish.
Enchilada sauce may be made in advance.

1 dozen corn tortillas
oil for frying
2 lbs. chicken breasts
3 Tbsp. olive oil
1/2 cup sliced stuffed green olives
1/2 cup chopped green onions
1 Tbsp. garlic salt
2 large ripe tomatoes, diced
1-1/2 cups shredded Monterey
    Jack cheese
green chili sauce
1 pint dairy sour cream
1/2 cup toasted dried
    pumpkin seeds

Saute tortillas in hot oil in a large skillet, turning frequently until browned but not crisp. Drain on paper toweling. Set aside. Skin, bone and cut raw chicken into bite-size chunks. Saute lightly in olive oil about 10 minutes until cooked through. Stir in olives, onions, garlic salt, tomatoes and 1/2 cup Jack cheese. Simmer 5 minutes. Spoon filling onto center of tortillas and roll. Place in 13 x 9 x 2 inch baking pan. Top with Green Chili Sauce and sprinkle with remaining Jack cheese. (May be prepared to this point early in the day, covered and refrigerated until ready to bake.) Bake uncovered in preheated 325 degree oven 30 to 35 minutes. Top with sour cream and pumpkin seeds to serve. Makes 6 servings.

GREEN CHILI SAUCE

1 cup chopped green onions
1 cup chunked green bell peppers
1 clove garlic
1 4-oz. can Ortega green chili
    peppers
1 7-oz. can green chili salsa
3 12-oz. cans peeled tomatillos
1/4 cup olive oil
1/2 cup chopped parsley

Combine onions, bell peppers, garlic, drained chili peppers and green chili salsa in blender. Drain and add 2 cans tomatillos. Add 1 can tomatillos with liquid. Blend smooth. Simmer in olive oil in a large skillet 30 minutes. Blend in parsley.

Virginia Golding (Mrs. John G.)

CHICKEN ENCHILADAS

4 whole chicken breasts
few celery tops and leaves
1-1/2 cups water
pinch of oregano
salt and pepper to taste
small onion, minced
1 7-oz. can green chili sauce
1 can cream of chicken soup
1 can cream of mushroom soup
1 cup milk
1 doz. tortillas, cut into 1-inch
    strips
1/2 lb. Longhorn cheese
1/2 lb. Jack cheese, grated

Simmer chicken, celery and seasonings with 1-1/2 cups water until tender. Save broth. Cool; bone and cut into bite-size pieces. Combine soup, milk, chili sauce and onions in bowl. Butter 11-3/4 x 7-1/2 x 1-3/4 inch baking dish. Put in 4 Tbsp. chicken broth; layer some tortillas, then some chicken, then some sauce. Do this about 3 times, ending with sauce. Top with grated cheese. Cover with foil and refrigerate for 24 hours. Bake at 350 degrees, covered, for 30 minutes and then for 30 minutes uncovered.

Noble Dillard

GLOSSY SATIN ORIENTAL CHICKEN

3 Tbsp. soy sauce
1 Tbsp. sugar
3 Tbsp. sherry wine
1/2 tsp. salt
dashes of pepper
1/2 tsp. Accent
1 tsp. grated fresh ginger
1 clove garlic, minced
3 to 4 lbs. chicken breasts and/or
    thighs, or equivalent in boned
    chicken breasts
1 Tbsp. oil for frying
3/4 cup chicken broth
5 to 8 large dried Oriental
    mushrooms
1-1/2 Tbsp. cornstarch
1 tsp. sugar
1/2 cup chicken broth
dash Accent

1. Rinse chicken, drain; dry well. Mix first 8 ingredients and marinate chicken for 30 minutes.
2. Heat wok to high heat; add oil. Slosh around. Add chicken; brown well. Turn often.
3. Add 3/4 cup broth and mushrooms which have been soaked in warm water for 15 minutes and squeezed dry. Cover and simmer over low heat for 1/2 hour.
4. Place on platter. Skim off excess fat from juices in wok, if necessary.

Mix cornstarch, 1 tsp. sugar, 1/2 cup chicken broth and Accent, and blend with remaining juices in wok. Cook until transparent. Replace chicken in wok. Mix carefully. Reheat. Serve garnished with parsley. Serves 4.

Virginia Golding (Mrs. John G.)

ORIENTAL CHICKEN STIR-FRY

1/4 cup salad oil
3 chicken breasts, skinned, boned
    and cut into 1-inch squares
3 cups broccoli florets
1 medium green pepper, cut into 1-
    inch squares
1/2 lb. mushrooms, sliced
3 Tbsp. thinly-sliced scallions
1 cup chicken broth
3 Tbsp. dry sherry
1 Tbsp. cornstarch
1 Tbsp. soy sauce
1/2 tsp. liquid hot pepper
1/3 cup cashew nuts
hot rice

In wok or skillet, heat oil. Add chicken. Cook, stirring constantly, until chicken turns white. Remove from skillet. Place broccoli, pepper, mushrooms and scallions in skillet; add more oil, if necessary. Cook 3 minutes, stirring constantly. In small bowl, mix broth, sherry, cornstarch, soy sauce and pepper sauce. Return chicken to skillet. Add sauce and stir until thick. Top with cashews and serve with rice. Serves 4.

Georgia Miller (Mrs. George)

STIR-FRIED CHICKEN OR TURKEY BREAST
This is great with a fruit salad!

6 boneless chicken breast halves,
or equivalent uncooked
turkey breast
3 Tbsp. butter
1 medium onion, chopped
1/2 large green pepper, chopped
1 10-oz. can chicken broth
1 1-lb. bag Japanese-style frozen
vegetables
salt and pepper to taste
cornstarch to thicken (optional)
soy sauce (optional)

Cut chicken or turkey breast into bite-size pieces. Saute onion and green pepper in butter. Add chicken broth and meat. Poach this mixture until tender (about 15 minutes) in covered frying pan. Remove lid and add bag of Japanese vegetables. Heat thoroughly, leaving vegetables on the crisp side. Add salt and pepper. If desired, add 1 Tbsp. corn starch, which has been mixed with a small amount of water, to thicken. Serve over cooked rice and offer soy sauce. Serves 4 to 6.

Mayree Kay Miller (Mrs. J.J.)

CHICKEN ORISSA
A mildly-seasoned chicken dish from India

1 3-lb. chicken, cut up and skin
removed
3 Tbsp. oil, divided
2 medium onions, chopped
5 cloves garlic
1 cup fresh coriander leaves
(cilantro)
1 Tbsp. chopped fresh ginger root
1/2 cup grated coconut
(unsweetened)
1 Tbsp. ground cumin
1 Tbsp. ground coriander
2 cardamon pods (whole)
1/2 tsp. ground cinnamon
1/2 tsp. ground cloves
salt and pepper to taste
1/2 cup water
1 Tbsp. lemon juice

Saute onions in 2 Tbsp. oil until onions are golden. In another pan dry roast coconut, ground cumin and ground coriander over medium heat for 2 minutes. Stir to prevent scorching. In blender grind all ingredients, except chicken, cardamon pods, salt and pepper. In large pot saute in 1 Tbsp. oil the cardamon pods and the blended onion-spice mixture over moderate heat for about 5 minutes. Stir frequently. Add chicken, salt and pepper and stir to mix. Cover and cook over moderate heat for 5 minutes. Add 1/2 cup water and cook, covered, over low heat until chicken is done, about 45 minutes. Before serving, add 1 Tbsp. lemon juice and stir. Serve with rice. Makes 4 servings.

Beverly Patnaik (Mrs. P.K.)

CHICKEN ITALIAN

*This recipe came from New Mexico. The Governor's wife recommended
lettuce wedges with Thousand Island type dressing with it.*

3 large chicken breasts
3 large chicken thighs and legs
salt, pepper and flour

SAUCE:
1 10-oz. can Campbell's Cream of
*   Onion soup*
2/3 cup evaporated milk
1/2 cup shredded Cheddar cheese
1/2 tsp. salt
1/8 tsp. pepper
1 4-oz. can sliced, drained
*   mushrooms*
1/2 cup sliced water chestnuts
1 10-oz. pkg. frozen green beans,
*   thawed*

Coat chicken with flour after salting and pep-
pering. Melt 1/4 cup butter in 9 x 13 inch baking
dish in 425 degree oven. Arrange chicken in the
dish, single layer. Bake at 425 degrees for 30
minutes. Turn chicken and continue baking for
15 to 20 minutes. Remove from oven and drain
fat. Reduce heat to 325. Combine the ingredients
for the sauce. Spoon over the chicken. (This sauce
should be ready when the chicken comes from the
oven.) Cover with foil. Bake an additional 30
minutes or just until beans are barely tender when
pierced with fork. Serves 6.

Gensie

ITALIAN CHICKEN PARMESAN

Similar to Veal Parmesan but uses less expensive chicken breasts.

5 chicken breasts, skinned,
*   deboned*
3 Tbsp. butter
3 cloves garlic, minced
1 medium onion, chopped
1 No. 2 can tomatoes (2-1/2 cups)
1-1/4 tsp. salt
1/2 tsp. pepper
1/4 tsp. thyme
1 8-oz. can tomato sauce
2 eggs
1 cup seasoned Italian
*   bread crumbs*
1 cup Parmesan cheese, divided
10 small slices mozzarella cheese
salad oil

Cut chicken breasts in half, making 10 pieces.
Salt and pepper lightly. Saute onions and garlic
in butter; add tomatoes, salt and pepper. Run
knife through tomatoes to cut up large pieces.
Simmer 5 minutes. Add thyme and tomato sauce;
simmer 20 minutes. Beat eggs. Mix together
bread crumbs and 1/2 cup Parmesan cheese. Dip
each chicken piece in egg, then coat well with
crumbs. Saute on both sides in hot oil in skillet
until golden brown, adding oil as needed. Put
sauteed chicken pieces in a well-greased 13 x 9
inch baking dish. Pour 2/3 of the tomato sauce
over the chicken. Top each piece with a slice of
mozzarella cheese. Pour rest of sauce over cheese.
Sprinkle with remaining half cup of Parmesan
cheese. Bake at 350 degrees, uncovered, for 30
mintues. Serves 5 or 10.

Ellen Knott (Mrs. B.F.)

PIZZA CHICKEN

1 envelope Shake 'n' Bake
  barbecue style mix
1 tsp. oregano
1 pkg. Pick of the Chix or
  equivalent chicken pieces
  (3 breasts, 3 thighs
  3 drumsticks)
shredded mozzarella cheese

Place Shake 'n' Bake in bag. Moisten chicken and shake as directed on package. Place in 13 x 9 pyrex dish and sprinkle with oregano. Bake 50 to 55 minutes. Sprinkle with cheese and bake 5 minutes longer or until cheese melts. Yield: 9 pieces.

Linda Brown (Mrs. William B.)

CHICKEN TETRAZZINI

I serve this with Elegant Molded Fruit, Pineapple Pickles, hot biscuits and Lemon Tarts (see index).

6 lbs. chicken breasts
1 Tbsp. salt
2 tsp. onion salt
1 tsp. celery salt
1/4 cup butter
9 Tbsp. all-purpose flour
4 cups chicken broth
1 cup heavy cream
3/4 lb. Velveeta, cut in chunks
1 1-lb. can ripe olives, pitted, sliced
  and drained
1 8-oz. can mushroom slices,
  drained; or 1 lb. sauteed fresh
  mushrooms
1 3-oz. pkg. toasted, slivered
  almonds
3 Tbsp. finely-minced onion
3 Tbsp. minced green pepper
3 Tbsp. minced celery
pepper to taste
12 oz. thin noodles

Simmer chicken breasts in 1 Tbsp. salt, 2 tsp. onion salt and 1 tsp. celery salt (reserve broth). Cut meat into bite-size pieces and set aside. Heat butter in large saucepan and gradually blend in flour. Slowly add 4 cups chicken broth, then cream. Stir over low heat until mixture has thickened. Add Velveeta and stir until melted. Combine with chicken and all other ingredients except noodles. Boil noodles in any remaining chicken broth mixed with water; drain well and stir into chicken mixture. Turn into 2 3-quart rectangular casseroles and refrigerate until ready to bake. Bake at 350 degrees until bubbly and heated through. Leftovers may be frozen. Serves 10.

NOTE: For best results, do not make any substitutions or add anything; follow recipe exactly, except that slightly less chicken may be used, as desired.

Virginia Golding (Mrs. John G.)

CHICKEN TETRAZZINI

1 hen, boiled and cut into bite-size pieces
1 7-oz. pkg. spaghetti
1 large onion, diced
1 green pepper, diced
1 cup celery, diced
1/4 cup butter
2 10-3/4 oz. cans cream of mushroom soup
grated cheese (about 2 cups)
1/2 to 1 cup slivered almonds

Cook spaghetti in chicken stock (remove and save 1/2 cup of the stock). Saute onion, green pepper and celery in butter until soft. Grease the bottom of a 2-1/2 quart casserole. Cover with half of the chicken and half of the onion/celery mixture. Salt this to taste and sprinkle 1/4 cup of chicken stock over mixture, then one can of mushroom soup. Make another layer using the remainder of the chicken, cooked spaghetti, vegetable mixture, stock and soup. Top with grated cheese and almonds. Bake, covered, at 375 degrees for 30 to 45 minutes. Serves 8. Can make ahead and refrigerate.

La McLeod (Mrs. J.A.)

CHICKEN OR TURKEY AND HAM TETRAZZINI

8 oz. can mushroom stems and pieces
2/3 cup chopped onion
1/2 cup butter
1/3 cup flour
3-1/2 cups chicken broth
1 cup half-and-half
2 cups diced chicken or turkey
2 cups diced cooked ham (good quality)
1/2 cup dry vermouth
1 tsp. salt
1/8 tsp. pepper
1 cup grated Parmesan cheese
1 lb. thin spaghetti
paprika

Drain mushrooms, saving liquid. Saute onion in butter in saucepan until onion is soft, not brown. Add mushrooms. Remove from heat; stir in flour. Gradually add chicken broth, cream and mushroom liquid. Cook and stir until thickened. Remove from heat; add chicken or turkey, ham, vermouth, salt, pepper and cheese.

Cook spaghetti as directed on package. Combine spaghetti and chicken mixture in 4 to 5 quart baking dish. Top with grated Parmesan cheese and paprika. Bake 30 to 40 minutes at 375 degrees until bubbling. Serves 10 to 12 — maybe more.

Beverly Hance (Mrs. James)

VARIATION:
Substitute 1/2 to 1 lb. bacon, cooked and cut up, for the ham.
Substitute 1 Tbsp. sherry for the vermouth.
Add 1/2 cup fresh chopped parsley.
Add poultry seasoning to taste.

Peggy Buchanan (Mrs. D. Douglas)

OLD ENGLISH CHICKEN PIE

2 small onions, chopped
3 to 4 stalks celery, cut on diagonal
1 chicken, or 1/2 turkey breast
8 oz. brick cheese (grated), divided
8 oz. Muenster cheese (grated), divided
1 pint medium cream sauce (see index)
1 9-inch deep-dish pie shell, baked

Cook chicken or use leftover turkey breast; pull apart in small pieces. Make a medium cream sauce seasoned with salt and pepper (1 pint). Add onions, celery and 1/2 cheese. Add chicken last. Put into baked deep-dish pie shell and top with rest of cheese. Bake 20 minutes at 400 degrees. Serves 6.

Becky Rencher (Mrs. Edwin R., Jr.)

YUMMY CHICKEN PIE

2 chicken fryers, cooked, deboned, cut into bite-size pieces
3 pie shells
1 box pie crust mix
1 egg yolk
1 can cream of celery soup
1/2 can chicken broth
1/2 cup chopped onion
salt and pepper

Cook fryers, skin and debone. Cut in medium pieces; divide into 3 portions and place a portion in each shell. Sprinkle onions on top of chicken; salt and pepper well. Mix soup and broth, pour over chicken.
Prepare crust on top of pie, prick with fork. Beat egg yolk and brush tops of pies. Makes 3 pies. Can freeze before baking.

Lea Bennett (Mrs. G.G.)

VARIATION:

1 chicken, cooked and deboned, cut into bite-size pieces
1-3/4 to 2 cups broth
1 can cream of celery soup
1 stick butter, softened
1 cup self-rising flour
3/4 cup milk
salt and pepper to taste

Place chicken pieces in a 13 x 9 pyrex dish; pour combined broth and soup on top. Sprinkle with salt and pepper. Mix softened butter, flour and milk together and pour over previous layer. Bake at 350 degrees for 40 minutes until crust is brown. Serves 6.

CHICKEN SOUFFLE

8 slices Pepperidge Farm bread,
    crust removed
4 cups cooked chicken, chopped
mayonnaise
10 slices Cheddar cheese
4 eggs
2 cups milk
1/2 tsp. salt
small jar pimiento, chopped
1 can mushroom soup
1 can celery soup
1 small can mushrooms
1 can water chestnuts, sliced
bread crumbs or rice krispies

Line buttered 3-quart baking dish with bread. Cover with chopped chicken. Cover chicken with a thin layer of mayonnaise. Add layer of thin-sliced Cheddar cheese. Beat together eggs, milk and salt. Pour over casserole ingredients and mash down lightly with back of spoon. Combine soups and pimientos. Add mushrooms and water chestnuts. Spread over top. Cover with foil and refrigerate overnight. Remove from refrigerator and let come to room temperature, or place on cookie sheet in oven (keeps the dish from cracking). Bake 1 to 1-1/4 hours at 325 degrees. Sprinkle with crumbs or rice krispies 15 minutes before done. Serves 8 to 10.

Charlotte Arrendel (Mrs. C.W.)

CREAMED CHICKEN AND SHRIMP
Nice company dish for a small group

2 sticks butter
1 bunch spring onions (4), chop-
    ped with some green tops
1 clove garlic, minced
1/2 to 1 lb. fresh mushrooms,
    sliced
8 Tbsp. flour
2 cups chicken broth
2 cups half-and-half
1/2 cup fresh parsley,
    finely chopped, OR
8 tsp. dried parsley
2 cups cooked, cubed chicken
    (see index)
2 lbs. cooked shrimp
salt and pepper to taste
rice or pastry shells, OR
toast points or Holland rusks
paprika

In very large skillet or electric fry pan melt butter; add onions, garlic and mushrooms and cook just until soft. Stir in flour, chicken broth and half-and-half. Stir constantly, adjusting heat if necessary, until thickened. Add parsley, chicken, shrimp, and salt and pepper to taste. Serve on rice, baked pastry shells, toast points or Holland rusks. Sprinkle with paprika. Serves 12.

Ellen Knott (Mrs. B.F.)

CHICKEN-CHEESE WHEEL

This is a great hors d'oeuvre or light meal. Very filling.
Leftovers are good for lunches!

CRUST:
1 pkg. dry yeast
2/3 cup warm water
2 to 2-1/2 cups plain flour
1/2 tsp. sugar
1/2 tsp. salt
2 Tbsp. oil

FILLING:
2 beaten eggs
2 cups shredded Swiss cheese
   (8 oz.)
2 cups chopped, cooked chicken
   (may use canned)
1/4 cup dry parsley
2 Tbsp. chopped green
   chili peppers, or more
1/4 tsp. paprika
1/8 tsp. onion powder (optional)

GLAZE:
1 beaten egg
1 Tbsp. water
1 tsp. poppy seeds

Soften yeast in water. Sift together 1 cup of flour, the sugar and salt. Beat in yeast and oil. Stir enough of remaining flour in to make moderately stiff dough. Turn out onto floured surface and knead 5 to 8 minutes or until smooth and elastic. Place in greased bowl, turning dough over once to grease both surfaces. Cover and let rise until double — approximately 1 hour. (I place my dough in cold oven along with a large pan of hot water underneath the dough.) Punch dough down. Divide in half. Cover and let rest for 10 minutes. Roll each portion onto a floured surface to a 13-inch circle. Place one circle on greased pizza pan.

FILLING:
Combine all ingredients for filling and spread over dough. Place remaining dough over top. Trim and flute edges. Prick top with fork several times. Cover lightly with foil and bake in preheated 400 degree oven for 55 minutes.

Remove from oven and top with mixture of egg, water and poppy seeds. Return to oven and bake *uncovered* 15 to 20 minutes longer. Cool and cut in wedges. Yum! Yum! Serves 8 to 10.

Linda Rodman (Mrs. M.L.)

CHICKEN-SHRIMP FLORENTINE

4 Tbsp. butter, divided
4 chicken breasts, skinned
1/2 lb. shrimp, peeled
   and deveined
1/2 to 1 cup white wine
salt, pepper, garlic powder
2 pkgs. frozen chopped spinach
1 8-oz. pkg. cream cheese
2 Tbsp. butter
2 Tbsp. Parmesan cheese
1 can mushroom soup
1 can celery soup
1/2 tsp. Italian seasoning
   or oregano
pan drippings from broiling
   chicken
1/2 cup seasoned bread crumbs,
   or a mixture of crumbs and
   Parmesan cheese

Sprinkle chicken with salt, pepper and garlic powder. Place in baking pan. Dot with 2 Tbsp. butter and pour generous amount of wine over all. Broil in oven until done. About 5 minutes before removing chicken, add shrimp to pan. Remove from oven and debone chicken when cooled. Reserve pan juices.

Boil spinach according to package directions. Drain thoroughly. Put 2 Tbsp. butter and cream cheese in saucepan and cook on low heat until melted. Remove from heat and add spinach and Parmesan cheese.

Grease 2-quart round casserole dish. Spread spinach mixture over bottom; then top with the chicken (cut into bite-size pieces).

Mix soups, seasonings and pan drippings from chicken and blend over low heat. Pour over casserole. You may refrigerate at this point if desired.

Preheat oven to 350 degrees and top casserole with bread crumbs. Bake for about 20 minutes or until bubbly. Serves 4 to 6.

NOTE: To serve 6 to 8, add 1 or 2 more chicken breasts.

Barbara B. Vereen
The Riverside Cookbook

DABNEY'S BRUNSWICK STEW

1 whole chicken fryer
3 lbs. lean pork, Boston butt or
   shoulder
2 1-lb. cans tomatoes
2 1-lb. cans cream-style corn
1 cup regular-style catsup
Tabasco and Worcestershire sauce
   to taste
3 Tbsp. brown sugar
juice of 3 lemons
1 large onion, chopped
2 1-lb. cans shoe peg corn

Place meats in heavy container. Pour in water to have meats covered only half way up. Simmer until tender. Save stock. Pull and cut meat from bones and put through coarse blade of food grinder. Return meat to cooking container; add stock and other ingredients except shoe peg corn. Cook about 3 hours, stirring often. Add shoe peg corn and cook 30 minutes more. Yield: 1-1/2 to 2 gallons.

NOTE: I use my 8-quart crock pot.

Teny Sugg (Mrs. W.C.)

HOT BROWNS

4 or 5 slices of bread, toasted
(may be cubed first)
2 cups cooked chicken or turkey
chunks (or slices to cover
toast)
mushrooms (optional)
tomato slices (optional)
fried bacon (optional)

CHEESE SAUCE:
1 cup milk
2 Tbsp. butter or margarine
2 Tbsp. flour
1/4 tsp. salt
1/2 tsp. Worcestershire sauce
dash dry mustard
1 cup grated sharp Cheddar cheese

In oven-safe individual dishes or plates, place toasted bread. Cover with chicken or turkey and then cover with cheese sauce. One or more of the optional additions can be added before or after the cheese sauce.

CHEESE SAUCE:
Melt butter in top of double boiler. Add flour and salt. Add milk, and stir constantly until thickened. Stir in Worcestershire sauce, mustard and cheese and heat until cheese is melted. After cheese sauce has been added, place dishes in 300 to 425 degree oven and heat until bubbly. Can be held in oven, depending on temperature used.

NOTE: To make Welsh Rarebit, use cheese sauce, but substitute 1/4 cup beer for 1/4 cup of the milk.

The Committee

BAKED CHICKEN ALMOND SANDWICHES

1 can mushroom soup
3/4 cup milk, divided
2 Tbsp. minced onions
1 can water chestnuts, sliced
1 small jar pimientos, chopped
2 heaping cups cooked, chopped
chicken
salt, pepper, paprika to taste
3 Tbsp. flour
16 slices Pepperidge Farm bread,
crusts trimmed
4 eggs, beaten
5 Tbsp. milk
1 large bag potato chips
1 cup sliced almonds,
more if desired

Mix first 6 ingredients plus seasonings to taste with 1/2 cup milk. Mix flour with 1/4 cup milk; stir into chicken mixture. Cook until thick. Place 8 slices of bread in 13 x 9 inch casserole. Cover with chicken mixture. Place remaining bread on top. Refrigerate overnight. Cut sandwiches in half. Dip in beaten egg mixed with 5 tablespoons milk. Roll in crushed potato chips. Place on cookie sheet. Sprinkle with sliced almonds. Bake at 350 degrees for 30 minutes. Makes 8 sandwiches.
NOTE: May also wrap in foil and freeze. While frozen, dip in egg mix, then in crushed potato chips. Bake at 325 for 45 minutes. May serve with a well-seasoned cream sauce.

Ellen Knott (Mrs. B.F.)

BARBECUE CHICKEN

2 chicken fryers, cut up, or 8
    quarters
1 stick butter or margarine
1/2 pint cider vinegar
1 9 oz. jar prepared mustard
2 Tbsp. Worcestershire sauce
1 Tbsp. salt
1 Tbsp. pepper
1 Tbsp. red pepper

Wash chicken, pat dry with paper towels. Melt butter in vinegar in large pot. Add remaining ingredients, except chicken. Dip chicken pieces in sauce; cook on grill. Brush chicken frequently with remaining sauce. Cook until tender — about 1 hour. Quarters may take a little longer. Serves 6 to 8.

NOTE:
If you have a microwave oven, you can partially cook the chicken before finishing it on the grill.

Donna Hanna (Mrs. R.T.)

BARBECUED CHICKEN

1 3-to-3-1/2 lb. ready-to-cook-
    frying chicken
oil for browning
1 medium onion
2 Tbsp. Mazola oil
2 Tbsp. vinegar
2 Tbsp. brown sugar
1/4 cup lemon juice
1 cup catsup
3 Tbsp. Worcestershire sauce
1/2 Tbsp. prepared mustard
1 cup water
1/2 cup chopped celery
salt

Brown chicken in hot oil as you would in frying chicken, but just to brown. Then brown onions in 2 Tbsp. Mazola oil; add remaining ingredients and simmer for 30 minutes. Pour over chicken. Bake uncovered in slow oven (325 degrees) for 1 hour. Serves 6.

Tiffany Rankin (Mrs. Wilton)

SQUINT'S CHARCOAL CHICKEN

1 stick margarine
1 tsp. Worcestershire sauce
juice from 3 lemons, OR
6 Tbsp. concentrated lemon juice
1/2 tsp. hot sauce, Tabasco or
    Texas Pete
1/2 cup water
1/4 cup brown sugar
8 chicken quarters

Combine sauce ingredients in saucepan and heat on low. Brown both sides of chicken pieces on grill (skin side up first). This takes about 15 minutes a side over low heat. Baste with sauce and turn every 15 minutes for an hour or longer if necessary. Fire should be low, not flaming.

John G. Thomas

SMOKED TURKEY ON COVERED GRILL

We smoke all of our holiday turkeys outside.

12-pound turkey, thawed,
 giblets removed
1/2 cup salad oil
1/2 cup salt
1 cup vinegar
1/4 cup pepper
2 Tbsp. dried parsley

Rinse turkey with water and pat dry. Combine salad oil and salt and put on bird, allowing 1/3 for cavity. Build indirect fire (coals on one side, meat on the other). Use drip pan under rack underneath turkey. When coals are ready, put turkey in, close cover and adjust vents. For even browning, change position of bird once or twice. After 1 hour, baste with vinegar, pepper and parsley mixture (use barbecue brush). For moistness, fill a small tin can with water and put on rack with turkey. Since charcoal fires vary, test for doneness by wiggling legs. Average time is 4 to 5 hours for a 12-pound bird. Let cool 1/2 hour before slicing. Meat will be pinkish which is the color of smoked meat. Great for sandwiches, too.

Shirley Snead (Mrs. H.T.)

ROAST GOOSE WITH CHESTNUT STUFFING

One frozen goose
salt
pepper
2 cups boiling watter

STUFFING:
1/2 Tbsp. finely chopped shallot
3 Tbsp. butter
1/4 lb. sausage
12 mushrooms, finely chopped
1 cup chestnut puree
1/3 cup stale bread crumbs
1/2 Tbsp. finely chopped parsley
1/2 tsp. salt and pepper

Clean goose and stuff with chestnut stuffing. Truss and pour boiling water over bird. Sprinkle with salt and pepper. Place breast up on rack in shallow roasting pan and cover. Roast at 325 degrees about 25 to 30 minutes per pound. Prick legs to release fat. To brown, remove cover for last 15 minutes.

STUFFING: Cook shallot with butter 5 minutes, add sausage and cook 2 minutes. Then add mushrooms, chestnut puree, parsley and salt and pepper. Heat to boiling point. Remove from heat; add bread crumbs. Cool before stuffing goose.

Betty Holland (Mrs. Calvin)

ROAST TURKEY

*1 fresh, 20-lb. turkey, not self-
     basting*

PASTE:
2 Tbsp. salt
1 Tbsp. pepper
2 Tbsp. garlic salt
4 Tbsp. paprika
3/4 Tbsp. poultry seasoning
hot water

STUFFING:
1-1/2 lbs. Ritz crackers, crushed
2 to 3 cups celery, chopped
2 to 3 onions, chopped
2 lbs. mushrooms, sliced
1 carrot, peeled and grated
2 eggs
some cranberries (optional)
salt and freshly-ground pepper
2 sticks butter
1 Tbsp. finely-chopped parsley
*1 can water chestnuts,
     finely chopped*

BASTING LIQUID:
1 cup water
1 cup white wine
1 stick butter, melted

The day before, clean turkey well with water and paper towels. Combine paste ingredients in small bowl. Add enough hot water to make a very thick paste. Rub this paste all over the turkey, inside and out. Cover pasted turkey with foil and place in refrigerator overnight. The next morning, prepare stuffing.

In a large skillet melt 1/2 stick of butter and saute onions and celery, adding more butter if needed. Saute until vegetables are tender but not brown — about 8 minutes. Place crushed crackers in large bowl and add sauteed onions and celery along with any remaining butter in skillet. Mix together; add remaining stuffing ingredients. Mix well and stuff turkey, including neck cavity. (Put remainder of stuffing in casserole to be cooked separately.) Preheat oven to 325 degrees. Place turkey in roasting pan. Combine basting ingredients and pour all of the mixture over the turkey. Cover turkey loosely with foil and roast for 7 hours or until juices run clear when thigh is pricked with a fork. Baste during roasting time with juices in bottom of pan. Pour juice in bowl for gravy, as is.

Tonia Fuller (Mrs. Edwin)

TURKEY AND STUFFING

One 15-lb. fresh turkey

STUFFING:
1 lb. margarine
1 large onion, chopped
1 cup celery, chopped
1 apple, grated
1 cup ground chestnuts (optional)
1 tsp. prepared mustard
salt and pepper to taste
3 boxes croutons (12 cups)
1 tsp. rosemary, crushed
1 tsp. savory, crushed
1/2 tsp. sage, or
   1 tsp. poultry seasoning
1 egg
salad oil or melted shortening
1/3 cup red currant jelly
1 Tbsp. butter

Preheat oven to 450 degrees. Melt one pound margarine and add onion, celery, apple, chestnuts, mustard, salt and pepper, croutons, rosemary, savory and sage. Saute until all the ingredients are well mixed. Cool and add well-beaten egg.

Place stuffing in turkey in pan in oven. Immediately reduce heat to 325 degrees. Cook 20 minutes per pound. Cover breast of turkey with cheesecloth soaked in unsalted oil or melted butter. One hour before cooking time is over, glaze with currant jelly mixed with 1 Tbsp. butter.

Stella Thurston (Mrs. Doc J.)

CORNISH HENS

Serve with a wild rice casserole and a cranberry salad.

6 Cornish hens, about 1-1/4 lb.
   each
3/4 cup butter
3/4 cup dry white wine
3 Tbsp. dried tarragon, divided
6 peeled cloves garlic
salt and pepper
garlic salt
1 bunch watercress, if available

Preheat oven to 450 degrees. Make sauce of butter, wine and 1 Tbsp. tarragon. Inside each hen place 1 clove garlic, 1 tsp. dried tarragon, 1/4 tsp. salt, 1/8 tsp. pepper. Sprinkle liberally with garlic salt. Roast at 450 degrees in open pan without rack. Baste with sauce. Birds should be done in 35 to 45 minutes — when brown and tender. Pour dripping over birds when serving. Serves 6.

Virginia Golding (Mrs. John G.)

QUAIL ON THE GRILL
Must pick up and eat with fingers

12 quail (or 2 quail per person)
1-1/2 quarts water
6 oz. melted butter
6 oz. teriyaki sauce
1 tsp. garlic powder
1 tsp. onion powder
1 tsp. salt
1 tsp. pepper

Drop frozen quail into boiling water seasoned with garlic powder, onion powder, salt and pepper. Reduce heat and cook for 15-20 minutes. Remove from heat and let sit until 1 hour before suppertime. Make sauce of butter and teriyaki sauce. Drain birds and let sit in sauce for about 1 hour, turning often. Grill over charcoal fire about 5 to 6 minutes, turning once so the birds brown evenly. Serves 6. Good with brown or wild rice.

Shirley Snead (Mrs. Henry T.)

QUAIL IN RED WINE SAUCE
A delicious way to prepare the game your hunter brings home

6 quail
brandy
flour
6 Tbsp. butter
2 cups mushrooms
1/4 cup melted butter
1 cup consomme
1 cup red wine
1 stalk celery, quartered
salt and pepper to taste
juice of two oranges

Rub quail with brandy and flour. Saute in butter for 10 minutes. Saute mushrooms; add mushrooms to quail. Add wine, consomme, celery, salt and pepper. Cover and simmer 30 minutes. Stir in orange juice before serving. Six servings.

Sandy Hamilton (Mrs. C.E.)

Seafood

CIOPPINO
Seafood Stew

1 lb. fish, fresh or frozen
1/2 lb. shrimp, fresh or frozen
5 oz. whole clams, canned or fresh
1 cup onions, chopped
1 cup green pepper, chopped
2 garlic cloves, minced
1/4 cup olive oil
1-lb. 12-oz. can tomatoes (28 oz.)
1 15-oz. can tomato puree
1 cup red table wine
1-1/2 tsp. salt
1/2 tsp. basil, crumbled
1/4 tsp. pepper
1/4 cup chopped parsley

Thaw fish and cut into serving pieces. Drain clams, reserving liquid. Saute onion, green pepper and garlic in olive oil in large kettle until soft but not browned. Add reserved clam juice, tomato puree, wine, salt, basil and pepper. Cover and simmer 10 minutes. Add fish and shrimp. Cover and simmer 20 minutes. Add drained clams and parsley. Heat. Serve in deep bowls with crusty bread. Serves 6 to 8.

Judy Ranson (Mrs. R.C.)

CASSEROLE SAINT JACQUES
Expensive, but a marvelous company dish

2 lbs. fresh scallops
1 cup dry white wine
1 small onion, sliced
1 Tbsp. snipped parsley
2 tsp. lemon juice
1/2 tsp. salt
4 Tbsp. butter
6 Tbsp. all-purpose flour
2 cups half-and-half
4 oz. Gruyere cheese (grated)
dash black pepper
1 lb. fresh crab meat (regular)
8 oz. cooked shrimp
1 4-oz. can sliced mushrooms, drained
1-1/2 cups soft bread crumbs
1 Tbsp. melted butter

Bring the first 6 ingredients to boiling in a saucepan. Simmer for 5 minutes. *Drain, reserving 1 cup liquid.* Make a white sauce with the next 3 ingredients and add the 1 cup reserved liquid. Cook over medium heat until it thickens. Remove from heat and add cheese and pepper. Pick crab meat well and remove any bits of shell; add crab meat to sauce. Add shrimp and mushrooms. Spoon into 9x13 baking dish and cover with buttered bread crumbs. Bake at 350 degrees for 25-30 minutes. Serves 6 to 8.

Kay D. Roberson (Mrs. G. Don)

CRAB MEAT-SHRIMP CASSEROLE

This is a very favorite recipe to serve special guests.

1 lb. crab meat, fresh backfin
    (picked over)
1/2 lb. cleaned, cooked shrimp
    (cook only slightly)
2 small cans sliced mushrooms
2 small onions, sliced
1 cup soft bread crumbs
4 Tbsp. flour
4 Tbsp. butter
juice of 1/2 lemon (sprinkled over
    seafood)
coffee cream to supplement mush-
    room liquid to make 2-1/2
    cups
4 Tbsp. sherry

Simmer mushrooms and onions in mushroom liquid about 15 minutes, drain and reserve liquid. Melt butter, add flour, blend well; add the 2-1/2 cups liquid (cream and mushroom liquid combined). Stir and cook over low heat until smooth and thickened. Add mushrooms, onions, bread crumbs and sherry to sauce. Add seafood and blend. Turn into buttered flat 2-qt. casserole. Sprinkle with toasted bread crumbs and dot with butter. Bake in 350 degree oven for 25 to 30 minutes. Can be prepared ahead. Can be frozen. Serves 6.

Virginia Golding (Mrs. John G.)

CRAB-SHRIMP CASSEROLE

Easy, make-ahead casserole

1 can cream of mushroom soup
1 can cream of celery soup
1 pt. sour cream
1 can French-fried onion rings
2 cans crab meat
1 lb. shelled, cooked shrimp
2 rounded Tbsp. grated Parmesan
    cheese
slivered almonds

Combine first 6 ingredients and pour into 2-qt. casserole. Sprinkle with cheese and slivered almonds. Bake at 300 degrees for 1 hour. Can be made ahead of time. Serves 4-6.

Dale O. Yaged (Mrs. David)

If it is to be fried, fish should be brushed with lemon rind or juice. This protects the natural flavor and cuts the fat needed for frying.

SEAFOOD LASAGNA

8 lasagna noodles
1 cup chopped onions
2 Tbsp. butter or margarine
1 (8 oz.) cream cheese, softened
1-1/2 cup cream-style cottage
    cheese
1 beaten egg
1 tsp. dried basil, crushed
1/2 tsp. salt
pepper
2 cans condensed cream of mush-
    room soup
1/3 cup milk
1/3 cup dry white wine
1 to 1-1/2 lbs. cooked shrimp
1 (7-1/2 oz.) can crab, drained,
    flaked
1/4 cup grated Parmesan cheese
1/2 cup (2 oz.) grated sharp cheese

Cook lasagna noodles according to package directions; drain. Arrange 4 noodles in bottom of greased 9x13 inch baking dish. Cook onions in butter until tender; blend in cream cheese. Stir in cottage cheese, egg, basil, salt and pepper. Spread half on top of noodles. Combine soup, milk and wine. Stir in shrimp (halved) and crab; spread half over cottage cheese layer. Repeat layers. Sprinkle with Parmesan cheese. Bake uncovered in 350 degree oven for 40 minutes. Top with sharp cheese and bake for another 5 minutes. Let stand 15 minutes before serving. Serves 8-10. (I have made this lasagna using 2 lbs. shrimp and eliminating the crab.)

Georgia Miller (Mrs. George)

SEAFOOD STRATA

8 slices white bread
1 cup mayonnaise
1 cup chopped onion
1 cup chopped celery
1 cup chopped green pepper
salt and pepper to taste
1 lb. crab meat (can be canned)
1 can shrimp, drained
1 can tuna, drained
4 eggs
3 cups milk
1 can mushroom soup
grated Cheddar cheese

Spread crumbs from 4 slices of bread in bottom of greased baking dish. Mix all ingredients up to egg and spread over bread. Cover with 4 slices of bread. Mix eggs and milk well. Pour over all. Bake at 325 degrees for 15 minutes. Remove. Spoon soup over top. Sprinkle with cheese. Bake 45 minutes longer.

Ada Offerdahl (Mrs. John)

SEAFOOD SUPREME

1/2 cup butter
1/2 cup chopped onion
1/2 cup chopped celery
1/2 cup chopped green pepper
2/3 cup flour
1/2 tsp. salt
1/2 tsp. garlic salt
dash Tabasco sauce
dash cayenne pepper
1 cup milk
1 cup half-and-half
1 10-oz. can frozen cream of
    shrimp soup, or Campbell's
    shrimp soup
1/2 lb. fresh crab meat, picked, or
1 can (7-3/4 oz.) crab meat,
    drained and picked
1/3 lb. fresh shrimp, cooked and
    cut in small pieces, or 1 can
    (4-1/2 oz.) tiny shrimp, rinsed
    and drained
1 can (5 oz.) water chestnuts,
    drained and sliced
1 can (4 oz.) mushroom pieces,
    undrained
TOPPING:
3 Tbsp. butter, melted
1/2 cup grated Cheddar cheese
3/4 cup seasoned Italian bread
    crumbs
paprika

Melt butter and add onion, celery and green pepper. Saute until just tender. Stir in flour, salt, garlic salt, Tabasco sauce and cayenne pepper. Add milk and cook until thick, stirring constantly. Stir in soup and mix well. Add remaining ingredients and pour into large greased casserole or 8 greased seafood shells or ramekins. Cook with topping at 350 degrees for 30 minutes for casserole or 20 minutes for ramekins, or until bubbly.

TOPPING: Combine ingredients and sprinkle on top of casserole. Sprinkle with paprika.

Ellen Knott (Mrs. B.F.)

WILD RICE SEAFOOD CASSEROLE
Nice for a crowd

2 cups cooked long-grain white
rice
2 cups cooked wild rice
2 cans (10-3/4 oz.) cream of
shrimp soup (Campbell's)
3/4 cup whole milk
1/4 tsp. nutmeg
1 tsp. seasoned salt
1/8 tsp. cayenne pepper
1 small green pepper, minced
1 small onion, minced
1 cup diced celery
1 4-oz. can sliced mushrooms,
drained
1 5-oz. can water chestnuts,
drained and sliced
1 can (7-1/2 oz.) crab meat
2 lbs. cooked whole shrimp
2 Tbsp. butter

Combine the two rices after cooking. Saute lightly the green pepper, onion, celery and mushrooms in butter. Blend soup with milk. Add rice, seasonings, sauteed vegetables, water chestnuts, shrimp and crab. Pour mixture into buttered casserole dish. Sprinkle with paprika. Bake at 350 degrees for 30 minutes or until bubbly. Can be made ahead. Serves 10 generously.

La McLeod (Mrs. J.A.)

STUFFED CLAM SHELLS
Really delicious!

1 cup crushed Ritz crackers
1-1/2 cups minced clams, including liquid
2 tsp. grated Parmesan cheese
1/4 stick melted butter or
margarine
1 small grated onion
lots of garlic powder

Mix by hand and stuff into clam shells. Can freeze before or after cooking. Bake for 20 mintues at 350 degrees.
Note: Doubles or triples nicely. Can be used as an appetizer or an entree.

Pat Nesbit (Mrs. W.M.)

CHESAPEAKE CRAB CAKES

1 lb. backfin crab meat, well
  picked
1/2 cup chopped celery
1/2 cup chopped onion
1 Tbsp. bacon grease
2 Tbsp. chopped fresh parsley
1/3 cup mayonnaise
1/2 tsp. Old Bay Seasoning
1/2 tsp. Worcestershire sauce
1/8 tsp. Tabasco
3 Tbsp. melted butter
salt and pepper to taste
2 to 3 slices bread, toasted
1 Tbsp. oil

Saute celery and onion in 1 Tbsp. bacon grease. Combine crab meat with next 7 ingredients; add celery and onions. Mix thoroughly. Make crumbs of toasted bread slices; add to crab meat mixture, making sure there are enough crumbs to hold mixture together. Form into patties and fry at medium heat in 1 Tbsp. cooking oil. Serves 6 to 8.

Kathleen Boyce (Mrs. R.N.)

CRAB MEAT CORN CASSEROLE

5 Tbsp. butter
5 Tbsp. flour
1 tsp. salt
1/2 tsp. pepper
2-1/2 cups half-and-half
2 eggs, well beaten
4 or 5 drops Tabasco sauce
1/2 chopped medium-sized onion
1 cup whole kernel corn (Niblets),
  drained
2 cups crab meat (Harris)
1 cup buttered bread crumbs

Make rich cream sauce with first 5 ingredients. Remove from heat. Add sauce to eggs. Add Tabasco sauce, onions, corn and crab meat. Put into buttered casserole. Cover with buttered bread crumbs. Bake 50 to 60 minutes at 325 degrees.

Stephany Alphin (Mrs. R.L.)

CRAB MEAT CASSEROLE
So easy and so good!

1 lb. fresh crab meat
6 Tbsp. melted butter or mar-
    garine
2 Tbsp. butter
1 Tbsp. prepared mustard
2 eggs, beaten
1 Tbsp. Worcestershire sauce
1/4 cup green pepper, chopped
1 pt. sour cream
bread crumbs

Saute green pepper in 2 Tbsp. margarine or butter. Combine crab meat, eggs, melted butter, Worcestershire sauce, mustard, sour cream and green pepper. Pour into 1-1/2 qt. buttered casserole. Cover with bread crumbs and bake for approximately 30-40 minutes at 350 degrees or until light and fluffy. Serves 4.

Sally Gaddy (Mrs. C.E.)

CRAB CASSEROLE
Easy but elegant

6 oz. crab meat, frozen or canned,
    rinsed
2 hard-boiled eggs, chopped
4 oz. water chestnuts, sliced
4 slices bread, broken
1 cup coffee cream, or half-and-
    half
1 cup mayonnaise
salt and pepper to taste
Worcestershire sauce to taste
1 3-oz. can French-fried onions
    (we prefer Durkee)

In a large bowl mix together all ingredients except onion rings. Place in a 9x13 inch casserole. Bake in a preheated 325 degree oven for 25 minutes or until hot and bubbly. Add onion rings, and bake another 5 minutes, or until onion rings are golden brown. Serves 4 to 6.

Catherine Willis (Mrs. Bart)

To enhance the flavor, add lemon or lime juice to white sauce for fish.

CRAB SUPPER PIE

1 cup shredded Swiss cheese (4 oz.)
1 unbaked 9-inch pie shell
1 (7-1/2 oz.) can crab meat,
    drained and flaked
2 green onions, sliced
3 beaten eggs
1 cup half-and-half cream
1/2 tsp. salt
1/2 tsp. grated lemon peel
1/4 tsp. dry mustard
dash mace
1/4 cup sliced almonds

Sprinkle cheese evenly over bottom of pie shell. Top with crab meat. Sprinkle with onion. Combine remaining ingredients. Pour over crab meat. Top with almonds. Bake at 325 degrees for 45 minutes or until set. Let stand 10 minutes before serving. Serves 6.

Anne Mooney (Mrs. William)

SEAFOOD PIE

1 can crab meat, shrimp or tuna
    (I use crab)
1 cup chopped celery
2 Tbsp. green pepper, chopped
1/4 tsp. salt
2 Tbsp. grated onion
2 eggs, beaten
1 cup mayonnaise
1 Tbsp. lemon juice
1/2 cup toasted bread crumbs
1/2 cup shredded Cheddar cheese
1 unbaked pie shell

Combine all ingredients except 2 Tbsp. crumbs and cheese. Mix lightly and put into pie shell. Sprinkle with crumbs and cheese. Place on cookie sheet. Bake 25 minutes at 350 degrees or until firm. Serves 6.

Libby Morrison (Mrs. Jack)

"CHARLOTTE'S" CRAB-SPAGHETTI CASSEROLE

1/3 of 9 oz. box thin spaghetti
1 can condensed cream of mush-
room soup
1 can mushrooms, drained
(optional)
3 Tbsp. butter
1 cup milk
1/2 lb. Cheddar cheese, grated
1 lb. fresh crab meat (picked)
1/8 tsp. pepper
sherry to taste
Worcestershire to taste

Cook spaghetti in boiling water until tender. Drain. To prepare cheese sauce heat soup, stir until smooth, add butter, milk, 3/4 of the cheese, mushrooms, sherry and Worcestershire. Place in a greased pyrex casserole, and sprinkle remaining cheese on top. Bake at 400 degrees for 30 minutes. Serves 6.

Barby Goode (Mrs. David T.)

BAKED OYSTERS
Serve with tomato pudding and tossed salad.

2 Tbsp. butter
1 cup fresh white bread crumbs
made from about 3 slices of
French bread
1 tsp. finely-chopped garlic
2 Tbsp. finely-chopped fresh
parsley
2 dozen fresh oysters
3 Tbsp. freshly-grated imported
Parmesan cheese
2 Tbsp. butter, cut in tiny pieces

Preheat the oven to 450 degrees. Choose an ovenproof platter or shallow baking and serving dish that is just large enough to hold the oysters in one layer (about 8x10 inches). Butter the dish generously. In a heavy 8-inch skillet, melt 2 Tbsp. butter over moderate heat. When the foam subsides, add the fresh, white bread crumbs and the garlic, and toss them in the butter for 2 or 3 minutes, or until they are crisp and golden. Stir in the finely-chopped parsley. Spread about 2/3 cup of the bread-crumb mixture in the bottom of the buttered baking dish and arrange the oysters over it in one layer. Mix the rest of the bread crumbs with the grated cheese and spread on the oysters. Dot with bits of butter. Bake on the top shelf of oven for 12 to 15 minutes.

Gensie

OYSTER PIE
"We always serve this at Thanksgiving and Christmas."

1 stick butter
1 box Oysterette crackers
1 cup milk
1 egg
Worcestershire sauce
1 pint oysters (more if desired),
drained—reserve juice

Place a layer of crackers in bottom of 1-1/2 qt. pyrex bowl. Melt stick of butter and pour a little over crackers. Put some of the oysters on top of the crackers and repeat layers. Combine the egg, milk, Worcestershire sauce and juice from oysters. Pour over the oysters and bake at 400 degrees for 30 minutes. Serves 6 to 8.

Jane McColl (Mrs. H.L.)

OYSTER MUSHROOM PIE
Great dish to serve with the traditional Thanksgiving dinner

1 cup sliced mushrooms
1/3 cup butter
1/3 cup flour
2 cups milk
1/2 cup oyster juice
1 pint oysters
1/2 tsp. salt
1/8 tsp. pepper
dash nutmeg
1/2 tsp. celery salt
pastry or pie dough

Cook mushrooms in butter for 3 minutes. Stir in flour. When smoothly blended, gradually add milk and oyster juice. Bring to boiling point, stirring constantly, and cook until smooth. Add oysters and seasonings and turn into baking dish. Top with any pastry, cutting slits to allow for escape of steam. Bake in hot oven (450 degrees) for 15 or 20 minutes. Serves 4 to 6.
Note: More oysters and mushrooms may be used for thicker filling. I use one cup half-and-half and 1 cup milk.

Nancy Langston (Mrs. J.T.)

SCALLOPED OYSTERS

1 qt. oysters
4 slices bread
1/2 cup melted butter
1/2 tsp. salt
2 Tbsp. sherry (optional)
1 tsp. white pepper
4 Tbsp. cream
1 tsp. Worcestershire sauce
dash cayenne pepper
1/4 cup oyster liquid

Go over oysters carefully for pieces of shells. Drain, reserving 1/4 cup liquid. Toast bread and crumble (about 2 cups); toss bread crumbs in melted butter. Sprinkle a layer of crumbs in the bottom of a shallow, greased 9x9 inch baking dish. Add a layer of oysters, another layer of crumbs, another layer of oysters. Mix together the salt, sherry, pepper, cream, Worcestershire sauce, cayenne pepper and oyster liquid and pour over oysters. Add the rest of crumbs over top of casserole. Bake 30 minutes at 425 degrees. Serve hot. Serves 8.

Stella Thurston (Mrs. Doc J.)

MISS MARY'S SCALLOPED OYSTERS

A Christmas dinner favorite—nutmeg adds a delicate taste

3 (12 oz.) cans stewing-size oysters
saltines
salt, pepper and nutmeg
butter
milk

Grease a 9x13 inch baking dish. Put thin layer of crumbled saltines in the bottom. Top with layer of oysters (about 1-1/2 cans). Sprinkle oysters with salt, pepper and nutmeg. Top with lots of butter, then another thin layer of saltines; then oysters, salt, pepper, nutmeg and butter, and another layer of crackers. Pour milk over this until milk bubbles to the top. Top with paprika. Bake at 350 degrees until set and light brown crust forms—about 30-40 minutes. Serves 10.

Peggy Buchanan (Mrs. D. Douglas)

WILD RICE AND OYSTER CASSEROLE

2 cups wild rice (no substitute)
1/4 lb. melted butter
salt and pepper to taste
hot pepper sauce
4 dozen oysters (1 qt.)
1 can cream of chicken soup
1 cup light cream
1-1/2 Tbsp. onion powder
3/4 tsp. thyme
1-1/2 Tbsp. curry powder
1/4 cup hot water

Cook and drain rice according to directions on package. Add butter and toss the rice until thoroughly mixed. Place half the cooked rice in the bottom of a large shallow baking dish. Place a layer of well-drained raw oysters on top of rice. Season the oysters with salt and pepper and hot pepper sauce. Place rest of cooked rice on top of them. Heat cream of chicken soup in a saucepan. Add cream. In 1/4 cup hot water, dissolve onion powder, thyme and curry powder. Pour this mixture over oysters and rice. Bake for 45 minutes in a 300 degree oven. Garnish with parsley. Serves 10 to 12 as a side dish or 6 as an entree.

Gayanne Mraz

COQUILLE ST. JACQUES

"This is our house specialty and is easy to fix the morning before a dinner party. It is a gourmet's seafood delight!"

1 lb. scallops
2 Tbsp. minced onion
1 Tbsp. butter
1 Tbsp. lemon juice
3/4 tsp. salt
1/8 tsp. marjoram leaves
dash paprika
3/4 cup white wine
1/4 lb. fresh mushrooms,
   chopped (1-1/2 cups)
1/3 cup butter
1/4 cup flour
1 cup whipping cream
2 Tbsp. snipped parsley
1 Tbsp. butter
1/3 cup dry bread crumbs

Cut scallops, cube and wash. In medium saucepan, cook and stir onion in 1 Tbsp. butter until tender. Add scallops, lemon juice, salt, marjoram, paprika and wine. Simmer uncovered 10 minutes. Add mushrooms, simmer 2 minutes. Drain liquid from mixture and save. Melt 1/3 cup butter in saucepan over low heat. Blend in flour. Cook over low heat, stirring until smooth. Remove from heat. Stir in reserved liquid and cream. Heat to boiling, stirring constantly. Boil and stir 1 minute. Stir in parsley. Reserving 1/2 cup sauce in saucepan, pour remaining over scallop mixture. Heat through. Immediately spoon scallop mixture into 6 baking shells. Spread each with 1 Tbsp. reserved sauce. Melt 1 Tbsp. butter in small skillet. Add bread crumbs, stirring until brown. Place shells on cookie sheet. Set oven at broil or 550 degrees. Broil 5 inches from heat for 5 to 8 minutes or until brown and bubbly. Sprinkle with the bread crumbs before serving. Finis! Serves 6.

Maryann R. Berry (Mrs. W.P.)

WOOTEN'S SCALLOPS

1/2 lb. scallops per person
1 Tbsp. self-rising flour per half-
   pound of scallops
2/3 Tbsp. sherry per half-pound
   of scallops
dash garlic salt
dash salt
lemon juice

Wash scallops. Butter casserole dish. For each half pound of scallops used, add 1 Tbsp. flour and mix. Add sherry, garlic salt and salt. Butter generously and sprinkle with lemon juice. Bake at 350 degrees for 25 minutes.

Dickie Tyler (Mrs. J.D.)

SHRIMP CASSEROLE SUPREME

"From an old cook book"

1/2 lb. fresh mushrooms, sliced
2 Tbsp. butter
1 onion, chopped
2 or 3 fresh tomatoes, peeled and
    chopped
1/2 cup half-and-half cream
2 Tbsp. flour
salt, pepper, paprika
sherry
3 lbs. shrimp, cooked, peeled and
    deveined

Saute mushrooms in butter. Add onion and tomatoes and simmer for a few minutes. Mix cream with flour and add to saute mixture. Add salt, pepper, paprika and sherry to taste. Add shrimp. Pour into buttered casserole, cover with bread crumbs and dot with butter. Bake for 20 or 25 minutes at 350 degrees. Serves 8.

Mary Beth Collins (Mrs. Kenneth)
Elena Giblin (Mrs. Richard)

EASY SHRIMP CASSEROLE

1 can shrimp (more if desired)
1/2 cup chopped celery
1/2 cup green bell pepper,
    chopped
1/2 cup uncooked rice
1/2 cup water
1/2 cup mayonnaise
1 can mushroom soup
2 tsp. Worcestershire sauce
grated cheese
buttered crumbs

Mix all ingredients except cheese and crumbs; place in 2-qt. casserole with cover. Bake 30 minutes at 350 degrees. During last 5 minutes of cooking time, top with cheese and buttered crumbs. (May turn on broil for *just* a minute!) Serves 6.

Dottie Grier (Mrs. R.N.)

SHRIMP CASSEROLE

1 lb. New York cheese, grated
1 can tomato soup
2 cups cooked rice
2 lbs. cooked and cleaned shrimp
3/4 stick butter
1 cup celery, chopped
1 green pepper, chopped
1 medium onion, chopped
1 Tbsp. Worcestershire sauce

Saute celery, onions and pepper in butter. In a bowl mix rice, cheese, Worcestershire sauce and soup together. Add sauteed vegetables and shrimp. Put in a 9x13 casserole; bake at 350 degrees for 40 minutes. Serves 6.

Pam Houser (Mrs. E.E.)

SPECIAL SHRIMP CASSEROLE

A seafood dish with broccoli that is economical

1 cup medium-sized cooked
   shrimp (or more)
1 10 oz. pkg. frozen broccoli
   spears
1 10-3/4 oz. can condensed cream
   of mushroom soup
1/4 cup milk
sherry to taste
1/2 cup shredded Cheddar cheese
1 cup toasted bread crumbs
2 Tbsp. melted butter
   or margarine

Peel, devein and cut shrimp in halves. Cook broccoli according to package directions, until almost tender. Heat soup in saucepan with milk and sherry; stir until smooth. Stir in shrimp. Arrange layer of broccoli, soup mixture and cheese in a shallow baking dish. Sprinkle with bread crumbs and spoon melted butter over top. Bake at 350 degrees for 20-25 minutes. Serves 4.

Kathleen Golding Boyce (Mrs. R.N.)

SHRIMP CASSEROLE ELEGANTE

An elegant casserole to serve your guests

1/2 cup butter
1/2 cup green peppers, chopped
1/2 cup onions, chopped
1/2 cup celery, chopped
2/3 cup flour
1/2 tsp. salt
1/2 tsp. garlic salt
1/4 tsp. paprika
1/16 tsp. cayenne pepper
1 cup shrimp soup
2 cups milk
7 or 8 oz. crab meat
5 oz. water chestnuts, sliced
4 oz. mushrooms, undrained
1-1/2 lbs. shrimp

Melt butter and saute pepper, onions and celery. Mix together flour, salt, garlic salt, paprika and pepper. Stir in milk; add to butter sauce; stir until thick. Add 1 cup shrimp soup. In a separate bowl, combine shrimp, crab meat, water chestnuts and mushrooms. Put in bottom of casserole dish. Cover with sauce. Bake at 350 degrees for 30 to 35 minutes. Serves 6 to 8.

Linda Miller (Mrs. W.R.)

GOLDEN SHRIMP CASSEROLE

5 slices bread
6 Tbsp. melted butter, divided
1/2 cup sliced mushrooms
2 cups peeled, cooked, deveined
    shrimp
2 cups shredded processed
    American cheese
3 eggs, beaten
2 cups milk
1/2 tsp. salt
dash pepper
dash paprika

Cut bread into 1/2 inch cubes. Brown bread cubes in 4 Tbsp. butter. Remove from skillet and set aside. Cook mushrooms in 2 Tbsp. butter for about 10 minutes. In a buttered 1-1/2 qt. casserole alternate layers of bread cubes, mushrooms, shrimp and cheese. Combine eggs, milk and seasonings. Pour over layers. Place casserole dish in a pan of hot water and bake at 350 degrees for 1 hour and 15 minutes. Serves 6.

Nancy Wohlbruck (Mrs. Everett L.)

SHRIMP 'N' CHEESE CASSEROLE

6 slices day-old bread
1 lb. shrimp, cooked, shelled and
    deveined
1/2 lb. Cheddar cheese, diced
1/4 cup melted butter
3 eggs, beaten
1/4 tsp. dry mustard
salt, pepper and cayenne to taste
2 cups milk

Remove crusts and cube bread. In a buttered 2-1/2 qt. casserole, layer bread, shrimp and cheese, making at least 2 layers of each. Pour melted butter over. Combine eggs, mustard and seasonings to taste. Stir in milk, and pour over layers in casserole. Cook at 350 degrees for 1 hour. Serves 4 to 6.

B. J. Miller (Mrs. H.F., III)

SHRIMP AND CHICKEN CASSEROLE
A very nice combination

2 Tbsp. butter
1/2 cup chopped onions
3 Tbsp. flour
salt and pepper to taste
1 can (4 oz.) sliced mushrooms
1/4 cup sherry
half-and-half cream
2 cups cooked chicken breasts, cut
    in bite-sized pieces
2 cups cooked shrimp
1 can (5 oz.) water chestnuts,
    drained and sliced
1 small jar diced pimientos
1 cup grated Muenster cheese
1-1/2 cup bread crumbs
butter, paprika

Melt butter in large skillet. Add onions and cook just until softened. Stir in flour, salt and pepper. Drain the mushrooms, reserving liquid. Combine the sherry with the reserved mushroom liquid and add enough half-and-half cream to equal 1-1/2 cups liquid. Add to the flour and onions. Cook over medium heat, stirring constantly, until mixture is smooth. Add the chicken pieces, shrimp, mushrooms, water chestnuts and pimiento. Mix gently. Pour mixture into a well-buttered 2 qt. casserole. Top with the cheese and bread crumbs. Dot generously with butter. Sprinkle with paprika. Bake for 35 to 45 minutes in a 350 degree oven. Serves 4. Doubles or triples nicely.

The Committee

SHRIMP CREOLE

2 lbs. unpeeled raw shrimp
1 medium onion, chopped
1 small green pepper, chopped
1/2 cup celery, sliced
1/4 cup salad oil
2 Tbsp. flour
1 (16 oz.) can tomatoes
1 (16 oz.) can tomato sauce
1/8 tsp. garlic powder
1 bay leaf
1 tsp. salt
2 tsp. chili powder
3 dashes hot sauce
1 cup tomato juice

Cook shrimp and peel. Saute onions, green pepper and celery in oil. Add flour and stir until smooth. Add tomatoes (cut up), tomato sauce and seasonings. Simmer about 20 minutes; then add shrimp and tomato juice; simmer 20 to 30 minutes. Serve over rice. Serves 6.

Caren Hollenbeck (Mrs. J.I.)
Liz Medearis (Mrs. W.F., Jr.)

SHRIMP FLORENTINE

3 pkgs. (10 oz.) chopped spinach
3 lbs. cooked shrimp
1/2 cup butter
1/2 cup flour
3 cups whole milk
1 cup white wine
1/2 cup chopped scallions
salt, pepper, paprika
2 cups shredded Cheddar cheese

Drain and thaw spinach. Spread spinach in a 9x13 inch baking dish or 2 small 8-inch square dishes and top with shrimp. In saucepan, melt butter, stir in flour. Add milk, wine and scallions. Cook until sauce bubbles and thickens. Add salt and pepper to taste and paprika for color. Pour sauce over shrimp; sprinkle with cheese. Bake uncovered at 350 degrees for 35 minutes or until bubbly. Can make ahead. Can be frozen. If frozen, bake 1 hour or until bubbly. Serves 8.

La McLeod (Mrs. J.A.)

SHRIMP FROMAGE SHERRILL

A nice seafood casserole for a crowd

2-1/2 to 4 cups cooked shrimp
  (2 to 3 pounds), peeled and
  deveined
1 12-oz. pkg. shell macaroni
1/4 cup butter
3 cloves garlic, crushed
1 cup chopped mushrooms
3 Tbsp. chopped onion
1 can Campbell's cream of shrimp
  soup
1/2 cup milk
10 oz. shredded Cheddar cheese
4 oz. shredded Mozarella cheese
2 Tbsp. Parmesan cheese
1/2 cup sour cream
1/2 cup cottage cheese
paprika
bread crumbs

Heat the butter in a skillet. Add the garlic, chopped mushrooms and chopped onions. Cook until soft. Heat the soup with the milk. Stir in Cheddar, Mozarella, and Parmesan cheeses. Stir until blended. Mix sour cream and cottage cheese. Stir into soup-cheese mixture along with shrimp and macaroni which has been cooked according to package directions. Put into 5 qt. casserole. Top with bread crumbs and sprinkle with paprika. (If shrimp are large, cut them in half.) Bake, uncovered, 30 to 40 minutes at 350 degrees. Serves 12.

Ellen Knott (Mrs. B.F.)

SHRIMP ISOBEL

1 cup diced celery
1/2 cup diced green pepper
1/2 cup chopped onion
3 Tbsp. butter
1 can mushroom soup
2/3 cup milk
salt and pepper to taste
1-1/2 lbs. shrimp, cooked and
  deveined
1 tsp. lemon juice
1/2 cup chopped parsley
1/4 lb. sharp cheese, grated
toasted slivered almonds
cooked rice

Saute celery, onion, and pepper in butter just until tender. Add soup, milk, cooked shrimp, salt and pepper to taste. Bring to a boil. Reduce heat, add lemon juice and simmer. Add parsley and cheese. Stir. Garnish with toasted slivered almonds. Serve on rice. serves 6.

Max Ussery

SHRIMP AND MUSHROOM CASSEROLE

4 cans mushrooms, drained
1/2 cup butter
2 lbs. cooked shrimp
3/4 cup catsup
4 cups cooked rice
    (1 cup uncooked)
1 lb. grated sharp Cheddar cheese
1 (14-1/2 oz.) can evaporated milk
2 to 3 tsp. Worcestershire sauce
salt and pepper

Saute mushrooms in butter. Add cooked rice, cooked shrimp and cheese. Combine milk, catsup, Worcestershire, salt and pepper to taste. Add to shrimp mixture and pour into casserole. Bake 45 minutes at 350 degrees. Freezes well. If frozen, thaw before cooking. Serves 10-12. You may halve or double this recipe.

Nancy Langston (Mrs. J.T.)

SHRIMP NEWBERG

1 can frozen cream of shrimp
    soup, thawed
2/3 cup evaporated milk
2 oz. shredded Cheddar cheese
1/3 cup mayonnaise
1/4 cup dry sherry
4 oz. noodles, cooked
5 oz. or more boiled shrimp

Mix shrimp soup and evaporated milk; heat to boiling. Remove from heat and add cheese and mayonnaise. Stir until cheese melts. Blend in sherry, noodles and shrimp. Bake in lightly greased 1-1/2 qt. casserole 25 minutes at 350 degrees. Serves 4.

Kathy Howe

ORIENTAL SHRIMP WITH PINEAPPLE
Ideal buffet entree

4 (20 oz. each) cans pineapple
    chunks in natural juice,
    drained and reserved
1-1/4 qts. pineapple juice (from
    drained chunks and aug-
    mented with other pineapple
    juice)
1-1/2 cups vinegar
1/2 cup Kikkoman soy sauce
3/4 cup corn starch
1 tsp. ginger
1/2 cup water
6 oz. brown sugar
2 large green peppers, cut into
    1-inch squares
1-1/2 lbs. onion, peeled and cut
    into rings
5 lbs. cooked shrimp

Mix pineapple juice, vinegar and soy sauce and bring to a boil. Blend corn starch, ginger and water and stir into hot liquid. Saute pepper, onion rings and add, along with the shrimp, to the hot mixture. When heated throughout, serve over rice. If desired, top with chinese noodles. Serves 24.

The Committee

SHRIMP PERLO

2 lbs. shrimp
1 cup raw rice
1-1/2 cups water
1 tsp. salt
3 or 4 slices bacon
1 medium onion, minced
1 Tbsp. butter
black pepper to taste (1 tsp.
    or more)

Shell and devein shrimp. Fry bacon, remove and crumble into bits (save the fat). Put all ingredients in a heavy pot with a tight lid. Bring to a boil, reduce to low simmer, and cook, covered, for 40-45 minutes, stirring once or twice. (If more shrimp are used, reduce amount of water; shrimp release water when cooking. Also, do not use more than one cup of rice; efforts to double this recipe are disappointing because the rice becomes mushy.)

This recipe is a variation of a fisherman's stew recipe from Florida years ago. Shrimp were among the cheapest forms of seafood then. Unlike most shrimp dishes, this one is not sensitive to overcooking. In fact, it will not be affected adversely if it is not served for an hour or so after it is cooked. Serves 4 or more.

Pat Gatlin (Mrs. Leon)

SHRIMP BOILED IN BEER

3 lbs. green shrimp, uncooked,
    washed
1 can beer
1 pint vinegar
juice of half a lemon
3 Tbsp. salt
1 package Zatarain's Shrimp and
    Crab Boil (3 oz. bag)
1 quart water
melted butter

Put all ingredients except shrimp into a large cooking container on top of stove. Bring mixture to a boil and boil for 3 minutes to blend flavors. Add shrimp and let come to a boil again, watching closely as it will boil over quickly. Turn heat down so that mixture continues a very slow boil and cook for 15 to 20 minutes. Pour liquid off and peel your own shrimp. Dip in butter. Serve hot or cold.

Ben Knott

GRILLED SHRIMP

Easy and delicious!

2 lbs. large shrimp in shell
1 cup salad oil
1 cup lemon juice
2 tsp. Italian salad dressing mix
2 tsp. seasoned salt
1 tsp. seasoned pepper
4 Tbsp. brown sugar
4 Tbsp. soy sauce
1/2 cup chopped green onion

Wash shrimp thoroughly; drain on paper towels. Mix together salad oil, lemon juice, salad dressing mix, salt and pepper. Place shrimp in bowl and pour in the marinade. Put in refrigerator and marinate 2 to 4 hours, stirring occasionally. Lift shrimp from marinade with slotted spoon and place on grill about 6 inches from hot coals. Grill for about 10 minutes, turning once and brushing with marinade. Pour remaining marinade into pan. Stir in brown sugar, soy sauce and onion. Heat to serve as a dip for shrimp. When very large shrimp are used they will not fall through the grill. Can use a metal-handled rack used for chicken, etc.—the kind that can be clamped together. Place as many rows as rack will hold and clamp tightly. Grill as above. Serves 4-5.

Judy Gainer (Mrs. R.S.)

EASY, DELICIOUS SAUTEED SHRIMP

1 stick butter
2 lbs. raw shrimp, peeled and
     deveined
garlic salt
2 Tbsp. dry vermouth
sprinkling of Parmesan cheese
sprinkling of parsley

Put butter into a large skillet (or electric frying pan) over medium heat. As butter melts, add shrimp. Stir with a large spoon and sprinkle liberally with garlic salt. The shrimp are done when they turn pink. This takes only a few minutes and can be done at the table in a chafing dish. Add dry vermouth, Parmesan cheese and parsley and heat again, briefly. Serves 4 to 5.

Gayanne Mraz

SHRIMP SCAMPI

Elegant and simple. Guests love to smell this last-minute dish cooking!

1/2 cup melted butter
24 jumbo shrimp, peeled and
     deveined
3 cloves garlic, minced
2 Tbsp. parsley, chopped
2 Tbsp. dry white wine
1 Tbsp. lemon juice
salt and pepper to taste

Heat butter and garlic in large skillet; add shrimp and saute on both sides until done (about 5 minutes). Pour off pan drippings through strainer into a small saucepan. Add remaining ingredients and cook over high heat for 1 minute. Pour sauce over shrimp and serve immediately. Serves 4.

Hilda Rutherford (Mrs. N.A.)

DELICIOUS SHRIMP SOUFFLE

12 slices white bread
2 cups cooked shrimp
1/2 lb. sharp cheese, grated
    (2 cups)
4 cups milk
4 eggs, beaten
1 tsp. salt
1/8 tsp. pepper
1 Tbsp. chopped parsley
1 Tbsp. dry mustard
1/4 cup chopped onion
1/2 cup finely chopped green
    pepper
1/4 cup melted butter.

Trim crusts from bread; cut into cubes. Arrange half of bread cubes in greased flat (9x13) casserole. Top with grated cheese. Cover with remainder of bread cubes. Combine remainder of ingredients. Pour over top. Chill overnight in refrigerator, covered. Bake at 350 degrees, covered, for 1 hour or until set. Let stand 10 minutes before cutting. Serves 8-10.

Note: Crab or lobster may be subtituted for shrimp.

Anne Thrift (Mrs. Charles)

LEE'S SHRIMP/WILD RICE CASSEROLE

One more really fabulous shrimp recipe

1/2 lb. cooked shrimp, split
    lengthwise
1 box Uncle Ben's long-grain and
    wild rice
1 can cream of mushroom soup
1 can cream of celery soup
2 tsp. chopped onion
2 tsp. chopped green pepper
2 tsp. chopped celery
1 Tbsp. Worcestershire sauce
1 Tbsp. lemon juice
2 Tbsp. melted butter
1/2 tsp. salt
1/2 tsp dry mustard
1/2 tsp. pepper

Cook rice as per instructions. Combine all ingredients. Place in greased 9x13 inch casserole. Bake at 350 degrees for 30 to 40 minutes. Serves 6.

Nancy Wohlbruck (Mrs. Everett L.)

SHRIMP AND SAUSAGE DINNER

Gather your friends for a great beach meal. Serve with green salad or slaw.

2 lbs. raw shrimp, washed
2 lbs. Hillshire Farm beef sausage,
    cut in 2-inch lengths
6 ears of corn-on-the-cob, shucked
    and cleaned
1 pouch Shrimp Spice and Crab
    Boil

Place large pot of water on stove. Add Shrimp Spice and Crab Boil. Bring to a boil; add sausage and let boil 5 minutes. Add corn and boil 7 to 10 minutes longer. Add shrimp and cook 3 to 5 minutes (until shrimp turns pink and tests done). Spread newspapers on table and serve with melted butter and/or cocktail sauce. Serves 6.

Jane Ives (Mrs. Claude L.)
Linde Mullis (Mrs. W.F.)

BEER BATTER FOR FISH OR SHRIMP

1 cup Bisquick
1/2 tsp salt
1 egg
1/2 cup beer
2 or 3 Tbsp. Bisquick
fish fillets or peeled shrimp

Combine first 4 ingredients for batter. Wash and pat dry fish or shrimp. Sprinkle with 2 to 3 Tbsp. Bisquick. Dip into batter. Drop into deep fat. Brown quickly. Drain on paper towels. Serve immediately. Delicious! These are not greasy and have a delicate crust.

Ben Knott

NANTUCKET BAKED BLUEFISH

Delicious recipe for any dark, strong-flavored fish

2 lbs. bluefish fillets
1/2 cup mayonnaise
1-1/2 cups sour cream
salt and pepper
2 Tbsp. chopped chives
3 Tbsp. lemon juice

Place fillets in buttered baking dish. Mix sour cream, mayonnaise, chives and lemon juice with salt and pepper to taste. Spread over fish. Bake at 375 degrees for 30 minutes. Serves 4.

Patricia Bone (Mrs. S.K.)

BAKED STUFFED FISH FILLETS

1/2 cup chopped mushrooms
1/4 cup sliced green onions
1/2 lb. shrimp (fresh, if possible)
1/4 cup minced parsley (fresh, if possible)
2 10-oz. fresh fillets (or 1 large), flounder, red snapper, sea trout . . .
2 Tbsp. or more fine bread crumbs
2 Tbsp. mayonnaise
butter
lemon juice
salt
pepper

In a skillet saute chopped mushrooms and onions in 2 Tbsp. of butter for 5 minutes; add the shrimp, shelled, deveined (if you like), and chopped into small pieces. Cook this mixture over medium heat just until shrimp turn pink. Remove pan from heat and stir in parsley, mayonnaise, 2 Tbsp. of bread crumbs, and salt and pepper to taste. Set aside. With a very sharp knife cut a pocket in each fish fillet; place fillet on a counter or board, hold it in place firmly with one hand, and carefully slice horizontally through the fillet, taking care not to cut quite all the way to the outside. When finished, the fillet should look like a thin pocketbook. Sprinkle each fillet inside and out with lemon juice, a little salt and pepper, and place them on a lightly greased baking dish, skin side down. Stuff the pockets with the shrimp mixture. Press edges of pocket together and sprinkle each fillet with a light coating of bread crumbs followed by 1 Tbsp. grated Parmesan cheese. Dot top of each fillet with small dabs of butter (or sprinkle melted butter over them). Bake in preheated 425 degree oven until just done (about 20 minutes). Do not overcook. Serve with lemon slices. Serves 4.

Pat Gatlin (Mrs. Leon)

MARIE'S FLOUNDER
Different and easy!

flounder fillets, skinned
mayonnaise
Kosher pickle juice, Claussen brand
lemon pepper
salt and pepper
lemon juice
paprika

This recipe has no specific proportions. Add pickle juice to mayonnaise until it is the consistency of pancake batter. Then add lemon pepper, salt, pepper and lemon juice. Spread over fillets of flounder that have been skinned. Top with paprika. Bake until flounder is flaky.

Georgia Miller (Mrs. George)

FLOUNDER PARMESAN

2 lbs. flounder or other fish fillets
1 cup sour cream
6 Tbsp. grated cheese (Parmesan)
1 Tbsp. minced fresh onion
1 Tbsp. lemon juice
1/2 tsp. each: garlic salt, red pepper, parsley, paprika

If fish is frozen, thaw completely. Arrange fillets in single layer in shallow, buttered baking dish. Combine other ingredients except paprika and spread over fillets. Bake in preheated 375 degree oven for 10-15 minutes, or until fish flakes easily. Sprinkle with paprika before serving. Serves 8.

Nancy Crutchfield (Mrs. Edward E., Jr.)

BAKED SALMON CROQUETTES
The good taste of salmon without frying

1 15-oz. can salmon
milk
1/4 cup butter
2 Tbsp. chopped onion
1/3 cup flour
1/2 tsp. salt
1/4 tsp. pepper
1 Tbsp. lemon juice
1 cup bread crumbs (or corn flakes) divided

Pick over and drain salmon; reserve liquid. To liquid add milk to make 1 cup. Saute onion in butter on low heat for a few minutes; add flour and stir constantly until smooth. Add milk mixture gradually. Stir in salt and pepper; set aside. Combine lemon juice with 1/2 cup finely crushed bread crumbs or corn flakes. Add to prepared salmon along with white sauce. Mix well and cool. Shape into croquettes or patties and bake on lightly greased cookie sheet at 400 degrees for 25 to 30 minutes. Yield: 6 croquettes. Note: Make be baked in a loaf pan.

Betty Dale Archer (Mrs. John M.)

SALMON TERIYAKI
Great for the grill

1/4 cup vegetable oil
2 Tbsp. lemon juice
2 Tbsp. soy sauce
1/2 tsp. dry mustard
1/2 tsp. ginger
1/8 tsp. garlic powder
4 fresh salmon steaks

Marinate salmon for at least 2 hours, turning to marinate both sides. Drain before broiling. Broil 5 minutes. Turn over; brush with marinade. Broil 5 minutes longer or until fish flakes near bone. Serves 4.

Dale Yaged (Mrs. David)

SALMON MOUSSE

Good as a luncheon entree or an hors d'oeuvre

1 envelope unflavored gelatin
2 Tbsp. lemon juice
1 med. onion, minced
1/2 cup boiling water
1/2 cup Hellman's mayonnaise
1/4 tsp. paprika
1 tsp. dried dill
1 lb. can salmon, drained and
 picked
1 cup heavy cream
1 cup celery, finely chopped
sauce for salmon mousse

Place gelatin, lemon juice, onion and boiling water in blender. Process 10 seconds. Add mayonnaise, paprika, dill and salmon which has been drained and picked of bones and dark skin. Blend briefly. Remove cover and add 1/2 of the cream at a time. Blend briefly after each addition. Blend all together for 30 seconds. Add celery last, stirring with long spoon to mix. Pour into oiled mold and chill until set. Unmold and serve with sauce as main course or as an hors d'oeuvre with crackers.

SOUR CREAM DILL SAUCE FOR SALMON MOUSSE

2 cups dairy sour cream
2 tsps. capers
2 tsps. lemon juice
1 tsp. dill
1/2 tsp. salt
1/8 tsp. pepper

Combine and chill. Serve as an accompaniment for Salmon Mousse.

Ellen Knott (Mrs. B.F.)

HOT TUNA SANDWICH

2 7-oz. cans tuna, drained and
 flaked
1/2 cup mayonnaise
1/4 cup sour cream
1/4 cup parsley
1 Tbsp. lemon juice
1/2 tsp. garlic salt
6 sesame seed buns
1/4 lb. Swiss cheese, thinly sliced

Combine first 6 ingredients. Place tuna mixture in buns with the Swiss cheese. Wrap in foil. Bake at 350 degrees for about 25 minutes.

Virginia Golding (Mrs. John G.)

CAPTAIN'S CASSEROLE

1 can cream of mushroom soup
1/2 cup milk
2/3 cup Cheddar cheese, grated
1-1/3 cup minute rice
1/2 tsp. oregano
dash pepper
1 can (1 lb.) whole tomatoes
1 cup water
1/2 onion, thinly sliced
2 cans (6-1/2 oz. each) Star Kist
    tuna
1/3 cup stuffed olives, sliced
1 can small green peas
1/2 cup potato chips, crushed

Heat soup, milk and cheese until cheese is melted, stirring occasionally. Combine rice, oregano and pepper in greased 1-1/2 qt. shallow baking dish. Drain tomatoes, reserving 1/2 cup juice. Stir juice and water into rice. Slice tomatoes and arrange most of tomatoes on rice. Add onion, tuna, olives and peas. Pour on sauce. Sprinkle with potato chips. Arrange remaining tomatoes on top. Bake at 375 degrees for 20 to 25 minutes. Makes 6 generous servings.

Caroline Gray (Mrs. B.K.)

TUNA BAKE

Ideal for Sunday night supper

1 med. can tuna (7 oz.)
1 2-1/2 oz. jar mushrooms
1 small can LeSeur peas
1 2-oz. jar pimientos
1 8-oz. carton sour cream
2 Tbsp. butter
2 Tbsp. flour
salt and lemon pepper
bread crumbs

Preheat oven. Place butter in pyrex and place in oven just long enough to melt. Blend flour into butter. In colander drain tuna, mushrooms, pimiento and peas. Place in pyrex. Add sour cream, salt and lemon pepper. Fold in gently, top with crumbs. *Place pyrex in pan of hot water.* Bake at 350 degrees for 30-40 minutes. Serves 3-4.

Teny Sugg (Mrs. Wm. C.)

TUNA CASSEROLE

2 cups Brownberry Seasoned
    Croutons
2 cans light or white tuna
2 cups (or less) thinly-sliced celery
1 cup Miracle Whip or
    mayonnaise
1/2 cup slivered, toasted almonds
2 Tbsp. lemon juice
2 tsp. instant onion
1/4 tsp. salt
1 cup Cheddar cheese, grated

Combine all ingredients except one cup of croutons and cheese. Pour into a 1-1/2 qt. baking dish. Top with croutons and cheese. Bake at 350 degrees for 15 minutes or until bubbly. Serves 4 to 6.
Note: Can substitute 2 cups chopped chicken in place of the 2 cans of tuna.

Jean Bridges (Mrs. D. T., Jr.)

Breads

M.E.Wellborn

ANGEL BISCUITS

They melt in your mouth. Can be pre-baked and frozen. I keep them in my freezer and pop them into the oven. Guests think I've baked all day.

1 pkg. activated dry yeast
2 or 3 Tbsp. warm water
5 cups plain flour
3 to 5 Tbsp. sugar
1 Tbsp. baking powder
1 tsp. salt
1 cup shortening
1 tsp. soda
2 cups buttermilk

Dissolve yeast in warm water. Sift flour, sugar, salt, baking powder and soda together. Cut in shortening. Stir in yeast mixture and buttermilk. Roll out on floured board and cut out with biscuit cutter; brush tops of biscuits with melted butter. Bake in 400 degree oven for 10 to 20 minutes, or until golden brown.

NOTE: This dough will keep refrigerated for several days, but you must allow biscuits to rise before baking if dough has been refrigerated. Prebake all biscuits at one time, then refrigerate or freeze them, and finish them up at serving time in a 400 to 500 degree oven. When prebaking, be careful just to bake until biscuits have "set up" but not browned, about 5 or 6 minutes. Makes 4 to 6 dozen.

Libby Morrison (Mrs. Jack)

MILE-HIGH BISCUITS

Handy to have in the freezer when unexpected guests arrive at mealtimes.

3 cups all-purpose flour
1/4 cup sugar
1 Tbsp. plus 1 tsp. baking powder
1/2 tsp. cream of tartar
3/4 tsp. salt
1/2 cup shortening
1 egg beaten
1 cup plus 2 Tbsp. milk

Combine dry ingredients in mixing bowl. Cut in shortening until mixture resembles coarse crumbs. Add egg and milk all at once; mix until dough forms a ball. Turn dough out on lightly-floured surface and knead 10 to 12 times. Roll out to 3/4 inch thickness; cut with floured 2-1/2 inch biscuit cutter. Place on ungreased baking sheet and freeze. When biscuits have been frozen, they may be stored in a plastic bag in the freezer until needed.
To bake frozen biscuits, place on lightly-greased baking sheet; bake at 475 degrees for 12-15 minutes or until light brown. Makes 1 dozen biscuits.

Joan BeLasco (Mrs. J.J.)

CHEESE BISCUITS

1/2 cup margarine, softened
1/4 lb. sharp Cheddar cheese, grated (room temperature)
dash cayenne pepper or Tabasco
1-1/2 cups self-rising flour

Cream the margarine, cheese and cayenne pepper well. Add flour and work in well, at first with fork, then with hands. It should be a smooth ball. Pinch off dough and roll into balls according to desired size. Press across one way, then the other with fork dipped in flour, or flatten with hand or bottom of flour-dipped glass. Bake in 350 degree oven on ungreased cookie sheet for 10 to 15 minutes. Watch—do not brown.

Ellen Knott (Mrs. B.F.)

PERFECT BISCUITS

2 cups sifted all-purpose flour
1/2 tsp. salt
4 tsp. baking powder
1/2 tsp. cream of tartar
2 tsp. sugar
1/2 cup butter or margarine
2/3 cup milk

Preheat oven to 425 degrees. Sift flour and then resift into bowl with dry ingredients. Work in butter with pastry blender until all blended. Add milk *all at once*, mixing lightly with fork. Roll out on lightly floured board. Cut with biscuit cutter. Bake on *greased* cookie sheet 12 to 15 minutes. Makes about 18 biscuits.

Margery Marcus (Mrs. R.A.)

ALABAMA BUTTERMILK ROLLS

1 pkg. yeast
2 Tbsp. warm water
1 cup buttermilk
4 to 6 cups flour
2 Tbsp. sugar
1 tsp. salt
1 tsp. soda
1 tsp. baking powder
4 Tbsp. shortening
1 cup buttermilk (additional)

Place yeast in warm water. Add buttermilk; let stand. Sift flour, sugar, salt, soda and baking powder. Add shortening, yeast, buttermilk mixture and 1 more cup buttermilk. Add more flour if needed for a soft dough. Grease another large bowl well, place dough in the bowl, and turn so dough gets grease on all sides. Cover well until it rises—about 1 hour. Put on counter and knead well. Form into balls and place in large pan (9 x 13 inches, or larger). Let rise again. Bake at 200 degrees for 10 minutes (so it won't fall). Turn up to 300 degrees until cooked and browned (will leave sides of the pan). Makes 35 to 60 rolls.

Judy Ranson (Mrs. R.C.)

FRENCH COFFEE ROLLS

1/3 cup butter, softened
1/2 cup sugar
1 egg
1/2 cup sour cream
1-1/2 cups flour
1-1/2 tsp. baking powder
1/2 tsp. salt
1/2 tsp. cinnamon
2/3 cup pecans (or walnuts), finely chopped

Cream butter and sugar. Add egg; beat well. Mix in sour cream. Sift together dry ingredients. Fold into butter mixture; add pecans. Fill small muffin tins (1-1/2 inch) 2/3 full. Bake at 350 degrees for 15 minutes. Remove from tins. While still hot brush with melted butter and roll in a mixture of cinnamon and sugar. These freeze nicely. Makes 3 dozen muffins.

Jean Bridges (Mrs. D.T., Jr.)
Sonja Edwards (Mrs. W.D., Jr.)

ICE BOX ROLLS

1/2 cup shortening
1/3 cup sugar
1 egg
1 pkg. dry yeast
1/3 cup lukewarm water
1 tsp. sugar
2 tsp. salt
4 cups flour
1 cup lukewarm water

Cream the 1/2 cup shortening and 1/3 cup sugar; add 1 egg. Dissolve the yeast in 1/3 cup lukewarm water. Add the sugar. Sift the salt with the flour; add alternately with 1 cup lukewarm water to creamed mixture to make soft dough. Knead briefly and allow to rise until doubled. Knead down and form rolls. Brush tops with butter and let rise until doubled. Bake in preheated 425 degree oven 12 to 15 minutes.

NOTE: Mixture can be stored in refrigerator after first rising. Make rolls and proceed as directed above.

Ruth Boyce (Mrs. William)

APRICOT BREAD

1 cup dried apricots
1/2 cup hot water
1 cup sugar
1 cup brown sugar, packed
3 cups flour
1/2 tsp. soda
2 tsp. baking powder
1/2 tsp. salt
3 eggs, beaten
1 cup sour cream
1 cup pecans, chopped

Cut apricots in pieces and soak in hot water while preparing bread. Sift together dry ingredients, add eggs, stir in sour cream and pecans. Add the undrained apricots. Put in 2 well-greased loaf pans. Bake in 300 degree oven for 45 minutes to 1 hour. Check after 45 minutes. Good with cream cheese. Makes 2 loaves.

Ellen Knott (Mrs. B.F.)

SOUR CREAM DINNER ROLLS

1 cup sour cream
1/2 cup sugar
1 tsp. salt
1/2 cup margarine, melted
1/2 cup warm water
2 pkgs. dry yeast
2 eggs
4 cups unsifted all-purpose flour

Scald sour cream. Stir in sugar, salt and melted margarine. Cool to lukewarm. Measure warm water into a large warmed bowl. Sprinkle yeast over mixture and stir until dissolved. Add lukewarm sour cream mixture, eggs and flour. Mix until well blended. Cover tightly and refrigerate overnight. Turn dough onto a lightly-floured board and divide into quarters. Roll each piece into a circle. Cut each circle into 12 wedge-shaped pieces. Roll up each cut piece beginning with wide end. Place on greased baking sheets. Cover lightly and let rise in a warm place, free from drafts until double in bulk. Bake at 375 degrees about 15 minutes. Brush with melted butter. Makes 4 dozen rolls.

Libby Morrison (Mrs. Jack)

APPLE-HONEY NUT BREAD

4 eggs
2 cups sugar
1 cup oil
2 tsp. vanilla
3/4 cup honey
2 Tbsp. apple cider
1 tsp. baking powder
1 tsp. soda
1 tsp. salt
1 tsp. cinnamon
1 tsp. nutmeg
3 cups flour
2 cups grated apples
1 cup coconut
1 cup raisins
1 cup nuts

Combine eggs, sugar and oil. Mix well. Add the vanilla, honey and cider and beat well. Sift together the dry ingredients and add to the sugar mixture. Stir in apples, coconut, raisins and nuts. Pour into 2 well-greased and floured 9 x 5 inch loaf pans. Bake at 325 degrees for 1 hour or until tests done. Makes 2 loaves.

Sandra Sue Jennings (Mrs. William)

BANANA BREAD

2 large bananas (very ripe)
1-/2 cup melted butter
   (or margarine)
1-1/2 cups flour
3/4 tsp. salt
1 cup sugar
1 tsp. baking soda
1 egg
nuts (optional)

Beat egg and add sugar, butter and bananas (mashed). Add this to the flour, soda and salt which have been sifted together. After mixing, put in loaf pan and bake at 350 degrees for 45-50 minutes, or until it begins to leave the sides of the pan. Makes 1 loaf.

Sally Gaddy (Mrs. C.E.)

Similar recipes submitted by
Judy Ranson (Mrs. R.C.)
Carole Goodwin

BEER BREAD

3 cups self-rising flour
3 Tbsp. sugar
12 oz. can beer, warm
2 to 3 Tbsp. butter, melted

Combine all ingredients except butter; stir just until blended. Pour into a well-greased loaf pan and bake at 375 degrees for 30 to 35 minutes. Brush with melted butter. Best served from oven. Can bake in a 2-quart greased pyrex dish. Test for doneness.

VARIATION: Beer Muffins:
Substitute 4 cups Bisquick for 3 cups self-rising flour. Use remaining ingredients, mix as above and fill greased muffin tins 2/3 full. Bake at 400 degrees 20 to 25 minutes or until done. Two dozen muffins.

Ellen Knott (Mrs. B.F.)

CARROT BREAD

2 cups flour
2 tsp. soda
1/2 tsp. salt
2 tsp. cinnamon
1-1/2 cups sugar
1-1/2 cups oil
2 Tbsp. vanilla
3 eggs
2 cups grated carrots
1/2 cup raisins (optional)
1/2 to 1 cup chopped walnuts

Sift first 5 ingredients together in large bowl. Add all other ingredients except carrots, raisins and nuts. Beat on medium speed until well blended. Fold in carrots, raisins and nuts. Pour batter into 2 well-greased and floured 9 x 5-inch loaf pans. Bake at 325 degrees for 1 hour or until tests done. Good with cream cheese. Makes 2 loaves.

Myrtle Ussery (Mrs. A.M.)

CELERY ROLLS IN A LOAF

1 loaf unsliced French bread
1 cup softened butter
   (the real thing!)
2 tsp. celery seed
1/2 tsp. salt
1/2 tsp. paprika
dash of cayenne

Trim crusts from top, sides, and ends of loaf. Cut down through center of loaf lengthwise, almost to bottom crust. Cut at 1-inch intervals crosswise almost to the bottom crust. Mix together other ingredients and spread over entire surface of cuts. Place on baking sheet, cover with waxed paper and refrigerate. Bake uncovered at 400 degrees for 15 to 18 minutes. Serves 8.

Anne Thrift (Mrs. Charles, III)

EASY CHEESE LOAF
So good yet so easy!

1 loaf unsliced bread (Harris-
   Teeter or a bakery)
1/2 lb. butter
1/2 lb. Old English Processed
   Cheese Spread (1-1/2 jars)

Have butter and cheese at room temperature. Beat in electric mixer until creamy. Cut crusts from top and sides of bread and slice into 1/2 inch slices. Spread each slice on both sides with cheese mixture. Stack together and tie string around to hold. Cover loaf with remaining cheese mixture. Put into jelly roll pan or other rimmed pan. Bake at 325 degrees for 30 minutes. Can put together several hours before baking and serving.

Kathy Walker (Mrs. Andrew W.)

EASY CHEESE BREAD

3-3/4 cups Bisquick
1-1/4 cups shredded sharp cheese
1 Tbsp. poppy seeds
1 beaten egg
1-1/2 cups milk

Combine first 3 ingredients; add egg and milk. Mix just to blend and then beat vigorously for 1 minute. Turn into well-greased 9 x 5 x 3 inch loaf pan. Sprinkle with additional poppy seeds. Bake at 350 degrees 50 to 60 minutes. Remove from pan and cool on rack.

Ellen Chason (Mrs. Lynn)

CURRY CHEESE BREAD
This goes well with chicken dishes.

1 Tbsp. shortening
1/4 cup chopped onion
1 egg, beaten
1/2 cup milk
1-1/2 cups Bisquick
2 Tbsp. curry powder
1 cup shredded sharp processed
    American cheese
2 tsp. sesame seeds or caraway
    seeds
2 Tbsp. butter

Cook onion in shortening until tender. Combine milk and egg. Stir together Bisquick and curry powder; add egg mixture and stir only until dry ingredients are moistened. Add onion and half of cheese. Spread into baking dish. Sprinkle remaining cheese and seeds on top. Drizzle with melted butter. Bake at 400 degrees for 20-25 minutes. Serve warm. Serves 8.

Susan Murfee (Mrs. D.G.)

ONION AND CHEESE PARTY BREAD

3/4 cup chopped onion
1 Tbsp. shortening
1 egg, slightly beaten
1/2 cup milk
1-1/2 cups Bisquick
1 cup (4 oz.) sharp Cheddar
    cheese, grated
1 Tbsp. poppy seeds
2 Tbsp. butter, melted

Preheat oven to 400 degrees. Saute onion in shortening until tender. Mix egg and milk and blend in Bisquick. Add onion and half of cheese. Spread dough into greased 8 x 1-1/2 inch round baking dish. Sprinkle top with remaining half of cheese and poppy seeds. Drizzle melted butter over the top. Bake for 25 minutes or until bread tests done. Serve hot with butter.

Jean Boiter

HERB BUTTER BREAD

1 large loaf French or Italian bread
1 stick butter, softened
1 tsp. dried parsley flakes
1/4 tsp. oregano
garlic salt to taste
seasoned salt to taste
grated Parmesan cheese

Cut bread into one-inch slices diagonally. Blend all ingredients except Parmesan cheese. Spread slices on both sides with butter mixture and reshape into a loaf. Wrap in foil, shaping like a boat. Leave the top open and twist both ends. Sprinkle generously with cheese. Heat 15 to 20 minutes in a 350 degree oven.

The Committee

GRAND SUSIE MILLER'S CRANBERRY NUT BREAD
These can be made ahead of time and frozen. Good Christmas presents

2 cups flour
1 tsp. salt
1-1/2 tsp. baking powder
1/2 tsp. baking soda
1 cup sugar
1 beaten egg
2 Tbsp. melted butter
2 Tbsp. hot water
1/2 cup orange juice
grated rind of one orange
1 cup raw cranberrries, cut in
   halves
1/2 cup chopped pecans

Sift dry ingredients. Add egg, melted butter, orange juice, rind, and hot water. Stir until well mixed. *Do not beat.* Stir in berries and nuts. Pour batter into greased and floured loaf pans. For one large loaf, bake at 325 degrees for 1 hour and 10 minutes (check before time is up). For 2 smaller loaves bake at 325 degrees for 45 minutes. While hot, wrap in aluminum foil and store immediately in refrigerator for 24 hours. May then be frozen or eaten. Keep refrigerated.

B.J. Miller (Mrs. H.F., III)
Anne Zeola (Mrs. John)

GINGERBREAD WITH WARM CARAMEL SAUCE

1 cup molasses
2 tsp. baking soda
1 tsp. cinnamon
1 tsp. ginger
1/4 tsp. nutmeg
1/2 cup sugar
1/2 cup melted butter
2 cups flour
1 cup boiling water
2 eggs (beaten separately)

SAUCE:
2 egg yolks
1 cup cream
1 lb. light brown sugar
1 Tbsp. butter
1 tsp. vanilla
1/8 tsp. salt

Mix molasses, soda and spices. Add sugar, butter, flour and water. Beat well. Add egg yolks and fold in whites. Pour in greased 8-cup mold or loaf pan. Bake at 350 degrees for 35 to 40 minutes. For the sauce, combine egg yolks, cream and sugar. Cook in double boiler until creamy. Add butter. When it cools a little add the vanilla and salt. Toasted pecan pieces may be added.

Barbara Stutts (Mrs. Clyde)

LEMON TEA BREAD

2 cups unsifted all-purpose flour
1-1/2 tsp. baking powder
1/4 tsp. salt
1/2 cup butter or regular
    margarine
1 cup sugar
2 eggs
1/3 cup milk
1/2 cup chopped walnuts
2 tsp. grated lemon peel

SYRUP:
1/4 cup lemon juice
1/3 cup sugar

Lightly grease 9 x 5 x 3 inch loaf pan. Preheat oven to 350 degrees. Sift flour with baking powder and salt; set aside. Beat butter with 1 cup sugar in large bowl until light and fluffy. Add eggs one at a time, beating after each until light and fluffy. Beat in flour mixture alternately with milk beginnning and ending with flour mixture; beat just until combined. Stir in nuts and lemon peel. Turn batter into prepared pan. Bake 55 to 60 minutes or until cake tester comes out clean. Make syrup by combining lemon juice and sugar. Cook, stirring, 1 minute, or until syrupy. Pour evenly over bread as soon as it is removed from the oven. Let cool in pan 10 minutes. Remove to wire rack; let cool completely. Makes 1 loaf.

Kay Roberson (Mrs. G. Don)

QUICK MARMALADE BREAD
"Delicious hot with butter or cold with cream cheese, but best with Honey Spread"

3 cups all-purpose flour, unsifted
    (reserve 1/4 cup for nuts)
3-1/2 tsp. baking powder
1 tsp. salt
1 cup sugar
1 tsp. cinnamon
1 egg, well beaten
3/4 cup milk
2 Tbsp. vegetable oil
1 cup chopped walnuts
3/4 cup orange marmalade

Sift flour, baking powder, salt, sugar and cinnamon into a large bowl. Beat egg and add milk. Pour egg and milk mixture into dry ingredients and mix well. Add oil, nuts that have been dusted with reserved flour, and marmalade. Spoon into greased loaf pan and let stand for 30 minutes. Bake in a preheated 350 degree oven for 1 hour or until bread tests done. Cool in pan for 10 minutes. Remove from pan and continue cooling on wire rack. Yield: 1 (9 x 5 x 3-inch) loaf. Best served with Honey Spread

HONEY SPREAD
1/2 cup margarine or butter,
    softened
1/2 cup honey

Let butter come to room temperature. Beat with honey until fluffy. Use as spread on Marmalade bread or any bread.

Ellen Knott (Mrs. B.F.)

303

MONKEY BREAD

Great for children to make!

4 cans refrigerator biscuits
    (10 each)
3/4 cup sugar
1 tsp. cinnamon

SYRUP:
1 cup brown sugar
3/4 cup butter
1/2 tsp. cinnamon

Cut biscuits in quarters and shake in bag with cinnamon and sugar. Put into greased Bundt pan. If desired, put 1/2 cup chopped pecans in bottom of pan before putting in biscuits.

Combine syrup ingredients and bring to a boil. Pour over top of biscuits. Bake at 350 degrees for 40 to 50 minutes. Put drip pan under Bundt pan to protect oven, as syrup may run over.

Grace McBride (Mrs. J.W.)

MARGARET'S OATMEAL RAISIN BREAD

2-1/4 cups all-purpose flour
3/4 cup quick-cooking oats,
    uncooked
1/4 cup whole bran cereal
3/4 cup firmly-packed brown
    sugar
4 tsp. baking powder
1 tsp. salt
1-1/2 tsp. ground cinnamon
1/2 tsp. ground cloves
2 eggs, beaten
1-1/2 cups milk
1/2 cup vegetable oil
1 cup raisins

TOPPING:
1/3 cup quick-cooking oats,
    uncooked
1/4 cup firmly-packed brown
    sugar
1 Tbsp. butter, melted

Combine first 8 ingredients in a large bowl. Combine eggs, mik and oil. Make a well in the center of the dry ingredients, pour in egg and milk mixture and stir until moistened. Stir in raisins. Pour into a lightly-greased and floured 9 x 5 x 3 inch loaf pan. Combine remaining ingredients; sprinkle over batter and press gently. Bake at 325 degrees for 70 minutes or until a wooden pick inserted in center comes out clean. Cool in pan 10 minutes; remove to cooling rack. Cool completely. Makes 1 loaf.

Marge Browning

AUNT LENA'S DATE LOAF
Favorite at Christmas

3/4 cup flour
3/4 cup sugar
2 tsp. baking powder
1/2 tsp. salt
3 eggs
1 tsp. vanilla
3/4 lb. pecan halves
3/4 lb. pitted dates

Combine flour, sugar, baking powder and salt. Beat eggs and vanilla. Add to flour mixture. Stir in pecans and dates — work in well. Bake in brown-paper lined loaf pan at 250 degrees for 2 hours. Makes 1 loaf.

Shirley Snead (Mrs. Henry T.)

POPOVERS

3 eggs
1 cup milk
1 cup flour
3 Tbsp. butter, melted
salt
bacon (crumbled)
spices, etc. (optional)

Preheat oven to 450 degrees. Grease popover pan (or custard cups). In blender, mix eggs, milk, flour and butter. Cover and process until smooth. Heat popover pan. Spoon 1/3 or more cups batter (about 2/3 full) into each cup. Bake 15 minutes. Reduce heat to 375 degrees and bake 30 minutes more, until brown. *Do not open oven!* Serve immediately. Can add bacon or various spices.

Dot Nicholls (Mrs. T.H.)

ONION-SWISS CHEESE SQUARES
*For the person who **thinks** she can't make breads, this unusually delicious dish always gets raves!*

8 medium onions, sliced
1/4 cup margarine
2-1/2 cups enriched self-rising flour
1/2 cup grated Parmesan cheese
1/3 cup shortening
1 to 1-1/4 cups milk
1 cup (4 oz.) shredded Swiss cheese

Fry onions in margarine until soft. Set aside. Sift together flour and Parmesan cheese. Cut in shortening until flour resembles coarse crumbs. Blend in milk, to make a thick batter. Spread into a greased 10-1/2 x 15-1/2 inch pan. This simple-to-fix dough may be refrigerated at this point, for an hour — or a day! When ready to bake, cover with Swiss cheese, then top with sauteed onions. Bake at 450 degrees for 18 to 20 minutes until the dough is crisp and golden. Serve warm. Makes 24 servings.

Betty Harkey (Mrs. E.L.)

POPPY SEED BREAD

3 cups flour
2-1/2 cups sugar
1-1/2 tsp. baking powder
1-1/2 tsp. salt
3 eggs
1-1/2 cups Crisco oil
1-1/2 cups milk
1-1/2 Tbsp. poppy seeds
1-1/2 tsp. each vanilla, almond and
    butter flavoring

GLAZE:
3/4 cup confectioners' sugar
1/2 tsp. each vanilla, almond and
    butter flavoring
1/4 cup orange juice

Mix together all batter ingredients. Beat 2 minutes. Bake in 2 greased and floured loaf pans. Combine glaze ingredients and pour over bread right out of the oven. Let cool before taking out of pans. Makes 2 loaves.

Pam Houser (Mrs. E.E.)

PUMPKIN TEA BREAD
This recipe came from a friend—it's always good.

3 cups flour
3 cups sugar
2 cups pumpkin
3 eggs
1 cup oil
1 tsp. nutmeg
1 tsp. ground cloves
1 tsp. cinnamon
1 tsp. baking soda
1 tsp. baking powder
1/2 tsp. salt
1 cup nuts (optional)
2/3 cup raisins (optional)

Add measured amount of sugar to oil; mix well. Add pumpkin and eggs. In a separate bowl, mix spices and flour well. Add to liquid mixture. Pour into ungreased angel food cake pan. Bake at 350 degrees for about 1 hour and 15 minutes, or until knife comes out clean.

Elizabeth Fox (Mrs. E.J.)

RAISIN SPICE BREAD

1 cup oatmeal
1/2 cup butter (no
    substitute
1 cup boiling water
1-1/2 cup plain flour
1 tsp. baking soda
1 tsp. cinnamon
1/2 tsp. salt
1/2 tsp. nutmeg
2 eggs
2 cups brown sugar
1/2 cup raisins
1 tsp. vanilla
1 cup pecans, chopped

In a large bowl, place oatmeal, butter and water and let set for 20 minutes. Sift together flour and spices. Add salt and soda and pour into oatmeal mixture. Blend well, adding eggs, sugar, vanilla, nuts and raisins. Bake in two greased loaf pans for 45 minutes at 350 degrees. Makes 2 loaves. May be frozen.

Jackie Plott (Mrs. C.W.)

CHEESE FLOWERPOTS

Make a big hit with children. Different

butter for pots
waxed paper
1-1/4 cups water (120 degrees)
3 Tbsp. butter
2 Tbsp. honey
4 large eggs
1 egg white
7 cups all-purpose flour
2 envelopes yeast
1 Tbsp. sugar
2 tsp. salt
1 tsp. baking powder
2 cups shredded medium
    Cheddar cheese
1 egg yolk, beaten
poppy seeds

Preheat oven to 375 degrees. Wash, grease and bake pots 5-10 minutes. Regrease and bake 5-10 minutes more. Cool. Butter well and line sides with buttered waxed paper. Do not line bottom. Combine water, butter and honey. Beat in 4 eggs and egg white, 3-1/2 cups flour, yeast, sugar and salt; mix well. Add baking powder and other flour (1/2 cup at a time). Beat until soft dough. Mix in cheese.

Turn onto floured board and knead 10 minutes. Put into greased bowl, turning to coat. Cover with damp towel. Let stand in warm place until doubled. Punch and let rise again until doubled. Punch once more — knead about 2 minutes and divide into 4 parts. Knead and separate into 10 small balls. Layer in pots with last ball in center. Cover and let rise. Preheat to 425 degrees.

Brush with egg yolk and poppy seeds. Put foil on rack and bake pots 10 minutes. Lower to 375 degrees and bake 25-30 minutes. Cover tops if browning becomes too fast. Makes 4 flowerpot loaves.

Dot Nicholls (Mrs. T.H.)

STRAWBERRY-NUT BREAD

2 cups all-purpose flour
1 tsp. baking soda
1 tsp. salt
1 Tbsp. ground cinnamon
2 cups sugar
4 eggs, beaten
1-1/4 cups vegetable oil
2 cups thawed, sliced frozen
    strawberries
1-1/4 cups chopped pecans

Combine dry ingredients. Add eggs, oil, strawberries and pecans. Stir just until all ingredients are moistened. Spoon batter into 2 well-greased loaf pans. Bake at 350 degrees for 60 to 70 minutes, until cake tests done. Cool in pans 5 minutes; remove to wire rack to cool. Freezes well. Makes 2 loaves.

Linda Miller (Mrs. W.R.)

SPICED ZUCCHINI BREAD
Makes nice Christmas gifts.

3 cups all-purpose flour
2 tsp. soda
1 tsp. salt
1/2 tsp. baking powder
1-1/2 tsp. cinnamon
3/4 cup chopped nuts
3 eggs
2 cups sugar
1 cup vegetable oil
2 tsp. vanilla
2 cups coarsely-shredded zucchini
1 8-oz. can crushed pineapple,
    drained well

Combine flour, soda, salt, baking powder, cinnamon and nuts; set aside. Beat eggs lightly in a large mixing bowl; add sugar, oil and vanilla and beat until creamy. Stir in zucchini and pineapple. Add dry ingredients, stirring only until dry ingredients are moistened. Spoon batter into 2 well-greased 9 x 5 x 3 inch loaf pans. Bake at 350 degrees for 1 hour. Cool 10 minutes before removing from pans. Makes 2 loaves.

Georgia Miller (Mrs. George)

BATTER BREAD
This is an easy stir-together yeast bread with no kneading.

2-1/2 cups unsifted plain flour
2 Tbsp. sugar
1 tsp. salt
1 pkg. active dry yeast
1 cup milk
2 Tbsp. shortening
1 egg

Thoroughly mix flour, sugar, salt and yeast in large bowl. Heat milk and shortening until warm. Add egg to flour mixture. Stir in milk. Beat 300 strokes until batter leaves side of bowl. Cover. Let rise in warm place 1/2 to 1 hour. Grease loaf pan. Stir batter down; place in pan. Let rise until double in size, 1/2 to 1 hour. Preheat oven to 350 degrees. Bake 40 minutes or until lightly browned. Remove bread from pan immediately and cool on rack. Makes 1 loaf.

Ann Morris (Mrs. Roy)

BUTTERMILK BREAD
My favorite white bread

1 cup buttermilk
3 Tbsp. sugar
2-1/2 tsp. salt
1/3 cup butter
1 cup warm water
1 pkg. or 1 Tbsp. yeast
1/4 tsp. ginger
1 tsp. sugar
5-3/4 cups sifted flour
1/4 tsp. baking soda

Scald buttermilk (it will appear curdled); stir in the sugar, salt and butter. Cool to lukewarm. Measure the warm water into large mixing bowl with the ginger, sugar and yeast. Stir and let stand until it bubbles. Add the lukewarm milk mixture. Stir in 3 cups sifted flour and the baking soda. Beat until smooth and elastic.

Add the remaining 2-3/4 cups flour; use a little more or less, depending on the flour, to make a dough that has a rough, dull appearance and is a bit sticky. Turn the dough out on a lightly-floured board and knead until smooth and elastic, about 8 to 10 minutes. Form into a ball and put into a greased bowl, turning to grease all sides.

Cover with a clean damp cloth and let rise in a warm place, free from draft, for about 1 hour, or until doubled in bulk. Punch down, turn out on a lightly-floured board and let rest for about 15 minutes. Divide the dough in half. Shape into loaves and place in 2 greased bread pans, 9 x 5 x 3. Cover and let rise in a warm place, free from draft, about 1 hour, until doubled in bulk. Bake in a moderate oven, 375 degrees for 30 to 35 minutes. Makes 2 loaves.

Gensie

PUMPKIN BREAD
These make great gifts for your neighbors and friends. Very moist!

3 cups sugar
4 eggs, beaten
1 cup corn oil
1 can pumpkin (16 oz.)
3-1/2 cups flour
1 tsp. baking powder
2 tsp. baking soda
2 tsp. salt
1 tsp. allspice
1/2 tsp. ground cloves
1 tsp. cinnamon
1 tsp. nutmeg
1 cup chopped nuts (optional)
1 cup water

Mix all ingredients and pour into 3 greased and floured loaf pans. Bake 45 minutes at 350 degrees. Freezes well.

Carolyn Adams (Mrs. G.B.)

CROISSANTS

Use as is, or with beef, brie and herb butter—heated—for a delicious sandwich.

1 pkg. yeast
3/4 cup lukewarm milk
2 cups sifted flour
1/2 tsp. salt
1/2 cup sweet butter
1 egg yolk

Dissolve yeast in milk. Sift together flour and salt; stir in yeast. Knead until smooth and elastic. Place in greased bowl, grease top and let rise until doubled. Roll dough out in long strip, dot with bits of butter and fold in thirds. Turn to open edge. Pat and roll into another long strip; fold in thirds, wrap in waxed paper and chill. Repeat this process 2 more times.

On the fourth time, roll dough about 1/8 inch thick. Do not fold. Cut into triangles; brush tip with beaten yolk mixed with a little water. Roll from wide end to tip. Press to seal and shape into half moons.

Place on well-greased cookie sheets. Cover with waxed paper. Let rise until doubled.

Brush tops with egg yolk. Bake in preheated 425 degree oven for 20 to 25 minutes. Serve hot. Makes 16-18. Freezes well.

Dot Nicholls (Mrs. T.H.)

"FAKE CROISSANTS"

1 pkg. dry yeast
1 cup warm water
3/4 cup evaporated milk
1-1/2 tsp. salt
1/3 cup sugar
1 egg
5 cups flour, divided
1/4 cup butter, melted and cooled
1 cup butter, unmelted
egg glaze (1 egg beaten with
    1 Tbsp. water)

Soften yeast in water; add milk, salt, sugar, egg and 1 cup flour. Beat until smooth; add melted butter. Cut unmelted butter into remaining flour until dough resembles size of kidney beans; stir into yeast mixture until flour is moistened. (Do not overbeat as butter must remain kidney bean size.) Chill overnight. Divide dough into 4 parts; roll each part into a 17-inch circle. Cut each into 8 wedges. Roll from wide side to point and curve into crescent forms. Let rise 2 hours at room temperature under a towel. Brush with egg glaze. Bake in preheated 325 degree oven for 30 to 35 minutes. Makes 32 croissants.

Mary Cloran (Mrs. Martin T.)

CUISINART BREAD

Quick, easy and so delicious—while you're at it, make 2 loaves.

2-3/4 cups unbleached flour
1 pkg. dry yeast
2 Tbsp. sugar
1 tsp. salt
2 Tbsp. Carnation non-fat
   dry milk
2 Tbsp. wheat germ (optional)
1 cup water (110 degrees)
2 Tbsp. salad oil

Put all dry ingredients in Cuisinart bowl and mix to blend. Add water and oil and mix for 1 minute. (Dough will form a lump and will bump around in the bowl but don't panic: it's doing your kneading for you). While mixing add flour if dough is too sticky: it *should* be slightly sticky. Place dough in oiled bowl, turn once, cover with damp cloth and let rise for 1 hour (or until double in bulk) in 80-90 degree oven (middle rack) over a pan of water placed on lowest rack. Remove from rising-place and punch dough down and pull away from sides. Let rest 15 minutes. Let rise, covered as above and in oven as above, in oiled loaf pan for 30 minutes. Brush top gently with melted butter. Bake at 400 degrees 20 to 23 minutes or until done. Test for doneness—tap top of loaf to hear "hollow"sound. Enjoy! Makes 1 loaf.

Nancy Little (Mrs. T.M.)

SALLY LUNN

1 pkg. dry yeast
1/4 cup warm water
1 cup milk
1/2 cup butter or margarine
1/4 cup sugar
4 cups sifted self-rising flour
4 eggs

Dissolve yeast in warm water. Heat milk until almost simmering. Stir butter or margarine into hot milk until melted. Into large mixing bowl measure sugar. Stir in milk mixture until sugar dissolves. Cool to lukewarm. Stir in 1-1/2 cups flour and beat until smooth—about 1 minute by electric mixer or 150 strokes by hand. Beat in yeast and eggs. Stir in enough of the remaining flour to make a stiff batter. Beat until batter is smooth and elastic—about 1 minute by electric mixer or 150 strokes by hand.
Cover and let rise in warm place until light and bubbly—about 1 hour. Meanwhile, grease a 9 inch tube pan. Stir batter down and turn into greased pan. Cover and let rise in warm place until doubled—about 30 minutes. Preheat oven to 350 degrees.
Bake 25 to 30 minutes or until cake tester comes out clean. Immediately remove from pan onto wire rack. Serve as warm as possible. Makes a 9-inch tube pan bread.

Anne Jones (Mrs. Richard A.)

PARSLEY SPIRAL BREAD

1 cup scalded milk
2 Tbsp. sugar
2-1/2 tsp. salt
1/4 cup shortening
1 cup lukewarm water
2 pkg. yeast
7 cups sifted flour
melted butter

FILLING:
2 cups chopped parsley
2 cups chopped scallions
1 clove minced garlic
2 Tbsp. butter
2 eggs, lightly beaten
3/4 tsp. salt
pepper, Tabasco

Add sugar, salt and shortening to milk. Stir. Cool to lukewarm. Add yeast to water and dissolve. Mix with milk. Add 4 cups flour; stir and beat. Add remaining flour; stir until damp. Rest 10 minutes. On floured surface, knead until smooth. Put into greased bowl, grease surface, cover and let rise until double. Punch down. Grease loaf pans. Cut dough in half. Shape each into ball and roll into rectangle 1/4 inch thick and 9 inches wide. Brush with beaten egg. Spread filling to 1 inch from edges. Roll like jelly-roll. Pinch edges to seal. Put in pans with seam side down. Brush with melted butter. Cover and let rise about 1 hour. Preheat oven to 400 degrees. Cut gashes in tops of loaves. Bake 1 hour. Turn out and cool slightly. Makes 2 loaves.

FILLING: Cook parsley, scallions and garlic in butter until wilted—not browned. Reduce to half. Cool. Save 2 Tbsp. eggs to brush loaves, add rest to parsley. Season with salt, pepper and Tabasco to taste.

Dot Nicholls (Mrs. T.H.)

DILLY BREAD
This recipe was given to me by a friend.

1 pkg. dry yeast
1/4 cup warm water
1 cup creamed cottage cheese, heated to lukewarm
2 Tbsp. sugar
1 Tbsp. instant onions
1 Tbsp. margarine
2 tsp. dill seeds
1 tsp. salt
1/4 tsp. soda
1 unbeaten egg
2-1/4 cups flour

Soften yeast in warm water. Combine cottage cheese with next 6 ingredients. Add unbeaten egg and yeast mixture. Add flour to form a stiff ball. Knead briefly. Turn into a well-greased loaf pan. Let rise until double in size.
Bake at 350 degrees for 40 to 50 minutes. Brush with butter and sprinkle with salt. Makes 1 loaf.

Betty Harkey (Mrs. E.L.)

RYE-PUMPERNICKEL

2 cups warm water (105 to 115
    degrees)
1/4 tsp. ginger
1 tsp. sugar
1 pkg. dry yeast (1 Tbsp.)
1 Tbsp. salt
1 Tbsp. honey
4 cups sifted all-purpose flour
2 cups unsifted rye flour
1 Tbsp. each: Postum, cocoa
1 tsp. instant coffee
1 Tbsp. caraway seeds
cornmeal
cold water

In a large mixer bowl, mix together warm water, yeast, sugar, ginger and honey. In a separate bowl, mix together the all-purpose flour, rye flour, salt and caraway seeds, Postum, cocoa and instant coffee.

Stir in four cups of the flour mixture into the yeast mixture. Beat for 5 minutes. Gradually add the rest of the flour mixture. Knead on a floured pastry board until the mixture is smooth. Place dough in a large, lightly-greased bowl; cover with a damp cloth. Put into your cold oven with a pan of hot water on the shelf below it. Let rise until double in bulk. Punch down and turn out onto a lightly floured board or pastry cloth. Knead until smooth.

Shape dough into a round loaf and place on a lightly greased cookie sheet that has been dusted with cornmeal. Let stand for 5 minutes. Slash the top of dough to form an X and brush with cold water. Place the bread on the middle rack of a cold oven with a pan of boiling water on the bottom rack. Turn on the oven to 400 degrees and bake 50 to 60 minutes or until bread sounds hollow when lightly tapped on the bottom or side. Cool on a wire cake rack. Cut with a serrated knife. Makes 1 loaf.

Sometimes I leave the bread in the oven to rise, about 10 minutes before I turn on the oven. You can try it both ways and see which does the better for you. The Postum, cocoa and coffee are for color. The Postum gives a nice nutty flavor.

Gensie

Both salt and sugar act best when a small amount of one is added to the predominant use of the other.

313

HONEY WHOLE WHEAT BREAD

5 cups warm water (110 degrees)
2 pkgs. active dry yeast
6 Tbsp. shortening
1/4 cup honey
4 cups whole wheat flour
1/2 cup instant potatoes
1/2 cup instant dry milk
1 Tbsp. salt
6-1/2 to 8 cups white flour

Combine 1/2 cup water and yeast in a bowl. Stir to dissolve yeast. Melt shortening in 6-quart saucepan; remove from heat. Add honey and remaining water. Mix whole wheat flour, instant potatoes, dry milk and salt. Add to saucepan. Beat until smooth. Add yeast mixture and beat until smooth. Then with a wooden spoon mix in enough white flour to make a dough that cleans the pan. Knead on lightly-floured board until smooth and satiny, and small blisters appear — 8 to 10 minutes.

Place in greased bowl; turn dough so top is greased. Cover; let rise in warm place (85 degrees) until doubled, 1 to 1-1/2 hours. Punch down dough; divide into thirds; cover and let rest 5 minutes. Shape into 3 loaves. Place in greased 9 x 5 x 3 inch pans; brush with melted shortening. Cover; let rise until doubled — 1 hour. Bake in hot oven (400 degrees) about 50 minutes. Cover with foil "tent" if browning too quickly. Remove from pans; cool on wire rack. Makes 3 loaves. Freezes well.

Janice Privette (Mrs. G.D.)

BEST MISSISSIPPI CORN BREAD
This is the best corn bread I've ever had!

1 cup corn meal (white bolted, stone ground)
1 cup flour, white, unbleached
2 tsp. baking powder
1 tsp. sugar
1/2 cup butter (1 stick)
pinch salt
2 cups buttermilk
2 eggs
chopped onion (1 small to medium)

Mix together and pour into 10 x 10 x 2 inch Corning ware baking dish and bake at 400 degrees for 30 to 45 minutes. Serves 6.

Marsha Cagle (Mrs. P.C.)

MY OWN 100% WHOLE WHEAT BREAD

2 pkg. dry yeast (2 Tbsp.)
1/2 cup warm water
1 tsp. sugar
1/4 tsp. ginger
1-1/2 cups milk, scalded
6 Tbsp. butter
3/4 cup warm water
3/4 cup honey
4 tsp. salt
7 to 8 cups whole wheat flour (be
   sure it is bread flour; I like
   Elams or Deaf Smith)

Dissolve yeast in 1/2 cup warm water with sugar and ginger in the large mixer bowl. Heat milk, take off the stove and add butter. When it melts, add the water and honey. It should be just warm. Pour into the large bowl with the yeast; add the salt and 5 cups whole wheat flour. Beat until it gets stretchy (about 5 minutes). Gradually add the flour either by kneading it in on a floured board or by dough hook.

Put into greased bowl, cover with damp tea towel and put in a warm place to rise until double in bulk (2 hours). This makes 3 medium sized loaves. Grease your loaf pans.

When double in bulk, punch down dough. Turn out on floured board. Make into 3 loaves and put in greased pans to rise again. When the loaves reach the top of the pans (40 minutes), bake in 375 degree oven for 25 to 30 minutes. When the loaves come from the oven, take immediately out of the pans and put on cake rack to cool. Grease tops with butter. When *completely cold* put in zip-lock bags or wrap in foil or freezer paper.

Gensie

STONE-GROUND SOUTHERN CORNBREAD

1 cup **stone ground** plain corn
   meal (Note: Finely ground
   meal does **not** result in the
   same crumbly texture as
   stone ground meal)
1 tsp. baking powder
1/4 tsp. soda
1/2 tsp. salt
1 Tbsp. sugar
1/4 cup cooking oil
1 egg
1 cup buttermilk

Place oil in skillet in hot oven. Sift together dry ingredients. Stir in egg and buttermilk until well mixed. Add *hot* oil and mix well. Pour batter into hot skillet. Bake until brown (30-35 minutes) at 400 degrees. Makes 8 servings.

Vernie Pickens (Mrs. F.O.)

MISSISSIPPI CORN BREAD MUFFINS

1/2 cup oil
1 cup sour cream
1 8-1/2 oz. can cream-style corn
1 cup plain corn meal
2 tsp. baking powder
1-1/2 tsp. salt
1 tsp. sugar
2 eggs, beaten

Mix first 3 ingredients. Stir in remaining ingredients. Pour batter into large, well-greased muffin tins. Makes 12 muffins. If making corn bread, bake in well-greased 9-inch square pan and then cut squares to desired size. For muffins bake at 375 degrees for 20 to 25 minutes or until done. For bread, bake 35 minutes or until done.

Arnita Kee
Laura Roddey (Mrs. J.H.)

VARIATION: Use 1 cup self-rising corn meal instead of plain corn meal, baking powder, salt and sugar. Add 1 medium onion, chopped. Proceed as directed.

Newley Lindsey (Mrs. R.L.)

VARIATION: Use 3 eggs instead of 2, 1 tsp. salt and 1 12-oz. box Flako Corn Muffin Mix instead of corn meal, baking powder and sugar.

Wynne McLean (Mrs. Malcolm)

CORN MUFFINS

These muffins are so moist and have such a tasty corn flavor, they will melt in your mouth.

1 8-oz. carton sour cream
1 8-1/2 oz. can cream-style corn
1/2 cup salad oil
1 cup self-rising corn meal
1/2 tsp. salt
1 heaping tsp. baking powder
2 eggs

Combine all ingredients except eggs, and mix well. Add eggs and mix well again. Fill greased muffin tins 2/3 full. Bake at 375 degrees 20-25 minutes until golden brown.

Janis Rikard (Mrs. W.L)

SOUTHERN CORNBREAD

2 cups self-rising cornmeal
2 cups buttermilk
2 eggs
1/2 tsp. soda
4 Tbsp. bacon drippings

Combine cornmeal, buttermilk, eggs and soda. Mix well. Heat bacon drippings in a heavy 10-inch skillet. Pour half of hot drippings into cornmeal mixture and mix well. Pour batter into hot skillet and bake at 425 degrees for 30 minutes. Serves 8.

Nancy Wohlbruck (Mrs. Everett L.)

DOC THURSTON'S BEST HUSHPUPPIES

1 cup cornmeal
1/3 cup flour
1 tsp. sugar
1 Tbsp. fat
2 pinches salt
1 Tbsp. baking powder
1 well-beaten egg
onion
cayenne pepper
vegetable oil

Mix dry ingredients. Add egg and melted fat and enough cold beer or water to make a paste (beer is better). Add onion and cayenne pepper to taste. Drop by spoonfuls into skillet with hot oil. Fry until golden brown. Drain on paper towels.

NOTE: Grated onion, dehydrated onion, onion powder or juice may be used, or a touch of garlic.

Stella Thurston (Mrs. Doc J.)

ANN'S MEXICAN SPOON BREAD

1 cup yellow cornmeal
1 tsp. salt
1/2 tsp. soda
3/4 cup milk
1/3 cup oil
2 eggs
1 17-oz. can cream-style corn
4 oz. diced green chilies (drained)
2 cups shredded sharp
    Cheddar cheese

Combine cornmeal, salt and soda. Stir in milk and oil; add eggs and corn. Spoon half of mixture into 1-1/2 quart casserole.
Sprinkle half of cheese and half of chilies. Repeat. Bake at 350 degrees for 45 minutes. Serves 8.

NOTE: I use only half the amount of chilies as many people do not like "hot" dishes.

Betty Holland (Mrs. Calvin)

317

RUBY'S SPOONBREAD

1 cup corn meal (white water-
    ground), measured after
    sifting
2 cups scalding water
1 cup milk
3 tsp. baking powder
2 eggs, beaten
1 tsp. salt
1 Tbsp. sugar
2 Tbsp. Wesson oil

Mix all ingredients well and pour into a well-greased 2-quart baking casserole. Bake for 1 hour at 350 degrees. Serves 4.

Dickie Tyler (Mrs. J.D.)

SOUTHERN SPOON BREAD

I found this recipe on a cornmeal bag one summer at the beach when cooking seafood and have used it ever since.

4 cups milk
2 cups enriched self-rising corn
    meal
3 Tbsp. butter or margarine,
    melted
4 eggs, **well** beaten

Mix the milk and the cornmeal mix. Scald and cook in the top of a double boiler or very heavy saucepan until the consistency of "mush" (about 8 minutes). Fold *well-beaten* eggs into the mixture. Add butter. Pour into a well-greased 2-quart baking dish. Bake in 400 degree oven for 45 minutes or until set. Serve hot from dish with lots of butter.

NOTE: For an extra nice touch, put melted butter in bottom of baking dish and sprinkle with coarsely-ground black pepper.

Ellen Knott (Mrs. B.F.)

BLUEBERRY MUFFINS

These muffins are very moist and delicious.
Great for breakfast!

2 eggs
1/2 cup melted butter
1 cup sugar
1 cup sour cream
2 cups all-purpose flour
1 tsp. baking powder
1/4 tsp. baking soda
1/2 tsp. salt
1 cup blueberries

Mix eggs, butter, sugar and sour cream. Sift dry ingredients together, then add blueberries. Fold blueberry and flour mixture into the egg mixture until blended. Spoon batter into greased muffin tins and bake at 375 degrees for 25 minutes. Makes 12 large muffins.

Judith Kennedy (Mrs. Richard L.)

SKYLINE'S APPLE MUFFINS
Great for breakfast, brunch or ladies luncheon

1/3 cup sugar
1 Tbsp. butter (room temperature)
1-1/2 cup brown sugar, firmly
    packed
2/3 cup vegetable oil
1 egg
1 cup buttermilk
1 tsp. baking soda
1 tsp. salt
1 tsp. vanilla
2-1/2 cups sifted all-purpose flour
1-1/2 cups diced, peeled apples
1/2 cup chopped pecans

In small bowl combine white sugar and butter. Mix until crumbly; set aside. In a larger bowl combine brown sugar, oil and egg. In another bowl combine buttermilk, soda, salt and vanilla. Blend flour into brown sugar mixture, alternately with buttermilk mixture. Stir just until ingredients are blended — do not overmix. Fold in apples and pecans. Pour into greased and floured muffin pans. Sprinkle sugar mixture on top. Bake for about 30 minutes at 325 degrees. Makes 24 muffins.

Blair Chewning (Mrs. John)

ENGLISH MUFFINS

1 cup hot water
1/2 cup scalded milk
2 tsp. sugar
1 tsp. salt
1 pkg. yeast
2 Tbsp. lukewarm water
4 cups flour, sifted before
    measuring
3 Tbsp. shortening

Combine 1 cup water, milk, sugar and salt. When lukewarm add yeast, dissolved in water, and beat 2 cups flour into mixture. Cover with damp cloth and let rise until it collapses (about 1-1/2 hours). Beat in shortening. Add rest of flour. Mix well. Let rise until doubled. Place on lightly-floured board. Press until 3/4 inch thick. Fill muffin rings 1/2 full — or cut into 3-inch round rings. Let rise. Cook until light brown at 350 degrees for about 1/2 hour. You may need to turn them. They freeze beautifully, are fun to make and much better than purchased ones. Yield: about 16 muffins.

Dot Nicholls (Mrs. T.H.)

JO'S LITTLE BREADS
Easy, quick and delicious

1/2 cup self-rising flour
1/2 stick butter or margarine,
    melted
1/2 cup sour cream

Mix together and put in greased tiny-cup muffin tin. Fill half full and bake at 450 degrees for 15 minutes. Serve piping hot. Makes 12 but everybody will want at least three. Recipe doubles easily.

Frances Evans (Mrs. D.O.)

EASY BLUEBERRY MUFFINS

2 cups Bisquick
1/4 cup sugar
1/2 tsp. cinnamon
1 cup sour cream
1 unbeaten egg
1 cup fresh or frozen blueberries
sugar

Mix first 5 ingredients until well blended. Add fresh or frozen blueberries and divide dough into muffin pans. Sprinkle with sugar and bake at 425 degrees for 20 minutes. Makes 12 large muffins.

Dale Yaged (Mrs. D.)

ALWAYS-READY BRAN MUFFINS

I make miniature muffins (cook for 8-10 minutes) for morning coffee, or to serve with luncheon salad plates.

3 cups All Bran
1 cup boiling water
1/2 cup butter or margarine
1/2 cup white sugar
1/2 cup packed brown sugar
2-1/2 tsp. soda
1 tsp. salt
2 cups buttermilk
2 beaten eggs
2-1/2 cups unbleached flour
1 cup raisins (plumped in boiling water)
1/2 cup chopped nuts (optional)

Combine 1 cup bran with 1 cup boiling water. Stir to mix and let steep. Cream butter and sugars. Add beaten eggs, steeped bran, rest of bran, dry ingredients and buttermilk. Stir until mixed well. Add raisins and nuts. Put batter into glass or plastic *covered* container and keep in refrigerator at least 12 hours before baking. Will keep for 6 weeks. Bake as needed in well-greased muffin tins at 375 degrees for 15 minutes. I cook muffins, freeze them and use a few at a time.

Peggy Young (Mrs. John A.)

Similar recipes by:
Linda Miller (Mrs. W.R.)
Janis Rickard (Mrs. W.L.)

FEATHER-LIGHT MUFFINS

A delicious plain muffin easily varied by adding blueberries.

1/4 cup sugar
1/4 cup soft shortening
1 egg
1-3/4 cup sifted, unbleached flour
4 tsp. baking powder
1/2 tsp. salt
1 cup milk

Mix sugar and shortening. Blend in egg. Sift together the flour, baking powder and salt. Stir into first mixture alternately with the milk. Fill greased muffin cups 2/3 full. Bake at 375 degrees until golden brown, 20 to 23 minutes. Serve hot. When using blueberries, fill cups 1/3, put blueberries in, fill cup to 2/3. Makes 12 muffins.

Nancy Little (Mrs. T.M.)

FIVE-FRUIT MUFFINS

1 17-oz. can fruit cocktail
1-3/4 cups sifted all-purpose flour
1/3 cup sugar
2 tsp. baking powder
3/4 tsp. salt
1/2 tsp. cardamon
2 eggs, beaten
1/4 cup melted butter
1 Tbsp. grated lemon rind
1/4 cup chopped walnuts

Drain fruit cocktail, reserving syrup. Measure syrup and add enough water to make 2/3 cup, if necessary. Sift together flour, sugar, baking powder, salt and cardamon. Stir in syrup along with eggs, butter and lemon rind.

Mix only until all dry ingredients are moistened. Stir in fruit and walnuts. Fill well-greased muffin tins 2/3 full. Bake at 400 degrees for 20 to 25 minutes, then remove from pan after a few minutes and cool thoroughly on wire rack. To store left-over muffins, wrap in foil and keep in refrigerator or freezer. Makes 12 3-inch muffins.

Ellen Knott (Mrs. B.F.)

MARGUERITE MUFFINS

2 eggs
1 cup brown sugar
1/2 cup flour
1/2 tsp. salt
1 cup chopped pecans
1/4 tsp. baking powder

Slightly beat 2 eggs, add next ingredients in order listed. Mix well and fill buttered muffin tins 3/4 full. Bake at 350 degrees until mixture begins to leave sides — 8 to 12 minutes. Makes 12 muffins. May be frozen.

Kathy Howe

MYSTERY MUFFINS
Can be done at the last minute!

1 cup self-rising flour
1/2 cup milk
3 Tbsp. mayonnaise

Mix all ingredients. Fill greased muffin cups half full. Bake at 425 degrees for 20-25 minutes. Serves 9.

Dottie Grier (Mrs. R.N.)

ORANGE MUFFINS

1/3 cup margarine
1/3 cup sugar
1 egg, beaten
1 Tbsp. grated orange rind
1-1/2 cups flour
1 Tbsp. baking powder
1/4 tsp. salt
1/4 cup milk
1/4 cup orange juice

Cream margarine and sugar. Blend in beaten egg and orange rind. Sift together flour, baking powder and salt, add alternately with milk and orange juice, mixing well after each addition. Grease muffin pan and fill 2/3 full. Bake in hot oven (400 degrees) for 15-20 minutes. Makes 1 dozen muffins.

Georgia Miller (Mrs. George)

PECAN MUFFINS

1 cup sugar
2 cups flour
1/4 tsp. salt
2 tsp. baking powder
1/2 cup melted shortening
   or butter
4 tsp. cinnamon
1 cup chopped pecans
1 cup milk
2 eggs, beaten

Sift dry ingredients together. Add nuts. Mix together milk, melted shortening and beaten eggs. Combine dry and liquid ingredients quickly with little stirring. Bake in muffin tins in hot oven (425 degrees) for 15 minutes. Yield: 12 muffins.

Shirley Snead (Mrs. Henry T.)

OATMEAL MUFFINS

2 cups quick-cooking (not instant)
   rolled oats
2 cups buttermilk
1 cup brown sugar
2 eggs
2 cups flour (mix whole wheat
   and regular)
2 tsp. baking powder
1 tsp. soda
1/2 tsp. salt
1 cup vegetable oil

Add oats to buttermilk. Let stand 1 hour. Add brown sugar, eggs, and flour that has been sifted with baking powder, soda and salt. Stir well and add oil. Bake in greased muffin tins *without* liners at 400 degrees for 15 minutes or until done. Batter can be stored in the refrigerator for up to 3 weeks. Freezes well.

Susan Murfee (Mrs. D.G.)

POPPY SEED MUFFINS

1-1/2 cups biscuit mix (like
    Bisquick)
1/2 cup sugar
1 Tbsp. poppy seeds
3/4 cup raisins
1 egg, beaten
3/4 cup commercial sour cream
1 tsp. vanilla

Mix all ingredients together and divide into 12 muffin tin sections. Bake at 400 degrees for 20 minutes. Yields 1 dozen.

Marsha Cagle (Mrs. P.C.)

PUMPKIN MUFFINS

1-2/3 cups sifted flour
1/4 tsp. baking powder
1 tsp. baking soda
1/4 tsp. salt
1 tsp. pumpkin pie spice
1/8 tsp. ground cloves
1/3 cup raisins
1/3 cup butter (melted)
1/3 cup water
1-1/2 cups sugar
2 eggs
1 generous cup canned
    pumpkin

Mix wet ingredients thoroughly, then add dry ingredients until blended. Bake in greased muffin tins at 350 degrees until golden brown — about 35 minutes.

Virginia Golding (Mrs. John G.)

WHOLE WHEAT MUFFINS

1 cup whole wheat flour, unsifted
1 cup unbleached flour, unsifted
1/4 cup sugar
4 tsp. baking powder
pinch of salt
2 eggs. beaten
1/4 cup Mazola oil
1 cup milk
1/2 cup chopped pecans
    (optional)
1/2 cup blueberries (optional)

Mix dry ingredients together. Mix liquid ingredients together. Pour liquid ingredients into a "well" made in dry ingredients. Stir together; stir in pecans or blueberries, if desired. Pour into greased muffin tins. Bake in pre-heated 425 degree oven for 15 minutes.

VARIATION: Corn Muffins:
Substitute corn meal for the whole wheat flour. Omit pecans or blueberries. Otherwise, follow above recipe exactly.

Mayree Kay Miller (Mrs. J.J.)

SPOON BREAD MUFFINS

Made in individual servings, rather than the traditional manner.

2 cups water
1 cup sifted cornmeal
1 tsp. salt
2 tsp. sugar
1/8 tsp. pepper
3/4 stick butter
1 cup cold milk
3 beaten eggs
2 heaping tsp. baking powder

Mix water, sifted cornmeal, salt, sugar and pepper in top of double boiler. Stir until thickened to oatmeal consistency. Remove from heat and add butter, stirring until melted. Stir in the cup of cold milk. Beat baking powder in eggs and add to cornmeal mixture. Mix well. Pour into glass custard cups, well greased with Crisco. Place on cookie sheet and bake at 350 degrees for 45 minutes to 1 hour. Makes 8 to 10.

NOTE: *Do not bake in metal muffin tins.* Recipe will not turn out well.

Wilhelmina Cunningham (Mrs. J.A.)

ALMOND COFFEE CAKE STRIPS

This delicious coffee cake will look like it came from a bakery.

2 cups flour (divided)
1 Tbsp. cold water
3 unbeaten eggs
1 cup butter, divided (do not use
    margarine)
1 cup water
1/2 tsp. almond extract

GLAZE:
1 cup confectioners' sugar
1/2 tsp. vanilla extract
4 tsp. cream
3 tsp. butter
1/4 cup sliced almonds (sprinkle
    on glaze)

Sift 1 cup flour into a bowl. Add 1/2 cup (one stick) softened butter. Blend the butter into the flour as you would do for a pie crust. Add 1 Tbsp. cold water. Toss lightly. Take half the dough and pat it out firmly into a strip 3 x 8 inches on a lightly-greased cookie sheet. Pat the rest of the dough out on the other end of the cookie sheet into a strip like the first one.

In a pan, heat to boiling the remaining 1/2 butter with 1 cup water. Beat in 1 cup flour. Remove from heat.

Add eggs, one at a time; beat after each addition. Add almond extract. Cool mixture slightly, then spread over the two 3 x 8 inch strips of pastry. Bake approximately 60 mintues in a 350 degree oven. Cool until slightly warm.

GLAZE: Mix together all glaze ingredients except almonds. Cover warm pastry with glaze and sprinkle with almonds. Freezes beautifully.

Anne Zeola (Mrs. John)

EASY CARAMEL COFFEE CAKE

1 box yellow cake mix (regular, not "pudding")
1 box vanilla pudding (not instant)
6 oz. butterscotch morsels
1 cup pecans, chopped
2 cups milk

Cook pudding according to package directions; let cool. Stir cooked pudding into dry cake mix and mix well. Pour into greased, floured 9 x 13 inch pan. Top with morsels and nuts. Bake at 350 degrees for 20-25 minutes. Cut. Serves 8-10.

Pam Allen (Mrs. John R.)

CHOCOLATE CHIP COFFEE CAKE

1 stick butter, softened
1 cup sugar
2 eggs, beaten
1 tsp. vanilla extract
1 cup sour cream
2 cups flour
1 tsp. baking powder
1 tsp. baking soda

TOPPING:
6 oz. chocolate chips
1/2 cup finely-chopped nuts
1 tsp. cocoa (Hershey's)
1/4 cup sugar

Cream butter and sugar; add eggs and vanilla. Mix together flour, soda and baking powder. Alternate some flour mixture, then sour cream into the butter, sugar and egg mixture until all the flour and sour cream has been used. In a greased tube pan put half of the batter and half of the topping. Finish off with rest of batter and topping. Bake at 350 degrees for 50 to 60 minutes.

Georgia Miller (Mrs. George)

LAZY LADY'S COFFEE RING

1 Tbsp. softened margarine
1/2 cup orange marmalade
2 Tbsp. chopped pecans
1 cup firmly-packed brown sugar
1/2 tsp. cinnamon
2 10-oz. cans refrigerated buttermilk flaky biscuits
1/2 cup melted margarine

Preheat oven to 350 degrees. Grease a 12-cup Bundt pan or a 3 qt. ring mold with 1 Tbsp. margarine. Place teaspoonsful of orange marmalade in pan. Sprinkle with nuts. In small bowl, combine brown sugar and cinnamon. Set aside. Separate biscuits. Dip them in melted margarine; then in sugar mixture. Stand biscuits on edge in pan, spacing evenly. Sprinkle with remaining sugar and drizzle with rest of margarine. Bake near center of oven until brown, about 30-40 minutes. Cool upright in pan for 5 minutes. Invert onto serving plate. Pull apart. Must be done immediately before serving. Serves 8.

Jean Webb (Mrs. F.A.)

DOODLE SNAP

Made with ingredients you always have in the house.

1 cup sugar
1 Tbsp. corn oil (Mazola
  or similar)
1 egg
1 cup milk
2 cups all-purpose flour
2 tsp. baking powder
1/2 tsp. salt
brown sugar
cinnamon
butter

Mix first 7 ingredients and pour into a greased and floured 9-inch square pan. Sprinkle the top with brown sugar, then cinnamon. Dot butter all around the top—approximately every 1-1/2 to 2 inches. Everywhere there is butter, it melts and makes the brown sugar and cinnamon go down into the cake. Too much butter makes it all go to the bottom—not enough butter and the top stays powdery. You may need to experiment with the brown sugar, cinnamon and butter to get it the way you like; but using a stick of butter, I cut a pat 1/8 inch thick, then cut that into fourths, and dot the fourths about 1-1/2 inches apart all over the top. Bake at 375 degrees for approximately 20 minutes. Yield: 16 2-inch square pieces.

Wynne McLean (Mrs. Malcolm)

CREAM CHEESE COFFEE CAKE

Coffee, brunch or breakfast treat. Dough is refrigerated overnight.

1 tsp. salt
1/2 cup sugar
1 cup sour cream, scalded
1 stick margarine, chopped up
2 pkgs. yeast
1/2 cup warm water
1 tsp. sugar
2 eggs
4 cups plain, unsifted flour

FILLING:
1 lb. cream cheese, soft
2 tsp. vanilla extract
3/4 cup sugar
1/8 tsp. salt

GLAZE:
1 cup powdered sugar
1 tsp. vanilla
2 Tbsp. milk

Heat together salt, sugar and sour cream; then add 1 stick margarine. Set aside. Sprinkle 2 pkgs. yeast over 1/2 cup warm water; add 1 tsp. sugar to proof. Add sour cream mixture. Beat in 2 eggs, add 4 cups flour (add 3 cups at once and stir in 4th cup). Cover and let it refrigerate overnight. Next day, roll into four 8 x 12 inch shapes and spread with filling mixture. (Combine all filling ingredients.) Roll up jelly-roll fashion and put on greased, foil-covered cookie sheets (2 per cookie sheet). Cut through tops of pastry with scissors (hold scissors tips perpendicular to pastry). Let rise in warm oven until double in bulk (1 to 2 hours). Bake at 375 degrees for 10-15 minutes. Brush with glaze immediately after baking. Make glaze by combining sugar, vanilla and milk in a small mixing bowl. This coffee cake freezes very well. Yield: 4 jelly rolls.

Sharon Edge (Mrs. W.S.)

OVERNIGHT CRUNCH COFFEE CAKE

2 cups sifted all-purpose flour
1 tsp. baking powder
1 tsp. baking soda
1 tsp. cinnamon
1/2 tsp. salt
2/3 cup butter
1 cup sugar
1/2 cup firmly-packed brown
    sugar
2 eggs
1 cup buttermilk (or sour milk)

TOPPING:
1/2 cup packed brown sugar
1/2 cup chopped nuts
1/2 tsp. cinnamon
1/4 tsp. nutmeg

Sift together dry ingredients in separate bowl. Cream together butter, sugar and 1/2 cup brown sugar. Add eggs, alternating dry and wet ingredients. Beat with mixer on medium speed until smooth. Pour into greased and floured 13 x 9 x 2 inch pan. Combine topping mix and pour over batter. Refrigerate at least 8 hours for full flavor. Bake at 350 degrees for about 45 mintues (check after 30 minutes). Serve hot.

Marsha Cagle (Mrs. P.C.)

EASY PINEAPPLE COFFEE CAKE

1 box yellow cake mix (Duncan
    Hines), divided
1 cup brown sugar, packed
3/4 cup walnuts, chopped
1/2 stick butter, firm
3 eggs
1-1/2 cups sour cream
1 tsp. almond flavoring
1 1-lb. 4 oz. can crushed pine-
    apple, drained

Mix together 2/3 cup of the dry cake mix, brown sugar, walnuts and butter. Cut with pastry cutter until crumbly; reserve. Beat together eggs, sour cream, flavoring and remaining cake mix. Spread half of cake batter in a greased and floured 9 x 13 inch baking container. Top with half the pineapple and sprinkle with half the brown sugar mixture. Spoon remaining batter over brown sugar mixture. Spread gently with spoon. Top with remaining pineapple and sprinkle with remaining brown sugar mixture. Bake at 350 degrees for 55 to 60 minutes. Makes 16 to 20 pieces.

NOTE: For a nice change, use 1 can cherry pie filling instead of pineapple and spread over first half of batter. Top with 1/2 crumb mixture, remaining batter as above and other half of crumb mixture. Bake at 350 degrees for 50 to 60 minutes or until done.

Ellen Knott (Mrs. B.F.)

SOUR CREAM COFFEE CAKE I

1/2 cup butter
1 cup sugar
2 eggs
1 tsp. vanilla
2 cups flour, sifted
2 tsp. baking powder
1 tsp. baking soda
1-1/2 cups sour cream
1/2 tsp. salt

TOPPING:
3/4 cup brown sugar
2 tsp. cinnamon
3/4 cup chopped nuts

Cream butter and sugar together. Add eggs, salt and vanilla. Sift flour; add baking soda and baking powder. Blend in dry ingredients, alternating with the sour cream.
Pour mixture into greased 9 x 13-inch pan. Alternate one layer of mixture and then one layer of topping, ending with mixture. Sprinkle remaining topping on top of the cake. Bake at 350 degrees for 35 minutes. May be frozen until needed. Serves 16.

Sandy Chase (Mrs. E. R.)
Pat Viser

BEST CREPE BATTER

These are marvelous to have on hand, ready to fill with either a gourmet combination or just leftovers!

1-1/8 cups flour
1/8 tsp. salt
4 eggs
2-2/3 Tbsp. cognac
1-1/3 tsp. grated lemon rind
2-2/3 Tbsp. melted butter
1-1/8 cup regular milk (not skim or 2%)

Sift dry ingredients together. Add eggs one at a time. Whisk well after each addition until no lumps are present (can use electric mixer at low speed). Add cognac, lemon rind and butter and gradually whisk in the milk. The batter should now have the consistency of thin cream. Let batter rest 1 to 2 hours. Cook crepes until lightly brown in crepe pan or electric crepe maker. As cooked, keep warm in low oven with foil over top of plate. If cooking to store in freezer, stack on plate while preparing the rest. Store with waxed paper between crepes. Then wrap well with foil and put into freezer.

VARIATION: For dessert crepes, sweeten batter by adding 4 tsp. sugar.

Nancy Little (Mrs. T. H.)

SOUR CREAM COFFEE CAKE II

3 cups flour
3 cups sugar
2 sticks butter or margarine
6 eggs
1 cup sour cream
1/4 tsp. baking soda
1 tsp. vanilla extract or anise

NUT MIXTURE:
1 cup chopped walnuts or pecans
1/4 cup sugar
2 Tbsp. cinnamon
1 cup butterscotch chips

First mix together sour cream and baking soda; set aside. Cream butter and sugar in mixer, adding eggs one at a time. Then add to the butter mixture, the sour cream and flour, alternating each time. Add flavoring last; do not overbeat. Set the batter aside.

Mix all of the nut mixture ingredients together; set aside. Place half of the nut mixture in bottom of a 10-inch tube pan, greased with Crisco, sprayed with Pam, and dusted with flour. Pour half of the batter over mixture. Then add remaining nut mixture. Pour remaining batter into pan. Bake cake at 350 degrees for 1-1/2 hours.

Aphroula Anderson (Mrs. Jimmie)

BUTTERMILK PANCAKES

My mother's recipe—our regular Saturday morning breakfast

2 cups flour
2 tsp. baking powder
1 tsp. salt
1/2 tsp. baking soda
4 Tbsp. sugar
2 well-beaten eggs
2 cups buttermilk
2 Tbsp. vegetable oil

Sift flour before measuring. Resift with dry ingredients. Beat eggs until very light. Add buttermilk and oil to eggs and mix. Add that mixture to dry ingredients and stir only until all flour is moistened. Batter will be lumpy. Bake on hot griddle. Serves 6.

Julia Warner (Mrs. C.E.)

COMPANY PANCAKE

1/2 cup flour
1/2 cup milk
2 eggs, lightly beaten
1/4 tsp. salt
pinch nutmeg
1 cup fruit—blueberries, apples,
    etc. (optional)
4 Tbsp. butter
juice of 1/2 lemon
powdered sugar

Preheat oven to 450 degrees. Blend together first 5 ingredients. Beat lightly, folding in fruit, if desired. In ovenproof skillet (12-inch) melt butter. When butter is very hot, pour in batter. Bake 15 minutes or until golden brown. Sprinkle generously with powdered sugar and return to oven briefly. Sprinkle with lemon juice and a dusting of sugar. Serve immediately from skillet, with maple syrup, jam, jelly or marmalade. Doubles nicely.

Ellen Knott (Mrs. B.F.)

PEACH BLOSSOM WAFFLES

4 eggs
1-1/2 cups buttermilk
1 tsp. almond extract
2 Tbsp. sugar
1 cup chopped peaches,
    fresh or canned
2 cups Bisquick
1/2 cup butter, melted

Beat eggs until light in large bowl of electric mixer. Add remaining ingredients and beat until blended. Ladle batter onto center of hot waffle iron and spread to cover surface. Bake until steaming stops. Serve hot with butter and syrup. Makes 12 waffles.

Betty Holland (Mrs. Calvin)

EASY BREAKFAST PUFF

1/4 cup butter
1/2 cup flour
1/2 cup milk
2 eggs, beaten
pinch of nutmeg

TOPPING:
1/2 lemon
marmalade
powdered sugar

Melt butter in 8-inch skillet on top of stove. In a bowl mix (do not beat) flour, milk, eggs and nutmeg. Batter will not be smooth. Pour into skillet and immediately place in preheated 425 degree oven for 15 to 20 minutes. Remove from oven when puffy and golden brown. Squeeze lemon over the puff. Spread orange marmalade over the puff; then sprinkle with powdered sugar.

Betty Bradley

FLUFFY FRENCH TOAST

3 slices dry bread (2 to 3 days old,
    cut 3/4 inch thick)
2 eggs
1/2 cup cream
pinch of salt
dash of nutmeg
1/4 cup cooking oil
confectioners' sugar
hot maple syrup

Trim crusts off bread and cut each diagonally. Beat eggs well; add cream, salt and nutmeg. Soak bread pieces, a couple at a time, in mixture until they absorb it thoroughly. In a skillet heat oil and fry bread on both sides until golden brown. Drain briefly on paper towels. Place bread on ungreased baking sheet in a 400 degree oven for about 5 minutes to puff up. Serve on heated plates. Sprinkle with sugar and serve with heated syrup. Serves 2.

Sophie Godwin

Cakes

ANGEL FOOD DELIGHT

1 medium-sized angel food cake
1/2 cup Kuhlua liqueur
3/4 cup heavy cream, whipped
5 small chocolate almond bars,
    crushed
1/2 cup slivered almonds, toasted

Make 24 small holes in cake. Fill holes evenly with Kuhlua and pour remainder over cake. Refrigerate chocolate almond bars for 2 hours and then crush into crumbly mixture. Add crushed bars to whipped cream and ice cake with the chocolate cream mixture. Toast almonds (watch carefully). Sprinkle on cake. Chill. Serves 10-12.

Ellen Knott (Mrs. B.F.)

COCONUT BAVARIAN CUSTARD CAKE
This cake is elegant yet light. A truly delicious dessert.

1 cup sugar
2 Tbsp. flour
4 eggs, separated
1 tsp. vanilla extract
2 cups milk
1 pkg. unflavored gelatin
1/4 cup cold water
1 cup heavy cream, whipped
1 large angel food cake, broken
    into bite-size pieces
1 cup heavy cream, whipped
    (for frosting)
1 pkg. frozen coconut
sherry

Sprinkle broken-up cake with sherry—set aside. Mix sugar, flour and egg yolks, add vanilla and blend well. Stir milk into mixture and blend thoroughly. Cook over low heat, stirring constantly until thickened (about 10 to 12 minutes). Stir in gelatin that has been soaked in cold water. Blend until gelatin is thoroughly dissolved—set mixture aside to cool. When cool, fold in the first cup of whipped cream and the stiffly beaten egg whites. In a large greased tube pan, alternate layers of broken cake pieces and sauce, ending with layer of sauce. Chill in refrigerator for at least 24 hours. When ready to serve, turn cake out onto serving platter. Frost with second cup of whipped cream. Sprinkle generously all over with coconut. Serves 12 to 14.

Peggy Buchanan (Mrs. D. Douglas)

ELEANOR'S COCONUT ICE BOX CAKE

Light dessert—very good!

1 angel food cake
2 cups milk
1 cup sugar
4 egg yolks
2 Tbsp. flour
1 envelope plain gelatin
1/2 cup cold water
4 egg whites
2 (6 oz.) pkgs. frozen coconut
1/2 pt. whipping cream
1/4 cup sugar

Crumble cake into small pieces and put into 9 x 13 x 2 cake pan. Heat milk, sugar, egg yolks, and flour until it coats the spoon. Soften gelatin in water and add to custard. Let cool. Beat egg whites until stiff. Add to custard. Mix in one package coconut. Pour over cake. Set aside. Whip 1/2 pint cream with 1/4 cup sugar. Pour over custard. Add the second package of coconut on top of cake. Refrigerate. Cut into squares. Serves 12-16.

Betty Holland (Mrs. R.C.)

HEAVENLY ANGEL CAKE

1 envelope Knox unflavored
    gelatin
1/4 cup cold water
1 cup maple syrup
1 pint whipping cream
1 cup coconut, flaked and toasted
1/3 cup slivered almonds, toasted
1 angel food cake, your favorite
    recipe or bought

In a small glass container, soften gelatin in water. Bring maple syrup to a boil and add gelatin, stirring well to dissolve. When thickened to the consistency of egg whites (can refrigerate to hasten thickening) fold in the whipped cream. Chill until mixture begins to stiffen. Spread on angel food cake. Toast coconut and almonds (watch carefully, burns easily), and sprinkle on cake.

Lea Bennett (Mrs. G.G.)

ICEBOX PINEAPPLE ANGEL FOOD CAKE

The perfect dessert after a heavy meal

1 angel food cake
2 (3 oz. each) pkgs. lemon Jello
1 (8 oz.) can crushed pineapple,
    undrained
juice and grated rind of 1-1/2
    lemons
1-1/2 pt. whipping cream, or 3
    pkgs. Dream Whip, whipped
mandarin oranges
pineapple pieces

Using pineapple juice and lemon juice in the liquid, prepare Jello using speed set directions. When Jello gets slightly thick, mix in drained pineapple and grated rind. Fold in 1 pt. whipping cream (or 2 pkgs. Dream Whip). Break up angel food cake into small pieces and fold into pineapple mixture. Put all into lightly oiled tube pan. Allow to jell and season for 24 hours. Garnish with additional whipped cream, mandarin oranges and pineapple pieces.

The Committee

APPLESAUCE DATE CAKE

2 cups flour
2 tsp. baking soda
1 tsp. cinnamon
1/2 tsp. allspice
1/2 tsp. nutmeg
1/4 tsp. salt
2 eggs
1 cup light brown sugar, firmly packed
1/2 cup butter or margarine, softened
2 cups hot applesauce
1 cup chopped dates
3/4 cup coarsely chopped pecans or walnuts

CREAM CHEESE FROSTING
1 pkg. (3 oz.) cream cheese, softened
1 Tbsp. butter or margarine, softened
1 tsp. vanilla extract
2 cups sifted confectioners' sugar

Grease well and flour a 9 x 9 x 2 inch baking pan. Into large bowl of electric mixer, sift flour with baking soda, cinnamon, allspice, nutmeg and salt. Then add eggs, brown sugar, butter and 1 cup hot applesauce. At low speed beat just until ingredients are combined. At medium speed beat 2 minutes longer, occasionally scraping sides of bowl. Add remaining hot applesauce, dates and pecans, and beat 1 minute. Pour batter into prepared pan. Bake in preheated 350 degree oven for 50 minutes or until cake tester inserted comes out clean. Let cool in pan 10 minutes. Remove from pan and let cool on wire rack. Frost top of cooled cake with Cream Cheese Frosting.
To prepare frosting:
In bowl of electric mixer, combine cream cheese, butter and vanilla. With mixer at low speed beat until smooth and fluffy. Gradually add confectioners' sugar and continue beating at medium speed until fluffy. Freezes nicely. Yield: 9 squares.

Ellen Knott ('Irs. B.F.)

LISA'S APPLE CAKE WITH RUM BUTTER GLAZE

Excellent for a coffee or as a dessert. Very moist and delicious!

1-1/2 cups oil
2 cups sugar
3 cups sifted flour
3 eggs
1 tsp. cinnamon
1 tsp. salt
1 tsp. soda
1 tsp. vanilla extract
16 oz. can apple pie filling
1 cup chopped nuts

GLAZE:
1/3 cup butter
2 cups confectioners' sugar
2 Tbsp. white rum
2 Tbsp. hot water

Beat together oil, sugar, flour, eggs, cinnamon, salt, soda and vanilla. Add apple pie filling and nuts. Stir until mixed. Pour into a greased and floured tube pan (10-inch). Bake at 350 degrees for 1 hour and 30 minutes.
GLAZE: Melt butter in saucepan. Blend in rum and hot water, mix in sugar. Glaze cooled cake. Freezes well. Serves 10.
Note: For best flavor, make 2 days ahead to age.

Lynn Wheeler (Mrs. Joseph G.)

CAROLINA APPLE CAKE

1-1/2 cups cooking oil
2 cups sugar
4 eggs, beaten
3 cups all-purpose flour
1 tsp. soda
1 tsp. salt
2 tsp. vanilla extract
1 tsp. cinnamon
3 cups peeled, diced apples
1 cup chopped nuts

GLAZE No.1:
1-1/2 sticks butter
1 cup brown sugar
1/4 cup milk
vanilla to taste

GLAZE No. 2:
1 cup confectioners' sugar
juice of 2 lemons

Mix oil, sugar and eggs together. Sift flour, soda, salt and cinnamon together and add to egg mixture. Mix thoroughly. Add vanilla, apples and nuts. Pour into greased, floured tube pan. Bake at 350 degrees approximately 1 hour. Remove from pan, cool and use glaze No. 1: Boil first 3 ingredients slowly for 10 minutes, add vanilla. Cool and pour over cake. OR pour cake mixture into greased and floured 9 x 13 pan. Bake in preheated 300 degree oven 1 hour and 20 minutes. Use glaze No. 2: mix sugar and lemon juice and pour over cake while hot.

Virginia Golding (Mrs. John G.)
Bonnie Phillips (Mrs. H.M.)

FRUIT COCKTAIL CAKE
Nice and moist

2 cups all-purpose flour
2 cups sugar
2 eggs
1 cup oil
2 tsp. soda
1/4 tsp. salt
1 17-oz. can fruit cocktail,
    undrained

TOPPING:
1 cup margarine
1 cup sugar
1 cup evaporated milk
1/2 cup chopped pecans
1 cup shredded coconut
1 teaspoon vanilla extract

Combine all ingredients in large bowl and beat 5 minutes. Pour into greased and floured 13 x 9 x 2 inch pan. Bake at 375 degrees for 45 minutes. Pour topping on cake. Allow cake to cool 2 hours before cutting.
TOPPING: Combine margarine, sugar, and evaporated milk in large saucepan; boil for 10 minutes (be careful or mixture will overflow). Remove from heat; add pecans, coconut and vanilla and pour on cake while topping is hot. Serves 12-15.

Ellen Knott (Mrs. B.F.)

AMBROSIA CHIFFON CAKE

5 egg yolks
1 cup egg whites (8 or 9 eggs)
2-1/4 cups sifted cake flour
1-1/2 cups sugar
1 Tbsp. baking powder
1 tsp. salt
1/2 cup oil
1/4 cup water
1/2 cup fresh orange juice
1 Tbsp. grated orange rind
1/2 tsp. cream of tartar
1 cup flaked or shredded coconut

ORANGE SATIN FROSTING
2 egg whites
1-1/2 cups sugar
1-1/2 tsp. light corn syrup
1/2 cup orange juice
dash of salt
1 tsp. grated orange rind
8 large marshmallows, cut in
    pieces
yellow food color

Bring eggs to room temperature. Sift flour with 1 cup sugar, baking powder and salt. Measure into mixing bowl the egg yolks, oil, water, orange juice and rind. Add sifted dry ingredients. Beat until smooth, about 1/2 minute at low speed or 75 strokes by hand. Add cream of tartar to egg whites. Beat until soft peaks form. Gradually add remaining 1/2 cup sugar, beating until mixture stands in very stiff peaks. Do not underbeat. Fold coconut into egg whites with a rubber spatula. Then gently fold egg yolk mixture into whites. Pour into ungreased 10 inch tube pan. Bake at 325 degrees for 1 hour or until surface springs back when touched lightly. Invert pan to cool. A good way is to place tube pan over inverted funnel or turn upside down and place on the neck of a bottle. When cool, loosen sides with a knife and turn out onto cake plate.

FROSTING: Combine in top of double boiler the egg whites, sugar, corn syrup, orange juice and salt. Beat one minute with electric or rotary hand beater. Cook over boiling water, beating constantly until mixture forms peaks (about 7 minutes). Remove from heat. Add marshmallows, orange rind and enough yellow food coloring to tint delicately. Beat 2 minutes until partially cooled. Spread over top and sides of cake. Can decorate with coconut.

Ellen Knott (Mrs. B.F.)

BANANA CAKE

1/2 cup butter or margarine
1 cup sugar
2 eggs
1 cup (2 to 3) very ripe mashed
    bananas
1/2 cup sour cream
2-1/4 cups flour
1 tsp. baking powder
1 tsp. baking soda
3/4 tsp. salt
1 tsp. vanilla

Cream butter and sugar. Beat in eggs one at a time. Add bananas and sour cream. Sift remaining ingredients together. Add to creamed mixture. Butter and flour a 10-inch tube pan. Pour in batter. Bake at 350 degrees until golden brown, about 50 minutes. Cool 5 minutes, turn out on rack.

Lillie Huss

APRICOT BRANDY CAKE
A never-fail cake

1/2 cup butter
1/2 cup margarine
3 cups sugar
6 large eggs
3 cups all-purpose flour
1/2 tsp. salt
1/4 tsp. soda
1 cup sour cream
1/2 tsp. lemon extract
1 tsp. orange extract
1/4 tsp. almond extract
1/2 tsp. rum extract
1 tsp. vanilla extract
1 cup apricot brandy (from local
ABC store)
FROSTING:
4 cups 10X powdered sugar
6 Tbsp. melted **butter**
1 tsp. vanilla extract
1/4 cup apricot brandy

Cream butter and margarine until light colored. Add sugar in thirds. Cream again until light and fluffy. Add eggs one at a time, beating well after each. Beat for another 3 minutes after the last egg is added. Add salt and soda to flour. Combine sour cream and the extracts. Add flour mixture and flavored sour cream alternately to the batter. Blend well. Fold in the apricot brandy. Bake in well-greased and floured 10-inch tube pan at 375 degrees for 70 minutes or until cake tests done. Cool for 15 minutes in pan; remove to cooling rack.

FROSTING: Make frosting by combining all ingredients; beat well. Apply to cooled cake with spatula and hands. It's the consistency of Play-doh and is easy to mold by hand. Cake can be frozen after baking but before icing. Serves 20-24.

Kay Roberson (Mrs. G. Don)

BANANA SPLIT CAKE

2 cups graham cracker crumbs
3 sticks margarine
2 cups confectioners' sugar
1 tsp. vanilla extract
4 or 5 bananas
1 large can crushed pineapple,
drained
1 16-oz. container Cool Whip
chocolate syrup
chopped pecans
maraschino cherries, halved

1st LAYER: Mix graham cracker crumbs and 1 stick of melted margarine. Press into 9 x 13 buttered dish.
2nd LAYER: Beat together until fluffy confectioners' sugar, 2 sticks softened margarine and vanilla. Spread over first layer.
3rd LAYER: Slice bananas. Place evenly over second layer.
4th LAYER: Drain and spread evenly over third layer a large can of crushed pineapple.
5th LAYER: Spread a large container of Cool Whip over fourth layer.
6th LAYER: Drizzle any amount of chocolate syrup over fifth layer.
7th LAYER: Sprinkle chopped pecans over sixth layer.
8th LAYER: Dot with maraschino cherry halves.

Caroline Carriker (Mrs. John H.)
Lea Bennett (Mrs. G.G.)

BANANA CHOCOLATE CHIP CAKE

This is a super moist cake that always gets raves.

1/4 cup margarine, melted
1 cup sugar
2 eggs
1 tsp. vanilla or rum extract
3 mashed ripe bananas
1/4 cup sour cream
1 tsp. baking soda
1 tsp. baking powder
1/2 tsp. salt
1-1/2 cups flour
3/4 cup chocolate chips
1/2 cup nuts

Melt margarine. Blend with sugar and eggs. Add flavoring and mashed bananas. Add sour cream alternately with dry ingredients. Beat on low speed until blended. Add nuts and chips. Pour into well-greased tube pan. Bake at 350 degrees for approximately 40 minutes. If wrapping for the freezer, remove from pan while slightly warm and wrap immediately in foil. Serves 10.
NOTE: I put leftover, mushy bananas in the freezer and use them up in this cake.

Paula Klein (Mrs. R.A.)

BLACKBERRY JAM CAKE

Every Kentucky family has their "secret" recipe. This is ours.
I hope Mama doesn't kill me.

1 cup butter (not margarine)
2 cups white sugar
4 egg yolks
1 cup blackberry jam
3 cups flour
1/2 tsp. salt
1/2 tsp. nutmeg
1/2 tsp. cloves
1 tsp. cinnamon
1 tsp. soda (rounded a little)
1 cup buttermilk
1 cup pecans, chopped
4 egg whites

CARAMEL ICING
1 1-lb. box light brown sugar
3/4 cup half-and-half
3/4 cup butter (not margarine)

Let butter and eggs come to room temperature. Cream butter and sugar. Add egg yolks one at a time. Gradually add jam. Sift flour, spices and soda together. Add alternately with buttermilk. Add pecans. Beat egg whites until stiff but not dry and fold in by hand. Bake at 325 degrees for 30 to 40 minutes in 3 greased and floured 9-inch cake pans. Test with toothpick for doneness. Cool and frost with caramel icing.

CARAMEL ICING: Stir all icing ingredients over medium heat until mixture forms a soft ball in a small cup of ice water. Do not use candy thermometer. Beat by hand until proper consistency to spread on cake. It is helpful to have your husband's arm in reserve. As icing thickens it will lose its shiny appearance. Spread icing between layers and on top of cake. If it become difficult to spread add a few *drops* of hot water. This cake keeps well.

Laura McMaster (Mrs. J.C.)

BLUEBERRY PUDDING CAKE

1 pt. blueberries, washed and
    drained
1 Tbsp. lemon juice
3/4 cup sugar
1/4 cup butter
1 cup all-purpose flour
1/2 tsp. salt
1 tsp. baking powder
1/2 cup milk

TOPPING:
1 cup sugar
1 Tbsp. cornstarch
1/2 tsp. salt
1 cup boiling water

Put berries in a greased 8-inch square pan. Sprinkle with lemon juice. Cream sugar and butter. Add dry ingredients and milk to sugar and butter mixture. Stir well and spread the mixture (or batter) over berries.

TOPPING: Combine the first 3 ingredients in the topping mixture. Sprinkle over batter. Pour 1 cup of boiling water over the top. Bake at 375 degrees for 45 to 60 minutes. Delicious served warm with ice cream. Serves 6-8.

Beverly Michaux (Mrs. Roy H.)

DIVINE CHOCOLATE CAKE

The cinnamon gives it a different flavor.

2 cups flour
2 cups sugar
1 tsp. cinnamon
1 cup margarine
1/4 cup cocoa
1 cup water
2 eggs, beaten
1/2 cup buttermilk (or 2 Tbsp.
    cider vinegar added to 6
    Tbsp. milk
1 tsp. vanilla extract
1 tsp. baking soda

FROSTING:
1/4 cup margarine
3 Tbsp. milk
2 Tbsp. cocoa
1 tsp. vanilla extract
1 tsp. cinnamon
1/2 box confectioners' sugar

CAKE: Sift flour, sugar and cinnamon together. In a pan just boil margarine, cocoa and water. Add that to the flour mixture. Add other ingredients in order listed. Mix well and pour into greased and floured 9 x 13 pan. Bake at 400 degrees, 25-30 minutes or until toothpick comes out clean.

FROSTING: Melt margarine. Add next 4 ingredients, mixing well. Gradually blend in powdered sugar. Slightly more sugar may be needed. Spread over the cake while still warm. Serves 16 to 20.

Guerry Russell (Mrs. Don J.)

BROWN SUGAR PRALINE CAKE

1 cup buttermilk
1/2 cup butter or margarine
2 cups brown sugar
2 Tbsp. cocoa
1/4 tsp. salt
1 tsp. soda
2 cups flour
2 eggs
1 tsp. vanilla extract

TOPPING:
1 stick butter or margarine
1 cup brown sugar
6 Tbsp. cream (can use evaporated milk)
1 cup chopped pecans

Warm buttermilk and margarine; add sugar while mixture is still warm. Mix cocoa, salt and soda with flour. Add eggs to buttermilk mixture, then add dry ingredients. Mix well and add vanilla. Bake in a greased 9 x 13 x 2 pan at 350 degrees for 25 minutes. While cake is baking prepare topping. Cream butter and sugar together; add cream and chopped pecans. Spread evenly over baked cake while cake is still warm. Place under broiler only until bubbly. Watch carefully—burns easily. Serve in squares with whipped cream or ice cream. Serves 12.

Linda Hawfield (Mrs. Ben)
Nancy Wohlbruck (Mrs. Everett L.)

HEAVENLY HASH CAKE

4 eggs
2 cups sugar
2 sticks butter, room temperature
1-1/2 cups self-rising flour
4 Tbsp. cocoa
1-1/2 cups chopped pecans
1 tsp. vanilla extract
1 pkg. large marshmallows

ICING:
1 box confectioners' sugar
4 Tbsp. cocoa
8 Tbsp. evaporated milk
4 Tbsp. melted butter, room temperature

Beat the eggs slightly and add sugar. Blend well and stir in the softened butter. Sift flour with cocoa and add to egg mixture. Add pecans and vanilla. Stir well. Pour into well-greased and floured 13 x 9 x 2 inch pan. Bake approximately 30 minutes at 350 degrees or until done. Cut 1 package of large marshamallows in halves and place cut side down on hot cake immediately. Top with icing.

ICING: Combine all ingredients and stir until smooth. Pour over hot cake covered with marshmallows. When cooled, cut into squares. Serves 12-15.

Penny Gregory (Mrs. C.D., Jr.)
Lucy Anderson (Mrs. D.L.)

CHOCOLATE RUM CAKE SUPREME

1 cup unsifted cocoa
2 cups boiling water
2-3/4 cups sifted flour
2 tsp. baking soda
1/2 tsp. salt
1/2 tsp. baking powder
1 cup butter
1-1/4 cups granulated sugar
1-1/4 cups brown sugar
4 eggs
1-1/2 tsp. vanilla extract
1 tsp. almond extract

FILLING:
1 cup heavy whipping cream
1/4 cup unsifted confectioners'
    sugar
1 tsp. vanilla extract

ICING:
1 6-oz. pkg. semi-sweet
    chocolate bits
1/2 cup half-and-half
1 cup butter
2-1/2 cups unsifted confectioners'
    sugar
1 Tbsp. vanilla extract
2 Tbsp. light rum

Combine cocoa with water until smooth and let it cool. Sift dry ingredients together. Heat oven to 350 degrees and grease and flour 3 8-inch cake pans. In a large bowl, mix, at high speed, the butter, eggs, sugar and vanilla and almond extracts until light. At low speed add alternately flour mixture (first and last) and cocoa mixture. Bake 25-30 minutes, remove from pans, and let cool thoroughly.

Whip cream with sugar and vanilla. Put between both layers.

Combine chocolate morsels, cream, and butter over medium heat until smooth. Remove from heat and beat in confectioners' sugar, vanilla and rum. Beat over ice water until stiff enough to spread. Frost whole cake and store in refrigerator at least an hour before serving.

The Committee

CHOCOLATE BUTTERMILK CAKE

Our favorite birthday cake!
My children like chocolate icing and I prefer butter cream icing.

2-1/4 all-purpose flour (sift before
    measuring)
1-3/4 cups plus 2 Tbsp. sugar
2/3 cup Crisco shortening
1 tsp. salt
1 tsp. soda
1-1/4 cups buttermilk
3 eggs
2-1/2 squares melted
    unsweetened chocolate

Mix together first 6 ingredients; beat for 3 minutes. Add eggs and chocolate; beat for 3 minutes. Bake at 350 degrees in 2 greased 9-inch pans for 25 to 30 minutes or 3 greased 8-inch pans for about 25 minutes. See index for Chocolate Icing or Butter Cream Icing.

Julia Warner (Mrs. C.E.)

FUDGE CAKE
A very special cake

3/4 cups butter or margarine
2-1/4 cups sugar
1-1/2 tsp. vanilla extract
3 eggs
3 cups sifted cake flour
3 1-oz. squares unsweetened
   chocolate, melted
1-1/2 tsp. baking soda
3/4 tsp. salt
1-1/2 cups ice water

DATE CREAM FILLING:
1 cup milk
1/2 cup chopped dates
1 Tbsp. flour
1/4 cup sugar
1 egg, beaten
1/2 cup chopped nuts
1 tsp. vanilla extract

FUDGE FROSTING:
2 cups sugar
1 cup light cream
2 (1-oz.) squares unsweetened
   chocolate, grated

Cream butter, sugar and vanilla with mixer. Add eggs and melted chocolate. Beat well. Sift dry ingredients; add alternately with water to chocolate mixture. Pour batter into 3 greased and floured 8-inch layer pans. Bake at 350 degrees for 30-35 minutes. Cool. Put layers together with Date Cream Filling. Frost with Fudge Frosting.

DATE CREAM FILLING: Combine milk and dates in top of a double boiler. Combine flour and sugar and add beaten egg, blending until smooth. Add to hot milk. Cook, stirring until thick. Cool. Stir in nuts and vanilla. Spread between layers.

FUDGE FROSTING: Combine all ingredients in heavy saucepan. Boil over medium high heat 3 minutes without stirring. Reduce heat and continue to cook until it reaches soft ball stage (238 degrees). Cool. Beat until creamy and of spreading consistency. Add cream if too thick. Spread on sides of cake first and a little over top edge. Frost top last.

Ellen Knott (Mrs. B.F.)

FRENCH CHOCOLATE CAKE
Easy to prepare and incredibly rich

1 lb. sweet or semi-sweet chocolate
1 tsp. water
1 Tbsp. flour
1 Tbsp. sugar
2/3 cup soft butter
4 eggs, divided
1 cup whipped cream

Melt chocolate and water in double boiler over hot, not boiling, water. Remove from heat. Stir in flour, sugar, and butter and blend thoroughly. Beat egg yolks well and gradually add to chocolate mixture. Beat egg whites until stiff and gently fold into batter. Pour into 9-inch cake pan which has been lined with waxed paper. Bake in preheated 425 degree oven for 15 minutes *only*. Cake will stiffen when cool. When cold, remove from pan and sprinkle with confectioners' sugar. Top with whipped cream. Cut into thin slices to serve. Serves 10 to 12.

Sally McMillen

CHOCOLATE DELIGHT CAKE

The cake is made out of the icing! Most delicious chocolate cake you'll ever eat

1 8-oz. cream cheese
1 3-oz. cream cheese
2 sticks butter or margarine
2 lbs. confectioners' sugar
1/4 cup water
1 4-oz. bar German chocolate
1/4 cup Crisco
3 eggs
2-1/4 cups plain flour
1 tsp. soda
1 tsp. salt
1 cup buttermilk
1 tsp. vanilla extract
nuts (optional)

Blend 1 8-oz cream cheese and 1 3-oz. cream cheese, 2 sticks butter or margarine. Add 2 lbs. powdered sugar, 1/4 cup water, 1 bar German chocolate, melted. Divide in half. Set aside one half. Into the other half add 1/4 cup Crisco, 3 eggs, 2-1/4 cups plain flour, 1 tsp. soda, 1 tsp. salt, 1 cup buttermilk, 1 tsp. vanilla extract. Bake in 3 well-greased pans at 350 degrees for 35 minutes. Spread the other half of icing over layers after they are cool. Nuts may be added.

Libby Morrison (Mrs. Jack)

FUDGE CAKE WITH COCONUT-CREAM CHEESE CENTER

A large, dark chocolate cake—travels well

2 cups sugar
1 cup oil
2 eggs
3 cups all-purpose flour
3/4 cup cocoa
2 tsp. soda
2 tsp. baking powder
1-1/2 tsp. salt
1 cup hot water or coffee
1 cup buttermilk
1 tsp. vanilla extract
1/2 cup chopped nuts

FILLING:
8 oz. cream cheese, softened
1/4 cup sugar
1 tsp. vanilla extract
1 egg
1/2 cup flaked coconut
6 oz. chocolate chips

Beat first 4 *filling* ingredients until smooth. Stir in coconut and chocolate chips. Set aside. In large bowl, blend sugar, oil and eggs; beat 1 minute at highest mixer speed. Sift together next 5 ingredients; then in separate bowl combine next 3 ingredients. Add these ingredients, alternating dry and wet, to sugar, eggs and oil (except for filling and nuts). Beat 3 minutes and add nuts. Into greased 10 to 12 inch tube pan pour half of batter. Spoon filling over batter. Top with remaining batter. Bake at 350 degrees for 70 to 75 minutes. Freezes well. Serves 16.

Phyllis Mahoney (Mrs. J.C.)

SOUR CREAM CHOCOLATE CAKE
This is a very rich, moist cake.

3 oz. baking chocolate
1/2 cup butter
1 cup boiling water
2 cups light brown sugar
2 cups flour
1-1/2 tsp. soda
1 tsp. salt
2 eggs
1/2 cup sour cream
1 tsp. vanilla extract

Combine chocolate, butter and boiling water; stir until melted. Combine brown sugar, flour, soda and salt in large mixing bowl. Gradually add chocolate mixture, beating until thoroughly combined. Blend in eggs, sour cream and vanilla; beat 1 minute at medium speed. Pour into greased and floured 13 x 9 x 2 pyrex pan or two 9-inch cake pans. Bake at 350 degrees for 35-45 minutes. Inserted toothpick will come out clean when done.

Stephanie Fletcher (Mrs. D.H.)

TEXAS SHEET CAKE

2 sticks butter or margarine
1 cup water
4 Tbsp. cocoa
2 cups all-purpose flour
2 cups sugar
1/2 tsp. salt
1 tsp. baking soda
1/2 cup sour cream
2 beaten eggs
1 tsp. vanilla extract

FROSTING:
1 stick butter or margarine
6 Tbsp. milk
4 Tbsp. cocoa
1 tsp. vanilla
1 box confectioners' sugar
1 cup chopped nuts

Bring butter, water, and cocoa to a boil in a saucepan. Set aside. Sift flour, sugar, salt, and soda together in a mixing bowl and add heated mixture. Beat well and add sour cream and eggs. Add vanilla and beat for one minute. Pour into a greased jelly roll pan (12-1/2 x 10-1/2 x 1 inches). Bake at 350 degrees for 20 to 25 minutes.
FROSTING:
Meanwhile, for frosting, bring to a boil the butter, milk and cocoa. Stir in sugar, vanilla and nuts. Pour over cake right out of the oven and let cool until set. This cake travels well; carry it right in the pan, cut in squares and serve. Serves 24.

Donna Hanna (Mrs. R.T.)

Variation: 1/2 cup buttermilk and 1 Tbsp. vinegar may be substituted for the sour cream.

*Similar recipes were submitted by
Sharon Edge (Mrs. W.S.)
Caren Hollenbeck (Mrs. J.I.)
La McLeod (Mrs. John A., Jr.)
Carolyn Tomlin (Mrs. M.G.)*

When creaming butter and sugar together, rinse the bowl in very hot water first; the two will cream faster.

COCOA-WALNUT BROWNIE LOAF

3/4 cup butter
3/4 cup packed brown sugar
3/4 cup granulated sugar
1 tsp. vanilla
2 eggs
1-3/4 cups unsifted all-purpose
  flour
1/2 cup Hershey's cocoa
1 tsp. baking powder
1/2 baking soda
1 8-oz. container plain yogurt
  (room temperature)
1 cup walnuts or black walnuts,
  coarsely chopped

COCOA FUDGE FROSTING

1/4 cup butter
1/4 cup Hershey's cocoa
1-1/2 cups powdered sugar
3 Tbsp. milk
1/2 tsp. vanilla
walnuts, coarsely chopped

Cream butter, sugar and vanilla. Add eggs one at a time, beating until mixture is light and fluffy. Combine dry ingredients. Add to creamed mixture in thirds alternately with yogurt. Stir in chopped walnuts. Pour into greased and floured 9 x 5 x 3 inch loaf pan. Bake at 350 degrees for 65 to 70 minutes or until cake springs back (top may be cracked). Cool in pan 10 minutes. Frost with Cocoa Fudge Frosting. If freezing is desired, do so before icing. Ice when ready to use.

FROSTING: Melt butter. Combine with cocoa, sugar, milk and vanilla. Beat until smooth and creamy, adding more sugar if necessary for spreading consistency. After cake is frosted, decorate top with chopped walnuts.

Kay Roberson (Mrs. G. Don)

KARIDOPITA

Greek nut cake—nice served warm with syrup

1-1/2 cups sugar
3 eggs
1 cup Wesson oil
*1 cup sour milk
2 cups flour
1 tsp. cloves
1 tsp. cinnamon
3 tsps. baking powder
1/2 tsp. baking soda
1 cup chopped nuts

SYRUP

2 cups sugar
1 cup water
2 Tbsp. lemon juice
cinnamon stick
4 whole cloves

Butter and flour a 13 x 9 inch pan. Beat eggs; add sugar and oil. Beat until creamy. Sift all dry ingredients together. Add dry mixture alternately with sour milk. Stir in nuts. Pour batter in pan and bake at 350 degrees for 35 to 45 minutes, or until done. Test with toothpick. Cool. Slice into 20 serving pieces. While cake is cooling, combine syrup ingredients in saucepan and boil gently for 7 minutes. Pour evenly over cooled cake. Serves 20.

*Note: If sour milk is not available, you may use 1 cup milk plus 1 tablespoon vinegar or lemon juice.

The Committee

FIG PRESERVE CAKE

A recipe from the deep South

2 cups flour
1 tsp. salt
1 tsp. nutmeg
1 tsp. ground cloves
1-1/2 cup sugar
1 cup oil
1 cup fig preserves (I chop these in
 blender)
1 Tbsp. vanilla extract
1 tsp. cinnamon
3 eggs
1 tsp. soda
1 cup buttermilk
1/2 cup nuts

SAUCE:
1/4 cup buttermilk
1/2 cup sugar
1-1/2 tsp. vanilla
1/4 tsp. soda
1-1/2 Tbsp. cornstarch
1/2 stick butter

Mix all dry ingredients. All oil, eggs, milk, figs and nuts. Beat well after each addition. Pour into prepared tube pan and cook for 1 hour and 15 minutes at 325 degrees.

SAUCE: Mix all sauce ingredients and bring to a boil. Pour over cake while still warm and in pan.

Virginia Golding (Mrs. John G.)

INDIVIDUAL FRUIT CAKES

Nice to have on hand or to give at Christmas

1 lb. butter
3 cups sugar
14 eggs (unbeaten)
5 cups flour
1 cup rum
2 tsp. baking powder
2 tsp. vanilla
2 tsp. lemon flavoring
2 tsp. almond flavoring
2-1/2 lbs. candied pineapple
2-1/2 lbs. candied cherries
2-1/2 lbs. nuts

Cream butter and sugar well. Add eggs, one at a time. Mix thoroughly. Sift flour and baking powder together. (Reserve 1 cup for coating nuts and fruits.) Add remaining flour, alternately with rum to sugar mixture. Blend well. Add flavorings. Add fruits and nuts, which have been chopped and coated with the 1 cup flour. Blend. Spoon into small-size fluted paper baking cups. Press together closely in shallow pan and bake at 275 degrees for about 30-45 minutes. Separate the cups so batter will bake through and through, using additional pans so cups may be spread out and separated. Continue baking until done — about 20 more minutes. Cool on racks. Makes about 150 tiny cakes.

Nancy Elmore

LINDA'S CHRISTMAS FRUIT CAKE

1 lb. butter
1 lb. dark brown sugar
6 eggs, separated
4 cups all-purpose flour, divided
2 cups chopped pecans
1 8-oz. container red candied cherries, chopped
1 8-oz. container green candied cherries, chopped
1 tsp. baking powder
1-1/2 oz. lemon extract

Beat egg whites until fluffy and set aside. Cream brown sugar and softened butter until smooth. Add egg yolks and blend. Add 2 cups flour, baking powder and lemon extract. Mix 2 cups flour with cherries and pecans. Slowly add to creamed mixture. Add egg whites to batter and cream until smooth. Pour into greased and floured tube pan. Let stand 8 hours before cooking. Bake at 250 degrees for 3-1/2 hours.

Linda Miller (Mrs. W.R.)

JAPANESE FRUIT CAKE
"Traditional Christmas Cake"

1 cup butter
2-1/2 cups sugar
1/2 cup milk
6 eggs, beaten
4 cups flour
1/4 tsp. salt
1 tsp. ground cloves
1 tsp. ground allspice
1 tsp. ground cinnamon
2 tsp. baking powder
1 cup chopped nuts
1 cup seedless raisins

FILLING:
2 cups sugar
1 cup water or coconut milk
1-3/4 cups cake batter
juice and grated rind of 2 lemons
1 grated or 2 cans coconut
1 cup chopped nuts
3 Tbsp. melted butter
1/4 cup chopped candied cherries
1/4 cup chopped candied pineapple

Cream butter and sugar; add milk. Beat well. Add beaten eggs. Combine dry ingredients and mix into batter. Add nuts and raisins. Reserve 1-3/4 cups of batter for filling. Bake in 3 8-inch cake pans at 375 degrees for 25 minutes.

Prepare filling by combining sugar and water and boil until slightly syrupy. Add the reserved cake batter and lemon juice and rind. Cook until thickened, stirring constantly. Add coconut, nuts, butter, and candied fruits. Spread between layers and on top of cooled cake.

Myrtle B. Ussery (Mrs. A.M.)

MRS. D. J. THURSTON SR.'S FRUIT CAKE

1/4 lb. citron
1/4 lb. lemon peel
1/4 lb. orange peel
1/2 lb. cherries
1/2 lb. nuts
1/2 lb. dates
1/2 lb. pineapple
1/2 lb. seeded raisins
1/4 lb. dry coconut
1/2 lb. butter
1/2 cup sugar
1/2 cup honey
5 eggs
2 cups flour
1 tsp. allspice
1/2 tsp. nutmeg
1/2 tsp. cloves
1 tsp. salt
1 tsp. baking powder
6 Tbsp. brandy

Dredge chopped fruit in 1/4 cup flour. Sift remaining flour with dry ingredients. Cream butter and sugar; add honey. Add well-beaten eggs. Add dry ingredients and brandy alternately. Pour batter over fruit and mix. Pour lightly into greased 10-inch tube pan, having 3 layers of waxed paper lining bottom. Bake 4 hours at 250 degrees. Have 2 cups water in pan underneath cake while baking. Remove from pan when cool. Wrap well. Store in a cool place.

Stella Thurston (Mrs. Doc J., Jr.)

ENGLISH CHRISTMAS CAKE
Even people who don't like fruit cake will love this cake!

1-3/4 cups coarsely chopped
    candied cherries
1-3/4 cups coarsely chopped
    candied pineapple
3 cups broken pecans
1 lb. white raisins
6 Tbsp. brandy (I prefer apple
    brandy)
1 cup butter
2-1/4 cups sugar
6 eggs
4 cups sifted flour
1-1/2 tsp. salt
1/2 tsp. baking powder
1-1/2 tsp. cinnamon
1 tsp. nutmeg

Line a 10-inch tube pan with foil. Mix fruits, nuts and 1/4 cup brandy together and let stand. Cream butter; add sugar, beat until light and fluffy. Mix eggs one at a time, beating well. Sift flour and dry ingredients. Divide in half. Stir 1/2 of flour in fruit and nut mixture. Coat well. Stir 1/2 of flour in egg mixture with 2 Tbsp. brandy. Mix fruit and batter *well*. Pour into pan and bake 3 hours and 45 minutes at 275 degrees. (Place pan of water in bottom of oven to keep cake moist.) Cool 5 minutes and remove from pan. Carefully remove aluminum foil. Cool cake on wire rack. Wrap in brandy-soaked cheesecloth and store in an airtight container. This cake should be made several weeks before it is to be cut. It can be made several months ahead. It helps to cut this cake with a very thin, sharp knife.

La McLeod (Mrs. John A., Jr.)

PETER PAUL MOUNDS COCONUT CAKE
Testers recommend this cake!

LAYERS:
2 cups sugar
1 cup Crisco
1 cup plain flour
1 cup self-rising flour
5 eggs
1 cup milk
2 tsp. vanilla extract

FILLING:
1 cup sugar
1 cup milk
1 bag frozen coconut (12 or 14 oz.)
12 large marshamallows
1 tsp vanilla extract

FROSTING:
2 cups sugar
1 can condensed milk
2 to 3 Tbsp. cocoa
1 stick margarine
confectioners' sugar

LAYERS: Cream sugar and Crisco thoroughly. Blend in eggs one at a time. Sift flours and add alternately with milk. Add vanilla extract. Beat for 3 minutes. Pour into 3 greased and floured 9-inch cake pans. Bake at 325 degrees until done — about 25 minutes. Make filling while layers are cooking.

FILLING: Boil sugar and milk together for 5 minutes. Add marshmallows and stir until melted. Remove from heat; add coconut and vanilla. When layers are done, stack as you remove from oven, putting filling between layers.

FROSTING: Cook sugar, milk, cocoa and butter over medium heat — stirring constantly. Cook until thickened. Add sifted confectioners' sugar until spreading consistency. Frost cake.

The Committee

QUEEN ELIZABETH CAKE
A favorite date cake

1 cup chopped dates
1 cup boiling water
1 tsp. baking soda
1 cup sugar
1/2 tsp. salt
1/4 cup margarine
1-1/2 cups flour
1 egg, beaten
1/2 cup chopped nuts

TOPPING:
5 Tbsp. brown sugar
2 Tbsp. margarine
5 Tbsp. cream
nuts
coconut

Pour the boiling water over the dates and soda. Stir and let stand while combining the remaining batter ingredients. Add date mixture, blend well, and bake in greased 9 x 13 pan for 35 minutes at 350 degrees. Spread with topping while cake is warm and still in pan.

TOPPING: Mix brown sugar and margarine. Add cream. Mix well. Spread on warm cake (in pan) and sprinkle with nuts and/or coconut. Cut as brownies after cake is cool. Serves 20 to 24.

Susan Murfee (Mrs. D.G.)

LEMON CHEESE CAKE

3 cups flour, sifted
3-1/2 tsp. baking powder
1-3/4 cups sugar
1/2 lb. butter, softened
3/4 cup milk
6 egg whites
1 tsp. vanilla extract

LEMON CHEESE FILLING
3/4 cup sugar
4 Tbsp. butter
1 Tbsp. cornstarch
*2 large lemons, juice and rind,
    grated (thin skin lemons)
6 egg yolks

NEVER-FAIL
WHITE ICING:
2 cups sugar
1/2 cup water
2 egg whites
8 marshmallows, cut up
1 tsp. vanilla extract

Sift flour and baking powder together. Cream butter and sugar. Add flour and milk alternately. Beat egg whites and fold into batter. Grease pans and line with waxed paper. Divide batter into 3 pans. Bake at 350 degrees for 25 minutes.

FILLING: Mix sugar and butter, cornstarch, juice and rind in top of double boiler. Add well-beaten egg yolks. Cook until thick. Let this cool completely before spreading. Do not spread it too near the edge of cake. This makes enough for 3 layers.

ICING: Combine sugar and water in saucepan and place on cold burner. At the same time, beat egg whites in electric mixer. When eggs are almost stiff, add marshmallows. At this time, turn heat on under sugar and water. When it first starts to boil, add 6 Tbsp. of syrup to egg mixture while they are beating. Turn beater off until syrup on stove spins a thread or 238 degrees on candy thermometer. Then resume beating while pouring in the syrup. Beat until spreading consistency. Add vanilla. Do not overbeat. Spread on top and sides of cake.
*Note: Thin skin lemons have more juice and are not bitter.

Ellen Knott (Mrs. B.F.)

LEMON PUDDING CAKE

4 eggs, separated
1/3 cup lemon juice
1 tsp. grated lemon rind
1 Tbsp. melted butter
1-1/2 cups sugar
1/2 cup sifted flour
1/2 tsp. salt
1-1/2 cups milk
whipped cream (optional)

Let ingredients reach room temperature. Beat together egg yolks, lemon juice, lemon rind and butter with rotary beater until thick and lemon-colored. Combine sugar, flour and salt. Add dry ingredients alternately with milk, beating well after each addition. Beat egg whites until stiff. Blend into yolk mixture on low speed of electric mixer. Pour into 8-inch square baking dish. *Set in pan of hot water.* Bake at 350 degrees for 45 minutes. May serve with whipped cream. Serves 6-9.

Helen Burns (Mrs. J. Gordon)

GREAT-GRANDMOTHER BOWDEN'S
LEMON DRIZZLE CAKES
Lemon Delicious! Makes 2 cakes

5-1/4 sticks butter, softened
5-1/8 cups sugar
5-1/8 cups flour, sifted 3 times
pinch salt
pinch baking powder
1-1/2 cups Carnation milk
11 large eggs
2 Tbsp. lemon extract

LEMON DRIZZLE:
2 cups 10X powdered sugar
juice and grated rind of 2 lemons

Cream together well the butter and sugar. Mix in flour, salt, baking powder, milk, and lemon extract. Add eggs one at a time, beating well. Pour into 2 generously greased and floured tube cake pans. Bake 2 hours in a 300 degree preheated oven. Place several sheets paper towels covered with waxed paper on 2 large round plates. Invert hot cakes onto plates. Mix powdered confectioners' sugar, lemon juice and grated rind. If too thin, add more sugar. Drizzle over hot cakes. The more drizzle, the better! Makes 2 cakes. Freezes well.

B. J. Miller (Mrs. H.F., III)

SWEET POTATO CAKE
When I bake this one, I could eat the whole thing!

1-1/2 cups cooking oil
2 cups sugar
4 eggs, separated
4 Tbsp. hot water
2-1/2 cups flour, sifted
3 tsp. baking powder
1/4 tsp. salt
1 tsp. each: ground cinnamon and
    nutmeg
1-1/2 cups grated raw sweet
    potatoes
1 cup chopped nuts
1 tsp. vanilla extract

COCONUT FROSTING:
1 13-oz. can evaporated milk
1 cup sugar
1 stick butter
3 egg yolks
1 tsp. vanilla extract
1-1/2 cup flaked coconut
1 cup chopped pecans

Combine oil and sugar; beat until smooth. Add egg yolks and beat well. Add water and then dry ingredients that have been sifted together; stir in potatoes, nuts and vanilla and blend and beat thoroughly. Beat egg whites until stiff and fold carefully into mixture. Turn batter into three 8-inch greased and floured or paper-lined layer cake pans and bake in 350-dgress oven 25 to 30 minutes. Cool on rack and frost with coconut frosting made by combining milk, sugar, butter, egg yolks and vanilla in saucepan. Cook over medium heat about 12 minutes, stirring constantly, until mixture thickens. Remove from heat and add coconut and nuts. Beat until cool and of spreading consistency. Spread between layers, and on top of cake. Serves 12.

Gensie

BECKY'S PUMPKIN CAKE

A delicious dessert in the fall of the year

1 pkg. Spice Cake mix
1 1-lb. can (2 cups) solid-pack
   pumpkin
1-1/2 tsp. soda
2 eggs
1/3 cup water
3/4 cup currants (optional)
1/2 tsp. each ginger, instant coffee
   and cinnamon

PENUCHE TOPPING:

1 cup whipping cream
1/4 cup brown sugar
1 tsp. vanilla extract
1/2 to 1 tsp. rum flavoring

Heat oven to 350 degrees. In a large mixer bowl combine all cake ingredients. Beat 30 seconds on low and then 4 minutes on medium. Pour batter into greased and floured 13 x 9 x 2 inch baking pan. Bake 45 minutes. Serve warm with Penuche Cream Topping

TOPPING: Beat cream, gradually adding sugar, vanilla and rum flavoring. Beat until stiff. Serve cake in squares with a large spoon of whipped topping. Serves 12.

Gensie

OATMEAL CAKE

1 cup quick-cooking oatmeal
1-1/2 cups hot water
1-1/2 cups plain flour
1 cup white sugar
1 cup brown sugar
1 tsp. soda
1/2 tsp. salt
1 tsp. cinnamon
2 eggs
1/2 cup oil or margarine

TOPPING

1 stick butter or margarine
1 cup brown sugar
1/2 cup evaporated milk
1 tsp. vanilla extract
8 oz. coconut
1/2 cup chopped pecans

Pour boiling water over oatmeal; let stand while mixing cake. Sift flour, soda, salt and cinnamon and pour into eggs, oil and sugars. Mix well. Add oatmeal; mix. Pour into greased and floured 9 x 13 inch pan and bake 30-40 minutes at 350 degrees.

While cake is baking, mix milk and sugar; add margarine. Cook, stirring constantly, until thick. Add coconut, nuts and vanilla. Spread on hot cake. Serves 20-24.

Sharon Edge (Mrs. W.S.)

PECAN PRALINE CAKE
Great to take on "tailgate picnics"

1 cup buttermilk
1 stick margarine
2 eggs
2 cups packed brown sugar
2 cups flour
1 tsp. soda
2 tsp. vanilla extract

TOPPING:
1 stick margarine
1 cup brown sugar
1 cup chopped pecans
1 small can crushed pineapple (drained)

Warm buttermilk and margarine together in a saucepan. Mix eggs and brown sugar and add to buttermilk mixture. Then add flour, soda and vanilla. Beat well and pour into a greased 9 x 13 inch pan. Bake at 375 degrees for 25 minutes. While cake is cooking, combine all topping ingredients and boil for 2 minutes. Spread topping on cake while cake is still hot. Serves 16 or more.

Barbara Stutts (Mrs. Clyde)

GLORY BE CAKE
This recipe is from Boston—uses tea!

2 cups all-purpose flour
2 tsp. baking powder
2 cups granulated sugar
1 cup salad oil
3 eggs
1 8-oz. junior-size jar prunes (with tapioca)
1 tsp. each powdered allspice, nutmeg and cinnamon
1 cup white raisins (sprinkled with flour before turning into batter)
1 cup chopped nuts
1 Tbsp. instant tea

Pour all ingredients into large bowl and stir with a spoon until well mixed. Turn into greased and floured tube pan. Bake at 350 degrees for 65 minutes or until done. Let cool 15-20 minutes before turning out. Freezes well. Serves 24.

Laura H. Tipps

If you wish to substitute honey for sugar in a recipe, use half the amount called for and reduce the amount of liquid by 3-1/2 tablespoons per cup of honey.

NETTIE'S PINEAPPLE UPSIDE-DOWN CAKE

8 Tbsp. butter, softened and divided
1/2 cup light brown sugar (packed)
3/4 cup granulated sugar
1 egg
1-1/2 cups flour
1-1/2 tsp. baking powder
1/4 tsp. salt
1/2 cup milk
1 tsp. vanilla extract
1   15-1/2 oz. can crushed pineapple, drained

Melt *4 Tbsp.* butter in iron skillet on top of stove. Add brown sugar. Arrange drained pineapple over sugar and butter. Cream together *4 Tbsp.* butter and white sugar until light. Add egg and vanilla; beat until fluffy. Sift dry ingredients; add alternately with 1/2 cup milk and beat for 2 minutes. Spread over pineapple/sugar mixture in skillet. Bake at 350 degrees for 40-45 minutes. Invert on plate immediately. May freeze while still warm. Serves 8-10.

Peggy Young (Mrs. John A.)

MOCK SPONGE CAKE

A versatile cake—can be ready in forty-five minutes.

2 eggs
1 cup sugar
1/4 tsp. salt
1 tsp. vanilla extract
1 Tbsp. butter
1 cup flour, unsifted
1 tsp. baking powder

Grease and flour a 9-inch square pan or use a 12-muffin tin with paper liners. Beat the eggs with a rotary or electric beater until very light. Beat in sugar, salt and vanilla. Melt 1 Tbsp. butter in 1/2 cup boiling milk, Mix together flour and baking powder and beat into egg mixture very quickly. Bake at 350 degrees for cake for 25 to 35 minutes, and at 400 degrees for 18 to 20 minutes for cupcakes. Good to use as shortcake for strawberries or peaches. While cake is still warm, it may be topped with a frosting made by combining 1/2 cup confectioners' sugar, orange or lemon flavoring (also peel if available), and enough milk to make a rather thin consistency. Pour over cake.

Note: 2 9-inch layer pans or a 13 x 9 inch pan may be used. Recipe doubles nicely.

Eileen Antonelli (Mrs. G.A.)

MOM'S SPONGE CAKE
A light cake—goes well with fresh fruit

4 eggs
1 cup sugar
1/2 cup water
1/2 tsp. vanilla extract
1/2 tsp. almond extract
1 cup flour
1 tsp. baking powder
pinch of salt

Beat 4 egg yolks. Add sugar slowly, then water (at room temperature). Flavor with vanilla and almond extracts. Add flour, baking powder and salt. Beat thoroughly. Fold in 4 beaten egg whites. Bake at 350 degrees for 35-40 minutes, in *ungreased* angel cake pan. Invert and cool for about 1 hour. Loosen at sides and remove from pan. Powdered sugar is good on top—better than frosting. Serves 12. Freezes well.

Marilyn Williams (Mrs. R.G.)

WILLIAMSBURG ORANGE CAKE

2-3/4 cups cake flour
1-1/2 cups sugar
1-1/2 tsp. baking soda
3/4 tsp. salt
1-1/2 cups buttermilk
1/2 cup butter, softened
1/4 cup shortening
3 eggs
2 tsp. vanilla extract
1 cup golden raisins, chopped
1/2 cup chopped nuts
1 Tbsp. grated orange peel
Butter Frosting

BUTTER FROSTING
1/2 cup soft **butter**
3 cups sifted confectioners' sugar
3 to 4 Tbsp. orange-flavored
    liqueur (or can use fresh
    orange juice)
2 tsp. grated orange peel

Preheat oven to 350 degrees. Grease and flour 13 x 9 x 2 inch baking pan. Measure all ingredients into a large mixing bowl. Blend one-half minute at low speed, scraping bowl constantly. Beat 3 minutes on high speed, scraping bowl occasionally. Pour into prepared pan. Bake 45 to 50 minutes or until cake tester comes out clean. Cool, then frost by combining butter and sugar. Stir in liqueur and orange peel. Beat until smooth. Spread on cake.

Ellen Knott (Mrs. B.F.)

VANILLA WAFER CAKE

2 lbs. vanilla wafers (crushed very fine)
1/2 lb. butter or margarine
2 cups sugar
6 eggs
1/2 cup milk
2 cups coconut
2 cups chopped pecans

Crush vanilla wafers until very fine and put aside. Cream butter and sugar together until light. Add eggs, one at a time. Then add vanilla wafers, milk, coconut and nuts. Bake in greased tube pan for 2 hours at 275 degrees.
NOTE: The batter becomes very thick and stiff. It is recommended that you mix by hand after the eggs have been added.

Patricia Davis (Mrs. J.A.)

1 - 2 - 3 - 4 CAKE

Very easy to make—can use with fruit and ice cream or eat plain.
An old favorite, given to me by my grandmother

1 cup Crisco
2 cups sugar
3 cups flour
4 eggs
1/2 tsp. salt
1/2 tsp. soda
1/2 tsp. baking powder
*1 cup buttermilk
2 Tbsp. lemon extract

TOPPING
juice of 1 lemon
juice of 1 orange
2-1/2 cups confectioners' sugar

Combine all ingredients and beat in mixer for 4 minutes. Pour into greased and floured bundt pan. Bake 1 hour at 350 degrees, or until done. Mix juice of lemon and orange. Add confectioners' sugar. Remove cake and pour topping over. Return to oven for 5 minutes (optional). Freezes well.

I buy powdered buttermilk and use according to directions

Betty Holland (Mrs. R.C.)

To measure less than 1 cup solid shortening, pour cold water (the amount being the difference between the amount of shortening called for and one cup) into measuring cup and add shortening until water reaches the top of the cup. Example: if recipe calls for 1/3 cup shortening, put 2/3 cup water into cup and add shortening to fill. Pour off water before using shortening.

BEST CHOCOLATE POUND CAKE
This is a family favorite birthday cake.

2 sticks butter
2 cups sugar
4 eggs
1/2 cup sifted cocoa
2 cups plain flour
1 tsp. baking powder
dash of salt
2/3 cups sweet milk (homog-
enized, not canned milk)
1 tsp. vanilla

Cream thoroughly the butter and sugar. Add eggs, one at a time, beating well after each addition. Mix the cocoa with the flour, baking powder and salt. Add alternately to batter with the milk and vanilla. Begin and end with flour mixture. Pour into a greased and floured tube pan and bake at 300 degrees for 1 hour and 20 minutes or until the cake tests done. Frost with Chocolate Icing. Cake freezes well.

CHOCOLATE ICING:
1-1/2 cups sugar
1 tsp. vanilla
1 egg
3 squares chocolate
pinch of salt
1/2 cup cream
1/2 stick butter

ICING: Mix sugar, cream, salt, vanilla and egg. Cook and stir for 7 minutes after mixture comes to a boil over medium heat. Remove from heat and add chocolate and butter. Beat until firm — about 30 minutes. Frost Chocolate Pound Cake. Serves 15-20.

Carolyn Bailey (Mrs. J.M.)

BOURBON POUND CAKE

1 lb. butter
3 cups sugar
8 eggs, separated
6 Tbsp. bourbon
2 tsp. vanilla extract
2 tsp. almond extract
3 cups flour, sifted
1-1/2 cups ground pecans

Separate eggs; beat whites until stiff and set aside. Grease and *paper*, then flour a 10-inch tube pan. Place half the nuts in bottom of the pan. Cream butter and sugar until light and fluffy. Beat in egg yolks one at a time. Add bourbon and flavorings. Mix in flour gradually. Fold in beaten egg whites. Pour batter into pan and top with remaining nuts. Bake at 300 degrees for 1-1/2 hours.

Hilda Rutherford (Mrs. N.A.)

Do not double the amount of salt when doubling a recipe for cakes, cookies and fruit desserts. Use the amount for a single recipe.

BROWN SUGAR POUND CAKE

1 box golden brown sugar
1 cup granulated sugar
3 sticks butter, softened
5 eggs
3 cups all-purpose flour
1/2 tsp. salt
1 tsp. baking powder
1 tsp. vanilla extract
1 tsp. maple flavoring
1 cup milk
1 cup chopped nuts (optional)

Cream sugars and butter well. Add eggs, 1 at a time, beating well after each. Mix flour, salt and baking powder together. Add flavorings to milk. Add flour and milk mixture alternately to batter, starting and ending with flour and beating just to blend. Add nuts. Put in greased and floured 10-inch tube pan. Bake at 350 degrees for 1 hour to 1-1/4 hours, or until toothpick comes out clean. Cool before frosting. See index for Caramel Frosting

Kay Cline

CAMDEN POUND CAKE

This cake was sold at the Woman's Exchange in Camden, S. C. for many years.

2 cups Wesson Buttery Flavor Oil
6 eggs
2 cups flour
2 cups sugar
2 tsp. almond flavoring
1/2 tsp. vanilla extract
1 tsp. baking powder
1/4 tsp. salt

Beat all ingredients very slowly until blended, then beat rapidly for 10 minutes. Pour into greased and floured tube pan. Bake for 1-1/2 hours at 300 degrees. Turn out onto floured waxed paper.

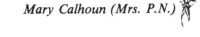

Mary Calhoun (Mrs. P.N.)

CREAM CHEESE POUND CAKE

The right cake for that special occasion

1-1/2 cups chopped pecans
1-1/2 cups butter (or margarine), softened
1 8 oz. pkg. cream cheese, softened
3 cups sugar
6 eggs
3 cups sifted cake flour
dash of salt
1-1/2 tsp. vanilla extract

Sprinkle 1/2 cup pecans in a greased and floured 10-inch tube pan; set aside. Cream butter and cream cheese; gradually add sugar, beating until light and fluffy. Add eggs, one at a time, beating well after each addition. Add flour and salt, stirring until combined. Stir in vanilla and remaining 1 cup pecans. Pour batter into prepared pan. Bake at 325 degrees for 1-1/2 hours, or until a wooden pick inserted in center comes out clean. Cool in pan 10 minutes. Turn out and cool on a rack.

Joan Belasco (Mrs. J.J.)

GOMMA'S COCONUT POUND CAKE

2 sticks butter
1/2 cup Crisco
3 cups sugar
6 eggs
1/2 tsp. almond extract
1 tsp. coconut flavoring
3 cups all-purpose flour
1 cup milk
1 can flaked coconut

Cream butter, shotening and sugar until light and fluffy. Add eggs, one at a time, beating well after each addition. Add flavorings, then add flour and milk alternately, beating well. Stir in coconut. Spoon batter into a greased and floured 10-inch tube pan, or a bundt pan. Bake at 350 degrees for 1 hour and 15 minutes. *Cool* in pan at least 15 minutes before removing!

Nancy Sibley (Mrs. W.A.L., Jr.)

MRS. HASTINGS' POUND CAKE

1/2 lb. butter
1/2 cup vegetable shortening
3 cups sugar
1 cup milk
6 eggs
1 tsp. baking powder
3-1/2 cups flour
salt
1-3/4 tsp. vanilla extract
3/4 tsp. lemon extract
1/4 tsp. almond flavoring

Cream butter, shortening and sugar until light and fluffy. Add eggs, one at a time, beating well after each addition. Sift dry ingredients together and add alternately with milk. Add pinch of salt and flavorings, and blend well. Pour into large tube pan (10-12 inch) that has been greased well and floured. A thick aluminum pan is preferable as it helps form a nice crust. Bake at 325 degrees for approximately 1-1/4 hours or until tests done.

Betty Francis (Mrs. David L.)

MRS. BURK'S MILLION DOLLAR POUND CAKE

This is the cake to bake if you want to impress dinner guests or to say Happy Birthday to a friend, or take as a house-warming gift—it's beautiful.

3 cups sugar
1 pound butter, softened
6 eggs
4 cups all-purpose flour
3/4 cup milk
1 tsp. almond extract
1 tsp. vanilla extract

Bring butter and eggs to room temperature. Combine sugar and butter; cream until light and fluffy. Add eggs, one at a time, beating well after each addition. Add flour to creamed mixture alternately with milk, beating well after each addition. Stir in flavorings. Pour batter into a well-greased and floured 10-inch tube pan. Bake at 300 degrees for 1 hour and 40 minutes or until cake tests done. Freezes nicely.

Dee Dee Grainger (Mrs. Isaac B., III)

POUND CAKE
An old family favorite

1 lb. butter (or 1/2 lb. butter and
    1/2 lb. margarine)
2-2/3 cups sugar, divided
3-1/2 cups flour
8 eggs
6 Tbsp. coffee cream
1 tsp. vanilla extract

Separate eggs — beat whites until stiff. To egg whites add 6 Tbsp. sugar (from 2-2/3 cup sugar called for) and beat until dissolved. Place whites in refrigerator. Cream butter and remaining sugar. Beat until light. Add egg yolks, two at a time. Add flour and coffee cream alternately at lowest speed on mixer. Fold in egg whites and vanilla. Bake at 300 degrees for 1 hour and 25 minutes. (Use 1 tube pan or 2 loaf pans — grease pans and line bottoms with greased waxed paper.)

Nancy Harper (Mrs. Robert M.)

POUND CAKE

1 cup milk
3 cups sugar
3 cups flour
5 eggs if extra large, or 6 large
1/2 lb. margarine
1/2 cup Crisco
1 tsp. lemon extract
1 tsp. almond extract
1 tsp. vanilla extract

Bring eggs and margarine to room temperature. Put all ingredients in mixing bowl. Beat for 1 minute on low speed and for 4 minutes on medium-high. (You can't seem to overbeat.) Bake at 325 degrees in a greased and floured 10-inch tube pan for 1 hour to 1-1/2 hours until done when tested. Let cool on rack until cake comes away from sides of pan.

Mary Sue Milton (Mrs. Cecil)

VARIATION: To make "Chocolate Pound Cake" add 5 Tbsp. sifted cocoa and 1 tsp. vanilla extract to above ingredients. Omit lemon and almond extract. Bake according to directions given above.

Jean Bridges (Mrs. D.T., Jr.)

To remove cake layers or cookies left in pan too long, return to 350 degree oven for 2 minutes, then remove food from pan immediately.

POUND CAKE

2 sticks butter or margarine
2 cups sugar
5 eggs
2 cups all-purpose flour, sifted
1 tsp. vanilla extract
1/2 tsp. mace
juice of 1/2 lemon

Bring butter to room temperature. Cream butter and sugar. Gradually add eggs and sifted flour. Beat for 5 minutes until light and creamy. Add vanilla, mace and lemon juice. Blend well. Grease and flour bundt pan and bake at 325 degrees for 1 hour and 15 minutes, or until done.

Jocelyn Rose (Mrs. L.L., Jr.)

VARIATION: To make "Papa's Pound Cake," add 1 pinch of nutmeg and 1/2 tsp. lemon extract to above ingredients. Omit mace and juice of 1/2 lemon. Bake according to directions given above.

Nancy Gribble (Mrs. Rex. N., Jr.)

LEMON AND ORANGE POUND CAKE

2 sticks butter, softened
2 cups sugar
6 eggs, room temperature
2 cups flour
juice of 1 large orange
1 tsp. almond extract
1 tsp. lemon extract

ICING:
juice of 1 lemon
1 tsp. grated lemon peel
2 Tbsp. orange juice
1 cup confectioners' sugar
3 or 4 jiggers Cointreau

Cream butter, add sugar and cream again. Add eggs, one at a time, mixing well after each addition. At lowest speed, add flour gradually. When all is added, turn to medium speed and beat for 10 minutes. Add 2 Tbsp. orange juice and both extracts. Pour mixture into a greased and floured bundt pan. Bake in a pre-heated oven at 350 degrees for about 1 hour. For the first 30 minutes of cooking put a pan of water under the cake. Turn out and ice while still hot.
FOR ICING: Combine all ingredients except Cointreau, adding more sugar if needed for thickness. Sprinkle liqueur over cake, then spread icing over warm cake. Keep covered — wait a few hours to serve.

The Committee

AUNT VIRGINIA'S OLD FASHIONED POUND CAKE

3 cups cake flour (or all-purpose)
1/2 tsp. baking powder
1/8 tsp. salt (or 1 tsp. if all
    margarine is used)
3 sticks butter or margarine (or
    mixture of the two)
3 cups sugar
6 eggs
1 cup milk
1 tsp. vanilla extract
1 tsp. lemon extract

Sift together flour, baking powder and salt; set aside. Cream butter and sugar thoroughly. Add eggs, 1 at a time, beating well after each addition. Add flour mixture and milk alternately, beginning and ending with flour. Do not overmix. Stir in extracts. Pour into a greased and floured tube pan. Cut through middle of batter with rubber scraper or wooden spoon. Bake at 325 degrees for 90 minutes. Ice with "Never Fail Icing." (See index.)

Barby Goode (Mrs. David J.)

GOLDEN BANANA LIQUEUR CAKE

1 pkg. Golden Butter Cake Mix
    (Duncan Hines)
1 large pkg. banana pudding (not
    instant type)
1/2 cup banana liqueur
1/2 cup water
1/2 cup Crisco Oil
1/2 cup pecans, chopped
4 eggs

GLAZE:
1 cup sugar
1/4 cup water
1/4 cup banana liqueur
1 stick butter

Grease and flour bundt pan. Sprinkle pecans in bottom of pan. Mix remaining cake ingredients at low speed until well blended. Beat 4 minutes at medium speed. Pour batter over nuts. Bake at 325 degrees for 55 minutes. Remove from oven and cool 5 minutes. Prick top of cake with cake tester. Saturate with glaze.

GLAZE: Combine all glaze ingredients in saucepan. Bring to a boil and boil for 3 minutes, stirring constantly. Spoon over cake until fully absorbed. Can be frozen. Serves 16.

Jean Bridges (Mrs. D.T., Jr.)

To store leftover egg yolks: Cover with cold water and keep in refrigerator. Drain and use within 3 days. Whites will keep in refrigerator, covered, for about 10 days.

CAROLINA CHESS CAKE

1 box Duncan Hines yellow cake
   mix
1 stick butter, softened
1 egg
1/2 cup chopped pecans

TOPPING:
2 eggs
1 8-oz. pkg. cream cheese,
   softened
1 box confectioners' sugar
1 tsp. vanilla extract
1 tsp. lemon extract

Blend together cake mix, softened butter and egg. Press into a well-greased 9 x 13 inch pan. Mix together remaining ingredients. Beat 3 to 4 minutes with an electric mixer until creamy and smooth. Pour over cake mixture. Bake at 350 degrees for 40-45 minutes or until tests done. Serves 15.

Kathy Demas (Mrs. R.C.)

CHOCOLATE CHIP CAKE

1 pkg. yellow cake mix (Duncan
   Hines)
1/2 cup oil
1 4-1/8 oz. pkg. instant chocolate
   pudding
8 oz. sour cream
4 eggs
1/4 cup rum or brandy
1 tsp. vanilla extract
6 oz. pkg. chocolate chips
1 cup chopped pecans

Mix first seven ingredients; beat 3 to 4 minutes. Add chocolate chips and pecans. Blend well. Pour into well-greased bundt or tube pan. Bake for 1 hour at 350 degrees. Check for doneness. Let cool in pan. Remove and dribble confectioners' sugar icing over cake (see index). Freezes well. Serves 20.

Susan Murfee (Mrs. D.G.)

CHOCOLATE CREAM TORTE

1 pkg. devil's food cake mix
   (Duncan Hines)
1 pint whipping cream
1/4 cup sugar
1 tsp. vanilla
1 cup finely-chopped walnuts,
   divided
almond liqueur

Using 8 or 9 inch greased and floured cake pans, make and cool cake as directions on box indicate. Whip cream until thick. Add sugar, vanilla and 3/4 cup nuts. Stir. Split each layer of cake into two equal parts. Brush top of each layer lightly with liqueur, then spread on whipped cream. Continue with all four layers, including top layer, but not on the sides of cake. Garnish with a ring of nuts and chill in refrigerator. Serves 12.

Mary McElveen (Mrs. G.A., III)

ICE BOX COCONUT CAKE
Perfect coconut cake for a crowd

1 box Duncan Hines Butter Cake mix
1 small box Instant Vanilla Pudding
1 small can evaporated milk
1 16-oz. carton Cool Whip
2 6 oz. pkgs. frozen coconut
4 eggs
vanilla extract
coconut flavoring
1/2 cup sugar

Prepare butter cake mix according to directions on box, but use 4 eggs and milk instead of water. Add 1/2 pkg. coconut to the batter. Divide batter into 2 pans 13 x 9 x2 inches. Bake according to directions. While cake is baking pour evaporated milk into a 2-cup measuring cup and finish filling with water to 1-1/2 cup mark. Pour into pan and bring to boil. Remove from heat. Add 1/2 cup sugar, 1/2 tsp. vanilla and 1/2 tsp. coconut flavoring. Mix well. While cakes are still hot, punch holes in cakes with toothpick, then pour the milk mixture over the 2 cakes. Let cool. Mix instant pudding according to directions on package. Spread evenly over cakes. Top with Cook Whip, then sprinkle with coconut. Keep refrigerated. Makes two 9 x 13 inch cakes. Freezes nicely.

Sonja Edwards (Mrs. W.D., Jr)

HOLIDAY CRANBERRY CAKE
Best served right out of the oven

1 1-lb. 3 oz. pkg. lemon cake mix
1 3 oz. pkg. cream cheese, softened
3/4 cup milk
4 eggs
1-1/4 cup ground cranberries
1/2 cup walnuts, chopped
1/4 cup sugar
1 tsp. mace (optional)
confectioners' sugar (optional)

Blend cake mix, cream cheese and milk; beat with mixer 2 minutes at medium speed. Add eggs; blend and beat for 2 additional minutes. Thoroughly combine cranberries, walnuts, sugar and mace; fold into cake batter. Pour into a well-greased and floured 10-inch tube or bundt pan. Bake in moderate oven (350 degrees) for 1 hour or until done. Remove from pan. Cool 5 minutes. Cool on wire rack. Dust with confectioners' sugar if you wish.

Virginia Golding (Mrs. John G.)

When recipes call for lemon juice, leave the lemons out for a few days until soft; then refrigerate them. You will get twice as much juice and they will be easier to squeeze.

COCONUT CHOCOLATE CAKE

1 pkg. coconut almond or coconut
  pecan frosting mix
1 pkg. German's chocolate or
  fudge cake mix
1 cup water
1/2 cup vegetable oil
4 eggs
1 cup semi-sweet chocolate
  morsels

Generously grease 10-inch bundt or tube pan. Sprinkle entire pan with about 1 Tbsp. sugar; then coat pan with about 1/4 cup dry frosting mix. In bowl of electric mixer combine 1 cup dry frosting mix, package of cake mix, water, oil and eggs. Blend until moistened. Beat 4 minutes at medium speed. Pour 1/3 of batter into prepared pan. Sprinkle with 1/2 cup dry frosting mix and 1/2 cup chocolate morsels. Repeat with another 1/3 batter, 1/2 cup frosting mix and 1/2 cup chocolate morsels. Cover with remaining batter and sprinkle with remaining frosting mix. Bake in preheated 350 degree oven for 45 to 55 minutes until toothpick in center comes out clean. Cool in pan 15 minutes; remove from pan. Cool completely. Freezes nicely. Yield: 1 10-inch bundt cake.

Ellen Knott (Mrs. B.F.)

COOL WHIP COCONUT CAKE
This is a hit even with non-coconut lovers.

1 box yellow cake mix (Duncan
  Hines is best)
2/3 cup canned evaporated milk
1 box powdered sugar
1 tsp. vanilla extract
1 tsp. coconut flavoring

ICING:

2 6 oz. pkgs. frozen coconut
1 16-oz. container Cool Whip
maraschino cherries (optional)
pineapple slices (optional)

Prepare cake mix as directed but add coconut flavoring. Bake in a 9 x 13 x 2 inch pan (or tube pan). As soon as the cake is done, stick holes in the top and pour in filling which is made by combining the milk, powdered sugar, vanilla and coconut flavoring. (The more holes, the better.) Sprinkle 1/2 pkg. of coconut (thawed) on cake. Then spread on Cool Whip with spatula. Sprinkle rest of coconut on top of the Cool Whip. May decorate with cherries or pineapple. Serves 12-16.

Lin Tillman (Mrs. L.W.)

LAYERED DELIGHT

1 22-oz. can cherry pie filling
1 15-1/4 oz. can crushed pine-
    apple, undrained
1 pkg. Duncan Hines yellow cake
    mix
2 sticks melted butter or
    margarine
1 3-1/2 oz. can flaked coconut
1 cup chopped pecans
whipped topping (Dover Farms is
    best)

Layer as listed, in a greased 9 x 13 x2 inch pyrex
dish. Bake at 325 degrees for 1 hour. Serve warm
with whipped topping. Serves 8-10.

Pam Allen (Mrs. John R.)
Mayree Kay Miller (Mrs. J.J.)

LEMON SEVEN-UP CAKE

A very moist cake! Keep in refrigerator.

1 box Duncan Hines lemon
    cake mix
1 3-3/4 oz. box instant pineapple
    pudding mix (or pistachio)
4 eggs
3/4 cup Crisco oil
1 12-oz. can 7-Up or other lemon-
    lime beverage

FILLING AND FROSTING:
1 1-lb. 4 oz. can crushed pineapple
    with juice
1 stick margarine
1 1-/2 cups sugar
2 eggs
2 Tbsp. flour
1 can coconut or 1 pkg. frozen
    coconut

For cake, mix first 5 ingredients *by hand.* (Do not
use mixer.) Grease and flour 3 8-inch layer cake
pans. Spoon mixture evenly into pans and bake
at 325 degrees for 30 minutes.
For filling and frosting, combine first 5 ingredients. Cook in double boiler over medium heat,
stirring constantly.   When thick, add coconut.
Fill and frost cakes while warm to retain
moisture.

Dottie Grier (Mrs. R.N.)

Place a piece of rye bread in a covered container
with brown sugar to prevent lumping.

MANDARIN CREAM CAKE AND ICING
One of *the best* "box-mix" cakes

1 box yellow cake mix (Duncan Hines)
1/2 cup vegetable oil (Crisco)
4 eggs
1 11 oz. can mandarin oranges and juice.

ICING:
1 3-oz. pkg. instant vanilla pudding
1 1-lb. 4-oz. can crushed pineapple and juice
1 8-oz. carton Cool Whip

Put cake mix, oil, eggs, oranges and juice into mixer bowl. Mix until smooth, but *no longer.* Pour into 3 well-greased and floured 8-inch cake pans. Bake at 325 degrees for about 15 minutes or until cake tests done. (Don't overcook.) Allow to cool for a few minutes in the pan, then turn out. Cool thoroughly before icing.

ICING: Place instant pudding in a bowl. Add pineapple and juice and mix well. Fold in Cool Whip, mixing just until blended. Spread between cake layers and on top. Refrigerate.

Myrtle Ussery (Mrs. A.M.)

PEANUT BUTTER PUDDING CAKE
Tastes like a Reese's peanut butter cup!

1 pkg. (2 layer size) yellow cake mix (Duncan Hines)
1 pkg. (3-3/4 oz.) vanilla instant pudding
4 eggs
1 cup water
1/4 cup oil
1 cup crunchy peanut butter

Combine all ingredients. Blend, then beat at medium speed for 4 minutes. Pour into greased and floured 10-inch tube pan. Bake at 350 degrees for 55 to 60 minutes. Cool in pan 15 minutes. Remove. Frost with your favorite chocolate icing.

Lynn Wheeler (Mrs. Joseph)

WINE CAKE

*1 box Duncan Hines yellow cake or pudding cake mix
1 3-3/4 oz. pkg. instant lemon pudding mix
3/4 cup Crisco oil
3/4 cup cream sherry (Gallo)
4 eggs
1 scant Tbsp. grated nutmeg
confectioners' sugar

Beat all ingredients, except confectioners' sugar, 5 minutes. Pour into greased and floured tube pan. Cook 50 to 60 minutes at 325 degrees. (If using pudding cake mix, cook for a longer time.) Cool 5 minutes. Turn onto cake plate and sift confectioners' sugar on top.

NOTE: If pudding cake is used, the cake will not be very pretty, but will have a moist, marvelous flavor.

Virginia Golding (Mrs. John G.)

SIMPLY DIVINE CAKE

1 cup sour cream
1 pkg. yellow cake mix (Duncan
   Hines)
1 3-3/4 oz. pkg. instant vanilla
   pudding
4 eggs
1/2 cup salad oil
4 Tbsp. granulated sugar
3 Tbsp. brown sugar
3 Tbsp. flour
1 Tbsp. cocoa
1 tsp. cinnamon
1/2 pkg. chocolate chips (3 oz.)

Mix first 5 ingredients with electric mixer for 10 minutes. Add the rest of the ingredients except for chocolate chips. Mix for 1 more minute. Stir in chocolate chips. Bake in tube pan for 1 hour at 350 degrees. Serves 10.

Dale Yaged

RON'S FAVORITE CUPCAKES

1 stick butter
1 cup sugar
2 eggs, beaten until thick
2 cups cake flour
3 tsp. baking powder
1/2 tsp. salt
3/4 cup milk
1 tsp. vanilla extract

Work butter until soft. Gradually add sugar and cream until smooth. Beat eggs until thick and add to butter mixture. Sift flour, baking powder and salt together. Stir flour mixture into butter mixture alternately with milk flavored with vanilla extract. Begin and end with dry ingredients. *Do not beat!* Put paper liners in muffin tins and fill 2/3 full. Bake at 375 degrees for 20 to 25 minutes. Frost with a favorite frosting. Yield: 18 cupcakes.

Margery Marcus (Mrs. R.A.)

PETE'S TRAVELING CUPCAKES

4 squares semi-sweet chocolate
2 sticks butter
1-3/4 cups chopped pecans
1-3/4 cups sugar
4 large eggs, beaten
1 cup plain flour
1 tsp. salt

Melt chocolate and butter in pan, add nuts and stir until well coated. Beat eggs, stir in sugar, then chocolate mixture. Add salt and stir in flour. Stir with fork until completely mixed. Fill greased baking cups 2/3 full. Bake at 325 degrees for 30-35 minutes.

Georgia Miller (Mrs. George)

BROWNIE CUPCAKES
"Unbelievably good!"

1 stick butter
1-1/2 sq. unsweetened chocolate
1 cup sugar
2/3 cup flour
1 tsp. vanilla
2 eggs, beaten
1/2 cup black walnuts, chopped
frosting, below

Melt butter and chocolate in double boiler. Beat eggs, add sugar, flour, vanilla, melted butter and chocolate. Stir in walnuts. Pour into paper baking cups, placed in muffin tins, and bake 12 minutes in 350 degree oven. Do not overbake. Frost while hot.

FROSTING

2 Tbsp. butter
1 square chocolate
1/2 box 10X powdered sugar
black coffee

Melt butter and chocolate and add to the powdered sugar with coffee enough to make frosting a spreading consistency. Refrigerate. Makes 18 cupcakes.

Doris Walker (Mrs. James E.)

BLACK BOTTOM CUPCAKES
These stay moist for several weeks.

8 oz. cream cheese, room
   temperature
1 egg
1/3 cup sugar
1/8 tsp. salt
1 cup semisweet chocolate chips
1-1/2 cups all-purpose flour
1 cup sugar
1/4 cup cocoa
1 tsp. baking soda
1/2 tsp. salt
1 cup water
1/3 cup vegetable oil
1 Tbsp. white vinegar
1 tsp. vanilla

Line muffin tins with cupcake papers. Using wooden spoon, blend cream cheese, egg, sugar and salt in mixing bowl. Carefully fold in chocolate chips, set aside. Combine dry ingredients in another bowl and mix well. Add remaining ingredients and blend thoroughly. Fill cupcake papers about 3/4 full with batter. Drop 1 heaping tablespoon cream cheese mixture into center of each. Bake at 375 degrees for 35 to 40 minutes. Yield: 18 cupcakes.

Frances J. Brackett (Mrs. Martin L., Jr.)

BUTTER FROSTING

1/4 cup butter or margarine
2 cups sifted confectioners' sugar
2 egg yolks
1 tsp. vanilla
1 Tbsp. cream

Thoroughly cream butter and sugar. Stir in unbeaten egg yolks and vanilla. Add cream as frosting becomes thick. Will frost tops and sides of two 8-inch layers.

Note: More confectioners' sugar may be added for desired consistency.

BUTTER FROSTING VARIATIONS

Orange Butter Frosting:
Substitute orange juice for cream, and grated peel of 1 orange for vanilla.

Chocolate Butter Frosting:
Add 1-1/2 1-oz. squares un-sweetened chocolate, melted, after first 1/4 cup sugar has been added; stir until well blended.

Coffee-Cocoa Frosting:
Sift 3 Tbsp. cocoa and 1/4 tsp. instant coffee with sugar.

Lemon-Banana Frosting:
Substitute 3 Tbsp. mashed banana and 1 Tbsp. lemon juice for cream and vanilla.

The Committee

BUTTER CREAM ICING

1-1/2 sticks soft butter
1-1/2 boxes confectioners' sugar
pinch of salt
1-1/2 tsp. vanilla extract
enough milk for spreading
(approx. 1/2 cup)

Beat butter, sugar and salt together. Add liquid and beat until smooth and creamy. If too thick, add milk; if too thin; add sugar.

Julia Warner (Mrs. C.E.)

"NEVER FAIL" ICING

2-1/2 cups sugar
1/2 cup light corn syrup
1/2 cup water
dash salt
2 egg whites, slightly beaten
1 tsp. vanilla extract

Mix first 4 ingredients together in pan. Cook until soft ball stage is reached on candy thermometer. Pour 4 Tbsp. of mixture over 2 stiffly-beaten egg whites and beat well, using electric mixer. Continue cooking syrup to 260 degrees. Then pour slowly over egg whites, beating continuously. When about half of the syrup has been poured, it may then be poured more rapidly. Add 1 tsp. vanilla extract. Continue beating until stiff enough to spread. If too stiff, stir in hot water, a Tbsp. at a time, until right consistency is reached.

Barby Goode (Mrs. David J.)

CARAMEL FROSTING

1 stick butter
1 cup brown sugar, firmly packed
1/4 cup milk
3 cups sifted confectioners' sugar

Melt butter in saucepan; add brown sugar. Boil over low heat, stirring constantly. Add milk and, still stirring constantly, bring to a boil again. Remove from heat, beat 4 minutes. Add the sifted confectioners' sugar and beat until spreading consistency. May add milk if too thick. Ices one 10-inch tube pan cake or 2-layer 8-inch cake, or one 13 x 9 sheet cake.

Ellen Knott (Mrs. B.F.)

GLORIA FLETCHER'S MOCHA ICING
I have modified this old family recipe to be used with my food processor.

1 box confectioners' sugar
1 stick butter
1 tsp. instant coffee (dissolved in
  1 tsp. hot water)
5 - 6 Tbsp. cocoa
5 - 6 Tbsp. evaporated milk
  (or cream)
1/4 cup chopped pecans or
  walnuts (optional)

Allow butter to reach room temperature. (This step may be shortened if you own a microwave oven that can soften butter.) Put butter into processor bowl and process until creamed. Add sugar, coffee dissolved in hot water, 5 Tbsp. of cocoa (6 Tbsp. if you like extra chocolate flavor) and 5 Tbsp. evaporated milk or cream. Process until well blended and until creamy spreadable texture is achieved. Add extra milk or cream if necessary. This recipe will ice one 13 x 9 x 2 inch cake or one 9-inch double-layer cake. Increase by 1/2 if you like thick icing. Sprinkle iced cake with nuts.

Stephanie Fletcher (Mrs. D.H.)

CHOCOLATE ICING FOR SHEET CAKE

1 stick butter
2 cups sugar
1 small can evaporated milk
dash of salt
1 6-oz. pkg. chocolage chips
1 tsp. vanilla

Put first 4 ingredients in heavy sauce pan. Bring to a boil (not on high heat) and let boil for 5 to 7 minutes. Remove from heat and add chocolate chips and vanilla and mix well. Pour on warm sheet cake.

Linda Brown (Mrs. W.B.)

YUMMY CHOCOLATE ICING

This is rich and good! Can also be used warm as chocolate sauce.

2 cans Eagle brand milk
4 squares unsweetened chocolate
1 tsp. vanilla extract
1/4 tsp. salt
2 Tbsp. water

Combine milk with salt and water. Add squares of chocolate. Cook over boiling water until thick. Remove from heat. Add vanilla.

Ann Thrift (Mrs. Charles B., III)

CONFECTIONERS' ICING

milk or cream
2 cups confectioners' sugar
dash salt
1 tsp. vanilla extract

Add sufficient milk or cream to confectioners' sugar to make spreading consistency. Add dash salt and 1 tsp. vanilla.

Ellen Knott (Mrs. B.F.)

LEMON FROSTING

1-3/4 cups sifted confectioners'
  sugar
1/4 cup melted butter or
  margarine
1/4 cup lemon juice
1 Tbsp. cream
1/8 tsp. grated lemon peel
1-3/4 cups sifted confectioners
  sugar

Combine 1-3/4 cups sugar with butter, lemon juice, cream, and lemon peel; beat until smooth. Add remaining 1-3/4 cups sugar; beat until of spreading consistency. Will frost tops and sides of two 9-inch layers or 1 angel food or tube-pan cake.

Virginia Golding (Mrs. John G.)

SEVEN-MINUTE FROSTING

2 egg whites
1-1/2 cups sugar
1-1/2 tsp. light corn syrup OR
1/4 tsp. cream of tartar
1/3 cup cold water
dash salt
1 tsp. vanilla extract

Put all ingredients except vanilla in double boiler. Beat 1 minute with electric mixer. Cook over boiling water, beating constantly with rotary or electric beater until mixture forms peaks, about 7 minutes. Remove from heat; add vanilla; beat until of spreading consistency.

Will frost tops and sides of two 9-inch layers or one 10-inch tube cake.

For a smaller amount, use half of all ingredients; cook about 4 minutes. Will frost top of 13 x 9 inch loaf cake; or top and sides of a 9-inch tube cake; or tops of 12 cupcakes.

Coconut Frosting:
Frost cake; sprinkle at once with 1-1/2 cups moist, shredded coconut. Toast or tint coconut, if desired.

Peppermint Frosting:
Color 1 recipe Seven-minute Frosting shell pink and add a few drops of oil of peppermint.

Chocolate Seven-minute Frosting: Add three 1-ounce squares unsweetened chocolate, melted and cooled, to frosting just before spreading on cake. Fold in; do not beat.

Pineapple Parfait Frosting:
Substitute syrup from canned pineapple for water. Omit vanilla; add 1 tsp. grated lemon peel. Garnish with pineapple cubes.

Ivory Frosting:
Substitute 1/4 cup brown sugar for 1/4 cup granulated sugar.

The Committee

CHOCOLATE ICING

1 stick soft butter
1/8 tsp. salt
1 16-oz. box confectioners' sugar, divided
4 squares unsweetened chocolate, melted
6 Tbsp. milk
1 tsp. vanilla extract

Beat butter, salt and 1 cup sugar until light and fluffy. Blend in chocolate; then add remaining sugar alternately with milk and vanilla extract. Beat until smooth and creamy.

Julia Warner (Mrs. C.E.)

Cookies & confections

CHOCOLATE PEANUT BUTTER BUCKEYES
Reese's Peanut Butter Cups "taste"

1/2 cup butter or margarine,
  softened
2 cups crunchy peanut butter
1 box confectioners' sugar
1 tsp. vanilla
4 cups Rice Krispies
8 oz. Hershey bar
1 6-oz. pkg. semi-sweet
  chocolate chips
1/2 bar paraffin

Blend together all ingredients except the Hershey bar, chocolate chips and paraffin. Form mixture into small balls. In top of double boiler, melt Hershey bar, chocolate chips and paraffin. Dip balls into chocolate mixture. Place on waxed paper to dry. Keep chocolate mixture over hot water while dipping balls. May be refrigerated or frozen. Yields 6-8 dozen, according to desired size.

VARIATION: Omit Rice Krispies and Hershey bar, and reduce paraffin to 1/4 bar. Make as above for a more "chocolate-peanut-buttery" version.

Sally Gray
Del Fox (Mrs. J. B.)

MILLIONAIRE CHOCOLATE PECAN CLUSTERS
This one may put Russell Stover "out of business."

1/2 cup Land o' Lakes butter
7 oz. jar marshmallow creme
1-1/2 lbs. Hershey kisses (better
  buy 2 lbs. if your kids are
  going to peel the papers off!)
13 oz. can evaporated milk
5 cups sugar
6 cups pecans, broken up
  (optional)
1 to 2 cups Bit of Brickle bits
  by Nestle, toffee flavor
  (optional)

Put kisses and marshmallow creme in bowl. Combine milk, sugar and butter in saucepan and bring to boil. Turn down to low heat and cook 8 minutes, stirring constantly. Pour this hot milk mixture over kisses and marshmallow in bowl, and stir. This melts instantly but starts "setting up" fast. Stir in nuts and brickle bits. Drop with spoon onto waxed paper or foil and cool before removing. If the chocolate sets up too fast for you, call the neighborhood kids and give them each a spoon to drop from too. Yields about 100 pieces.

Lin Tillman (Mrs. L. W.)

CHOCOLATE PECAN CANDY

1 7-oz. jar marshmallow creme
1-1/2 lb. Hershey bars (break into small pieces)
5 cups sugar
1 13-oz. can evaporated milk
1/2 cup butter
2 cups chopped pecans or black walnuts

Place marshmallow creme and Hershey bars in a large bowl; set aside. Combine sugar, milk and butter in a saucepan. Bring mixture to a boil; then cook 8 minutes. Pour over marshmallow creme and Hershey bars, stirring well until blended. Pour mixture immediately into a buttered 9 x 13 inch pan. Cool before cutting into squares.

Hilda Hemby (Mrs. T.E., Jr.)

GOLD NUGGET FUDGE

Flecks of orange peel and dates give this a different taste.

2 Tbsp. butter
2 cups sugar
1 cup milk
1/4 tsp. salt
1 tsp. vanilla extract
1/2 cup finely-chopped dates
1 Tbsp. grated fresh orange peel
1 cup chopped walnuts

Melt butter in 3-quart saucepan. Rotate pan to coat sides. Add sugar, milk and salt, blending well. Stir constantly while cooking rapidly to the soft-ball stage of 236 degrees. Remove from heat. Stir in vanilla, dates, orange peel and walnuts. Set in cold water to cool; then beat until thick and creamy. Pour immediately into buttered 8-inch square pan. Cut into squares. Makes about 1 pound.

Virginia Golding (Mrs. John G.)

MARVELOUS FUDGE

The best!

4-1/2 cups sugar
1/8 tsp. salt
3 Tbsp. butter
1 13-oz. can evaporated milk
1 tsp. vanilla extract
12 oz. semisweet chocolate bits
12 oz. German's sweet chocolate, broken into small pieces
2 7-oz. jars marshmallow creme for a mild Swiss chocolate taste
2 cups chopped nuts

Bring first 4 ingredients to a boil in a large saucepan over medium heat. Boil for 6 minutes. Remove from heat, add vanilla and pour boiling syrup over remaining ingredients. Beat until all chocolate is melted. Pour out onto buttered marble slab or waxed paper or into large pans (You need a large area to pour it out.) Allow candy to set for 3 hours before cutting. Yield: about 4 pounds of fudge.

Susan Knott

MICROWAVE FUDGE

1 lb. box confectioners' sugar
1/2 cup cocoa
1/4 tsp. salt
1/4 cup milk
1 Tbsp. vanilla
1/2 cup butter
1 cup chopped nuts

In a 1-1/2 quart casserole stir sugar, cocoa, salt, milk and vanilla until partially blended. (Mixture is too stiff to blend thoroughly.) Put butter over top in center of the dish. Place in microwave at high speed for 2 minutes, or until milk feels warm on bottom of dish. Stir until smooth. If all the butter has not melted in cooking, it will as mixture is stirred. Blend in nuts. Pour into an 8 x 4 x 3 pan that has been lined with waxed paper. Chill for 1 hour in your refrigerator.

Jean Bridges (Mrs. D. T.)

WHITE CHOCOLATE FUDGE
Very good and colorful

3 cups sugar
1 cup evaporated milk
3/4 stick butter
1 16-oz. jar marshmallow creme
12 oz. white chocolate, cut into
    small pieces
1 cup chopped pecans
1 4-oz. jar candied cherries,
    drained and chopped

Bring sugar, milk and butter to a boil over low heat, stirring constantly. Cook to 237 degrees (use a candy thermometer). Remove from heat, add marshmallow creme, white chocolate, nuts and cherries. Stir until marshmallow creme and chocolate are melted. Pour into a 9 x 13 inch buttered pan. Cool before cutting. Yields 6 dozen candies.

Pam Allen (Mrs. John)

HAYSTACKS

1-1/2 pounds white chocolate
1 11-oz. bag pretzel sticks, broken
1 12-oz. can salted peanuts
    (pecans, almonds, walnuts
    may be substituted)

Melt chocolate over boiling water in top of double boiler. Add combined pretzels and peanuts to melted chocolate. Drop by teaspoonfuls onto waxed paper. Reheat over hot water if mixture hardens too quickly.

VARIATIONS:
1. Pretzels may be omitted and all nuts added to the chocolate.
2. 1-1/2 cups smooth or crunchy peanut butter may be added instead of pretzels and peanuts. Complete as above.

Marilyn Lea (Mrs. Scott)

HOLLY LEAVES

These are great for Christmas. An easy thing to do with children

40 large marshmallows
1 stick margarine
1 tsp. vanilla
1 tsp. green food coloring
1 box red hot cinnamon candies
4-1/2 cups corn flakes

Mix first 3 ingredients in double boiler until melted. Add food coloring, then corn flakes. Drop by spoonfuls onto waxed paper. Decorate each with 2-3 red hots. Let dry thoroughly for 1-2 days on waxed paper. Store in air-tight container.

NOTE: Can also shape into circles like wreaths and decorate with red hots or red and green cherries.

Yvonne Rayburn (Mrs. C. Richard, Jr.)

PEANUT BRITTLE

Makes a good Christmas gift

2 cups sugar
1 cup white Karo syrup
1/2 cup water
1 tsp. salt
2 Tbsp. soda
4 cups red skin raw peanuts

Mix sugar, syrup and salt. Add boiling water; stir well. Boil until it spins a thread. Add large peanuts. Stir, almost constantly, until liquid turns dark amber color. Remove from stove. Add soda, stirring well, and pour out on buttered marble slab. Spread with wooden spoon slightly. (Can be done on 2 well-buttered heavy cookie sheets.) Cool until hardened and no longer sticky to touch. Break into bite-sized pieces. Yields 2-1/2 pounds.

Dot Nicholls (Mrs. T.H.)

NEW ORLEANS PRALINES

1 cup firmly-packed dark or light
  brown sugar
1 cup granulated sugar
3 Tbsp. butter
5 Tbsp. boiling water
1 cup chopped pecans
1 tsp. vanilla extract

Combine sugars, butter and water in a heavy 2-quart saucepan. Let mixture come to a rolling boil over medium heat, *stirring constantly*. Boil one minute; remove from heat. Add pecans and vanilla extract and beat for about 2 minutes. Drop *quickly* by tablespoons onto waxed paper or aluminum foil before mixture sets. Wrap pralines individually in plastic wrap or aluminum foil. Store in covered container.

Ellen Knott (Mrs. B.F.)

EASY TOFFEE

1-3/4 cups sugar
1/8 tsp. cream of tartar
1 cup heavy cream
1/2 cup butter
1 tsp. rum or other fruit flavoring
6 Tbsp. chopped almonds and/or
Hershey bars (optional)

Place sugar and cream of tartar in deep saucepan which is rounded at the bottom. Add cream and boil a few minutes, stirring with a wooden spoon. Add butter, boil to soft crack stage (290 degrees on candy thermometer), stirring all the time. Add 1 tsp. rum or any fruit flavoring. Pour into buttered pan. Cut into squares. May add almonds or let Hershey bars melt on top.

Carol Gatewood

ENGLISH TOFFEE

1 box. brown sugar
1 lb. butter
12 (1.05 oz.) Hershey Milk
Chocolate bars
1 pkg. sliced almonds

Butter large cookie sheet with sides. Heat together brown sugar and butter. Cook this to hard-crack stage (300 degrees), approximately 15 minutes, stirring constantly. Pour into cookie sheet and immediately lay Hershey bars covering toffee mixture. Spread smoothly and sprinkle almonds on top. Cool in refrigerator; break into pieces. Yields 3 pounds.

Pat Nesbit (Mrs. W.M.)

TURTLES
Everybody's favorite, especially children's

1/2 lb. caramels
2 Tbsp. heavy cream
1 cup pecan halves
1/2 pkg. chocolate chips

Melt caramels in cream over hot water. Cook for 10 minutes. Place nuts on waxed paper in threes. Spoon caramel mixture over nuts leaving tips showing. Let set for about 30 minutes. Melt chocolate over hot water. Cool until lukewarm. Spread over caramels.

Myrtle Ussery (Mrs. A.M.)

APPLESAUCE RAISIN BARS

2 cups applesauce
1 cup butter
2 cups sugar
2 cups raisins
2 tsp. baking soda
3 cups flour
2 tsp. cinnamon
1 tsp. nutmeg

CREAM CHEESE
FROSTING:
3 oz. cream cheese, softened
1/2 cup butter softened
1 tsp. vanilla
powdered sugar

For bars: In a 2-quart saucepan, heat applesauce, butter, sugar and raisins until butter melts; add soda, stir and cool. Sift dry ingredients and add to applesauce mixture. Spread on a greased jelly roll pan. Bake at 350 degrees for 25 minutes; cool. For frosting: Cream butter and cream cheese. Add vanilla and enough powdered sugar to spread easily. Frost cooled applesauce mixture and cut into squares.

Linda Miller (Mrs. W. R.)

BLACK AND WHITE BARS
The best "bar cookie"—with a distinctive almond flavor

1 cup butter or margarine
1-1/2 tsp. vanilla
2 cups sugar
4 eggs
2 cups sifted plain flour
1/2 tsp. salt (sifted into flour)
1 cup chopped nuts
2 squares unsweetened chocolate, melted

FROSTING:
1 box confectioners' sugar
6 level Tbsp. cocoa
6 Tbsp. margarine
1 tsp. almond extract
6 Tbsp. liquid coffee, brewed or instant
1 cup chopped nuts

Cream butter, vanilla and sugar together until light and fluffy. Add eggs, one at a time, beating well after each addition. Add flour and salt and mix until blended. Stir in nuts. Divide batter in half; add cooled chocolate to one part. Drop batter alternately into greased, waxed-paper lined 15 x 10 x 1 inch pan. Run knife through batter several times to marbelize. Bake in 350 degree oven for about 20 minutes. Do not overcook. Turn out on rack to cool. Remove paper. Frost and cut into squares — larger ones for dessert with coffee, smaller ones for bars. Yields 96 small bars.

FROSTING: Mix ingredients together until smooth. Add nuts last.

Ellen Knott (Mrs. B. F.)

378

BUTTERMILK BROWNIES

2 cups sugar
2 cups flour
1 tsp. soda
1/2 cup buttermilk
2 eggs
1 tsp. vanilla extract
1/2 tsp. salt
2 sticks margarine
4 Tbsp. cocoa

ICING:
7 Tbsp. margarine
4 Tbsp. cocoa
5 Tbsp. buttermilk
1 1-lb. box powdered sugar
1 tsp. vanilla
1 cup chopped pecans

For brownies, bring salt, margarine and cocoa to a boil. Pour over dry ingredients in a large mixing bowl. Add buttermilk, eggs and vanilla. Mix well. Bake at 350 degrees in a greased and floured jelly-roll pan for 20-25 minutes. While brownies are baking, prepare icing.

In a saucepan, mix together margarine, cocoa and buttermilk. Bring to boil. Remove from heat and gradually add powdered sugar, mixing well. Stir in vanilla and pecans. Spread over brownies while hot. When cool, cut into squares.

Alice Nance (Mrs. James A.)

BUTTERSCOTCH BROWNIES

1-1/2 cups melted butter
4 cups light brown sugar
2 cups flour
2 tsp. baking powder
1 tsp. salt
4 eggs
2 tsp. vanilla
2 cups pecans, chopped

Cream sugar, vanilla and butter. Add eggs, one at a time, beating after each one. Add mixed sifted dry ingredients, then pecans and vanilla. Mix and put into 9 x 13 inch buttered pan. Bake 25 minutes at 350 degrees, or until tests done. Cut when cool. Yields 2 to 3 dozen brownies. Freezes well.

Louise Hardman (Mrs. John D.)
Laura H. Tipps

CHOCOLATE CHIP BROWNIES

2/3 cup melted butter
1 box dark brown sugar
3 eggs
2-3/4 cups sifted flour
2-1/2 tsp. baking powder
1/2 tsp. salt
2 tsp. vanilla extract
1-2 cups chopped pecans (I use 2)
1 12-oz. pkg. chocolate bits

Add melted butter to brown sugar and beat well. Add eggs and vanilla and blend. Combine flour, baking powder and salt; add to sugar mixture. Mix well. Add nuts and chocolate bits. Spread in greased pan 15 x 10 x 1 inch. Bake at 325 degrees for 30 minutes. Do not overbake. Cool and cut into squares. Makes about 48 brownies. Can be frozen.

Julia Warner (Mrs. C.E.)
Missy Bridges

CREME DE MENTHE BROWNIES

4 oz. unsweetened baking
   chocolate
1 cup margarine
4 eggs
2 cups sugar
1/2 tsp. salt
1 tsp. vanilla extract
1 cup flour, sifted

FILLING:
1/2 cup margarine
4 cups sifted confectioners' sugar
1/4 cup evaporated milk
1/4 cup creme de menthe

TOPPING:
6 oz. chocolate chips
4 Tbsp. margarine
3 Tbsp. water

Melt chocolate and margarine over water in top of double boiler; cool slightly. Beat eggs in mixing bowl until light and fluffy. Beat in sugar gradually. Add remaining ingredients including chocolate mixture. Beat 1 minute. Pour into well-greased 13 x 9 inch pan. Bakes at 350 degrees for 25 minutes. Do not overbake. Base will be "fudgy." Cool before spreading with filling.

To prepare filling, beat together margarine and sugar. Gradually add milk and creme de menthe. Mixture will be light and fluffy. Spread over base and chill 1-1/2 hours.

For topping, melt chocolate chips and margarine over water. Mix and spread over filling. Chill. Store in refrigerator. Freezes well. Yields about 5 dozen.

Ellen Knott (Mrs. B.F.)

FOOLPROOF BROWNIES

1/2 cup Wesson oil
2 eggs
1 cup sugar
1/2 cup flour
1 tsp. baking powder
6 Tbsp. Hershey's cocoa
1/2 tsp. salt, if desired
1/2 tsp. vanilla extract
   (not imitation)
1/2 cup chopped pecans
powdered sugar

Beat eggs, add sugar. Sift, then add other dry ingredients. Add oil, vanilla and nuts and combine thoroughly. Bake in shallow 8 x 9 inch pan at 325 degrees for 20-25 minutes (test for doneness the way you test a cake, and add a couple of minutes on damp days). Sprinkle with powdered sugar and enjoy. Yields 16 brownies.

Boyd Davis (Mrs. R.A.)
Faye Thurston (Mrs. W.H.)

LEE'S BLOND BROWNIES

2 sticks butter, melted
1 box (1 lb.) dark brown sugar
3 eggs
3 cups self-rising flour
1 tsp. vanilla
12 oz. pkg. semi-sweet chocolate
    chips
1 cup pecans, chopped

Cream butter and brown sugar, adding one egg at a time. Add flour, vanilla, chocolate chips and pecans. Line a 9 x 13 pan with tinfoil. Spread mixture in pan and bake at 350 degrees for 20 to 25 minutes. Cut before completely cool. For thinner brownies use one 9 x 13 inch pan and one 8 x 8 inch pan.

Nancy Wohlbruck (Mrs. Everett L.)

LIBRARY BROWNIES

1 pkg. Duncan Hines
    Brownie Mix

FROSTING:
1 Tbsp. butter
1/2 cup sifted powdered sugar
1-1/2 tsp. cream
1/2 tsp. peppermint extract
green food coloring (optional)

GLAZE:
2 Tbsp. butter
3 Tbsp. chocolate chips

Prepare brownie mix according to package directions. Let cool. Cream 1 Tbsp. butter, powdered sugar, cream and peppermint extract until fluffy. Spread over cooled brownies and refrigerate to set. For the glaze, melt together butter and chocolate chips. Pour over frosting, tilting so it spreads evenly. Refrigerate before cutting. Serve at room temperature.

Nancy Little (Mrs. T.M.)

QUICK BROWNIES

2 cups sugar
1/2 cup cocoa
1 stick margarine, melted
4 large eggs
1 tsp. vanilla
1-1/4 cups plain unsifted flour
1/2 cup nuts (optional)

Grease a 9 x 13-inch pan. Mix sugar and cocoa; add margarine, eggs, vanilla, flour and nuts. Pour into greased pan. Cook for 20 minutes at 350 degrees. Cut into squares while hot. Yields 20 to 24 brownies.

Caroline Gray (Mrs. B.K.)

TWENTY-SEVEN MINUTE BROWNIES

4 1-oz. squares unsweetened
    baking chocolate
3/4 cup margarine or butter
1-1/2 cups sugar
3 eggs
1-1/2 tsp. vanilla, or more
3/4 cup flour
nuts (optional)

Melt chocolate. Cream butter and sugar; add eggs and mix. Blend in rest of ingredients. Bake in greased 8 x 8 inch pan at 350 degrees for 27 minutes. Makes 16 to 20 brownies.

Beverly S. Hance (Mrs. James)

SENSATIONAL SUGAR COOKIES

1 cup butter, softened
1 cup sugar
1 cup confectioners' sugar
1 cup vegetable oil
2 eggs
1-1/2 tsp. vanilla
4-1/4 cups flour
1 tsp. cream of tartar
1 tsp. baking soda
1/2 tsp. salt
granulated sugar

Cream butter and sugars. Add oil and eggs, mixing well. Blend in remaining ingredients except sugar. Dough should be covered and chilled several hours or overnight to make handling easier. Roll dough into small balls the size of walnuts and place on lightly-greased cookie sheets. Lightly grease the bottom of a glass, dip in granulated sugar and press each ball flat. Bake 12 to 15 minutes at 350 degrees.

NOTE: For a fun activity in the kitchen with children, roll dough 3/16 inch thick. Place hand lightly on dough; trace around hand with pastry wheel. Bake 6-8 minutes. Cool and decorate as desired.

Kathleen Boyce (Mrs. R.N.)

SALTED PEANUT CRISPS

1-1/2 cups packed brown sugar
1/2 cup butter or margarine,
    softened
1/2 cup shortening
2 eggs
2 tsp. vanilla
3 cups flour
1/2 tsp. salt
1/2 tsp. baking soda
2 cups salted peanuts

Heat oven to 375 degrees. Combine first 5 ingredients; mix well. Stir in remaining ingredients. Drop dough by rounded teaspoonfuls about 2 inches apart onto lightly greased cookie sheet. Flatten with greased bottom of glass dipped in sugar. Bake until golden brown, 8 to 10 minutes. Remove from cookie sheet immediately. Yields 6 dozen cookies.

Betty Boyd (Mrs. Basil)

CHOCOLATE PEPPERMINT BARS

LAYER 1:
2 oz. unsweetened chocolate
1/2 cup butter
2 eggs
1 cup sugar
1/2 cup sifted flour
1/2 cup chopped almonds
    (optional)

LAYER 2:
1-1/2 cups powdered sugar
3 Tbsp. butter or margarine
2 to 3 Tbsp. cream
1 tsp. peppermint extract

LAYER 3:
3 oz. unsweetened chocolate
2 Tbsp. butter

For layer 1: Melt chocolate and butter; cream eggs and sugar. Add flour and chocolate mixture. Mix well. Bake in greased 8 x 8-inch pan at 350 degrees for 20 minutes. Then turn oven off and bake 5 minutes more.

For layer 2: Cream sugar and butter. Blend in cream and peppermint extract. Spread on cooled first layer. Refrigerate until chilled.

For layer 3: Melt chocolate and butter and pour over peppermint layer. Chill. Cut into small squares. Yields 24 to 30 bars.

Dixie L. Denney (Mrs. T.E.)

CHOCOLATE SHERRY CREAM BARS

BASE:
4 squares unsweetened chocolate
1 cup butter
4 eggs
1 cup sifted flour
1 tsp. vanilla
2 cups sugar

FILLING:
1/2 cup margarine,
    room temperature
4 cups sifted confectioners' sugar
1/4 cup half-and-half cream
1/4 cup sherry
1 cup chopped pecans

TOPPING:
1 6-oz. pkg. semi-sweet
    chocolate chips
3 Tbsp. water
4 Tbsp. butter

BASE: Melt chocolate with butter. Cool. Beat eggs until light and creamy. Add sugar and vanilla and beat until well blended. Beat the cooled chocolate into the egg mixture and stir in the flour and vanilla. Pour into greased 9 x 13 inch pan and bake at 350 degrees for 25 minutes. Do not overcook. Chill in refrigerator.

FILLING: Beat margarine and sugar until creamy. Beat in cream and sherry. Stir in chopped nuts. Spread over chilled cake.

TOPPING: In saucepan, melt chocolate chips, butter and water. Spread over filling. Cut into bars. Makes 3 dozen.

Judy Ranson (Mrs. R.C.)

CZECHOSLOVAKIAN BAR COOKIES

Spreading last layer of dough takes a little time, but it's worth the effort.

1 cup butter
1 cup sugar
2 egg yolks
2 cups sifted plain flour
3/4 cup nuts, chopped
1/2 cup Smuckers Strawberry
   Preserves

Cream butter and sugar well. Add egg yolks and beat well. Add flour and nuts. Spread half of dough in 8 or 9-inch greased pan. Spread with preserves. Drop remaining dough on top of preserves with a tablespoon. Spread evenly over top. Bake at 325 degrees for 45 minutes or until brown. Cool completely. Cut in squares and roll in powdered sugar. Yields 16 squares. These freeze well.

La McLeod (Mrs. J.A.)

DATE AND NUT BARS

These are moist and chewy!

1/2 cup butter
1 cup sugar
1 egg
1 tsp. vanilla
1 cup chopped walnuts
1 cup chopped dates
1-1/2 cups applesauce
1/2 tsp. cinnamon
1/4 tsp. cloves
2 cups flour
2 tsp. baking soda

Cream together butter and sugar. Add egg and vanilla; mix well. Sift flour with spices. Add dry ingredients, dates and nuts; beat. Add applesauce last. Spread in greased and floured square baking pan. Bake at 350 degrees for 30 minutes. Cool. Cut into squares. Sprinkle with powdered sugar. Keep covered or they will dry out quickly. Makes 20 squares.

Mary Ann Falciani (Mrs. R.B.)

ENERGY BARS

A nutritious snack or dessert for those bag lunches we seem to fix every day!

1/2 cup peanut butter
1/2 stick margarine
2-1/2 cups Cheerios
1-1/2 cups Rice Krispies
1/2 lb. (40) marshmallows
1/2 cup raisins
1/2 cup peanuts
1 cup chocolate chips (optional)

Melt peanut butter, margarine and marshmallows in top of double boiler over hot water. Place cereals, raisins and peanuts in a large bowl. Stir in peanut butter mixture and blend well. Butter a 9 x 13 inch pan and use waxed paper to press mixture evenly into pan. Cut into bars when cool.

Hilda Rutherford (Mrs. N.A.)

ELEGANT TOFFEE SQUARES

1 cup margarine, room
    temperature
1 cup light brown sugar
1 egg
1 tsp. vanilla
2 cups sifted flour
6 oz. pkg. *real* chocolate chips, or 3
    to 4 (8 oz.) milk chocolate
    bars
1/2 tsp. salt
1/2 cup chopped pecans
    or walnuts

Cream margarine and sugar until fluffy. Add egg and vanilla; beat thoroughly. Sift the flour with the salt, add by spoonfuls to above and beat until blended. Spread batter, which will be stiff, evenly in a jelly-roll pan. Bake at 350 degrees for 15 minutes. Remove from oven, put chocolate chips or chocolate bars on top. Return to oven for 1 more minute. Remove and immediately spread chocolate evenly over batter (a spatula works well). Sprinkle with nuts. Cut into bars while warm but don't remove from pan until chilled. Store in refrigerator. Yields 4 to 5 dozen.

Jean Bridges (Mrs. D. T., Jr.)
Nancy Little (Mrs. T. M.)

GRAHAM CRACKER RUM BARS

FIRST MIXTURE:
1-1/2 sticks butter
1 cup sugar
1 egg
1-1/2 cups milk

SECOND MIXTURE:
1 cup angel flake coconut
1 cup chopped pecans
1-1/2 cups fine graham cracker
    crumbs

ICING:
1/2 stick butter, room
    temperature
1/2 box (1-1/2 cups) 4X powdered
    sugar
2 tsp. or more rum extract
a little dark rum to thin, if needed

Mix first mixture in deep saucepan. Bring to a boil, stirring constantly. Allow to boil 2 minutes. Set aside while you line a large jelly-roll pan (15 x 10 inches) with whole graham crackers, row after row. Now add the second mixture to the first mixture in the saucepan. Stir until just blended and then spoon or pour over crackers on cookie sheet. Now top with another layer of graham crackers. Press lightly as you go. Prepare a *thin* icing with icing ingredients. Beat until smooth and ice the top of last layer of graham crackers. Cover with foil and refrigerate for 24 hours. Cut into small squares to serve. Yields about 96 bars.

Virginia Golding (Mrs. John G.)

LEMON SQUARES

1 cup butter
2-1/2 cups flour
1/2 cup confectioners' sugar
6 Tbsp. lemon juice
4 Tbsp. flour
3/4 tsp. baking powder
1/4 tsp. salt
2 cups sugar
4 eggs, beaten
additional confectioners' sugar

Mix together first 3 ingredients. Press together in greased 9 x 13 inch pan. Bake at 350 degrees for 20 minutes. Mix remaining ingredients and pour over the baked crust. Bake an additional 25 minutes. Dust with additional confectioners' sugar. Cool and cut into squares or bars.

Eileen Antonelli (Mrs. G. A.)

VARIATION: For crust use only 2 cups flour, with butter and confectioners' sugar. Press into 2 greased 8 x 8 pans. For topping, increase salt to 1/2 tsp., increase flour to 6 Tbsp., add grated rind of 1 lemon and omit baking powder. Otherwise follow preceding directions exactly.

Beverly Hance (Mrs. James)

LEMON-COCONUT SQUARES
A 5-star recipe!

CRUST:
1-1/2 cups sifted flour
1/2 cup brown sugar
1/2 cup butter, softened

FILLING:
2 eggs, beaten
1 cup brown sugar, firmly packed
1-1/2 cups flaked or shredded
    coconut
1 cup chopped nuts
2 Tbsp. flour
1/2 tsp. baking powder
1/4 tsp. salt
1/2 tsp. vanilla

FROSTING:
1 cup confectioners' sugar
1 Tbsp. melted butter
juice of 1 lemon

Mix together all crust ingredients; pat firmly into a well-buttered 9 x 13-inch pan. Bake in a 275 degree oven for 10 minutes.
For the filling, combine all ingredients and spread on top of baked mixture. Bake 20 minutes in moderate 350 degree oven.
Combine frosting ingredients and spread over filling while warm. Cut into squares. Makes 24 squares.

The Committee

MAPLE WALNUT BARS

1 egg
1/2 cup sugar
1/3 cup melted butter
1/2 cup self-rising flour
1 tsp. maple flavoring
1 cup English walnuts, coarsely
    broken
1/2 cup chopped raisins

Beat egg; add sugar and blend; add melted butter, flour, flavoring, walnuts and raisins and blend until mixed. Spread evenly on greased 8-inch square pan, approximately 2 inches deep. Bake in 350 degree oven for 30 minutes. Cool in pan then cut into squares with very sharp knife. Store in covered container. Yield: 16 large or 20 small squares.

Debbie White (Mrs. David)

GLAZED MINCEMEAT BARS

3/4 cup sugar
2 eggs
1/4 cup butter or margarine,
    softened
1-3/4 cups mincemeat
1 cup chopped nuts
1-1/2 cups sifted flour
1/2 tsp. salt
1/2 tsp. cinnamon
1/4 tsp. baking soda

ORANGE GLAZE:
2 cups sifted confectioners' sugar
2-1/2 Tbsp. milk
1 tsp. grated orange rind

Combine sugar, eggs and butter in a bowl and beat until creamy. Add mincemeat and nuts. Mix well. Sift together and blend in flour, salt, cinnamon and baking soda. Pour into greased 15 x 10 x 1 inch pan. Bake at 350 degrees for 25 to 30 minutes.
Combine in bowl confectioner's sugar, milk and orange rind; stir until blended and smooth. Spread on baked mixture while warm. Cool. Cut into 3 x 1 inch bars. Makes 50 bars.

Sue Anderson (Mrs. R.D.)

VARIATION: For Pineapple Glazed Mincemeat Bars use only 3/4 cup mincemeat and add 1/2 cup crushed pineapple, undrained, to batter ingredients. Bake as above. For glaze, combine 2 cups sifted confectioners' sugar and 2 Tbsp. hot pineapple juice. Ice as above. Cut into squares.

Ellen Knott (Mrs. B.F.)

When cutting sticky foods such as marshmallows, dried or candied fruits, dip kitchen shears into sugar or hot water periodically while cutting.

JANE'S MUD HEN BARS

Friends' favorite-they call them "dirty chickens."

1/2 cup shortening or butter
1 cup sugar
1 egg, whole
1-1/2 cups flour
1 tsp. baking powder
2 tsp. vanilla
1/4 tsp. salt
1 cup chopped nuts (optional)
1 cup semisweet chocolate chips
3 eggs, separated
1-1/2 cups miniature
  marshmallows
1 cup light brown sugar

Preheat oven to 350 degrees. Cream shortening and sugar. Beat in the whole egg and 2 egg yolks. Sift flour, baking powder and salt together. Combine the two mixtures; blend thoroughly; add vanilla. Spread batter in 9 x 13 inch pan. Put nuts, marshmallows and chocolate pieces over the batter. Beat 3 egg whites until stiff; fold in brown sugar. Spread over top. Bake 30-40 minutes. Cut into bars. Makes approximately 32.

Betsy Knott

NO-NAME COOKIE BARS

This was served at 1982 graduation reception with raves from everyone.

1/2 cup butter
1/2 cup confectioners' sugar
2 egg yolks
1 cup flour
1/2 cup thick apricot preserves
1/2 cup thick pineapple preserves

COCONUT MERINGUE:
2 egg whites
1/2 cup sugar
1/2 cup flaked coconut

Mix butter, sugar and egg yolks thoroughly. Stir in flour. Press and flatten mixture to cover bottom of ungreased 13x9x2-inch pan. Bake at 350 degrees for 10 minutes. Remove from oven and spread with preserves which have been mixed together. Cover with meringue (which has been made by beating 2 egg whites until frothy, then gradually adding 1/2 cup sugar and beating until stiff and glossy, and then folding in coconut). Return to oven and bake about 20 minutes longer until meringue is golden brown. Cool slightly and cut into squares. Yields 4 dozen.

Teresa Fletcher (Mrs. Herbert M.)

OOEY-GOOEY BUTTER BARS
Easy!

1 pkg. yellow, lemon, chocolate,
    Swiss chocolate or pound cake
    mix (or yellow or lemon
    pudding cake mix — I use
    lemon pudding cake mix)
1 stick butter, melted
1 egg
1 cup coconut
1/2 cup chopped nuts
1 8-oz. pkg. cream cheese
2 eggs
1 1-lb. box powdered sugar
1-1/2 tsp. vanilla extract or 1 tsp.
    almond extract; or 2 tsp.
    lemon extract if using lemon
    cake mix; or 2 tsp. vanilla and
    2 tsp. cocoa added to
    powdered sugar mixture if
    using chocolate cake mix

Mix first 3 ingredients together. Press mixture into a greased 13 x 9 x 2 inch pan. Sprinkle the coconut and chopped nuts over this. Mix together cream cheese, 2 eggs, powdered sugar and extract. Spread this over nut and coconut layer. Bake at 350 degrees for 35 minutes. Cool and cut into small squares. Makes about 36 bars.

NOTE: If using pound cake mix, cook 40 to 45 minutes.

Jean Boiter
Judy Ranson (Mrs. R.C.)
Noble Dillard

"BABY RUTH" COOKIES

3-1/2 cups flour
1 tsp. salt
1 tsp. soda
1-1/2 cups sugar
1 cup butter or margarine
2 eggs
2 tsp. vanilla
6 "Baby Ruth" candy bars (1.2
    oz.), cut in small pieces

Blend flour with salt and soda in small bowl. Gradually add sugar to butter in mixing bowl; cream until light and fluffy. Add eggs and vanilla; beat well. Blend in dry ingredients gradually; mix thoroughly. Stir in candy pieces. Chill dough for easy handling. Drop by tablespoon onto lightly greased baking sheet. Bake at 375 degrees for 10 to 12 minutes until golden brown. Makes about 6 dozen.

Betty Holland (Mrs. Calvin)

BOURBON BALLS

1 cup vanilla wafers, rolled fine
1 cup chopped pecans
1 cup powdered sugar
2 Tbsp. cocoa
1-1/2 Tbsp. corn syrup
1/4 cup bourbon
powdered sugar

Combine first 4 ingredients. Add corn syrup and bourbon to dry ingredients. Add a few more drops of bourbon if the mixture is too dry to form balls. Roll into balls and roll each ball in powdered sugar. Yields about 40 balls. Store in covered container in refrigerator.

Ellen Knott (Mrs. B.F.)

BREAKFAST TAKE-ALONGS

This is an excellent source of protein.

2/3 cup margarine
2/3 cup sugar
1 egg
1 tsp. vanilla
3/4 cup all-purpose flour
1/2 tsp. soda
1/2 tsp. salt
1-1/2 cups Quaker Oats (quick or
    old fashioned), uncooked
1 cup (4 oz.) shredded Cheddar
    cheese
1/2 cup wheat germ
6 slices bacon, cooked and
    crumbled

Beat together margarine, sugar, egg and vanilla until well blended. Add combined flour, soda and salt; mix well. Stir in oats, cheese, wheat germ and bacon. Drop by rounded teaspoonfuls onto greased cookie sheet. Bake at 350 degrees for 12 to 14 minutes or until edges are golden brown. Cool 1 minute on cookie sheet and remove to wire cookie rack. Store in covered container.
This can easily and quickly be done in a Cuisinart. Yields approximately 4 dozen.

Yvonne Rayburn (Mrs. C. Richard, Jr.)

BUTTERSCOTCH THINS

6 oz. Butterscotch Morsels
1/2 cup butter
2/3 cup light brown sugar, firmly
    packed
1 egg
1-1/3 cups flour
3/4 tsp. baking soda
3/4 tsp. vanilla

Melt the butterscotch morsels and butter in double boiler or a heavy metal pan. Remove from heat. Beat in brown sugar and egg. Stir in flour, baking soda and vanilla. Chill. Roll into 12-inch roll and wrap in waxed paper. Dough hardens and softens quickly. If too hard, let it remain at room temperature. Slices better when hard. Slice very thinly, watch your oven as they can burn easily. Dough can be frozen. Yields 10-12 dozen.

Elieen Antonelli (Mrs. G.A.)

CHEESE DELIGHTS

3/4 cup soft butter
1 lb. extra-sharp cheese, grated
2 cups all-purpose flour
1 tsp. salt
1 tsp. cayenne pepper
dates, cut in half lengthwise
pecan halves

Mix softened butter with cheese. Add flour, salt and pepper; combine well. Roll dough into balls, the diameter of a quarter. Make a depression in the middle of each ball. Place a date half in each depression. Cover with pecan half. Make sure cheese comes up and molds slightly around edges of pecan. Bake at 350 degrees for 10 to 12 minutes.

Kathy Howe

CHEESE WAFERS
Easy! Spicy!

10 oz. sharp cheese, grated
1 cup sifted flour
1 tsp. baking powder
1/4 tsp. red pepper
3/4 stick softened margarine
1 cup cornflakes, crushed
    (not crumbs)
1/2 tsp. Worcestershire sauce
1/4 tsp. paprika
1/2 tsp. salt

Mix all ingredients together thoroughly. Make dough into balls, 1/2 tsp. each. Place on cookie sheet. Flatten with fork. Bake in preheated oven at 300 degrees for 20 minutes or less. Store in airtight container until ready to use. Yields 5 to 6 dozen wafers.

Nancy Harper (Mrs. Robert M.)

CHOCOLATE BON BONS
An easy cookie recipe that looks hard to make when served!

1 pkg. coconut pecan or coconut
    almond frosting mix
1/2 cup butter or margarine
2 tsp. water
1 6-oz. pkg. chocolate chips
1 Tbsp. Crisco

Put the frosting mix and butter and water into a bowl. Mix with a fork and form into one-inch balls. Place on ungreased cookie sheet and chill for 15 minutes. Melt the chocolate chips with the Crisco over a low heat. Dip the balls into the chocolate and return to the pan and chill again. These freeze well.

Anita Shapiro (Mrs. Marvin)

CHOCOLATE CRINKLES

2 cups granulated sugar
1/2 cup vegetable oil
4 oz. melted unsweetened
    chocolate (cool)
2 tsp. vanilla
4 eggs
2 cups flour
2 tsp. baking powder
1/2 tsp. salt
1/2 cup powdered sugar

Mix granulated sugar, oil, chocolate and vanilla. Mix in eggs, one at a time. Stir in flour, baking powder and salt. Cover and refrigerate at least 3 hours. Heat oven to 350 degrees. Shape dough by rounded teaspoonfuls into ball. Roll in powdered sugar. Place about 2 inches apart on greased cookie sheet. Bake until firm — 10 to 12 minutes. Yields 6 dozen cookies.

Virginia Golding (Mrs. John G.)

CRISP CHOCO-CHIP COOKIES

This is a terrific cookie—stays crisp and is economical to make.

1 cup margarine
1 cup white sugar
1 cup dark brown sugar
2 eggs
2 cups sifted flour
1 tsp. soda
1/2 tsp. baking powder
1/2 tsp. salt
1 cup Rice Krispies
1 cup regular rolled oats
2 tsp. vanilla
1 (6 oz.) pkg. chocolate chips
    or raisins
1/2 to 3/4 cup chopped pecans
    or walnuts

Blend margarine and sugars in large bowl. Add eggs and beat until fluffy. Sift together flour, soda, salt and baking powder. Add to other ingredients and blend. The mixture will be stiff to mix. By hand, stir in Rice Krispies, rolled oats, vanilla, chocolate chips and nuts. Drop by spoon onto cookie sheet. Bake at 375 degrees for 12-15 minutes until lightly browned. Remove from cookie sheet immediately, before cookie becomes crisp. Raisins may be substituted for chocolate chips.

Katherine Moore (Mrs. Peter)

GINGERBREAD MEN

Great for children to decorate

1/2 cup butter, softened
3/4 cup sugar
1 egg, beaten
1/4 cup molasses
juice of 1/2 orange
3-1/2 to 4 cups all-purpose flour
1/2 tsp. salt
1 tsp. soda
1 tsp. ground ginger
raisins
decorator candy
decorator icing

Cream butter and sugar; beat in eggs. Add molasses and orange juice to creamed mixture. Combine dry ingredients and blend into creamed mixture. Chill dough about 1 hour or until stiff enough to handle. Work with half the dough at a time; store remainder in refrigerator. Roll dough between two pieces of waxed paper to 1/4 to 1/8 inch thickness. Cut with a 4 or 7-inch gingerbread man cutter, and remove excess dough. Place greased cookie sheet on top of gingerbread men; invert and remove waxed paper. Press raisins into dough and decorate with cake candies. Bake at 350 degrees for 10 minutes. Cool 1 minute. Remove to rack to finish cooling. Makes 2 dozen 4-inch or 1 dozen 7-inch cookies.

Noble Dillard

MILLER FAMILY CHRISTMAS ROCKS
*This is an excellent recipe to make for a cookie exchange
since it makes so many cookies.*

1-1/2 cups brown sugar
1 cup butter
3 eggs
pinch of salt
2-1/2 cups flour, sifted
1 tsp. cinnamon
1-1/2 tsp. soda, dissolved in
   1/4 cup boiling water
1 box seeded raisins

In a *large* mixing bowl cream butter and sugar. Beat eggs until foamy. Add eggs to butter/sugar mixture and mix thoroughly. Add sifted flour, cinnamon and salt. Add soda and water   Mix thoroughly. Add nuts and raisins. Drop by small tablespoonfuls onto greased cookie sheets. Bake in moderate oven (325 degrees) until light brown and tops look slightly dried, approximately 8-10 minutes. Makes about 10 dozen.

B. J. Miller (Mrs. H.F., III)

DAD'S FAVORITE COOKIES
Makes large, chewy cookies

1 cup butter, softened
1 cup sugar
1 cup brown sugar
1 egg
1-1/2 cup rolled oats (regular
   or quick)
1-1/2 cups flour
1 tsp. baking powder
1 tsp. baking soda
1 tsp. nutmeg
1-1/2 tsp. allspice
1 tsp. vanilla
2 Tbsp. molasses
1 cup coconut
1/4 cup wheat germ (optional)

Mix ingredients together in order listed. Mix well. Roll into small balls and place on ungreased cookie sheet 2 inches apart. Bake at 350 degrees until brown, about 12 minutes. Yields 4 dozen. Can be frozen after baking.

Susan Rielly (Mrs. P.C.)

HEALTH SNACKS

1-1/2 cups peanut butter
1/4 cup carob powder
1/2 lb. chopped almonds, toasted
1 cup dates or raisins
3 tsp. vanilla extract
1/2 cup honey
sesame seeds

Mix well. Form into balls. Roll each ball in toasted sesame seeds. These may be refrigerated to last longer. They may also be frozen.
NOTE: If dates are used, they should be cut into pieces.

Margaret L. Pitts

ICE BOX COOKIES

1 cup shortening
2 cups brown sugar, packed
2 eggs
1 cup chopped nuts
1 tsp. soda
3-1/2 cups flour
1 tsp. salt

Cream shortening and sugar. Add eggs and beat well. Sift dry ingredients together and add to creamed mixture. Make into several rolls and roll in waxed paper. Place in refrigerator overnight. Slice thinly and bake on greased cookie sheet at 350 degrees for 10 to 15 minutes. Makes 8 dozen cookies.

Virginia Golding (Mrs. John G.)

KATCHY'S COOKIES

1 stick butter
1 stick margarine
1/4 cup sugar
chopped pecans (as many as you want)
Keebler graham crackers (1 box makes 2 batches)

Use cookie sheet with sides. Break apart graham crackers and line the cookie sheet as closely as you can with crackers. Boil butter, margarine and sugar for 3 minutes. Pour over crackers evenly. Sprinkle with nuts. Bake at 275 degrees for 15 minutes. Remove from cookie sheet to waxed paper while still warm.

Mary Sue Patten (Mrs. Robert)

KIFLI PASTRY

Must prepare dough the night before baking. Serve at Christmas time.

6 egg yolks
1 cup sour cream
1 lb. margarine
4 cups flour
1 tsp. vanilla

FILLING:
1 lb. ground pecans
1 lb. powdered sugar
1 tsp. vanilla
6 egg whites

Mix dough ingredients together; roll into 100 balls and refrigerate overnight. Next day roll each ball into a circle. Mix filling ingredients and put a small amount of filling on each circle and roll up. Bake at 350 degrees until light brown, about 10-12 minutes. Yields 100 cookies.

Sharon Edge (Mrs. W.S.)

LUMBERJACK COOKIES

Dough keeps in refrigerator several days—bake as needed.

1 cup sugar
1 cup shortening (margarine)
1 cup dark molasses
2 eggs
4 cups flour
1-1/2 tsp. baking soda
1 tsp. salt
2 tsp. cinnamon
1 tsp. ginger

Cream sugar and shortening, add molasses and eggs, then dry ingredients. Have on hand a small bowl of sugar. Dipping the fingers into the sugar, pinch off a ball of cookie dough, about walnut-sized. Dip a ball into the sugar, arrange on a greased cookie sheet. Bake at 350 degrees for 15 minutes. These freeze well. Yields 4 dozen soft cookies.

Sandy Chase (Mrs. E.R.)

M & M COOKIES

Probably our favorite cookie—always crisp!

1 cup shortening
1 cup brown sugar
1 cup granulated sugar
2 tsp. vanilla
2 eggs
2-1/4 cups sifted all-purpose flour
1 tsp. soda
1 tsp. salt
1 cup plain M & M candies

Blend shortening and sugars. Beat in vanilla and eggs. Sift remaining dry ingredients together; add to the sugar and egg mixture. Mix well. Stir in M & M's. Drop from teaspoon onto greased cookie sheet. Bake at 375 degrees for 10 to 12 minutes, until golden brown. Makes about 60 to 100 cookies depending on size. We like them fairly thick (60 cookies) or you can make them smaller (100 cookies) if you are cooking for quantity.

Betsy Knott

CHOCOLATE MACAROONS

2 oz. unsweetened chocolate
1 14-oz. can sweetened condensed
    milk
2 cups finely-shredded coconut
1 cup chopped nuts
1 Tbsp. strongly-brewed coffee
1 tsp. almond extract
1/4 tsp. salt

Preheat oven to 350 degrees. In a large, heavy saucepan, combine the chocolate and milk and cook over medium heat, stirring briskly with a whisk until thick and glossy. Remove from heat and add remaining ingredients, stirring with a wooden spoon to blend.

Drop the chocolate mixture by small teaspoonfuls onto a greased baking sheet, about an inch apart. Bake 10 minutes or until the bottoms are set. Do not overbake. The macaroons should have a soft, chewy texture. Transfer to waxed paper to cool. Yields 5 dozen macaroons.

The Committee

DOT'S CHRISTMAS COOKIES

1/4 cup sugar
1 cup soft butter (no substitute)
2 cups sifted flour
2 tsp. vanilla
2 cups chopped pecans
powdered sugar

Cream together sugar and butter. Add flour, chopped nuts and vanilla. Roll into balls a little larger than a marble (easier if dough is chilled). They will get somewhat larger as they cook. Bake at 300 degrees on ungreased cookie sheet for 30-35 minutes. While the cookies are hot, roll in powdered sugar. After they cool, roll a second time. Yields 5 dozen.

Julia Warner (Mrs. C.E.)

GREAT-GRANDMOTHER GRAVES' CHRISTMAS COOKIES
Festive-looking holiday cookies that taste really good without being too sweet.

1 cup sugar
1 cup butter
2 eggs
2 cups dry oatmeal
2 cups flour, sifted
6 Tbsp. sweet milk
1/2 tsp. baking soda
1/2 tsp. cinnamon
1 cup pecans or walnuts, chopped
1/2 cup red cherries, chopped
1/2 cup green cherries, chopped
red and green cherries cut in halves
    to garnish

Cream butter and sugar. Beat in eggs. Add sweet milk gradually and flour which has been sifted with soda and cinnamon. Mix in oatmeal, nuts, and chopped cherries. Drop by small Tbsp. onto lightly-greased cookie sheets. Garnish each cookie with either half a green or half a red cherry. Bake in a quick oven, but not too hot — about 350 degrees — until light brown and tops look slightly dried, approximately 8 to 10 minutes. Makes 5 to 6 dozen cookies.

B. J. Miller (Mrs. H.F., III)

GOBS

4-1/2 cups flour
2 tsp. soda
1/2 tsp. baking powder
1/2 tsp. salt
1/2 cup cocoa
2 cups sugar
1/2 cup shortening
2 eggs
1 cup sour milk or buttermilk
1 tsp. vanilla
1 cup boiling water

FILLING:
2 cups milk
6 Tbsp. flour
3/4 cup Crisco
3/4 cup sugar
1 tsp. vanilla

Sift together flour, soda, baking powder, salt and cocoa. Cream together sugar, shortening and eggs. Add dry ingredients to creamed mixture; then add sour milk, vanilla and water. Drop by tablespoon onto ungreased pan and bake at 350 degrees for 15 minutes or until done. For filling, mix milk and flour until smooth and cook until thick. Let cool. Beat Crisco and sugar for 5 minutes and then add flour and milk mixture, one spoonful at a time, and beat 5 more minutes until fluffy. Add vanilla. Put 2 cookies together with filling between.

Linda Rodman (Mrs. M. R.)

GRANDMOTHER'S HERMIT COOKIES

These are very soft. Recipe is 50 years old, at least!

1 cup Crisco
2 cups brown sugar (lightly packed)
2 eggs, room temperature
1/2 cup cool black coffee
3-3/4 cups flour
1 tsp. soda
1 Tbsp. cinnamon
1 tsp. ground ginger
1 tsp. nutmeg
1 tsp. allspice
2 Tbsp. sorghum
2 cups raisins
1 cup chopped pecans

Cover raisins with hot water and set aside. Thoroughly cream shortening and brown sugar. Add eggs and beat well. Beat in coffee. Stir together flour, soda, cinnamon, ginger, nutmeg and allspice; add to creamed mixture along with sorghum. Stir just to mix. Drain raisins well. Add raisins and nuts to the cookie mixture. Stir to mix. Drop from tablespoon 2 inches apart on lightly greased cookie sheet. Bake for only 8 minutes in 375 degree oven. *Secret:* don't over-bake. May freeze after baking. Makes 3 dozen.

Mandy Martin

FRUIT CAKE COOKIES
A Christmas tradition

1 stick butter
1 cup honey
3 eggs
3 cups flour
1/4 cup orange juice or sherry
1/2 tsp. soda
4 cups broken pecans
6 slices dried pineapple, cut up
2 cups date pieces
1 box (1 lb.) golden raisins

Cream together honey and soft butter. Add eggs, one at a time, then add remaining ingredients. Drop by teaspoon onto greased cookie sheet. Bake at 300 degrees for approximately 15 minutes. Yields lots of cookies! These freeze well.

Carolyn Adams (Mrs. G.B., Jr.)

COCONUT MACAROONS

2 egg whites
dash salt
1/2 tsp. vanilla
2/3 cup granulated sugar
1 3-1/2 oz. can (1-1/3 cups)
  flaked coconut

Beat egg whites with dash of salt and the vanilla until soft peaks form. Gradually add sugar, beating until stiff. Fold in coconut. Drop by rounded teaspoon onto greased cookie sheet. Bake at 325 degrees for about 20 minutes until lightly browned. Makes 1-1/2 dozen.

Janice Privette (Mrs. G.B.)

MERINGUE CRUNCH COOKIES
A little different from most meringue cookies

3 egg whites
1 cup sugar
pinch of salt
1 tsp. vanilla
1-1/2 cups Capt. Crunch cereal
1/2 cup chopped nuts
1/2 cup flaked coconut
1/2 cup chocolate chips

Preheat oven to 350 degrees. In a large bowl beat egg whites until foamy. Keep beating while you slowly add sugar, salt and vanilla. Beat until stiff. Fold in cereal slowly; add nuts, chocolate chips and coconut; stir until well coated. Line cookie sheet with foil and drop mixture by slightly rounded teaspoonful. Place in oven and turn off heat. Do not open until oven is cold—at least 3 hours. Makes 50 cookies.

Georgia Miller (Mrs. George)

MELT-IN-THE-MOUTH COOKIES

1/2 cup butter
1 cup brown sugar (packed)
1 tsp. vanilla
1 egg
3/4 cup sifted flour
1 tsp. baking powder
1/2 tsp. salt
1/2 cup chopped nuts (optional)

Cream butter; add sugar, vanilla and egg. Beat until light and fluffy. Add dry ingredients and nuts. Drop by scant teaspoonful onto ungreased cookie sheet. Bake in preheated 400 degree oven for about 5 minutes. Cool 1/2 minute before removing to rack. Cool.

Gini Osborne (Mrs. Wallace)

ABEGWEIT OATCAKES

A coffee or teatime shortcake—not very sweet. Can cut into different shapes for different occasions.

2 cups all-purpose flour
1-1/2 cups quick rolled oats
1/3 cup granulated sugar OR
1/2 cup lightly packed brown
  sugar
1 tsp. salt
1/2 tsp. soda
3/4 cups shortening or butter
1/2 cup water or milk

Cream shortening, add sugar, then dry ingredients and 1/2 cup milk or water. (May use a little less water—dough should just cling together.) Stir in oats. Roll in 3 portions, very thin. Cut into 2 inch squares or desired shapes. Place 1 inch apart on ungreased baking sheet in a 375 degree oven for 10-15 minutes. Yields 4 to 5 dozen. May wrap and freeze after cooking.

Peggy D. Young (Mrs. John A.)

BEST OATMEAL COOKIES

A wholesome, natural cookie

1-1/2 cups regular oats
2 cups firmly-packed brown sugar
3/4 cup shortening
2 eggs
2-1/4 cups all-purpose flour
1 tsp. soda
1 tsp. baking powder
1 tsp. ground cinnamon
1 tsp. ground cloves
1 tsp. ground nutmeg
1/3 cup buttermilk
1 tsp. vanilla extract
1 cup chopped dates
1 cup chopped pecans
1 cup raisins

Toast oats under broiler, stirring frequently to avoid scorching; set aside. Cream sugar, shortening and eggs until light and fluffy. Combine flour, soda, baking powder, cinnamon, cloves and nutmeg; add to creamed mixture, alternating with buttermilk. Stir in vanilla. Add oats, dates, pecans and raisins. Mix thoroughly. Drop by teaspoonfuls onto greased cookie sheets. Bake at 375 degrees for 10 minutes. Yields 7 dozen.

Peggy Buchanan (Mrs. D. Douglas)

OATMEAL LACE COOKIES

1 cup quick oats
1 cup sugar
7 Tbsp. melted butter
2 Tbsp. flour
1 egg, slightly beaten
1/4 tsp. baking powder
1/4 tsp. vanilla
dash salt

Beat egg in medium bowl. Melt butter. Mix all ingredients until moistened. Take a small 1/2 tsp. batter and put very far apart on foil-lined cookie sheet, shiny side up. Bake at 350 degrees for 7 to 8 minutes in center of oven. WATCH—they brown easily. Remove foil with cookies on it and let cool completely before removing. They will peel right off the foil. Yields 4 dozen.

Susan Justice (Mrs. M.E.)

POTATO CHIP COOKIES
Children love these!

1 lb. butter at room temperature
   (not margarine)
1 cup sugar
1-1/2 cups crushed potato chips
3 cups flour
2 tsp. vanilla

Cream butter and sugar on medium speed of electric mixer for 15 minutes. Mixture will be very creamy. Gradually stir in flour and vanilla until well blended. Fold in crushed potato chips. Drop from teaspoon onto ungreased cookie sheet. Bake at 350 degrees for 12 minutes. Sprinkle powdered sugar over warm cookies.

Mandy Martin

POUND CAKE COOKIES
A lovely cookie for a morning coffee or afternoon tea

2-1/2 sticks real butter (a
   necessity)
1 cup sugar
2 egg yolks
3 cups flour, sifted
1 tsp. vanilla
pecans (whole or pieces) or
   cherry halves

Cream butter and add sugar gradually. Add egg yolks one at a time. Add flour gradually. Add flavoring last. Drop by teaspoons on ungreased cookie sheet and bake at 350 degrees for 12 to 15 minutes. Garnish before baking with cherries or pecans — pieces or halves. Yields 5 to 6 dozen cookies.

Myrtle Ussery (Mrs. A.M.)

PUDDING COOKIES
Very easy—fun to decorate

3/4 cup Bisquick
1 egg
1/4 cup salad oil
1 3-oz. pkg. Jello **Instant** Vanilla
    Pudding Mix

Combine all ingredients. Mix together. Drop by teaspoonfuls onto ungreased cookie sheet. Flatten each cookie. Top with pecan, Hershey kisses, M & M's, or raisins. Bake at 350 degrees for about 6 minutes. Makes about 20 cookies.

Pat Viser

REESE'S PEANUT BUTTER COOKIES

1 roll Pillsbury Sugar Cookie
    dough
1 bag Reese's miniature peanut
    cups (35 cups)

Cut sugar cookie roll in 1-inch slices. Quarter each slice. Using miniature muffin pans and miniature paper cups, place quarter slices in cups Bake at 350 degrees for 15 minutes. While still hot and puffy put Reese's peanut cups in center of sugar cookie. Yields 3 dozen.

Janet Miller
Jeanne Golding

SALTED PEANUT COOKIES
Cookies when you need a lot

2 eggs, beaten
2 cups brown sugar, firmly packed
1-1/2 cups butter or margarine,
    melted
1-1/2 cups salted peanuts,
    chopped
2-1/2 cups sifted flour
1 tsp. baking soda
1 tsp. baking powder
1/2 tsp. salt
3 cups rolled oats
1 cup corn flakes

Beat eggs; add sugar and mix well. Stir in butter, then peanuts, and mix. Sift together flour, soda, baking powder and salt. Combine with oats and corn flakes. Combine with egg mixture and stir well to mix. Drop tablespoons of dough on greased baking sheet. Bake in hot oven (400 degrees) 8 to 10 minutes. Makes 6 dozen.

Sophie Godwin

SCOTTISH SHORTBREAD

This is the best shortbread we have ever had—even in Scotland.

1/2 lb. butter, softened (no
    substitutes)
3 cups all-purpose flour
1/2 cup sugar

Put ingredients into a bowl, remove your rings, wash your hands, and dig in—mixing with your hands until the dough becomes a round ball with no crumbs. Do not use a mixer. The warmth of your hands makes the dough better.

Pat the dough evenly in the bottom of a 9 x 13 inch pan. Prick all over with a fork (approximately every 1/2 inch or less).

Bake in preheated 325 degree oven for 30-35 minutes or until the edges show the slightest tint of brown. Remove from oven, and while hot, sprinkle the top with granulated sugar.

Cut into pieces and place on a wire cake rack. Put the cookie-filled rack in a preheated 275 degree oven and bake for 30 minutes more. This second cooking makes a hard, yet crisp, cookie.

Wynne McLean (Mrs. Malcolm)
Mary Kay Greig (Mrs. John H.)

WEDDING COOKIES
(Kourabiedes)

2 cups clarified butter
1 cup powdered sugar
2 egg yolks
1 whole egg
1 oz. anisette, or
    1-1/2 tsp. vanilla
1 tsp. soda
1 cup toasted almonds,
    chopped fine
4-1/2 cups sifted flour
2 boxes confectioners' sugar

Beat butter and sugar until creamy, about 15 minutes. Add 1 whole egg and egg yolks, flavorings and almonds, beating until well blended. Remove from beater, and gradually add sifted flour to make a soft dough.

Pinch off pieces of dough and shape carefully into various designs—crescent, round, etc. Place on ungreased cookie sheet 1 inch apart. Bake in oven at 375 degrees for 15 minutes, or until very lightly brown. Allow to cool slightly before removing from cookie sheet. Carefully place on a flat surface which has been sprinkled with confectioners' sugar. Sprinkle confectioners' sugar over cookies. Cool. Makes 5 dozen.

Aphroula Anderson (Mrs. Jimmie)

Desserts

ALMOND CREAM PUFF RING

This takes some time, but is worth it!

1 cup water
1/2 cup butter or margarine
1/4 tsp. salt
1 cup flour
4 eggs

ALMOND CREAM FILLING:
1 3-3/4 pkg. vanilla instant
*   pudding*
1-1/4 cups milk
1 cup cream, whipped
1 tsp. almond extract

CHOCOLATE GLAZE:
1/2 cup semi-sweet chocolate
*   pieces*
1 Tbsp. butter or margarine
1-1/2 tsp. milk
1-1/2 tsp. light corn syrup

FOR PUFF PASTRY: In a 2-quart saucepan over medium heat, heat water, butter and salt until butter melts and mixture boils. Remove saucepan from heat. With wooden spoon, vigorously stir in flour all at once until mixture forms a ball and leaves side of saucepan. Add eggs to flour mixture, one at a time, beating after each addition, until mixture is smooth and satiny. Cool mixture slightly. Preheat oven to 400 degrees. *Lightly* grease and flour large cookie sheet. Using 7-inch plate as a guide, trace a circle in flour on cookie sheet. Drop batter by Tbsp. into 10 mounds, inside circle to form ring. Bake ring 40 minutes until golden. Turn off oven; let ring remain in oven 15 minutes. Remove ring from oven; cool on wire rack. When ring is cool, slice horizontally in half with long serrated knife. Prepare almond-cream filling; spoon into bottom of ring. Refrigerate. Prepare chocolate glaze. Spoon over top of ring.

ALMOND CREAM FILLING: Prepare one 3-1/2 or three 3-3/4 oz. packages vanilla flavor instant pudding and pie filling as label directs, but using only 1-1/4 cups milk. Fold in 1 cup whipping cream, whipped, and 1 tsp. almond extract.

CHOCOLATE GLAZE: In double boiler over hot, not boiling, water (or in heavy 1 quart saucepan over low heat) heat 1/2 cup semi-sweet chocolate pieces with 1 Tbsp. butter or margarine, 1-1/2 tsp. milk and 1-1/2 tsp. light corn syrup until smooth, stirring occasionally.

Joan B. BeLasco

Instant and Delicious
Divide coffee ice cream into serving dishes. Pour Creme de Cocoa over, to taste. Garnish with Cool Whip and nuts, if desired. *Fran Shafter*

ANGEL SURPRISE DESSERT

1-1/2 cups milk
1 3-oz. pkg. cream cheese,
    room temperature
1 3-3/4 oz. pkg. instant vanilla
    pudding mix
4 cups angel food cake cubes
1 13-1/4 oz. can crushed
    pineapple, drained
1 2-oz. pkg. dessert topping mix or
    small carton of Cool Whip

In small mixing bowl, gradually blend milk into cream cheese, beating until smooth. Add pudding mix and beat at low speed until smooth and slightly thickened, about 2 minutes. Pour pudding mixture over angel food cake cubes, stirring to coat. Turn into 8 x 8 x 2-inch baking dish. Spread drained pineapple over top. Spread whipped topping or Cool Whip over all. Chill several hours or overnight before serving. Serves 6. Recipe doubles easily.

Linda Dowd (Mrs. J. Kenneth)

ANNAPOLIS ANGEL FOOD DESSERT
Hard to resist!

2 bags chocolate bits
6 tsp. warm water
3 eggs, separated
3 Tbsp. powdered sugar
1/2 cup chopped walnuts
1-1/2 cups whipping cream
1 unfrosted angel cake
    (9-1/2-inch)

Melt chocolate bits in top of double boiler. Add water and stir to mix. When all is melted and mixed, remove from fire. Beat egg yolks with powdered sugar and add to chocolate mixture slowly. Add chopped nuts. (Don't give up. This is usually hard to mix!) Beat egg whites until stiff and fold into above mixture. Whip cream and fold it in. Place frosting in refrigerator for 12 hours. Cut angel cake horizontally into 3 layers. Cover each layer with frosting. Reassemble cake; frost top and sides and place in refrigerator another 12 hours. Serves 12.

The Committee

HEAVENLY PISTACHIO DESSERT
Great for bridge dessert—light

2 small (3 oz.) pkgs. Instant
    Pistachio Pudding
1 large (12 oz.) Cool Whip, thawed
1 angel food cake, sliced
3 cups milk
1/4 cup sliced almonds

Prepare pudding according to package directions, using 3 cups milk. Fold into pudding 1/2 of the Cool Whip. Place 1/2 of cake slices in bottom of 9 x 13 pan. Cover with 1/2 of pudding mixture. Repeat with remaining cake slices and rest of pudding. Top with remainder of Cool Whip. Sprinkle almonds over top. Refrigerate overnight. Serves 16.

Mandy Martin

BUTTERSCOTCH TOFFEE HEAVENLY DELIGHT

1-1/2 cups whipping cream
1 can (5-1/2 oz.) butterscotch
  syrup (topping)
1/2 tsp. vanilla extract
1 unfrosted angel cake (9-1/2 inch)
3/4 lb. English toffee, crushed (put
  through food grinder using
  largest blade)

Whip cream until it starts to thicken. Add butterscotch syrup and vanilla slowly and continue beating until thick. Cut cake horizontally into 3 layers. Spread the butterscotch mixture on the layers and sprinkle each generously with crushed toffee. Put cake back together again and frost the top and sides with butterscotch mixture and sprinkle them, too, with toffee. Place cake in the refrigerator and chill for a minimum of 6 hours. Serves 12.

Ellen Knott (Mrs. B.F.)

HENNY'S ANGEL FOOD DESSERT

3 eggs, separated
1 cup sugar
2 cups milk
1-1/2 envelopes unflavored
  gelatin
1 cup heavy cream, whipped
1 small angel food cake, broken
  into small pieces
1 cup coarsely chopped pecans
1 8-oz. can crushed pineapple
1 6-oz. bottle maraschino cherries
1 cup heavy cream, whipped,
  for icing
1 can angel flake coconut
  (optional)

Mix beaten egg yolks with milk and sugar. Bring to boil. Add gelatin, softened in 1/4 cup cold water. When cool, fold in stiffly beaten egg whites. When cold, fold in 1 cup whipped cream. Add remaining ingredients. Pour mixture into angel food cake pan. Refrigerate until set. Unmold on platter and ice with another cup of whipped cream, sweetened to taste. Sprinkle with coconut. Serves 12.

Ellen Knott (Mrs. B.F.)

When whipping well-chilled cream, sprinkle the cream with a few drops of lemon juice before whipping. It speeds up the work and gives the whipped cream more body.

FRESH LEMON CHARLOTTE RUSSE

4 eggs, separated
1/2 cup lemon juice
1/8 tsp. salt
1 envelope unflavored gelatin
1-1/2 cups sugar, divided
3 Tbsp. butter
1-1/2 tsp. grated lemon rind
1 tsp. vanilla extract
12 ladyfingers, split in half
    lengthwise
1 cup whipping cream, whipped
sweetened whipped cream
    (optional)

Combine egg yolks, lemon juice and salt in top of double boiler. Mix well. Stir in 1 cup sugar and the gelatin. Cook over simmering water about 10 minutes or until thickened, stirring constantly. Add butter, lemon rind and vanilla, stirring until butter melts. Chill mixture until partially thickened. Arrange ladyfingers around bottom and sides of 9-1/2 inch spring form pan. Set aside. Beat egg whites until soft peaks form. Gradually add remaining sugar and continue beating until stiff peaks form. Fold whipped cream and gelatin mixture into egg whites. Spoon into prepared pan. Cover and chill 4 to 5 hours or until firm. Garnish with sweetened whipped cream if desired. Serves 8.

Nancy Wohlbruck (Mrs. Everett L.)

HOLIDAY TRIFLE

Make the Trifle in a glass bowl so that you can see the layers.

1 pound cake (bought or
    homemade)
1 10-oz. pkg. frozen raspberries,
    thawed
1 10-oz. pkg. frozen strawberries,
    thawed
1 cup sherry or rum (more
    if desired)
1 3-oz. box strawberry Jello
1 3-oz. box raspberry Jello
1/2 pint whipping cream
2 envelopes Bird's custard
sliced almonds

Slice pound cake and sprinkle with sherry or rum. Mix strawberry and raspberry jello and make according to package directions. Chill until firm. Whip cream and sweeten to taste — refrigerate. Make custard of 2 envelopes Bird's custard and 3-1/2 cup milk and 6 Tbsp. sugar and prepared according to directions, or use 4 cups of any custard of your choosing (thin custard).
Layer trifle starting with pound cake followed by frozen raspberries, 1/2 of Jello, 1/2 of custard, pound cake, frozen strawberries, rest of Jello, rest of custard. Top with whipped cream. Top with almonds just before serving.

Pat Vinroot (Mrs. Robert)

Heat lemons before extracting juice for twice as much juice.

IRISH TRIFLE

1 pkg. ladyfingers
1 small jar raspberry jam (not jelly or preserves)
6 Tbsp. sherry wine
2 bananas, sliced
1 can (16 oz.) sliced peaches, drained
2 eggs, separated
2 Tbsp. sugar
1 cup milk
1 3-oz. pkg. raspberry gelatin
1/2 pt. whipping cream

Split ladyfingers in half; sandwich with jam. Arrange in base of glass casserole dish. Sprinkle sherry over the ladyfingers. Next, layer the bananas and the peaches. Make gelatin according to package directions and pour over fruit. Place in refrigerator to set. Mix together egg yolks and sugar. Warm the milk and stir into the egg mixture until well blended and return to saucepan to cook egg and milk mixture over low heat. Do not allow to simmer. Remove from heat when mixture is thick enough to coat back of a wooden spoon. Pour over congealed gelatin mixture and allow to set. Before serving, whip the cream with the egg whites until it forms soft peaks. Spread over trifle. Refrigerate any leftovers. Serves 8.

Jane Riley (Mrs. J.C.)

PASADENA PEACH DELIGHT

1 pkg. ladyfingers (about 10)
peach brandy
2 pkgs. frozen sliced peaches (semi-thawed)
1/2 pint whipping cream
1 tsp. sugar
4 or 5 drops vanilla *or* almond extract
slivered almonds, toasted

Line bottom and sides of ice cube tray with split ladyfingers. Moisten ladyfingers with brandy but do not saturate. Arrange partly-thawed peach slices over ladyfingers. Whip cream, adding sugar and flavoring. Top the dessert with whipped cream. If you wish to be extra fancy, sprinkle top of whipped cream with toasted slivered almonds. Cover ice tray with waxed paper and freeze for at least 6 hours. Remove from freezer 20 minutes before serving. When serving, cut across tray to form narrow slices. Serves 8.

Mary Frances Gray (Mrs. Gene)

RITZY PEANUT BUTTER STACKS
A real conversation piece!

Ritz crackers
crunchy peanut butter
white chocolate

Spread peanut butter between 3 Ritz crackers. Melt chocolate over hot water in top of double boiler. Spoon over stacks, scraping up excess and spoon over again.

Eleanor Minor (Mrs. William)

WHISKEY ICE BOX CAKE

2 envelopes gelatin
1/2 cup cold water
1/2 cup boiling water
6 eggs. separated
7 or 8 Tbsp. whiskey
1 cup sugar
1 tsp. lemon juice
1 pint whipping cream
3 pkgs. ladyfingers, split

Soak gelatin in cold water. Then add boiling water and dissolve. Beat egg yolks until thick. Add whiskey very slowly. Beat in the sugar. Add lemon juice. Stir in gelatin and chill a short time. Whip cream and fold it in. Beat egg whites and fold in. Line sides and bottom of a spring form pan (about 12 inches) with split ladyfingers. Pour the mixture in slowly. When about half way, put in layer of ladyfingers. Then, when filled, place a layer of ladyfingers on top in a design. Chill overnight in the refrigerator. Serves 12.

Virginia Golding (Mrs. John G.)

IGLOOS
Great for bridge!

1 stick butter, creamed
1 cup sugar
1 cup ground raisins
1 cup chopped pecans
1 large can crushed pineapple,
    drained
Nabisco butter cookies
1/2 pint whipping cream, whipped
    and seasoned
1 can angel flake coconut

Mix first 5 ingredients well. Stack 3 cookies and spread mixture between each. Cover with whipped cream and sprinkle with coconut. Refrigerate. Serves 15.

Libby Morrison (Mrs. Jack)

CHIPS AND MAC DELIGHT
So simple the donor is ashamed to sign her name!

Jack's Chips 'n Mac Cookies
milk
whipped cream or non-dairy
    substitute
chopped nuts (optional)

Dip cookies one at a time lightly in milk and line the bottom of a deep serving dish. Cover cookies with a 1/2 inch layer of whipped cream. Add another layer of dipped cookies, covering with another layer of whipped cream, until serving dish is full. May add nuts sprinkled on top of whipped cream if desired. Place in refrigerator for 24 hours or in freezer for 2 hours before serving. Tastes like a chocolate macaroon pudding.

Anonymous

BAVARIAN CREAM CHEESECAKE

I get requests for this recipe whenever I serve it.

38 ozs. cream cheese, softened
2 cups sugar
1/2 cup sour cream
7 eggs, room temperature
1/2 tsp. vanilla
pinch of salt
2-1/2 cups graham cracker crumbs,
    to make crust
1/2 cup butter, softened
1/4 cup sugar

Make graham cracker crust according to directions on crumb package and line bottom of spring form pan. Grease sides of pan thoroughly with butter. Mix cream cheese until creamy, add sugar and blend well. Add eggs one at a time, beating until thoroughly mixed. Add sour cream, salt and vanilla and mix well. Pour batter into crust up to 1 inch from rim. (Cake will rise considerably while cooking.) Smooth or tap lightly to remove air bubbles. Bake at 300 degrees until edges are lightly browned (60-70 minutes). Center of cake will still look soft. Cool completely on rack; then refrigerate until served.

Donna K. Alpert (Mrs. Eric D.)

CHEESE CAKE

A very old recipe

1/4 cup melted butter
1 lb. cream cheese, softened
2 or 3 eggs (enough for 1/2 cup)
1-1/2 cups graham cracker
    crumbs
1/2 cup sugar
3/4 tsp. vanilla

TOPPING:
1 6-oz. carton sour cream
1/4 cup sugar
1 tsp. vanilla

Preheat oven to 375 degrees. Combine butter and graham cracker crumbs. Press into bottom of a 9 x 3-inch spring form plan and up the sides about 1/2 inch. Beat cream cheese, sugar, eggs and vanilla until smooth. Pour into pan and bake for 20 minutes. Remove from oven and allow to cool 15 minutes. Increase oven heat to 475 degrees. At the end of the 15 minutes cooling period, spread topping evenly over cake. Bake at 475 degrees about 12 minutes until firm but not brown. Cool. Refrigerate 5 or 6 hours before serving. Can glaze if desired.

Jean Bridges (Mrs. D.T., Jr.)

MOCHA MOUSSE CHEESECAKE

1 cup graham cracker crumbs
1/2 stick butter
2 Tbsp. sugar
1/2 tsp. cinnamon
3 8-oz. pkgs. cream cheese, room temperature
3/4 cup sugar
3 eggs
1 8-oz. pkg. semisweet chocolate squares
2 Tbsp. whipping cream
1 cup sour cream
1 tsp. instant expresso powder (instant coffee) dissolved in 1/4 cup hot water, then cooled
1/4 cup coffee liqueur
2 tsp. vanilla

Butter sides of 8 inch spring form pan. Combine first 4 ingredients. Press evenly into bottom of pan. Preheat oven to 350 degrees. Beat cream cheese until smooth. Add sugar, while mixing. Add eggs one at a time. Beat on low speed until smooth.
Melt chocolate with whipping cream over boiling water, stirring frequently until smooth. Add to cheese mix, blending well. Mix in sour cream, cooled coffee and liqueur. Add vanilla and beat well. Turn into pan and bake 45 minutes (center will be a bit soft but will firm up). Refrigerate at least 12 hours.

Georgia Miller (Mrs. George)

FABULOUS CHEESECAKE
Best around!

2 8-oz. pkgs. soft cream cheese
1 lb. creamed cottage cheese
1-1/2 cups sugar
4 eggs, slightly beaten
3 Tbsp. cornstarch
3 Tbsp. flour
1 tsp. vanilla
1/2 cup butter, melted
1 pint sour cream

Grease 9-inch spring form pan. Preheat oven to 325 degrees. Beat cream cheese and cottage cheese together at high speed. Gradually beat in sugar and eggs. At low speed, beat in cornstarch, flour and vanilla. Add melted butter and sour cream. Beat just until smooth. Pour into pan. Bake 1 hour and 10 minutes. Turn off oven, let cake stand for 2 hours. Remove from oven. Let cake cool completely. Refrigerate. To serve, remove sides. Serves 10-12.

Mary Kay Hight (Mrs. William)

STRAWBERRY CHEESECAKE

CRUST:
1-1/2 cups graham cracker
crumbs
1/2 cup corn flake crumbs
1/2 cup butter, softened
1 Tbsp. sugar

FILLING:
3 pkgs. (8 oz.) cream cheese,
softened
1 pkg. (3-oz.) cream cheese,
softened
1 pint sour cream
1-1/2 cups sugar
3 eggs
2 tsp. vanilla

STRAWBERRY GLACE:
1 box (10 oz.) frozen strawberries,
thawed and mashed
1 Tbsp. cornstarch
red food coloring

STRAWBERRY TOPPING:
1/4 cup sugar
1 Tbsp. water
red food coloring
16 to 20 large strawberries

Combine all crust ingredients thoroughly. Press onto bottom and sides of an 8-inch spring form pan. In electric mixer beat together cream cheese and sugar thoroughly. Add sour cream, eggs and vanilla, and beat until well blended. Pour filling into crust and bake in 350-degree preheated oven for 1 hour and 15 minutes. Do not open oven door. Leave in oven until completely cool.

Combine all strawberry glace ingredients together in saucepan. Cook over medium heat, stirring, until thickened. Cool completely and pour on top of cooled cheesecake in its pan. In saucepan combine sugar, water and red food coloring. Bring to boil. Coat fresh strawberries in mixture and place on top of strawberry glace, points up. Refrigerate. Can freeze before adding strawberry glace and whole strawberries. Wrap well to freeze. Defrost in refrigerator for about 12 hours and then add glace and strawberries. Do not remove cheese cake from spring form pan until ready to serve. Serves 10-12.

The Committee

TINY CHEESECAKES

3 large pkgs. cream cheese
1 full cup sugar
4 eggs
1 tsp. vanilla
1 tsp. lemon juice
1 cup sour cream
2 Tbsp. sugar
graham cracker crumbs

Beat ingredients until creamy — about 15 minutes. Grease tiny muffin tins heavily with Crisco. Fill with graham cracker crumbs and pat around sides. Pour out excess. Fill with cheese mixture (not quite full). Bake 8-10 minutes at 350 degrees. Let cool and spread tops with 1 cup sour cream mixed with 2 Tbsp. sugar. Return to oven for 5 minutes. Cool. Makes about 5 dozen.

Anne Jones (Mrs. Richard A.)

MOCK CHEESECAKE
This is very easy and very rich.

1 can lemon ready-to-spread frosting
1-1/4 cup graham cracker crumbs (about 16 crackers)
2 Tbsp. sugar
1/4 cup butter or margarine, melted
1 cup small curd creamed cottage cheese
1 cup dairy sour cream

Heat oven to 350 degrees. Mix graham cracker crumbs and sugar in bowl. Add butter and mix thoroughly. Reserve 3 Tbsp. for topping. Press remaining mixture firmly and evenly on bottom of a 9 x 9 x 2-inch square pan. Bake 10 minutes. Cool. In small mixer bowl, combine frosting, cottage cheese and sour cream. Beat on high speed until blended, about 1 minute. Pour into crumb-lined pan; sprinkle with reserved crumbs. Freeze overnight. If desired, garnish with strawberries, peaches, small bunches of seedless grapes or other fruit. Serves 9 to 12.

Dee Dee Grainger (Mrs. Isaac B.)

ULTIMATE CHEESECAKE
This is Craig Claiborne's favorite cheesecake (New York Times food critic).

1/3 cup graham cracker crumbs, approximately
2 lbs. cream cheese, room temperature
1/2 cup heavy cream (whipping cream)
4 eggs
1-3/4 cups sugar
1 tsp. vanilla extract
dash lemon extract
blueberry pie filling (optional)

Preheat oven to 300 degrees. Butter inside of 8 x 3 inch spring form pan. Sprinkle inside with graham cracker crumbs, and shake crumbs around bottom and sides of pan until coated. Place the cream cheese, cream, eggs, sugar, vanilla and lemon extracts in a large bowl. Start beating at low speed and, as ingredients blend, increase to high. Beat until smooth (it will not have to be completely smooth). Pour batter into pan and shake pan gently to level. Cook at 300 degrees for 2 hours. Turn off oven and let cake sit 1/2 hour more. May spread blueberry pie filling on top. Serves 8 to 12.

Helen Burns (Mrs. J. G.)

PETITE CHERRY CHEESECAKES

1 lb. cream cheese, softened
3/4 cup sugar
2 eggs
1 Tbsp. lemon juice
1 tsp. vanilla
24 vanilla wafers
1 can (21 oz.) cherry pie filling

Beat together the cheese, sugar, eggs, lemon juice and vanilla until light and fluffy. Line muffin pan with paper baking cups. Place a wafer in bottom of each. Fill cups about 2/3 full of cheese mixture. Bake at 375 degrees for 15 to 20 minutes, or just until set. Top each with one tablespoon of pie filling. Yield: 2 dozen.

Jane Craven (Mrs. J.C.)

BLUEBERRY DREAM DESSERT

CRUST:
1 cup plain flour
1 stick margarine, melted
3/4 cup pecans, chopped
1/4 cup brown sugar

FILLING:
8 oz. cream cheese, softened
1 envelope Dream Whip (I prefer
    Dream Whip to frozen
    toppings)
1 tsp. vanilla
3/4 cup sugar

TOPPING:
1 pint blueberries
1/2 cup sugar

Mix together berries and sugar; bring to a boil and cook 2 minutes. Let cool while preparing crust and filling.
CRUST: Mix and pat flour, margarine, pecans and sugar into bottom of 9 x 13 inch pyrex dish. Bake at 350 degrees for 25 minutes. Cool.
FILLING: Mix cheese with sugar, add vanilla. Make Dream Whip; fold into cream cheese mixture. Spread on cooled crust. Using pierced spoon, place cooked berries on top, reserving blueberry juice for pancakes, etc. Refrigerate dessert. Serves 16 to 20.

Sharon Edge (Mrs. W.S.)

BERRY DESSERT

2 3-oz. pkgs. cream cheese,
    softened
1 cup dairy sour cream
2 Tbsp. brown sugar
1 quart fresh strawberries
1/4 cup packed brown sugar

In a bowl beat cream cheese until fluffy. Add sour cream and the 2 Tbsp. brown sugar; beat until smooth. Halve berries and arrange evenly in bottom of a shallow 8-inch round broiler-proof dish. Spoon cream cheese mixture over berries. Sieve remaining 1/4 cup brown sugar evenly over cream cheese mixture. Broil 4 to 5 inches from heat for 1 to 2 minutes or until sugar turns golden brown. Serve hot. Serves 8.

Ellen Knott (Mrs. B.J.)

CHOCOLATE DELIGHT

CRUST:
1 cup sifted flour
1 stick butter or margarine,
softened
1 cup chopped nuts (reserve some
for top)

FILLING:
1 8-oz. pkg. cream cheese,
softened
1 cup confectioners' sugar
1 9-oz. carton Cool Whip, divided
2 3-3/4 oz. pkgs. instant chocolate
pudding
3 cups milk

Combine all crust ingredients until crumbly. Pat into a 9 x 13 inch pan or baking dish. Bake at 325 degrees for 25 minutes. Cool.
FILLING: Mix cream cheese and confectioners' sugar and blend in 1 cup of the Cool Whip. Spread carefully on crust. Prepare pudding according to directions on the package and spread over cream cheese filling. Spread remaining Cool Whip on top and sprinkle with reserved nuts. Chill, cut in squares and serve. This freezes well. Serves 15 to 20.

Lucy Anderson (Mrs. D. L.)
Sandy Hamilton (Mrs. C. E.)

VARIATIONS: For Butter Pecan Dessert, substitute 2 3-3/4 oz. packages of butter pecan instant pudding for the 2 3-3/4 oz. packages of chocolate instant pudding in the filling. Prepare as directed.
For Lemon Delight, substitute 2 3-3/4 oz. packages of lemon instant pudding for the 2 3-3/4 oz. packages of chocolate instant pudding in the filling. Prepare as directed. May also use butterscotch pudding.

CHOCOLATE VELVET DESSERT
Resembles a chocolate cheesecake, but is nice to be able to prepare further ahead of time.

1-1/2 cups finely-crushed
chocolate wafers
1/3 cup melted margarine
1 8-oz. cream cheese, softened
1/2 cup sugar, divided
1 tsp. vanilla
2 eggs, separated
6 oz. semi-sweet chocolate
morsels, melted
1/2 cup whipping cream
chopped pecans

CRUST: Mix chocolate wafers with margarine. Press into 9 x 13 inch pyrex dish. Bake at 325 degrees for 10 minutes. Cool.
FILLING: Mix cream cheese with 1/4 cup sugar. Add vanilla. Stir in egg yolks and melted chocolate. Cool. Beat egg whites until soft peaks form. Fold in cream which has been whipped with 1/4 cup sugar. Gently fold egg white/cream mixture into chocolate mixture. Marbleize. Pour into cooled crust. Sprinkle with nuts. Freeze. Remove from freezer a few minutes before serving. Serves 8-10.

Jean Webb (Mrs. F. A., III)

APPLE CRISP

1 can (21 oz.) apple pie filling
1 can (20 oz.) pie sliced apples
8 Tbsp. butter
brown sugar
cinnamon
1/2 to 3/4 box apple and spice
   cake mix, or spice cake mix

Mix apple pie filling and pie sliced apples together in greased 12 x 8 x 2 inch baking dish. Cut butter into small slices. Place over top of apple mixture and mix through. Sprinkle heavily with brown sugar and cinnamon. Sprinkle cake mix over the top. Bake in preheated 350 degree oven for one hour. Best served warm, not hot. Can make early in day and reheat for 10 minutes in 350 degree oven. Serve with vanilla ice cream. Serves 6 to 8.

Katherine Moore (Mrs. Peter F.)

APPLE DUMPLING DELIGHT, WITH SAUCE
A family favorite. Rich dessert

DOUGH:
2 cups flour
3/4 cups milk
6 Tbsp. Crisco
4 level tsp. baking powder
1 tsp. salt

FILLING:
5 apples, peeled and sliced
4 Tbsp. sugar
2 tsp. cinnamon

SYRUP:
3 cups water
3 Tbsp. butter
2-1/4 cups sugar

Stir together flour, baking powder and salt. Cut Crisco into flour mixture with pastry blender. Stir in milk. Roll out dough as for biscuits. Shape dough into large rectangle. Set aside.
Mix filling ingredients well and sprinkle over the dough. Roll up dough with apple mixture like a jelly roll. Then slice into 8 slices and place in a buttered 9 x 13 inch pan. Make syrup by mixing all syrup ingredients and bring to a boil. Pour over dough slices. Bake at 375 degrees for 40 minutes. Serve warm. Serves 8.

Mandy Martin

When melting chocolate, it is important to keep moisture from coming in direct contact with the chocolate because moisture will cause chocolate to stiffen.

OUR DELIGHT

From "The Old House on Mocking Bird Lane," Dallas, Texas

CRUST:
2 cups self-rising flour
2 sticks butter, melted
1 cup chopped pecans

FILLING, 1st Layer:
1-1/4 cup whipping cream
1/2 cup sifted confectioners' sugar
4 oz. cream cheese,
room temperature
2nd Layer:
2 3-3/4 oz. boxes instant vanilla
pudding
2-1/2 cups milk
3rd Layer:
1 banana sliced
4th Layer:
1 cup whipping cream
1/2 cup chopped pecans, toasted
5th Layer:
1/2 cup flaked coconut, toasted

CRUST: Position rack in lower third of oven. Preheat oven to 350 degrees. Combine all crust ingredients, pat into a 9 x 13 inch dish. Bake for 25 minutes. Cool

Filling, *1st layer:* Beat all ingredients together well; spread evenly over crust. Cover and chill.
2nd layer: Whisk (beat) pudding with milk until thickened. Spread evenly over cream cheese layer. Cover and chill again.
3rd layer: Thinly slice a banana and arrange in a single layer over pudding.
4th layer: Whip cream and fold in pecans; spread over bananas.
5th layer: Sprinkle with toasted coconut and chill thoroughly. Keep covered. Serves 16 to 20.

Libby Morrison (Mrs. Jack)

FROZEN STRAWBERRY DESSERT

Very different—like an ice cream with crunch

1/2 cup margarine
1/4 cup brown sugar
1 cup flour
1/2 cup chopped nuts
2 egg whites
2/3 cup sugar
1 Tbsp. lemon juice
16. oz. frozen sliced strawberries,
thawed
1/2 pint whipping cream, whipped

In a saucepan, melt margarine; stir in brown sugar, flour and nuts. Spread mixture on a greased cookie sheet. Bake in a preheated oven (350 degrees) for 20 minutes. Reserve 1/3 of crumb mixture for topping; pat remaining 2/3 mixture into the bottom of a greased 9 x 13 inch pan; set aside. In a large mixing bowl, beat egg whites until stiff; slowly add sugar and lemon juice. Beat for 10 to 15 minutes on high speed. Continue beating while adding strawberries. Fold in whipped cream. Swirl mixture in prepared crust, and top with reserved crumb mixture. Freeze until 20 minutes before serving time; cut into squares. Serves 12.

Catherine Willis (Mrs. Bart)

THREE-LAYER DREAM DESSERT

First layer:
2 cups crushed pretzels
3 Tbsp. sugar
1-1/2 sticks margarine, melted
Second Layer:
1 8-oz. pkg. cream cheese,
　softened
1 cup sugar
1 8-oz. carton Cool Whip
Third Layer
1 6-oz. pkg. strawberry Jello
2 cups boiling water
1 6-oz. can crushed pineapple,
　drained

Mix together all ingredients in first layer; spread in a 9 x 13 inch pan. Bake at 350 degrees for 15 to 20 minutes. Cool. Beat cream cheese and sugar together; fold in Cool Whip and spread on crumbs. Chill. Mix together strawberry Jello and water until gelatin is dissolved. Add pineapple and let thicken. Spread over cream cheese mixture and refrigerate. Serves 16 to 20.

Lillie Huss

BABY RUTH DESSERT SQUARES
Very Rich!

4 cups quick-cooking oatmeal
1 cup white corn syrup
1 cup light brown sugar
2/3 cup margarine
1/4 cup chunky-style peanut
　butter
2 tsp. vanilla
1 12-oz. pkg. semi-sweet chocolate
　chips
2/3 cup chunky-style peanut
　butter
1/4 bar cooking paraffin
1 cup chopped peanuts

Mix together oatmeal, corn syrup and brown sugar in mixing bowl. Set aside. Melt margarine and pour over oatmeal mixture. Mix well. Add 1/4 cup chunky peanut butter and vanilla. Mix well and pat into greased 9 x 13 inch pan. Bake at 350 degrees for 12 minutes. Cool.

TOPPING: Melt chocolate chips with 2/3 cup chunky peanut butter and paraffin. Stir in chopped peanuts. Spread over cooled crust. Let cool completely and cut into squares.

Mandy Martin

STRAWBERRIES MELBA

1 to 1-1/2 quarts fresh
　strawberries
2 to 3 boxes fresh raspberries, OR
　3 pkgs. frozen raspberries
sugar
whipped cream
Kirsch or Grand Marnier

Wash and hull strawberries. Puree fresh raspberries or drain frozen raspberries. Flavor with a little sugar. Spoon over strawberries. Serve with sweetened whipped cream flavored with Kirsch or Grand Marnier.

Ada Offerdahl (Mrs. John)

417

APPLE BROWN BETTY

Our favorite family dessert! Easy!

4 cups pared, sliced tart apples
1/4 cup orange juice
1 cup sugar
3/4 cup sifted all-purpose flour
1/2 tsp. cinnamon
1/4 tsp. nutmeg
dash salt
1/2 cup butter

Place sliced apples in buttered 2-quart flat casserole dish. Sprinkle with orange juice. Combine sugar, flour, spices and salt. Cut in butter until mixture is crumbly. Sprinkle over apples. Bake at 375 degrees for 45 minutes or until apples are tender and topping is crisp. Serve warm with whipped cream, hard sauce or ice cream. Serves 6.

Virginia Golding (Mrs. John G.)

APPLE KUCHEN

This may also be made with peaches or pears.

1/2 cup butter, softened
1 pkg. yellow cake mix (Betty Crocker if you can get it)
1/2 cup flaked coconut
1 can (20 oz.) **pie-sliced** apples, well drained, or 2-1/2 cups sliced pared baking apples
1/2 cup sugar
1 tsp. cinnamon
1 cup sour cream
2 egg yolks

Heat oven to 350 degrees. Cut butter into dry cake mix until crumbly. Mix in coconut. Press mixture into ungreased 13 x 9 x 2 inch pyrex baking dish, building up dough slightly at the edges. Bake 10 minutes.
Arrange apple slices on warm crust. Mix sugar and cinnamon and sprinkle on apples. Blend sour cream and egg yolks; drizzle over apples (topping *will not* completely cover apples). Bake 25 minutes or until edges are light brown. Serves 12 to 15.

Kay Roberson (Mrs. G. Don)

PEACH DELIGHT

You'll make this over and over and over . . .

1 box yellow cake mix
1-1/2 sticks margarine, room temperature
1 large can sliced peaches
1/2 cup sugar
1 tsp. cinnamon
3 egg yolks, beaten
16 oz. sour cream

Put cake mix into a bowl. Add softened margarine; mix well. Press into the bottom of a 9 x 13 inch pan. Drain the peach slices and place on top of crumb mixture. Mix 1/2 cup sugar and cinnamon. Sprinkle on top of peaches. Add sour cream to the beaten egg yolks; pour over peaches. Bake at 325 degrees for 40 minutes. Serves 10.

Ellen Knott (Mrs. B.F.)

JOLLY JELLO AND YUMMY YOGURT
Very nutritious snack or dessert!

JELLO:
*1 5-1/4 oz. box Jello (raspberry is
    our favorite)*
1 quart buttermilk
2 cups water
Cool Whip to "dab" on top
    OR
YOGURT:
1 3-oz. box Jello
*3 or 4 cups buttermilk
1 cup water

**JELLO DIRECTIONS: Boil 2 cups water and
add to Jello. Stir until melted and cool. Add
buttermilk. Refrigerate until it "gels." Serve cold
with whipped cream or Cool Whip. Serves 8.**

**YOGURT DIRECTIONS: Boil 1 cup water and
add to Jello. Stir until melted and let cool. Add
buttermilk and put into one large or several small
containers. Refrigerate until it "gels." Makes 5
8-oz. cups.
*4 cups makes yogurt runny like Bryers — 3 cups
makes yogurt creamier, like Sealtest.**

Frances Fennebresque (Mrs. J.C.)

CHERRY-ALMOND CREAM
Elegant but easy

1 (21 oz.) can cherry pie filling
*1 (14 oz.) can sweetened
    condensed milk*
*1/4 cup chopped blanched
    almonds, toasted*
1 cup whipping cream
1/8 tsp. almond extract
*toasted chopped almonds for
    decoration, if desired*

**Line 14 or 15 muffin cups with fluted paper
baking cups or set aside 14 or 15 small individual
molds. In a medium bowl, combine pie filling and
sweetened condensed milk. Stir in 1/4 cup
almonds. In a small bowl, whip cream until soft
peaks form. Stir in almond extract. Fold into
cherry mixture. Spoon into paper-lined muffin
cups or individual molds. Cover with foil or
plastic wrap. Place in freezer; freeze until firm, 2
to 4 hours. To serve, peel off paper, arrange on a
platter. Decorate with additional almonds, if
desired. Makes 14 or 15 servings.**

The Committee

Instant and Delicious
Soften 1/2 gallon good vanilla ice cream. With
electric mixer blend in 8 or 9 oz. container of Cool Whip
and 3/4 cup Creme de Menthe. Refreeze in parfait glasses
(or large flat container and serve in squares).

Georgia Miller (Mrs. George)

AMBROSIA
Serve at Thanksgiving and especially at Christmas.

1 dozen large navel oranges
1 6-oz. jar frozen coconut,
   thawed
1 small jar maraschino cherries,
   cut in halves (optional)
1/4 cup sugar

Cut oranges in halves. Scoop out "meat"leaving membranes. Hold over a bowl so that juice and meat will be saved. Gently mix coconut, cherries, and sugar into orange meat and juice. Refrigerate, allowing sugar to be absorbed.

NOTE: This is an old Southern recipe. No other kind of fruit is added in the traditional ambrosia.

VARIATION: Use 6 oranges, 6 bananas cut in small pieces, and one 8-1/4 oz. can crushed pineapple (drained), plus other ingredients above. Combine as directed. 12 to 14 servings.

Patricia S. Padgett (Mrs. F.L.)
Stella Thurston (Mrs. Doc J.)

STRAWBERRIES ROMANOFF
My guests always ask for the recipe.

*2 qts. fresh strawberries
granulated sugar
1 pt. vanilla ice cream, softened
1/2 pt. cream, whipped
juice of 1 lemon
1 oz. Bacardi rum
2 oz. Cointreau

Sprinkle berries lightly with sugar and chill for at least an hour. Whip ice cream slightly and fold in whipped cream. Add lemon juice and liqueur. Pour over chilled berries in a glass bowl. Toss lightly so as not to damage the strawberries. Refrigerate for several hours before serving.

*NOTE: Never place strawberries in a pan of water to wash! Wash individually, then cap, then place on paper towels to dry. Serves 10.

Beverly Keller (Mrs. Guy)

YOGURT SURPRISE
This is so simple, but so good, when you need an emergency dessert.

1 8-oz. container peach yogurt
1 8-oz. container red raspberry
   yogurt
1 9 to 12 oz. container of Cool
   Whip
1 1-lb. 4-oz. can crushed
   pineapple, well drained
1/2 cup nuts (optional)

Press juice out of pineapple. Blend ingredients together and refrigerate until time to serve. Serves 4 to 6.

Gensie

CHOCOLATE AMARETTO MOUSSE

CRUST:
1 cup crushed Nabisco (Famous)
  chocolate wafers
1/4 cup melted butter
2 Tbsp. sugar
2 Tbsp. finely-ground almonds

FILLING:
1 pkg. (12 oz.) semi-sweet
  chocolate chips
3/4 cup whipping cream
6 eggs, separated
3 Tbsp. Amaretto
1/2 tsp. almond extract
2 Tbsp. sugar
1/3 cup seedless red raspberry jam
  (Village Market)

Use a spring form pan to make crust. Bake at 350 degrees for 7 minutes. Then, put chocolate chips in food processor using steel blade (blender can be used but it is not as successful). Heat whipping cream until it comes to a boil and put in food processor. While food processor is running add egg yolks, one at a time. Add Amaretto and almond extract. Blend until smooth; let cool to room temperature. In a bowl beat egg whites until peaks form, adding sugar slowly. Fold together egg whites and chocolate mixture. Spread raspberry jam over crust. Spoon mousse mixture over raspberries. Cover, and put in freezer until firm. Return to refrigerator one hour before serving. Can be served with whipped cream. Serves 12.

Georgia Miller (Mrs. George)

CHOCOLATE ORANGE MOUSSE

12 (1 oz.) squares semi-sweet
  chocolate
2 tsp. grated orange rind OR
  2 tsp. orange extract
1/2 cup firmly packed
  brown sugar
4 egg yolks
4 eggs
2 Tbsp. orange juice
2 cups whipping cream, whipped
additional whipping cream

Melt chocolate over hot water in top of double boiler. Cool. Combine orange flavoring or rind, sugar, egg yolks and eggs in blender, and blend until light and foamy. Add chocolate and orange juice; blend well. Fold in whipped cream. Pour into small wine glasses or individual serving dishes. Chill until set. Garnish with additional whipped cream and mandarin orange slices, if desired. Serves 10.

Shirley Benfield (Mrs. R. H.)

QUICK CHOCOLATE MOUSSE
A quick dessert for family or guests

6 oz. chocolate chips
2 eggs
3 Tbsp. very strong hot coffee, or
    1 or 2 Tbsp. Cointreau, rum,
    Grande Marnier or vanilla
3/4 cup scalded milk

Blend all the ingredients at high speed for two minutes. Pour mixture into 4 dessert cups and chill for several hours.

Beverly Michaux (Mrs. Roy H.)
Mary Lou Scholl (Mrs. Ken)
Anne and Louis Szymanski

FROZEN STRAWBERRY MOUSSE
Quick, easy and elegant!

1 pint sour cream
1 16 oz. box frozen strawberries,
    thawed
1 cup sugar
1 Tbsp. vanilla extract

Do not drain thawed strawberries. Combine all ingredients. Beat well and pour into 2 ice cube trays. Freeze. Cover with foil or plastic wrap. Serve in small portions. Garnish with fresh or frozen strawberries.

Beverly Hance (Mrs. James)

POTS A LA CREME ELEGANTS
Easy, easy chocolate mousse

1 6-oz. pkg. semi-sweet
    chocolate pieces
6 eggs, separated
2 tsp. vanilla extract
1-1/2 pts. whipping cream
1 tsp. instant coffee powder
1 1-oz. square semi-sweet
    chocolate (optional)

In double boiler, over hot, *not boiling*, water, melt chocolate pieces; remove from heat. With spoon, beat in egg yolks and vanilla. In small bowl, with electric mixer at high speed, beat egg whites until stiff but not dry; fold into chocolate mixture. Spoon this pot a la creme mixture into six 6-oz. wine glases or glass bowls. Refrigerate at least 4 hours.
Before serving: whip cream; add instant coffee to cream. Spoon a portion on each dessert. With vegetable parer, scrape curls from semi-sweet chocolate square onto each pot a la creme, as a garnish. (You can use chocolate sprinkles — it has the same effect.)
This is Soooo good — and easy!

Sallie Wooten (Mrs. F.M.)

MOTHER'S CHOCOLATE ECLAIRS
An easy dessert—tastes better than bakery-made

1 pkg. ladyfingers
1 8-oz. carton whipping cream
sugar to taste

ICING:
2 cups powdered sugar
4 Tbsp. melted butter
4 Tbsp. cocoa
1/2 tsp. vinegar
5 or 6 Tbsp. boiling water
1 tsp. vanilla extract

Split ladyfingers. Beat whipping cream, adding sugar to taste. Put whipped cream (about 1-1/2 inches thick) on top of each ladyfinger. Be sure whipped cream is even and smooth. Put top back on ladyfinger. Place all on a cookie sheet. Beat all icing ingredients by hand with a spoon until smooth and of icing consistency. Refrigerate for 1 hour. Spoon over each ladyfinger, using a knife to get what has dripped on pan, and using it to ice next ladyfinger. Refrigerate until icing has hardened. Remove ladyfinger with a spatula.

Dee Dee Grainger (Mrs. Isaac B.)

ECLAIR DESSERT

2 3-3/4 oz. pkg. Instant French
    Vanilla pudding
3 cups milk
1 9-oz. carton Cool Whip
1 1-lb. box graham crackers
2 squares unsweetened baking
    chocolate
3 Tbsp. butter
2 Tbsp. white corn syrup
1 tsp. vanilla
1-1/2 cup confectioners' sugar
3 Tbsp. milk

Butter the bottom of 9 x 13 inch pan. Line pan with whole graham crackers. Mix pudding with 3 cups milk. Beat at medium speed for 2 minutes. Blend in Cool Whip. Pour half of the mixture over the graham crackers, then place a second layer of crackers over the pudding. Pour the remaining pudding mixture over and cover with more crackers. Refrigerate for 2 hours. Frost with the following mixture:
Melt chocolate with 3 Tbsp. butter. Add corn syrup, vanilla, confectioners' sugar and milk. Beat all ingredients until smooth; spread over chilled graham cracker and pudding mixture. Refrigerate 24 hours before serving. Serves 12.

Anne Morris (Mrs. Roy)

Instant and Delicious
Mix softened pineapple sherbet with Creme de Menthe to taste (not too much Creme de Menthe). Spoon into sherbet glasses or other suitable containers and freeze. Delicious dessert, served with a cookie after an Oriental meal.   *Gensie*

FRENCH PUDDING
Must be made in advance—better than strawberry shortcake.

2 cups vanilla wafer crumbs,
  divided
1 stick butter or margarine,
  softened
1/2 cup sugar
1 egg, beaten
1 cup whipped cream, sweetened
  to taste, divided
1 pkg. frozen strawberries, OR
  1 pint fresh strawberries
  (best), divided
1 cup pecans, chopped, divided

Grease bottom of an 8 x 8 inch square pan. Sprinkle 1 cup crumbs over the bottom. Mix together the butter, sugar and beaten egg in top of double boiler. Heat until thickened, stirring constantly. Pour half of this mixture over crumbs, add a layer of half of the strawberries, a layer of half the nuts, and half the whipped cream. Repeat but end with crumbs and nuts. Refrigerate for 24 hours. Serves 8.

Libby Preston (Mrs. James)

MOLDED FRENCH CREAM
This dessert is especially spectacular and delicious topped with sugared, fresh strawberries, peaches or blueberries. Don't expect leftovers!

1 cup sour cream
1 cup heavy cream
3/4 cup sugar
1 envelope gelatin (unflavored)
1/4 cup water
1 8-oz. pkg. cream cheese
1/2 tsp. vanilla

Lightly oil one 4-cup mold. Combine sour cream and heavy cream in a saucepan. Beat in sugar; place pan over *very low* heat to warm. Sprinkle gelatin over water in a cup to soften, place cup in hot water to dissolve and liquify. Stir into warm cream mixture and remove from heat. Beat cream cheese until soft. Stir in cream mixture and vanilla. Blend thoroughly. Pour into mold. Refrigerate until firm. Unmold by dipping mold into warm water for 10 seconds; then invert and shake gently onto serving plate. Return to refrigerator until serving time.

Stephanie Fletcher (Mrs. D.H)

CRANBERRY DESSERT SALAD
Good at Christmas with turkey and chicken dishes

1 can whole cranberry sauce
2 Tbsp. lemon juice
1/2 pint heavy cream, whipped
1/4 cup confectioners' sugar
2/3 cup chopped nuts
1/2 cup crushed pineapple,
  drained

Combine cranberry sauce and lemon juice. Pour into refrigerator tray. Blend together remaining ingredients and spread over cranberry mixture. Freeze. Serves 8.

Stephany Alphin (Mrs. R.L.)

FROZEN FRUIT CUP
Great in summer for a brunch. Can serve as dessert or salad.

1 cup orange juice (frozen is fine)
2 Tbsp. lemon juice
3/4 to 1 cup sugar
1 cup crushed pineapple (can be a little more)
2 mashed bananas
1 small bottle ginger ale

Mix all ingredients thoroughly and freeze either in a 9 x 13 inch pan or a 3-quart mixing bowl. Best if thawed slightly before serving. It is like a fresh fruit sherbet or ice so is nice scooped out and served in pretty bowls. Serves 6.

Marg Barnes (Mrs. R. W.)

LEMON BISQUE
Easy, light dessert

1 (13 oz.) can very cold evaporated milk
juice of 3 or 4 lemons
sugar to taste
graham cracker crumbs

Whip milk; then add lemon juice and sugar. The amount of sugar and lemon used really depends on personal taste.

Line shallow container with cracker crumbs and spread whipped mixture over this. Cover with more crumbs and freeze. Cut into squares to serve. (Allow the bisque to stand out of freezer a few minutes before serving. This makes cutting easier.) Serves 6.

Liz Lowry (Mrs. W. F.)

FROZEN LEMON CREAM

1 egg, well beaten
1/4 cup lemon juice
1/2 cup sugar
1/8 tsp. salt
1 tsp. shredded lemon peel
1/2 tsp. vanilla
2-3 drops yellow food coloring
1/4 cup melted butter or margarine
1/2 cup brown sugar, packed
pinch of nutmeg
1/2 cup chopped nuts
3 cups corn chex crushed to 3/4 cup
3/4 cup grated coconut
1 cup heavy cream, whipped

Line bottom and sides of loaf pan with waxed paper, extend paper over sides. Combine egg, lemon juice, sugar, salt and lemon peel. Heat and stir over hot, not boiling, water, until mixture coats spoon—about 12-15 minutes. Remove from heat. Stir in vanilla and food coloring. Cool thoroughly.

Combine butter, brown sugar and nutmeg. Add nuts and chex crumbs. Mix until evenly blended. Save 3/4 cup crumb mix for topping. Press remaining crumbs into prepared pan. Fold coconut and whipped cream into cooled lemon mixture. Spoon into pan. Top with reserved crumbs. Press crumbs together tightly, cover or wrap in foil. Freeze 6 hours or overnight. Serves 8.

Myrtle Ussery (Mrs. A. M., Sr.)

FROZEN LEMON DESSERT

3 eggs, separated
2/3 cup sugar
1 lemon rind, grated
5 Tbsp. lemon juice
1 cup heavy cream
30 vanilla wafers crushed, divided

Beat egg white until stiff, then add sugar slowly. Beat egg yolks separately, add lemon juice and rind. Fold mixture into egg whites. Beat cream until whipped and fold into egg mixture. Sprinkle half of vanilla crumbs in bottom of 8 x 8 inch pan. Pour mixture into pan with crumbs. Sprinkle top with vanilla crumbs. Freeze. Makes 9 servings.

Bobbie Davis (Mrs. Claude T.)

MACAROON-FUDGE LOAF
For ease in slicing, place loaf in refrigerator about 15 minutes before serving.

12 (2-inch) chewy macaroons
1 (4-oz.) pkg. sweet baking
   chocolate
2 eggs
4 cups sifted powdered sugar
1 tsp. vanilla extract
1/2 cup chopped pecans
1 cup whipping cream

Line an 8 x 4 inch loaf pan with waxed paper, letting paper extend over edges. Grease waxed paper with soft butter or margarine. Use your fingers to crumble macaroons into small pieces. Press half of crumbled macaroons on bottom of waxed paper lined pan; reserve remaining macaroon crumbs. Refrigerate lined pan about 15 minutes. Place chocolate into top of double boiler. Melt over simmering water; set aside. In a large bowl, beat eggs. Stir in powdered sugar, melted chocolate and vanilla; beat until smooth. Stir in pecans. Spoon into chilled macaroon-lined pan. In a small bowl, whip cream until soft peaks form. Fold in reserved macaroon crumbs. Spoon over chocolate filling. Cover pan with foil or plastic wrap. Place in freezer; freeze until firm, 4 to 5 hours. To unmold, grasp waxed paper and lift molded loaf from pan; remove paper. Cut in cross-wise slices. Makes 8 to 10 servings.

Kathleen Boyce (Mrs. R. N.)

RUSSIAN MINT PIES

*Guests always go back for more. Can be prepared well in advance
and removed from the freezer when needed.*

1 cup butter
2 cups sifted powdered sugar
4 squares unsweetened chocolate,
    melted
4 eggs
1 tsp. peppermint extract
2 tsp. vanilla extract
18 vanilla wafers
1 cup heavy cream, whipped
chopped nuts, cherries
18 cupcake papers

Cream butter and sugar. Blend in melted chocolate. Add eggs and beat well, then blend in flavorings. Put a vanilla wafer into cupcake paper. Fill 3/4 full with chocolate mixture. Place a dollop of whipped cream on top and sprinkle with nuts and top with a cherry. Freeze in muffin tins to keep shape and store in plastic bags after frozen. (This recipe can be cut in half, if desired.) Serves 18.

Linda Hawfield (Mrs. Ben)

AMARETTO FREEZE

1/3 cup amaretto liqueur
1 Tbsp. brown sugar
1 quart vanilla ice cream
whipped cream
maraschino cherries

Combine amaretto and brown sugar and stir until dissolved. Combine ice cream and amaretto mixture in container of electric blender or food processor and process until smooth. Pour into 4 parfait glasses and freeze. Garnish with whipped cream and cherry. I serve with Pepperidge Farm cookies — Cappuccino, Pirouettes, etc. Serves 4.

Kay Roberson (Mrs. G. Don)

FROZEN BING CHERRY DESSERT

1 can pitted bing cherries
1/2 cup Bourbon whiskey
1/2 cup pecans
15 almond macaroons
1/2 gallon vanilla ice cream

Soak cherries with juice in Bourbon overnight. Crush macaroons; soften ice cream and add rest of ingredients. Mix well. Freeze in shallow molds or shallow freezing tray.
NOTE: You may need to order macaroons from bakery in advance.

Ann Lester (Mrs. W. C.)

CHERRIES JUBILEE

1 large can black pitted cherries
2 Tbsp. sugar
1 Tbsp. cornstarch
1/2 cup cognac
vanilla ice cream

Drain cherries. Mix sugar and cornstarch; add enough cherry juice to make a smooth paste. Stir into the rest of the juice and simmer in chafing dish or sauce pan. Cook, stirring constantly, for 3 minutes. Add cherries; remove from heat. Add cognac and ignite. Serve flaming cherries and sauce over good vanilla ice cream. Serves 3 or 4.

Phyllis Mahoney (Mrs. J.C.)

COFFEE CRUNCH PARFAITS

1 quart coffee ice cream,
    slightly softened
1 (2-1/4 oz.) pkg. slivered al-
    monds, chopped and toasted
2 (7/8 oz.) English toffee candy
    bars, crushed
1/2 cup chocolate syrup
1 (4 oz.) carton frozen whipped
    topping, thawed
8 maraschino cherries with stems

Spoon 1/4 cup ice cream into each of eight 4-oz. chilled parfait glasses; freeze 30 minutes. Layer 1/2 Tbsp. each of almonds, crushed candy and chocolate syrup. Repeat layers of ice cream, almonds, candy and chocolate. Cover and freeze until firm. Top each parfait with whipped topping and a cherry. Serves 8.

Brenda Monteith (Mrs. James)

ICE CREAM CRUNCH

2-1/2 cups crisp rice cereal (Rice
    Krispies)
1 can (3-1/2 oz.) flake-type
    coconut
1 cup coarsely chopped pecans
1/2 cup butter, melted
3/4 cup firmly-packed
    brown sugar
1/2 gallon vanilla ice cream

Spread rice cereal, coconut, pecans and melted butter in jelly roll pan, and bake at 300 degrees for 30 minutes. Stir mixture occasionally to brown evenly. Add brown sugar to hot mixture and blend in.

Pat 1/2 the mixture in bottom of 9 x 12 x 2 inch rectangular dish. Cut ice cream into one inch slices and place solidly over crunchy mixture. Press rest of crunchy mixture on top of ice cream. Cover dish with foil and freeze a minimum of 6 hours. Cut into squares and top with hot fudge sauce (see index). Serves 12.

Jeanne Golding

HOMEMADE ICE CREAM

I try other ice cream recipes and always come back to this one.

4 eggs, well beaten
2-1/2 cups sugar
1 tall can evaporated milk
1 pint light cream
2 tsps. vanilla
1/2 tsp. salt
2 cups fruit (peaches, strawberries, bananas)
enough milk to make a gallon

Beat eggs and sugar together. Add canned milk and cream and fruit, and enough milk to make one gallon. Freeze in turn-type freezer. Makes one gallon of ice cream. Serves 8-10.

Ellen Knott (Mrs. B.F.)

FRESH LIME SHERBET

2 cups milk
1 cup sugar
juice of 3 limes
1 cup heavy cream, whipped

Mix milk and sugar. Stir lime juice into milk mixture very slowly. Freeze. Fold whipped cream into frozen mixture. Freeze again, stirring occasionally to prevent it from becoming icy. A few drops of green food coloring may be added to milk in first mixture. Creamy and delicious! Makes about 1 quart.

Fran McCoy

SCRUMPTIOUS MOCHA ICE CREAM DESSERT

24 Oreo or Hydrox chocolate cream sandwich cookies, crushed
1/3 cup butter, melted
1/2 gallon coffee ice cream
3 oz. unsweetened chocolate
2 Tbsp. butter or margarine
1 cup sugar
dash of salt
2 5-1/2 to 6 oz. cans of evaporated milk
1/2 tsp. vanilla extract
1-1/2 cups heavy cream, whipped
1-1/2 oz. Kahlua liqueur
powdered sugar to taste
1/2 to 3/4 cup chopped nuts

Combine cookie crumbs and butter and press into the bottom of a buttered 9 x 13 inch pan. *Refrigerate.* When chilled, spoon on softened ice cream. *Freeze.* Melt chocolate and butter. Add sugar, salt and milk. *Boil*, stirring until thickened. Remove from heat and add vanilla extract. *Chill*; spread on top of ice cream. *Freeze.* Whip cream. Add Kahlua and powdered sugar to taste. Spread over chocolate layer and sprinkle with chopped nuts. *Freeze.* Serves 25.

NOTE: An excellent variation is to use peppermint stick ice cream, garnished with cookie crumbs or shavings of semi-sweet chocolate.

Marilyn Lea (Mrs. Scott C.)

PEPPERMINT ICE CREAM

1 quart milk
1 lb. peppermint candy
1 pint half-and-half
1 pint whipping cream, whipped

Combine milk and candy. Cover and refrigerate 12 hours. Combine candy mixture, half-and-half, and whipped cream. Pour into freezer canister of a 1-gallon ice cream churn. Freeze. Let ripen at least 1 hour.

Jane McColl (Mrs. H.L.)

GRAPENUT PUDDING

1 tsp. grated rind of lemon
4 Tbsp. margarine
1 cup sugar
2 egg yolks, well beaten
3 Tbsp. lemon juice
2 Tbsp. flour
4 Tbsp. Grapenuts
1 cup milk
2 egg whites, well beaten

Cream margarine and add sugar. Add egg yolks, lemon rind and lemon juice. Fold in flour, grapenuts and milk; then fold in beaten egg whites. Pour into open-face baking dish (approximately 6 x 10); place in a pan of water and bake 40 minutes in 350 degree oven. When serving, dig deep for sauce on bottom.

Katherine Moore (Mrs. Peter)

Similar recipe submitted by:
Eileen Antonelli (Mrs. George A.)

HAWAIIAN PUDDING
So easy—so rich.

2 cups vanilla wafer crumbs
1 stick melted margarine or butter
5 sliced bananas
1 cup sweetened condensed milk
1/3 cup lemon juice
1 small can crushed pineapple,
    drained
1 small carton Cool Whip
1 small can coconut
1/2 cup chopped nuts
1 small jar cherries

Mix vanilla wafer crumbs and butter. Line bottom of 10 x 10 pan; add in layers: bananas, condensed milk and lemon juice mixed, pineapple, Cool Whip, coconut, nuts and cherries. Chill 2 to 3 hours.

Max Ussery

MOLDED CUSTARD

1 quart milk, scalded
12 eggs, slightly beaten
1-1/2 cups sugar, divided
1/4 tsp. salt
1 tsp. vanilla extract

Melt to caramelize 1/2 cup of sugar in a heavy skillet and then pour into bottom of a tube pan. Scald milk. Combine eggs, salt and remaining cup of sugar. Add scalded milk slowly, stirring constantly to prevent curdling. Add vanilla extract and mix well. Pour custard mixture over caramelized sugar glaze and bake at 350 degrees for 1 hour or until knife inserted in center of custard comes out clean.

IMPORTANT: Place tube pan in a pan of hot water in oven while baking. (I use a 10 x 15 inch pan with water in it and heat it while the oven is preheating.) Cool custard and refrigerate. When ready to serve, unmold upside down so that caramel glaze frosts custard.

Betty Forlidas (Mrs. Phillip)

SPANISH FLAN WITH CARAMEL SAUCE
Elegant dessert; very light. A favorite—rather easy!

1 cup sugar
4 large eggs
1 can condensed milk
1 cup water
2 tsp. vanilla
1/2 tsp. salt

Put sugar in heavy pan over medium-high heat. Stir sugar as soon as it begins to brown, then stir constantly. Pour into 10-inch round glass baking dish and cool. Beat eggs just to mix. Blend in milk, water, vanilla and salt and beat until mixed. Pour egg mixture over caramelized sugar. Place baking dish in pan of hot water and bake at 350 degrees for 1 hour. Cool and refrigerate. To serve, invert on platter and let caramelized sugar flow down sides of custard.

Mandy Martin

Combine thoroughly 1/2 gallon good vanilla ice cream, softened, with 1/2 to 3/4 jar of Roberson's Ginger Marmalade (Reid's). Spoon into sherbet glasses and freeze. Delicious dessert, served with a cookie after an Oriental meal.

Gensie

CHESTNUT SOUFFLE
This is an elegant, easy dessert.

6 whole eggs
4 egg yolks
1/2 cup sugar
6 Tbsp. rum
1-1/2 cups sweetened chestnut
    puree (in gourmet section)
1-1/2 cups heavy cream
3 Tbsp. gelatin

Combine eggs, yolks and sugar in a bowl and beat with electric mixer until very light and thick. Soften gelatin in rum and dissolve over boiling water. Add to eggs and beat well. Fold in puree and beat again. Last, carefully fold in whipped cream and turn into 1-1/2 quart souffle dish which has a waxed paper collar. Chill several hours and remove collar before serving. Decorate with whipped cream. Serves 6-8.

Anna Stanley (Mrs. V.E., Jr.)

LEMON SOUFFLE
This is a lovely and light dessert.

1 can (13 oz.) chilled
    evaporated milk
1/2 cup sugar
1 3-oz. pkg. lemon Jello
3 lemons, juice and rind
3 drops yellow food coloring

SAUCE:
1 10-oz. pkg. thawed frozen
    raspberries
1/3 jar Raffeto Melba Sauce

Dissolve the lemon Jello in 1 cup boiling water and set aside to cool. Beat the chilled milk in very large bowl until thick and frothy. Slowly add sugar, beating until thick. Stir in Jello gradually. Stir in lemon juice, lemon rind and food coloring. Pour into large souffle dish or 3-quart glass dish. Refrigerate overnight. Serve with melba sauce and raspberries. Serves 8.

Margery Marcus (Mrs. R.A.)

ANNEMARIE'S FROZEN LEMON SOUFFLE

8 eggs
1 cup sugar
2 pkgs. unflavored gelatin,
    dissolved in the juice of
    1 lemon
1/2 cup fresh lemon juice
1 Tbsp. grated lemon rind
2 cups heavy cream, whipped to
    soft peaks

Beat the eggs and sugar in a mixer bowl for about 10 minutes, until light and creamy. Add the dissolved gelatin to the rest of the lemon juice and add this slowly to the beaten eggs, along with the grated lemon rind. Fold in the whipped cream and pour into a souffle dish prepared with a waxed paper collar around the dish. Put in the freezer for two hours; remove the paper collar and decorate with whipped cream put through a pastry bag, lemon slices and mint.

The Committee

FROZEN GRAND MARNIER SOUFFLE
WITH HOT STRAWBERRY SAUCE

SOUFFLE:
1 quart vanilla ice cream
8 tsp. Grand Marnier liqueur
4-5 almond macaroons, crumbled
1 cup heavy cream, whipped
2/3 cup chopped almonds, toasted
1/2 cup powdered sugar

SAUCE:
2 pkgs. (10 oz.) frozen sliced
*   strawberries, thawed*
8 tsp. Grand Marnier liqueur
1 pint fresh whole strawberries
*   for garnish*

Prepare souffle: Soften ice cream slightly. Stir in crumbled macaroons and Grand Marnier. Fold whipped cream into ice cream mixture. Spoon into 6-cup metal mold. Sprinkle surface lightly with almonds and powdered sugar. Cover with plastic wrap and freeze a minimum of 4 to 6 hours.

Prepare sauce: Heat the thawed strawberries; stir in Grand Marnier.

To serve: Wrap mold several seconds in hot damp towel. Loosen edge with spatula and turn out on cold platter. Can refreeze for several hours at this point. Garnish with fresh strawberries. Cut into 8 portions and pass hot strawberry sauce in sauce boat to pour over frozen souffle. This recipe increases nicely. Serves 8.

Ellen Knott (Mrs. B. F.)

BROWNIE JELLY
A light "fairy-like" dessert to serve after a heavy meal

1-1/2 cups sugar
1 cup boiling water
1 Tbsp. unflavored gelatin
1/2 cup water
2 cups fresh orange juice
*   (may use frozen)*
juice of 1 lemon
1 cup cream, whipped

Dissolve gelatin in 1/2 cup cold water. Boil sugar and water for 5 minutes; add dissolved gelatin. Mix well and let cool. Add orange and lemon juices; blend and pour into freezing tray. Freeze about 4 hours. Cover with a layer of whipped cream. Slice and serve frozen. Very good to serve after a heavy meal. Serves 6.

Betty Boyd (Mrs. Basil)

Instant and Delicious
Divide good vanilla ice cream into serving dishes.
Pour Bailey's Irish Cream over to taste.　　　*Gensie*

433

🌿 INSTANT DELICIOUS DESSERT TOPPINGS

Top a chilled slice of pineapple with a scoop of pineapple sherbet. Make a slight indentation on top of sherbet and pour in 2 or 3 Tbsp. Creme de Menthe.

Top coffee ice cream with grated semi-sweet chocolate.

Top a serving of vanilla ice cream with several Tbsps. Cointreau.

Top mocha ice cream with hot chocolate sauce.

Top lime sherbet with crushed chocolate bits.

Top a sauce of fresh raspberries with several Tbsps. commercial sour cream. Top sour cream with 1/2 Tbsp. brown sugar.

Mix peeled fresh lime wedges with lime sherbet and top with a dollop of heated Bacardi Rum.

Into coffee ice cream, stir chopped rind of orange and chocolate kisses or chocolate chips.

Mix pineapple sherbet with pieces of finely chopped, candied ginger.

Mix a few slivers of candied or fresh orange peel with chocolate ice cream and pour a little Cointreau and Triple Sec over the top.

Decorate lemon sherbet with sections of canned, drained tangerines or mandarin oranges. Heat and reduce the can's syrup, add a little bourbon and pour over the sherbet.

Moisten ground almonds with apricot brandy and mix with peach ice cream.

Slosh Tia Maria over vanilla ice cream and sprinkle with coconut.

Pour some Cointreau over ice cream or sherbet and then spoon a dollop of marmalade, preserves or Nesslerode over the top.

ALL OF THE ABOVE SHOULD BE SERVED WITH A VERY GOOD COOKIE OR CAKE, SUCH AS POUND CAKE.

The Committee

Pastry

M.E. Wellborn

BUTTERMILK PIE

6 eggs, beaten
1 cup butter, melted
1/2 cup flour
3-1/2 cups sugar
1 tsp. salt
1 cup buttermilk
2 tsp. vanilla
2 9-inch unbaked pie shells

Preheat oven to 350 degrees. Add butter to eggs. Combine dry ingredients and add to egg mixture. Blend in buttermilk and vanilla. Pour into pie shells. Bake 45 minutes.
VARIATION: Add 2 Tbsp. grated orange peel to buttermilk mixture for a nice Orange-Buttermilk pie.
NOTE: To keep crust from being soggy, brush with unbeaten egg white just before pouring in custard.

Ellen Knott (Mrs. B.F.)

COFFEE PIES

This recipe makes two pies.

1 lb. marshmallows
2 cups (or less) hot, strong coffee
1 pint heavy cream
1 tsp. vanilla extract
2 graham cracker crumb crusts

Melt marshmallows in coffee; cool. Add vanilla extract and fold in cream that has been whipped. Fill crusts and refrigerate.
VARIATION: After the marshmallows have melted and cooled, add some dark rum instead of vanilla extract (about 1/4 cup rum). This variation is better with a little less coffee.

Margaret L. Pitts

BIG MARGARET'S ICE BOX PIE

This pie is so easy to make, and so elegant!

1 9-inch frozen pie crust (deep
    dish)
1 medium-size container
    Cool Whip
1/2 stick butter, softened at room
    temperature
3/4 cup powdered sugar
1 tsp. almond extract
any fresh fruit as strawberries,
    peaches or bananas, sliced

Cook pie shell according to directions and cool slightly. Mix together 1/2 stick butter, powdered sugar and almond extract until creamy. Spread mixture evenly in bottom and up sides of the pie shell. Fill pie shell with enough sliced fruit to cover. Spread Cool Whip on top and garnish with one slice of the fruit in the center. Serves 6 to 8.

Dee Dee Grainger (Mrs. Isaac B., III)

COFFEE KAHLUA PIE

Oreo cookies
2 Tbsp. melted butter
1 pint vanilla ice cream, softened
1 pint coffee ice cream, softened
1/3 cup Kahlua
chocolate shavings (optional)

Crush 1/2 pkg. Oreo whole cookies. Mix with 2 Tbsp. butter and press into pie plate. Cool. Mix ice creams and Kahlua and spoon over crust. Freeze. Chocolate shavings may be sprinkled on top. Yields 1 pie.

Trudy Nix (Mrs. Ray)

KAHLUA PIE II
A coffee lover's treat

1 9-inch pie shell, baked
4 egg yolks
1/2 cup sugar
2 1-oz. squares semi-sweet
    chocolate
1/4 cup water
1 envelope unflavored gelatin
1/4 cup water
1/4 cup Kahlua
1-1/4 cups whipping cream
2 Tbsp. sugar
2 egg whites
chopped toasted almonds

Prepare pie shell. Beat yolks in top of double boiler. Add 1/2 cup sugar. Simmer, stirring until sugar is dissolved. Melt chocolate with 1/4 cup water in small saucepan. Add to yolks. Cook and stir until thick. Soften gelatin in 1/4 cup cold water. Add to chocolate mixture. Stir and remove from heat. Add Kahlua. Put into bowl of ice water to cool. Beat cream and sugar. Fold in 1/2 the cream, then fold in the stiffly-beaten egg whites. Save extra cream. Pour into shell; chill. Top with remaining cream as decoration, along with almonds. Do not freeze. Serves 6 to 8.

Dot Nicholls (Mrs. T.H.)

OATMEAL PIE

2 beaten eggs
2/3 cup melted margarine
2/3 cup sugar
2/3 cup white corn syrup
2/3 cup oatmeal
1/4 tsp. salt
1 tsp. vanilla
1/2 cup chopped pecans
1 unbaked pie shell

Mix well — pour into unbaked pie shell and bake 1 hour at 350 degrees.

Mary Kay Greig (Mrs. John H.)

VINEGAR PIE

1 cup sugar
2 eggs
2 tsp. vinegar
pinch salt
1 stick margarine
1 tsp. vanilla

Cream all together and pour into 1 large unbaked pie shell or 10 tart shells. Bake at 350 degrees for 30 minutes for 1 pie or 12 to 15 minutes for tarts.

Ann Copeland (Mrs. E.H., Jr.)

YOGURT PIE

1 8-oz. pkg. cream cheese
2 large eggs
1/2 cup sugar
1 tsp. vanilla extract
1 Tbsp. cornstarch
1/4 cup milk
1 8-oz. container plain yogurt
1 9-inch unbaked graham cracker
   crust

At high speed beat together until smooth cream cheese, eggs, sugar and vanilla. Stir together cornstarch and milk until smooth; stir into cream cheese mixture; fold in yogurt, pour into crust. Bake in preheated 350 degree oven until center is set — 35-40 minutes. Top with fruit if desired. Serves 8.

Kathleen Boyce (Mrs. R.N.)

ACAPULCO MOCHA PIE

35 chocolate cookies, crushed
   (1-1/2 cups)
3 Tbsp. butter, melted
1 pt. coffee ice cream, slightly
   softened
1/2 cup chocolate fudge ice cream
   topping, room temperature
1 cup whipping cream
2 Tbsp. coffee liqueur

In a small bowl, combine cookie crumbs and butter. Reserve 1/4 cup crumb mixture. Press remaining crumb mixture over bottom and up sides of a 9-inch pie plate. Refrigerate about 30 minutes. Spread softened ice cream over chilled crust. Spoon fudge topping evenly over ice cream. Cover with foil or plastic wrap. Place in freezer; freeze until firm, about 3 hours. In a small bowl, whip cream until soft peaks form. Gradually beat in liqueur until blended. Spread evenly over top of frozen pie. Sprinkle with reserved cookie crumbs. Cut into wedges; serve immediately or return completed pie to freezer until served. Makes 6 servings.

Georgia Miller (Mrs. George)

BROWNIE MINT PIE
A great way to use some of those Girl Scout Cookes!

14 chocolate mint cookies
3 egg whites
dash of salt
3/4 cup sugar
1/2 tsp. vanilla
1/2 cup chopped pecans
sweetened whipped cream or
    Cool Whip

Chill cookies. Roll with rolling pin between waxed paper to make crumbs. Beat egg whites until foamy and add salt. Gradually beat in sugar until stiff peaks form. Add vanilla and fold in crumbs and nuts. Spread evenly in 9-inch pie plate. Bake at 325 degrees for 35 minutes. Cool thoroughly and spread whipped cream or Cool Whip over pie. Chill and garnish with shaved chocolate. May be prepared ahead. Serves 8.

Hilda Rutherford (Mrs. N.A.)

ANNE'S GRASSHOPPER PIE

24 Oreo cookies, crushed
1/4 cup melted butter
1/4 cup green creme de menthe
7 oz. jar marshmallow creme
2 cups whipping cream, whipped

Combine crushed cookies and butter and press into spring form pan, reserving some crumbs to sprinkle on top. Mix together creme de menthe and marshmallow cream. Fold 2 cups whipped cream into creme de menthe mixture. Spread on cookie crust and sprinkle with reserved crumbs. Freeze. Serves 8 to 10.

Betty Bradley

CARIBBEAN FUDGE PIE
Sinfully delicious

1/4 cup butter
3/4 cup firmly-packed
    brown sugar
3 eggs
1 (12 oz.) pkg. semi-sweet
    chocolate morsels, melted
2 tsp. instant coffee powder
1 tsp. rum extract
1/4 cup all-purpose flour
1-1/2 cups chopped pecans,
    divided
1 unbaked pie shell
whipped cream

Cream butter and sugar and add the eggs one at a time. Add melted chocolate morsels, instant coffee, run extract and 1 cup pecans. Pour into pastry shell. Sprinkle with remaining pecans. Bake on the bottom shelf of the oven at 450 degrees for 5 minutes; then lower the temperature to 275 degrees and bake another 40 minutes. Cool and serve topped with whipped cream. Yields 1 pie, or 7 to 8 servings.

Gensie

MARGARITA PIE

1 cup finely crushed pretzels
3 Tbsp. sugar
1/4 cup butter, melted
2/3 cup sugar
1 (1/4 oz.) envelope unflavored
  gelatin
1 cup milk
2 egg yolks, beaten
1/4 cup lime juice
1/4 cup tequila
2 Tbsp. Triple Sec
1 cup whipping cream
2 egg whites
lime slices, if desired

In a small bowl, combine pretzel crumbs, 3 Tbsp. sugar and butter. Press over bottom and up side of a 9-inch pie pan; refrigerate. In a medium saucepan, combine 2/3 cup sugar and gelatin. Gradually stir in milk and beaten egg yolks. Cook and stir over low heat until slightly thickened and mixture coats a metal spoon. Cool to room temperature. Stir in lime juice, tequila and Triple Sec. In a small bowl, whip cream until soft peaks form. Fold into custard mixture. Refrigerate until mixture mounds when dropped from a spoon, 30 to 45 minutes. In a small bowl, beat egg whites until stiff but not dry. Fold into partially set custard mixture. Spoon evenly into chilled pie shell. Cover with foil or plastic wrap. Place in freezer; freeze until firm, 3 to 4 hours. Place in refrigerator about 15 minutes before serving time. To serve, cut into wedges; decorate with lime slices, if desired. Makes 6 servings.

Virginia Golding (Mrs. John G.)

CHOCOLATE ANGEL PIE

2 egg whites
1/8 tsp. salt
1/8 tsp. cream of tartar
1/2 cup sugar
1/2 cup small pecan pieces
1/2 tsp. vanilla extract
1 pkg. Baker's German's sweet
  chocolate
3 Tbsp. hot water
2 tsp. vanilla extract
2 cups whipping cream
3 Tbsp. sugar

Beat egg whites until frothy. Continue beating and add salt, cream of tartar and sugar gradually, beating until stiff. Fold in pecans and vanilla. Carefully spread on well-buttered 10-inch pie tin. Bake 55 minutes at 300 degrees. Cool.
To make filling, melt chocolate and hot water in top of double boiler over hot water. Set in cold water to cool to room temperature. Whip one cup of the whipping cream with 1 tsp. vanilla extract. Fold into chocolate mixture and spread in crust. Whip remaining cup of whipping cream with remaining tsp. of vanilla plus 3 Tbsp. sugar. Spread on top of pie. Decorate with chocolate curls made by scraping a sharp knife along a block of baking chocolate. Chill 2 to 3 hours. Do not make a day ahead.

Betty Bradley

MRS. MAC'S CHOCOLATE PIE

1 cup sugar
1/3 cup flour
1/3 cup cocoa
dash salt
1-2/3 cups milk
3 eggs, separated
6 Tbsp. sugar
1 9-inch pie shell, baked
1 tsp. vanilla extract
1-1/2 Tbsp. butter

Mix together sugar, flour, cocoa and salt in top of double boiler. Add milk and egg yolks and mix thoroughly. Place over slow-boiling water and cook until thick (pudding consistency), stirring all the time. Remove from heat, add vanilla extract and butter and stir. Pour into baked pie shell. Top with meringue and put into a cold oven set at 325 degrees; bake until meringue is light brown. Recipe doubles nicely. Serves 6.

MERINGUE: Beat the egg whites in electric mixer until frothy. Gradually add the 6 Tbsp. sugar, 1 Tbsp. at a time, and continue beating until stiff peaks can be made. When topping pie, be sure to spread meringue all the way to the edge of pie crust to seal it.

Mary McElveen (Mrs. G. A., III)

CHOCOLATE CHESS PIE

1 9-inch pie shell, unbaked
1-1/2 cups sugar
3 Tbsp. cocoa
1/4 cup margarine, melted
2 eggs, slightly beaten
1/8 tsp. salt
1 (5.33 oz.) can evaporated milk
1 tsp. vanilla extract
1/2 to 3/4 cups pecans, chopped
   (optional)

Prepare unbaked pie shell. Mix sugar, cocoa and margarine. Stir well. Add eggs, beat with electric mixer for 2-1/2 minutes. Add salt, milk and vanilla. Stir in pecans, if desired. Pour filling into pie shell. Bake at 350 degrees for 35 to 45 minutes. Serves 6 to 8.

Shirley Benfield (Mrs. R. H.)
Kathy Busby (Mrs. H. T.)
Sandra Sue Jennings (Mrs. William)

CHOCOLATE CHIP TOLL HOUSE PIE

2 eggs
1/2 cup unsifted plain flour
1/2 cup sugar
1/2 cup packed brown sugar
1 cup butter, melted and cooled
1 6-oz. pkg. chocolate chips
1 cup chopped nuts
1 9-inch unbaked pie shell
whipped cream or ice cream

Preheat oven to 325 degrees. In large bowl beat eggs until foamy; beat in flour, sugar and brown sugar until well blended. Blend in melted butter, chocolate chips and nuts. Pour into pie shell and bake at 325 degrees for 1 hour. Remove from oven, serve with ice cream or whipped cream. Makes 1 pie.

NOTE: If crust browns too quickly, cover with foil for rest of baking time.

Pam Allen

FUDGE PIE

2 oz. bitter chocolate
1 stick margarine
2 eggs
1 cup sugar
1/4 cup sifted flour
1 tsp. vanilla extract

Melt together chocolate and margarine. Remove from heat and add sugar, flour, eggs and vanilla until blended. Pour into a greased 9-inch pie plate. Bake at 350 degrees for 30 to 45 minutes. Serve with whipped cream.

Maria Blount (Mrs. J.A)

BUSY LAWYER'S CHOCOLATE CHIP PECAN PIE

1 cup sugar
1/2 cup plain flour
2 eggs, beaten
1 stick butter, melted
2 tsp. vanilla extract
1 cup chopped pecans
1 cup chocolate chips
whipped cream

Combine sugar and flour. Add eggs, butter and vanilla. Fold in pecans and chocolate chips. Pour into unbaked pie shell and bake at 325 degrees for 30 minutes. Serve hot or cold. Top with whipped cream if desired.

The Committee

FOOLPROOF CHOCOLATE PIE
Very rich!

1 6-oz. pkg. Nestle's semi-sweet
    chocolate bits
2 Tbsp. milk
2 Tbsp. sugar
4 large eggs, separated
1 tsp. vanilla extract
1 baked 10-inch pie shell

TOPPING:
1/2 pint whipping cream
3 Tbsp. powdered sugar
1/2 tsp. vanilla

Melt chocolate, milk and sugar in a double boiler over medium heat, stirring until smooth. Set pan in cold water and keep stirring and scraping from sides of pan until slightly cooled. Add egg yolks one at a time, beating with hand mixer after each addition. Whip egg whites until stiff but not dry. Stir vanilla and beaten egg whites into chocolate mixture. Pour into baked pie shell and chill 1-1/2 hours or longer before adding topping.
Whip 1/2 pint whipping cream until thick and add 3 Tbsp. confectioners' sugar and 1/2 tsp. vanilla. Spread over pie. Keep chilled. May grate chocolate over whipped cream for garnish. Yields 1 10-inch pie or 8 to 10 servings.

Kay Roberson (Mrs. G.D.)

KENTUCKY HORSE RACE PIE

4 whole eggs
3/4 cup white sugar
1/4 cup brown sugar
1 tsp. vanilla extract
2 Tbsp. bourbon
1 cup white corn syrup
1 stick melted butter
1 Tbsp. flour
1 cup chopped pecans or walnuts
1 cup chocolate chips
1 unbaked 10-inch pie shell

Beat the eggs, add to them the sugars, vanilla, bourbon, corn syrup, butter and flour. Mix well. Distribute nuts and chips in the bottom of the pie shell. Pour the filling on top. Bake for 45 minutes at 325 degrees. Best served warm. Garnish with whipped cream. Serve small slices, very rich! Serves 8 to 10.

Nancy Kiser (Mrs. James)

EASY CHOCOLATE MOUSSE PIE

*1-1/2 cups chocolate wafer
    crumbs
1 cup blanched almonds, lightly
    toasted and chopped
1/3 cup sugar
3/4 stick butter, softened
1/2 pint heavy cream
5-1/2 ounces Hershey's chocolate
    syrup
1 Tbsp. confectioners' sugar

In a bowl combine wafer crumbs, almonds, sugar and butter. Pat mixture firmly in bottom and sides of a well-buttered 9-inch pie pan. Bake in preheated 375 degree oven for 10 minutes. Cool. Whip cream, adding syrup just before cream stiffens. Add sugar, pour into crust and sprinkle a few crumbs on top. Freeze. Remove from freezer 10 minutes before serving. Can be made several days ahead. Serves 6 to 8.
*One 8-1/2 oz. box of chocolate wafers equals 2-1/2 cups of chocolate wafer crumbs.

Ellen Knott (Mrs. B.F.)

STRAWBERRY COBBLER

2 cups sliced berries
1-1/2 cups sugar, divided
1 stick margarine
3/4 cup flour
2 tsp. baking powder
dash of salt
3/4 cup milk

Melt the margarine in a deep dish. Mix one cup of the sugar with the berries. Make a batter with remaining ingredients. Pour batter over the margarine. Do not stir. Add the berries. Do not stir. Bake at 350 degrees for 1 hour.

Barbara Stutts (Mrs. Clyde)

CHERRY VALLEY COBBLER
Different twist for cherry cobbler

2 (1-lb. 5 oz.) cans cherry
    pie filling
1/2 cup chopped pecans or
    walnuts
1 tsp. cinnamon
1/2 tsp. nutmeg
1 Tbsp. finely-grated fresh lemon
    peel
1 cup biscuit mix
1 Tbsp. sugar
1/3 cup milk
cream, whipped cream or dairy
    sour cream

Preheat oven to 450 degrees. Mix pie filling, pecans, cinnamon, nutmeg and lemon peel with a rubber spatula in a 9-inch round cake pan. Bake for 15 minutes. Meanwhile blend biscuit mix, sugar and milk with a fork in a small bowl. Remove cherry mixture from oven; drop topping by small teaspoonfuls onto cherries. Return to oven and bake 15 to 18 minutes more. Serve warm with cream. Makes 6 to 8 servings.

Virginia Golding (Mrs. John G.)

UPSIDE-DOWN APPLE PECAN PIE

2 Tbsp. soft butter
1/3 cup brown sugar, packed
3 cups pecan halves
6 cups sliced apples
3/4 cup sugar
2 Tbsp. flour
1 tsp. cinnamon
1/2 tsp. nutmeg

Line 9-inch pie pan with tinfoil (13-inch circle), leaving 1-inch overhanging edge. Spread butter over bottom and sides of foil. Press pecan halves round-side down in butter. Gently pat sugar into butter. Prepare pastry for 9-inch 2-crust pie. Ease one crust into pan. Combine rest of ingredients, pile mixture into crust, cover with crust, seal and flute edges. Prick crust to allow steam to escape. Bake 10 minutes at 450 degrees; 35 to 40 minutes at 375 degrees, until apples are tender. Remove from oven and let stand 5 minutes. Invert on serving dish.
NOTE: Turn up overhanging edge of foil to catch juice during cooking.

Joan BeLasco (Mrs. J.J.)

Pie crusts will be glossy if brushed with a little milk before baking.

APPLE NUT PIE

1/2 cup flour
3/4 cup sugar
1/4 tsp. salt
1 tsp. baking powder
1/2 cup nuts
1 tsp. vanilla extract
1 egg, beaten
1 cup diced apples

Combine ingredients in order given. Mix and beat well. Spread in 8-inch pie tin, greased. Bake at 350 degrees for 25 minutes. Serve warm or cold with whipped cream. Serves 6.

Dixie L. Denney (Mrs. T.E.)

EASY GRATED APPLE PIE
This is delicious with ice cream.

2 cups grated apples, unpeeled
1 stick butter or margarine
1 cup sugar
1 egg, beaten
1/2 tsp. cinnamon
1/2 tsp. allspice
1 deep-dish pie crust, unbaked, or
    2 regular pie crusts, unbaked

Grate apples and set aside. In saucepan melt butter. Add sugar, egg, cinnamon and allspice. Fold in apples and stir until well mixed. Pour into unbaked pie shell. Bake 1 hour at 350 degrees. If frozen crusts are used this will make 2 regular pies or one deep dish pie.

Libby Morrison (Mrs. Jack)

HONEY APPLE PIE

5 tart apples, peeled and sliced
1/2 cup sugar
3 Tbsp. flour
1/3 cup whipping cream
1/2 cup honey
1/2 tsp. cinnamon
1/4 tsp. nutmeg
3 Tbsp. butter
2 unbaked pie crusts

Line pie pan with half of pastry, using your favorite pastry recipe for a 2-crust pie. Sprinkle 1 Tbsp. each of sugar and flour in bottom of pastry shell. Combine remaining sugar and flour, whipping cream and honey. Pour over apples and mix lightly. Arrange apple mixture in pastry shell. Sprinkle cinnamon and nutmeg over apples. Dot with butter. Cut strips 1/2 inch wide from remaining pastry. Make lattice top and flute edges. Bake at 400 degrees for 40-45 minutes. Makes 6 servings.

Ellen Knott (Mrs. B.F.)

BLENDER COCONUT PIE

2 cups milk
4 eggs
1/2 cup Bisquick
1/2 cup sugar
1 6-oz. pkg. frozen, flaked coconut
3 Tbsp. melted butter
1 tsp. vanilla extract

Blend all ingredients on low speed of blender for 1 minute. Pour mixture into buttered 9-inch pie plate. Bake at 375 degrees for 35 to 40 minutes or until pie is set. Serves 6 to 8.

Linda Brown (Mrs. W.B.)

PEGGY'S PERFECT COCONUT PIE

4 eggs
1-1/2 cup milk
2-1/2 Tbsp. flour
1-1/2 cups sugar
1/4 cup melted butter
1 large can angel flake coconut (3-1/2 oz.), or 1 pkg. (6 oz.) frozen
1 tsp. vanilla extract

Mix flour and sugar together. Beat milk and eggs together. Add small amount of liquid mixture to dry ingredients. When smooth, stir in remaining liquid. Stir in melted butter and vanilla. Add coconut and pour into 2 pie shells. Bake at 350 degrees for 35-40 minutes. Crimp tinfoil around edges of pie shells before baking. This keeps the edges from browning before pie is done. Yields 2 pies. (Eat one and give one away.)

Peggy Young (Mrs. John A.)

MOTHER'S COCONUT-PINEAPPLE PIE
A very rich pie made quickly for a busy day dessert!

2 9-inch unbaked Pet Ritz pie shells
1-1/2 cups sugar
1 stick softened butter or margarine
4 large eggs, well beaten
1 8-1/4 oz. can crushed pineapple, drained
1 3-1/2 ounce can coconut

Cream butter and sugar. Add well-beaten eggs. Mix together with drained pineapple and coconut. Pour into 2 unbaked pie shells. Bake at 350 degrees for 40-45 minutes or until set. Yields 2 pies.

Linda Dowd (Mrs. J. Kenneth)

JAMBOREE FRUIT PIE (OR TARTS)

2 cups sugar
2 sticks butter
5 eggs
1 cup chopped pecans
1 cup chopped raisins **or**
   1 cup chopped dates
1 cup coconut
1 tsp. vanilla extract
1 Tbsp. vinegar

Cream sugar and butter. Add eggs. Add remaining ingredients. Put into 2 unbaked pie shells *or* 18 tart shells. Bake pies 35-40 minutes, or tarts 25 minutes at 325 degrees.

Carolyn Bailey (Mrs. J.M.)
Patricia Davis (Mrs. J.A.)

CONCORD GRAPE PIE
This recipe came from my husband's New England family.

4 cups concord grapes, washed
   and pulled from stems
1-1/4 cups sugar
3 Tbsp. flour
1 egg, beaten well
pastry for 2-crust 9 or 10-inch pie

Separate pulp from skins, putting pulp in saucepan. Heat until pulp is soft. Press through sieve to remove seeds. Add skins to pulp. Combine sugar and flour, then the egg. Add to the pulp and skins. (At this point it may be frozen.)
Pour into pie shell, dot with butter and cover with top crust. Bake in preheated oven at 425 degrees for 20 minutes. Reduce heat to 350 degrees and bake 20-30 minutes more.

Guerry Russell (Mrs. Don J.)

LEMON CHESS TARTS (OR PIE)
An old family recipe

1 stick butter
5 eggs
2 cups sugar
1 Tbsp. cornmeal or flour
juice of 3 lemons
grated rind of 2 lemons
16 Bama tart shells

Melt butter and mix with all other ingredients. Pour into 16 Bama tart shells and bake at 325 degrees for 20 to 25 minutes.
For pie, pour into 2 regular or 1 deep-dish 9-inch shell and bake at 375 degrees for 35 to 45 minutes.

Virginia Golding (Mrs. John G.)
Phyllis Mahoney (Mrs. J.C.)

LEMON ANGEL PIE

3 egg whites
1/4 tsp. cream of tartar
1 cup sugar

FILLING:
8 egg yolks
1-1/2 cups sugar
1/2 cup fresh lemon juice
rind of 1 lemon, grated
2 cups heavy cream, whipped

Beat egg whites until frothy. Add cream of tartar and beat until soft peaks form. Gradually add sugar, beating until very thick and glossy. Shape meringue into a well-buttered 9-inch pie plate. Bake at 275 degrees for 1 hour and 5 minutes. Cool in oven with door shut. This can be done overnight with the filling being prepared the next day. Can also be baked in a 2 quart baking dish. Beat egg yolks well, adding sugar gradually. Add juice and rind and cook in top of double boiler over hot water until very thick. Refrigerate to cool. Whip cream, divide in half, and spread half on meringue shell. Spread the cooled filling over this, and cover with rest of whipped cream. Sprinkle grated rind on top. Refrigerate 2 to 3 hours before serving. Serves 6 to 8.

Wynne McLean (Mrs. Malcolm)

BEST-EVER LEMON PIE

1-1/4 cup sugar
6 Tbsp. cornstarch
2 cups water
1/3 cup lemon juice
3 eggs, separated
3 Tbsp. butter
1-1/2 tsp. lemon extract
2 Tbsp. vinegar
1 baked 9 or 10 inch pie shell

NEVER FAIL MERINGUE:
1 Tbsp. cornstarch
2 Tbsp. cold water
1/2 cup boiling water
3 egg whites
6 Tbsp. sugar
1 tsp. vanilla extract
pinch of salt

Mix sugar and cornstarch together in top of double boiler. Add 2 cups water. Combine egg yolks with lemon juice and beat. Add to rest of mixture. Cook over boiling water until thick. Add lemon extract, butter and vinegar. Stir thoroughly. Pour into pie shell and let cool. Cover with meringue as follows:
MERINGUE: Blend cornstarch and cool water in saucepan. Add boiling water and cook, stirring until clear and thickened. Let stand until cold. With an electric beater, beat egg whites until foamy. Then gradually add sugar and beat until stiff. Turn mixer to low speed, add salt and vanilla. Slowly beat in cold cornstarch mixture. Turn mixer to high and beat well. Spread over pie filling. Bake 10 minutes at 350 degrees. Yields 1 pie.

Mary Robinson (Mrs. R.F.)

TRIPLE LEMON PIE

1 cup water
2 Tbsp. cornstarch
1/4 tsp. salt
1 tsp. grated lemon rind
4 Tbsp. flour
3/4 cup sugar
1/2 cup cold water
3 egg yolks
1 Tbsp. butter
4 Tbsp. lemon juice

MERINGUE:
3 beaten egg whites
1 tsp. lemon juice
6 Tbsp. sugar

Boil 1 cup water, sugar, salt and lemon rind. Add flour and cornstarch mixed with 1/2 cup water. Cook slowly for 5 to 10 minutes stirring constantly. Add beaten egg yolks and cook 2 minutes. Remove from heat and add butter and lemon juice, stirring well. Cool slightly. Pour into baked 9-inch pie shell. Make meringue by beating egg whites stiff and gradually adding 6 Tbsp. sugar, a little at a time. Add lemon juice last. Brown 15 minutes at 350 degrees.

Frances Sanders (Mrs. Robert)

LEMON TARTS
This is one of my favorite desserts for a buffet or open house.

1 cup shortening (1/2 butter)
1 cup granulated sugar
1 egg, unbeaten
1 tsp. almond extract
2-1/2 cups flour

FILLING:
juice of 3 lemons
grated rind of 2 lemons
1 cup sugar
2 Tbsp. flour
2 Tbsp. butter
4 egg yolks
whipped cream

Combine ingredients in top of double boiler. Cook until thick, stirring occasionally. Cool and spoon into pastry shells, made as follows: Cream shortening, add sugar and cream well. Add egg and extract. Add the flour to make a stiff dough. Pinch off a small ball of dough and place it in the center of tin and press dough evenly on inside of tin with thumb, spreading as thin as possible. Place filled tins (with pastry only) on cookie sheet. Bake in moderate oven (375 degrees) for 15 minutes or until golden brown. Cool before removing from tins. To remove, invert the tin and tap gently. (Clean tins with a dry cloth — never wash!) Top tarts with a dab of whipped cream.

M. L. Reese (Mrs. Wm. N.)

ORANGE AND LEMON TASSIES

2 sticks butter
2 3-oz. pkgs. cream cheese
2 cups sifted flour
1 tsp. grated orange rind
1 tsp. grated lemon rind

FILLING:
1 egg, beaten
3/4 cup light brown sugar
1 Tbsp. butter
pinch salt
1 tsp. vanilla extract
few nuts, broken

Blend softened butter and cheese together until creamy. Add flour, 1/2 cup at a time, blending well each time. Add lemon and orange rind. Make little round balls of the pastry, and put each ball into a *tiny* muffin tin and spread with your thumb to make a cup. Then put your filling in it and sprinkle your nuts on top. Bake in ungreased tins for 25 minutes at 325 degrees.

Jocelyn Rose (Mrs. L.L., Jr.)

LIME JELLO PIE

2 cups pineapple juice
1 cup sugar
1 3-oz. pkg. lime Jello
1 large can evaporated milk,
    refrigerated

CRUMB CRUST:
1 large box vanilla wafers, crushed
1 stick butter, softened

Heat pineapple juice to boiling. Put in sugar and lime Jello and stir until dissolved. Refrigerate and congeal. Whip the above mixture and then add the can of *chilled* evaporated milk which has also been whipped. Fold together and pour into crumb crusts and chill before serving. Better if made a day ahead.
CRUST: Mix vanilla wafer crumbs thoroughly with butter. Press firmly into two 8-inch pie shells.

Doris Edwards (Mrs. Mark)

PEACH PIE
A different type of Peach Pie that is simple and delicious

1 9-inch deep-dish pie crust
1/2 stick butter, softened
3/4 cup powdered sugar
4-5 drops almond extract
6 peaches, peeled and sliced
1 small carton Cool Whip

Cook the crust according to package directions and cool. Cream together sugar and butter; spread over pie crust. Mix together the sliced peaches and almond extract and pour into crust. Ice the pie with Cool Whip. Refrigerate for 1 to 2 hours.

Genevieve Cummings (Mrs. T.E.)

BLUSHING PEACH PIE
Unusual combination—red cinnamon candies and peaches

Pastry for 9-inch, 2-crust pie
2 cans (29 oz. each) peaches, sliced and drained
1 cup sugar
1/4 cup all-purpose flour
1/4 cup red cinnamon candies
3 Tbsp. butter or margarine

Heat oven to 425 degrees. Prepare crust. Mix peaches, flour, sugar and candies. Turn into pastry-lined pie plate. Dot with margarine. Cover with top crust. Make slits in it; seal edges and flute. Double tinfoil into a square large enough to set pie on, pulling edges of foil up around piecrust and crimping over the top to keep juices from bubbling over into oven. This will not hurt crust. Bake until golden brown and juices are bubbling through slits in top crust, 40 to 50 minutes.

Ellen Knott (Mrs. B.F.)

CHITOSE CREAMY PEACH PIE
We got this recipe from a friend while stationed in Japan with the Air Force, 25 years ago!

unbaked deep-dish pie shell
3 cups sliced peaches
1 cup cream
3/4 cup sugar
1/4 cup flour
1/4 tsp. salt
1/4 tsp. nutmeg

Combine dry mixture, add to peaches and toss to coat thoroughly. Pour into pie shell. Pour cream over top. Bake at 400 degrees 35-45 minutes or until firm. Especially good served warm, or can cool before serving.

NOTE: I sometimes use 4 cups of peaches and put mixture into two 8 or 9 inch pie shells.

Jane W. Lucas (Mrs. R.T.)

FROZEN PEACH PIE

2 baked pie shells (9-inch frozen)
4 cups sliced fresh peaches
1 cup sugar
1/2 cup lemon juice
1 can condensed milk
1 9-oz. container Cool Whip

Sprinkle sugar over peaches and let stand while you mix the remaining ingredients. Add lemon juice to condensed milk and fold in Cool Whip. Add peaches; mix all together and put into baked pie shell and freeze. Serves 12.

Babs Merrill (Mrs. Jack)

PINEAPPLE PIE

1/3 cup sugar
1 Tbsp. cornstarch
1 9-oz. can crushed pineapple
1 8-oz. pkg. cream cheese
1/2 cup sugar
1 tsp. salt
2 eggs
1/2 cup milk
1/2 tsp. vanilla extract
1/2 cup chopped pecans
1 baked 9-inch pie shell

Blend 1/3 cup sugar, cornstarch and pineapple. Cook until thick and clear. Cool. Mix cream cheese, 1/2 cup sugar, salt, eggs (one at a time, stirring well after each), milk and vanilla extract. Spread cooled pineapple mixture into baked pie shell. Pour cream mixture on top and sprinkle with chopped pecans. Bake at 400 degrees for 10 minutes. Reduce heat to 325 degrees and continue to bake for 50 minutes. Cool. Serves 6 to 8.

Judy Beise (Mrs. D.W.)

PINEAPPLE TORTE

3 egg whites
1/2 tsp. baking powder
1/8 tsp. salt
1 cup sugar
11 graham cracker sections,
    crushed
1 cup crushed pineapple, drained
1/2 cup pecans or walnuts,
    chopped
Cool Whip or whipped cream

Combine egg whites, baking powder and salt, and beat until frothy. Add sugar gradually and beat until stiff. Fold in crushed graham crackers, drained pineapple and nuts. Spread in an 8-inch pie pan and bake at 350 degrees for 30 minutes. Cut in wedges and serve with Cool Whip or whipped cream.

Georgia Miller (Mrs. George)

FROZEN RASPBERRY PIE

If you are a raspberry fancier you'll love this pie.

1 (10 oz.) pkg. frozen raspberries
1 cup sugar
2 egg whites, room temperature
1 Tbsp. lemon juice
dash salt
1 cup whipping cream, whipped
1/4 cup blanched, sliced
    toasted almonds
1 baked 9-inch pie shell

Thaw raspberries. Reserve a few for garnish if desired. Toast almonds by spreading on a cake pan and heating in a 300 degree oven until barely beige in color. Watch closely because the nuts burn easily.

Combine raspberries, sugar, egg whites, lemon juice and salt. Beat 15 minutes or until fairly stiff. Fold in whipped cream and almonds. Mound in baked pie shell. Freeze until firm. Garnish with reserved raspberries.

NOTE: If you make your own pie crust, add 1/2 tsp. almond extract to pastry for a delicious almond pie shell.

Ellen Knott (Mrs. B.F.)

451

FRESH STRAWBERRY PIE
Terrific summertime pie!

CRUST:
1-1/2 cups flour
1/2 tsp. salt
2 Tbsp. sugar
1/2 cup vegetable oil
2 Tbsp. milk

FILLING:
1 cup sugar
1 cup water
3 Tbsp. cornstarch
2 Tbsp. white Karo syrup
3 Tbsp. strawberry Jello
1 quart fresh strawberries
whipped cream (optional)

CRUST: Mix ingredients until you can form an oily ball. Press into pie plate. Bake at 400 degrees for about 12 minutes.

FILLING: Boil first four filling ingredients until smooth and thick. Add 3 Tbsp. strawberry Jello. Cool until lukewarm. Arrange 1 quart fresh strawberries in shell. Pour filling over strawberries. Chill at least 3 hours. Garnish with whipped cream if desired. Serves 6.

Mary Kay Hight (Mrs. Wm.)
Rickey Springs (Mrs. Eli B., Jr.)

PUMPKIN CHIFFON PIE
A light and lively version of this holiday favorite!

CRUST:
1-1/2 cups graham crackers
(18 crackers, crushed)
1/3 cup sugar
1/2 cup melted butter

FILLING:
3 beaten egg yolks
3/4 cup brown sugar
1-1/2 cups canned pumpkin
1/2 cup milk
1/2 tsp. salt
1 tsp. cinnamon
1/2 tsp. nutmeg
1/2 tsp. ginger
1 envelope plain gelatin
1/4 cup cold water
3 egg whites, beaten stiffly
1/4 cup granulated sugar
honey

CRUST: Combine ingredients and press into 9 inch pie plate. Chill for 45 minutes.

FILLING: Combine egg yolks, sugar, pumpkin, milk, salt and spices. Cook in top of double boiler, stirring, until thickened. Add gelatin which has been soaked in the cold water, and stir until blended. Chill until partially set. Beat egg whites, adding sugar gradually. Beat until stiff and then fold into gelatin mixture. Pour into pie crust and chill several hours or overnight. Garnish with whipped cream and drizzle honey over in a very fine stream. Yields one pie.

Nancy Little (Mrs. T.M.)

FROZEN PUMPKIN PIE

This is a marvelous Thanksgiving dessert. The filling may also be served as ice cream atop mincemeat pie. I always double the recipe and put into a 12-3/4 x 9 x 2 inch pan and serve by cutting into squares.

1 cup canned pumpkin
1/2 cup packed brown sugar
1/2 tsp. salt
1/2 tsp. ginger
1/2 tsp. cinnamon
1/4 tsp. nutmeg
1 quart French vanilla ice cream

CRUST:
1 cup finely chopped pecans
1/2 cup ground ginger snaps
1/4 cup sugar
1/4 cup soft butter

FILLING: Beat pumpkin, brown sugar, salt and spices with beater several minutes. Stir in softened ice cream. Pour into crust, freeze overnight. Remove from freezer about 15 minutes before serving. Top with whipped cream, if desired.

CRUST: Combine pecans, cookie crumbs, sugar and butter; press into the bottom of a 9-inch pie pan. Bake at 450 degrees for 5 to 7 minutes. Serves 6 to 8.

Virginia Golding (Mrs. John G.)

FROZEN PEANUT BUTTER PIE

1 (ready-crust) crust
1/3 cup peanut butter
1 cup confectioners' sugar
1/2 tsp. vanilla extract
4 oz. cream cheese
1/2 cup cold milk
1 cup heavy cream
chocolate curls or nuts

Chill crust. In bowl combine cream cheese, peanut butter, milk and sugar. Beat until smooth. In separate bowl whip cream and vanilla (with chilled beaters). Gently fold together whipped cream and cream cheese mix. Pour filling into prepared crust. Freeze several hours until firm. Garnish with Dover Farm whip plus 3/4 cup sugar and chocolate curls or nuts.

Noble Dillard

SURPRISE PIE

1 quart chocolate ice cream, softened
6 oz. smooth peanut butter
4 oz. Cool Whip
1 graham cracker pie shell

Blend the ingredients together well. Pour mixture into the graham cracker pie crust. Freeze until ready to serve. Serves 6.

Kathy Evans

ALMOND TART ANNA

1 cup blanched almonds
3/4 cup sugar
3/4 cup heavy cream
1 tsp. orange-flavored liqueur
1/8 tsp. almond extract
1/8 tsp. salt
1 recipe for pate brisee, to which
   you add 1/2 tsp. vanilla
   extract and 1/8 tsp. almond
   extract, or unbaked pie shell

Mix ingredients for filling and let stand for 15 minutes. Spoon mixture into shell and bake in preheated 400 degree oven for 30 to 40 minutes or until top is caramelized. Transfer to rack, let cool; cut into serving pieces. Serves 6.

Mary Lou Bethune (Mrs. W.H.)

PEANUT PIE
Very rich—similar to pecan pie, but different!

1 9-inch unbaked pie shell
3 eggs
1 cup sugar
3 Tbsp. melted margarine
1 cup light corn syrup
1 tsp. vanilla
1-1/2 cup salted peanuts
dash cloves, nutmeg
   and cinnamon

Beat eggs and blend in sugar, margarine and syrup. Add spices and vanilla. Stir in peanuts and pour into pie shell. Bake at 325 degrees for 45 minutes or until center tests set. Serves 6.

Jackie Plott (Mrs. C.W.)

ANGEL PECAN PIE
Good for company

3 egg whites
1 cup plus 2 Tbsp. sugar
2 tsp. vanilla extract
1 cup Ritz cracker crumbs
1-1/2 cup chopped pecans
1 cup whipping cream
1/4 tsp. almond flavoring

Beat egg whites until foamy. Add 1 cup sugar a little at a time. Add 1 tsp. vanilla. Mix cracker crumbs and 1 cup pecans. Fold into meringue. Spoon mixture into an 8-inch pie pan to form shell. Make peaks around edge. Bake at 350 degrees for 30 minutes. Cool. Mix cream, 2 Tbsp. sugar, 1 tsp. vanilla and 1/4 tsp. almond extract. Whip until thick and shiny. Spoon into cold pie shell. Sprinkle remaining nuts on top. Serves 6 to 8.

Mary Lou Lindsey

BEST EVER PECAN PIE
Easy!

1 cup white Karo syrup
1 cup sugar
1/4 cup butter or margarine (soft)
3 eggs, beaten
1 tsp. almond extract
1 tsp. vanilla extract
1 cup chopped pecans
1 9-inch unbaked pie crust

Mix syrup, sugar and butter together. Add eggs and extracts. Fold in pecans. Pour into unbaked pie crust. Bake at 350 degrees for 45 minutes. Serves 6 to 8.

Susan Murfee (Mrs. D.G.)

PECAN PIE

2 9-inch unbaked pie shells
1 stick butter or margarine, melted
1 lb. brown sugar
4 eggs, beaten
2 Tbsp. self-rising corn meal
2 tsp. water
2 tsp. vanilla extract
2 cups pecans, chopped

Melt butter, add remaining ingredients in order given. Blend well. Pour into 2 unbaked pie shells. Bake at 300 degrees for 45 minutes. Serves 16. Freezes well.

Tonia Fuller (Mrs. E.W.)
Betty Cobb (Mrs. J.O.)

PECAN TASSIES

1 cup butter or margarine, softened
6 oz. cream cheese, softened
2 cups flour
1/2 cup butter, softened
1 cup sugar
1 egg, lightly beaten
1-1/2 cups chopped pecans
1 cup chopped dates
1 Tbsp. vanilla extract
1/8 tsp. salt
confectioners' sugar

Preheat oven to 350 degrees. In a large bowl, combine the first three ingredients. Mix until well blended. Divide the dough into 4 equal parts, then separate each part into 12 balls. Place the balls in the 2-inch sections of 4 ungreased, miniature muffin tins. Using your thumb and forefinger, press each ball into its cup, working the dough evenly up the sides to the rim.
Cream the remaining 1/2 cup butter with sugar. Add the remaining ingredients and mix well. Divide among the unbaked shells, filling each completely.
Bake until golden brown, about 30-40 minutes. Cool on racks before removing the tarts from their tins. When serving, sprinkle with confectioners' sugar. Yields 48 tarts.

The Committee

WALNUT PIE

1 9-inch unbaked pie shell
3 eggs
1/2 cup firmly-packed
    brown sugar
1 cup light corn syrup
1/2 stick butter, melted
1 tsp. cinnamon
1/4 tsp. salt
2 tsp. vanilla
1 cup broken English walnuts

Beat eggs in a medium-sized bowl. Add remaining ingredients except nuts in the order listed. Blend well. Stir in nuts. Pour into unbaked pie shell. Bake 50 minutes on the lowest shelf in a 375 degree oven. Bake until just set or until filling shakes slightly. Cool before serving. Good made ahead. Serves 8 to 10.

The Committee

EASY PIE CRUST

2 cups flour
1-1/2 tsp. salt
1/2 cup corn oil
1/4 cup cold milk

Combine all ingredients; stir with a fork to blend. Form a ball and divide into 2 parts. Roll out to desired form. For a baked pie shell, bake in a hot oven (475 degrees for about 10 minutes).

Mrs. Kay Roberson (Mrs. G. Don)

PIE CRUST FOR TWO 9-INCH PIES

1 stick margarine plus
    1/3 cup Crisco
1/4 cup boiling water
1 Tbsp. milk
1 tsp. salt
2-1/4 cups sifted plain flour

Cut all ingredients together. Divide in half, roll out and fit into 2 pie plates — or use one roll for top of 2-crust pie.

Carolyn Bailey (Mrs. J.M.)

NEVER-FAIL PIE CRUST

3 cups flour
1-1/2 tsp. salt
1-1/4 cups shortening
1 egg, well beaten
4-5 Tbsp. water
1 Tbsp. cider vinegar

Mix flour and salt together. Cut in shortening until crumbly, using a pastry blender or a fork. Beat egg and stir in water and vinegar. Add to the flour mixture, blending well. Divide into 4 equal parts. I form them into "patties." Place double waxed paper between each pattie, put into plastic bag or container and freeze until needed. Stays well in refrigerator 2-3 weeks. Yields 4 single 8 to 10 inch crusts.

Guerry Russell (Mrs. Don J.)

Sauces & accompaniments

M.E. Wellborn

BUTTERED APPLESAUCE

3 lbs. apples, peeled, cored
* and quartered*
1-1/2 cups water
1/2 stick butter (no substitute)
1 tsp. cinnamon
1 tsp. grated fresh lemon rind
1 cup sugar

Cook apples and water until apples are tender. Stir in remaining ingredients with wire whisk, combining until nearly smooth. Serve warm. Makes 2-1/2 pints. Especially good with ham or pork chops.

Betty Bradley

APRICOT CASSEROLE

1 large or 2 small cans apricots
1 cup brown sugar
2 Tbsp. lemon juice
1 stick margarine
1 cup Ritz crackers, crushed

Drain apricots for about 1 hour. Place in flat casserole dish with cup side up. Fill each with brown sugar. Pour lemon juice over top and marinate overnight. Top with Ritz cracker crumbs. Pour melted margarine over all apricots. Bake 1 hour at 300 degrees.

Bobbie Davis (Mrs. Claude)
Liz Deal (Mrs. Maurice)

LEMON CURD

This recipe was given to me by my mother-in-law who lived in Scotland—she served it with their High Tea, usually on bread. However, I much prefer it with pound cake.

1 stick butter
grated rind of 1 lemon
juice of 3 lemons
1-1/2 cups sugar
3 whole eggs
3 additional egg yolks
tiny pinch of salt

Melt butter slowly over hot water in double boiler with lemon juice and rind. Beat all eggs, add sugar and salt. Stir the butter into the lemon juice mixture, stirring rapidly over hot water until thick and shiny. Cool. Keeps for several weeks if covered and stored in refrigerator.

Mary Kay Greig (Mrs. John H.)

QUICK SPICED PEACHES

2 cans (1 lb., 13 oz.) peach halves
1-1/2 cups sugar
1 cup cider vinegar
4 3-inch cinnamon sticks
2 tsp. whole cloves

Drain syrup from peaches and set aside for use in another dish. Combine remaining ingredients. Bring to a boil. Lower heat and simmer 10 minutes. Pour over peaches and chill before serving.

Mary Louise Douglas (Mrs. Ben, Jr.)

COLD SPICED FRUIT

Serve in individual crystal compotes for a colorful and delicious side dish.

1 to 2 unpeeled oranges, sliced
    thinly and seeded
1 20-oz. can pineapple chunks
1 16 oz. can sliced peaches
1 16-oz. can apricot halves
1 29-oz. can pear halves
1 cup sugar
1/2 cup vinegar
3 sticks cinnamon
5 whole cloves
1 3-oz. pkg. cherry Jello

Cut orange slices in half; place in saucepan and cover with water. Simmer until rind is tender; drain well and set aside. Drain canned fruits well, reserving all of the pineapple juice and half of the peach and apricot juices. Combine reserved juices, sugar, vinegar, cinnamon, cloves and Jello, simmer 30 minutes. Combine fruits and pour hot juice mixture over fruit. Refrigerate at least 24 hours before serving. Serves 15.

Jane W. Lucas (Mrs. R.T.)

PINEAPPLE CHEESE CASSEROLE

1 (20 oz.) can pineapple chunks,
    drained (reserve juice)
1-1/2 cups grated Cheddar cheese
1/2 bag miniature marshmallows
1/2 cup sugar
2 Tbsp. cornstarch
1 egg, beaten

Drain pineapple chunks, reserving juice. Layer pineapple, grated cheese and marshmallows in a greased pyrex pie plate. Make topping by mixing reserved pineapple juice, sugar, cornstarch and egg in a small saucepan. Cook over medium heat until thick. Pour topping over layered casserole. Let stand at room temperature for at least one hour. Then cook at 325 degrees until it bubbles, approximately 20-25 minutes. Serves 6 to 8.

Alice Nance (Mrs. James A.)

PEAR CHUTNEY

A nice Christmas thought for a neighbor.

7 to 8 cups peeled, cored and diced
    green pears
1 lb. light brown sugar
2 cups cider vinegar
1 onion, chopped
1 cup raisins
2 oz. crystallized ginger, chopped
1 clove garlic, finely chopped
cayenne pepper to taste
2 tsp. salt
1 tsp. cinnamon
1/2 tsp. ground cloves
2 tsp. mustard seeds

Combine all the ingredients in a heavy kettle. Bring to a boil and simmer gently until mixture is thick, about 1 hour. Pour into hot sterilized jars and seal. Store in a cool, dark, dry place. Serve with chicken curry. Also a nice accompaniment for meats. Makes about 2-1/2 pints.

Woody Clark (Mrs. Jerry)
Cathy Bradford (Mrs. W.Z.)

CINNAMON JELLY

Pretty red jelly for Christmas giving.

1 qt. bottled or canned apple juice
1 pkg. powdered fruit pectin
4-1/2 cups sugar
2 Tbsp. red cinnamon candies

Combine juice and pectin in large saucepan. Bring to full rolling boil. Add sugar and cinnamon candies, stirring constantly; return to boil. Boil 2 minutes. Remove from heat. Let boiling subside and skim. Pour into hot jars; seal. Makes 7 half-pints.

Janice Privette (Mrs. G.D.)

PINEAPPLE PEPPER JELLY

This is even better than regular pepper jelly!

2-1/4 cups pineapple juice
3/4 cup cider vinegar
5-1/2 cups sugar
1 Tbsp. chopped red bell pepper or
*   1 tsp. crushed red chili*
*   pepper*
1 bottle liquid pectin (Certo)

Combine and mix juice, vinegar, sugar and pepper in large saucepan. Bring to a boil over high heat, stirring constantly. Stir in pectin; bring to a full, rolling boil. Boil for one minute, stirring all the while. Remove from heat. Pour into sterilized jars. Seal or cover with paraffin. Yield: 6 to 8 small jars.

Margaret L. Pitts

YELLOW SQUASH PICKLES

Enjoyed even by non-pickle lovers. Half-pint jars make nice little gifts.

2 lbs. yellow summer squash
2 small onions
1/4 cup salt and water
2 cups vinegar
2 cups sugar
1 tsp. celery seed
2 tsp. mustard seed

Slice squash and onions. Cover with salted water; let stand 2 hours. Drain squash and onions. Bring other ingredients to boil and pour over squash; let stand 2 more hours. Bring squash mixture to full boil for 5 minutes. Pour into hot jars and seal. Makes about 6 half-pint jars of pickles.

Brenda Monteith (Mrs. James D.)

HOT CURRIED PEACHES

12 fresh peaches (2 per person)
1/4 cup butter, melted
3/4 cup light brown sugar
2 Tbsp. cornstarch
1-1/2 tsp. curry powder

Peel peaches, cut in halves; remove pits and place in a 2-quart casserole, cut side up. Blend remaining ingredients and pour over peaches. Bake at 350 degrees for 40 minutes. Serves 6.

Liz Medearis (Mrs. W.F., Jr.)

ZIPPY SAUCE FOR GREEN VEGETABLES
Spruces up tired vegetables!

1 cup mayonnaise
2 hard boiled eggs
3 Tbsp. lemon juice
2 Tbsp. minced onion
1 tsp. Worcestershire sauce
1 tsp. prepared mustard
1/4 tsp. garlic salt
dash of bottled hot pepper sauce

Chop eggs. Combine all ingredients. Heat and stir over low heat just until mixture is hot through. Can be made ahead and heated prior to serving. Makes 8 to 10 servings.

Beverly Michaux (Mrs. Roy)

BORDELAISE SAUCE
This sauce enhances the most delectable cuts of beef and can also dress up cheaper cuts and left-over slices.

3/4 cup fresh mushrooms, sliced
2 tsp. butter
4 tsp. cornstarch
1 cup beef broth
1 tsp. dried, crushed tarragon
  leaves
1 Tbsp. lemon juice
3 Tbsp. red wine

In small saucepan, cook mushrooms in butter until tender (about 4 minutes). In cup, combine cornstarch and beef broth. Blend into mushrooms and cook and stir until mixture boils. Add remaining ingredients and a dash of pepper. Simmer about 5 minutes. Serve on filet mignon, prime rib or roast beef. Can be made ahead and refrigerated. Makes about 1 cup.

Maryann R. Berry (Mrs. W.P.)

MAYONNAISE

2 egg yolks
1 tsp. salt
1 tsp. sugar
1 tsp. dry mustard
1/4 tsp. paprika
dash of cayenne
1 Tbsp. vinegar
3 Tbsp. lemon juice
2 cups cold salad oil
1 Tbsp. hot water

Put 2 egg yolks into the small bowl of electric mixer and beat until thick — about 1/2 minute. Beat in salt, sugar, mustard, paprika, cayenne, vinegar and lemon juice. Gradually add, a few drops at a time, the 2 cups cold salad oil. When mix begins to thicken, add oil more rapidly. At the last, beat in 1 Tbsp. hot water. Store in a covered 2-cup container in refrigerator.

Gensie

QUICK AND EASY CHEESE SAUCE
Delicious served over green vegetables!

1 (5.33 oz.) can evaporated milk
grated Cheddar cheese

Pour milk into small saucepan. Heat over low heat. Add grated cheese, using the amount needed for desired consistency. Cook and stir over low heat until cheese melts and sauce begins to thicken. Will thicken more as sauce cools.

Martha M. Goodwin (Mrs. W.B.)

HOLLANDAISE SAUCE

3 egg yolks
2 Tbsp. lemon juice
1/4 tsp. salt
1/4 tsp. cayenne pepper
1/2 cup melted butter
   (no substitute)

Combine egg yolks, lemon juice, salt and cayenne pepper in mixing bowl. Beat well with electric mixer. Gradually add melted butter in a steady stream while continuing to mix just until blended and thickened. May keep warm over a pan of hot water. Makes about 1 cup.

Kathy Howe

CREAM OR WHITE SAUCE

THIN SAUCE	MEDIUM SAUCE	THICK SAUCE	SOUFFLE BASE
1 Tbsp. flour	1-1/2 Tbsp. flour	2 Tbsp. flour	3 Tbsp. flour
2 Tbsp. butter	2 Tbsp. butter	2 Tbsp. butter	3 Tbsp. butter
1 cup milk	1 cup milk	1 cup milk	1 cup milk
salt, pepper	salt, pepper	salt, pepper	salt, pepper

Melt butter in saucepan over medium heat or in double boiler. Blend in flour, using wire whisk or slotted spoon. Continue stirring while slowly adding milk, salt and pepper. Cook until right consistency.

Ellen Knott (Mrs. B.F.)

FLANK STEAK MARINADE

garlic salt
2 oz. Bourbon
1 oz. soy sauce
2 oz. Worcestershire sauce
1 oz. oil

Rub meat with garlic salt. Pour marinade over meat. Turn every hour. (If the meat is small enough to put into a large ziploc bag and seal, it isn't necessary to turn as often.) Marinate 3 to 5 hours. Cook meat on grill over medium heat 7 minutes on each side. Delicious!

Pat Vinroot (Mrs. Robert)

GARLIC CHEESE SPREAD
Easy—modified from a steak-house recipe in Savannah, Ga.

1 (8 oz.) pkg. Velveeta cheese,
  room temperature
1 (8 oz.) pkg. cream cheese,
  room temperature
1/4 cup evaporated milk
1/4 tsp. garlic powder,
dash of salt
dash of pepper

Mix all ingredients at once in bowl. Pour into desired serving dish. Refrigerate until ready to use. Great as a spread on bread (particularly French), baked potatoes or steak. Makes about 2 cups.

Patricia Padgett (Mrs. F.L.)

TOPPING FOR BAKED POTATOES

1 stick melted, cooled butter
1/2 cup Parmesan cheese
1/2 to 3/4 cup mayonnaise
1 tsp. Worcestershire sauce

Mix all ingredients together. Serve on hot baked potatoes. Makes enough topping for about 8 potatoes.

Jean Bridges (Mrs. D.T.)

HOME MADE CURRY POWDER
This is so much better than comercially prepared mix.

3 tsp. turmeric
2 tsp. cumin
4 tsp. coriander
1 tsp. ground ginger

Mix and store in tightly capped bottle.

Margaret L. Pitts

BARBECUE SAUCE

1 (32 oz.) bottle catsup
1 bottle water
1 cup salad oil
1/4 cup dried onion
1/4 cup Worcestershire sauce
1/3 cup brown sugar
1/3 cup French's mustard
1/2 cup lemon juice
1 Tbsp. salt
1 tsp. pepper

Simmer all ingredients for 15 minutes. Pour over boiled or baked beef roast (sirloin tip is good) or cooked pork roast which has been pulled into small pieces. Simmer in large pot on top of stove for 30 minutes. Enough sauce for approximately 6 lbs. of beef or pork.

Eleanor Minor (Mrs. William)

BARBECUE SAUCE FOR CHICKEN
For those who like a sauce without tomatoes!

1 cup vinegar
4 Tbsp. olive oil
2 tsp. chili powder
1 tsp. Tabasco sauce
1 tsp. black pepper
2 Tbsp. Worcestershire sauce
2 crushed garlic cloves, **or**
   1 tsp. garlic powder
2 Tbsp. prepared mustard
2 Tbsp. grated lemon peel
juice of 2 lemons
2 Tbsp. salt
2 Tbsp. sugar

Mix all ingredients and simmer 15 minutes. Marinate chicken in sauce and then grill outside. Brush sauce on chicken pieces frequently.

Kay Roberson (Mrs. G. Don)

LEMON BARBECUE SAUCE

1 small clove garlic or
   garlic salt
1/2 tsp. salt
1/2 cup salad oil
1/2 cup lemon juice
2 Tbsp. onion, finely chopped
1/2 tsp. black pepper
1/2 tsp. thyme

Mash clove garlic with salt in a bowl. Add remaining ingredients. Blend well and brush over chicken several times during cooking. You can marinate chicken in sauce a couple hours before cooking. If possible, allow sauce to stand over-night. Makes about 1 cup.

Ann Copeland (Mrs. E. H., Jr.)

SPAGHETTI SAUCE

1 lb. hamburger
1 to 1-1/2 tsp. garlic salt
1-1/2 tsp. onion salt
1 28-oz. can tomatoes, mashed
2 6-oz. cans tomato paste
2 tomato-paste cans water
1/2 tsp. salt
1/4 tsp. pepper
1 Tbsp. sugar
1 Tbsp. oregano
1/2 tsp. parsley flakes

Brown hamburger. Drain excess grease. Add remaining ingredients, mixing well. Simmer, covered, for 30 minutes (or until ready to serve). Can be frozen. Serves 5 to 6.

Vivian Stanley (Mrs. J.S.)

CREAMY COCKTAIL SAUCE

1 cup Hellman's mayonnaise
3 Tbsp. catsup
1 Tbsp. Worcestershire sauce
1 clove garlic, crushed
1 tsp. Tabasco sauce
1 tsp. salt
1/2 tsp. pepper
2 Tbsp. grated onion
juice of 1 lemon

Combine all ingredients. Good with shrimp or crab. Makes 1-1/2 cups.

Doris Walker (Mrs. James E.)

PRALINE SAUCE

1-1/2 cups light brown sugar, packed
2/3 cup white Karo syrup
4 Tbsp. butter
1 (5.33 oz.) can evaporated milk
1/2 tsp. vanilla extract
pecans, chopped

Mix first 3 ingredients and bring to a boil. Remove from heat and cool. When lukewarm, add milk and vanilla; blend well. Store in jar in refrigerator. Serve warm (can be reheated often) or cold over ice cream. Makes about 3-1/2 cups.

Betty Holland (Mrs. Calvin)

FRESH FRUIT SALAD SAUCE

1/2 cup sugar
salt to taste
1 orange
1 lemon
2 beaten eggs
4 tsp. cornstarch
1 cup pineapple juice
8 oz. cream cheese, softened

Grate orange and lemon, using 1/2 tsp. of peel. Squeeze juice. Combine all ingredients except cream cheese. Cook until thick in the top of a double boiler. Chill. Whip cream cheese, fold in chilled mixture. Serve over fresh fruit. Makes about 2-1/2 cups.

Ellen Knott (Mrs. B.F.)

ELEGANT BUTTERSCOTCH SAUCE

Dress this up with a little toasted coconut and serve over real vanilla which you've placed in a meringue, and you have something special!

1 egg yolk
4 Tbsp. water
1/3 cup white Karo syrup
5 Tbsp. real butter
2/3 cup brown sugar (dark
   works better)

Beat slightly with a fork: 1 egg yolk and 4 Tbsp. water. Add 5 Tbsp. butter, 2/3 cup brown sugar, 1/3 cup white Karo syrup. Cook over low heat, stirring until it boils (10 to 15 minutes). Then place in top of a double boiler over hot water to ripen —about 30 minutes. (Turn element to "low after water boils.)

Boyd Davis (Mrs. R.A.)

RASPBERRY SAUCE

1 10-oz. pkg. frozen raspberries,
   thawed
2 Tbsp. sugar
1 Tbsp. orange liqueur
1 tsp. lemon juice

Using an electric blender, blend the thawed raspberries with their syrup at high speed until thoroughly pureed and slightly frothy. Stir in the other ingredients. Pour over vanilla ice cream for a delightful parfait. Serves 4.

VARIATION: Clean and cap 1-1/2 qts. fresh strawberries. Add 1/4 to 1/3 cup sugar. Put in a bowl and stir. Chill in refrigerator for 6 hours. Then cover with the Raspberry sauce and serve.

Ellen Knott (Mrs. B.F.)

CREME DE MENTHE SAUCE

1 cup pineapple preserves
1/2 cup orange marmalade
1/2 cup blanched slivered
   almonds
1/2 cup green creme de menthe

Mix first three ingredients well. Blend in creme de menthe. Serve over vanilla ice cream. Makes 6 servings.

Ellen Knott (Mrs. B.F.)

FUDGE SAUCE I

3 squares unsweetened chocolate
1/4 cup butter
1 cup confectioners' sugar
6 Tbsp. heavy cream
2 tsp. vanilla extract
1 to 2 Tbsp. Grand Marnier
   (optional)

In a saucepan, over low heat, melt chocolate and butter, stirring constantly with a whisk. When melted, beat in sugar. Add 3 Tbsp. cream and continue beating with whisk. When well-blended, beat in remaining cream. Add vanilla extract and Grand Marnier. Makes 2 cups. Keeps well in the refrigerator.

The Committee

HOT FUDGE SAUCE II
So rich but so good! When reheating, if too thick, add a little cream.

2 Tbsp. butter
2 squares chocolate
1 cup sugar
1 small (5-1/3 oz.) can
   evaporated milk

Melt butter and chocolate in a saucepan over low heat. Add sugar and evaporated milk and stir until blended, about 10 minutes. Makes approximately 1 cup.

Caren Hollenbeck (Mrs. J.I.)

Similar recipes submitted by:
Barby Goode (Mrs. David J.)
Nancy Little (Mrs. T.M.)

JEZEBEL SAUCE

1 10-oz. jar pineapple preserves
1 10-oz. jar apple jelly
1 4-oz. jar Coleman's mustard
6 Tbsp. prepared horseradish

Mix all ingredients well 24 hours before using. Refrigerate. Will keep 2 weeks. Serve with cold turkey or roast beef. Marvelous as an hors d'oeuvre with cream cheese and crackers.

Libby Morrison (Mrs. Jack)

Classic Recipes
from Clubs & Restaurants

Marie Edith Wellborn

ENTRECOTE LINDBERG
Slug's Thirtieth Edition

This recipe can be used for any number of guests as each steak is prepared individually.

10 oz. closely-trimmed New York
    Strip sirloin steaks
salt
finely-ground black pepper
Dijon mustard
finely-minced yellow onions
flour
cooking oil

Take steak and sprinkle with salt and pepper. Lightly spread dijon mustard on top of steak then cover with the minced onions and pat into top. Sprinkle flour on top and pat to form a sold layer. (Flour must stay dry, but don't over-flour.) Preheat skillet on high and add 1 Tbsp. of oil. Carefully place steak, flour side down, in oil. (Caution! Watch for splattering grease.) Turn heat to medium and saute steak until edges are golden brown. Turn steak over using a spatula to keep onions from separating from steak. Let simmer until desired degree of doneness is reached. If you like it well done, cover and let simmer.

To enhance flavor serve on a bed of your favorite bordelaise sauce.

Owner, Slug Claiborne

CHILLED CUCUMBER SOUP A LA GIEL
Slug's Thirtieth Edition

2 medium cucumbers
1/4 tsp. salt
2-1/2 pounds sour cream
1 to 2 cups milk
dash Worcestershire sauce
1 oz. lemon juice
pinch white pepper
1/2 chicken bouillon cube
1/2 tsp. dried dill weed

Peel cucumbers and slice in half; remove seeds. Cut each half into four long slices and then cut all slices into 1/4 inch pieces. Sprinkle the salt over the cucumbers; mix lightly. Let stand 30 minutes. Place sour cream in a bowl and slowly mix in the milk until you arrive at a consistency of a cream soup. The milk must be added by sight and not by accurate measure. Add Worcestershire, lemon juice, dill weed and white pepper to sour cream mixture. Dissolve bouillon cube in two teaspoons of water and add to mixture. Drain cucumbers and mix thoroughly with sour cream mixture. Chill for 3 hours and serve in chilled bowl with a slice of fresh cucumber for garnish. Yield 1/2 gallon or 8 cups.

Owner, Slug Claiborne

SEAFOOD GUMBO
Hotel Charlotte

1 pound okra, sliced
1/4 cup shortening
2 Tbsp. flour
1 onion, chopped
1 bunch green onions, chopped
1/2 cup celery, chopped
1 can (10-1/2 oz.) tomatoes
parsley, chopped
1 bay leaf
1/2 tsp. thyme
2 quarts water
1 lb. shrimp
1/2 lb. crab meat (or 1 doz. crabs)
1/2 pint oysters

Saute okra in 2 Tbsp. shortening until it ceases to "rope"—about 20-40 minutes.

In another pan, prepare roux with remaining shortening and flour. Brown this mixture slowly, stirring frequently. When roux is dark brown, add onions and celery and cook about 5 minutes. Add all other ingredients (except seafood) and simmer for at least one hour. Salt and pepper to taste.

Add peeled raw shrimp (and cooked, cleaned and halved crabs—if whole crabs are used). Simmer 30-45 minutes more.

Add oysters (if these are used) and simmer 10-15 minutes more—or until the oysters are curled at edges.

If crab meat is used, stir in at end. Serve over cooked white rice. Serves 6.

(Gumbo is better if prepared ahead of time and refrigerated overnight. Seafood amounts and types may be varied to taste.)

Chef and Owner Danny Royer

VEAL PICCATA
Valentino's

1-1/2 lbs. fresh veal cut into 2 oz.
   medallions
1/2 cup drawn butter
1 cup white Rhine wine
juice of 2 whole lemons
1-1/2 cups chicken broth, with
   pinch of chicken base
flour seasoned with white pepper
   and salt

Pound veal into thin medallions. Individually flour each piece of veal. Saute medallions in butter until lightly browned on both sides. Add white wine, juice of two lemons and chicken broth. Simmer for approximately 2 minutes. Remove veal from skillet and boil gravy down until slightly thickened and pour over medallions. Garnish with fresh chopped parsley. Serves 4.

William P. Georges, Owner

CHICKEN WITH DUMPLINGS
Anderson's Restaurant

1 plump chicken

DUMPLINGS:
2 cups flour
4 tsp. baking powder
1/2 cup milk
2 Tbsp. shortening
1 tsp. salt

Dress chicken, cut in pieces. Place in saucepan, cover with boiling water. Add 1 tsp. salt and 1/4 tsp. pepper. Cover. Simmer slowly until chicken is tender. Prepare dumpling dough.
Sift flour, measure, and sift with salt and baking powder. Cut in shortening with 2 spatulas. Add milk until thick drop batter is obtained. Drop by teaspoonfuls into boiling broth. Cover. Boil 12 minutes. Serve at once.

Jimmy Anderson

CREAM OF CHICKEN SOUP
Moxie's

5 lb. diced chicken meat
1-1/2 gallon hot water
1/2 stalk celery
2 diced carrots
1 diced white onion
1/2 tsp. white pepper
1 dash Tabasco
1 quart half-and-half
1/2 lb. margarine
2 oz. chicken base
ROUX:
1 lb. margarine
3 cups flour

Add ingredients in order given, starting with the water. Bring soup to between 170 and 180 degrees. This will allow spices to dissolve and take effect. At this time add roux mixture to thicken soup. After roux has been added in, add the diced chicken meat. Allow to simmer for 15 minutes. Makes approximately 2 gallons.

Chef Betty Young

MUD PIE
Barley & Rye

7 ounces Oreo Cookies
1/4 lb. butter, melted
1/2 gallon coffee ice cream
fudge topping
whipped cream

Crush cookies and mix with melted butter. Press cookie mixture into a 9-inch pie pan. Let crust stand in freezer for 1 hour. Let ice cream soften somewhat; then mix in blender to make a soft ice cream consistency. Spread ice cream in crust and freeze overnight. Before serving, top with a purchased fudge topping and whipped cream.

FLOWER SHRIMP
Shun Lee Palace

1 cup vegetable oil
7 oz. shrimp, peeled and cleaned
6 oz. fresh broccoli
1 oz. sliced water chestnuts
1/2 oz. sweet pepper
1 Tbsp. vegetable oil
1/4 tsp. chopped ginger
1 clove garlic, halved
1 Tbsp. cooking wine
5 Tbsp. chicken broth
3/4 tsp. sugar
3/4 tsp. salt
dash white pepper
1 Tbsp. corn starch
1/4 cup cold water
1/2 tsp. sesame oil

Heat 1 cup oil in wok until very hot. Add vegetables, water chestnuts and shrimp. Saute about 2 minutes until shrimp turn pink. Drain shrimp and vegetables and place on heated platter; discard oil or save for future use. In wok put 1 Tbsp. fresh oil and heat. To this add ginger and garlic and cook for 1 minute. Discard garlic. Add broth, salt, sugar, pepper, wine and blend well. Mix cornstarch and water to make a paste. Add this to wok and continue cooking until slightly thickened. Return vegetables and shrimp to wok; stir to mix. Add sesame oil around outer edges of wok. This gives a subtle flavor to shrimp and vegetables. Mix well and serve with rice.

Frank Yaw, Owner

VEAL OSCAR
Silver Cricket

2 lbs. veal
1 lb. frozen or 2 lbs. fresh
  asparagus
1 lb. Alaskan king crab leg pieces
2 tsp. lemon juice
1/2 ounce brandy
hollandaise sauce

Dredge veal in flour; saute in clarified butter. After turning veal, add crab meat pieces. Flambe with brandy and lemon juice. Remove from pan. Place on serving dish. Cover veal with crab meat, asparagus and hollandaise sauce. Serves 4.

POTATO CAKES
Epicurean Restaurant

10 lbs. potatoes (about 11 big
  Idaho), boiled, peeled and
  mashed
8 eggs
1 large onion, finely chopped
1 cup parsley, finely chopped
3 cups cracker meal (reserve 1 cup)
4 tsps. salt
white pepper to taste

Mix all ingredients together. Form into balls or use ice cream scoop. Roll in cracker meal and deep fry. Yield: approximately 25 to 30 potato cakes.
NOTE: You can add more onion to this recipe if desired. Easy to halve for a smaller quantity.

VINAIGRETTE
Dikadee's Front Porch

2 Tbsp. mustard powder
2 Tbsp. warm water
3 Tbsp. salt
4 Tbsp. sugar
2 tsp. black pepper
2 tsp. garlic powder
1/3 cup onion, minced
1/4 cup tarragon leaves
1/4 cup parsley leaves
1-1/2 cups vinegar
1/2 cup lemon juice
1-1/2 quarts salad oil.

Blend mustard with water. Let stand 10 minutes. Add remaining seasonings and mix well. Add oil. Mix and let stand overnight.

Chef and Owner Nick Collias

LIMA CASSEROLE
Carolina Inn, Chapel Hill, N.C.

1-1/2 lbs. ground beef
1 large onion, chopped
2 tsp. chili powder
2 cups good white sauce
2 1-lb. cans lima beans, drained
1-1/2 cups mushroom soup
3 cups buttered toasted bread
  crumbs
1 cup grated sharp cheese
1 can mushrooms, sliced
salt and pepper to taste

Line large buttered casserole with toasted bread crumbs. Saute onions and ground beef and cover crumbs with layer of meat, beans and sauce. Add salt and pepper to taste. Sprinkle mushrooms over sauce, then light layer of crumbs. Repeat until casserole is filled and covered with crumbs and cheese. Bake for 35 minutes at 350 degrees. Serve very hot. Serves 10 to 12.

PEANUT BUTTER PIE
Eli's on East, Ltd.

1 cup powdered sugar
2 cups peanut butter
1/4 cup cornstarch
2/3 cup sugar
1/4 tsp. salt
3 egg yolks
2 cups milk
2 Tbsp. butter

Mix powdered sugar and peanut butter until it looks like Bisquick. Cook next 6 ingredients in double boiler until it thickens.
Spread half of peanut butter mixture in cooked pie shell. Then custard mixture and remaining peanut butter mixture over the custard mixture. Top with meringue made with 3 egg whites or whipped cream.

Owners, Bob and Karen Smoots

PORK NORMANDE
7th Street Coach House

4 boneless pork chops or
    tenderloin of pork slices
2 medium onions, sliced into
    1/2 inch cubes
4 medium apples, cored, sliced
    and cubed
salt and pepper
1/2 stick butter
apple brandy
apple cider

In a medium skillet, saute salted and peppered pork in butter until brown. Add brandy and ignite. When flame dies down, remove pork from pan. Add onions and saute until soft. Return pork to the pan and add the apples. Add enough cider to barely cover the pork. Cover and cook over medium heat until liquid is reduced in half. Serve with noodles or Austrian Spatzle.

Chef and Owner Jerry Conner

SCALLOPS CEVICHE
Myers Park Country Club

1 pound scallops
1 carrot, sliced julienne
3 stalks celery, sliced thin
1 cup olive oil
1/2 cup lime juice
1/2 tsp. sugar

Mix together olive oil and lime juice and add a pinch of salt and pepper and 1/2 tsp. sugar. Pour over the raw scallops and marinate for 3-4 hours until snowy white. Add the carrot and celery and serve on a bed of spinach.

Although the scallops are never exposed to heat, they are in essence "cooked" by the acid in the marinade.

This dish is perfect as a small summer appetizer or salad. Serves 4-6.

Chef Barry Love, C.W.C.

TENDERLOIN BITS AND CRUNCHY VEGETABLES
Myers Park Country Club

3-4 oz. oil
4 cups coarsely cut vegetables: red
    onions, zucchini, bell pepper,
    broccoli florets, celery
1 tsp. tarragon
1 Tbsp. chives
1 clove garlic
1 tsp. cracked pepper
1 lb. beef tenderloin cut into 1 inch
    chunks
2 oz. Brandy or Cognac
1 cup beef stock or consomme

Heat the oil in a skillet and stir-fry the vegetables quickly; remove. Then cook the tenderloin that has been dusted with flour. Brown the meat. Add the brandy and flame; add the stock and simmer until thick. Stir in cooked vegetables. Serve over rice or noodles.

Chef Barry Love, C.W.C.

BAKED SCAMPI
Quail Hollow Country Club

2 lb. shrimp (shelled and
    deveined)—tails on
2-1/2-3 cups dry bread crumbs
1/4 cup melted butter
1 Tbsp. chopped tarragon
1 Tbsp. chopped sweet basil
1 tsp. thyme leaves
2 Tbsp. fresh chopped parsley
4 Tbsp. minced garlic (can use
    granulated garlic)
juice of 2 lemons
1 cup dry white wine
salt and pepper

Sprinkle layer (1/4 inch) of bread crumbs in 6 individual casserole dishes. Arrange shrimp on top of crumbs. Mix together herbs and garlic; sprinkle over shrimp. Sprinkle with lemon juice and about 2 Tbsp. wine in each casserole. Top with bread crumbs; drizzle with butter. Bake at 500 degrees until bubbling around edges and has a solid crusty seal of buttered crumb topping — about 15-20 minutes. Serve immediately with green salad, crusty bread and buttered spinach. Check to see if crumbs begin to darken too quickly — cover loosely with sheet of foil. Serves 6.

Chef Guy Thomas

ZUCCHINI-BEEF SOUP
Quail Hollow Country Club

1/4 cup butter
2 lb. tenderloin or sirloin tips
    (1-inch cubes)
2 cups chopped onion
6 cups zucchini
6 cups chopped, peeled tomatoes
1 cup flour
2 cloves garlic, minced
1 qt. beef stock or bouillon
2 qts. chicken stock or bouillon
1/2 cup tomato paste
2 cups sherry wine
1 tsp. each: thyme, basil, nutmeg,
    black pepper
salt to taste

Saute onion and zucchini; add beef and garlic, stirring frequently. Add 1 cup flour, cook 5 minutes, add tomatoes, beef and chicken stock, tomato paste. Stir well, simmer 20 minutes on medium-low heat.

Add sherry, spices and salt; simmer 10 minutes. If you desire a thicker soup, mix 1 cup cornstarch to two cups water, stir well and add to soup (stirring until desired thickness is achieved). Makes one gallon.

Chef Guy Thomas

ALASKAN SHRIMP SALAD
Carmel Country Club

2 lb. peeled and cooked Alaskan
    Shrimp (squeeze all excess
    liquid)
1/2 cup green onions
4 oz. diced pimiento
1/2 cup diced celery
1 cup mayonnaise
1/2 tsp. mustard
1/2 tsp. Worcestershire sauce
salt and pepper
parsley, fresh
3 hard boiled eggs
black olives
1/2 head shredded lettuce
radishes and tomatoes

Mix shrimp, mayonnaise, chopped green onions, chopped celery, diced pimientos and mustard in a bowl. Add Worcestershire sauce, salt and pepper to taste. Line the shredded lettuce on platter or in bowl and arrange shrimp salad nicely on it. Garnish with egg slices or wedges, tomato wedges, black olives, radishes and fresh parsley. Serves 6.

Chef Hans Lohrer

PARFAIT GRAND MARNIER
Carmel Country Club

1-1/2 cups (12 oz.) sugar
1/2 cup water
6 egg yolks
1 quart heavy whipping cream
1/2 cup (4 oz.) Grand Marnier

Boil the sugar with a little water in a small pot and cook to soft ball stage (230 to 240 degrees). Have the egg yolks in a mixing bowl; then pour the hot liquid sugar into the mixing bowl with the eggs and mix until well blended. Keep mixing until cold.

In another bowl, whip up the quart of heavy whipping cream until stiff. Now combine everything into the whipped cream, including the Grand Marnier. Spoon the mixture into a 9 x 4 inch springform or 10 x 4 x 4 inch bread pan and freeze until next day. When ready to use, cut in desired portions and garnish with whipped cream. Serve immediately. Serves 6 or more.

Chef Hans Lohrer

CURRIED CHICKEN AND RICE SALAD "CALCUTTA"
Charlotte City Club

2 chicken breasts
2 cups cooked rice
1/2 cup mayonnaise
1-1/2 tsp. curry powder
1 small apple
2 slices pineapple
1 banana
1/4 onion
1/2 green pepper
1 stalk celery
2 Tbsp. raisins
1 Tbsp. coconut
1/2 tsp. salt

Cook chicken breasts, remove skin. Cut chicken into small chunks. Rinse cooked rice in cold water. Add rice to chicken. Dice all other ingredients and combine. Add curry powder to mayonnaise; stir, then mix it with the other ingredients. Serve on lettuce bed garnished with grapefruit section, pineapple rings, and shredded coconut. Chopped peanuts or mango chutney may be added if available. Serves 6.

Chef Jean Lampel

CRAB MEAT OR SCALLOPS AU GRATIN
Charlotte City Club

1 lb. fresh backfin crabmeat (or scallops slightly cooked in wine and butter)
1/4 cup dry sherry
1 tsp. butter
2 cups Bechamel sauce
salt, black pepper to taste
heavy cream (optional)
Parmesan cheese
paprika

In a skillet, melt the butter, add crumbled crab meat (check for pieces of shell). Add sherry, salt, pepper. When warm, add Bechamel sauce, let simmer a few minutes, add cream if too thick. Pour into a casserole dish, sprinkle with some Parmesan cheese and paprika and butter. Bake in oven, or brown under broiler.

BECHAMEL SAUCE
(Basic White Sauce)

2 tsp. butter or margarine
4 tsp. flour
2 cups milk
salt, pepper, nutmeg

Melt butter, add flour, mix well. Let cook 2 to 3 minutes. Set aside to cool. Boil milk, add salt, pepper and nutmeg to taste. When flour mixture (roux) is cool, pour milk over mixture and mix with a whip. Set over heat, mix well until mixture boils and thickens. Let simmer 5 to 10 minutes, stirring occasionally. Strain, if necessary, and keep warm. Butter or margarine may be sprinkled on top to avoid skim forming. Serves 4 to 6.

Chef Jean Lampel

JELLIED MADRILENE
Charlotte Country Club

12 ounces tomatoes
1 quart consomme
1 Tbsp. unflavored gelatin
1/3 cup beet juice
4 tsp. grated white onions
4 paper-thin lemon slices

Crush tomatoes, cook until there's only half as much as you had when you started, add consomme. Soften gelatin in beet juice, add a little hot consomme to beet juice when gelatin has been added; stir until gelatin is dissolved. Add to hot tomato mixture; stir, chill until set. Once chilled, beat or cut, serve in chilled soup cups. Top with lemon slice and grated onions.

Chef Joe Deas, C.E.C.

SOUP COMBINATIONS
Charlotte Country Club

Cream of mushroom mixed with cream of chicken, then add fresh chopped parsley.

Tomato soup mixed with chicken and rice. Add a little saffron.

Cream of asparaguus soup mixed with cream of celery, add diced ham; croutons or chives.

Vegetable soup mixed with beef noodle soup. Add slices of scallion or celery for garnish.

Boola-Boola
Equal amounts of strained green turtle soup with puree of pea soup. Put cooked peas in blender, add bouillon and dried basil, marjoram, rosemary, thyme, bay leaf, smallest amount possible of anise.

Mix cream of tomato soup with puree of split peas; add diced apples. Garnish with chives or dipped lemon slices or paprika.

Chef Joe Deas, C.E.C.

In a Class by Itself

HUEVOS RANCHEROS

6 huevos
6 tortillas
Aceite o manteca
5 tomates
1 cebolla
2 ajies picantes
cilantro
2 dientes de ajos

Fria tortillas en aceite, colo
sobre una bandeja, ponga
un huevo frito enc
cada una y les ec
encima salsa pre
Salsa: Picar los to
cebolla, chiles, aj
Sazonelos con s
no se cocina. S
las ta
calien

GUACAMOLE

3 aguacates
2 tomates
1 cebolla
Salsa picante al gusto
1 cucharada cilantro
2 cucharadas aceite
sal y pimienta

Machaque l
añada l   tes,
y
con la   eite
enta. Sirva   sal y
cortadas como   las
y   te

SAUCE BECHAMEL

llumez le gas
osez la casserole d

3 c   a sou
de be   Ajoute
cuille   de farir
glang   la cuil
la   cui
Ajoutez doucement en
tournant avec le fouet
1½ tasse de lait froid
Mettez 4 pincees de sel
Laissez cuire 5 minutes.

BANANE FONDUES

Allumez le four
Mettez-y 2 bananes
K   ez le four pour
20 minutes. Sortez les
bana   du four
Po   un assiette
du dessus.
5   pou   l'interieur
de chaq e banane
ave   cuilleres à
café de sucre en
poudre.
Mangez a la cuillere.

ARTICHOKE MOUSSAKA

1/4 cup butter
2 large onions, minced
2 lbs. ground veal
2 to 3 large garlic cloves, minced
1/2 cup dry red wine
2 tomatoes, peeled, seeded
    and chopped
1/2 cup parsley
1/2 tsp. cinnamon
1/2 tsp. nutmeg
1 cup toasted pine nuts
    (optional)

1/4 cup butter
1/2 cup minced onions
1/4 cup flour
3 cups milk, room temperature
1/4 cup sherry
1 tsp. salt

2 eggs, beaten
2 cups Ricotta cheese
1/8 tsp. nutmeg

1/2 cup bread crumbs
24 artichoke bottoms or crowns,
    drained and rinsed
1 cup Kisseri cheese
1/2 cup Parmesan cheese

Heat butter in a 12 inch skillet. Add onions and saute until lightly browned. Add veal and garlic and cook until meat loses red color. Add wine, tomatoes, parsley, cinnamon and nutmeg. Taste for seasoning. Add pine nuts if desired.

For sauce, melt butter in 3-qt. saucepan. Add onions and saute until lightly browned. Remove from heat and blend in flour. Return to heat and cook until flour mixture simmers. Add milk slowly, stirring constantly to blend thoroughly. Add sherry and salt; simmer, stirring constantly with a whisk, until mixture is thickened.

Stir 3 Tbsp. sauce into meat mixture. Combine remaining sauce with eggs, Ricotta and 1/8 tsp. nutmeg.

Preheat oven to 350 degrees. Oil a 3-qt. rectangular casserole; sprinkle with bread crumbs. Arrange 12 artichoke bottoms atop crumbs. Cover with half of meat mixture. Spread with half of the Kisseri cheese. Dust with half the Parmesan. Repeat for second layer, using remaining ingredients. Bake 1 hour until top is golden brown. Remove from oven and allow to set for 10 to 15 minutes. Cut into squares.

May be prepared 1 day ahead and stored in refrigerator. Reheat before serving, allowing about 15 minuntes additional baking time. Serves 8 to 10

Georgia Miller (Mrs. George)

PINEAPPLE PICKLES
These pickles seem to enhance any chicken or ham entree.

1 (29 oz.) can pineapple chunks
3/4 cup cider vinegar
1 cup granulated sugar
6 whole allspice berries
3 whole cloves
1 (3-inch) stick cinnamon
1 tsp. powdered coriander seed
dash salt
2 tsp. tiny red cinnamon candies
    (or food coloring)

Drain pineapple, reserving 3/4 cup of the syrup. Put the 3/4 cup syrup and all ingredients except pineapple chunks and coloring into a large saucepan. Cook uncovered for 15 minutes. Add pineapple chunks and bring to a brisk boil; cook for 5 minutes. Remove from heat, add coloring if desired. Cool, pour into jar with tight-fitting cover and refrigerate at least 24 hours before serving. Serve very cold in a pretty bowl.

Virginia Golding (Mrs. John G.)

PARTY PAELLA (COSTA DEL SOL—ESPANA)

1 cup white rice
1 7-oz. pkg. R.M. Quigg's Yellow
    Rice Mix
3 pieces chicken cut into bite-sized
    pieces
3 pork chops cut into bite-sized
    pieces
1/2 cup flour seasoned with salt
    and pepper
1 doz. shrimp in shells
2 8-oz. cans minced clams
3/4 cup white wine
2 green peppers
1 garlic clove
1 small jar pimiento
2 whole lemons
1 can black olives, pitted
1/2 cup vegetable oil
1/2 cup cooked green beans, fresh
    or frozen
1/2 cup cooked green peas, fresh
    or frozen

Shake yellow rice in a sieve (dry) to eliminate excess saffron. Boil or steam along with white rice until almost done, according to package directions.

While rice is cooking, dip meats into flour mixture and fry slightly in oil in a heavy skillet or paella pan, along with mashed garlic clove. Remove from pan.

Cut green pepper into strips, salt and fry in same oil until soft.

Add drained rice to pan along with meat, beans, peas, pimientos, salt and pepper (to taste).

In a small pan, simmer clams and juice in 3/4 cup white wine and add to mixture.

Lay fresh shrimps on top of paella. Add black olives and pimientos and cover with heavy lid or aluminum foil. Steam for 20 minutes or until shrimps are cooked. Add water if necessary.

When done, decorate with fresh cold lemon rounds. Serves 6.

Gwen D. Rogers (Mrs. R.A.)

RAHM SCHNITZEL—VEAL CUTLETS WITH MUSHROOMS

2 lbs. veal cutlets, cut into slices
    1/4 inch thick
1 cup lemon juice
salt
freshly-ground black pepper
flour
4 Tbsp. butter
4 Tbsp. vegetable oil
1 cup fresh mushrooms,
    thinly sliced
1/2 cup heavy cream

In a glass dish, marinate cutlets in lemon juice for 1 hour, turning them every 20 minutes. Remove from juice; pat dry with paper towels. Salt and pepper generously; dip in flour and shake off excess. In a heavy skillet, heat butter and oil over high heat; add cutlets. Cook for 1 or 2 minutes on each side, using tongs to turn them. Lower heat to medium and cook for 5 to 6 minutes longer on each side. Place them on a platter in a 200 degree oven to keep warm. Pour off all but a thin film of fat, add mushrooms to the skillet and cook for 3 or 4 minutes over medium heat. Pour in cream and bring to a boil, stirring in any brown bits that cling to the pan. Cook briskly until cream thickens enough to coat a spoon lightly. Taste for seasoning; pour over cutlets to serve. Serves 4.

Noble Dillard

PROVENCAL SUPPER WITH AIOLI SAUCE

6 whole artichokes, cooked
12 small red potatoes, steamed
1/2 lb. asparagus
1/2 lb. green beans
1/2 lb. baby carrots
6 small wedges red cabbage
6 small zucchini, cut in sticks
1/2 pint cherry tomatoes
1/2 lb. mushrooms
6 hard-boiled eggs, quartered
1-1/2 lbs. large shrimp
AIOLI SAUCE:
1 egg
2 tsp. tarragon vinegar
1 tsp. Dijon mustard
2 or 3 peeled cloves garlic
1/2 tsp. sea salt
pinch cayenne
1/2 cup safflower oil
1/2 cup olive oil

Double Aioli Sauce recipe and place in bowl set in the middle of a large serving plate. Cook and peel shrimp. Surround bowl with vegetables, eggs and shrimp. The cooked artichokes and potatoes may be served either hot or cold, and the asparagus, green beans and carrots can be served either raw or steamed until tender-crisp.

To make Aioli Sauce: Place all except oils in blender and blend until smooth. With motor running, remove top and pour oil into blender in a slow, steady stream. Blend until it makes a thick mayonnaise. Refrigerate, covered, until serving time. Yield: 1/2 cup. If you are not a garlic lover, you will find this sauce very strong. You may prefer a home-made mayonnaise, seasoned with curry powder. Makes 6 to 8 generous servings.

Ada Offerdahl (Mrs. John)

ROANOKE BEEF TENDERLOIN

A gourmet classic. This is the recipe of Mr. Harrison Hale, a well-known caterer from Roanoke, Virginia.

1 well-trimmed whole beef
    tenderloin
1 Tbsp. ground thyme
1 tsp. white pepper
1 Tbsp. Lawry's Seasoned Salt
1 tsp. garlic salt
1/4 tsp. oregano
1 tsp. salt
1/4 cup Worcestershire sauce
1 cup water

Place beef on large sheet of aluminum foil and rub thyme into beef. Mix pepper, seasoned salt, garlic salt and oregano; sprinkle over beef and roll beef over foil to pick up remaining dry ingredients just sprinkled. Wrap beef in foil and refrigerate for 12 hours. Remove 2 hours before cooking. Place beef in cooking pan and sprinkle with salt and Worcestershire sauce. Add 1 cup water to the pan and cook 35 minutes at 400 degrees — rare to medium-rare — the only way to cook a tenderloin!

Ellen Knott (Mrs. B.F.)

CHICKEN SALTIMBOCCA

6 chicken breasts
6 thin slices prosciutto, cut in half
12 pieces Mozzarella cheese, about 3/4 inch square
12 pitted black olives, cut in half
1 tsp. MSG
1 tsp. pepper
1/2 cup flour
1 egg
3 Tbsp. milk
2 cups fine cracker crumbs
1/2 cup butter
2 cloves garlic, finely minced
1/2 cup chopped parsley
butter and olive oil in equal parts, to cover bottom of a skillet to a depth of 1/4 inch

Bone, skin and halve chicken breasts. With a mallet pound each one thin between 2 sheets of waxed paper. Place half a piece of prosciutto, a piece of mozzarella cheese and 2 olive halves on each breast. Sprinkle with MSG and pepper. Fold side over to cover filling, and press edges firmly together.

Flour each breast. Beat egg slightly, adding milk. Dip both sides of chicken breasts into egg mixture; dip into bread crumbs. Chill for at least 1/2 hour. Melt 1/2 cup butter in a small saucepan. Add chopped garlic and parsley; keep warm until the chicken is cooked.

Heat butter and olive oil in a skillet until hot. Cook in skillet on medium high. saute chicken quickly, turning once to cook the other side.

Remove to heated serving dish; pour warm garlic-parsley butter sauce on top and serve at once. Serves 6.

Virginia Golding (Mrs. John G.)

RIPE TOMATO PICKLE
A good way to use ripe tomatoes when you have lots in the garden.

24 ripe tomatoes
8 large onions
2 bunches celery
2 hot peppers
1 lb. brown sugar
1-1/2 cups vinegar
2 Tbsp. salt

Scald tomatoes and skin. Dice tomatoes into large pot. Chop onions, celery and peppers finely (use gloves for these). Add to tomatoes along with vinegar, sugar and salt. Cook slowly (uncovered) until slightly thickened—about 1-1/2 hours. Put into sterilized jars. Put tops on and submerge in simmering water for 10 minutes. Makes 8 to 10 pints.

Anna Stanley (Mrs. Verner)

FLORENTINE CREPE CUPS

These make wonderful hors d'oeuvres if tiny muffin tins are used.

CREPES:
3 eggs, slightly beaten
2/3 cup plain flour
1/2 tsp. salt
1 cup milk

FILLING:
1-1/2 cups (6 oz.) shredded
    sharp cheddar cheese
3 Tbsp. flour
3 eggs, slightly beaten
2/3 cup mayonnaise
10-oz. pkg. frozen chopped
    spinach, thawed
4-oz. can mushrooms, drained
8 or 10 slices bacon, cooked
    and crumbled
1/2 tsp. salt
dash of pepper

Combine eggs, flour, salt and milk; beat until smooth. Let stand 30 minutes. For twelve crepes, pour two tablespoons batter into hot lightly-greased 8-inch skillet. Cook on one side, only, until underside is lightly browned.

Toss cheese with flour, add remaining ingredients, mix well. Fit crepes into greased muffin pan, fill with cheese mixture. Bake at 350 degrees, 40 minutes or until set. Garnish with crumbled bacon.

NOTE: To fill tiny muffin tins, I make large crepes and cut circles with scissors for small cups.

Sallie Wooten (Mrs. F.M.)

MARCHAND DU VIN SAUCE

1/2 cup butter
1/3 cup mushrooms
1/2 cup minced ham
1/2 cup chopped shallots
1/2 cup finely chopped onion
2 cloves minced garlic
2 Tbsp. flour
1/8 tsp. pepper
dash cayenne
3/4 cup beef stock
1/2 cup red wine

Finely chop mushrooms and saute in butter with ham, shallots, onion and garlic. Add flour and spices. Brown about 6-7 minutes, stirring constantly. Blend in stock and wine. Cover and simmer over low heat about 30 minutes. Stir occasionally. Makes 1-1/2 cups. Can be made ahead and reheated; freezes nicely. Delicious on Eggs Hussard, steak or veal. Also good on chicken breast over ham.

Dot Nicholls (Mrs. T.H.)

CHARTREUSE

1 lb. green beans
2 yellow summer squash
2 zucchini
2 large carrots
1/4 cup green peas
1/2 cup Brussels sprouts
1/2 cup cauliflower florets
6 cabbage leaves
salt and pepper
soft butter
1-1/2 cups mashed potatoes
1/4 cup clarified butter

Cut ends off beans. Scrape carrots and cut same length and size as beans. Slice zucchini and squash thinly. Parboil beans, squash and other vegetables separately in boiling water. Drain each and season with salt and pepper.

Use 6-inch diameter souffle dish spread *thickly* with butter. On outside edge, put border of peas. Inside dish, put outer circle of overlapping squash and inner circle of overlapping zucchini. Stand alternate slices of beans and carrots upright on peas. Trim ends even with mold (use scissors). Cover bottom and sides with mashed potatoes. Press down firmly. Cover with leaf or leaves. On top of the cabbage, make an outer circle of sprouts and an innner circle of cauliflower. Add another layer of squash and zucchini. Pour melted, clarified butter on top. Cover once more with cabbage and more potatoes (you may need extra potatoes). Fill to rim. Bake at 350 degrees for 20 minutes. Remove and turn mold out on serving plate. Variety of vegetables can be changed. This is tedious but worth it. Besides, it's fun!

Gertie, the Evil Witch

REMOULADE SAUCE
Serve over cold shrimp or as a vegetable dip.

3 cups mayonnaise
1 jar Zatarian's mustard
3 eggs
2 cloves garlic, crushed
1/2 onion
2 Tbsp. Worcestershire sauce
1 Tbsp. lemon juice
1 Tbsp. vinegar
2 Tbsp. anchovy paste
1 Tbsp. horseradish sauce
1 Tbsp. Sherry

Boil eggs and grate. Grate 1/2 onion or slice 4 green onions, including some tops. Mix all of the ingredients in a glass jar until well blended and store in refrigerator. Yields 5 cups.

Dee Dee Grainger (Mrs. Isaac B.)

COOKING WITH CLASS
9502 Providence Road
Charlotte, North Carolina 28277-8695

Please send _____ copies of **COOKING WITH CLASS** at $20.00 per copy ($16.95
plus $3.05 for postage & handling). Enclosed is my check for $ _____
(N.C. residents add $1.02 sales tax for each book).

If this is a gift, card should read: _____

_____

Name: _____

Address: _____

City: _____ State: _____ Zip: _____

Make checks payable to: **CLS PARENTS' COUNCIL**
Proceeds from the sale of this book are returned to *Charlotte Latin School* through
projects of The Parents' Council.

- -

If you enjoy the recipes in **COOKING WITH CLASS,** you must try **COOKING WITH
CLASS - A SECOND HELPING!** Over 900 delicious new recipes!

COOKING WITH CLASS - A SECOND HELPING
9502 Providence Road
Charlotte, North Carolina 28277-8695

Please send _____ copies of **COOKING WITH CLASS - A SECOND HELPING** at $20.00
per copy ($16.95 plus $3.05 for postage & handling). Enclosed is my check for
$ _____ (N.C. residents add $1.02 sales tax for each book).

If this is a gift, card should read: _____

_____

Name: _____

Address: _____

City: _____ State: _____ Zip: _____

Make checks payable to: **CLS PARENTS' COUNCIL**
Proceeds from the sale of this book are returned to *Charlotte Latin School* through
projects of The Parents' Council.

I would like to see this marvelous cookbook in the following stores:

Store Name _____

Address _____

City _____ State _____ Zip _____

Store Name _____

Address _____

City _____ State _____ Zip _____

I would like to see this marvelous cookbook in the following stores:

Store Name _____

Address _____

City _____ State _____ Zip _____

Store Name _____

Address _____

City _____ State _____ Zip _____